ELIHU BURRITT LIBRARY
CENTRAL CONNECTICUT STATE UNIVERSITY
NEW BRITAIN, CONNECTICUT 06050

The United States in East Asia

This bibliography was conceived and compiled from the periodicals database of the American Bibliographical Center by editors at ABC-Clio Information Services.

Jessica S. Brown, Managing Editor
Susan K. Kinnell, Assistant Editor

Pamela R. Byrne

The United States in East Asia

A Historical Bibliography

ABC-Clio Information Services
Santa Barbara, California
Denver, Colorado
Oxford, England

Library of Congress Cataloging-in-Publication Data
Main entry under title:

The United States in east Asia.
   Includes index.
   1. East Asia—Relations—United States—Bibliography.
   2. East Asia—Relations—United States—Abstracts.
   3. United States—Relations—East Asia—Bibliography.
   4. United States—Relations—East Asia—Abstracts.
   I. ABC-Clio Information Services.
   Z3001.U65 1985 (DS518.8) 016.3034'8273'05 85-7545
   ISBN 0-87436-452-3

Copyright © 1985 by ABC-Clio, Inc.

All rights reserved. No part of this publication may be reproduced, stored in a retrieval system, or transmitted in any form, or by any means, electronic, mechanical, photocopying, recording, or otherwise, without the prior written permission of ABC-Clio, Inc.

This book is Smyth sewn and printed on acid-free paper to meet library standards.

ABC-Clio Information Services, Inc.
2040 Alameda Padre Serra, Box 4397
Santa Barbara, California 93140-4397

Clio Press Ltd.
55 St. Thomas Street
Oxford, OX1 1JG, England

Manufactured in the United States of America.

ABC-CLIO RESEARCH GUIDES

The ABC-Clio Research Guides are a new generation of annotated bibliographies that provide comprehensive control of the recent journal literature on high-interest topics in history and the related social sciences. These publications are compiled by editor/historians and other subject specialists who examine article entries in ABC-Clio Information Services' vast history data base and select abstracts of all citations that relate to the particular topic of study.

Each entry selected from this data base—the largest history data base in the world—has been reviewed to ensure consistency in treatment and completeness of coverage. The subject profile index (ABC-SPIndex) accompanying each volume has been evaluated and revised in terms of the specific subject presented to allow precise and rapid access to the entries.

The titles in this series are prepared to save researchers, students, and librarians the considerable time and expense usually associated with accessing materials manually or through online searching. ABC-Clio's Research Guides offer unmatched access to significant scholarly articles on the topics of most current interest to historians and social scientists.

ABC-CLIO RESEARCH GUIDES

Pamela R. Byrne, Executive Editor
Jessica S. Brown, Managing Editor
Susan K. Kinnell, Assistant Editor

1.
World War II from an American Perspective
1982   ISBN 0-87436-035-8

6.
Crime and Punishment in America
1983   ISBN 0-87436-2

2.
The Jewish Experience in America
1982   ISBN 0-87436-034-x

7.
The Democratic and Republican Parties
1983   ISBN 0-87436-364-0

3.
Nuclear America
1983   ISBN 0-87436-360-8

8.
The American Electorate
1983   ISBN 0-87436-372-1

4.
The Great Depression
1983   ISBN 0-87436-361-6

9.
The Weimar Republic
1984   ISBN 0-87436-378-0

5.
Corporate America
1983   ISBN 0-87436-362-4

10.
The Third Reich, 1933-1939
1984   ISBN 0-87436-379-9

11.
The Third Reich at War
1984   ISBN 0-87436-393-4

14.
The United States in East Asia
1985   ISBN 0-87436-452-3

12.
American Family History
1984   ISBN 0-87436-380-2

13.
The Sino-Soviet Conflict
1985   ISBN 0-87436-382-9

LIST OF ABBREVIATIONS

A.	Author-prepared Abstract	*Illus.*	Illustrated, Illustration
Acad.	Academy, Academie, Academia	*Inst.*	Institute, Institut-.
Agric.	Agriculture, Agricultural	*Int.*	International, Internacional, Internationaal, Internationaux, Internazionale
AIA	Abstracts in Anthropology		
Akad.	Akademie		
Am.	America, American	*J.*	Journal, Journal-prepared Abstract
Ann.	Annals, Annales, Annual, Annali	*Lib.*	Library, Libraries
Anthrop.	Anthropology, Anthropological	*Mag.*	Magazine
Arch.	Archives	*Mus.*	Museum, Musee, Museo
Archaeol.	Archaeology, Archaeological	*Nac.*	Nacional
Art.	Article	*Natl.*	National, Nationale
Assoc.	Association, Associate	*Naz.*	Nazionale
Biblio.	Bibliography, Bibliographical	*Phil.*	Philosophy, Philosophical
Biog.	Biography, Biographical	*Photo.*	Photograph
Bol.	Boletim, Boletin	*Pol.*	Politics, Political, Politique, Politico
Bull.	Bulletin	*Pr.*	Press
c.	century (in index)	*Pres.*	President
ca.	circa	*Pro.*	Proceedings
Can.	Canada, Canadian, Canadien	*Publ.*	Publishing, Publication
Cent.	Century	*Q.*	Quarterly
Coll.	College	*Rev.*	Review, Revue, Revista, Revised
Com.	Committee	*Riv.*	Rivista
Comm.	Commission	*Res.*	Research
Comp.	Compiler	*RSA*	Romanian Scientific Abstracts
DAI	Dissertation Abstracts International	*S.*	Staff-prepared Abstract
		Sci.	Science, Scientific
Dept.	Department	*Secy.*	Secretary
Dir.	Director, Direktor	*Soc.*	Society, Societe, Sociedad, Societa
Econ.	Economy, Econom-.		
Ed.	Editor, Edition	*Sociol.*	Sociology, Sociological
Educ.	Education, Educational	*Tr.*	Transactions
Geneal.	Genealogy, Genealogical, Genealogique	*Transl.*	Translator, Translation
		U.	University, Universi-.
Grad.	Graduate	*US*	United States
Hist.	History, Hist-.	*Vol.*	Volume
IHE	Indice Historico Espanol	*Y.*	Yearbook

CONTENTS

LIST OF ABBREVIATIONS.............................vi
INTRODUCTION vii
ABSTRACTS
1. General 1
2. China... 27
3. Hong Kong 112
4. Japan 113
5. Korea (North and South) 197
6. Taiwan.......................................222
SUBJECT INDEX...................................229
AUTHOR INDEX 293

USER'S GUIDE TO THE INDEXES

All titles in this series use ABC-Clio Information Services' unique Subject Profile Index (ABC-SPIndex) and an author index. The following abstract is found in this volume:

Abstract

940. Tsuchimochi, Gary H. THE TREND OF RESEARCH ON EDUCATIONAL REFORM UNDER THE AMERICAN OCCUPATION OF JAPAN WITH PARTICULAR REFERENCE TO DOCTORAL DISSERTATIONS IN THE U.S. *Asian Profile [Hong Kong] 1982 10(2): 129-142.* Surveys US doctoral dissertations on educational reform in Japan under US occupation. Dissertations of the 1950's were often written by American officers having direct personal experience with their subject of research. During the 1960's interest in the subject waned but was stimulated in the late 1970's by the publication of Robert E. Ward and Frank J. Shulman's *The Allied Occupation of Japan, 1945-1952: An Annotated Bibliography of Western-Language Materials,* 1974. Table, 27 notes, biblio. J. Powell

---

In this Subject Index, each index entry is a complete profile of the abstract and consists of one or more subject, geographic, and biographic descriptors, followed by the dates covered in the article. These descriptors are rotated so that the complete subject profile is cited under each of the terms in alphabetical order. Thus, indexing for the abstract shown above is located in five different places in the index:

Subject Index

Dissertations. Educational Reform. Historiography. Japan. Military Occupation. 1950-80. *940*
Educational Reform. Dissertations. Historiography. Japan. Military Occupation. 1950-80. *940*
Historiography. Dissertations. Educational Reform. Japan. Military Occupation. 1950-80. *940*
Japan. Dissertations. Educational Reform. Historiography. Military Occupation.
Military Occupation. Dissertations. Educational Reform. Historiography. Japan. 1950-80. *940*

A dash replaces second and subsequent identical leading terms. Cross-references in the form of *See* and *See-also* references are provided. Refer also to the notes at the head of the Subject Index.

Chou En-lai *See* Zhou Enlai.
Foreign Aid *See also* Economic Aid; Military Aid.

The separate Author Index lists the name of the author and abstract number.

Author Index

Tsai Wei-ping 120 520 521
Tsien Tsuen-hsuin 127 522
Tsou, Tang 522
Tsuchimochi, Gary H. 940
Tsumoda, Jun 941

INTRODUCTION

The history of trans-Pacific relations between the United States and the nations of East Asia involves a long and complex intermingling of bilateral and multilateral, regional and international alignments. US diplomatic, cultural, and social influences upon China, Hong Kong, Japan, the Koreas, and Taiwan have been significant since the early commercial and missionary activities of the late-18th and 19th centuries. During the past two decades strategic, economic, and political relations between East Asia and the United States have been transformed in the wake of changing international conditions. The normalization of Sino-American relations, the dominance of modernizing factions in post-Mao Chinese foreign policymaking, the convergence and divergence of US and Japanese economic interests, and the cautious attempts at rapprochement between the two Koreas are but a few of the factors that have caused major diplomatic shifts.

As a subject for scholarship, US-East Asian relations have been reinterpreted during the 20th century in response to international and domestic political changes. During the 1960's and 1970's the opening of heretofore inaccessible American political and military records and the "eclipse of domestic political controversy over the loss of China and the conduct of the Korean War"[1] gave rise to new revisionist interpretations of and approaches to US policy in Asia. As major Asian Studies programs emerged to address the need for systematic analysis of the region's unique development, critiques of the prewar and immediate postwar scholarship posed new questions about the effects of Western cultural, political, and linguistic biases.

To achieve bibliographic control of a major portion of this vast body of recent historical writing, *The United States in East Asia* provides comprehensive access to journal articles on the subject published from 1973 to 1984. The 1,176 article abstracts in this work are compiled from ABC-Clio's vast history database of nearly 400,000 records.

The bibliography is organized geographically in six chapters. The first chapter covers general articles discussing multilateral relations among the United States and two or more countries in the region, or with the region as a whole. Subsequent chapters for each East Asian nation include entries on bilateral relations with the United States. Although the historical period of the subject matter covered extends from the beginning of relations in the late 18th century, the bulk of the material concentrates on 20th-century political and cultural relations. The work includes literature on the Open Door policy, American missionary activities, US economic intervention in the region, the Korean War, the Pacific War with Japan (1941-45), arms sales to Taiwan, and US-East Asian finance and trade. Abstracts are organized alphabetically by author in each chapter.

The journal articles abstracted in this bibliography have been selected from the ABC-Clio history database, which surveys over 2,000 journals in some 40 languages from over 80 countries. The principal strength of this database's coverage of US-East Asian relations is in the literature published since 1973 in the United States, Canada, Eastern Europe, Western Europe, and the USSR. There are also a number of abstracts of articles published since 1973 in Indian, Australian, Taiwanese, Japanese, and Hong Kong Journals. (A reprint list of the periodicals covered in the ABC-Clio history database is available free upon request from ABC-Clio's Customer Services Department.)

Additional subject access to the abstracts and brief annotations in this book is through ABC-SPIndex—one of the most advanced and comprehensive indexing systems yet developed. Editors have taken great care to eliminate inconsistencies and ambiguities in the index, while achieving subject access to the highest degree of specificity possible by tailoring the index to the particular subject of this bibliography.

Many individuals contributed to publication of this volume. Pamela R. Byrne, Executive Editor of the ABC-Clio Research Guides, had overall responsibility for the creation of this volume and provided guidance essential to its production. Jessica S. Brown, Managing Editor, and Susan K. Kinnell, Assistant Editor, performed all editorial tasks, including extensive work on the index, conceptualization and definition of the scope of the topic, and coordination of all production of the book. The Data Processing Services Department, under the supervision of Ken Baser, Director, and Deborah Looker, Production Supervisor, ably manipulated the database to fit editorial specifications. Tanya Cullen, Production Assistant, created the unique cover design.

We are immensely grateful to the worldwide community of scholars who wrote the abstracts that constitute this volume. Without their timely and unfailing efforts, this contribution to the scholarship of US-East Asian relations would not have been possible.

Jessica S. Brown
Managing Editor

---

[1] Burns, Richard D., ed. *Guide to American Foreign Relations since 1700,* Chapter 27, "United States and East Asia, 1941-1953," Michael H. Hunt, contributing editor, p. 795 (Santa Barbara: ABC-Clio, 1983).

1

GENERAL

1. Ahn, Byung-Joon. THE U.S.-JAPAN-PRC TRIANGLE AND THE BALANCE OF POWER IN NORTHEAST ASIA. *Korea and World Affairs [South Korea] 1979 3(2): 163-182.*

2. Anderson, David L. BETWEEN TWO CULTURES: FREDERICK F. LOW IN CHINA. *California History 1980 59(3): 240-254.* Frederick F. Low, successful gold rush businessman, served as a California congressman and as state governor out of loyalty to the Union cause. In 1869 he was appointed minister to China. Low believed that peace and cooperation could lead to amicable relations between East and West, despite such incidents as the Tientsin massacre of 21 June 1870. Disillusionment set in, however, when Low went to Korea to ask for redress for the alleged murder of the crew of a wrecked American ship. An American squadron was forced to destroy five Korean forts, a diplomatic defeat which changed Low's views on relations with the Orient. Similar questions involving protocol in China finally resulted in his resignation in 1874. Not a gunboat diplomatist, Low at the end of his service predicted that Chinese-Western relations would embody hostility and violence rather than cooperation. Photos, 40 notes. A. Hoffman

3. Arnold, Joseph C. OMENS AND ORACLES. *US Naval Inst. Pro. 1980 106(8): 47-53.* Since 1945, it has become increasingly apparent that the military's use of information provided by various sources must improve. The Battle of the Bulge, the Chinese Communist entry into the Korean War, and the Soviet introduction of missiles into Cuba in the early 1960's are but three of the most recent failures of US military intelligence agencies to evaluate information properly. Once gathered, intelligence has been neither properly nor promptly interpreted. The United States must devise a way of ascertaining an enemy's capabilities, and should discard its policy of trying to determine enemy intentions. Secondary sources; 4 photos, 3 notes.

4. Beaumont, Roger A. RAPIERS VERSUS CLUBS: THE FITFUL HISTORY OF "SMART BOMBS." *J. of the Royal United Service Inst. for Defence Studies [Great Britain] 1981 126(3): 45-50.* In World War II, the Germans began using "glide bombs" with striking results during the Italian campaign, and sank several major Allied combat vessels with the new weapon. The United States developed controlled glide bombs late in the war, using them with considerable success in Europe and Asia. Successful strikes continued in both Korea and in Vietnam. Surprisingly, development of these weapons

consistently faltered after 1943, not necessarily due to budgets, but because of security constraints, misguided tactical assumptions, and resistance to change, even though use of guided "smart bombs" promised reduced aircraft and aircrew losses. Based on RAF documents, official histories, and secondary sources; table, photo, 31 notes. R. E. Bilstein

5. Beer, Lawrence W. AMERICAN APPROACHES TO EAST ASIA. *Colorado Q. 1973 22(1): 5-25.* Discusses misinformation and misunderstanding in the United States about East Asia, especially Korea, China, Japan, and Vietnam. American perspectives on East Asia require considerable change and updating. International education is a national necessity. There are means within the country's educational structure to achieve this. B. A. Storey

6. Benaerts, Pierre. NOUVEAU PARTAGE OU GRAND AFFRONTEMENT EN AFRIQUE [A new division or great confrontation in Africa]. *Écrits de Paris [France] 1976 355: 38-49.* Surveys the political situation in Africa, emphasizing the determining role of the United States, the USSR, and China.

7. Ben-Zvi, Abraham. SURPRISE ATTACKS AS A RESEARCH FIELD. *Peace Res. Rev. [Canada] 1979 8(4): 1-79.* Analyzes literature on nations' responses to surprise attacks and examines three specific cases of inadequate response to crisis: Pearl Harbor, the outbreak of the Korean War, and the outbreak of the October War.

8. Blechman, Barry M. and Powell, Robert. WHAT IN THE NAME OF GOD IS STRATEGIC SUPERIORITY? *Pol. Sci. Q. 1982-83 97(4): 589-602.* In 1981, Eugene V. Rostow stated, during the hearings confirming his nomination as director of the US Arms Control and Disarmament Agency, that an example of the utility of strategic superiority was the manner in which the Korean War was ended by a "nuclear hint from President Eisenhower." However, by his own admission, this threat was viable only because the United States was in a superior strategic position to the USSR. Therefore, unilateral strategic superiority may be an effective negotiating instrument, but there has been no unilateral superiority since the mid-1960's, when the USSR achieved rough strategic parity with the United States. With the present large arsenals and mutual devastation capabilities, the concept of strategic superiority is obsolete. Furthermore, Rostow's statement does not take into account that the USSR and China agreed to US terms more from a threat of general escalation than from any covert atomic threat. Primary sources; 26 notes. J. Powell

9. Bootsma, N. A. NEDERLAND OP DE CONFERENTIE VAN WASHINGTON, 1921-1922 [The Netherlands at the Washington Conference, 1921-22]. *Bijdragen en Mededelingen betreffende de Geschiedenis der Nederlanden [Netherlands] 1978 93(1): 101-126.* The Netherlands exerted little influence at the Washington Conference and felt that the big powers had not fully recognized its interest in the Far East. The Four-Power Treaty which was concluded at the conference between the United States, France, Japan, and Great Britain seemed to have weakened the Dutch position. Dutch Foreign Minister Hermann Adriaan van Karnebeek suggested that the nine powers at

the conference promise to recognize the status quo in the Pacific or recognize each others territorial rights. The four powers did agree to respect Dutch territory in the Far East although that promise was not embodied in a treaty. 74 notes. G. D. Homan

10. Buhite, Russell D. "MAJOR INTERESTS": AMERICAN POLICY TOWARD CHINA, TAIWAN, AND KOREA, 1945-1950. *Pacific Hist. Rev. 1978 47(3): 425-451.* Traditional geopolitical categories, which define China, Taiwan, and Korea as peripheral interests for the United States, are too facile to serve as the basis for an understanding of American foreign policy. Recently opened documents suggest that after 1945 US officials came to think of these areas in terms of a middle category between vital and peripheral: "major interests." The expansion of American power and military presence after World War II created this new category of interests. American officials did not merely bow to public pressure; they believed containment of communism in Asia was a major American interest after 1945. Officials were concerned about American credibility and the "lesson" of World War II, which dictated that the United States could permit no single hostile power to dominate Asia. At first only China was a major interest; Korea and Taiwan became so after the "loss" of China. Based on documents in *Foreign Relations,* 1946-50; 39 notes.
W. K. Hobson

11. Butera, J. L. RESCUE CONCEPTS, BEFORE AND AFTER. *Aerospace Hist. 1974 21(1): 8-11.* "Evaluates the impact and validity of US military rescue concepts before, during, and after World War II, Korea, and Vietnam."
S

12. Chan, F. Gilbert. CHINA'S REUNIFICATION AND THE TAIWAN QUESTION: THE SEEDS OF NATIONALISM: A BIBLIOGRAPHICAL SURVEY. *Can. Rev. of Studies in Nationalism [Canada] 1982 9(Biblio): 1-21.* Annotated bibliography of works published in English since 1972. 22 notes. R. Aldrich

13. Chan, Jeffery Paul; Chin, Frank; Inada, Lawson; and Wong, Shawn. RESOURCES FOR CHINESE AND JAPANESE AMERICAN LITERARY TRADITIONS. *Amerasia J. 1981 8(1): 19-32.* Criticizes the lack of study of Chinese and Japanese American literature, suggests several themes for investigation, and cites source materials. 4 notes. E. S. Johnson

14. Chang, Shu Yuan. CHINA OR TAIWAN: THE POLITICAL CRISIS OF THE CHINESE INTELLECTUAL. *Amerasia J. 1973 1(2): 47-81.* Reports the results of questionnaires concerning political attitudes sent to 750 Chinese students and 750 Chinese professionals in the United States in May 1970.

15. Chang, Y. C. U.S. RELATIONS WITH COMMUNIST CHINA. *Issues and Studies [Taiwan] 1977 13(11): 1-20.* US relations with the People's Republic of China (PRC) from 1949 to President Richard Nixon's 1972 visit were turbulent and they have not markedly improved. The major area of disagreement is the status of Taiwan and of the Republic of China (ROC). If

the United States should "derecognize" the ROC and abrogate the mutual defense treaty, it will lose credibility as an ally and possibly drive Taiwan into the Soviet Union's camp. The United States cannot afford to normalize relations with the PRC at any cost. Presented to the Asian American Assembly for Policy Research at the City College of New York on 30 April 1977. 63 notes. A. N. Garland

16. Chary, Srinivas. AN ANALYSIS OF INDO-AMERICAN RELATIONS: CHESTER BOWLES' VIEWS. *Indian J. of Am. Studies [India] 1980 10(1): 3-9.* Compares the cold war views of Chester Bowles and Jawaharlal Nehru concerning the best way to seek a stable balance of power. Bowles emphasized the importance of the Sino-Indian competition in the broader context of the East-West struggle, while Nehru emphasized the need to buttress the democratic and developmental infrastructure in India rather than the need to try militarily to contain China by an alliance of undemocratic and weak Asian states. Covers 1949-54. 17 notes. L. V. Eid

17. Ch'en, Ts'un-kung. LIEH CH'IANG TUI CHUNG KUO CHIN YÜN CHUN HUO TI FA TUAN [The first prohibition of arms sale to China]. *Bull. of Inst. of Modern Hist., Acad. Sinica [Taiwan] 1974 4(1): 315-349.* From 1919 to 1929, Great Britain, Spain, Portugal, the United States, Russia, Brazil, France, and Japan enforced a prohibition of arms sale to China. The move was initiated by the United States and was ostensibly to help China to end her civil wars. The real reason was primarily to break Japan's monopoly of arms trade in China. The author describes the background and events that led to the prohibition and analyzes the motives of the principal countries. He suggests that the prohibition prolonged instead of shortened the civil wars and that it severely crippled China's internal security and defence. Based on documents in the Foreign Office Files, Wai-chiao tang (China), the US Foreign Relations series, and secondary works in English, Chinese, and Japanese; 200 notes. C. C. Brown

18. Cheong, W. E. CHINA HOUSES AND THE BANK OF ENGLAND CRISIS OF 1825. *Business Hist. [Great Britain] 1973 15(1): 56-73.* Describes the financial structure of the China trade and its ramifications in Hong Kong, India, Manila, Latin America, the United States, and England. The Bank of England crisis of 1825 was but one of a number of crises affecting China houses 1823-27. Follows particularly two houses, Magniac and Co. and Yrissari and Co., the first international, the second regional, through unpublished company records (location unspecified). 7 tables. B. L. Crapster

19. Chi, Madeleine. CHINA AND UNEQUAL TREATIES AT THE PARIS PEACE CONFERENCE OF 1919. *Asian Profile [Hong Kong] 1973 1(1): 49-61.* Analyzes China's failures to achieve its goals in the Paris Peace Conference in 1919. The allied powers encouraged China to seek territorial control over the Shantung Peninsula and the annulment of the unequal treaties. Japan had seized German holdings in China during World War I and in the unequal treaties, imposed extraterritoriality, spheres of influence, and foreign control over customs, postal, and trading authorities. Japan prevailed in its claims for the former German special concessions in China and in the Pacific

islands north of the equator. To secure the establishment of the League of Nations Woodrow Wilson yielded in his initial support for Chinese diplomatic positions. British and French diplomats were unwilling to yield any imprerial prerogatives. Refusing to sign the humiliating Versailles Peace Treaty, the Chinese delegates resigned. Based on official diplomatic documents and secondary sources; 71 notes. S. H. Frank

20. Cho, Soon Sung. THE CHANGING PATTERN OF ASIAN INTERNATIONAL RELATIONS: PROSPECTS FOR THE UNIFICATION OF KOREA. *J. of Internat. Affairs 1973 27(2): 213-231.* As relations among the great powers ease, the two Koreas, fearful of being isolated pawns, move toward unification. South Korea follows the US in modifying its anticommunism and in seeking better relations with China and the USSR. Japan is warming to both Koreas, but would like to economically annex the South. North Korea wants immediate settlement of major problems; the South prefers a gradual approach. Talks have bogged down in a mutual distrust that will pass with time and contact, if the Korean people desire it. R. D. Frederick

21. Clark, Malcolm, Jr. THE BIGOT DISCLOSED: 90 YEARS OF NATIVISM. *Oregon Hist. Q. 1974 75(2): 108-190.* A history of bigotry in the Pacific Northwest, illustrated in the nativism of the period on the religious, social, and political scenes. Extreme religious sectarianism was evident at a very early date, exemplified by strong anti-Catholicism. The treatment of Chinese laborers was equally shameful, and became the subject of inflammatory journalism and oratory. Henry Francis Bowers and his American Protective Association brought bigotry into the political arena, followed in turn by the Guardians of Liberty, the I.W.W., and the revived Ku Klux Klan under the leadership of Edward Young Clark. The latter organization had phenomenal growth and influence in the 1920's, with Fred L. Gifford becoming the political boss of Oregon. Despite the Klan's demise, nativism unfortunately is not dead. 17 photos, 179 notes. R. V. Ritter

22. Clough, Ralph N. NORMALIZATION AND AFTER: RELATIONS WITH THE UNITED STATES. *Int. J. [Canada] 1979 34(4): 668-679.* The Taiwan issue was bypassed rather than resolved in the final diplomatic relations normalization agreement, announced in December 1978, between the Peoples Republic of China and the United States. Important differences over Taiwan remain, but the more valuable Washington and Tokyo connections are to China, the less likely it is to risk jeopardizinng them by attempting to take over Taiwan by force. M. J. Wentworth

23. Clubb, O. Edmund. AMERICA'S CHINA POLICY. *Current Hist. 1981 80(467): 250-253, 280-281.* Describes Sino-American relations since World War II, focusing on US policies vis-à-vis China and Taiwan since 1971.

24. Cohen, Warren I. COLD WARS AND SHELL GAMES: THE TRUMAN ADMINISTRATION AND EAST ASIA. *Rev. in Am. Hist. 1983 11(3): 430-436.* Reviews Robert J. McMahon's *Colonialism and Cold War: The United States and the Struggle for Indonesian Independence, 1945-1949* (1981), Russell D. Buhite's *Soviet-American Relations in Asia, 1945-1954* (1982), and

Robert M. Blum's *Drawing the Line: The Origin of the American Containment Policy in East Asia* (1982), which recall policies whereby preoccupation with Europe caused the United States to slight East Asian problems.

25. Cornelius, Wanda and Short, Thayne R. "WHEN TIGERS FLEW IN CHINA." *Am. Hist. Illus. 1979 14(1): 40-42.* Discusses shoulder patches designed for the American Volunteer Group and the 23rd Fighter Group depicting Flying Tigers, a popular image derived from their air defense in China against the invading Japanese, 1930's-45.

26. Dallek, Robert. LIMITED INFLUENCE: AMERICAN OPINION LEADERS AND EAST ASIA. *Rev. in Am. Hist. 1979 7(3): 401-405.* Review article on Warren I. Cohen's *The Chinese Connection: Roger S. Greene, Thomas W. Lamont, George E. Sokolosky, and American-East Asian Relations* (New York: Columbia U. Pr., 1978) emphasizes the import of international affairs and public opinion in forming American foreign policy toward China and Japan, 1900's-40's, and the relative lack of influence among apparent opinion leaders Greene, Lamont, and Sokolosky.

27. Davies, John Paton. AMERICA AND EAST ASIA. *Foreign Affairs 1977 55(2): 368-394.* Reviews 200 years of US relations with East Asia, an area which has at times appeared alien, exotic, and even irrelevant to Americans. Yet, as the scene of four major wars involving the US, East Asia has also received the "greatest outpouring of American altruism." The results have been physically and psychologically costly. We have learned the limits of American power, and the mutability of alliances and enmities. Perhaps the best thing that has come to America from East Asia is not wealth, ideas, or arts, but that which we so long resisted—Japanese and Chinese immigrants. The author was an American Foreign Service officer, 1931-54. W. R. Hively

28. Davis, Clarence B. LIMITS OF EFFACEMENT: BRITAIN AND THE PROBLEM OF AMERICAN COOPERATION AND COMPETITION IN CHINA, 1915-1917. *Pacific Hist. Rev. 1979 48(1): 47-63.* After World War I began, Japan and the United States invested in China. Great Britain, having less investment capital and encountering difficulty in financing the war effort in Europe, sought to restrain American and Japanese moves to increase their economic interests in China without jeopardizing their aid in defeating Germany. British diplomacy between 1915 and 1917 sought to play Japan and the United States against each other in order to protect British economic and political interests in China, while at the same time maintaining a limited cooperation among all three nations. 62 notes. R. N. Lokken

29. Dick, Everett N. THE ADVENTIST MEDICAL CADET CORPS AS SEEN BY ITS FOUNDER. *Adventist Heritage 1974 1(2): 18-27.* The Adventist Medical Cadet Corps was founded in 1934 by the author to train Adventist boys to serve in the Army medical department, if conscripted, in order to avoid the moral difficulties encountered with arms bearing and Sabbath observance in the service; covers World War II and Korean War service.

30. Diebel, Terry L. A GUIDE TO INTERNATIONAL DIVORCE. *Foreign Policy 1978 (30): 17-35.* The United States should be pragmatic enough to view the termination of security commitments as a viable and not necessarily unscrupulous policy. New realities make old promises irrelevant and dangerously restrictive. Periodic analyses of the costs and benefits of ending an agreement, rather than of the agreement itself, should determine decisions. If termination is indicated, careful procedures in accomplishing it can minimize unfavorable repercussions. President Jimmy Carter is approaching this issue wrongly, for he is publicly reinforcing the expendable commitment to Taiwan, while abruptly and undiplomatically weakening the critically important one to South Korea. Note. T. L. Powers

31. Diem, Bui. A NEW KIND OF WAR IN SOUTHEAST ASIA. *Asian Affairs: An Am. Rev. 1979 6(5): 273-281.* The author, a former Republic of Vietnam ambassador to the United States, analyzes the historical roots of conflict among the nations of Southeast Asia and the probabilities of renewed hostilities in the future. The Vietnamese invasion of Cambodia and the retaliatory Chinese invasion of Vietnam were turning points in the history of world Communism in terms of the balance of power (including Soviet and US interests) and in the attraction of Communism in general. The dominant factor is no longer East versus West, but Chinese versus Soviet Communism, with Vietnamese nationalism as the fulcrum between Southeast Asia and the rest of the world. Primary sources. R. B. Mendel

32. Dingman, Roger. STRATEGIC PLANNING AND THE POLICY PROCESS: AMERICAN PLANS FOR WAR IN EAST ASIA, 1945-1950. *Naval War Coll. Rev. 1979 32(6): 4-21.* Plans developed between World War II and the Korean war influenced strategic thinking about war in East Asia for the following quarter century. A consideration of how and why they were developed may be useful to the contemporary strategic planner and other military professionals. J

33. Dobbs, Charles M. AMERICAN MARINES IN NORTH CHINA, 1945-1946. *South Atlantic Q. 1977 76(3): 318-331.* To stall a communist takeover in north China in October 1945, 50,000 US soldiers of the Marine Amphibious Corps were sent in to accept the surrender of the 500,000 Japanese soldiers there. Quickly occupying ports, railroads, and the cities of Peking, Tsinan, and Tientsin, the marines settled into garrison duty. Both the Nationalists and the Communists soon began harrying the marines: the Communists by guerilla attacks, the Nationalists by demands for control of American-held areas. The Japanese troops were actually pressed into active service while they awaited repatriation, which was accomplished by mid-1946. Embarassed now by Soviet heckling, bewildered by the byzantine situation of the Chinese civil war, and confronted by the demands of US Senators Allen Ellender and Hugh Butler for their removal, the marines were slowly withdrawn by early 1947. 30 notes. W. L. Olbrich

34. Donnelly, J. B. PRENTISS GILBERT'S MISSION TO THE LEAGUE OF NATIONS COUNCIL, OCTOBER, 1931. *Diplomatic Hist. 1978 2(4): 373-387.* The appearance on 16 October 1931 of Prentiss B. Gilbert,

US Consul at Geneva, at an emergency session of the Council of the League of Nations, created high hopes that war between Japan and China, which had broken out on the night of 18-19 September, could be checked. Gilbert was under orders from Secretary of State Henry L. Stimson to join in calling for peace under the aegis of the Kellogg-Briand Pact to which the United States was a signatory (it had not signed the League Covenant). The pact was indeed invoked, but when the session ended on 24 October, little concrete progress toward peace had been made. A series of bad transatlantic telephone connections between Stimson and Gilbert, and the former's sensitivity to isolationist criticism at home hampered the American effort. Based on archival and other primary sources; 71 notes. L. W. Van Wyk

35. Dorwart, Jeffery M. JAMES CREELMAN, THE *NEW YORK WORLD* AND THE PORT ARTHUR MASSACRE. *Journalism Q. 1973 50(4): 697-701.* Describes James Creelman's sensational coverage of the Port Arthur massacre of the 1894-95 Sino-Japanese War for the *New York World.*

36. Dorwart, Jeffery M. PROVIDENCE CONSPIRACY OF 1894. *Rhode Island Hist. 1973 32(3): 91-96.* Summarizes a scheme developed by certain Rhode Island businessmen to supply China with a new weapon—perhaps some form of torpedo—to destroy the Japanese navy in the Sino-Japanese War of 1894-95. The incident suggests that Rhode Islanders may have sought solutions to their economic problems in foreign adventures. Based on documents in the National Archives, the Houghton Library (Harvard University), newspapers, and secondary accounts. P. J. Coleman

37. Dorwart, Jeffery M. THE UNITED STATES NAVY AND THE SINO-JAPANESE WAR OF 1894-1895. *Am. Neptune 1974 34(3): 211-218.* During the Sino-Japanese War the United States concentrated a large force of warships in the Far East and landed military forces on the Asian mainland. Throughout the war, however, "Navy commanders resisted diplomats, missionaries and politicians in their attempts to entangle American military forces in East Asian politics." Based on primary sources; 18 notes. G. H. Curtis

38. Dorwart, Jeffery M. WALTER QUINTIN GRESHAM AND EAST ASIA, 1894-1895: A REAPPRAISAL. *Asian Forum 1973 5(1): 55-63.* Reexamines the contributions of Walter Quintin Gresham to American foreign policy by discussing his approach to the Korean crisis of 1895 and the Sino-Japanese War of 1894-95. Primary sources; 50 notes. R. B. Orr

39. Dove, Kay L. RESOURCES ON CHINA, JAPAN, AND KOREA WITHIN THE PRESBYTERIAN HISTORICAL ARCHIVES IN PHILADELPHIA. *Ch'ing-shih Wen-t'i 1980 4(3): 130-134.* The Presbyterian Historical Society of Philadelphia contains considerable scholarly resources of interest to Asianists. Organized in 1852, the society preserved church history and as such became a repository for missionary reports, letters, journals, and artifacts, including, "the lapdesk of the first American Presbyterian missionary to be martyred in China." J. R. Pavia, Jr.

40. Edgerton, F. Van. THE CARLSON INTELLIGENCE MISSION TO CHINA. *Michigan Academician 1977 9(4): 419-432.* Chronicles the events of an intelligence mission performed for Franklin D. Roosevelt by Evans Carlson in China during the war with Japan, 1937-38.

41. English, H. Edward. OCEAN OF OPPORTUNITY? THE PACIFIC CONCEPT IN FOREIGN POLICY. *Int. Perspectives [Canada] 1976 (2): 10-14.* Discusses the US' reevaluated trade and economic relations with the industrialized nations of the Pacific region, specifically Japan, Australia, and New Zealand, in light of the failure of the Vietnam War, 1968-70's.

42. Etzold, Thomas H. FROM FAR EAST TO MIDDLE EAST: OVEREXTENSION IN AMERICAN STRATEGY SINCE WORLD WAR II. *US Naval Inst. Pro. 1981 107(5): 66-77.* Examines US errors in handling Far Eastern problems that might be repeated in the Middle East. Chief among those errors was the failure to commit an adequate amount of naval resources. 6 photos, map.   A. N. Garland

43. Gaddis, John Lewis. RECONSIDERATIONS: WAS THE TRUMAN DOCTRINE A REAL TURNING POINT? *Foreign Affairs 1974 52(2): 386-402.* Critics and defenders of the Truman Doctrine agree on two points: Truman's comments marked a turning point in U.S. foreign policy, and U.S. involvement grew out of that. The policy was in keeping with precedents. In spite of the administration's pronouncements, it had neither the intention nor the capability of policing the world. The policy of treating Communism as a monolith began with proof (Korea, 1950) that Communism was militarily aggressive. Until that point, one must distinguish between the *language* of the Truman Doctrine and the actual *policies* carried out by that administration. Based on U.S. Government publications, other primary works, and secondary works; 35 notes.   R. Riles

44. Gay, James Thomas. SOME OBSERVATIONS OF EASTERN SIBERIA, 1922. *Slavonic and East European Rev. [Great Britain] 1976 54(135): 248-261.* Lieutenant John Marie Creighton, an American naval intelligence officer, was assigned to two coastal settlements, on southern Kamchatka and the Bering Sea, to observe local developments and any possible Japanese interventionist moves. His reports to the US State Department are presented from papers in the National Archives in Washington. Map, 13 notes.
    R. E. Weltsch

45. Gayn, Mark. THE PROBLEMS OF TRANSITION TO A SETTLEMENT IN VIETNAM. *Internat. Perspectives [Canada] 1973 (1): 14-19.* The agreement between Washington and Hanoi will reduce an international conflict to a local civil war. The realignment of priorities by China, the United States, and the USSR meant an end to their direct involvement.   L. S. Frey

46. Ginneken, Jaap van. BACTERIOLOGICAL WARFARE. *J. of Contemporary Asia [Sweden] 1977 7(2): 130-152.* The United States began research into biological warfare in World War II. After the war the American military may have been assisted by Japanese such as Shiro Ishii, who had been involved

in the development of bacteriological weapons during the war. Although the US government claimed not to have used bacteriological warfare during the Korean War, outbreaks of disease and the appearance of unusual insects in North Korea and northeastern China during the Korean conflict, in addition to confessions from captured US airmen, make the American claim suspect. An investigation was made in 1952 by the International Scientific Commission for the Investigation of the Facts concerning Bacterial Warfare in Korea and China, but its conclusions were not decisive, and a serious investigation still needs to be performed. Based on secondary sources in English.

K. W. Berger

47. Goldstein, Jonathan. PREFACE TO THE ISSUE, "GEORGIA'S EAST ASIAN CONNECTION, 1733-1983." *West Georgia Coll. Studies in the Social Sci. 1983 22: ix-xii.* In addition to the post-1865 migrations of Chinese to Georgia and travel by Southerners in the Orient, trade has been an important factor in relations between Georgia and East Asia.

48. Gordon, Bernard K. THE UNITED STATES AND ASIA IN 1982: YEAR OF TENTERHOOKS. *Asian Survey 1983 23(1): 1-10.* US foreign policy in East Asia failed to resolve dissatisfaction with Japan on trade and defense matters or the continuing worry about the stability of relations with China. There was also unease among the ASEAN and other smaller states regarding the direction and consistency of the US role in East Asia. There were neither great losses for Asian policy nor important gains but there were some embarrassments and setbacks. Based on newspapers and radio broadcasts; 35 notes.

M. A. Eide

49. Gough, Barry M. JAMES COOK AND THE ORIGINS OF THE MARITIME FUR TRADE. *Am. Neptune 1978 38(3): 217-224.* Captain James Cook's last voyage opened a new branch of commerce quite by accident. Beginning in March 1778 in Nootka Sound, Cook's crews traded for curios and souvenirs along the northwest coast of North America, resulting in their acquisition of sea-otter pelts. Upon their arrival in Macao, China (November 1779), Cook's officers and crews discovered that the pelts were highly prized by the Chinese. Thus began the development of a profitable maritime fur trade along the rim of the Pacific basin. Based on published journals; 8 notes.

G. H. Curtis

50. Gumpel, Werner. DIE WIRTSCHAFTSPOLITIK DER UDSSR IM SPANNUNGSFELD ZWISCHEN CHINA UND USA [Economic policy of the USSR in the magnetic field between China and the USA]. *Osteuropa [West Germany] 1973 23(8): 572-584.* The USSR lacks sufficient capital for major resource development and is looking to the United States as a likely source, with West Germany and Japan as additional possibilities, and with oil and gas as prospective means of payment. China has been and may become again a useful trading partner supplying the Soviet Far East with needed foodstuffs and consumer goods. 11 notes.

R. E. Weltsch

51. Habibuddin, S. M. FRANKLIN D. ROOSEVELT'S ANTI-COLONIAL POLICY TOWARDS ASIA: ITS IMPLICATIONS FOR INDIA,

INDO-CHINA AND INDONESIA (1941-45). *J. of Indian Hist. [India] 1975 53(3): 497-522.* Examines the anticolonial policies of President Franklin D. Roosevelt with special emphasis on India, Indochina, and Indonesia. Roosevelt's support of Asian aspirations for national independence reflected a commitment to humanitarian ideals. The strategic importance of India after the Japanese capture of the British, French, and Dutch colonies in Asia prompted American officials to urge concessions from the British. Roosevelt wanted the imperialistic powers of Europe to follow the American example in the Philippines and grant independence to subject nationalities. By the end of World War II, however, American anticolonialist policy became passive, particularly after the publication of the William Phillips letter on India in the summer of 1944. War Department and Navy interests were opposed to any trusteeship system which would weaken American control of strategic islands in the Pacific Ocean. Although the Netherlands gave a wartime pledge of greater autonomy to its Asian colonies, neither France nor England indicated any willingness to liquidate overseas empires. Asian nationalists were inspired by the American president's continuing efforts in their behalf. Secondary sources; 105 notes. S. H. Frank

52. Haering, George. HOW TACTICAL AIR WORKS. *US Naval Inst. Pro. 1982 108(11): 60-65.* Argues from the experience of World War II, Korea, and Vietnam that to be successful a tactical air campaign must concentrate on one type of military target, recognize that technology changes tactical air warfare very little, remember that people will perform better than expected, and know that intelligence evaluation can be misleading. K. J. Bauer

53. Hardin, Thomas L. AMERICAN PRESS AND PUBLIC OPINION IN THE FIRST SINO-JAPANESE WAR. *Journalism Q. 1973 50(1): 54-59.*

54. Hartig, Thomas H. ROBERT LANSING AND EAST ASIAN-AMERICAN RELATIONS: A STUDY IN MOTIVATION. *Michigan Academician 1974 7(2): 191-199.* Examines Secretary of State Robert Lansing's foreign policy, particularly toward Japan, prior to World War I. S

55. Hayes, Harold B., III. THE IRON(IC) HORSE FROM NIKOLSK. *Military Rev. 1982 62(5): 18-28.* In the summer of 1918 the Bolsheviks were at war with the Poles, the Czechs, the White Russians, the Chinese, the Japanese, and indirectly the British. President Wilson decided to send 10,000 US Army troops under General William S. Graves to Siberia to maintain some order. They intervened in what would have otherwise been bloody massacres by the Japanese, and were instrumental in transporting by rail and protecting a peace delegation which entered Vladivostok in 1920, thereby peacefully eliminating the last White Russian stronghold. Based on official reports and a diary kept by Major Harold B. Hayes, the author's grandfather; 23 notes. J. Powell

56. Hinton, Harold C. THE UNITED STATES AND EXTENDED SECURITY COMMITMENTS: EAST ASIA. *Ann. of the Am. Acad. of Pol. and Social Sci. 1981 (457): 88-108.* In East Asia and the Western Pacific the United States faces an impressive recent Soviet military buildup, continuing and serious tension in Korea, a Japan that to date has not done much to put

itself in a viable defensive posture, and potential for further unrest in Southeast Asia. In the last year or two of the Carter administration, accordingly, a trend begun a decade earlier toward American military disengagement from the region was reversed. The Reagan administration is almost certain to maintain this reversal and to cultivate closer relations with South Korea and Taiwan than did its predecessor, while trying at the same time to establish a strategic relationship of some sort with China. Covers 1960-80. J/S

57. Holbo, Paul S. PRESIDENTS, PROFESSORS, AND ASIAN POLICY, 1899-1945. *Rev. in Am. Hist. 1980 8(2): 277-283.* Review essay of Noel H. Pugach's *Paul S. Reinsch: Open Door Diplomat in Action* (Millwood, N.Y.: KTO Pr., 1979), Michael Schaller's *The U.S. Crusade in China, 1938-1945* (New York: Columbia U. Pr., 1979), and Richard E. Welch, Jr.'s *Response to Imperialism: The United States and the Philippine-American War, 1899-1902* (Chapel Hill: U. of North Carolina Pr., 1979).

58. Holmes, John W. THE I.P.R. IN RETROSPECT: A REVIEW ARTICLE. *Pacific Affairs [Canada] 1974/75 47(4): 515-520.* Reviews *The Institute of Pacific Relations, Asian Scholars and American Politics* (Seattle: University of Washington Press, 1974) by John N. Thomas. Discusses the persecution of the Institute of Pacific Relations by the McCarran Committee in 1951-52, comparing the "conspiracy mentality" of that time to present public opinion on the Watergate trials. The IPR was viewed as a conspiracy and a tool of Moscow. By instilling fear and stirring up anti-intellectual hatreds, the China Lobby and others used IPR as a scapegoat for the fall of the Chiang Kai-shek government in China. S. H. Frank

59. Hoyt, Frederick B. GEORGE BRONSON REA: FROM OLD CHINA HAND TO APOLOGIST FOR JAPAN. *Pacific Northwest Q. 1978 69(2): 61-70.* Convinced that the United States could uplift underdeveloped areas of the world with its industrial might and foreign railroad construction, George Bronson Rea promoted America's brand of the Open Door Policy to keep European powers and Japan from monopolizing China's resources. By the 1920's, however, Rea became convinced that only a strong alliance between Japan and the United States could bring progress to China and save it from Communism. He ardently defended Japan's takeover of Manchuria and exercised considerable influence through his newspaper *Far Eastern Review* until his death in 1936. Primary sources; 2 photos, 31 notes. M. L. Tate

60. Hoyt, Frederick B. "WHEN A FIELD WAS FOUND TOO DIFFICULT FOR A MAN, A WOMAN SHOULD BE SENT": ADELE M. FIELDE IN ASIA, 1865-1890. *Historian 1982 44(3): 314-334.* Adele M. Fielde, a transitional figure, illustrates the changing emphasis of the Protestant mission movement from wives to single women as evangelists. Recounts Fielde's life, including her introduction to the Orient in 1865, her missionary work as an American Baptist in Siam, her assignment to Swatow in China in 1872, and her permanent return to the United States in 1890. The major focus of her life as both a missionary and reformer was the condition of women and the reformation of society. Primary sources; 63 notes. R. S. Sliwoski

61. Hsu, King-yi. AMERICA'S NATIONAL INTERESTS AND ITS CONTINUED SUPPORT OF THE REPUBLIC OF CHINA. *Issues & Studies [Taiwan] 1974 10(6): 69-77.* Discusses political, economic and strategic factors in US foreign policy toward China and Taiwan during the 1950's-70's.

62. Hsu, King-yi. SINO-AMERICAN RELATIONS AND THE SECURITY OF TAIWAN. *Asian Affairs: An Am. Rev. 1978 6(1): 48-66.* Explores the Taiwan issue as an obstacle to full diplomatic relations between Washington and Peking. Analyzes the Nixon and Ford administrations' formula for normalization and its ability to convince public opinion and Congress of its viability. Examines the Washington-Moscow-Peking triangular relationship, consequences for American business, Taiwan's security, the Peking regime, and international law. Primary and secondary sources; media and government reports; 81 notes. R. B. Mendel

63. Hungdah, Chiu. NORMALIZING RELATIONS WITH CHINA: SOME PRACTICAL AND LEGAL PROBLEMS. *Asian Affairs: An Am. Rev. 1977 5(2): 67-87.* Discusses problems in Taiwan-US-China relations: the 1972 Shanghai communiqué; the legal status of Taiwan as perceived by the participants and by international law and practice; the impact of normalization of relations; possible responses of Taiwan to US moves toward normalization with China. 16 notes. R. B. Mendel

64. Inoue, Shigenobu. REAGAN'S ASIA-PACIFIC POLICY. *Issues & Studies [Taiwan] 1981 17(9): 27-34.* The Reagan administration has shifted the United States from geopolitics to the ideological values of the John Foster Dulles (1885-1959) era. It is actively working to upgrade the defense of non-Communist nations in the Asia-Pacific area, while limiting relations with mainland China to the common interest of opposition to the Soviet Union. International think tanks on anti-communism, located in the United States and Taiwan, could provide important support to this policy. Based on U.S. documents and Chinese, Japanese, and U.S. media reports; 12 notes.
J. A. Krompart

65. Jan, George P. PUBLIC OPINION AND AMERICAN POLICY TOWARD THE SINO-JAPANESE WAR, 1937-1945. *Asian Profile [Hong Kong] 1979 7(4): 319-334.* This paper examines American mass public opinion on the Sino-Japanese War from 1937 to 1945 as well as American policy toward the war during the same period, in order to ascertain the relationship between the two. Public opinion polls dealing with the war are summarized chronologically with respect to American government policy on the same issues. There was general consistency between American policy and public opinion. Based on polls conducted by the American Institute of Public Opinion, Fortune Magazine, National Opinion Research Center, and Office of Public Opinion Research; 5 tables, 77 notes. J. Powell

66. Keatley, Robert. EAST ASIA: THE RECESSION ARRIVES. *Foreign Affairs 1983 61(3): 692-713.* During 1982, the East Asian nations' economic growth rate declined as exports to the Western industrialized nations decreased, resulting from the worldwide recession. This situation also contributed

to rising protectionist sentiment and the worsening of economic relations between the United States and Japan. The American call for Japan to increase its defense spending was resisted by the Japanese and the ASEAN nations. China sought to improve relations with the Soviet Union and with developing nations, while maintaining relations with the United States. 6 notes.

A. A. Englard

67. Kihl, Young Whan. CHANGING U.S.-JAPAN RELATIONS AND KOREAN SECURITY. *J. of Korean Affairs 1976 6(2): 31-39.* Surveys the foreign relations of Japan and the United States with Korea during the 20th century. After World War II, Japan generally followed the lead of the United States. President Richard M. Nixon's rapprochement with Peking in 1971 shifted the East Asian balance of power, and Japan began to enunciate an independent policy based on separate geographic, economic, and military considerations. South Korea is a "penetrated system" because of foreign influence on domestic policy. As interests and policies shift among the four powers (Russia, China, Japan, and the United States) the future of Korea becomes more uncertain. Based on news articles and secondary sources; 18 notes.

D. M. Bishop

68. Kil, Soong-Hoom. WASHINGTON-TOKYO-BEIJING RELATIONS IN THE POST-1978 YEARS. *Korea & World Affairs [South Korea] 1981 5(4): 537-557.* Analyzes the 1978 normalization of diplomatic relations between the United States, Japan, and China, focusing on the political implications of the Chinese economic modernization program.

69. Kim Won-Mo. AMERICAN "GOOD OFFICES" IN KOREA, 1882-1905. *J. of Social Sci. and Humanities [South Korea] 1975 (41): 93-139.* The Korean-American Treaty of 1882 contained a good offices clause on the model of the American-Chinese Treaty of 1858. With the ratification of the treaty, the United States recognized Korea's independence, but a review of American foreign policy decisions on Korea demonstrates a pattern of nonfulfillment of its obligations. The United States lent Korea no meaningful support during either the Sino- or Russo-Japanese wars and failed to recognize the pleas of various royal envoys after the Japanese established the protectorate in 1905. The flagrant breach of faith abandoned Korea to brutal Japanese overlordship. 170 notes.

D. M. Bishop

70. Knapp, Ronald G. and Hauptman, Lawrence M. CIVILIZATION OVER SAVAGERY: THE JAPANESE, THE FORMOSAN FRONTIER, AND UNITED STATES INDIAN POLICY, 1895-1915. *Pacific Hist. Rev. 1980 49(4): 647-652.* After Japan acquired Taiwan as a result of the Sino-Japanese War of 1895, the Japanese followed the example Americans had set in solving their Indian problem by using a moving line of frontier posts and punitive expeditions to gain control of the Formosan interior from hostile aborigines. The Japanese studied US Indian policy in formulating their own Formosan aboriginal policy, but drew from many other sources, especially the Chinese. Based on correspondence in the records of the Bureau of Indian Affairs and Department of State in the National Archives and other primary sources; 17 notes.

R. N. Lokken

71. Kosobud, Richard and Stokes, Houston. TRADE PEACE IN THE PACIFIC THROUGH A FREE TRADE AREA? *J. of Internat. Affairs 1974 28(1): 54-66.* Unless Japan's power to export and the US imbalance of payments are institutionally rearranged, the two could be forced into economic warfare since Japan and other Pacific powers are effectively excluded from the European economic community. The most likely solution is a Pacific free trade area which would feature regional agencies for trade and development, currency and payment, and investment. Due to US-USSR cooperation, China would decline membership, leaving the Pacific free trade area to US and Japanese domination. R. D. Frederick

72. Krause, Walter and Mathis, F. John. THE U.S. POLICY SHIFT ON EAST-WEST TRADE. *J. of Internat. Affairs 1974 28(1): 25-37.* With the rise of nonaligned nations and the death of Stalin in 1953, the Soviets launched a "trade-aid offensive" to challenge US dominance. By 1971 the United States realized its commonality of goals with the USSR and China and decided to join its western allies in trading with the East. The East seeks western technology, consumer goods, credit, and grain; the United States seeks better trade balances, reduced political tension, and possible access to Soviet raw materials. R. D. Frederick

73. Kulikov, V. I. PROBLEMA TAIVANIA V KITAISKO-AMERI-KANSKIKH OTNOSHENIIAKH [The Taiwan factor in Sino-American relations]. *Narody Azii i Afriki [USSR] 1980 (6): 131-137.* The establishment of diplomatic relations with China in 1979 and abrogation of the 1955 defense treaty with Taiwan did not affect American support for Taiwan's independence, thus precluding its unification with mainland China. While Chinese propaganda claims its treaty with the United States is a victory of Chinese foreign policy, the treaty, in fact, shows the Chinese government's purely pragmatic approach to the Taiwan problem, oblivious to the national interests of the Chinese people. 14 notes. N. Frenkley

74. Kupperman, Karen Ordahl. APATHY AND DEATH IN EARLY JAMESTOWN. *J. of Am. Hist. 1979 66(1): 24-40.* Uses an analogy between prison camps during World War II and the Korean War and the early Jamestown settlement to demonstrate the connection between nutritional diseases and psychological factors such as fear and despair. In both cases, malnutrition and psychological factors interacted to produce a withdrawal from life. Because nutritional diseases produce symptoms that appear psychological, both prisoners of war and early settlers would seem to be suffering from inexplicable melancholy. This was especially true in Jamestown, where a complex interaction between environmental and psychological factors produced high death rates between 1607 and 1624. 88 notes. T. P. Linkfield

75. LaFeber, Walter. ROOSEVELT, CHURCHILL, AND INDOCHINA, 1942-1945. *Am. Hist. Rev. 1975 80(5): 1277-1295.* During 1942-44 Franklin D. Roosevelt hoped to place the French colonies in Southeast Asia under an international trusteeship after the war. He further hoped that China would become the "policeman" in the area, and that the United States could work through China to stabilize and develop Southeast Asia. The president believed

that once this precedent was established and China became a great power, the British colonies would also be given their independence and opened to world trade. Roosevelt thought little of the French and strongly disliked the new French leader, General Charles de Gaulle. Fully realizing Roosevelt's plans, Winston Churchill and the British Foreign Office concluded by 1943 that they needed de Gaulle's cooperation if British interests in Asia and Europe were to be protected after the war. As they worked to undercut Roosevelt's policy, they were helped by European specialists in the US Department of State, who also wanted to restore French power, and, most important, by the near-collapse of the Chinese government in 1944. After the summer of 1944 Roosevelt gave up in large measure on Chiang Kai-shek, and as he did so (and as Southeast Asia became less important to American military strategy), he slowly allowed the French to return to Southeast Asia. Above all, Roosevelt wanted an orderly, non-revolutionary Southeast Asia open to Western interests. It was therefore not illogical that when his trusteeship plan failed, he allowed the colonial powers to reenter the area. A

76. Lee, Yur-Bok. AMERICAN POLICY TOWARD KOREA DURING THE SINO-JAPANESE WAR OF 1894-1895. *J. of Social Sci. and Humanities [South Korea] 1976 (43): 81-97.* The American government was opposed to the Japanese policy of domination in Korea, and it tried to exert a moral influence to restrain Japan during the Sino-Japanese War. Japan refused good offices tendered in accordance with the Korean-American treaty of 1882. At China's request, American diplomats in Tokyo and Peking played important roles in mediating between the two belligerents, but the United States refused to have any influence on the final treaty. Based on American, Japanese, Russian, and British diplomatic documents and secondary sources; 86 notes.

D. M. Bishop

77. Li, Victor H. TAIWAN AND AMERICA'S CHINA POLICY: AN INTRODUCTION. *Int. J. of Pol. 1979-80 9(4): 1-22.* The Taiwan question may be the major source of friction between the United States and the People's Republic of China (PRC). The United States normalized relations with the PRC without jeopardizing Taiwan's security or economic well-being. It has not defined Taiwan's status, but to maintain existing ties the United States will have to apply to Taiwan the concept of "a de facto entity with international personality." Internal changes are developing in Taiwan as its old "Mainlander" leadership dies off; if Taiwan moves toward independence, the United States may have to choose between support for self-determination and a possible rupture with the PRC. Covers 1972-79. Based on US government documents; 40 notes. R. E. Noble

78. Longmuir, D. Gordon. JAPAN AND CHINA: THE ROOTS OF A NEW ERA IN EAST ASIA. *Internat. Perspectives [Canada] 1973: 36-39.* Examines effects on Japanese foreign relations of the "China lobby" in Japan which favored "at least a two-China policy"; the "American decision to seek detente with China"; and the accession of Tanaka as prime minister. Even with the "establishment of diplomatic relations" with China in September 1972, problems remain. Reviews Japan's relations with Taiwan, Russia, and the United States and the border disputes with China. L. S. Frey

79. Meyer, Armin H. DETENTE WITH MAINLAND CHINA: THE VIEW FROM JAPAN. *Foreign Service J. 1974 51(11): 8-11.* Explains the causes for Japan's consternation at President Nixon's announcement of plans to visit China in 1971. S

80. Millar, T. B. THE "ASIAN QUADRILATERAL": AN AUSTRALIAN VIEW. *Australian Outlook [Australia] 1973 27(2): 134-139.* The idea of a multiple balance of power, an Asian quadrilateral composed of China, Japan, the Soviet Union and the United States cannot adequately explain the Asian situation. South Asia is an area of Sino-Soviet confrontation; Southeast Asia involves all four powers. In the northeast the quadrilateral comes closest to reality. The only fixed aspect is the Sino-Soviet split. E. Plumridge

81. Morley, James William. THE SEARCH FOR A NORMALIZATION FORMULA. *J. of Asiatic Studies [South Korea] 1977 20(2): 105-120.* Reviews the political and economic aftermath of the establishment of diplomatic relations between Japan and China in 1972, and assesses the prospects for normalization between China and the United States. The US-Taiwan relationship is the stumbling block. Paper presented at the Conference on Triangular Relations of Mainland China, the Soviet Union, and North Korea, Seoul, 23-25 June 1977. 5 tables, 2 notes. M. Elmslie

82. Morse, David B. EYE IN THE SKY: THE BOEING F-13. *Am. Aviation Hist. Soc. J. 1981 26(2): 150-168.* Describes the development and use of the Boeing F-13, the photoreconnaissance version of the B-29 Superfortress bomber, during 1944-54; the aircraft served with distinction during World War II and the Korean War.

83. Mughal, N. A. ANALYSIS OF AMERICAN CONGRESSIONAL AND PUBLIC OPINION ON THE MANCHURIAN CRISIS, 1931-33. *Pakistan Horizon [Pakistan] 1975 28(2): 24-47.* Analyzes American Congressional and public opinion during the Japanese attack on China.

84. Nagai, Yōnosuke. THE PITFALLS OF A PARTIAL PEACE. *Japan Interpreter [Japan] 1979 12(3-4): 289-309.* Examines the international security climate created by the conclusion of a Japan-China treaty, which would establish a "partial" peace in East Asia, excluding the USSR. The Japan-China alliance fits with the rise of anti-Soviet, "human rights" diplomacy in the United States, but it may unduly threaten the USSR and provoke unanticipated Soviet reactions. Discusses the development of US policy worldwide and its reflection in East Asia, the relationship of the antihegemony clause demanded by the Chinese to the constitution of Japan, and the economic consequences of a Sino-Japanese treaty. Article first appeared in *Chūō kōron* (May 1978), intended partly as a response to an earlier review of US policy by Sakamoto Yoshikasu, which is also to appear in translation in *Japan Interpreter.* S

85. Nuernberger, Richard. DIE CHINESISCHE FRAGE AUF DER PARISER FRIEDENSKONFERENZ 1919 [The Chinese question at the Paris peace conference of 1919]. *Festschrift für Hermann Heimpel* (Göttingen: Vandenhoeck & Ruprecht, 1971 1: 238-256). To obtain Japan's ratification of

the League of Nations treaty, President Wilson agreed to the absorption by Japan of German possessions in China. This decision rejected the policy of limiting Japan's influence by compelling the return of Shantung and Kiaochow to China and resulted in the loss of US prestige in the Far East after World War I. Based on the official publications of the Paris Peace Conference.

B. Alltman

86. Ogram, Ernest W., Jr. GEORGIA, ATLANTA, AND EAST ASIAN WORLD: AN ECONOMIST'S OVERVIEW OF INTERACTIONS SINCE WORLD WAR II. *West Georgia Coll. Studies in the Social Sci. 1983 22: 81-86.* Most East Asian countries have established a commercial presence in Georgia with headquarters in Atlanta, an international city, and Georgia firms, like Coca Cola, have made commitments in Asia.

87. Okita, Saburo. JAPAN, CHINA AND THE UNITED STATES: ECONOMIC RELATIONS AND PROSPECTS. *Foreign Affairs 1979 57(5): 1090-1110.* The countries of Asia are experiencing high levels of economic growth which will in all likelihood continue in the decades ahead. As the economic fortunes of Japan and the United States are closely interwoven, both nations must learn to solve their economic disagreements and coordinate their efforts to assist China to fulfill its ambitious developmental programs. The stability of the entire Pacific region is at stake.

M. R. Yerburgh

88. Olsen, Edward A. ASIAN PERCEPTIONS OF THE US-SOVIET BALANCE. *Asian Affairs: An Am. Rev. 1981 8(5): 263-280.* Examines the motives and methods of manipulation of China, Japan, North and South Korea, and Taiwan as each attempts to influence US policies in its favor, sometimes to the detriment of its neighbors, but usually for the regional good. Addresses the dilemma of how to be strong enough to protect themselves from Soviet intervention, yet not so strong as to provoke a lessening of US commitment to the area.

R. B. Mendel

89. Olsen, Edward A. CHANGING U.S. INTERESTS IN NORTHEAST ASIA. *World Affairs 1981 143(4): 346-365.* Describes US interest in Northeast Asia since the Korean War, the postwar reconstruction of Japan and South Korea, and the need of the United States to reevaluate its diplomatic and economic relations with these two nations.

90. Olsen, Edward A. THE NIXON DOCTRINE IN EAST ASIAN PERSPECTIVE. *Asian Forum 1973 5(1): 17-28.* Argues that the approach to East Asia expressed by the Nixon Doctrine is not new, but a reaffirmation of former guidelines. Discusses the application of the Nixon Doctrine to Vietnam, Korea, and Japan, assessing its success, failures, and prospects for the future. Primary and secondary sources; 31 notes.

R. B. Orr

91. Overholt, William H. PRESIDENT NIXON'S TRIP TO CHINA AND ITS CONSEQUENCES. *Asian Survey 1973 13(7): 707-721.* Discusses the diplomatic and foreign policy consequences of the United States-China rapprochement, particularly in relation to Japan.

S

92. Panda, Rajaram. SINO-US RELATIONS: THE TAIWAN FACTOR. *China Report [India] 1982 18(5): 3-16.* Despite the temporary easing of tensions in US-China relations, Chinese unease over US dealings with Taiwan is unlikely to be alleviated soon, an anomaly institutionalized in the Taiwan Relations Act (US 1979). The Taiwan issue is unlikely to push China to mend fences with the Soviet Union but the likelihood of deteriorating China's relations with the capitalist world cannot be ruled out. Regional and global stability, healthy US-China relations, and peace in East Asia would be enhanced by a solution of the Taiwan issue. 43 notes. J. V. Coutinho

93. Pant, H. G. INDIAN FOREIGN POLICY UNDER MRS. INDIRA GANDHI, 1966-71. *Pol. Sci. Rev. [India] 1974 13(1-4): 327-362.* An overview of Indian foreign policy toward the United States, the USSR, and communist China, 1946-71.

94. Park, Han Shik. CHINESE FOREIGN POLICY ORIENTATIONS AND THE KOREAN PENINSULA. *Korea & World Affairs [South Korea] 1980 4(2): 301-321.* Relates relevant domestic political situations to changes in China's foreign policy, 1950-80, focusing on its policies on Korea, and suggests that the desire for a status quo on the Korean peninsula might include the concept of cross-recognition, in which China would normalize relations with South Korea as would the United States with North Korea.

95. Park, Yung H. JAPAN'S PERSPECTIVES AND EXPECTATIONS REGARDING AMERICA'S ROLE IN KOREA. *Orbis 1976 20(3): 761-784.* For several years in the early 1970's, and because of Richard Nixon's visit to mainland China in 1972 and the apparent thaw in Seoul-Pyongyang relations that same year, Japan's attitude toward North Korea changed and Japanese industry rushed to take advantage of this new market. But by 1974, the situation in Asia had again changed, and while many Japanese industrial leaders wanted to continue business-as-usual with North Korea, they represented a minority and business relations, accordingly, have cooled. Today, Japans' leaders would like the United States to use its influence with China and the USSR to promote stabilization on the Korean peninsula, and would like to see the two-Korea status quo accepted for the immediate future. Japan also hopes that North Korea will ease its hard line toward South Korea so that Japanese industry will soon be able to resume its once-profitable relations with North Korea, while maintaining its good relations with South Korea. Based on a presentation at the international symposium held 6-7 February 1976 at Arizona State University, Tempe. 83 notes. A. N. Garland

96. Pearson, Alden B., Jr. A CHRISTIAN MORALIST RESPONDS TO WAR: CHARLES C. MORRISON, *THE CHRISTIAN CENTURY* AND THE MANCHURIAN CRISIS, 1931-33. *World Affairs 1977 139(4): 296-307.* Discusses *The Christian Century,* the most prominent and outspoken Christian periodical on the Japanese threat to peace during the crisis in Manchuria, and its editor, Charles C. Morrison, who had a significant role in determining American foreign policy.

97. Pelz, Stephen E. BIG OIL AND PEARL HARBOR. *Rev. in Am. Hist. 1976 4(1): 115-119.* Review article prompted by Irvine H. Anderson, Jr.'s *The Standard-Vacuum Oil Company and United States East Asian Policy, 1933-1941* (Princeton, New Jersey: Princeton U. Pr., 1975) which examines the interrelationship of American foreign investment in oil production in the Dutch East Indies and foreign policy toward East Asia.

98. Peragallo, James L. CHENNAULT: GUERRILLA OF THE AIR. *Aerospace Hist. 1973 20(1): 1-6.* Claire Lee Chennault and his band of American fliers fought the Japanese in China, 1937-45.   S

99. Pestana, Harold R. HISTORY OF GEOLOGY IN JAPAN AND NORTHERN ASIA: DOCUMENTS PUBLISHED BY THE UNITED STATES CONGRESS. *Japanese Studies in the Hist. of Sci. [Japan] 1974 13: 69-73.* Discusses some relatively unknown early geological and geographical works on Japan, China, Manchuria, and Siberia published, 1848-83, by the US Congress and generally not accessible to Japanese scholars.

100. Peters, Gayle; Goldstein, Jonathan; and Kirk, Merlin. HISTORICAL DOCUMENTS RELATING TO ASIAN-AMERICANS AND TO EAST ASIA IN THE ATLANTA REGIONAL ARCHIVES BRANCH. *West Georgia Coll. Studies in the Social Sci. 1983 22: 3-12.* The Atlanta archives, a branch of the US National Archives, contains data, reaching to the 18th century, from US agencies dealing with East Asia and with Asian Americans.

101. Petrov, D. JAPAN'S PLACE IN US ASIAN POLICY. *Int. Affairs [USSR] 1978 (10): 52-59.* Over the past two years, Japan has been encouraged to remilitarize and take a more active role in influencing Asian nations on behalf of the United States, which is blatantly using its Japanese allies to acquire closer ties with Peking and embark on an anti-Soviet course.

102. Phongpaichit, Pasuk. THE OPEN ECONOMY AND ITS FRIENDS: THE DEVELOPMENT OF THAILAND. *Pacific Affairs [Canada] 1980 53(3): 440-460.* Surveys the economic history of Thailand, especially the efforts of Great Britain, the United States, and finally Japan to develop an open economy. Although never formally colonized, Siam was opened to foreign trade in 1855 and operated a simple rural rice-exporting economy until the 1930's. Even with the advent of a constitutional monarchy in 1932, economic patterns continued much the same until the end of World War II. Capitalizing on the huge profits made in Thailand during the Korean War, the United States played the role of chief sponsor for a coalition of Chinese businessmen and Thai military and civil servants who held economic and political power. By the 1960's, Thailand became the regional headquarters for international organizations such as UNICEF, the Economic Commission for Asia and the Far East, UN Food and Agriculture Organization, and Southeast Asia Treaty Organization. The simple one-crop, rural economy shifted to an international, diversified, urban, and industrial model. During the 1970's Japanese business and investment interests also continued Thailand's economic development with an emphasis on the idea of an open economy. Secondary sources; 38 notes.
S. H. Frank

103. Poliakov, N. PUT' K BEZOPASNOSTI V INDIISKOM OKEANE I PERSIDSKOM ZALIVE [The road to security in the Indian Ocean and Persian Gulf]. *Mirovaia Ekonomika i Mezhdunarodnye Otnosheniia [USSR] 1981 (1): 62-73.* Focuses on the dramatic situation in this region where aggressive reactionary forces and the belligerent circles of the United States and China prevent creation of conditions favorable for making the region one of international stability and peace.

104. Ponnwitz, A. J. LIMITED WAR AND THE WAR POWERS RESOLUTION. *Marine Corps Gazette 1980 64(10): 35-41.* Discusses the US concept of limited war since the end of World War II, focusing on the Korean War, the Vietnam War, and most recently, the Russian invasion of Afghanistan in December 1979, and the passing of the War Powers Act (US, 1973) to insure that the Congress and the President agree collectively to enter and continue hostilities.

105. Porter, Gareth. THE GREAT POWER TRIANGLE IN SOUTHEAST ASIA. *Current Hist. 1980 79(461): 161-164, 195-196.* Before March-April 1978 China refrained from interfering in the struggle between Vietnam and Pol Pot's regime in Cambodia in an attempt to improve relations with the USSR, while the United States, urged by the Association of Southeast Asian Nations (ASEAN), who sensed Vietnam's desire for independence from Moscow, moved toward normalization of relations with Vietnam; that spring, however, the United States and Japan moved to form a strategic alignment with China against the Soviet Union, which led to a strengthening of ties between Vietnam and Moscow and to an intensification of hostilities between Cambodia and Vietnam.

106. Quo, F. Quei. JAPAN, CHINA AND THE U.S.: THE NEW TRILATERALISM OF ASIA. *Int. Perspectives [Canada] 1979 (Mar-Apr): 23-26.* The peace and friendship treaty between Japan and China, and the normalization of relations between China and the United States, have inaugurated a new era in the international politics of Asia. Reasons for the new scheme of things in the Far East include the failure of detente and internal conflicts within the two major ideological camps. The coalition among these three nations effectively controls Soviet ambitions in the area and should create conditions of peace and stability for the immediate future, but the theater of struggle for domination among the superpowers is likely to shift to Southeast Asia. Photo.
E. S. Palais

107. Rhee, T. C. JAPANESE-AMERICAN RELATIONS AND THE U.S.-CHINA DETENTE: WHAT BALANCE BETWEEN THE TWO? (PART II). *Asia Q. [Belgium] 1978 (4): 247-261.* Continued from a previous article (see abstract in this chapter). Speculates that, since the deaths of Chou En-lai and Mao Tse-tung, the People's Republic of China and the USSR could begin to resolve their differences, which might lead the way to Soviet recognition of Japanese claims to certain islands held by the USSR since 1945, and this, in turn, could result in a relaxation of tensions between the PRC and Japan, and thus the United States could find itself confronted by a very different and dangerous coalition of forces in the East.

108. Rhee, T. C. JAPANESE-AMERICAN RELATIONS AND THE U.S.-CHINA DETENTE: WHAT BALANCE BETWEEN THE TWO? *Asia Q. [Belgium] 1978 (3): 174-188.* Examines Japanese-American relations in light of : 1) US-China detente highlighted by the shift in global economic equilibrium of which OPEC is merely a symbol, 2) the emergence and consolidation of the Third World in direct challenge to traditional powers' dominance, 3) the decline of American military power relative to Soviet ascendancy and, 4) the resurgence of empassioned nationalisms. Concludes that the American "partnership" with Japan as the sole pivot in East Asia ought to be reconsidered and reduced for the sake of permanence of America's role in Asia and for regional stability. Based on Government documents, primary and secondary sources; 27 notes. Article to be continued. G. M. White

109. Rowe, David N. THE STATE DEPARTMENT WHITE PAPER: A SUGGESTED RESPONSE. *Issues & Studies [Taiwan] 1981 17(9): 35-59.* A discussion of the "White Paper on China": Department of State, *Relations with China, 1944-1949* (1949). This collection of documents was politically oriented toward promoting a military alliance between the United States and the Chinese Communists. Full disclosure of restricted materials, 1944-49, in government archives on Taiwan is necessary to refute the views contained in this volume, which still have an unfortunate influence on US politics.
J. A. Krompart

110. Saitō, Yoshifumi. THE NEW SITUATION IN ASIA. *Japan Q. [Japan] 1973 20(1): 30-38.* A brief review of the history of Asia since World War II, including an analysis of changing relations between Asian nations and the Great Powers and of Japan's role in Asia.

111. Sakamoto, Yoshikazu. MAJOR POWER RELATIONS IN EAST ASIA. *Bull. of the Atomic Sci. 1984 40(2): 19-24.* The new containment policy of the United States and the revived Cold War have created a new phase in Japan's relations with the United States, the USSR, and China.

112. Scalapino, Robert A. CHINA AND THE BALANCE OF POWER. *Foreign Affairs 1974 52(2): 349-385.* A basic desire for security has fashioned Chinese foreign affairs since the 1950's. Contemporary policy is to promote a strong US presence to counterbalance the USSR and to prevent Japan from dominating the area. Although China will continue to develop economic ties with Japan in order to balance Soviet power in Asia, it will not become dependent on Japan—or any other single nation. Its crucial relationship is continuing the US-USSR-China balance of power in Asia. Note. R. Riles

113. Scalapino, Robert A. THE US AND EAST ASIA: VIEWS AND POLICIES IN A CHANGING ERA. *Survival [Great Britain] 1982 24(4): 146-155.* Reviews US-USSR interaction since 1945, the strategic importance of East Asia, and the flexibility called for in alliances.

114. Scalapino, Robert A. U.S. POLICY IN ASIA. *Korea & World Affairs [South Korea] 1979 3(4): 471-484.* The power vacuum in Asia is dangerous for that region; the United States has responded by reversing its

withdrawal strategy and tilting toward China, but it should also engage in closer consultation with other states in the area.

115. Shaw Yu-ming. THE FLUX OF US-CHINESE AND US-KOREAN RELATIONS IN THE 1970'S. *Issues and Studies [Taiwan] 1977 13(2): 54-65.* Examines the foreign relations record, 1971-76; examines the differences in US relations with Taiwan and China on the one hand and Korea on the other and speculates on possible changes and accommodations which President Carter may need to make, 1976-77.

116. Smith, Gerard C. THE VITAL TRIANGLE. *World Today [Great Britain] 1974 30(4): 141-150.* "To aim only at revitalizing the Atlantic partnership would be an inadequate reply to the world's present needs. Broader trilateral co-operation could be one answer to the failure of the United Nations to promote a viable universal structure." J

117. Smith, M. J. J. F. D. R. AND THE BRUSSELS CONFERENCE, 1937. *Michigan Acad. 1981 14(2): 109-122.* Discusses the role of Franklin D. Roosevelt in undermining the Brussels Conference of the Nine Power Treaty signatories in 1937 in the context of the undeclared Sino-Japanese War and the imminent outbreak of World War II.

118. Smylie, Robert F. JOHN LEIGHTON STUART: A MISSIONARY IN THE SINO-JAPANESE CONFLICT 1937-1941. *J. of Presbyterian Hist. 1975 53(3): 256-276.* As President of Yenching University in 1937 when the Japanese occupied Peking and north China, John Leighton Stuart's unique outlook on China thrust him into the role of intermediary among the varying forces striving for dominance in China. He was disdainful of Chiang Kai-shek who obstinately refused to meet with Japanese officials and sympathized with liberal Japanese who saw the Sino conflict without purpose or end. In 1937-41, all parties in China had confidence in him, but because he was not a US diplomat, he received little sympathy from Roosevelt. Stuart urged an embargo on Japan, financial assistance to China, and settlement of anachronistic foreign rights in China, such as extraterritoriality. Based largely on documents in State Department Archives and the Franklin D. Roosevelt Library in Hyde Park; biblio., 64 notes. H. M. Parker, Jr.

119. Solomon, Richard H. EAST ASIA AND THE GREAT POWER COALITIONS. *Foreign Affairs 1982 60(3): 686-718.* Numerous events in 1981 created difficulties for US foreign policy in East Asia. Relations with China became strained, tensions developed in US-Japan relations, and disagreements among the Association of Southeast Asian Nations threatened to disrupt their unity. An effective US policy would be flexible and would regard Asia from a global and strategic viewpoint. 7 notes. A. A. Englard

120. Sormani, Piero. IL PROBLEMA DI TAIWAN E IL RAPPORTO CINA-STATI UNITI [The Taiwan problem and China-US relations]. *Mondo Cinese [Italy] 1981 9(1): 79-92.* Ronald Reagan's election has reopened the problem of Taiwan in Chinese-American relations and China's domestic policy.

Analyzes Beijing's strategy toward Taiwan and considers possible solutions of this historical and political conflict. J/S

121. Steeds, David. REAPPRAISING THE AMERICAN ROLE IN ASIA. *Int. Affairs [Great Britain] 1977 53(2): 255-268.* Review article prompted by recent studies on US foreign policy in East Asia since 1945 in the light of recent changes, such as the death of Mao and the change of the US administration. The works all stress the importance of maintaining the links between Japan and the United States, the potential dangers of the northeast Asian situation, and the difficulties of predicting the future course of Sino-American relations. Based on: A. Iriye, *The Cold War in Asia* (Englewood Cliffs: 1974), D. F. Lach and E. S. Wehrle, *International Politics in East Asia since World War II* (New York: 1975), H. C. Hinton, *Three and a Half Powers* (Bloomington: 1975), R. N. Clough, *East Asia and US Security* (Washington: 1975), R. N. Clough, A. D. Barnett, M. H. Halperin, and J. H. Kahan, *The United States, China and Arms Control* (Washington: 1975), and R. A. Scalapino, *Asia and the Road Ahead* (Berkeley: 1975). 48 notes.
P. J. Beck

122. Sutter, Robert G. U.S.-SOVIET-PRC RELATIONS AND THEIR IMPLICATIONS FOR KOREA. *Korea & World Affairs [South Korea] 1983 7(1): 5-20.* Based on the restrained attitudes of the major powers since the 1960's, no unnecessary risks will be taken and Korean reunification will require changes in North and South Korean policies.

123. Tikhvinskii, S. L. AMERIKANSKII AVTOR O POLITIKE PEKINA V VOSTOCHNOI AZII [An American author on China's policy in East Asia]. *Novaia i Noveishaia Istoriia [USSR] 1978 (6): 165-171.* Professor A. Doak Barnett analyzes Sino-Soviet, Sino-Japanese, and Sino-American relations. China's shift from political proximity with the USSR in the 1960's to extensive rapprochement with the West, Japan, and the United States after 1976 produced a surge in trade and cultural agreements. Many Sino-American contacts had existed since 1944, long before diplomatic relations were established (in 1972). Zbigniew Brzezinski's visit to Peking (in May 1978) and subsequently to Tokyo postdates Barnett's work. These, and the signing of a Sino-Japanese treaty (in August 1978) under US pressure, were a threat to the USSR and East Asia.
M. R. Colenso

124. Tolley, Kemp. LEARNING THEIR LINGO. *US Naval Inst. Pro. 1982 108(10): 70-72.* Experiences of Tolley as an ensign during 1935 while learning Russian in Harbin, Manchuria.
K. J. Bauer

125. Treadgold, Donald W. THE UNITED STATES AND EAST ASIA: A THEME WITH VARIATIONS. *Pacific Hist. Rev. 1980 49(1): 1-27.* Examines American ideas about China and Japan in three stages: Christianization, 1830-1910, introduction of democracy, 1900-50, and introduction of socialism since 1910. American missionaries did not know Oriental languages and culture. Chinese and Japanese resisted American efforts to influence them to be Christian and democratic. Orientals were more attracted to science and Marxism than to Christianity and American-style democracy. United States

policy in the Far East has seldom been made by people who understood the societal and cultural heritages of East Asia. This paper was the presidential address to the Pacific Coast Branch of the American Historical Association at its annual meeting in Honolulu in August 1979; 44 notes. R. N. Lokken

126. Tsai Wei-ping. AMERICAN THINKING ON THE SECURITY OF N.E. ASIA. *Issues and Studies [Taiwan] 1977 13(9): 1-8.* In the early 1950's, the United States concluded mutual defense treaties with the Republic of China, Japan, and the Republic of Korea. To many, the three treaties are considered "a tripod supporting the peace and prosperity of East Asia." If the United States abrogated any one of the treaties, the result on the East Asians would be devastating, especially if the United States "derecognized" the Republic of China in favor of "normalizing" relations with Communist China. It seems most Americans do not want to abrogate any of the treaties and will not hesitate to let their government officials know their feelings. Secondary sources; 7 notes. A. N. Garland

127. Tsien Tsuen-hsuin. TRENDS IN COLLECTION BUILDING FOR EAST ASIAN STUDIES IN AMERICAN LIBRARIES. *Coll. and Res. Lib. 1979 40(5): 405-415.* Among the many non-Western language area collections in American libraries, the East Asian collection was the earliest to be established. Its growth during the last two decades has been especially rapid and spectacular. Today some 100 individual collections contain nearly eight million volumes in exclusively indigenous languages with numerous editions written or printed centuries ago. With the increasing interest in the study of world civilizations, these once exotic materials have become an integral part of many research collections in American libraries and are of national and international significance. J

128. VanEdgerton, F. THE CARLSON INTELLIGENCE MISSION TO CHINA. *Michigan Academician 1977 9(4): 419-432.* Chronicles an intelligence mission for Franklin D. Roosevelt by Evans Carlson in China during the war with Japan, 1937-38.

129. Vernant, Jacques. LE "TRIANGLE" WASHINGTON, PÉKIN, TAÏPEH [The Washington, Peking, Taipei triangle]. *Défense Natl. [France] 1977 33(11): 123-129.* Reassesses the character of the relationship between the United States, the People's Republic of China, and Taiwan, in the light of Cyrus Vance's visit to Peking, 22-25 August 1977, with reference to the delicate diplomatic balance to be maintained due to the conflict between Peking and Taipei. Secondary sources; 4 notes.

130. Vidov, A. PEKIN I "NOVAIA" TAIVANSKAIA POLITIKA SSHA [Peking and the "new" US-Taiwanese policy]. *Aziia i Afrika Segodnia [USSR] 1982 (4): 16-18.* For the Chinese ruling elite, Taiwan was and remains a small issue in its bargaining with US imperialism; in holding forth on "uniting Taiwan with its homeland," Peking actually has no intention of eliminating a capitalist system in Taiwan.

131. Wakaizumi, Kei. JAPAN UND DIE AMERIKANISCHE PRÄSENZ IN SÜD-KOREA [Japan and the American presence in South Korea]. *Europa Archiv [West Germany] 1978 33(5): 125-134.* The decision of the Carter administration to withdraw American troops from South Korea can be seen as a return to the American policy toward Asia in the 19th and early 20th centuries, characterized by US resistance to the hegemony of any power without having troops stationed in that area.

132. Walker, Richard L. THE FUTURE OF U.S. TRANS-PACIFIC ALLIANCES. *Orbis 1975 19(3): 904-924.* Discusses aspects of US naval strategy and foreign policy in its Pacific Ocean alliance involving Japan, South Korea, the Philippines and Australia, 1951-70's.

133. Weinstein, Martin E. THE STRATEGIC BALANCE IN EAST ASIA. *Current Hist. 1973 65(387): 193-196, 225-226.* Reviews the effects of American foreign policy since 1968, in particular relations with Japan and China.
S

134. Whiting, Allen S. CHINA, AMERICA, AND THE KOREAN WAR. *Rev. in Am. Hist. 1981 9(4): 549-552.* Reviews William Whitney Stueck, Jr.'s *The Road to Confrontation: American Policy toward China and Korea, 1947-1950* (1981).

135. Wilhelm, Alfred D., Jr. THE NIXON SHOCKS AND JAPAN. *Military Rev. 1974 54(11): 70-77.* Discusses Japanese reaction to President Nixon's policy of detente with China, 1971-73.

136. Yoshizawa, Tetsutarō. KINDAICHŪ JIKEN TO NIHON NO CHŌSEN SEISAKU [The Kim Dao Jung case and the Japanese policy toward Korea]. *Ajia Afurika Kenkyū [Japan] 1973 13(11): 10-12.* The Kim Dae Jung case emphasized the actual importance of the Japanese role in South Korea. However, this is not only a result of the Japanese government's support of the Park Chung Hee regime, but results from President Nixon's "Two Koreas" policy, which places Japan in an important role regarding Korea.
H. Kawanami

137. Yu-ming Shaw. THE FLUX OF US-CHINESE AND US-KOREAN RELATIONS IN THE 1970'S. *Issues and Studies [Taiwan] 1977 13(2): 54-65.* Examines the legacy of foreign relations given the Carter administration, the differences in US relations with Taiwan and China on the one hand and Korea on the other, and speculates on possible changes and accommodations which Carter may need to make.

2

CHINA

138. Agnew, James B. COALITION WARFARE—RELIEVING THE PEKING LEGATIONS, 1900. *Military Rev. 1976 56(10): 58-70.* Questions the viability of military coalitions brought about by diplomatic alliances in the United States, Great Britain and Russia's joint participation in amphibious operations in the Boxer Rebellion in Eastern China in 1900.

139. Alexandrov, I. PEKING AND SOVIET-CHINESE RELATIONS. *Soviet Military Rev. [USSR] 1976 (9): 55-58.* Chinese foreign policy has aimed at inciting unrest throughout the world and putting the United States and the USSR at odds with one another, 1960's-76.

140. Alexeyev, I. MANOEUVRES OF THE PEKING DIPLOMACY. *Int. Affairs [USSR] 1974 (2): 26-33.* Analyzes the nature of Chinese diplomacy since the 1940's with particular emphasis upon US-Chinese relations and China's anti-Soviet designs since 1971.

141. Alexeyev, I. and Apalin, G. TWO PERIODS IN THE PRC'S HISTORY: TWO RESULTS (THE 25TH ANNIVERSARY OF THE PEOPLE'S REPUBLIC OF CHINA). *Int. Affairs [USSR] 1974 (11): 26-39.* Contrasts China's first 10 postrevolutionary years, characterized by successful application of the experience of the USSR in building socialism, with the last 15, marked by the recklessness of the Cultural Revolution and irresponsible international adventurism.

142. Allen, T. Harrell. U.S.-CHINESE DIALOGUE, 1969-72. *J. of Communication 1976 26(1): 81-86.*

143. Alpern, Stephen I. DIPLOMACY OF ADAPTABILITY: THAILAND'S CHANGING ATTITUDE TOWARD COMMUNIST CHINA. *Military Rev. 1974 54(3): 85-93.* With waning US influence in Southeast Asia, Thai leadership is likely to seek an accommodation with China while maintaining ties with the United States and the USSR.

144. Alpert, Eugene J. and Bernstein, Samuel J. INTERNATIONAL BARGAINING AND POLITICAL COALITIONS: U.S. FOREIGN AID AND CHINA'S ADMISSION TO THE U.N. *Western Pol. Q. 1974 27(2): 314-327.* Models the bargaining processes that determined the voting behavior and the nature of coalition formation on the issue of China's admission to the

UN, 1961-68, using US foreign aid as an independent variable in explaining voting patterns.

145. Alvarez, David J. THE DEPARTMENT OF STATE AND THE ABORTIVE PAPAL MISSION TO CHINA, AUGUST 1918. *Catholic Hist. Rev. 1976 62(3): 455-463.* The State Department's response to the establishment of diplomatic relations between China and the Vatican illuminates America's Far Eastern policy during World War I. Alarmed over the penetration of German influence into Siberia, the State Department intervened with the Chinese to block the reception of Monsignor Petrelli, a Germanophile, as papal nuncio. Concerned also with possible Japanese expansion into China, the Department cooperated with France to prevent the acceptance of any papal representative. France claimed a protectorate over Catholics in the Far East and the Department supported this claim in order to buttress European influence in China and counter Japanese influence. A

146. Alvi, Naheed. AFGHAN CRISIS—KABUL EFFORTS AT SOLUTION. *South Asian Studies [India] 1981 16(1): 85-93.* A review of the efforts of the legitimate government of Afghanistan to solve its problems with the reactionary forces within its borders and the imperialist powers seeking to exploit them. Pakistan, China, and the United States are the big offenders, the first mainly because of its long border with Afghanistan, which enables it to serve as a base from which the imperialists can launch their reactionary offensives. In return, Pakistan has been given quantities of military aid, which enables General Zia to maintain power and keep the masses of his nation subservient and oppressed. V. L. Human

147. Amin, Samir. UNIVERSALITY AND CULTURAL SPHERES. *Monthly Rev. 1977 28(9): 25-38.* Discusses the appeal of and resistance to the US, Soviet, and Chinese models of social organization, in different regions of the world.

148. Anderson, David L. ANSON BURLINGAME: REFORMER AND DIPLOMAT. *Civil War Hist. 1979 25(4): 293-308.* Anson Burlingame skyrocketed from Michigan frontiersman to Massachusetts Free-Soil stalwart and state senator. As US Representative from 1854, he wielded wide, effective Republican leadership. For that support, President Lincoln appointed him minister to China. Burlingame's personality, oratory, optimism, sensitivity, and boldness in furthering democracy helped him accomplish more than his more gifted rivals. These talents also caused him to grasp China's need for cooperative support in internal and external (diplomatic) reform and to carry through soundly and brilliantly. Proof was his appointment as first imperial envoy to the West, 1867-69. Based on family papers, State Department China Dispatches, and other sources; 56 notes. R. E. Stack

149. Anderson, David L. ANSON BURLINGAME: AMERICAN ARCHITECT OF THE COOPERATIVE POLICY IN CHINA, 1861-1871. *Diplomatic Hist. 1977 1(3): 239-255.* As US envoy to China in the 1860's Anson Burlingame (1820-70) was architect and defender of the cooperative policy. His efforts cast the United States into a leading policy role among

Western nations in Peking during that decade, largely because of his engaging personality and background as a crusader for the oppressed. Successors in the 1870's did not maintain his policy. 53 notes.

J. Tull

150. Anderson, David L. CHINA POLICY AND PRESIDENTIAL POLITICS, 1952. *Presidential Studies Q. 1980 10(1): 79-90.* The election of 1952 was the first presidential contest following the founding of the Communist People's Republic of China in 1949. The Korean War had drawn the United States and China into military conflict, causing much of the 1952 debate to turn on the "loss of China." A new and uncomfortable notion was born in 1952: the United States was no longer the omnipotent champion of democracy. US-Chinese relations were not restored to a friendly basis until the 1970's, when the United States withdrew from the Asian continent. 52 notes.

G. E. Pergl

151. Aplington, Henry, II. CHINA REVISITED. *Marine Corps Gazette 1973 57(7): 24-31.* Recalls the experiences of US Marines stationed in China from 1944 until the Chinese Communist victory of 1949.

152. Ardoin, Birthney and Hall, James L. AN ANALYSIS OF SOVIET AND CHINESE BROADCASTS CONCERNING U.S. INVOLVEMENT IN VIETNAM. *Southern Q. 1975 13(3): 175-180.* Evaluates 3800 assertions made in USSR and Chinese broadcasts between 1968 and 1973 to establish correlations. There is a difference in the intensity of negative assertions made about American involvement in the Vietnam War between 1968 and 1973. China's hostility was the greater of the two. 2 tables, 5 notes.

R. W. Dubay

153. Armentrout-Ma, L. Eve. A CHINESE ASSOCIATION IN NORTH AMERICA: THE PAO-HUANG HUI FROM 1899 TO 1904. *Ch'ing-shih wen-t'i 1978 3(9): 91-111.* Describes the rise and decline of the Pao-huang Hui Party in North America, founded by K'ang Yu-wei in Canada. The party grew rapidly, soon spreading over the North American continent and Hawaii. It emphasized the abuses the Chinese abroad endured, immigration policy, and the overthrow of the Manchu dynasty in China. The party's ideology was deliberately made broad, so that all could join, but the result was the development of factions and consequent struggling between them. The moderate, wealthier branch eventually triumphed, the masses of Chinese nationals slipped away, and the party's effective influence came to an end. 70 notes.

V. L. Human

154. Armstrong, Oscar V. OPENING CHINA. *Am. Heritage 1982 33(2): 40-49.* China trade began in 1784 when an American ship arrived at Whampoa Beach, the anchorage for Canton. Backed by Robert Morris, the voyage was chronicled by Samuel Shaw, who was put in charge of the business affairs of the *Empress of China*. Shaw's account describes Chinese trading customs and the problems and difficulties of this new trade. The trade became important to the economic life of the new nation as well as a stimulus to westward expansion. 9 illus.

J. F. Paul

155. Aronsen, Lawrence R. THE "NEW FRONTIER": POSTWAR PERCEPTIONS OF THE CHINA MARKET, 1943-1950. *Mid-America 1982 64(1): 17-32.* Traces the rise and demise of hopes for postwar trade with China. American businessmen hoped to forestall a postwar depression by increasing foreign markets, particularly in China, ignoring the lessons of the failure of Open Door diplomacy and economics in the early 20th century as well as the absence of a developed market, given China's failure to modernize. When the realities of Nationalist Chinese corruption and Communist takeover of China became manifest, American businessmen showed no hesitation in trading with the victors, in spite of increasingly prevalent American political ideology to the contrary. With Communist China's intervention in the Korean war, trade with mainland China was effectively cut off by legislation. Secondary sources; 58 notes. P. J. Woehrmann

156. Aspaturian, Vernon D. THE USSR, THE USA AND CHINA IN THE SEVENTIES. *Military Rev. 1974 54(1): 50-63.* Discusses the foundations of a post-Cold War world order being established by the United States, the USSR, and China in the 1970's, emphasizing the function of nuclear stalemate.

157. Auw, David C. L. COMMUNIST CHINA AND POWER CONFIGURATION IN THE ASIA-PACIFIC REGION. *Issues & Studies [Taiwan] 1983 19(10): 49-66.* During the past 30 years, Chinese policies in the Asian-Pacific area have varied from dependence on a military alliance with the USSR to the use of multiple options, including the "American card." There are several possibilities for future Chinese strategies, but complex international relations in the area make Peking's actions difficult to predict. Based on a paper presented at the 12th Sino-American Conference on Mainland China in Warrenton, Vermont, 9-12 June 1983; 15 notes. J. A. Krompart

158. Ballard, William T. STRATEGIC POWER: ON BALANCE. *Air U. Rev. 1973 24(4): 89-94.* Reviews Joseph I. Coffey's *Strategic Power and National Security* (U. of Pittsburgh Press, 1971), which analyzed U.S., Soviet, and Communist Chinese military strength. Concludes that U.S. military superiority has diminished in recent years. Note. J. W. Thacker, Jr.

159. Banno, Masataka. CHŌINGAKI-CHO "SANSHŪ NIKKI" (1896 NEN KAN) O YOMU: SHINMATSU NO ICHI-GAIKŌKA NO SEIYŌSHAKAI-KAN [Zhang Yinhuan's (Chang Yin-huan) *San-cho Diary*: a Chinese diplomat's view of Western social life in the late Ch'ing era]. *Kokkagakkai Zasshi [Japan] 1982 95(7-8): 101-122.* Examines the diary written by Zhang Yinhuan (1837-1900) during the period April 1886 to September 1889 while he was China's Minister to the United States, holding additional posts as Minister to Spain and Peru. In those days a diplomat was required to submit his diary to the prime minister's office after his three-year assignment. The diary recalls diplomatic negotiations among Zhang, his lawyer, John Watson Foster, and the US Secretary of State in a case involving Rock Springs, Wyoming Territory in September 1885. It also describes his visits to New York, Latin America (including Cuba), and Europe, and cultural differences observed while attending diplomatic receptions in Washington, D.C., which Zhang depicts as "a tiresome and even painful duty." 67 notes. M. Kawaguchi

160. Barié, Ottavio. STATI UNITI, CINA E ASIA ORIENTALE NEL SECONDO DOPOGUERRA [The United States, China, and East Asia since 1945]. *Mondo Cinese [Italy] 1983 11(1): 15-38.* Describes Chinese-American relations since 1945, and the major events and the strategic reasons that induced Americans to be directly interested in China. J/S

161. Barnett, Suzanne Wilson. TWO-WAY BRIDGES: EDUCATING NEW CHINA. *Hist. of Educ. Q. 1980 20(1): 101-108.* Review article of Philip West's *Yenching University and Sino-Western Relations, 1916-1952,* the history of Beijing (Peking) University's predecessor. American missionary groups consolidated four institutions in 1916 to form Yanjing (Yenching) University. John Leighton Stuart served as President of Yanjing during 1919-45. By the mid-1920's Yanjing was ranked among the top three universities in China. Wu Lei-Ch'uan was appointed chancellor in 1929 to help fulfill the American ideal of making Yanjing a two-way bridge connecting the peoples and governments of America and China. After the Communists took over China in 1949 and the United States froze Chinese assets during the Korean War, the university was dissolved. The modern Beijing University opened by Mao Zedong (Mao Tse-tung) occupied the former facilities of Yanjing. 11 notes. S. H. Frank

162. Baron, Michael L., comp. CHRONOLOGY OF EVENTS, 1947-1950. Borg, Dorothy and Heinrichs, Waldo, ed. *Uncertain Years: Chinese-American Relations, 1947-1950* (New York: Columbia U. Pr., 1980): 305-317.

163. Barsegov, Iu. and Nikol'skaia, E. "DIPLOMATIIA KANONEROK" V STRATEGII SOVREMENNOGO IMPERIALIZMA [Warship diplomacy in the strategy of modern imperialism]. *Mirovaia Ekonomika i Mezhdunarodnye Otnosheniia [USSR] 1981 (8): 97-100.* Examines the use of navies in the foreign policies of the United States and China during 1974-80.

164. Bays, Daniel H. POPULAR RELIGIOUS MOVEMENTS IN CHINA AND THE UNITED STATES IN THE NINETEENTH CENTURY. *Fides et Hist. 1982 15(1): 24-38.* Both Chinese sectarian and American popular religious movements stressed millenarianism and salvation, flourished in areas of fluid economic and social change, and shared a sense of community through a congregation of laity from which a charismatic leadership might emerge. The point at which those shared elements coalesced probably occurred in mid-century during the Taiping Rebellion (1850-64) and the Mormon movement. While both movements stressed attainable perfection through abstention from vice, the movement toward Christian utopianism which fostered many experimental communities in the United States never developed in China and instead created tensions in the political order. Due to a tradition of religious plurality and the separation of church and state, sectarianism was more acceptable in the United States and sects were able to complete the transition to denominations; by contrast, Chinese popular religion remained enclosed and alienated from the Confucian ethical system and the predominant elitist culture. Secondary sources; 28 notes. G. A. Glovins

165. Beers, Burton F. AMERICANS IN CHINA? SOME HISTORICAL PERSPECTIVES ON A CONTEMPORARY ENTHUSIASM. *South Atlantic Q. 1975 74(1): 1-11.* Current Sino-American cultural relations evoke national memories of earlier pre-World War II associations. But where Americans see a long history of unselfish endeavors by individuals and institutions to create a unified and well-educated China, the Chinese see cultural imperialism and foreign encroachment. For much of the 19th century China's best access to the West came through American missionary schools, periodicals, and books; over 7,000 Chinese received higher education in America before 1940. Yet the social upheaval and unrest which accompanied Western innovations and the American failure to respect Chinese culture has made the Chinese wary of new associations. Based on secondary sources; 4 notes. W. L. Olbrich

166. Beresford, Melanie; Catley, Bob; and Pilkington, Francis. AMERICA'S-PACIFIC RIM STRATEGY. *J. of Contemporary Asia [Sweden] 1979 9(1): 67-74.* United States foreign policy in the Pacific rim did not suffer a fatal blow as a result of the Vietnam War. The defeat in Vietnam awakened the United States to the futility of resisting nationalist uprisings by colonial people. Since the conflict, the United States has followed a policy of trying to integrate the economies of China and Vietnam into the world market economy. Secondary sources; 19 notes. R. H. Detrick

167. Berry, Mary and Shanker, Albert. THE POLITICS OF THINKING ABOUT CHINA. *Change 1978 10(2): 36-39, 64.* Presents the text of a speech by Mary Berry on Chinese education presented at the University of Illinois following her return from China where she studied the educational system, and the response of Albert Shanker, president of the American Federation of Teachers, disparaging her favorable impression of totalitarian education.

168. Bert, Wayne. CHINESE RELATIONS WITH BURMA AND INDONESIA. *Asian Survey 1975 15(6): 473-487.* Discusses the policy of China toward Burma and Indonesia before and after the Cultural Revolution, with regard to nonalignment, international Communism, and relations with the United States.

169. Best, Gary Dean. IDEAS WITHOUT CAPITAL: JAMES H. WILSON AND EAST ASIA, 1885-1910. *Pacific Hist. Rev. 1980 49(3): 453-470.* General James H. Wilson does not qualify as an expansionist, as some historians have portrayed him. He was interested in his own personal profit and prestige in China, but doubted that the United States would contribute significantly to China's progress. He preferred that China develop autonomously, helped by American economic advice. His attitudes toward United States-China relations shifted with changing conditions in East Asia, but he never advocated an American expansionist policy there. He did not consider the Philippine Islands a door to the China market, and did not support the open door policy. He was convinced that America's manifest destiny was in the western hemisphere. Based on the Wilson Papers in the Library of Congress and Wilson's published magazine articles; 43 notes. R. N. Lokken

170. Bickerton, Ian J. JOHN HAY'S OPEN DOOR POLICY: A RE-EXAMINATION. *Australian J. of Pol. and Hist. [Australia] 1977 23(1): 54-66.* Details the background to Secretary of State John Hay's China policy of 1899-1901 and suggests that recent revisionist interpretations are incorrect. Marilyn Young (1969) and Raymond Esthus (1959) deemed that the Open Door policy concerned commerce, finance, and politics, and suggested that, while the rhetoric stressed Open Door, in reality US policy soon became a pragmatic one of securing only equal access for US trade. An examination of the Philander C. Knox, Francis M. Huntington Wilson, Willard Straight, William Rockhill, and Hay Papers indicates that the Open Door and opposition to foreign spheres were consistently pursued. W. D. McIntyre

171. Billa, Krupadanam J. B. THE "NIXON SHOCK" AND ITS CONSEQUENCES: SINO-AMERICAN RECONCILIATION. *China Report [India] 1979 15(5): 51-61.* Examines the positive and negative factors in four areas—the United States-China-USSR relationship, financial claims, domestic politics, and the Taiwan issue—that were important in establishing improved relations between the United States and the People's Republic of China. 46 notes. S

172. Black, Gregory D. KEYS OF THE KINGDOM: ENTERTAINMENT AND PROPAGANDA. *South Atlantic Q. 1976 75(4): 434-446.* Uses the history of *The Keys of the Kingdom,* a 1944 20th Century-Fox movie about early 20th-century missionary life in China, to show the Office of War Information's (OWI) involvement in American wartime film industry. Only with the greatest persuasion could the filmmakers conceive of Chinese society in terms other than the mysterious East, but the stereotyping forced on them by the government agency was equally unrealistic. The OWI was promoting Franklin D. Roosevelt's concept of China as a fourth world power and obviously used this movie to improve relations between Washington and Chungking. Primary and secondary sources; 19 notes. W. L. Olbrich

173. Brach, Hans Günter. AMERIKANISCH-SOWJETISCHE BEZIEHUNGEN: VOM KALTEN KRIEG ZUR ENTSPANNUNG? AMERIKANISCHE ENTSPANNUNGSPOLITIK GEGENÜBER DER SOWJETUNION UND CHINA (I) [US-USSR relations: from Cold War to detente? US policies of detente toward the USSR and China, Part I]. *Neue Politische Literatur [West Germany] 1979 24(4): 513-548.* While immediate postwar armament developments were controlled by the United States and the USSR the explosion of the Chinese nuclear bombs and the increasing ideological differences between China and the USSR have changed the balance of world conflict. Richard Nixon's foreign policy changed the modalities and style of US foreign policy but not US goals. 127 notes. R. Wagnleitner

174. Bradford, Richard H. THAT PRODIGAL SON: PHILO MC GIFFIN AND THE CHINESE NAVY. *Am. Neptune 1978 38(3): 157-169.* Discusses Pennsylvania-born Philo Norton McGiffin's (1860-97) career in the Imperial Chinese Navy during 1885-95. McGiffin served in the Chinese Navy as an instructor and advisor soon after graduating from the US Naval Academy. During the 1st Sino-Japanese War he participated in several naval

engagements, including the Battle of the Yalu (September 1894) where he was wounded. Published sources; 45 notes. G. H. Curtis

175. Brady, Erika. FIRST U.S. PANDA, SHANGHAIED IN CHINA, STIRRED UP A RUCKUS. *Smithsonian 1983 14(9): 145-164.* Describes the expeditions of Floyd Tangier Smith and Ruth Harkness, competing to be the first to capture a live giant panda; details the subsequent controversy over Su Lin, the panda Harkness brought back to the United States from China.

176. Brahm, Heinz. DIE SOWJETUNION UND DIE VOLKSPREPUBLIK CHINA, 1949-1957 [The USSR and China, 1949-57]. *Österreichische Osthefte [Austria] 1978 20(2): 371-382.* The negative attitude of the United States toward China in 1949 forced the Chinese Communists to work more closely with the Soviet Union than their fear of Soviet hegemony would have indicated. After the revolts in Poland and Hungary, the Chinese Communist leadership began to openly develop a divergent political ideology. Secondary literature; 51 notes. R. Wagnleitner

177. Brandon, Donald. A NEW FOREIGN POLICY FOR AMERICA. *World Affairs 1975 138(2): 83-107.* The United States should pay more attention to domestic problems while exploiting the USSR-China rift by taking advantage of the reopened door to China in the 1970's.

178. Briggs, Philip J. CONGRESS AND THE COLD WAR: U.S.-CHINA POLICY, 1955. *China Q. [Great Britain] 1981 (85): 80-95.* Bipartisanship in foreign policy, the aftereffects of the McCarthy era, and John Foster Dulles's crusade against communism, combined to allow passage of the Formosa Resolution and the Mutual Defense Treaty with Taiwan in 1955. Based on US Government publications and the papers of John Foster Dulles and Herbert H. Lehman. J. R. Pavia, Jr.

179. Brown, Roger Glenn. CHINESE POLITICS AND AMERICAN POLICY. *Foreign Policy 1976 (23): 3-23.* Concludes that the United States should establish diplomatic relations with China as quickly as possible in order to best maintain the world equilibrium. Since 1969 Mao Tse-tung and Chou En-lai have directed Chinese policy away from expanded militarism and isolationism toward diplomatic ties with the United States. Although Chou is now dead and his deputy Teng Hsiao-ping has been purged, the possibility of close ties between the United States and China remains strong until the death of Mao. The intensifying succession struggle might then turn the Chinese to a policy of isolationism or accommodation with the Soviet Union. 10 notes.
C. Hopkins

180. Buck, Peter. ORDER AND CONTROL: THE SCIENTIFIC METHOD IN CHINA AND THE UNITED STATES. *Soc. Studies of Sci. 1975 5(3): 237-268.* Contrasts the understanding of science in the United States based on laissez-faire industrialization with that in China based on a methodology dictated by life-long crises in the 20th century.

181. Buhite, Russell D.   MISSED OPPORTUNITIES? AMERICAN POLICY AND THE CHINESE COMMUNISTS, 1949. *Mid-America 1979 61(3): 179-188.* It has been argued that the United States missed opportunities to establish friendly relations with Chinese Communists in 1949. Two such possibilities were an overture by Zhou Enlai (Chou En-lai) and an invitation to John Leighton Stuart to visit Beijing (Peking). State Department officials doubted Chou's sincerity and were also concerned with American domestic reaction. The Chinese were constrained by their Marxist-Leninist ideology and by Soviet pressure, to treat America as an enemy. It is not clear if such opportunities really existed. Based on State Department records, *Foreign Relations of the United States,* other primary, and secondary sources; 30 notes.

J. M. Lee

182. Bullard, Monte R.   THE US-CHINA DEFENSE RELATIONSHIP. *Parameters 1983 13(1): 43-50.* By the late 1970's, the United States and the People's Republic of China had moved militarily together mainly due to the perceived threat posed by the Soviet Union. Yet, this relationship has not developed as fast as it might have and is still tenuous due to a number of factors. From the Chinese standpoint, US support for Taiwan has been a problem. The Chinese military does not have a need for the advanced weapons that the United States could provide in its strategy of "people's" war nor can it currently digest such technology. The United States has had to take into account the concerns of its allies as well as its relationship with the Soviet Union. Both nations have also had to deal with the major ideological differences between them. Based on interviews with Chinese military and government officials and Defense Department documents; 34 notes.

L. R. Maxted

183. Buxbaum, David C.   AMERICAN TRADE WITH THE PEOPLE'S REPUBLIC OF CHINA: SOME PRELIMINARY PERSPECTIVES. *Columbia J. of Transnational Law 1973 12(1): 39-55.*

184. Cadart, Claude.   DU PROJET STRATÉGIQUE SINO-SOVIÉTIQUE AU PROJET STRATÉGIQUE SINO-AMERICAIN [From a Sino-Soviet to a Sino-American strategic concept]. *Études Int. [Canada] 1979 10(4): 757-796.* Reviews China's role as a world power especially in the last three decades. From 1949 to 1959, China's strategy was cooperation with the Soviet Union; during the next decade it looked to Europe for help to withstand confrontation of the United States in Vietnam and the USSR. During the third decade, China sought a liaison with the United States as a new vehicle for world influence. Discusses China's initiatives in this new direction from the Mao-Nixon talks to the effect of the Washington visit of Deng Xiaoping (Teng Hsiao-p'ing). Examines China's goal to have the two Pacific powers control the intervening trans-Atlantic continents. Despite China's design to establish an economic, diplomatic, military, and cultural entente with the United States, Washington only views Peking as an adjunct issue to the real contest for global superiority with the Soviet Union.

J. F. Harrington

185. Capie, Susan A.   JAMES B. ANGELL, MINISTER TO CHINA 1880-1881: HIS MISSION AND THE CHINESE DESIRE FOR EQUAL

TREATY RIGHTS. *Bull. of the Inst. of Modern Hist. Acad. Sinica [Taiwan] 1982 11: 273-314.* James B. Angell (1829-1916) was the US minister to China and chaired the Commission Plenipotentiary to revise the Burlingame Treaty of 1868 in 1880. Angell was moderate in his negotiation of the Immigration and Commercial Treaties, but underestimated his country's determination to limit Chinese immigration. The Chinese displayed both knowledge and skill in their conduct of these negotiations. Based on contemporary American and Chinese documents and other writings; 105 notes. J. A. Krompart

186. Carbonneau, Robert. THE PASSIONISTS IN CHINA, 1921-1929: AN ESSAY IN MISSION EXPERIENCE. *Catholic Hist. Rev. 1980 66(3): 392-416.* Examines the policy of inexperienced Passionist missionaries to Hunan, China, 1921-29, and studies their attempts at cultural and evangelical adaptation. Two factors dominated mission policy: the political and social conditions of China during the turbulent warlord period, and the desire for unity of lifestyle and ministry among the missionaries. Their views and experiences provide a means of understanding the policy of other missionaries to China in the 20th century. Based on correspondence and interviews. A

187. Chan, F. Gilbert. THE AMERICAN REVOLUTION AND THE RISE OF AFRO-ASIAN NATIONALISM; WITH SPECIAL REFERENCE TO SUN YAT-SEN AND THE CHINESE EXPERIENCE. *Asian Profile 1982 10(3): 209-219.* The American Revolution, as perceived by US-educated Afro-Asian elites, has served in the 20th century as a model for developing nations in Africa and Asia. However, these elites have been more concerned with national self-determination than individual liberty, and have not fully appreciated the "spirit of 1776," to the extent that this spirit stands for individual rights. Sun Zhongshan (Sun Yat-Sen) paid tribute to the American Revolution but did not rely on it exclusively for ideological inspiration. The anticolonial spirit of the American Revolution was not replicated in the Chinese Revolution, and many revolutionaries allowed their sympathies for China's traditional culture to prevent modernization. Americans who believed that the American model for revolution had been transplanted to China were mistaken. Lecture delivered at Clemson University, 12 February 1976. Secondary sources; 57 notes. J. Powell/S

188. Chan, K. C. THE ABROGATION OF BRITISH EXTRA-TERRITORIALITY IN CHINA 1942-43: A STUDY OF ANGLO-AMERICAN-CHINESE RELATIONS. *Modern Asian Studies [Great Britain] 1977 11(2): 257-291.* In 1929 the Nationalist government announced its intention of terminating extraterritoriality in China. Sino-British negotiations on the subject ended with the Japanese invasion in 1937, but recommenced in 1942 on the joint initiative of Britain and America, now allies of the Chinese. The United States succeeded in protecting its immigration policies. Britain, however, failed to secure guarantees for the freedom of British commerce in China. The treaty ending extraterritoriality was signed on 11 January 1943. Based on British archival materials released in 1972; 136 notes.
L. W. Van Wyk

189. Chan, K. C. THE ANGLO-CHINESE LOAN NEGOTIATIONS (1941-1944): A STUDY OF BRITAIN'S RELATIONS WITH CHINA DURING THE PACIFIC WAR. *Papers on Far Eastern Hist. [Australia] 1974 (9): 101-135.* Compares British and American policies toward China during World War II, with special reference to the financial state of Chiang Kai-shek's government.

190. Chan, King-yuh. WASHINGTON-PEIPING RELATIONS: THREE LEVELS OF ANALYSIS. *Issues and Studies [Taiwan] 1978 14(6): 53-76.* By the 1950's US foreign policy produced a stable and pro-American atmosphere in Northeast Asia which has been jeopardized by America's apparent acceptance of China's conditions for the establishment of diplomatic relations.

191. Chang, Hwa-Bao. A STUDY OF THE ATTITUDES OF CHINESE STUDENTS IN THE U.S. *Sociol. and Social Res. 1973 58(1): 66-77.* "Previous studies suggest that the most significant determinants of a foreign student's attitude toward the host country include the national status of his home country, the degree of his contact with Americans, the frustration he encounters during his sojourn, the length of time he has been in the United States, and his authoritarianism. This study found Chinese student attitudes toward the United States positively associated with contact with Americans, but negatively associated with authoritarianism. A U-curve hypothesis concerning attitude changes through time was partially supported. No association was found between a Chinese student's attitude and the perceived national status of his home country, or his degree of frustration." J

192. Chang, Parris H. PEKING'S STRATEGY AGAINST MOSCOW. *Asian Affairs: An Am. Rev. 1981 8(3): 131-147.* Analyzes the ebb and flow of relations among China, the USSR, and the United States since 1949. Discusses the Sino-Soviet alliance (1950's), the Sino-Soviet dispute (1960's), Sino-U.S. rapprochement (1980's), and the effects of these developments on Southeast Asia. Based on speeches, government documents, other primary sources; 19 notes. R. B. Mendel

193. Chang, Yü-fa. CHINA'S AGRICULTURAL IMPROVEMENT, 1901-1916: REGIONAL STUDIES ON THIRTEEN PROVINCES. Hou, Chi-ming and Yu, Tzong-shian, ed. *Modern Chinese Economic History: Proceedings of the Conference on Modern Chinese Economic History* (Taipei: Inst. of Econ., Academia Sinica, 1979): 135-156. Studies attempts to modernize agriculture in 13 Chinese provinces during the period from 1900 to 1920. Principal achievements were the dissemination of agricultural information, the organization of people interested in promoting agriculture, the establishment of agricultural experimental stations, and the expansion of economic crops. Despite improvements in flood control and irrigation, China still suffered from flood and drought during this period. Poverty and ignorance prevented the application of technological improvements in many instances. Lack of participation in the program by absentee landlords and by tenant farmers who were not inclined to invest their meager earnings in land that was not their own was another stumbling-block. Availability of human labor made mechanization relatively expensive and unnecessary. 88 notes. S

194. Chang Chung-tung. DR. SUN YAT-SEN'S PRINCIPLE OF LIVELIHOOD AND AMERICAN PROGRESSIVISM. *Chinese Studies in Hist.* 1982 15(3-4): 4-19. Sun Zhongshan (Sun Yat-sen) drew from both Chinese traditions and American progressivism in formulating his political, economic, and social philosophy. He shared much in common with such progressive reformers as Henry George and Edward Bellamy. Though critical of capitalism, Sun retained an optimistic view of human progress, and appreciated the reform movement in early 20th-century America. Based on Sun's works; 44 notes.
A. C. Migliazzo

195. Chari, P. R. US-USSR-CHINA INTERACTION: THE STRATEGIC PLANE. *China Report [India] 1976 12(1): 33-41.* The basis of the US-USSR-China triangular relationship is discussed from the Chinese perspective, emphasizing the centrality of US-USSR strategic parity while noting Chinese strategic inferiority. The balance within the triad system is a juxtapositioning of geopolitical, ideological, and military interests among different pairs of countries. China's nuclear growth threatens the stability of the existing order, for China's dependence on the United States to counter Soviet strength is only a passing phase. 15 notes.
S. F. Benfield

196. Cheng, Joseph Y. S. AN INTERPRETATION OF CHINA'S FOREIGN POLICY—THE POST CULTURAL REVOLUTION PHASE. *J. of Contemporary Asia [Sweden] 1976 6(2): 148-171.* Argues that the widely accepted view that the Sino-American detente was the result of Chinese fears of a Soviet military attack is too simplistic. If the Soviet Union was considering attacking China, it had its best opportunity during the Cultural Revolution. The improvement in Sino-American relations was more significantly influenced by internal consolidations in China after the Cultural Revolution, the Chinese perception of increasing American restraint, and the new ideological framework which placed the United States and the Soviet Union on an equal footing as superpowers. 92 notes.
K. W. Berger

197. Cheong, W. E. CHINA AGENCIES AND THE ANGLO-AMERICAN FINANCIAL CRISIS, 1834-1837. *Rev. Int. d'Hist. de la Banque [Italy] 1974 9: 134-159.* Following the collapse of the Great East India Houses of Calcutta in 1830-34, new commercial houses emerged in the Far Eastern trade, particularly in the China tea trade. These establishments differed from their predecessors in securing multiple agencies for accommodation, discounting, and credit, and in relying heavily on American commercial bills to finance the China trade in the mid-1830's. The vigor of this trade, the multiple financial agencies, and the end of the British East India Company's monopoly led to reckless credit expansion and commodity speculation in tea. The overstocking of tea and the tightening up of credit by the Anglo-American houses brought on a series of business failures. Based largely on primary sources, especially the Jardine Matheson Papers, and on secondary sources; 5 tables, 83 notes.
D. McGinnis

198. Chern, Kenneth S. POLITICS OF AMERICAN CHINA POLICY, 1945: ROOTS OF THE COLD WAR IN ASIA. *Pol. Sci. Q. 1976-77 91(4): 631-647.* Reviews the American foreign policy debate of 1945 over the question

of intervention in the civil war between the Nationalist and Communist Chinese. The Truman administration failed in its obligation to educate the American public about the near inevitability of Communist victory. J

199. Chih Meng. RECOLLECTIONS OF CHINESE-AMERICAN CULTURAL PERSONS: A SAMPLING. *Chinese Studies in Hist. 1977-78 11(2): 16-28.* Analyzes the characters and contributions of Chinese students returning from study in America, and American students returning from Chinese universities, 1911-36. These traveling students successfully bridged cultural gaps and contributed to both nations. Their great value at present is as teachers. The present Chinese-American cultural impasse has robbed a generation of students of first-hand knowledge, a shortcoming which returned students are equipped to overcome. V. L. Human

200. Chiu, Hung-dah. MEI KUO TUI CHUNG KUO FA LÜ TI YEN CHIU [The study of Chinese law in the United States]. *Ssu yü Yen (Thought and Word) [Taiwan] 1973 10(6): 406-408.* In the last 15 years, Chinese law has become a subject of research by American legal scholars. Their works are few but significant, and cover all aspects of laws, ranging from pre-Ch'ing times to the present. Their approaches are generally analytical, historical, and sociological. Only a few law schools offer relevant courses, and the problems in developing widespread interest in this field are the lack of funds, the language barrier, and the general conservatism of the American law schools. Secondary sources; 26 notes. C. C. Brown

201. Chou, S. H. CHINA'S FOREIGN TRADE. *Current Hist. 1976 71(419): 68-72, 84-88.* Discusses the prospects for trade between China and the United States in the 1970's, emphasizing the role of agricultural production, consumer goods, and industry and trends in China's trade since 1950.

202. Choudhury, Golam W. EMERGING U.S.-CHINA MILITARY COOPERATION: ITS IMPLICATIONS FOR THE BALANCE OF POWER IN ASIA. *Korea & World Affairs [South Korea] 1981 5(4): 558-580.* Traces the development of Sino-US military cooperation from the beginning of diplomatic normalization between the two countries in 1972, focusing on the implications of this cooperation for Asian politics, especially in Afghanistan, India, Pakistan, Vietnam, and Japan and on its impact on US-Soviet relations.

203. Chu, John. A COMPARISON OF TWO SYSTEMS OF SELECTING TALENTS. *Issues and Studies [Taiwan] 1973 10(2): 38-44.* Compares contemporary systems of talent selection in the United States and Communist China, praising the American dream of equal opportunity and condemning the tyranny of Communism.

204. Chu, Yung-Deh Richard. CHINESE SECRET SOCIETIES IN AMERICA: A HISTORICAL SURVEY. *Asian Profile [Hong Kong] 1973 1(1): 21-38.* Examines the history of Chinese tong societies in the United States. These organizations had their origins in the Hung-men societies organized in China to overthrow the Manchu rulers. The first wave of Chinese immigration to America came in the 1850's and the 1860's during the Gold Rush and the

building of the transcontinental railroad, and following the defeat of the Taiping rebels. The great majority of these Chinese were men who had virtually no family life and who turned to gambling, opium, and prostitution. When Irish mobs burned their residences and all levels of government imposed prejudicial laws against them, these Chinese immigrants turned to their secret societies. In the decades following 1870 many Chinese moved from California to the metropolitan areas of America and organized new tongs. Their identification with the anti-Manchu organizations in China continued, although their activities centered on local issues in America. In the years following World War II immigration and other restrictive laws have been amended and Chinese immigration has markedly increased. In New York City the Chinese population increased from 6,000 in the pre-World War II period to 12,000 in 1954, 30,000 in 1967, and 60,000 by 1972, with more than 100,000 in the greater New York metropolitan area. This new immigration has been not of single individuals but of urban families. Tongs have continued to provide assistance and protection for numbers of newly arrived Chinese. Based on interviews and secondary sources; 70 notes. S. H. Frank

205. Chyba, Christopher F. U.S. MILITARY-SUPPORT EQUIPMENT SALES TO THE PEOPLE'S REPUBLIC OF CHINA. *Asian Survey 1981 21(4): 469-484.* Early in 1980 the United States announced that it was prepared to sell some types of "nonlethal" military-related equipment to China, the most recent and dramatic step in a series of indications of increasing US-Chinese security ties, some of them clearly intended as a warning to the Soviets. Such sales are not likely to improve significantly China's defense against attack, nor are they likely to entice the Chinese leadership to maintain good relations with Washington. Rather than serving any beneficial purpose the offer to sell military-related equipment may have only detrimental effects, such as worsening Washington's relations with Moscow. Based on newspapers, radio broadcasts, and government documents. M. A. Eide

206. Clark, Ian. SINO-AMERICAN RELATIONS IN SOVIET PERSPECTIVE. *Orbis 1973 17(2): 480-493.* Discusses foreign relations between the United States, Russia, and China during the 1970's.

207. Clubb, O. Edmund. CHINA AND THE SUPERPOWERS. *Current Hist. 1974 67(397): 97-100, 134-135.* From an issue on the People's Republic of China, 1974. S

208. Clubb, O. Edmund; Cohen, Warren I., introd. CONSUL GENERAL O. EDMUND CLUBB ON THE "INEVITABILITY" OF CONFLICT BETWEEN THE UNITED STATES AND THE PEOPLE'S REPUBLIC OF CHINA, 1949-50. *Diplomatic Hist. 1981 5(2): 165-168.* A letter from O. Edmund Clubb, American consul general in Beijing in 1949, in which Clubb discusses two essays by Michael H. Hunt and Steven M. Goldstein (see entries in this chapter) which appeared in *Uncertain Years: Chinese American Relations, 1947-1950* (1980), a collection of essays resulting from a project organized by the East Asian Institute at Columbia University to examine newly available material from the archives of the US government and especially the collection of V. K. Wellington Koo, Chinese ambassador to the United States

during the period. Clubb finds fault with the thesis that the Sino-American hostility and the breach of 1949-50 were inevitable. Clubb's letter is published with an introduction. 3 notes. — J. V. Coutinho

209. Cohen, Warren I. AMBASSADOR PHILIP D. SPROUSE ON THE QUESTION OF RECOGNITION OF THE PEOPLE'S REPUBLIC OF CHINA IN 1949 AND 1950. *Diplomatic Hist. 1978 2(2): 213-217.* In response to a 1973 query from a historian, former Ambassador Philip D. Sprouse wrote that the Truman administration recognized the inevitability of a Communist victory in the Chinese civil war and the futility of continuing to send aid to the Kuomintang, because all materials sent would end up with the Communists eventually. The question of extending diplomatic recognition to the Communists was considered, but adverse public opinion, and especially congressional opposition, made such action hazardous and dictated the continuation of existing policy. China's entry into the Korean War ended any possibility that recognition would be offered. — T. L. Powers

210. Cohen, Warren I. HARRY TRUMAN, CHINA, AND THE COLD WAR IN ASIA. *Rev. in Am. Hist. 1978 6(2): 146-154.* Review essay of Stanley D. Bachrack's *The Committee of One Million: "China Lobby" Politics, 1953-1971* (New York: Columbia U. Pr., 1976), *The Origins of the Cold War in Asia* (New York: Columbia U. Pr., 1977) edited by Yonosuke Nagai and Akira Iriye, and Lewis McCarroll Purifoy's *Harry Truman's China Policy: McCarthyism and the Diplomacy of Hysteria, 1947-1951* (New York: New Viewpoints, 1976).

211. Cohen, Warren I. US, CHINA, AND THE COLD WAR IN ASIA, 1949-1979. *Centennial Rev. 1980 24(2): 127-147.* Traces the relationship between the United States and China from the post-World War II era to the diplomatic recognition of China. Throughout this period the possibility of formal relations between the two countries fluctuated, responding to world and internal crises. Dean Acheson early recognized the futility of continuing support for the Guomindang (Kuomintang) on Taiwan, but the Korean War and fears of a monolithic Communist structure dominated by the USSR escalated US distrust of the People's Republic. This distrust continued through the active involvement of the United States in Vietnam. Not until 1970 were active US efforts to normalize relations with China resumed. In the late 1970's, with assurances from Deng Xiaoping (Teng Hsiao-p'ing) that force would not be used against Taiwan, the United States at last recognized the People's Republic. If the major powers maintain a balanced perspective in US-Chinese-Soviet relations, warmer relations between them could result. — A. Hoffman

212. Coleman, Michael C. PRESBYTERIAN MISSIONARY ATTITUDES TOWARD CHINA AND THE CHINESE, 1837-1900. *J. of Presbyterian Hist. 1978 56(3): 185-200.* Focuses on Presbyterian missionary attitudes toward the Chinese from 1837 to the eve of the Boxer Rebellion in 1900. Over six decades the missionaries made little attempt to understand Chinese sociology—family relationships, sex roles, class structure—or Chinese economics, arts, and literature. One positive note is drawn: if the missionaries were predisposed to view Chinese civilization as heathen, and thus inferior,

they also saw the people as redeemable, as human beings full of potential. Based largely on periodicals and pamphlets found in the Presbyterian Historical Society, Philadelphia, Annual Reports of the Board of Foreign Missions of the Presbyterian Church and secondary materials; 46 notes.

H. M. Parker, Jr.

213. Combs, Cecil E.   A FORGOTTEN MISSION—THE KAILAN COAL MINE. *Aerospace Hist. 1983 30(1): 2-5.* Describes Cecil E. Combs's experiences on a mission involving six US Army Air Force B-24 bomber crews, that were brought from the Middle East just for this mission, which was against the Kailan coal mine in China, October 1942. At the time it was the longest bombing mission in the war and involved flying over difficult terrain in "quite hazardous conditions." The bombs hit the target; but because these crews were not permanently attached to the 10th or 14th Air Forces, they were quickly sent back to the Middle East and never received proper credit for this "forgotten mission." 4 illus.   J. K. Ohl

214. Cope, Jesse D.   AMERICAN TROOPS IN CHINA: THEIR MISSION. *By Valor and Arms 1975 1(2): 48-54.* Reprints an article from a 1931 journal in which a military man stationed in China with the US Army discussed the initial presence of American troops in China, 1898-1902.

215. Copper, John F.   SINO-AMERICAN RELATIONS: REACHING A PLATEAU. *Current Hist. 1982 81(476): 241-245, 277.* In 1972, Sino-American relations were full of hope, that hope was satisfied or disappointed primarily by fluctuations in US relations with Taiwan and the USSR.

216. Cortinovis, Irene E.   CHINA AT THE ST. LOUIS WORLD'S FAIR. *Missouri Hist. Rev. 1977 72(1): 59-66.* The 1893 exposition in Chicago encouraged St. Louis businessmen to plan for their World's Fair, in which China was one of 53 foreign countries displaying its arts and crafts. This was the first time China chose to display her wares before a large Western audience. Illus., 16 notes.   W. F. Zornow

217. Crone, Ray H.   THE UNKNOWN AIR FORCE. *Saskatchewan Hist. [Canada] 1977 30(1): 1-17.* An air training school for Chinese pilots and aeronautical engineers was operated in Saskatoon from May 1919 until mid-1922. The King Wah Aviation field, known to Saskatonians as "the Chinese airfield" was founded to aid the armies of Dr. Sun Yat-Sen's Nationalists. The first instructor, Douglas Fraser, of the Royal Air Force, taught a class of six starting in July 1919. Fraser was the brother-in-law of a Mr. Lee, an ardent member of the Chinese Nationalist League. Lee's friend, Stanley Bring Mah, was also active in the founding of the air school. Fraser's successor as instructor was Lt. Harry Lobb, a partner in Stan McClelland's aviation business. The first graduate of this school was Y. M. Lim On. 6 photos, 49 notes.   C. Held

218. Davidson, Frederic.   STRATEGIC ENGAGEMENT AND SINO-AMERICAN TRADE. *SAIS Rev. 1981 (2): 131-140.* Since the Nixon administration, US export control policy has been manipulated to satisfy

China's appetite for Western technology and to punish the USSR for forays into Afghanistan and Africa.

219. Davis, Clarence B. FINANCING IMPERIALISM: BRITISH AND AMERICAN BANKERS AS VECTORS OF IMPERIAL EXPANSION IN CHINA, 1908-1920. *Business Hist. Rev. 1982 56(2): 236-264.* There have been conflicting interpretations of the role played by British and American bankers in early 20th-century investments in China. Were they subordinating profits to the diplomatic aims of their respective nations, or were they aggressively pursuing their own interests and in the process manipulating government officials? The author rejects both views as too simplistic and contends there were "shared goals" between public and private policymakers. Both sought Chinese dependence on the West, though not at the cost of seriously impairing China's integrity. Based on American and British governmental documents and periodicals. C. J. Pusateri

220. Dean, Britten. SINO-AMERICAN RELATIONS IN THE LATE 19TH CENTURY: THE VIEW FROM THE TSUNGLI YAMEN ARCHIVE. *Ch'ing-shih Wen-t'i 1981 4(5): 77-107.* Tsungli Yamen holdings, now in Taiwan at the Academia Sinica, are extensive but incomplete because some documents remain in Beijing. Close study of reports from local officials indicate a still vital administrative structure during 1868-94 quite unlike that portrayed by many contemporary scholars. Table, 35 notes.
J. R. Pavia, Jr.

221. Dean, Britten. THE UNITED STATES AND CHINA: JOHN RUSSELL YOUNG AND THE RIGHT TO MANUFACTURE IN THE TREATY PORTS, 1882-1883. *Hsiang Kang Chung Wen Ta Hsüeh Chung Kuo Wen Hua Yen Chiu So Hsüeh Pao (J. of the Inst. of Chinese Studies of the Chinese U. of Hong Kong) [Hong Kong] 1980 11: 271-290.* Intense negotiation over whether foreigners had a right to engage in manufacturing in the treaty ports of China was triggered by an American's attempt to establish a cotton-yarn factory in Shanghai in 1882. Diplomat John Russell Young zealously presented the US view, but the Chinese, insisting on their sovereign rights, acquitted themselves well. Based on US documents and contemporary reports in *The North China Herald;* 87 notes. Chinese summary.
J. A. Krompart

222. Dean, Britten. THE UNITED STATES AND CHINA IN THE NINETEENTH CENTURY: AN INCIDENT IN THE CAREER OF MINISTER CHARLES DENBY. *Bull. of the Inst. of Modern Hist. Acad. Sinica [Taiwan] 1978 7: 611-625.* A disputed claim for indemnity from the Chinese government for injuries sustained by an American resident in China in 1889 is used as a case study for a reevaluation of Charles Denby, American envoy in Peking, 1885-1898. Argues that Denby's aggressive and high-handed conduct typified America's China policy, and that the Chinese officials were not as incompetent as customarily thought to be. Based on archival documents at the Institute of Modern History, Academia Sinica, Taipei, and dispatches in National Archives nos. 59, 92, Washington; 25 notes. C. C. Brown

223. Dean, David M. THE DOMESTIC AND FOREIGN MISSIONARY PAPERS: THE CHINA PAPERS: 1835-1951. *Hist. Mag. of the Protestant Episcopal Church 1973 42(3): 333-340.* A brief account of Episcopalian missionary activity in China, 1835-1951 and a listing of the papers from the Chinese missions now held in the Church Historical Society archives in Austin, Texas. S

224. Deane, Hugh. HERBERT HOOVER AND THE KAILAN MINES SWINDLE. *Eastern Horizon [Hong Kong] 1981 20(5): 34-38.* Traces Herbert Hoover's role in the British takeover of the Chinese Engineering and Mining Company, from the Boxer Rebellion of 1900 to the legal proceedings during his campaign in 1928, which called into question Hoover's involvement in the affair.

225. DeAngelis, Richard C. RESISTING INTERVENTION: AMERICAN POLICY AND THE LIN CH'ENG INCIDENT. *Bull. of the Inst. of Modern Hist. Acad. Sinica [Taiwan] 1981 10: 401-416.* In the spring of 1926, Chinese bandits took foreign travelers on the Tientsin-Pukow Railway as hostages. The official American response departed from a stated policy of nonintervention and avoidance of punitive demands, but remained less bellicose than that of other foreign governments. Based on American documents and other contemporary writings; 60 notes. J. A. Krompart

226. Dearing, Albin. VISITING CHINESE BIG WHEEL INSPIRED NEW YORK FURORE. *Smithsonian 1975 6(7): 87-93.* Portrays the excitement of New York City upon the visit of the "exotic" minister from China, Li Hung-chang, in 1896.

227. DeBary, William Theodore. THE MING PROJECT AND MING THOUGHT. *Asian Thought and Soc. 1976 1(2): 189-193.* Discusses the state of Ming studies in the United States: the publication of the Ming Biographical History Project of the Association for Asian Studies in 1960 which encouraged the compilation of basic biographical and bibliographical reference tools, the subsequent three conferences with Japanese and Chinese scholars which changed perceptions about Ming thought, and future areas in need of study.

228. deDubnic, Vladimir Reisky. THE GLOBAL REALIGNMENT OF FORCES AND THE INDOCHINA QUESTION. *Orbis 1974 18(2): 535-552.* Discusses foreign relations particularly with regard to China in the wake of the withdrawal of US troops from Vietnam, 1973. S

229. deDubnic, Vladimir Reisky. L'EUROPE ET LA NOUVELLE POLITIQUE DES ETATS-UNIS ENVERS LA CHINE [Europe and the new United States policy towards China]. *Rev. de l'Est [France] 1973 4(4): 183-205.* The geopolitical linkage between China and Europe is based on the fact that both are neighbours of an expanding Soviet Union. This linkage became relevant when China became a nuclear power and when the United States' diplomacy catapulted China into the international system. The United States' new China policy implies a more modest role for the two superpowers and from this Europe can only benefit. The European endorsement of the new

United States China policy is based on (1) interest in a new world balance of power system; (2) "third force" aspirations; (3) considerations of security; (4) "revanchist" sentiments in Eastern Europe; (5) considerations for strengthening peace. The United States' new policy strengthens China's overall position, which in turn alters the Soviet strategic situation. The fact that Moscow must reappraise its global strategy due to the Sino-American rapprochement is of vital interest to the countries of Eastern Europe. While China can currently contribute little to a change of the status quo in Europe, she is the only great power whose declared policy it is to assist in bringing about the end of Soviet supremacy over the socialist states. Western Europe is apprehensive of a United States-Soviet detente at the expense of Europe; but a United States-China detente is in the interest of Europe, for it may lead to a new world balance of power where Europe can assume a third force role, provided her integration advances.
J

230. deKeijzer, Arne J. CHINA IN THE SCHOOLS: DIRECTIONS AND PRIORITIES. *Asian Studies Professional Rev.* 1973 2(2): 26-34. A conference was held at Wingspread, Wisconsin, in June 1972 to implement ideas for teaching Chinese studies in secondary schools. Participants relied on *China: A Resource and Curriculum Guide* (U. of Chicago Press, 1972) for teaching suggestions and heard papers by Wilbur J. Cohen, former Secretary of Health, Education, and Welfare, and Thomas Collins of the Center for War/Peace Studies. Participants discussed the priority for China studies, the teacher as a client, teacher-scholar relations, media use in China studies, and multiorganizational cooperation and funding. Recommendations included the preparation of program packets, organization of conferences and workshops, improved teacher education programs on Asia, and strengthening the periodical *Focus on Asian Studies*.
R. H. Detrick

231. DeSimone, Silvio. DA NIXON A FORD: L'EVOLUZIONE DELLA POLITICA AMERICANA VERSO LA CINA, DALLA DOTTRINA DI GUAM AL DOPO VIETNAM [From Nixon to Ford: the evolution of American policy toward China from the Guam Doctrine to post-Vietnam]. *Mondo Cinese* [Italy] 1976 4(15): 85-123. Considers the history of the prospective in which the United States observed China, from the 1950's to the 1970's. Examines the internal reasons and the international objectives for the change in US policy, and outlines the content of the "about-face." Ascribes various motives to explain this normalization and the progressive abandonment of Taiwan on the part of the Americans, including the circumstance of strategic importance, and how for the United States China constitutes a cushion between itself and Soviet expansionism.
J

232. DeSimone, Silvio. DAL VIETNAM ALL'AFGANISTAN: SI DELINEA LA COOPERAZIONE MILITARE CINO-AMERICANA [From Vietnam to Afghanistan: toward Sino-American military cooperation]. *Mondo Cinese* [Italy] 1980 8(2): 15-34. Examines US-Chinese interaction in the Chinese invasion of Vietnam and the Soviet invasion of Afghanistan and the risks to the balance of power if the United States were to contribute substantially to China's military modernization.
J/S

233. Devane, Richard T. THE UNITED STATES AND CHINA: CLAIMS AND ASSETS. *Asian Survey 1978 18(12): 1267-1279.* The claims-assets issue in US-China relations began on 16 December 1950. It was one of a series of US responses to Chinese intervention in the Korean conflict. The State Department explained that it would be revoked when the People's Republic of China (PRC) "behaved properly." The Chinese responded by placing all American assets in China under the control of the government. The persistence of these sanctions is remarkable; the issue continues to affect US-China relations "even in this period of accommodation in the Pacific." Discusses problems of valuation; rapprochement; reasons for the delay; opportunity for settlement; resolution of the issue; and significance of settlement. It would have "important symbolic value in eliminating the vestiges of the Cold War. It is at once an important action and a relatively easy one." Table, 38 notes.
E. P. Stickney

234. Dial, Roger. IN SEARCH OF A NEW CHINA. *Pacific Affairs [Canada] 1976-77 49(4): 680-685.* Reviews three studies on China by Americans and comments on their "paradigmatic orthodoxy." In *The Chinese Calculus of Deterrence,* Allen S. Whiting analyzed three conflicts which pitted China directly against the United States. Claude A. Buss in his *China: The People's Republic of China and Richard Nixon* examined the prospects for a continuing detente with China. Chairman Mao was ubiquitous in the author's conceptual scheme. John K. Fairbank's *Chinese-American Interactions: A Historical Summary* called American intellectual inertia a dangerous hindrance to US dealings with East Asia.
S. H. Frank

235. Dillon, Linda D.; Burton, Bruce; and Soderlund, Walter C. WHO WAS THE PRINCIPAL ENEMY? SHIFTS IN OFFICIAL CHINESE PERCEPTIONS OF THE TWO SUPERPOWERS, 1968-69. *Asian Survey 1977 17(5): 456-473.* Attempts to measure the level of official Chinese hostility toward the United States and the USSR, 1968-69, and to determine whether there occurred a change in the perception of China's principal enemy during this period. Considers that 1968-69 was crucial in the development of Chinese foreign policy, for it spanned the last phase of the Cultural Revolution and the first stages in China's reaction to increasing threats in the international environment. The authors claim that China moved toward a stance which regarded the USSR as the principal enemy due to the impact of the Soviet invasion of Czechoslovakia in August 1968 and the fear of Soviet attack. Based on an analysis of hostile symbols in the *Peking Review;* 8 charts, 17 notes.
M. Feingold

236. Dingman, Roger. LOST CHANCE IN CHINA. *Rev. in Am. Hist. 1981 9(2): 252-259.* Review essay on *Uncertain Years: Chinese-American Relations, 1947-1950,* edited by Dorothy Borg and Waldo Heinrichs (1980), Kenneth S. Chern's *Dilemma in China; America's Policy Debate, 1945* (1980), and James Reardon-Anderson's *Yenan and the Great Powers: The Origins of Chinese Communist Foreign Policy, 1944-1946* (1980).

237. Dojka, John. THE YALE-CHINA COLLECTION. *Yale U. Lib. Gazette 1979 53(4): 211-216.* The Yale-in-China Association to develop and

maintain a Christian institution of higher learning was conceived in 1901, began its work in 1902, and ended its work in China in 1951 when its last representative crossed the border to safety in Hong Kong. Its archives and the papers of its officials constitute an important source of missionary work in China.
 D. A. Yanchisin

238. Dominguez, Jorge I. RESPONSES TO OCCUPATIONS BY THE UNITED STATES: CALIBAN'S DILEMMA. *Pacific Hist. Rev. 1979 48(4): 591-605.* This concluding essay in this issue's series of case studies of American military occupation in Cuba, Peking, and the Philippines between 1898 and 1903 discusses the conditions of resistance, modes of collaboration, inducements to collaborate, the role of elites in the societies of occupied countries, and the building of racist and class prejudices among both occupiers and occupied. 3 notes.
 R. N. Lokken

239. Donahue, William J. THE CALEB CUSHING MISSION. *Modern Asian Studies [Great Britain] 1982 16(2): 193-216.* Traces the history of American trade with China from 1784 and the effects of the dominance of the British East Indies Company in commerce in the Far East. Attention is directed to the events leading to, preparations for, and the conduct of the Caleb Cushing mission to China in 1844, with reference to the Xu Aman (Hsü A-man) incident, the treaty of negotiations, the significance of the commercial arrangements, and the limited power and prestige of the United States in China. An abbreviation of the Treaty of Wangxia (Wanghsia) is appended. Based partly on Senate documents; 91 notes.
 P. J. Durell

240. Donahue, William J. THE FRANCIS TERRANOVA CASE. *Historian 1981 43(2): 211-224.* Sino-American trade relations were disrupted in 1821 when sailor Francis Terranova of the *Emily* was accused of killing a Chinese woman. The subsequent accusations, trial, stoppage of trade, and execution of Terranova in October, 1821, recounted here in detail, went almost unnoticed in the United States. The incident represented the first conflict between the United States and China over extraterritoriality and it demonstrated the lack of American policy in the Pacific. The Chinese effectively held foreigners under control with economic threats, such as the abrupt termination of trade. Not until 1844 was the issue of legal jurisdiction resolved in favor of the United States. From then on the United States had jurisdiction over American nationals in China, an unequal treaty arrangement that lasted for the next 100 years. Primary sources; 58 notes.
 R. S. Sliwoski

241. Donaldson, Robert H. TRIANGULAR POLITICS: THE RULES OF THE GAME. *Pakistan Horizon [Pakistan] 1974 27(1): 3-10.* Discusses the current policies of the United States, the USSR, and China, each of which views the other two as a principal adversary. The threat of collusion between two nations to the disadvantage of the third keeps the situation in balance. From an address at the Pakistan Institute of International Affairs, 23 February 1974.
 H. M. Evans

242. Donneur, André. THE EMERGING NATIONAL ORDER. *Int. Perspectives [Canada] 1973 (Jul/Aug): 3-9.* Examines the world balance of

power, assessing the importance of the USSR, the United States, China, and Europe, 1945-73.

243. Drucker, Alison R.   WESTERN WOMEN AND THE ORIGINS OF THE WOMEN'S MOVEMENT IN TRANSITIONAL CHINA, 1840-1927. *Towson State J. of Int. Affairs 1976 11(1): 17-24.* Examines the influence of British and American cultural attitudes in elevating the social status of women in China from 1840 to 1927.

244. Dubinski, A. M.   PEREGOVORY "SOIUZNICHESKOI GRUPPY NABLIUDATELEI" SSHA S RUKOVODSTVOM KPK [The negotiations conducted by the US "Allied Group of Observers" with the CPC leadership]. *Voprosy Istorii [USSR] 1979 (1): 71-81.* Traces the activity of the American "allied group of observers," which arrived in Yenan in July 1944 and entered in contact with Mao Zedong, and his closest entourage. The special line of the CPC leadership in the person of Mao—their anti-Sovietism manifested already at that time—attracted the attention of American diplomats who tried to prevent the development of the national liberation revolution in China into the socialist revolution and to bar China's orientation to the Soviet Union. But the whole course of the Chinese revolution in 1945-49 thwarted the designs of American politicians. 47 notes.   J

245. Duke, David C.   ANNA LOUISE STRONG AND THE SEARCH FOR A GOOD CAUSE. *Pacific Northwest Q. 1975 66(3): 123-137.* Committed to humanitarian causes throughout her life, Anna Louise Strong initially received inspiration from Industrial Workers of the World activities and the Seattle General Strike of 1919. But it was in the USSR of the 1920's and 1930's that she found a new sense of achievement as organizer and writer. Never a doctrinaire Marxist and never fully recognized for her achievements in the Soviet Union, Ms. Strong gradually developed an affection for the Maoist brand of communism. Her praise of the Chinese model led to deportation from the Soviet Union in 1948. Though subsequently exonerated of the charges, she chose life in China as an activist writer until her death in 1970. Based on primary and secondary sources; 2 photos, 67 notes.   M. L. Tate

246. Duke, David C.   SPY SCARES, SCAPEGOATS, AND THE COLD WAR. *South Atlantic Q. 1980 79(3): 245-256.* Traces the paths of two American women, Agnes Smedley (d. 1950) and Anna Louise Strong (1885-1970), from the post-World War I period until their respective deaths. Smedley was quite enamored by the Communist movement in China, Strong by the Communist takeover in Russia. Strong was later deported from the USSR for not adhering precisely to the Communist line—a very disenchanting experience for her. Both became scapegoats for Americans and Russians who were looking for excuses for the failures that marked their Cold War ventures. Based on the Strong Papers, University of Washington Libraries, Seattle; Strong Papers, Swarthmore College Peace Collection, and the writings of Agnes Smedley; 28 notes.   H. M. Parker, Jr.

247. Dutt, Gargi.   CHINA AND THE SHIFT IN SUPER-POWER RELATIONS. *Int. Studies [India] 1974 13(4): 635-662.* Examines the implica-

tions of detente for China's foreign policy in the 1970's; assesses the impact of President Richard M. Nixon's visit to China in 1972.

248. Eckstein, Alexander. CHINA'S TRADE POLICY AND SINO-AMERICAN RELATIONS. *Foreign Affairs 1975 54(1): 134-154.* Examines fluctuating patterns of Sino-American trade and the foreign economic policy of the People's Republic of China. Great shifts have occurred there, and the political implications are significant because the Chinese depend upon the United States to deter Russian expansionism. There was no trade during 1951-71, followed by a largely agriculture export situation from the United States to China. The economic situation of the 1970's has hurt China's exports to the United States, and the absence of a most-favored-nation status for China has meant a full tariff levy on Chinese goods. Oil production will certainly have a favorable impact upon Chinese foreign exchange, but the lack of full diplomatic relations with the United States is a serious obstacle to the further development of trade. 3 tables, 11 notes. C. W. Olson

249. Eckstein, Alexander and Reynolds, Bruce. SINO-AMERICAN TRADE PROSPECTS AND POLICY. *Am. Econ. Rev. 1974 64(2): 294-299.* Describes the development of Communist China's foreign trade, 1952-72, and prospects for trade with the United States. From the American Economic Association's annual meeting in 1973.

250. Eggert, Gerald G. LI HUNG-CHANG'S MISSION TO AMERICA, 1896. *Midwest Q. 1977 18(3): 240-257.* Li Hung-Chang (1823-1901) represented China at the coronation of Tsar Nicholas II of Russia in 1896 and then returned to China by way of Europe and America. His visit raised great hopes among government officials and businessmen in each country that he visited, because of their growing interest in investing in the Orient. The country least affected by his visit was the United States, because President Cleveland and the people of the country generally viewed his visit as a curiosity. The country which in fact benefitted was Russia: closer ties between Russia and China were formed for economic and military reasons. Bibliographic note.
S. J. Quinlan

251. Emmerson, John K. CHINA-BURMA-INDIA. *Foreign Service J. 1977 54(10): 8-12; 54(11): 11-14.* Part I. Discusses battalions in the China-Burma-India Theater during World War II, 1941-43. Part II. Discusses his remembrances of fighting in the China-Burma-India Theater, 1944.

252. Evans, P. M. THE LONG WAY HOME: JOHN FAIRBANK AND AMERICAN CHINA POLICY 1941-72. *Int. J. [Canada] 1982 37(4): 584-605.* The career of Harvard Sinologist John K. Fairbank is a model of academic vocation committed to national service. During World War II, he advised the government on Chinese affairs. During 1946-50 he published widely on Sino-American relations, most notably his *The United States and China* (1948), which advocated recognition of the Chinese government and its admission to the UN. During the Cold War years, Fairbank's views were attacked as pro-Communist, and he dedicated his energies to scholarly pursuits. After 1960, Fairbank encouraged a cross-cultural understanding of Chinese and Vietnam-

ese attitudes and values rather than offering specific tactical or political advice. He helped bring about the normalization of Sino-American relations by advising that the Taiwan problem was not insurmountable. Based on Fairbank's published works; 42 notes.   J. Powell

253. Fabritzek, Uwe G.   DIE REAKTION IN OSTEUROPA AUF DIE CHINA-REISE NIXONS [East European reactions to Nixon's China trip]. *Osteuropa [West Germany] 1972 22(7): 497-506.* Four types of press response represented the Eastern European Communist attitudes: Czechoslovakia, Poland, and East Germany aggressively supported the Soviet anti-Chinese position; Bulgaria and Hungary kept their criticism of China within limits; Rumania and Yugoslavia welcomed the Chinese-American rapprochement; Albania ignored the Nixon trip altogether. 63 notes.   R. E. Weltsch

254. Feaver, John H.   THE CHINA AID BILL OF 1948: LIMITED ASSISTANCE AS A COLD WAR STRATEGY. *Diplomatic Hist. 1981 5(2): 107-120.* It is commonly assumed that public and congressional opinion forced the Truman administration to extend aid to the Nationalist regime in China and that the China Aid Bill of 1948 was due to the pressure of a loosely knit "China bloc" in both houses of Congress. Recently released government papers reveal that, though the China bloc did exert pressure, it was not the source of the administration's decision. The aid bill resulted from increasingly systematic calculations concerning the global strategic importance to the United States of the East Asian mainland, after the failure of the Marshall mission. Based on material listed in Declassified Documents Reference System; 26 notes.
    J. V. Coutinho

255. Fetzer, James.   SENATOR VANDENBERG AND THE AMERICAN COMMITMENT TO CHINA, 1945-1950. *Historian 1974 36(2): 283-303.* Senator Arthur H. Vandenberg had great influence on American policy toward China and its civil war. Studies his part in the "maintenance of an American commitment to Chiang Kai-shek, the form of this commitment, and the failure of the United States to disengage from Chiang's tottering regime." Questions can be raised about the appropriateness of the actions taken to achieve the ends desired, and Vandenberg's approach contributed much "which manifested this lack of vision." As a result an attachment to Chiang's government was maintained, a government which was "unwilling and unable to help itself effectively." 66 notes.   R. V. Ritter

256. FitzGerald, C. R.   CHINA AND SOUTH EAST ASIA AFTER VIETNAM. *Plural Societies [Netherlands] 1975 6(4): 3-16.* Analyzes China's relations with Southeast Asia, particularly after the Vietnam War, as they reveal the false premises upon which US intervention in Vietnam was based.

257. Forcier, Pierre and Srivastava, H. P.   CAMBODGE: MESURES SOCIO-ÉCONOMIQUES ET IMPLICATIONS POLITIQUES AU CAMBODGE DE 1963 À 1975 [Cambodia: socioeconomic measures and their political implications in Cambodia, 1963-75]. *Études Int. [Canada] 1975 6(2): 240-254.* Discusses the effect of American foreign aid on Cambodia, 1955-62, and emphasizes the economic and political impact caused by the rupture of this

aid in 1963. Notes Cambodia's increasing dependence on China subsequent to the rupture with the United States. Primary and secondary sources; 3 maps, 6 tables, 20 notes, biblio.   J. F. Harrington, Jr.

258. Fraser, Angus M. THE DEPARTMENT OF DEFENSE AND THE CHINESE THREAT. *US Naval Inst. Pro. 1974 100(2) 18-25.* The US Defense Department assesses Soviet and Chinese forces differently. Statements about Chinese forces and programs tend to be general: overall defense expenditures are probably high and burdensome, but not unbearably so; there has been remarkable progress in nuclear weapons development; "ground force improvements are unspectacular, but significant"; naval and aircraft construction looks to close-in defense; there is concern over having to operate on more than one front; and the Chinese high command is "transfixed by the Soviet presence along their long border and in the operational sense is moving to avert the disaster that major war with the Soviet Union would be." 7 photos.
A. N. Garland

259. Frost, Edwin C. CHINA CONVOY. *Aerospace Hist. 1983 30(1): 15-23.* Describes Edwin C. Frost's experiences commanding a US Army Air Force Air Transport Command truck convoy traveling the Ledo Road-Burma Road from India to China in June 1945. Drawn from various AAF units, the drivers and mechanics were generally inexperienced in this kind of work. But during the 12-day trip over mountainous jungle roads in monsoon season, they became veterans of the road and proved themselves capable of dealing with the numerous organizational and logistic problems, overcoming mechanical difficulties, and delivering the goods on time. 9 illus.   J. K. Ohl

260. Funnell, Victor C. CHINA AND ASEAN: THE CHANGING FACE OF SOUTH EAST ASIA. *World Today [Great Britain] 1975 31(7): 299-306.* Discusses US efforts to normalize relations with China and gains made by Association of South East Asian Nations (ASEAN) members in relations with Asia's great nuclear power.

261. Gabard, William M. JOHN ELLIOT WARD: A GEORGIA ELITIST IN THE CELESTIAL EMPIRE, 1858-60. *West Georgia Coll. Studies in the Social Sci. 1983 22: 53-62.* Dignity, firmness of purpose, and genuine concern for others helped John Elliot Ward to bring about diplomatic relations between the United States and China during a difficult period for the Chinese.

262. Garner, William V. SALT II: CHINA'S ADVICE AND DISSENT. *Asian Survey 1979 19(12): 1224-1240.* For some 20 years the Chinese have strenuously protested US-Soviet arms control negotiations; however, the USSR is now the target of their protests rather than the United States. Recent events have increased the importance of the "China factor" in US arms control policy, increasing the difficulty with which US policymakers reconcile Sino-Soviet policy with arms control and defense policies. US policymakers must decide whether national interests would be better served by the maintenance of current Soviet military superiority over China or by China's steady acquisition of more effective military capabilities against the Soviets. 44 notes.
M. A. Eide

263. Garver, John. CHINESE FOREIGN POLICY IN 1970: THE TILT TOWARDS THE SOVIET. *China Q. [Great Britain] 1980 (82): 214-249.* A shift by China toward the USSR in 1970 was forced by a military faction which was convinced the United States was being destroyed by political and economic stress as well as by military defeat. A more moderate group led by Zhou Enlai (Chou En-lai) also adopted this position to enlist the support of the military faction. 3 fig., 87 notes. J. R. Pavia, Jr.

264. Garver, John W. SINO-VIETNAMESE CONFLICT AND THE SINO-AMERICAN RAPPROCHEMENT. *Pol. Sci. Q. 1981 96(3): 445-464.* Discusses how China's support for North Vietnam's war effort from 1968 to 1973 was affected by Peking's rapprochement with the United States. In the 1973 peace negotiations China urged Hanoi to accept a compromise settlement with the United States. J

265. Gelm, George E. THE ADMIRALS AND THE VICEROY. *US Naval Inst. Pro. 1973 99(2): 82-84.* In 1907 the presence of four armored cruisers at Nanking and the skillful diplomacy of Rear Admiral Willard H. Brownson, commander of the US Armored Cruiser Squadron, convinced Tuan Fang, a powerful and corrupt Chinese viceroy, to call off a boycott of American goods in the five southern provinces of China. Excerpted from the journal of the author, gunnery officer on one of the cruisers. 3 illus.

J. K. Ohl

266. George, Brian T. THE STATE DEPARTMENT AND SUN YAT-SEN: AMERICAN POLICY AND THE REVOLUTIONARY DISINTEGRATION OF CHINA, 1920-1924. *Pacific Hist. Rev. 1977 46(3): 387-408.* Historians have failed to analyze the reasons for the State Department's distaste for Sun Yat-sen in the latter part of his career. The main reasons were the view that Sun's activities had a destabilizing effect which raised problems for the successful implementation of the US Open Door policy. Sun was not seen as a revolutionary and a nationalist, but as a megalomaniacal troublemaker who was primarily responsible for China's failure to unify peacefully and reform politically under warlord control. Based on documents in manuscript collections and National Archives and on published primary sources; 67 notes.

W. K. Hobson

267. Ghosh, Partha S. FROM RED SCARE TO [MC CARTHYISM]: BUILDING OF NATIONAL IMAGES: THE AMERICAN EXPERIENCE. *China Report [India] 1978 14(5-6): 27-46.* Changes in US anti-Communism, first against the USSR and then against the People's Republic of China as well, 1917-50, were due to shifting economic and political interest in the United States.

268. Ghosh, Partha S. PASSAGE OF THE SILVER PURCHASE ACT OF 1934: THE CHINA LOBBY AND THE ISSUE OF CHINA TRADE. *Indian J. of Am. Studies [India] 1976 6(1-2): 18-29.* Describes the activity of the congressional lobby in manipulating the passage of the Silver Purchase Act of 1934. Using the quite secondary issue of a depreciating China US trade as its most handy weapon, the China lobby pushed through this act over the

opposition of Franklin D. Roosevelt and Secretary of Treasury Henry Morgenthau. The silver purchase program enriched the act's promoters but it neither stabilized the Chinese currency nor revitalized the US-China trade. 54 notes.

L. V. Eid

269. Ghosh, Partha S. SINO-AMERICAN ECONOMIC RELATIONS, 1929-1939. *Int. Studies [India] 1976 15(3): 343-364.* Studies efforts at restoring Sino-American trade, which had reached an all-time high in 1928. After the crash of 1929, however, the price of silver, China's monetary base, fell sharply, and trade dropped correspondingly. United States silver interests lobbied to get an increase in government domestic silver purchases, ostensibly to help China; the result, however, was a drain on Chinese silver reserves. Trade was further hindered by Japan's invasion of China in 1937. Only World War II genuinely committed the United States to economic aid for China. 3 tables, 104 notes.

J. Tull

270. Ghosh, Partha S. SINO-AMERICAN ECONOMIC RELATIONS, 1784-1929: A SURVEY. *China Report [India] 1976 12(4): 16-27.* The disintegrating Chinese political situation in the 1830's prompted American merchants to pressure their government for a well-defined China policy that later became the foundation for a century of US economic interest in China. Events such as the American Civil War had their impact in shaping and directing US economic policies. While comparing the volume and quality of British and US trade with China, shifts in America's foreign policy toward China are portrayed as predicated upon US economic interests at given points in history. The author discusses the Open Door policy, the Consortium, and the Nanking Treaty. 4 tables, 77 notes.

S. F. Benfield

271. Ghosh, Suchita. THAILAND'S RELATIONS WITH THE U.S. AND CHINA: THE SEARCH FOR AN INDEPENDENT FOREIGN POLICY. *China Report [India] 1976 12(4): 46-57.* An analysis of Thai policy toward the United States in the 1950's and 1960's emphasizing Thailand's abandonment of a traditional neutral position in favor of a pro-American alignment in the mid-1960's in response to Communist aggression in Indochina. In the early 1970's Thailand shifted its policies in response to US withdrawal from Southeast Asia and normalization of relations with China. The necessity of maintaining good relations with its neighbors as well as a polarization of opinion in Southeast Asia over Sino-Soviet rivalry has necessitated Thailand's return to a neutralist policy. 19 notes.

S. F. Benfield

272. Giddes, Paul H., ed. CHINA'S FIRST OIL WELL: RECOLLECTIONS OF ROBERT D. LOCKE, TITUSVILLE OIL PIONEER. *Pennsylvania Hist 1980 47(1): 29-37.* In 1878, Robert D. Locke and A. P. Karns drilled China's first oil well on Taiwan. In 1940, Paul H. Giddens interviewed Locke, then 90 years old, regarding his trip from Titusville to Taiwan and his experiences there. Reprints the interview. 5 notes.

D. C. Swift

273. Goldstein, Johnathan. RESOURCES ON EARLY SINO-AMERICAN RELATIONS IN PHILADELPHIA'S STEPHEN GIRARD COLLEC-

TION AND THE HISTORICAL SOCIETY OF PENNSYLVANIA. *Ch'ing-shih Wen-t'i 1980 4(3): 114-129.* Identifies items dealing with early Sino-American trade to be found in Philadelphia. The Stephen Girard Collection is housed at Girard College and provides information on the commercial, social, and diplomatic history of late 18th- and early 19th-century China. The Historical Society of Pennsylvania has its own collection of China materials on subjects similar to those dealt with in the Girard Collection and covering essentially the same period. Illus., 19 notes. J. R. Pavia, Jr.

274. Goldstein, Steven M. CHINESE COMMUNIST POLICY TOWARD THE UNITED STATES: OPPORTUNITIES AND CONSTRAINTS, 1944-1950. Borg, Dorothy and Heinrichs, Waldo, ed. *Uncertain Years: Chinese-American Relations, 1947-1950* (New York: Columbia U. Pr., 1980): 235-278. Mao Zedong's (Mao Tse-tung's) "lean to one side" speech of June 1949 was not a benchmark in China's foreign policy, marking the end of a period of open-ended policy allowing for rapprochement with the United States, but a confirmation of the hard line that the Chinese Communists had been following since 1946.

275. Gough, Barry M. THE NORTH WEST COMPANY'S "ADVENTURE TO CHINA." *Oregon Hist. Q. 1975 76(4): 309-332.* Early in the European development of Canada, the economic promise of the Pacific and the China market drew explorers west. A focal point of the North West Company's interest in the China market and the Pacific was Astoria, "where furs were collected for export and where suppliers and trade items for the vast interior were received." In 1814 the *Isaac Todd* began taking all the furs from the Columbia River Basin to Canton and returning to England with tea on account for the East India Company. High costs were offset by the good prices received for the furs. Illus., map, 66 notes. E. P. Stickney

276. Graebner, Norman A. HENRY KISSINGER AND AMERICAN FOREIGN POLICY: A CONTEMPORARY APPRAISAL. *Australian J. of Pol. and Hist. [Australia] 1976 22(1): 7-22.* Henry A. Kissinger's diplomacy marked the first major change in American foreign policy since World War II. Instead of containing Communism he sought a stabilization of relations with Russia and China, based on the notion that they were essentially status quo powers. Until 1974 he achieved great popularity, but his sanctioning of wiretapping indicated flaws, and his neglect of the professionals demoralized the State Department. Although his reputation survived the Watergate crisis and Nixon's removal, critics noted that his success with Moscow and Peking stemmed largely from Russian and Chinese desire for better relations. His uniqueness lies in the fact that he was the first Secretary of State in three generations to think and act in political rather than judicial/moral terms. Documented from newspapers and periodicals. W. D. McIntyre

277. Graham, Edward D. SPECIAL INTERESTS AND THE EARLY CHINA TRADE: NEGATIVE MYTHS OF THE CANTON TRADE. *Michigan Academician 1973 6(2): 233-242.*

278. Gupta, Sisir. SINO-U.S. DÉTENTE AND INDIA. *Internat. J. of Pol. 1974 4(3): 89-99.*

279. Gupta, Surendra K. AMERICA'S CHINA POLICY AND MCCARTHYISM: THE CASE OF JOHN CARTER VINCENT. *China Report [India] 1981 17(5): 35-42.* Reviews Gary May's study of McCarthyism, *China Scapegoat: The Diplomatic Ordeal of John Carter Vincent* (1979) and the current resurgence of extremist anti-Soviet feeling in the United States. The account of Vincent's ordeal, ending in his unjust humiliation, may serve to remind Americans of the dangers of extremism. 7 notes. J. Cushnie

280. Harding, Harry. FROM CHINA WITH DISDAIN: NEW TRENDS IN THE STUDY OF CHINA. *Asian Survey 1982 22(10): 934-958.* The pronounced American fascination with the People's Republic of China (PRC) that lasted through most of the 1970's seems to be giving way to a more objective and even cynical view. There has also been a transformation in many of the intellectual assumptions that Americans make about the PRC, imposing Western standards to a higher degree. This reappraisal results from changes in the US political and intellectual climate, as well as from changes in the role China plays in American foreign policy and changes in the terms under which Westerners are able to visit the PRC. Westerners continue to adopt the official Chinese interpretations of society in the PRC. Based on memoirs and secondary sources. M. A. Eide

281. Harding, Harry. FROM CHINA, WITH DISDAIN: NEW TRENDS IN THE STUDY OF CHINA. *Issues & Studies [Taiwan] 1982 18(7): 12-39.* American attitudes toward China tend to swing between excessive praise and cynical scorn. In the 1970's Americans idealized China. Now the trend is to harsh criticism. A more realistic approach is in order. Based on a paper presented at the 11th Sino-American Conference on Mainland China, Taipei, 8-11 June 1982; 71 notes. J. A. Krompart

282. Hartgen, Stephen. HOW FOUR U. S. PAPERS COVERED THE COMMUNIST CHINESE REVOLT. *Journalism Q. 1979 56(1): 175-178.* Discusses coverage by four daily newspapers of the resignation of Patrick J. Hurley, US Ambassador to China, on 27 November 1945, and the battles between Chinese Nationalists and Communists in Manchuria of April-May 1946. The newspapers carried more interpretive articles on the Hurley resignation, a story originating in Washington, D.C., than they did on the fighting in Manchuria. Based on articles in the Atlanta *Constitution,* the Cleveland *Plain Dealer,* the Louisville *Courier-Journal,* and the Minneapolis *Tribune;* 7 notes. R. P. Sindermann, Jr.

283. Hartmann, Frederick H. THE DETENTE DEBATE. *Naval War Coll. Rev. 1977 30(1): 33-40.* A good portion of the comment, discussion and debate that has concerned detente has been as much the result of failure to define it precisely as it has been directed towards its substance. An accommodation or relaxation of political tensions accompanied by an increase in weapons systems might appear to be inconsistent with detente. However, the

Soviet Union is faced with two potential enemies, the United States and China, each of which it must consider when dealing with the other. J

284. Hartwell, Charles K., Mrs. MOBILE TO CHINA: A VALIANT WOMAN'S MISSION. *Alabama Rev. 1978 31(4): 243-255.* Describes Mary Horton Stuart's (1842-1926) early life in Mobile, Alabama, and the 39 years she spent as a Presbyterian missionary in Hangchow, Nanking, and Peking. Of her four sons, John L. Stuart became president of Yenching University and US ambassador to China, and Warren Stuart became president of Hangchow College. Primary and secondary sources; 48 notes. J. F. Vivian

285. Hawkins, John N. FRANCIS LISTER HAWKS POTT (1864-1947), CHINA MISSIONARY AND EDUCATOR. *Paedagogica Hist. [Belgium] 1973 13(2): 329-347.* Francis L. H. Pott, an Episcopalian missionary, was president during 1888-1941 of one of the most influential mission colleges in China, St. John's University in Shanghai. 45 notes, biblio. J. M. McCarthy

286. Heaton, William R., Jr. A NEW ERA OF US-CHINA RELATIONS. *Air Force Mag. 1973 56(3): 51-55.* America's relations with China are changing fundamentally, and peaceful accommodation between the two countries seems more likely than ever before.

287. Heimann, Bernhard. ZUR INTERVENTION DER USA WÄHREND DES BÜRGERKRIEGES IN CHINA 1945 BIS 1949 [US intervention in the civil war in China, 1945-49]. *Militärgeschichte [East Germany] 1982 21(3): 282-292.* Describes US expansionist policy in Asia in a period when it tried to convert the Guomindang regime in China into its chief ally in Asia. Describes the phases of US military intervention in the Chinese civil war up to the withdrawal of the US armed forces in 1949 and evaluates the USSR's assistance to the Chinese people and the People's Liberation Army, whose victory it made possible. Map; 59 notes. J/T (H. D. Andrews)

288. Heininger, Janet E. PRIVATE POSITIONS VERSUS PUBLIC POLICY: CHINESE DEVOLUTION AND THE AMERICAN EXPERIENCE IN EAST ASIA. *Diplomatic Hist. 1982 6(3): 287-302.* Spurred by Chinese nationalism, American missionaries stated their goal of building an indigenous church. Nonetheless, they slowed devolution through their attitude of superiority, rejection of Chinese values, doubts of Chinese abilities, and desire to retain control. Chinese reticence to assert themselves and willingness to rely on foreign subsidies contributed to the problem. The Congregationalist missionaries' standard of living and Chinese poverty made self-supporting missions impossible; inadequate training of Chinese Christians made self-propagation improbable. The mission experience is a microcosm of the American experience in the Far East. Based on the papers of the American Board of Commissioners for Foreign Missions and other primary sources; 40 notes. T. J. Heston

289. Heinrichs, Waldo. ROOSEVELT AND TRUMAN: THE PRESIDENTIAL PERSPECTIVE. Borg, Dorothy and Heinrichs, Waldo, ed. *Uncertain Years: Chinese-American Relations, 1947-1950* (New York: Columbia U. Pr., 1980): 3-12. Reports on the first session of the Conference on

Chinese-American Relations, sponsored by the East Asian Institute of Columbia University, at Mount Kisco, New York, 1978, devoted to US policy toward China 1944-48, discussing Franklin D. Roosevelt's postwar plans, Harry S. Truman's early Cold War policies, assistance to Jiang Jieshi (Chiang Kai-shek), and the Marshall mission.

290. Henry, Ernst. PEKIN-VASHINGTON [Beijing and Washington]. *Voprosy Istorii [USSR] 1980 (6): 100-111.* Traces the history of relations between China and the United States from 1944 to 1978. Even during the Korean War, when relations between the two countries were generally thought to be extremely poor, Mao Zedong and Zhou Enlai were plotting with representatives of the US government to present a united front against the "Polar Bear" even as Mao was hypocritically mouthing phrases pledging eternal friendship to the USSR. China has so far made more concessions than the United States in establishing the present cordial relations between the two superpowers, but in 1976 Geng Biao threatened to turn on the United States when the time was right. 61 notes. S

291. Henson, Curtis T., Jr. THE US NAVY AND THE TAIPING REBELLION. *Am. Neptune 1978 38(1): 28-40.* The Taiping Rebellion (1850-64) imposed severe burdens on the America East India squadron because the squadron was involved in "opening" Japan and making treaty revisions with China. Nevertheless, the US Navy "met its responsibilities in China, securing American interests." Primary sources; 39 notes. G. H. Curtis

292. Hettig, David and Pozzetta, George E. THE LOSS OF CHINA: A SELECTED BIBLIOGRAPHY. *Social Studies 1974 65(5): 214-217.* Bibliographical essay on Chinese-American relations. L. R. Raife

293. Hinton, Harold C. THE UNITED STATES AND THE SINO-SOVIET CONFRONTATION. *Orbis 1975 19(1): 25-46.* Discusses US military strategy and foreign policy regarding friction between the USSR and China, 1969-70's, emphasizing China's accusations of Soviet expansionism.

294. Holbraad, Carsten. THE TRIANGULAR SYSTEM. *Cooperation and Conflict [Norway] 1973 8(2): 81-90.* "The triangle of the United States, the Soviet Union, and China, though likely to represent only a stage in a transition from the duel of the original two super powers to a complex system of five or more powers, may be the dominant relationship of the seventies. Relations among the three powers will probably be a mixture of conflict and cooperation, though the mixture may not be the same on each side of the triangle. Stabilizing forces are at work in a great-power triad, but there are also sources of instability. A coalition of two powers against the third seems a distinct possibility." J

295. Holbrook, Francis X. BRAVE HEARTS AND BRIGHT WEAPONS. *Marine Corps Gazette 1973 57(11): 56-65.* Examines the contribution of three Marine Corps battalions in Peking, Tientsin, and Taku, during the Boxer Rebellion of 1900.

296. Hollander, Paul. THE IDEOLOGICAL PILGRIM: LOOKING FOR UTOPIA, THEN AND NOW. *Encounter [Great Britain] 1973 41(5): 3-15.* Compares the western intellectuals who made an "ideological pilgrimage" to the USSR in the 1930's with those who made similar journeys to Cuba, China, and North Vietnam in recent years. Notes that "in both periods many intellectuals were searching for a type of social order which they could enthusiastically endorse and contrast with the dispiriting state of affairs they deplored in their own countries." Analyzes the nature of intellectual alienation which produces such pilgrimages, the attractive characteristics of the "new societies" which act as goals, and the methods by which the pilgrims were deceived by "the selective presentation of reality" by their hosts. 23 notes.
D. H. Murdoch

297. Holloway, Bruce K. THE P-40. *Aerospace Hist. 1978 25(3): 136-140.* The author, a retired USAF General, describes the P-40 aircraft and his experiences in flying it in the 14th Air Force, the former American Volunteer Group (Flying Tigers), in China, 1942-43. Provides an informal exchange of correspondence between the editor of the *Aerospace Historian* and General Holloway regarding the aircraft. 2 photos.
C. W. Ohrvall

298. Hong, Zhu. AMERICAN LITERARY STUDIES IN NEW CHINA: A BRIEF REPORT. *Am. Studies Int. 1981 19(3-4): 43-48.* With brief exceptions in China, such as the Hundred Flowers period in 1956-57, the 1950's and 1960's were unfavorable for American literary studies, while the Cultural Revolution brought a complete blank. After the downfall of the Gang of Four in 1976, a major development began: universities started courses in American literature, translations—especially of living authors—multiplied, and the first Chinese history of American literature appeared. But the dogma of critical realism remains influential, causing a relative neglect of American classics in favor of popular fiction.
R. E. Noble

299. Hoya, Thomas W. THE CHANGING U.S. REGULATION OF EAST-WEST TRADE. *Columbia J. of Transnational Law 1973 12(1): 1-38.* Discusses the recent rapid increase in east-west trade, especially between the United States, the People's Republic of China, and the USSR.
S

300. Hoyt, Frederick B. THE LESSON OF CONFRONTATION: TWO CHRISTIAN COLLEGES FACE THE CHINESE REVOLUTION, 1925-1927. *Asian Forum 1976 8(3): 45-62.* Discusses how two American sponsored Christian colleges, Canton Christian College, and Yale-in-China, attempted to accommodate themselves to the Chinese Revolution, 1925-27. The critical factor proved to be the willingness and ability of the Chinese government to tolerate the schools and deflect antiforeign sentiment, not the attitudes of college administrators or their country's diplomats. 31 notes.
R. B. Orr

301. Hoyt, Frederick B. THE OPEN DOOR EMPIRE VIEWED AS A CHINESE DYNASTY. *Australian J. of Pol. and Hist. [Australia] 1976 22(1): 23-35.* An account of the American business empire in China, centered on Shanghai, in the 1920's. Instead of treating it as a branch of American

diplomatic history, Hoyt sustains an analogy with earlier Sino-foreign dynasties and traces it through the traditional cycle of rise, splendor, and fall. In place of the old scholar-gentry, who ruled with books and brushes, the open door empire was ruled by capitalist-engineers, whose books were capital and concrete. The scholar bureaucracy was succeeded by a commercial bureaucracy. Concentrates especially on the view of George Bronson Rea of the *Far Eastern Review,* and social life and attitudes of the "Shanghailanders." Documented from newspapers, monographs, and private papers.

W. D. McIntyre

302. Hoyt, Frederick B. THE OPEN DOOR LEADS TO RELUCTANT INTERVENTION: THE CASE OF THE YANGTZE RAPID STEAMSHIP COMPANY. *Diplomatic Hist. 1977 1(2): 155-169.* Lured by promises of profit and official US support, the owners of the Yangtze Rapid Steamship Company established their shipping firm in the Chunking-Inchang area "only to discover that their investment was neither welcome nor safe. As a result, they demanded diplomatic and military protection, which American diplomats recognized would compromise the major thrust of their Asian policy. From 1925 until 1936, officials of the United States government attempted to resolve potential tensions by controlling the actions of the company" but failed. Because of treaty obligations, US State Department and Navy personnel in China were compelled to provide protection; thus, the Yangtze Rapid bent American diplomacy to its needs. Consequently, protecting the American-owned company implied support for the Chinese Nationalists against the Communists, a foreign policy which contradicted the expressed desires of American diplomats. Based on primary sources; 41 notes.

G. H. Curtis

303. Hoyt, Frederick B. PROTECTION IMPLIES INTERVENTION: THE U.S. CATHOLIC MISSION AT KANCHOW. *Historian 1976 38(4): 709-727.* The American Catholic mission at Kanchow, China directly influenced American foreign policy from 1929 to 1932. During the Kuomintang era the mission, protected by the American flag, identified itself with the Chinese elite. In 1928 the Communists advanced on Kanchow. The missionaries remained in Kanchow seeking American diplomatic help, which forced the Nationalists to protect them. The State Department had two options: 1) persuade the missioners to evacuate or 2) protect the mission. Notes.

M. J. Wentworth

304. Hoyt, Frederick B. THE SUMMER OF '30: AMERICAN POLICY AND CHINESE COMMUNISM. *Pacific Hist. Rev. 1977 46(2): 229-249.* Events of the summer of 1930 were crucial in confirming in the minds of American diplomats that the Chinese Communists were "organized brigands" whose program was not an acceptable vehicle for Chinese nationalism. During that summer Communist forces attacked major urban areas. These attacks included threats to the lives and property of Americans. American policy in response to these clashes shifted from authorizing merely protection of life to protection of property. Based on manuscript collections in the National Archives, the Library of Congress, Mary Immaculate Seminary, the Hoover Institution, Princeton University, Yale University, and the Minnesota Historical Society, and on published primary sources; 42 notes.

W. K. Hobson

305. Hsin Kuo-ch'iang.   A STUDY OF THE "PEACE" POLICIES OF WASHINGTON, PEIPING AND MOSCOW. *Issues and Studies [Taiwan] 1972 8(9): 15-22.* The communique issued by Chou En-lai and President Nixon after Nixon's 1972 China trip and Leonid Brezhnev's 1972 speech to Soviet trade unionists committed all three to the pursuit of peace, but the word has a different meaning for each.

306. Hsing Kuo-ch'iang.   THE WASHINGTON-PEIPING-MOSCOW TRIANGLE FROM A STRATEGIC POINT OF VIEW. *Issues & Studies [Taiwan] 1973 9(12): 26-34.* Compares 20th-century foreign policy in the USSR and China with US foreign policy after 1945.

307. Hsu, King-yi.   THE IMPACT OF THE CURRENT TURBULENCE IN MAINLAND CHINA ON WASHINGTON-PEIPING RELATIONS. *Issues and Studies [Taiwan] 1974 10(12): 17-27.* Discusses the possible impact of ideological and political instability among Maoists on foreign relations between China and the United States, 1969-70's.

308. Hsueh, Chun-tu.   RUSSIA REVISITED: A NEW LOOK AT THE TRIANGULAR RELATIONS. *Int. Studies Notes 1982 9(3): 9-12.* Examines the changing relations between China, the United States, and the USSR.

309. Huan Xiang.   ON SINO-U.S. RELATIONS. *Foreign Affairs 1981 60(1): 35-53.* Relations between the United States and China have entered the stage where they can jointly endeavor to prevent Soviet expansion. Stronger relations could be achieved by removing such obstacles as US support for Taiwan, more diplomatic, scientific, technical, and cultural exchanges, and increased trade. 2 notes. A. A. Englard

310. Huang, Chia-mo.   MA-SHA-LI SHIH HUA TI HUO TUNG [The diplomatic activities of Humphrey Marshall]. *Bull. of Inst. of Modern Hist., Acad. Sinica [Taiwan] 1974 4(1): 293-314.* As US Commissioner to China, 1853-54, Humphrey Marshall was primarily concerned with maintaining and advancing American interest during the Taiping Rebellion crisis. The lack of a clear and consistent China policy in Washington forced Marshall to interpret events in his own way. After arriving in Shanghai, his attempts to reach Peking were thwarted by the Ch'ing Court and Commodore Matthew C. Perry, Commander of the US East India Squadron. When the Taiping Army seized Nanking, Marshall recommended American intervention to support the Ch'ing government. Unsupported, he then turned his attention to persuading Perry to send part of his fleet to Shanghai to safeguard American economic investments. Perry's refusal prompted Marshall to decide that American interest might best be served by recognizing the Taiping government. He was on the verge of going to Nanking when he was relieved of his post. Based on Diplomatic Instructions, China series and US Ministers to China series of the US National Archives, and secondary works in English and Chinese; 74 notes.
C. C. Brown

311. Huang, Robert Chu-kua.   CHUNG-KUNG SU-LIEN SHENG CHIH TE MAO TUN YÜ T'UNG I [Antagonism and unity in the Sino-Soviet

conflict]. *She Hui K'o-hsüeh Lun Ts'ung [Taiwan] 1976 25: 225-255.* Argues that the present Sino-Soviet dispute is quite spurious, since the foreign policies and actions of China and the USSR are in complete unison. The mutual abuse is irrelevant, the object of all the attacks being really the United States. The feigned antagonism is designed to bring about East-West reconciliation, to contend for Western economic and technological aid, and to isolate Taiwan. Based on articles in the *Herald Tribune* international edition, New York Times, and the *South China Morning Post,* 1966-75; 104 notes.

M. Elmslie

312. Huang Chia-mo. MA-SHA-LI SHIH HUA TI HUO TUNG [The diplomatic activities of Humphrey Marshall]. *Bull. of Inst. of Modern Hist., Acad. Sinica [Taiwan] 1974 4(1): 293-314.* As US Commissioner to China, 1853-54, Humphrey Marshall was primarily concerned with maintaining and advancing American interest during the Taiping Rebellion. The lack of a clear and consistent China policy in Washington forced Marshall to interpret events in his own way. After arriving in Shanghai, his attempts to reach Peking were thwarted by the Ch'ing court and Commodore Matthew C. Perry, commander of the US East India Squadron. When the Taiping army seized Nanking, Marshall recommended American intervention to support the Ch'ing government. Unsupported, he then turned his attention to persuading Perry to send part of his fleet to Shanghai to safeguard American economic investments. Perry's refusal prompted Marshall to decide that American interest might best be served by recognizing the Taiping government. He was on the verge of going to Nanking when he was relieved of his post. Based on Diplomatic Instructions, China series and US Ministers to China series of the US National Archives, and secondary works in English and Chinese; 74 notes.

C. C. Brown

313. Hunt, Michael H. AMERICANS IN THE CHINA MARKET: ECONOMIC OPPORTUNITIES AND ECONOMIC NATIONALISM, 1890's-1931. *Business Hist. Rev. 1977 51(3): 277-307.* Examines the success of private American business interests in the China market, 1890's-1931. The firms that were willing to invest heavily in both effort and money prospered. Governmental support was of little value, and the successful companies learned how to accommodate themselves to Chinese business practices, preferences, and nationalism. Secondary Chinese and American sources; 59 notes.

C. J. Pusateri

314. Hunt, Michael H. THE FORGOTTEN OCCUPATION: PEKING, 1900-1901. *Pacific Hist. Rev. 1979 48(4): 501-529.* During the Boxer Rebellion US Army occupation in Peking was assisted by Chinese collaborators. The American Army commander, Lieutenant General Adna Chafee, implemented programs of public health, relief, and justice to demonstrate the benevolent influence of the United States. The imperial government collaborated with the military occupation to regain control of the city. Through collaboration Americans and Chinese worked their way through a complex situation, but Americans did not understand the Chinese. Chafee believed that Asiatics respected only the power of might, and in 1901 applied in the Philippines the lessons he thought he had learned in Peking. Based on Chinese sources, US

archival and government documents, and secondary sources; 46 notes.

R. N. Lokken

315. Hunt, Michael H. MAO TSE-TUNG AND THE ISSUE OF ACCOMMODATION WITH THE UNITED STATES, 1948-1950. Borg, Dorothy and Heinrichs, Waldo. *Uncertain Years: Chinese-American Relations, 1947-1950* (New York: Columbia U. Pr., 1980): 185-233. Mao Zedong (Mao Tse-tung) and his associates on the eve of their civil war victory in 1948-49 suspended ideological assumptions and sought relations with the United States on the basis of China's best interests until US actions confirmed deep-seated anti-imperialist suspicions, which after mid-1949 served as the basis of Chinese foreign policy.

316. Hunt, Michael H. RESISTANCE AND COLLABORATION IN THE AMERICAN EMPIRE, 1898-1903: AN OVERVIEW. *Pacific Hist. Rev. 1979 48(4): 467-471.* Introduces the articles in this issue which focus on the problems involved in the construction of a new American empire, the interaction between American occupiers and foreign occupied in Cuba, the Philippines, and Peking, and the role of the US Army in governing alien peoples. 7 notes.

R. N. Lokken

317. Ijiri, Hidenori. CHŪKA JINMIN KYŌWAKOKU SEIRITSU ZENYA NO KOKUSAI KANKEI [Foreign relations on the eve of the establishment of the People's Republic of China]. *Ajia Kenkyū [Japan] 1981 28(1): 30-53.* Within the Communist Party of China in 1948-49, the moderates, led by Zhou Enlai (Chou En-lai), advocated rebuilding the nation by obtaining aid from capitalist countries. The radicals, led by Liu Shaoqi (Liu Shao-ch'i), desired aid solely from the USSR. The latter faction won. Meanwhile, the United States, which had intensified tension with the Soviet Union in Europe, did not dare to support the Chinese Communist Party. China was forced to adopt a pro-Soviet policy, but the Soviet Union under Stalin's leadership was not friendly to the new China. The alliance between the two countries became strained. Based on published US official documents; 68 notes.

E. Motono/S

318. Inglis, Alex I. PROLOGUE: THE CHANGING WORLD OF 1950-75. *Int. Perspectives [Canada] 1975 (6): 3-7.* Discusses political, economic, and military developments in foreign relations from 1950 to 1975, emphasizing Canada, the United States, the USSR, China, and the developing nations.

319. Israel, Jerry. "MAO'S MR. AMERICA": EDGAR SNOW'S IMAGES OF CHINA. *Pacific Hist. Rev. 1978 47(1): 107-122.* Edgar Snow (1905-72) was a member of the post-gunboat diplomacy generation and was prepared to see China in a new light. Snow's secularism led him to see missionary efforts with a jaundiced eye. He found Shanghai's materialism a caricature of the United States at its most tawdry. He made Peking his home, thus seeing China from the inside rather than from the treaty ports. Snow hoped to see America's democratic doctrines spread in China by American aid, trade, and education. He very strongly feared Japanese domination of China and throughout his career searched for an alternative. This search led him to

see the Communists increasingly sympathetically. Based on Snow's published writings; 47 notes.
                                                                    W. K. Hobson

320. Israel, Jerry. THE MISSIONARY CATALYST: BISHOP JAMES W. BASHFORD AND THE SOCIAL GOSPEL IN CHINA. *Methodist Hist. 1975 14(1): 24-43.* James W. Bashford, bishop of the Methodist Episcopal Church and missionary to China, saw the Pacific Ocean as the final stage in the development of civilization. He thought the United States had the ability to export its domestic success, particularly with social problems, including educational reform and women's rights. 85 notes.   H. L. Calkin

321. Israel, John and Hochman, Steven H. DISCOVERING JEFFERSON IN THE PEOPLE'S REPUBLIC OF CHINA. *Virginia Q. Rev. 1981 57(3): 401-419.* This article is subdivided into three short essays. Israel (pp. 401-406) describes his contacts with Chinese visitors to the University of Virginia since 1976 and his 1980 discovery of, and correspondence with, the Chinese historian Liu Zuochang (Liu Tso-ch'ang), apparently "China's sole Jefferson expert." Hochman (pp. 406-414) reviews Liu's "Thomas Jefferson's Ideas of Democracy" and finds it a surprisingly favorable assessment of Jefferson despite some biases and omissions. Israel (pp. 414-419) completes the trilogy with reflections on Marx and Jefferson in the People's Republic.
                                                                        O. H. Zabel

322. Jackson, Hermione Dannelly. WIFE NUMBER TWO: ELIZA G. SEXTON SHUCK, THE FIRST BAPTIST FOREIGN MISSIONARY FROM ALABAMA. *Baptist Hist. and Heritage 1974 9(2): 69-78.* Discusses the somewhat mysterious life of Eliza G. Sexton Shuck, wife of J. Lewis Shuck and a missionary with him from the Baptist Church to China, 1846-63.

323. Jaffe, Philip J. AGNES SMEDLEY: A REMINISCENCE. *Survey [Great Britain] 1974 20(4): 172-179.* Details Agnes Smedley's early attraction to radicalism, her life in China, dismissal by Chu Teh whom she worshipped, and her relationship to Richard Sorge, the Soviet spy, in Tokyo which later caused her much trouble in the five years preceding the McCarthy era and finally drove her to England where she died.   R. B. Valliant

324. Johnson, Sheila K. TO CHINA, WITH LOVE. *Commentary 1973 55(6): 37-45.* Holds fellow-traveling reports about China less dependent on facts than on the predispositions of the viewers.   S

325. Ju, Woo Jung. NATURE OF THE COLD WAR. *Asian Profile [Hong Kong] 1981 9(1): 71-79.* Discusses the history of the Cold War, with special emphasis on the Truman Doctrine and the balance of power between the USSR, the United States, and China. The United States must learn that revolutions and coups in various Latin American, African, and Asian countries are not due to Communist intervention. Furthermore, the United States must seek stronger relations with Communist China, even at the expense of losing Taiwan, if international order is to be maintained. Based on secondary sources; 3 notes.   J. Powell

326. Juhnke, James. MENNONITE MISSION IN CHINA: A PHOTOGRAPHIC ESSAY. *Mennonite Life 1979 34(2): 8-14.* H. C. and Nellie Schmidt Bartel founded the first Mennonite mission in China in 1901 at Caoxian (Tsaohsien). Between 1910 and 1914, Ernest and Maria Dyck Kuhlman and H. J. and Maria Miller Brown also founded China missions. The General Conference Mennonite Church took over the Brown mission at Kai Chow in southern Hubei (Hopeh) province in 1914. 19 photos. B. Burnett

327. Jundanian, Brendan F. GREAT POWER INTERACTION WITH AFRICA: AN AFRICANIST'S PERSPECTIVE. *Studies in Comparative Communism 1973 6(3): 319-325.* Comments on Bruce D. Larkin's *China and Africa, 1949-1970* (Berkeley: University of California Press 1971), and Helen Desfosses Cohn's *Soviet Policy Toward Black Africa: The Focus on National Integration* (New York: Praeger 1972) following a background discussion of the relationship of the United States, China, and USSR to the newly independent African nations. Both the USSR and China have increased ties with the elites of African countries and have exhibited a marked degree of pragmatism by recognizing the exceeding complexity of African politics. 4 notes. D. Balmuth

328. Kamachi, Noriko. AMERICAN INFLUENCES ON CHINESE REFORM THOUGHT: HUANG TSUN-HSIEN IN CALIFORNIA, 1882-1885. *Pacific Hist. Rev. 1978 47(2): 239-260.* An important Chinese scholar-official, Huang Tsun-hsien (1848-1905) served as consul general in San Francisco between 1882-85. The experience influenced greatly the formation of his reform ideas. His nationalism was deepened, but the racial prejudice and humiliation he endured in California undermined his earlier belief in the possibility of universal harmony. Huang learned to use the American court and administrative systems to his advantage and came to believe efficient administration was a major key to building a strong nation-state. Huang became critical of American democratic practices and egalitarian principles as sources of weakness for modern nations. Based on documents in the National Archives and published primary sources in Chinese and English; 51 notes.
W. K. Hobson

329. Katz, Naomi and Milton, Nancy. DAUGHTERS OF EARTH. *Monthly Rev. 1978 29(11): 41-45.* Reviews leftist Agnes Smedley's *Daughter of Earth* (New York, 1973) and *Portraits of Chinese Women* (New York, 1976); this American woman grew up on the frontier in great poverty, put freedom above love, and found herself with the Communists in China in the 1930's.

330. Keeton, Morris T. INTEGRATING EDUCATION AND PRACTICAL EXPERIENCE IN AMERICAN HIGHER EDUCATION. *Liberal Educ. 1977 63(2): 259-270.* Postsecondary integration of labor experience and education in the United States, compared to similar efforts made in China, are grossly inadequate; a national policy is needed to increase such integration, thus encouraging "responsibility and growth."

331. Kehoe, Barbara B. WILLIAM PATTERSON JONES, AMERICAN CONSUL TO CHINA, 1862-1868. *J. of the Illinois State Hist. Soc. 1980*

73(1): 45-52. William Patterson Jones (1831-86), American educator, founder, and later president of Northwestern Female College of Illinois, served for six years as American consul to China. He described such features of 19th-century China as port city life, education, superstitions, and gambling. Jones blamed Westerners for many of the contemporary problems of China. Based on personal diaries and lectures of Jones; 2 illus., 2 photos, 26 notes.

D. J. Maika

332. Keith, Ronald C. CHINA AND "TRILATERALISM." *Int. Perspectives [Canada] 1983 (July-Aug): 24-26.* The People's Republic of China regards both the USSR and the United States as imperialist members of the "First World," while viewing itself as a Third-World country. Although China's foreign policy allows for momentary political cooperation with one of the two superpowers at any given time, it has renounced "trilateralism," defined as global strategic cooperation between two of the parties against the third. 4 fig.

E. Palais

333. Kim, Samuel. AMERICA'S FIRST MINISTER TO CHINA: ANSON BURLINGAME AND THE TSUNGLI YAMEN (CHINESE FOREIGN OFFICE). *Maryland Hist. 1972 3(2): 87-104.* Describes the career of Anson Burlingame, who served as America's first resident minister to Peking during 1861-67. Concludes that Burlingame was successful in establishing a cooperative Chinese position toward America. This is attributed to Burlingame's effort to understand Chinese society, culture, and history. Burlingame papers and secondary sources; 74 notes.

G. O. Gagnon

334. Kim, S. S. BURLINGAME AND THE INAUGURATION OF THE CO-OPERATIVE POLICY. *Modern Asian Studies [Great Britain] 1971 5(4): 337-354.* Describes the role Anson Burlingame (1820-70), first resident American minister in Peking, 1861-67, played in the evolution and enunciation of the Cooperative Policy. Prior to Burlingame's arrival in China, Sir Frederick William Bruce, British envoy, had independently adopted and unilaterally followed the premises of the policy, but Burlingame was the catalyst in negotiating and formalizing the policy. Burlingame demonstrated the effectiveness of personal diplomacy and neutralized the British position in China. Summarizes the Cooperative Policy and enumerates its underlying assumptions. Primary sources; 67 notes.

K. A. Harvey

335. Kinter, William R. A STRATEGIC TRIANGLE OF "TWO AND A HALF POWERS." *Orbis 1979 23(3): 525-534.* Analyzes the effect of US recognition of China on Soviet-American relations, and the possible strategic effects. Discusses recent failures of US foreign policy, the Soviet view of the China-America relationship, Soviet opinions, and the risks and opportunities of the new situation. Concludes that the US relationship with China will succeed only if there is a fundamental change in strategic planning for the defense of the vital interests of the United States. Based on newspaper reports; 8 notes.

J. W. Thacker, Jr.

336. Kit-Ching, Chau Lau. JOHN KING FAIRBANK, ED., *THE MISSIONARY ENTERPRISE IN CHINA AND AMERICA. J. of Oriental*

Studies [Hong Kong] 1976 14(2): 190-193. Fairbank's *The Missionary Enterprise in China and America* (1974), the sixth work in the Harvard studies in American East Asian relations series, is the most comprehensive study ever published on the role of American missions in China. Part I examines the factors which helped mold the pattern of American missionary work. Part II studies the impact of US missionaries in China. Part III is concerned with the image of Chinese missions in American culture. Through this book and other publications, Harvard University has played a leading role in the postwar advancement in this field. 12 notes. J. Sokolow

337. Klein, Sidney. CHINA'S FOREIGN TRADE: THE AMERICAN CONTRIBUTION. *Military Rev. 1974 54(3): 55-59.* Analyzes trade between the United States and the People's Republic of China during 1972-73.

338. Koval, M. PRESENT-DAY US HISTORIOGRAPHY ON SINO-US RELATIONS BETWEEN 1928 AND 1937. *Far Eastern Affairs [USSR] 1981 (1): 101-112.* Current Chinese and American historians are actively falsifying Chinese history and the history of Sino-US relations.

339. Krebs, Edward S. HISTORY OF THE UNITED STATES-CHINA PEOPLE'S FRIENDSHIP ASSOCIATION OF ATLANTA. *West Georgia Coll. Studies in the Social Sci. 1983 22: 101-109.* Founded by three Maoist students in 1972, just prior to their own journey to China; the association is now active in promoting student exchange.

340. Kua, Michael Y. M.; Perrolle, Pierre M.; Marsh, Susan H.; and Berman, Jeffrey. PUBLIC OPINION AND OUR CHINA POLICY. *Asian Affairs: An Am. Rev. 1978 5(3): 133-147.* Collaborative effort discussing opinion polling of the general public by the Gallup and Harris organizations and that of "opinion leaders" by the US State Department. Examines past and present patterns, trends, and practical implications regarding various foreign policy decisions facing the Carter Administration. Primary and secondary sources; table, 12 notes. R. B. Mendel

341. Kuan, John C. PRINCIPAL ASPECTS IN WASHINGTON-PEIPING RELATIONS. *Issues and Studies [Taiwan] 1976 12(7): 9-34.* Examines US-China relations from three angles: the attitude of the USSR, the attitude of China, and the attitudes of US diplomatic and foreign policymaking circles, 1970-74.

342. Kubek, Anthony. CHINESE-AMERICAN RELATIONS DURING WORLD WAR II: DIPLOMATIC REPORTINGS BY THE SO-CALLED "OLD CHINA HANDS." *Issues and Studies [Taiwan] 1970 6(7): 16-25.* Identifies and summarizes key changes of US policy in China from the Open Door to intervention on behalf of the Chinese Communist Party. Gives detailed analysis of reports of John Stewart Service from Yenan in 1944, which were favorable to Mao Tse-tung and may have greatly influenced the change in US postwar policy. Text of author's address at Symposium on Modern China, St. John's University, New York, 25 July 1969. Based on US State Department records; 2 photos. L. J. Stout

343. Kubek, Anthony. INTRODUCTION OF *THE AMERASIA PAPERS: A CLUE TO THE CATASTROPHE OF CHINA. Issues and Studies [Taiwan] 1970 6(8): 81-92, (9): 72-89, (10): 69-81, (11): 76-90, (12), 7(1): 81-93, (2): 63-70, (3): 76-88.* Surveys the history of the relations between the Nationalists and the Chinese Communist Party, 1911-45, and the espionage case and subsequent Justice Department prosecution involving *Amerasia* magazine in 1945. Considers how influential John Stewart Service's reports from China were in changing US foreign policy. Service, diplomatic consultant to General Joseph W. Stilwell during World War II, was strongly opposed to Chiang Kai-shek's Nationalists and was favorable toward the Communist Party led by Mao Tse-tung. Mao was said to agree with multiparty rule and ready to compromise with the National Government. S

344. Lai, H. Mark. THE CHINESE LANGUAGE SOURCES BIBLIOGRAPHY PROJECT: PRELIMINARY FINDINGS. *Amerasia J. 1978 5(2): 95-107.* Source materials in the Chinese language are indispensable for the proper study of Chinese Americans, particularly since English-language sources often reflect the bias of the non-Chinese observer rather than the perspective of the Chinese themselves. The Asia American Studies Center of the University of California at Los Angeles has initiated a project to compile a bibliography of such sources and has uncovered a wealth of material. Decribes, in bibliographic format, a preliminary report on these materials. Covers 1854-1978.   T. L. Powers

345. Lampton, David M. THE U.S. IMAGE OF PEKING IN THREE INTERNATIONAL CRISES. *Western Pol. Q. 1973 26(1): 28-50.* Analyzes the relationship between US policy toward Communist China and the images of Communist China held by US foreign policymakers during the crises in Korea (1950), Indochina (1954), and Laos (1961-62).

346. Laptev, V. "KITAISKII FAKTOR" V POLITIKE AMERIKANSKOGO IMPERIALIZMA ["The Chinese Factor" in the policies of American imperialism]. *Mirovaia Ekonomika i Mezhdunarodnye Otnosheniia [USSR] 1982 (1): 25-35.* Focuses attention on the modern stage of American-Chinese relations, noting that the US motive is opposition to the USSR.
                                                                                                    J/S

347. Laughlin, C. H. FERRY FLIGHT. *Am. Aviation Hist. Soc. J. 1978 23(1): 51-59.* The author discusses his part in ferrying airplanes from Accra, Gold Coast, to Kunming, China, 1942.

348. Lazarev, V. I. IZ ISTORII SGOVORA MAOISTSKIKH LIDEROV S IMPERIALISTAMI SSHA [Collusion of Maoist leaders with US imperialists]. *Voprosy Istorii KPSS [USSR] 1980 (10): 74-86.* Surveys the history of collusion between Mao Zedong and the United States from the early 1930's with special emphasis on the period from 1936 to the 1950's. Mao sought American military and economic assistance through Edgar Snow in 1936 and other Americans invited to Yenan. Promises to break relations with Moscow and alter the political program of the Chinese Communist Party continued during World War II, as Mao looked primarily to the United States for help.

In 1949 Zhou Enlai (Chou En-lai) asked for US assistance so that China could follow an independent course, a proposal that foundered because of internal opposition, Soviet aid, and the Korean War. Later, however, a series of anti-Soviet deals were struck with the United States as Chinese policy increasingly represented the petit bourgeois nature of Maoist leadership. Based on memoirs and published documents; 56 notes. L. E. Holmes

349. Lazo, Dimitri D. THE MAKING OF A MULTICULTURAL MAN: THE MISSIONARY EXPERIENCES OF E. T. WILLIAMS. *Pacific Hist. Rev.* 1982 51(4): 357-383. The impact of experience in China on missionaries can be seen in the career of Edward Thomas Williams, a Disciples of Christ missionary in Nanjing (Nanking) during 1887-96. Missionaries found the Chinese language hard to master, and formed a stereotype of the Chinese as a heathen, superstitious, and immoral people. As Williams learned the Chinese language and culture, he abandoned the mission's prejudices against the Chinese. His scholarly work adapted him to Chinese society and made him a multicultural man, but so estranged him from his missionary colleagues that he resigned the mission in 1896. Thereafter he endeavored to teach the Chinese elite the intellectual virtues of Western civilization, and to show the West the virtues of Chinese civilization. From 1897 to 1918 he served in the State Department as a specialist in Chinese affairs. Based on Williams Papers, Bancroft Library, University of California, Berkeley, and other primary sources; 51 notes. R. N. Lokken

350. Ledovski, A. M. TAINYE KONTAKTY MAOISTOV I AMERI-KANSKOI DIPLOMATII V 1949 GODU [The Maoists' clandestine contacts with American diplomacy in 1949]. *Voprosy Istorii [USSR]* 1980 (10): 75-89. Highlights the clandestine contacts between US diplomacy and the Mao Zedong group in 1949 on the eve of the victorious Chinese Revolution. Washington tried to use nationalist elements in the Communist Party of China in order to save the Guomindang (Kuomintang) regime from utter defeat and to retain the positions of American imperialism in China. Mao Zedong and his closest associates were prepared to go to great lengths to seize political power in the country and strike a bargain with American imperialism for the sake of attaining their selfish aims. This conspiracy was thwarted by the victorious development of the people's revolution, which enjoyed broad international support from the forces of democracy and socialism and which relied on the USSR's internationalist assistance. J

351. Ledovsky, A. THE FIASCO OF US PLANS OF INTERVENTION IN CHINA AND ALIENATION OF MANCHURIA. *Far Eastern Affairs [USSR]* 1979 (1): 65-77. Discusses General Albert Wedemeyer's report to President Truman concerning US interests in China, ambitions in Taiwan, Nationalist defeats in Manchuria, and plots by "nationalistic renegades" in the Communist Party, including Mao Zedong and Zhou Enlai, to work with US imperialists against the better interests of the Chinese people and the USSR, 1946-49.

352. Lee, Chin-Chuan. THE UNITED STATES AS SEEN THROUGH THE *PEOPLE'S DAILY*. *J. of Communication* 1981 31(4): 92-101. Examines

the Beijing *People's Daily* as representative of Chinese mass media, which mirrored China's policy: as its attitude hardened against the USSR, it softened against the United States, and once diplomatic relations were normalized in 1979, though many US problems were portrayed, it expressed admiration for scientific and technological advance. Approximately 62% of the comments on US foreign policy were favorable. The *Southern Daily* was similar.

353. Lee, Sang-Chul. THE PACIFIC ORDER AND CHINA ATTITUDE. *Asian Profile [Hong Kong] 1980 8(2): 123-137.* Examines relations between China and the United States in the 20th century. A critical factor in the equation is a China strong enough to maintain independence from great power influence, yet able to benefit from their aid. A delicate balance exists in southeast Asia among the four major world powers with military, economic, and political commitments in the area. 91 notes. J. Cushnie

354. Levine, Steven I. CHINA POLICY DURING CARTER'S YEAR ONE. *Asian Survey 1978 18(5): 437-447.* Surveys US-Communist Chinese foreign relations and international trade and exchange programs in 1977. The former have been tentative explorations, with Taiwan an ever-present issue. Trade has dropped and exchange programs have not changed. The hesitation to negotiate could prove extremely unfortunate. 40 notes. J. Tull

355. Levine, Steven I. INTRODUCTION. Borg, Dorothy and Heinrichs, Waldo, ed. *Uncertain Years: Chinese-American Relations, 1947-1950* (New York: Columbia U. Pr., 1980): 181-183. Outline of scholars' major approaches to Chinese Communist Party foreign policy in order to provide a context for papers by Michael Hunt and Steven M. Goldstein that emerged from the Conference on Chinese-American Relations, Mt. Kisco, New York, 1978.

356. Levine, Steven I. A NEW LOOK AT AMERICAN MEDIATION IN THE CHINESE CIVIL WAR: THE MARSHALL MISSION AND MANCHURIA. *Diplomatic Hist. 1979 3(4): 349-375.* Chronicles George C. Marshall's efforts to mediate between the Nationalists and Communists to form one government. Marshall believed that only through political reform could a Communist takeover in China be prevented. He gave up on the Guomindang (Kuomintang) as a vehicle for reform and hoped that an American-style nonpartisan government made up of reformers from both Chinese factions could be formed. He failed to resolve China's political crisis but succeeded in removing China as an area of conflict in Soviet-American relations, keeping the USSR's political influence at a minimum by providing only limited American support for the Nationalists. 88 notes. S

357. Li, Victor H. UPS AND DOWNS OF TRADE WITH CHINA. *Columbia J. of Transnat. Law 1974 13(3): 371-380.* Discusses the rapid growth of US-China trade, 1970-73, and predicts future volumes of trade with China. S

358. Liang, Chin-tung. PATRICK HURLEY: THE CHINA MEDIATOR. *Bull. of the Inst. of Modern Hist. Acad. Sinica [Taiwan] 1977 6: 329-353.* Describes the attempts by General Patrick J. Hurley to mediate

between Jiang Jieshi (Chiang Kai-shek) and Mao Zedong while serving as US ambassador to China from 1944 to 1945. His pro-Chiang stance was consistently opposed by officers in the State Department, notably John Carter Vincent. US indirection in China policy strengthened Mao's demand for a coalition government, which Chiang resisted. Hurley resigned in 1945 and was replaced by General George C. Marshall. Based on documents in Tachi Archives, vol. 6, Foreign Relations of the United States, vol. 6-7, 1944-45; 83 notes. C. C. Brown

359. Liao, Hollis S. PUBLISHING TIES BETWEEN THE UNITED STATES AND COMMUNIST CHINA. *Issues & Studies [Taiwan] 1982 18(1): 49-63.* US and mainland Chinese publishers have recently promoted closer relations through book fairs and joint publications. Serious obstacles, including China's production of pirated editions and restriction of free and direct trade, still prevent real advantages for the West. Based on mainland publications and *Publisher's Weekly;* 60 notes. J. A. Krompart

360. Lien Chan. NEGOTIATION IN COMMUNIST CHINA'S FOREIGN POLICY TOWARD THE UNITED STATES. *Issues and Studies [Taiwan] 1975 11(2): 27-49.* Discusses the role of negotiations in China's diplomacy and foreign policy toward the United States in the 1960's and 70's, emphasizing aspects of Maoism.

361. Lin, Sein. SUN YAT-SEN AND HENRY GEORGE. *Am. J. of Econ. and Sociol. 1974 33(2): 201-220.* The tax and land ownership beliefs of Sun Yat-sen are explored, with special reference to the influence on him by Henry George. Based on secondary sources: 66 notes. W. L. Marr

362. Lin Kuo-hsiung. THE CULTURAL EXCHANGE BETWEEN WASHINGTON AND PEIPING. *Issues & Studies [Taiwan] 1973 9(4): 22-35.* Discusses how diplomacy between the US and China led to closer cultural relations from 1950 to 1972.

363. Lin Ming-te. YUAN SHIH-K'AI AND THE 1911 REVOLUTION. *Bull. of the Inst. of Modern Hist. Acad. Sinica [Taiwan] 1982 11: 347-361.* An examination of the events that brought Yuan Shikai (Yüan Shih-k'ai, 1859-1916) the presidency of the Chinese Republic in 1912. An important factor in Yuan's success was the support of Great Britain and the United States, who saw him as a strong man who could stabilize the chaotic situation. Based on contemporary writings and documents; 42 notes. J. A. Krompart

364. Linde, Gerd. DIEGO GARCIA [Diego Garcia]. *Marine Rundschau [West Germany] 1974 71(7): 389-396.* The island of Diego Garcia remains of high strategic value in the Indian Ocean. Examines history of this island, US policy in the Indian Ocean, Soviet interest in this area, Peking's attitude, and Indian protests. 6 illus., 50 notes. G. E. Pergl

365. Lindsay, Michael. UNITED STATES CHINA POLICY. *Australian Outlook [Australia] 1978 32(2): 182-204.* Speculates on US China policy since World War II. If American support had not been given to the Kuomintang in

the 1940's, the latter might have effected the type of reform pursued later in Taiwan and created a coalition with the Communists. Such a coalition might have maintained diplomatic relations with the United States and a seat in the UN. Failure to curb General MacArthur's statements during the Korean War was the major landmark in deteriorating relations, and subsequent irrationalities in US policy were due to the positivism and behavioralism of the American approach to truth. There are two possible outcomes to normalization and the Taiwan issue, abandonment of Taiwan or the conditioning of full diplomatic relations on acceptance of Taiwan's existence. The latter would increase China's respect for the United States. Documented from newspapers, monographs, and personal experience. W. D. McIntyre

366. Lindsay, Michael. U.S. RELATIONS WITH THE PEOPLE'S REPUBLIC OF CHINA. *Asian Affairs 1974 2(1): 18-28.* Explores problems of semantics and psychological differences between the Chinese and the United States, the Soviet Union, and other non-Asian countries since the 18th century and suggests ways to overcome them. Based on personal observations, Chinese documents and publications, and other primary and secondary sources; 2 notes. R. B. Mendel

367. Litvak, I. A. and McMillan, C. H. A NEW UNITED STATES POLICY ON EAST-WEST TRADE: SOME IMPLICATIONS FOR CANADA. *Internat. J. [Canada] 1973 28(2): 297-314.* Improved relations between the United States and the USSR and between the United States and Communist China will produce a freer climate for trade. Because this trade will be more competitive than that which Canadian business firms have enjoyed, they will have to be far better informed and more imaginative and aggressive in their commercial dealings with the East. 11 notes, appendix. R. V. Kubicek

368. Liu, Alan P. L. CONTROL OF PUBLIC INFORMATION AND ITS EFFECTS ON CHINA'S FOREIGN AFFAIRS. *Asian Survey 1974 14(10): 936-951.*

369. Liu, Paul. U.S.-CHINA RELATIONS: PERSPECTIVES AND PROSPECTS. *Michigan J. of Pol. Sci. 1981 1(1): 12-25.* Examines the Chinese view of the international system, the relationship of this view to US-China relations, and the Chinese strategic policy for the near future and its relation to China's modernization effort.

370. Lomykin, V. PRC-USA: SOME RESULTS AND PROBLEMS OF RAPPROCHEMENT. *Far Eastern Affairs [USSR] 1982 (1): 27-38.* Attempts at rapprochement between the People's Republic of China and the United States since the 1970's ignore the necessity to cooperate with the USSR in the solution of global problems.

371. London, Miriam and London, Ivan D. [THE OTHER CHINA]. THE OTHER CHINA: HUNGER: THE THREE RED FLAGS OF DEATH. *Worldview 1976 19(5): 4-11.* Postulates that the Three Red Flags movement of Mao Tse-tung, because of unrealistic Party zeal and ill-conceived agricultural projects, was responsible for a nationwide famine, 1960-62.
THE OTHER CHINA: HUNGER: THE CASE OF THE MISSING BEGGARS. *Worldview 1976 19(6): 43-49.*
THE OTHER CHINA: HOW DO WE KNOW CHINA? LET US COUNT THE WAYS... *Worldview 1976 19(7-8): 25-26, 35-37.* Speculates on the level of agricultural production, 1975-76.

372. Long, Charles H. THE LIBERATION OF THE CHINESE CHURCH: A MEMOIR OF THE REVOLUTION FROM A MISSIONARY POINT OF VIEW. *Hist. Mag. of the Protestant Episcopal Church 1980 49(3): 249-280.* Autobiographical account of Charles H. Long's trip to China in 1946 as a missionary of the Protestant Episcopal Church. Recounts what was to be part of "the end of the missionary era," to observe first-hand one of the greatest revolutions of modern times as it occurred. He shared briefly in the life of the Chinese church during its liberation from dependency and privilege over a three-year period. The liberation of the church began long before the arrival of the Communists, beginning when the Chinese clergy during World War II squarely faced the fact that they might never again be able to depend on American support. The "greatest obstacle to our coming back to China will not be the Communists but the Chinese Church itself." H. M. Parker, Jr.

373. Lovelace, Daniel. DEVELOPING ASIAN STUDIES CURRICULA FOR THE PUBLIC SECONDARY SCHOOLS: A REPORT FROM THE C.H.I.N.A. PROJECT. *Rocky Mountain Social Sci. J. 1974 11(1): 19-23.* Part of a symposium entitled "Interpreting Asia to Americans." Describes the results of one study unit written by Asian and American teachers for use by high school students. S

374. Luo Rongqu. SOME QUESTIONS REGARDING THE STUDY OF THE HISTORY OF SINO-AMERICAN RELATIONS AND U.S. HISTORY. *Chinese Studies in Hist. 1982-83 16(1-2): 8-38.* Chinese Marxist historians of the past have dismissed any detailed, analytic study of Sino-American relations as not worthy of attention because of the bourgeois nature of the United States. China's relationship with the United States, however, has been extremely complex. Therefore, systematic study of American history by Chinese scholars must be undertaken to understand the underlying bases for Sino-American relations since the 19th century and to facilitate understanding of the American culture and its people. Secondary sources; 21 notes.
A. C. Migliazzo

375. MacKinnon, Jan and MacKinnon, Steve. AGNES SMEDLEY (1892-1950). *Eastern Horizon [Hong Kong] 1980 19(8): 20-23.* American author Agnes Smedley was committed to proletarian internationalism, worked with Indian nationalists in the United States, spent years as a correspondent in

China and associated with the Chinese Communists and with satirist Lu Xun (Lu Hsün).

376. Mahajani, Usha. US-CHINESE DÉTENTE AND PROSPECTS FOR CHINA'S REHABILITATION IN SOUTHEAST ASIA. *Southeast Asia 1974 3(2): 713-739.* The Sino-American détente has affected the chances of rapprochement between China and the Soviet Union and China and India, prospects which were already dim when Nixon was inaugurated in 1971. China is interested in Southeast Asia; and, although Thailand, Singapore, Indonesia, and the Philippines currently favor nonofficial relations with China, none has precluded eventual diplomatic recognition. China is using bilateral and collective approaches designed to regain it a leadership role in Southeast Asia. In this effort China must compete with, among others, the Soviet Union. The result will be a deepening of the "cold war" between these two communist nations. The Sino-American détente has already benefitted from this communist feud in Southeast Asia. However, Southeast Asia will not be immune to the aftershock of rapprochement. Largely from newspapers and periodicals; 91 notes. R. H. Detrick

377. Mahler, Oldřich and Mikulín, Antonín. JADERNÉ ZBROJENÍ A ODZBROJENÍ [Nuclear armament and disarmament]. *Hist. a Vojenství [Czechoslovakia] 1979 28(4): 72-95.* Surveys the history of nuclear arms since the end of World War II, focusing on China—the fifth member of the nuclear club—and on the Soviet-American relationship in the era of nuclear disarmament. 36 notes. G. E. Pergl

378. Makela, Lee A. A SENATE INVESTIGATION INTO THE "FALL" OF CHINA: A ROLE-PLAYING EXERCISE. *Hist. Teacher 1978 11(4): 525-535.* Sets for students a mock Senate investigation of this historic problem. Provides extensive bibliography for a wide variety of potential witnesses ranging from Pearl Buck and Edgar Snow to George Marshall and General Albert C. Wedemeyer. Also includes possible variations for the game, a guide preparing a Senate committee report of its findings, and criteria for evaluation of individual student performance. L. C. Smith

379. Martellaro, Joseph A. SOME ASPECTS OF SINO-AMERICAN ECONOMIC RELATIONS: POST-1950. *China Report [India] 1982 18(4): 19-33.* With the Communist takeover in China in 1949 diplomatic and economic relations between China and the United States ceased. During the Kennedy-Johnson administrations the possibility of adopting a two-China policy arose, especially in light of the Sino-Soviet rift of 1960. In 1972 Nixon visited the People's Republic of China, opening the way for the establishment of diplomatic and economic relations. The Blumenthal-Jingfu agreement of March 1979 settled some standing claims-assets issues. Taiwan, however, continues to be a barrier to complete normalization. The future looks bright for US-Chinese relations, especially because China has large oil resources which can be developed by US technology. Based on secondary sources; 3 tables, 28 notes. J. Powell

380. Martin, Ben L.   THE NEW "OLD CHINA HANDS."
SHAPING A SPECIALTY. *Asian Affairs: An Am. Rev. 1975 3(2): 107-137.*
Part I. Discusses the views of China scholars. After 1944 liberal criticism of Nationalist corruption rose to flood proportions. In 1945 the State Department policy shifted to a more evenhanded treatment of the Nationalist government and Chinese Communists. A round table conference in Washington in 1949 led to eventual recognition of the new Chinese Communist government. The conservative campaign of the early 1950's was traumatic for the liberals who were temporarily terrorized in the McCarthy era. In the 1960's the study of China was funded by the Ford Foundation on a large scale, and "the expansion of the number and quality of area centers provided a basis for the beginning of a self-sustaining process of growth of the China specialty." 52 notes.
RESHAPING AMERICAN OPINION. *Asian Affairs: An Am. Rev. 1976 3(3): 185-208.* Part II. President Kennedy chose liberals for top posts relevant to China policy. By 1960 public opinion supported a change in American China policy. The Fulbright hearings showed that the Kennedy Administration was far below the country's willingness to adopt new approaches. "Over three fourths of all current specialists on contemporary China were produced in the 1960's," and they are overwhelmingly liberal. By 1971 there was little consensus for the isolation of Communist China. 35 notes.   E. P. Stickney

381. Mates, Leo.   CHINA AND EAST-WEST RELATIONS: THE THIRD POINT OF THE COMPASS. *Contemporary Rev. [Great Britain] 1984 244(1417): 73-76.* Considers the importance of China in East-West relations, emphasizing the Strategic Arms Limitation Talks, the deployment of Soviet and US nuclear missiles in Europe, and the inclusion of China in nuclear armament negotiations.

382. Matlock, Jack F.   US-SOVIET RELATIONS IN THE 1970S. *Survey [Great Britain] 1973 19(2): 132-139.* Emphasizes the changes in US-Soviet relations as of 1972, the number of agreements signed and negotiations in progress. Expects problems from two very different systems trying to get along and the Soviet intensification of their ideological struggle. The rise of China and economic difficulties have encouraged the USSR toward more cooperation. The United States must approach future cooperation with the USSR with strengthened ties with its allies, sufficient military strength, and an open mind. Summary of speech on 1 December 1972 at Conference on Soviet Foreign Policy in the Seventies. Part of a special issue on the future of Soviet foreign policy.   R. B. Valliant

383. Matsuda, Takeshi.   WILSON SEIKEN TO WALL STREET: TAIKA ROKKAKOKU SHAKKANDAN DATTAI MONDAI O CHŪSHIN TO SHITE [The Wilson administration and Wall Street]. *Seiyō Shigaku [Japan] 1979 (112): 1-17, (113): 33-43.* Examines the historical significance of President Woodrow Wilson's statement of 18 March 1913 withdrawing from the Sextuple Consortium to China. Considers the American Bankers group's attitudes toward Chinese loans during the Taft administration, and reviews Wilson's opposition to participation in the consortium. Emphasizes Wilson's

view that it was necessary to curtail the influences of international financial capitalists in Wall Street in order to open the Chinese door. Primary sources, including papers by Willard Straight and Thomas W. Lamont; 122 notes.

Y. Aoki

384. May, Gary. THE "NEW CHINA HANDS" AND THE RAPE OF THE CHINA SERVICE. *Rev. in Am. Hist. 1976 4(1): 120-127.* Review article prompted by E. J. Kahn, Jr.'s *The China Hands: America's Foreign Service Officers and What Befell Them* (New York: Viking Pr., 1975) which discusses the State Department Foreign Service officers stationed in China during the 1940's and the ambivalent attitudes they received, domestically.

385. Mayers, David. EISENHOWER'S CONTAINMENT POLICY AND THE MAJOR COMMUNIST POWERS, 1953-1956. *Int. Hist. Rev. [Canada] 1983 5(1): 59-83.* In the years of Eisenhower's first administration, the two major Communist powers were the USSR and China. Eisenhower continued the substance of Truman's foreign policy: status quo defense. His Secretary of State, John Foster Dulles, supported his policies wholeheartedly. Russia and China were allies, but it became increasingly evident that there were tensions in their relationship. Dulles sought to sever the Sino-Soviet alliance by activating strains and stresses within the Russian Communist empire so as to disintegrate it. He seized the opportunity to open informal relations with China in order to weaken its exclusive reliance on Russia, thus weakening Russian strength in Europe. American policy toward the alliance was not ultimately responsible for the demise of the Sino-Soviet partnershp, yet the Dulles-Eisenhower policy of containment by applied pressure was a contributing factor. Based on the Dulles Papers at Princeton University, the National Security Council file at the National Archives, and other primary and secondary sources; 80 notes.

H. M. Parker, Jr.

386. Mazuzan, George T. "OUR NEW GOLD GOES ADVENTURING": THE AMERICAN INTERNATIONAL CORPORATION IN CHINA. *Pacific Hist. R. 1974 43(2): 212-232.* A study of the founding in 1915 and the subsequent activities of the American International Corporation in its China operation. In 1916 and 1917, AIC attempted to capitalize on China's market potential contracting with the Chinese government. Examination of AIC's effort underscores some of the problems in Sino-American commercial relations. Frank A. Vanderlip, president and later chairman of its board, gave aggressive leadership, but the initial chance for success was subverted by AIC's own contracting methods, by protests from Britain, France, and Russia regarding encroachments, and an increased turning to lower-risk enterprises. 62 notes.

R. V. Ritter

387. McCabe, Carol. THE CHINA TRADE. *Early Am. Life 1982 13(3): 48-51, 60-62, 64, 66.* Discusses the production of porcelain in China, particularly in "the Porcelain City" of Ching-tê-Chên, during the 18th and early 19th centuries, focusing on the export of porcelain to America and the designs painted on this tableware.

388. McGee, Gale W. A CHINA POLICY FOR THE UNITED STATES. *South Atlantic Q. 1977 76(4): 424-437.* Reprint of 1954 article discussing US foreign policy toward China. Asserts that the United States should attempt soft and firm approaches to wean China away from the USSR and also away from a Chinese desire to dominate Asia. This dual approach means combining a "two-China" policy to contain the Communists and a series of economic lures to increase trade and encourage Chinese consumer growth.
W. L. Olbrich

389. Medvedev, Roy. THE USSR AND CHINA: CONFRONTATION OR DETENTE? *New Left Rev. [Great Britain] 1983 (142): 5-29.* Examines China's relations with the United States and the USSR; although foreign relations have stabilized with the two nations, it is not in China's interest to become a strong ally of either.

390. Mei, June. SOCIOECONOMIC ORIGINS OF EMIGRATION: GUANGDONG (KWANGTUNG) TO CALIFORNIA, 1850-1882. *Modern China 1979 5(4): 463-501.* Early Chinese emigration, especially to the more desirable destinations of Hawaii, California, and Australia, was largely voluntary. The first group of emigrants to California from China were for the most part of the merchant class, and most of the rest were of rural backgrounds, with few economic resources. Emigration was encouraged by domestic problems and labor shortages abroad, even though it was never supported by the Chinese government. Secondary sources in English and Chinese; 3 fig., 67 notes, ref.
K. W. Berger

391. Melby, John F. THE MARSHALL MISSION IN RETROSPECT: A REVIEW ARTICLE. *Pacific Affairs [Canada] 1977 50(2): 272-277.* Review article prompted by *Marshall's Mission to China, December 1945-January 1947: The Report and Appended Documents,* with an introduction by Lyman P. Van Slyke. The official report to President Truman of the fruitless effort of General George C. Marshall to avert a civil war in China was written by Philip D. Sprouse, who also wrote the same section in the China White Paper.
S. H. Frank

392. Melby, John F. SHADOWS ON THE TAPESTRY. *Internat. J. [Canada] 1973 28(2): 230-235.* Reviews three books about foreign powers trying to "get something out of" China for themselves while proclaiming their good intentions. The books are: John Paton Davies, Jr.'s *Dragon by the Tail: American, British, Japanese and Russian Encounters with China and One Another* (New York: Norton, 1972), Warren I. Cohen's *America's Response to China: An Interpretative History of Sino-American Relations* (New York: Wiley, 1971), and William H. Bueler's *U.S. China Policy and the Problem of Taiwan* (Boulder, Colo.: Assoc. U. Press, 1971). The reviewer was a U.S. foreign service officer who served in China during 1945-49.
R. V. Kubicek

393. Melis, Giorgio. EVOLUZIONE DELLA POLITICA ESTERA CINESE [The development of Chinese foreign policy]. *Mondo Cinese [Italy] 1978 6(4): 43-58.* A Party Central Committee circular of 20 July 1971 and a September 1971 *Red Flag* article marked the turning point in China's policy

toward the United States, and the 1 November 1977 article in the *Peoples Daily* sets the doctrinal frame for current foreign policy. J/S

394. Meserve, Walter J. and Meserve, Ruth I. THE STAGE HISTORY OF *ROAR CHINA!*: DOCUMENTARY DRAMA AS PROPAGANDA. *Theatre Survey 1980 21(1): 1-13.* Discusses production in Great Britain, the United States, Canada, and elsewhere, of the documentary drama *Roar China!* by Soviet poet and teacher Sergei Tretiakov (1892-1939), who wrote the play originally as a poem about the exploitation of China by Westerners, specifically based on an incident in 1924 in which Edwin C. Hawley of the British firm of Arnhold & Company of Shanghai was killed by Chinese junkmen who did not want foreign steamers interfering with Chinese junks along the Chang (Yangtze) River.

395. Metallo, Michael V. AMERICAN MISSIONARIES, SUN YAT-SEN, AND THE CHINESE REVOLUTION. *Pacific Hist. Rev. 1978 47(2): 261-282.* American missionaries greeted the 1911 Chinese Revolution optimistically, expecting it would improve prospects for the expansion of Christianity. Missionaries also expected the new China to model its political, social, and economic institutions after those of the United States. Sun Yat-sen was especially esteemed. The American business and diplomatic communities in China viewed the revolution far less positively, influencing the William Howard Taft administration's nonrecognition policy. Woodrow Wilson was more sympathetic to the missionary viewpoint, extending diplomatic recognition to China in May 1913. From 1913 on, American missionaries withdrew support from Sun Yat-sen and extended support to elements in China which stood for stability and order rather than for extending the revolution. Based on private papers of missionary societies, documents in the National Archives and Library of Congress, and missionary newspapers; 81 notes. W. K. Hobson

396. Meyer, Susan E. CANTON: MERCHANT'S OUTPOST IN THE ORIENT. *Art and Antiques 1980 3(1): 52-61.* Traces European and American trade with China, specifically in Canton, from the third-century Roman Empire through US trade with China in the mid-19th century, discussing the commodities most popular for trade then and now.

397. Miller, John R. THE CHIANG-STILWELL CONFLICT, 1942-1944. *Military Affairs 1979 43(2): 59-62.* After Pearl Harbor, China was granted Great Power status because America expected it to tie down much of the Japanese war machine and hoped to use Chinese bases for air and sea attacks against Japan. Lieutenant General Joseph W. Stilwell implemented American strategy in China. General Stilwell and Generalissimo Chiang Kai-shek disagreed, however, over many issues: strategy, supply, use of Chinese troops, air versus ground priorities, prosecution of the war, and use of Chinese Communist forces. "The real difficulty was that Stilwell expected more of Chiang than Chiang could deliver." 27 notes. A. M. Osur

398. Mills, William. TREATMENT OF FOREIGN POLICY ISSUES IN THE REGIONAL CHINESE PRESS. *Asian Survey 1981 21(7): 795-810.* Examines the degree of difference of opinion in newspapers in China through

content analysis of their coverage of Vice-President Mondale's 1979 visit, the 1979 announcement of Sino-Soviet talks, Richard Nixon's 1979 trip, the Soviet intervention in Afghanistan, Secretary of Defense Brown's trip in 1980, Vice-Premier Geng Biao's (Keng Piao) 1980 trip to the United States, and the 1980 Chinese response to a Reagan campaign statement in Taiwan. The diversity of opinion and coverage of these events reflects the growing attitude of frankness in the Chinese press. Based on newspaper accounts; 24 notes. J. Powell

399. Mingde, Tsou and Jun, Li. INTRODUCTION TO THE GENERAL SITUATION REGARDING RESEARCH IN CHINESE-AMERICAN RELATIONS. *Diplomatic Hist. 1981 5(3): 273-275.* Lists the divergent views of Chinese scholars on the following topics: the general appraisal of the history of Chinese-American relations, problems of methodology in the study of the subject, appraisal of the Open Door policy, and the question of friendship between Chinese and American people. Reprinted from the Shanghai *Jiefang Ribao* [Liberation Daily]. J. V. Coutinho

400. Miracle, Ralph. ASIAN ADVENTURES OF A COWBOY FROM MONTANA. *Montana 1977 27(2): 44-53.* Fred Barton, a cowboy from Montana, worked in the Shansi province of China, 1912-32, as a horse breeder; discusses his sociopolitical connections there.

401. Mishra, Pramod Kumar. CHINA POLICY: OLD PROBLEMS AND NEW CHALLENGES. *J. of the United Service Inst. of India [India] 1979 109(457): 287-291.* Reviews A. Doak Barnett's *China Policy: Old Problems and New Challenges* (1977). Following hostility during the 1950's, US-China relations improved greatly during the early 1970's due mainly to the perception on the part of Chinese leaders that the USSR was a greater threat than the United States. The fall of Vietnam slowed this rapproachement as the Chinese began to doubt US power in the face of Soviet hegemony. Many Chinese leaders also concluded that they had given up too much on the issue of Taiwan. L. R. Maxted

402. Molesworth, Carl and Moseley, H. Stephens. FIGHTER OPERATIONS OF THE CHINESE-AMERICAN COMPOSITE WING. *Am. Aviation Hist. Soc. J. 1982 27(4): 242-257.* Details the operations during World War II of the Chinese-American Composite Wing, an air unit of the Chinese Air Force under the command of the US Air Force, which was staffed by Americans and Chinese.

403. Moore, John Allphin, Jr. FROM REACTION TO MULTILATERAL AGREEMENT: THE EXPANSION OF AMERICA'S OPEN DOOR POLICY IN CHINA, 1899-1922. *Prologue 1983 15(1): 23-36.* The Open Door policy in the early 20th century was intended to encourage a strong independent China aided by foreign investment that would absorb increased American imports. There are two dominant views on where the policy went wrong. The realist argument, derived from a study by A. Whitney Griswold in 1938, sees the policy alternating between an aggressive/assertive approach and retreating/withdrawing approach whereby the integrity of China, which was to be a means to trade, became an end in itself creating other problems. The revisionist

argument, formulated by William Appleman Williams, sees the policy as a calculated, well-planned strategy that would allow the United States all of the benefits of an empire without any of the burdens of colonial administration. Present theory sees shortcomings in both arguments. Based on the Edward Mandell House Papers at Yale University Library, US Department of State Papers, and newspaper accounts; 8 photos, 79 notes. M. A. Kascus

404. Morken, Hubert. PROTECTING AMERICAN COMMERCE IN CHINA: WASHINGTON'S APPROACH TO URBAN CONCESSIONS, 1876-1885. *Historian 1977 40(1): 53-69.* By the mid-19th century Americans recognized the value of urban concessions (sections of port cities reserved for foreign residents and commerce) extracted from China by European nations. While not directly securing such leaseholds, the United States did seek to cooperate with other nations, chiefly the British, in governing and defending these holdings. Describes American trade policy, 1876-85, as the United States sought and obtained most-favored-nation status. M. S. Legan

405. Murray, Douglas P. EXCHANGES WITH THE PEOPLE'S REPUBLIC OF CHINA: SYMBOLS AND SUBSTANCE. *Ann. of the Am. Acad. of Pol. and Social Sci. 1976 (424): 29-42.* Since 1972, the United States has become one of China's principal exchange partners—despite the absence of formal diplomatic relations. The countries' differing social systems and goals are well reflected in the exchange process and the imbalance in flow of visitors. Although Americans of all backgrounds and viewpoints have visited China, formal exchanges of scholars have been heavily weighted in scientific and technical fields, and cultural projects in performing arts and sports—reflecting Chinese but not always US preferences. Exchanges cannot be entirely removed from politics despite their avowed people-to-people nature, and critical problems remain concerning reciprocity, substantive content, and integrity. J

406. Myers, Ramon H. and Metzger, Thomas A. SINOLOGICAL SHADOWS: THE STATE OF MODERN CHINA STUDIES IN THE U.S. *Australian J. of Chinese Affairs [Australia] 1980 (4): 1-34.* Summarizes trends in Chinese historiography as they have developed in the United States.

407. Nass, Matthias and Oldag, Andreas. THE DEBATE WITHIN NATO AND THE "CHINA CARD." *J. of Peace Res. [Norway] 1983 20(2): 107-127.* Examines the current political situation in NATO and possible forms of cooperation between Western Europe and China. There has been a recent trend toward increasing conflict within the alliances created in the aftermath of World War II. These conflicts arise when secondary powers, such as the Western European nations and China, redefine their security interests independently of the superpowers: the United States and USSR. J/S

408. Nastri, Anthony D. FOR WHOM THE BELL TOLLS. *US Naval Inst. Pro. 1983 109(11): 133-137.* Reminiscences of Wiley H. Smith, a Marine on the armored cruiser *Pittsburgh* at Shanghai, China, in 1927. Based on Smith's scrapbook. K. J. Bauer

409. Nayar, Baldev Ray. TREAT INDIA SERIOUSLY. *Foreign Policy 1975 (18): 133-154.* Since World War II, Indo-US relations have been marked by oscillations, but an underlying logic has prevailed, dividing the postwar years into four periods: 1) 1945-55, strained relations between the two countries develops as India refuses to subordinate itself to US goals and the United States refuses to consider India a great power in Asia; 2) 1955-62, a reversal in US policy as the USSR successfully courts Third World nations, resulting in increased US aid to India; 3) 1963-68, pro-Indian policies are pursued by both the United States and the USSR in an effort to contain China; 4) 1969-71, the Nixon administration's efforts to maintain US power results in the development of friendly relations with China as a lever against the USSR. As a consequence, Nixon strengthens Pakistan militarily against India. Inasmuch as the United States cannot successfully contain India, nor make it a satellite, the only realistic policy is to accommodate itself to India. Secondary sources; 3 notes. R. F. Kugler

410. Neufeld, Gabrielle and Santelli, James S. SMEDLEY BUTLER'S AIR CORPS: FIRST MARINE AVIATORS IN CHINA. *US Naval Inst. Pro. 1977 103(4): 48-59.* Despite some opposition in June 1927 from the naval commander in China, Admiral Clarence S. Williams, Brigadier General Smedley D. Butler, received permission to land US marine aviation squadrons in North China to support ground forces. Admiral Williams agreed to this move because he feared that a Chinese Nationalist takeover of North China might lead to violence against the various foreign colonies in the region. Butler created an air base at Hsin Ho, five miles from the mouth of the Hai River and only 15 minutes by air from Tientsin. The first Marine flights were made in July 1927 and they continued at an increased pace for the remainder of 1927 and the early part of 1928. By late November 1928 all of the Marine aviation units were out of China. In their 19 months in that country, the Marine aviators amassed more than 3,100 flying hours during a total of 4,565 flights. They suffered no injuries and counted only five crashes. Primary and secondary sources; 8 photos, 23 notes. A. N. Garland

411. New, Peter Kong-Ming and New, Mary Louie. THE LINKS BETWEEN HEALTH AND THE POLITICAL STRUCTURE IN NEW CHINA. *Human Organization 1975 34(3): 237-252.* Discusses the "barefoot doctor movement" in the People's Republic of China and its relation to Western medicine. S

412. Newman, John Michael, Jr. THE CHINESE SUCCESSION STRUGGLE: SINO-AMERICAN NORMALIZATION AND THE MODERNIZATION DEBATE. *Asian Affairs 1979 6(3): 164-186.* Analyzes the power struggle between Hua Kuo-feng and Teng Hsiao-p'ing regarding the pace and direction of modernization in today's China; the roles of the United States and the USSR in the modernization process; China's present and future rleationships with the United States, the USSR, and the rest of Asia; and China's role as an Asian power and US and Soviet perspectives on that role. Press and government primary and secondary sources; chart, 49 notes. R. B. Mendel

413. Newman, Robert P.   LETHAL RHETORIC: THE SELLING OF THE CHINA MYTHS. *Q. J. of Speech 1975 61(2): 113-128.* Analyzes the effects of ideas about China on US foreign policy and describes how these ideas became current.   S

414. Newman, Robert P.   THE SELF-INFLICTED WOUND: THE CHINA WHITE PAPER OF 1949. *Prologue 1982 14(3): 141-156.* Discusses the China White Paper issued by the Truman administration to explain why China went Communist. Outlines the preparation of the document, the reaction against it from the military establishment and elements in the government, and the decision to go public with it. The document consisted of 412 pages of narrative covering US-Chinese relations from 1944 to 1949, and 642 pages of documents as an appendix. The document was accompanied by a letter of transmittal prepared as a preface but published separately as well. Details the flaws of the document, criticisms leveled against it, and Peking's reaction to it. Based on US State Department's *Foreign Relations of the United States,* US Senate committee hearings, and correspondence; illus., 4 photos, 62 notes.
M. A. Kascus

415. Nikonov, A. and Faramazian. R.   OPASNYI KURS NAGNETANIIA VOENNOI NAPRIAZHENNOSTI [The dangerous course of escalating military tension]. *Mirovaia Ekonomika i Mezhdunarodnye Otnosheniia [USSR] 1981 (2): 47-59.* After stating the positive impact of détente, the main tendency in international relations in the 1970's, points out that the reactionary imperialist United States and China have launched a counteroffensive against détente.

416. Ninkovich, Frank.   CULTURAL RELATIONS AND AMERICAN CHINA POLICY, 1942-1945. *Pacific Hist. Rev. 1980 49(3): 471-498.* United States-China cultural relations were hampered by Guomindang (Kuomintang) politics and US failure to understand Chinese culture. The State Department originally emphasized extending practical assistance to China in technical fields, but the Guomindang politicized the technical training of Chinese students. American intellectuals opposed the technically oriented cultural program and the Guomindang's effort to modernize China without accepting Western liberal ideas. The State Department's later humanities-oriented cultural program was also obstructed by Guomindang politics. The US assumption that the diffusion of Western liberal ideas among Chinese intellectuals would result in a strong, democratic China resulted in intractable differences between the United States and China. Based on US State Department Papers, Papers of the American Library Association, and other primary sources; 46 notes.
R. N. Lokken

417. Nogee, Joseph L. and Spanier, John W.   THE POLITICS OF TRIPOLARITY. *World Affairs 1977 139(4): 319-333.* Assuming the equal power of the United States, the USSR, and China, discusses how US foreign policy might best promote peace and global stability, and the consequences of tripolarity on the international system.

418. Nossal, Kim Richard. CHUNGKING PRISM: COGNITIVE PROCESS AND INTELLIGENCE FAILURE. *Int. J. [Canada] 1977 32(3): 559-576.* Examines the perceptions of the government of China held by Canada's first ambassador to China, Victor Wentworth Odlum. Covers 1943-46. Primary sources; 52 notes. R. V. Kubicek

419. Ojha, Ishwer C. SINO-AMERICAN RAPPROCHEMENT: WHY WASN'T IT PREDICTED? *China Report [India] 1973 9(3): 53-57.* By 1968 both China and the United States had learned from the war in Vietnam that the two large nations would have to achieve some kind of detente, but books being written in 1970-71 still did not perceive this.

420. Oksenberg, Michel. A DECADE OF SINO-AMERICAN RELATIONS. *Foreign Affairs 1982 61(1): 175-195.* A historical account of the relations between the United States and China from 1969 through summer 1982. The relationship fluctuated as a result of changes in the domestic political situations in the two countries, changing strategy regarding the Soviet Union, and differences over the US-Taiwan relationship. US-China relations have become essential to both nations' national security. Based in part on the memoirs of Richard Nixon and Henry Kissinger; 12 notes. A. A. Englard

421. Oksenberg, Michel. ON LEARNING FROM CHINA. *Pro. of the Acad. of Pol. Sci. 1973 31(1): 1-16.* Discusses the importance of America's learning from China in social and economic reform.

422. Oliver, Lucile Cummings. LIFE IN THE ORIENT: SHANGHAI CHAPTER, DAUGHTERS OF THE AMERICAN REVOLUTION. *Daughters of the Am. Revolution Mag. 1978 112(3): 214-217.* The author relates her life, 1916-43, in Shanghai, China, and her activities in the local chapter of the Daughters of the American Revolution and with her husband, Jay C. Oliver, in the YMCA; accounts for the chapter activities, 1943-57, after most members moved to Pasadena, California following evacuation.

423. Oman, Ralph. YANKEES IN CHINA PORTS. *U.S. Naval Institute Proceedings 1972 98(10): 70-81.* Because US sailing men who went to China's east coast ports in the 18th and 19th centuries could not buy postcards of the ports they visited, could take no snapshots of themselves and the sights they had seen, and had no news photographs to point to, they turned to substitutes—paintings on glass or canvas, oil portraits, coffee cups, and porcelain plates. "The authors of this painted history were journeymen Chinese artists and artisans" who "worked to please the customer and to sell their wares." And although "they were not sticklers for accuracy, and their illustrations of the contemporary scene must be taken with a grain of skepticism, the distinctive art form they created furnishes a valuable permanent record of this era." Only one Western painter, George Chinnery, an Englishman, stayed long enough in China to exert any significant influence on the native painters. Chinnery lived in Macao from 1825 until his death in 1852, and his portraits were his more important works. 14 photos.
A. N. Garland

424. Ovendale, R. BRITAIN, THE UNITED STATES, AND THE RECOGNITION OF COMMUNIST CHINA. *Hist. J. [Great Britain] 1983 26(1): 139-158.* Great Britain's attitude toward the diplomatic recognition of Communist China in 1949-50 was governed by economic interests in China, the vulnerable position of Hong Kong, the attitudes of Commonwealth countries, and conflicts in Indochina. Foreseeing possible friction between China and the Soviet Union, Britain opted for recognition to keep "a foot in the door." American policy, however, was governed by domestic political factors, particularly after the Peking barracks incident and the beginning of the Korean War. For Britain, the importance of the Anglo-American special relationship meant policy had to take into account American sensibilities, but this did not prevent recognition of the Communists. Based on documents in the Public Record Office and on the *Foreign Relations of the United States;* 89 notes. D. J. Nicholls

425. Pacy, James S. BRITISH VIEWS OF AMERICAN DIPLOMATS IN CHINA. *Asian Affairs: An Am. Rev. 1981 8(4): 251-261.* Discusses the diplomatic qualities of American ambassadors to China (1920-46) as seen by their British counterparts. Based on candid confidential reports from British ambassadors to China and other primary sources; 39 notes. R. B. Mendel

426. Palmer, Norman D. SOUTH ASIA AND THE GREAT POWERS. *Orbis 1973 17(3): 989-1009.* Points out the interest of China, the United States and the USSR in South Asia in the 1970's.

427. Papageorge, Linda Madson. FEMINISM AND METHODIST MISSIONARY ACTIVITY IN CHINA: THE EXPERIENCE OF ATLANTA'S LAURA HAYGOOD, 1884-1900. *West Georgia Coll. Studies in the Social Sci. 1983 22: 71-77.* A devout Christian and feminist, Laura A. Haygood became a Methodist Episcopal Church (South) missionary in China and participated in feminist reforms of the missionary administration.

428. Paterson, Thomas G. IF EUROPE, WHY NOT CHINA? THE CONTAINMENT DOCTRINE, 1947-1949. *Prologue 1981 13(1): 19-38.* Discusses the central principle of American Cold War diplomacy, the Truman Doctrine of containment, and gives four reasons for the inconsistent application of the policy to Europe and China: 1) Europe was perceived to be the area where the Communist threat was the greatest; 2) China was considered to be too vast and unmanageable to allow massive US intervention; 3) Jiang Jieshi's (Chiang Kai-shek) regime was corrupt, inept, and resistant to US intervention; and 4) China did not qualify as a recipient of large-scale aid since one major requirement was that the recipient have the support of a large percentage of the indigenous population and be committed to self-help. Based on State-War-Navy-Coordinating Committee Records, Public Papers of the Presidents, US Congress Senate and House Committee Hearings, and newspapers; 13 photos, 104 notes. M. A. Kascus

429. Paulsen, George E. MISSIONARY CRITICISM OF THE TOLERATION CLAUSE IN REED'S TREATY OF 1858. *Monumenta Serica [West Germany] 1979-80 34: 65-76.* The Tientsin Treaty of 1858, negotiated by

Commissioner William B. Reed, was ratified by the Imperial Chinese government the following year. Among China's concessions to the United States was the formal acceptance of Christianity, as provided by Article XXIX, the "toleration clause," written by Reed's aid Samuel Wells Williams. American Chinese missionaries criticized the article, pointing out serious shortcomings in the Chinese version and discrepancies between it and the English version. This comparative study of the English and Chinese texts examines the underlying causes of the differences between them, mostly due to Willaims' omissions of language and incorporation of sentiments. Based on some private letters.

T. Parker

430. Paulsen, George E. OPENING THE YANGTZE DOOR. *Am. Neptune 1974 34(2): 103-122.* Explains why the Chinese government granted a concession to Great Britain which resulted in Vice Admiral Sir James Hope proclaiming the Yangtze River open to British trade in 1861. American diplomats, however, were unwilling to cooperate with British envoys in obtaining this concession before the Taiping Rebellion had been crushed. Based on government records and published sources; 48 notes. G. H. Curtis

431. Paulsen, George E. PETREL SHOWS THE FLAG. *Am. Neptune 1980 40(2): 100-107.* During 1895, antiforeign feeling rose in China and American consuls repeatedly requested visits by gunboats to intimidate the populace. The navy's view that the consuls were alarmist seemed to be supported by an uneventful cruise by the *Petrel* to Hankow made at the request of the consul in the city. For six months American diplomats and naval officers argued over the necessity of the trip and over who should decide when and where gunboats should be dispatched. When stability returned to China after the Sino-Japanese War and the leading men involved in the controversy were transferred elsewhere, the dispute died down. Based on documents in Area File 10 of the Naval Records Collection, National Archives, Washington; 15 notes. J. C. Bradford

432. Paulson, George E. OPENING THE YANGTZE DOOR. *Am. Neptune 1974 34(2): 103-122.* After the Chinese Government granted a concession to Great Britain, Vice Admiral Sir James Hope proclaimed the Yangtze River open to British trade in 1861. American diplomats, however, were unwilling to cooperate with British envoys in obtaining this concession before the Taiping Rebellion had been crushed. Based on government records and published sources; 48 notes. G. H. Curtis

433. Peeples, Dale H. WILLIAM L. SCRUGGS: A GEORGIAN AS UNITED STATES CONSUL IN CHINA, 1879-81. *West Georgia Coll. Studies in the Social Sci. 1983 22: 63-70.* William L. Scruggs was a reluctant but dedicated diplomat during his brief tenure in Zhenjiang (Chekiang), where he effectively filled the consulate but was frequently at odds with the Department of State.

434. Petukhov, V. PRC-USA: A THREAT TO PEACE AND SECURITY. *Far Eastern Affairs [USSR] 1980 (3): 55-68.* The United States, with its escalation of the arms race and rejection of detente, is playing into China's

hands, for China's overall strategy is to provoke an armed conflict between the United States and the USSR.

435. Pfaltzgraff, Robert L., Jr. CHINA, SOVIET STRATEGY, AND AMERICAN POLICY. *Int. Security 1980 5(2): 24-48.* Examines China's growing fear of the USSR, and the influence of that fear on the Chinese-US rapprochement during the 1970's.

436. Pfaltzgraff, Robert L., Jr. MULTIPOLARITY, ALLIANCES AND U. S.-CHINESE RELATIONS. *Orbis 1973 17(3): 720-736.* Discusses foreign relations between the United States, China, and the USSR in the 1970's.

437. Pickler, Gordon K. UNDERSTANDING THE SHIFTING CHINA SCENE. *Air U. R. 1974 25(5): 59-66.* Reviews John Paton Davies, Jr., *Dragon by the Tail: American, British, Japanese, and Russian Encounters with China and One Another* (New York: W. W. Norton, 1972), which emphasizes the years 1937-49 and US-Soviet policies. J. W. Thacker, Jr.

438. Pickler, Gordon K. THE USAAF IN CHINA, 1946-47. *Air U. R. 1973 24(4): 69-74.* Discusses the Army Air Force's airlift of Communist officials and their staffs and families from Nanking and other Nationalist cities to the Communist capital of Yenan in 1947. Based on interviews and secondary sources; 5 photos, 4 notes. J. W. Thacker, Jr.

439. Pilkington, Luann Foster. THE SHANGHAI PUBLISHING HOUSE. *Methodist Hist. 1979 17(3): 155-177.* The Methodist Episcopal Church, South, at the suggestion of missionaries of the church's China Mission, approved a publishing house in 1898. Almost immediately different viewpoints arose between the Southern Book Committee and the Mission board. By 1901 a site had been selected in China and a manager elected. After continuing conflict and many problems, the property of the publishing house was transferred to the Mission board in 1919. The next year the manufacturing division of the House was discontinued because the Asiatic printers could do the printing more cheaply. 2 illus., 36 notes. H. L. Calkin

440. Pillsbury, Michael. U.S.-CHINESE MILITARY TIES. *Foreign Policy 1975 (20): 50-64.* Reviews US relations with China and the Soviet Union. Calls for an end to a policy of "even-handedness" because China is not as large a security threat as the Soviet Union. Calls for the enhancement of Chinese defense capabilities by US military assistance without alarming the Soviet Union and endangering the US-Soviet detente. Secondary sources.
R. K. Kugler

441. Poropat, Liviana. LE GRANDI LINEE DEI RAPPORTI TRA R.P.C. E U.S.A. (1949-1971) [The main trends in the relations between the PRC and the USA (1949-71)]. *Mondo Cinese [Italy] 1976 4(14): 57-70.* The relations between the United States and the People's Republic of China have registered an about-face in these last few years which cannot be fully understood if they are not interpreted in the light of the history between the

two countries from 1949 to the reentry of China into the UN in 1971. Traces the history of those relations. Notes, biblio.   J/S

442. Porter, Gareth. THE DECLINE OF U.S. DIPLOMACY IN SOUTHEAST ASIA. *SAIS Rev. 1981 (1): 149-159.* Discusses American influence in Southeast Asia since the end of the Vietnam War, particularly during the Carter administration, with special reference to relations with Vietnam and China.

443. Poulose, T. T. SOME RECENT BOOKS ON DETENTE. *Int. Studies [India] 1974 13(4): 843-852.* Reviews four 1971-73 books dealing with the detente between the United States and Russia; includes the implications of detente for China and Richard M. Nixon's diplomacy.

444. Prisco, Sal. PAUL S. REINSCH, PROGRESSIVE ERA DIPLOMAT IN PEKING, 1913-1919. *Asian Forum 1979 10(1): 51-59.* Traces the career of Paul S. Reinsch, the US minister to China, 1913-19. Because of fear of Chinese political and economic instability, Reinsch directed his diplomatic efforts toward the establishment of a strong foundation for closer ties between the United States and China. 36 notes.   R. B. Orr

445. Prisco, Salvatore. A NOTE ON JOHN BARRETT'S CHINA POLICY. *Pacific Historian 1974 18(2): 47-54.* Examines the foreign policy recommendations (1898-99) of diplomat John Barrett concerning US-China relations. While not the author of the Open Door Policy, Barrett contributed toward its formulation and US protection of the commercial and political integrity of China. 23 notes.   C. W. Olson

446. Prybyla, Jan S. UNITED STATES TRADE WITH CHINA. *Current Hist. 1979 76(447): 209-213, 222-223.* Examines China's trade with the West since the early 19th century, particularly its US trade and suggests future possibilities.

447. Pugach, Noel H. AMERICAN SHIPPING PROMOTERS AND THE SHIPPING CRISIS OF 1914-1916: THE PACIFIC & EASTERN STEAMSHIP COMPANY. *Am. Neptune 1975 35(3): 166-182.* Because Sino-American trade experienced soaring shipping rates and a shortage of ships after the outbreak of World War I, US and Chinese officials supported efforts to launch a Chinese-American steamship line. Consequencly, the Pacific & Eastern Steamship Company was formed in 1915. The venture proved unsuccessful, however, owing to speculators and opportunists jockeying for control of the company and failing to honor their obligations. Primary and secondary sources; 38 notes.   G. H. Curtis

448. Pugach, Noel H. ANGLO-AMERICAN AIRCRAFT COMPETITION AND THE CHINA ARMS EMBARGO, 1919-1921. *Diplomatic Hist. 1978 2(4): 351-371.* Wartime demand had swollen the production capacity of British, European, and American aircraft manufacturers, so at the close of World War I they were looking urgently for new markets. China, ravaged by civil war, offered some opportunities, but the Arms Traffic Convention of 1919

created difficulties. The British Foreign Office assisted Vickers Ltd. in obtaining a very large contract on 1 October 1919. But it soon found itself threatened, on the one hand, with the collapse of the arms embargo if it let the contract stand, and, on the other, with legal liability for Vickers's losses if it forbade further deliveries. British verbal adroitness, in addition to lack of interest among American manufacturers in selling airplanes to the almost bankrupt Chinese, temporarily saved the day for Anglo-American cooperation and for the embargo. Primary sources; 40 notes. L. W. Van Wyk

449. Pugach, Noel. EMBARRASSED MONARCHIST: FRANK J. GOODNOW AND CONSTITUTIONAL DEVELOPMENT IN CHINA, 1913-1915. *Pacific Hist. Rev. 1973 42(4): 499-517.* Frank Johnson Goodnow's constitutional ideas were adopted in 1914 when Yüan Shih-k'ai became a presidential dictator. Goodnow felt that China needed a centralized government with a strong president in order to withstand internal disintegration and interference from foreign powers. In 1915 when asked for his opinions on various systems of government, Goodnow replied that monarchy was well-suited to China, and he advised Yüan to become emperor. He did not know that a well-organized movement favoring restoration of the monarchy in Yüan's person already existed. Goodnow's statements were used to partisan advantage. Yüan Shih-k'ai failed to gain the throne and when he died in 1916 China was thrown into civil war. Goodnow's good intentions were embarrassing but he continued to favor monarchy as more suitable than a republic for China. 58 notes. C. W. Olson

450. Pugach, Noel H. KEEPING AN IDEA ALIVE: THE ESTABLISHMENT OF A SINO-AMERICAN BANK, 1910-1920. *Business Hist. Rev. 1982 56(2): 265-293.* Occasionally, American and Chinese businessmen explored the possibilities of joint ventures and actually launched such projects. The example studied here is the Chinese-American Bank of Commerce which opened its doors in 1920. The background events reveal Americans anxious to penetrate the almost legendary "China market," and their Chinese counterparts who were seeking to gain access to American capital. Nevertheless, this venture ran into difficulty during the 1920's and was liquidated in 1929. Based largely on American records, especially diplomatic correspondence of the State Department in the National Archives; illus., 44 notes. C. J. Pusateri

451. Quester, George H. SOME ALTERNATIVE EXPLANATIONS OF SINO-AMERICAN DETENTE. *Internat. J. [Canada] 1973 28(2): 236-250.* Suggests the basis for *détente* had been in existence for some time and its timing was dictated by an eventual weariness on both sides of polemical confrontation and by propitious domestic developments. R. V. Kubicek

452. Ramachandran, K. N. US-USSR-CHINA-TRIANGLE: IMPACT ON SOUTHEAST ASIA. *China Report [India] 1976 12(1): 50-57.* Notes several basic political, economic, and military trends in the three powers' impact on Southeast Asia. Foremost is the complementary nature of US and Chinese policies at the expense of the Soviet Union. Secondly, the exacerbation of the Sino-Soviet conflict has resulted in volatile relations with Communist Southeast Asian countries. Certain advantages and cleavages of the Soviets and

Chinese with specific Communist countries are discussed in some detail with Hanoi portrayed as the only independent power in Southeast Asia. 9 notes.
S. F. Benfield

453. Ray, Dennis M. AN EXPERIMENT IN PEER GROUP GRADING AT AN AMERICAN UNIVERSITY: THE STUDENT AS PEASANT, OR LEARNING FROM TACHAI. *Teaching Pol. Sci. 1975 2(4): 454-460.* Discusses the value of applying the Chinese incentive system of the Tachai production brigade to student activity in the American classroom. S

454. Raymond, David A. COMMUNIST CHINA AND THE VIETNAM WAR. *Asian Affairs: An Am. Rev. 1974 2(2): 83-99.* China's foreign relations with North Vietnam have been cautious, due to its reluctance to defy the United States, its enduring distrust of the Soviets, and its wariness of cultivating influence among revolutionary governments; when the United States was finally able to recognize China's position, the conflict was resolved in 1973.

455. Record, Jane Cassels and Record, Wilson. TOTALIST AND PLURALIST VIEWS OF WOMEN'S LIBERATION: SOME REFLECTIONS ON THE CHINESE AND AMERICAN SETTINGS. *Social Problems 1976 23(4): 402-414.* Considers the women's liberation movements in China and the United States with primary reference to the ideological context and discusses issues such as liberation within capitalism and Maoism, the role of the state vis-à-vis the household, and private institutions, and its role in opening new doors. Consideration of ideological forces should be at the center of attempts to analyze developments in China.
A. M. Osur

456. Rhee, T. C. PEKING AND WASHINGTON IN A NEW BALANCE OF POWER. *Orbis 1974 18(1): 151-178.* Discusses US and Communist Chinese foreign policy goals in the 1970's.

457. Rice, Edward E. THE SINO-US DETENTE: HOW DURABLE? *Asian Survey 1973 13(9): 805-811.* Questions the durability of the rapprochement between China and the United States, because Chinese leadership was divided over the issue, some preferring to mend relations with the USSR.
S

458. Roberts, Stephen S. THE DECLINE OF THE OVERSEAS STATION FLEETS: THE UNITED STATES ASIATIC FLEET AND THE SHANGHAI CRISIS, 1932. *Am. Neptune 1977 37(3): 185-202.* The Japanese assault on Shanghai, January 1932, marked the decline in influence of the European and US navies stationed in China. The Western nations' confrontation with Japan "brought into the naval balance the entire Japanese navy," thus rendering ineffective the Western powers' small station fleets. The author focuses on the roles of the US Asiatic Fleet commander Admiral Montgomery Meigs Taylor and Secretary of State Henry L. Stimson, indicating "a fundamental disagreement between the two in their interpretation of the Far Eastern crisis." Based primarily on Admiral Taylor's papers and government records; 44 notes.
G. H. Curtis

459. Robinson, Thomas W. CHOICE AND CONSEQUENCE IN SINO-AMERICAN RELATIONS. *Orbis 1981 25(1): 29-51.* Examines the evolution in US-Chinese relations toward a defensive relationship aimed at the USSR. A deterioration in the American-Soviet balance of power, the Afghanistan crisis, and the US hope that a stronger relationship would promote post-Mao liberal pragmatism are the major reasons for this shift in American attitude. Discusses the good and bad reasons for Sino-American cooperation, the Chinese view of the relationship and the basis of their political strategy, and America's China policy in the context of US-Soviet relations. 3 notes. J. W. Thacker, Jr.

460. Rogers, Frank E. SINO-AMERICAN RELATIONS AND THE VIETNAM WAR, 1964-66. *China Q. [Great Britain] 1976 (66): 293-314.* Confronted with continuing escalation of conflict in Vietnam, the United States and China exploited subtle public statements and possibly confidential diplomatic contacts to prevent war. Statements, outwardly belligerent, contained carefully structured signs of potential agreement. Based on Chinese materials in translation and secondary English sources; 91 notes. J. R. Pavia, Jr.

461. Rosholt, Malcolm. TO THE EDSIN GOL: A WISCONSINITE'S JOURNEY IN INNER MONGOLIA, 1935. *Wisconsin Mag. of Hist. 1977 60(3): 197-227.* The author, a Wisconsin journalist, in the summer of 1935 journeyed 750 kilometers through desert and semiarid land from Kueilhua to the Edsin Gol (river) in Inner Mongolia. He journeyed via camel to the region to meet the Prince of the Torgut Mongols. 8 photos, 4 notes.

N. C. Burckel

462. Rowe, David N. THE NIXON CHINA POLICY AND THE BALANCE OF POWER. *Issues & Studies [Taiwan] 1973 9(8): 12-28.* Discusses the Nixon Administration's foreign policy of improving relations with China, 1969-72, to maintain the balance of power between the USSR and China and to take advantage of the hostility between the two Communist countries.

463. Rowe, David Nelson. GEN. GEORGE C. MARSHALL: STRATEGIST AND POLICY-MAKER. *Issues & Studies [Taiwan] 1974 10(4): 2-27.* Provides a study of General George C. Marshall's military career, focusing on his role as a strategist and drawing special attention to his ill-fated mission to China during 1945-47.

464. Rowe, David Nelson. TRENDS IN GRADUATE LEVEL EDUCATION ON CHINA IN THE UNITED STATES 1962-1974. *Issues and Studies [Taiwan] 1976 12(2): 12-52.* A statistical study of abstracts of the more than 1,200 American dissertations written 1962-74 on all phases of Chinese life. Charts prepared from this analysis detail the schools awarding degrees, their distribution by geography, and comparisons between public and private institutions. Based on 43 subject matter categories, the content of dissertations was analyzed statistically to discover trends in subject emphasis. Some results are evaluated as to possible implications. Through analysis of courses offered on China at five top institutions for the years 1962 and 1974, the report seeks to discover the changing interests among graduate students and faculty

concerning China. Based on *Dissertation Abstracts International,* primary sources, and catalogs; 6 charts, statistical summaries. J. C. Holsinger

465. Rubin, Julius. NOTES ON THE COMPARATIVE STUDY OF THE AGRICULTURE OF WORLD REGIONS. *Peasant Studies Newsletter 1973 2(4): 1-4.* Reports on three studies of agricultural growth: 18th-century frontiers in China and North America, central Russia in the 19th century, and the South of the United States in the 19th century, with reference to Ester Boserup's model. S

466. Rubinstein, Murray A. GO YE UNTO THE WORLD: THE DEFINING OF THE MISSIONARY'S TASK IN AMERICA AND CHINA, 1830-1950. *Bull. of the Inst. of Modern Hist. Acad. Sinica [Taiwan] 1981 10: 377-400.* 19th-century American missionary organizations, fired by Second Great Awakening Protestant theology, had an optimistic view of their representatives' task in China. Missionaries in the field, however, met official and unofficial resistance. Publication, education, and medicine were the major activities in which they had some success. 41 notes. J. A. Krompart

467. Rubinstein, Murray A. THE NORTHEASTERN CONNECTION: AMERICAN BOARD MISSIONARIES AND THE FORMATION OF AMERICAN OPINION TOWARD CHINA: 1830-1860. *Bull. of the Inst. of Modern Hist. Acad. Sinica [Taiwan] 1980 9: 433-453.* The American attitude toward the Chinese shifted from guarded admiration to contempt. The American Board of Commissioners for Foreign Missions, whose objective was to promote support for missionary activities among American Protestants, promoted a view of the Chinese as "perishing heathens." This image was reinforced by missionaries who lectured about China when they returned to the Northeast. Based on board publications and documents and other contemporary writings; 75 notes. J. A. Krompart

468. Rushkoff, Bennett C. EISENHOWER, DULLES AND THE QUEMOY-MATSU CRISIS, 1954-1955. *Pol. Sci. Q. 1981 96(3): 465-480.* Examines high-level decisionmaking in the Eisenhower administration during the Quemoy-Matsu crisis of 1954-55. Dwight D. Eisenhower's personal handling of the crisis was responsible for a relaxation in early 1955 of the American commitment to the defense of the offshore islands. J

469. Russell, Hilary. THE CHINESE VOYAGES OF ANGUS BETHUNE. *Beaver [Canada] 1977 307(4): 22-31.* In 1813 and 1815, Angus Bethune, a partner for the North West Company, led two trading expeditions to Canton. He carried mostly furs, and in return received Oriental foods, tea, and fireworks. Bethune touched at the Hawaiian Islands, the California coast, and Alaska. The Company was not pleased with the ventures. Expenses were too high, repairs costly, quarreling was common, and there was much bribery and red tape in China. The author details some of the contacts with officials in Hawaii, California, and China. 10 illus., map. D. Chaput

470. Salaff, Janet W. MORTALITY DECLINE IN THE PEOPLE'S REPUBLIC OF CHINA AND THE UNITED STATES. *Population Studies*

[Great Britain] 1973 27(3): 551-576. "The means by which the Chinese gained control over mortality between 1949 and 1959, and the diseases over which they gained control are compared with the mortality decline in the United States in the nineteenth century. The Chinese combined a high degree of social organization and a minimal amount of capital- intensive health fixtures as an immediate response to bettering health while relying on improved and widespread medical technology as the long-term solution. The major infectious diseases affecting infants and children were reduced first and most dramatically. China benefited from the medical discoveries of the developed nations, and popular organisation was crucial in disseminating information about the major infectious diseases and in immunising the people against them." J

471. Sánchez, G. Walter. EL TRIÁNGULO WASHINGTON-MOSCÚ-PEKÍN Y EL PROCESO DE DISTENSIÓN INTERNACIONAL [The Washington-Moscow-Peking triangle and the process of international detente]. *Estudios Int. [Chile] 1976 9(35): 65-117.* Examines the diplomatic, commercial, and political-military links among the United States, the USSR, and China, 1970-75, and their effects on the newly emerging pattern of international relations.

472. Sanders, Sol W. CHINOISERIE IN MOD CLOTHES. *Asian Affairs: An Am. Rev. 1978 4(2): 85-93.* Analyzes arguments for normalization of relations between Communist China and the United States. Discusses US "responsibility" under the Shanghai Communique (1972), US self-interest, US-China trade, the Republic of China on Taiwan, protocol, and the Moscow-Peking rivalry. Argues for the status quo in Sino-American relations. Secondary sources; note. R. B. Mendel

473. Scalapino, Robert A. UNCERTAINTIES IN FUTURE SINO-U.S. RELATIONS. *Orbis 1982 26(3): 681-696.* Examines the course of Sino-US diplomacy during 1949-82 and speculates on the directions that their relations will take. Despite the rapprochement between the United States and China during 1972-79, relations have cooled, especially since the inauguration of President Reagan. Although Taiwan is a major issue, domestic considerations (slow-down of the Chinese economy and widespread corruption), China's interest in the leadership of developing nations and its increased concern over US capabilities have played a role in this apparent shift of attitude.
J. W. Thacker, Jr.

474. Schaller, Michael. AMERICAN AIR STRATEGY IN CHINA, 1939-1941: THE ORIGINS OF CLANDESTINE AIR WARFARE. *Am. Q. 1976 28(1): 3-19.* During 1940-41 influential American officials worked closely with individuals and special interest groups associated with the Chinese Nationalist regime to develop at least two plans for clandestine military attacks on Japan. These schemes, using ostensibly private American aircraft and pilots, were developed outside of the State and War Departments. They had the effect of escalating the Japanese-American military confrontation and set precedents for the use of clandestine military means as an active element of American foreign policy. N. Lederer

475. Schaller, Michael. THE COMMAND CRISIS IN CHINA, 1944: A ROAD NOT TAKEN. *Diplomatic Hist. 1980 4(3): 327-331.* Contains the text of General George C. Marshall's draft of a proposed reply to Chinese Generalissimo Jiang Jieshi's (Chiang Kai-shek's) demand that General Joseph W. Stillwell be recalled from China. Marshall, who had selected Stillwell for the assignment, proposed that President Franklin D. Roosevelt rebut each point of Jiang's complaint and decline to remove Stillwell. Marshall's draft was rejected in favor of a more conciliatory response, and Stillwell was recalled as demanded. 4 notes. T. L. Powers

476. Schaller, Michael. SACO! THE UNITED STATES NAVY'S SECRET WAR IN CHINA. *Pacific Hist. Rev. 1975 44(4): 527-553.* The history of Naval Group China (later, Sino-American Cooperation Association, SACO) explains many of the apparent failures and contradictions of the US World War II China policy. From 1942 to 1945 SACO was the only American unit under effective Chinese control, supplying military aid, training, and political support to the Kuomintang. SACO bolstered the most reactionary and anti-Communist faction in the Kuomintang, under the leadership of General Tai Li, in contrast to the tactical moderation of US official policy, which was based on a fear of civil war and a desire to create a coalition in China that would subsume the Communists in an army and government dominated by Chiang Kai-shek. SACO owed its success in preventing American rapprochement with the Communists to the ultimate American strategic commitment to Chiang and to the shared conservative nationalism of American leaders outside the OSS. The significance of SACO lies both in its active role in stimulating the civil war in China and its commitment to the full logic of America's commitment to Chiang. Based on government documents at Federal Records Center (Suitland, Md.), Navy Operational Archives, the National Archives, and personal papers in six depositories; 81 notes. W. K. Hobson

477. Schloss, Ruth. ELIZA MCCOOK ROOTS: AN AMERICAN IN CHINA, 1900-1934. *Connecticut Antiquarian 1980 32(1): 10-25.* At age 30, Eliza McCook (1869-1934) of Hartford, Connecticut, traveled to China; there she and Logan H. Roots (d. 1945), whom she married in 1902, lived as Episcopalian missionaries (she until her death, he until 1937).

478. Schroeder, Paul E. THE OHIO-HUBEI AGREEMENT: CLUES TO CHINESE NEGOTIATING PRACTICES. *China Q. [Great Britain] 1982 (91): 486-491.* In October 1979 the Chinese province of Hubei (Hupeh) signed a commercial and cultural agreement with the state of Ohio. That the Chinese take this kind of sister-state arrangement seriously is indicated by the unexpected openness of the Chinese negotiators and by the ability of provincial Hubei officials to make binding agreements without involving Beijing. The Chinese have shown themselves to be flexible and eager to reach agreement with Ohio firms as well as ready to pay for patent rights. Based largely on the author's conversations with the leading members of the Hubei and Ohio negotiating and implementing teams; 5 notes. J. R. Pavia, Jr.

479. Schuhmacher, W. Wilfried. A NEW SOUNDING: TWO MARITIME FUR TRADE VESSELS. *Oregon Hist. Q. 1977 78(4): 355-356.*

Discovers, from records of ships' arrivals and departures at Cape Colony, information concerning the ships *Alexander* and *Betsy* not included in *A List of Trading Vessels in the Maritime Fur Trade, 1785-1825.* Explains why the *Alexander* was so long in making the homeward bound voyage from the Islands and China. Based on documents in the South Africa Library.

D. R. McDonald

480. Schwartz, Harry. THE MOSCOW-PEKING-WASHINGTON TRIANGLE. *Ann. of the Am. Acad. of Pol. and Social Sci. 1974 (414): 41-50.* Two major factors in the world scene must be considered in any analysis of current Soviet-American relations: 1) the United States and Western Europe are, today, at the nadir of their effective political, military and economic power; 2) the specter of war with the People's Republic of China is in the background of all Soviet thinking. What has actually happened in the last few years is a sort of competitive wooing of the United States by the Russians and the Chinese. Each country is worried that the United States will team up with the other: for, while the United States does not have the political will to do anything major on the world scene by itself, the combination of American technological power and either Chinese or Soviet political power raises the most awesome possibilities. Thus, the recent historic changes—including those accomplished by President Nixon and Secretary of State Kissinger—have issued from the opportunities created by the Soviet-Chinese split. However, both in China and in Russia very real questions are being raised about the wisdom of the policy of the past. In view of this danger, in addition to the prospect of a major Constitutional crisis in the impeachment and trial of the president of the United States, American foreign policy must be at maximum alert. J

481. Segal, Gerald. CHINA AND THE GREAT POWER TRIANGLE. *China Q. [Great Britain] 1980 (83): 490-509.* China's approach to foreign policy is essentially tripolar, seeing the United States, USSR, and China as the significant focal points. China's reaction to this has been unsophisticated in its refusal to mix cooperative and confrontational moves, especially in dealing with the USSR. Based on Chinese and other radio and press reports as well as papers in the John F. Kennedy Library; 74 notes. J. R. Pavia, Jr.

482. Seith, Alex R. CHINA ON OUR MINDS. *Contemporary Educ. 1974 45(3): 165-169.* Terms 20th-century US-Chinese relations a "tragedy of conflicting perceptions." One of nine articles on East Asian education. S

483. Service, John S. ONLY IN REJECTION COULD THERE BE VINDICATION... EXCERPTS FROM "LOST CHANCE IN CHINA." *Foreign Service J. 1974 51(3): 14-16.* The World War II dispatches of John S. Service reveal that the United States should have listened to the Foreign Service officer's advice regarding foreign policy toward Communist China in 1945.

484. Seth, S. P. CHINA'S FOREIGN POLICY—POST CULTURAL REVOLUTION. *Asia Q. [Belgium] 1976 (2): 137-155.* Examines China's foreign policy after the Cultural Revolution. The most singular breakthrough

was an evolving Sino-US power equation in the Asia-Pacific region. Based on newspapers, other primary, and secondary sources; 21 notes. G. M. White

485. Sewall, Arthur F. KEY PITTMAN AND THE QUEST FOR THE CHINA MARKET, 1933-1940. *Pacific Hist. Rev. 1975 44(3): 351-371.* Although Nevada's Senator Key Pittman in the 1930's used the argument that overseas expansion of the American economic system comprised the best means of economic recovery, he did so as a tactical device to win additional support for programs devised to raise the domestic price of silver. He achieved this end in an agreement signed at the World Economic and Monetary Conference in 1933 and in the Silver Purchase Act of 1934. When the domestic price of silver reached 77 cents, Pittman ceased to emphasize the need to increase exports to China, despite the fact that they were on the decline. Based on the Pittman Papers (Library of Congress), the Senate Foreign Relations Committee Papers, the F. D. Roosevelt Papers, published government documents, other published primary sources, and secondary sources; 75 notes.
W. K. Hobson

486. Shaw, Yu-ming. JOHN LEIGHTON STUART AND US-CHINESE COMMUNIST RAPPROCHEMENT IN 1949: WAS THERE ANOTHER "LOST CHANCE IN CHINA"? *China Q. [Great Britain] 1982 (89): 74-96.* The failure of Ambassador John Leighton Stuart to meet with Mao Zedong and Chou Enlai in the summer of 1949 has been regretted as a "lost chance" for Sino-American rapprochement. However, Stuart did contact Mao and Chou through an intermediary, Zhen Mingshu (Chen Ming-shu) during that summer. The stumbling blocks of continued US support for the Nationalists and China's "leaning to one side" prevented any agreement and make the "lost chance" an unlikely thesis. Based largely on Stuart's dispatches in *Foreign Relations of the United States, 1949;* 56 notes. J. R. Pavia, Jr.

487. Shen, I-Yao. A CENTURY OF AMERICAN IMMIGRATION POLICY TOWARD CHINA. *Foreign Service J. 1974 51(7): 10-12, 25.*

488. Shergin, S. O. DEIAKI TENDENTSII EKSPANSIONISTS'KOI POLITYKY SSHA V PIVDENNOSKHIDNIY AZII 1968-1979 RR. [Some tendencies of US expansionist policy in Southeast Asia, 1968-79]. *Ukraïns'kyi Istorychnyi Zhurnal [USSR] 1979 (12): 81-87.* US foreign policy in Southeast Asia was severely criticized by Leonid Brezhnev at the 25th Congress of the CPSU. The statements of US political leaders indicate that the lesson of Vietnam has not sunk in. The United States continues to assist reactionary regimes with military aid disguised as economic help. The establishment of diplomatic relations between the United States and China has not helped to preserve world peace. 28 notes. H. Diuk

489. Shewmaker, Kenneth E. THE GRENVILLE CLARK-EDGAR SNOW CORRESPONDENCE. *Pacific Hist. Rev. 1976 45(4): 597-602.* Surveys the general content of the Dartmouth College Library files of the correspondence between Grenville Clark and Edgar Snow relating mainly to the People's Republic of China and Sino-American relations. The correspondence occurs during 1963-67 and provides significant insights into the thinking

of the correspondents. Clark was an important worker for world peace and Snow was the only personal friend Mao Tse-tung had outside China. 9 notes.
R. V. Ritter

490. Shrewmaker, Kenneth E. THE LOST ALTERNATIVE: AMERICA AND CHINA, 1936-46. *Rev. in Am. Hist.* 1974 2(2): 282-289. Review article prompted by Paul A. Varg's *The Closing of the Door: Sino-American Relations, 1936-1946* (East Lansing: Michigan State U. Pr., 1973). Varg views the China tangle from the perspective of Washington, Chunking, and Yenan. Minimizing economic and missionary sentiment, he overemphasizes strategy and politics. Rightly critical of American obtuseness, Varg too fatalistically concludes the United States was incapable of significantly influencing China's course. 9 notes.
W. D. Piersen

491. Shuja, Sharif M. WESTERN INVOLVEMENT IN CHINA (1557-1949): CHALLENGE TO CHINESE SOVEREIGNTY. *Pakistan Horizon* [Pakistan] 1976 29(3): 33-47. Chronicles western involvement (primarily Great Britain and the United States), focusing on the interventions during the early 20th century, Sun Yat-sen's Revolution, and the power struggle between Chiang Kai-shek and Mao Tse-tung which led to the eventual accession of Mao Tse-tung to power at the head of the Chinese Communist Party in 1949.

492. Sim, Yawsoon. SINO-AMERICAN DETENTE: A NOTE ON AFRO-AMERICANS' VIEWS. *J. of Black Studies* 1974-75 (4): 77-85. Afro-Americans look with favor upon the improvement of Sino-American relations. Most Blacks believe that the United States should recognize China. They identify with the Chinese because they have faced discrimination in the United States as the Chinese have faced world discrimination. 3 notes, biblio.
K. Butcher

493. Singh, L. P. REGIONAL POWER VS. GLOBAL POWER IN ARMS CONTROL: INDIA, AMERICA AND NUCLEAR AFFAIRS. *India Q.* [India] 1979 35(3): 351-361. Examines India's role as a regional power determined to maintain its flexibility on nuclear policy by resisting nuclear safeguards that are proposed by any great power—but especially by the United States. Accordingly, India has retained its nuclear autonomy by following an independent course of action mainly to ensure its security in south Asia. By working closely with Canada to exchange peaceful nuclear technology, India alerts both China and America to the reality that India must remain a nuclear regional power. Covers 1951-78. US documents, secondary sources; 22 notes.
W. R. Johnson

494. Siu, Victoria M. BRIDGING THE CULTURAL GAP: JOHN RUSSELL YOUNG, MINISTER TO CHINA, 1882-1885, AS A CASE HISTORY. *Asian Profile* [Hong Kong] 1982 10(4): 387-394. John Russell Young demonstrated astute diplomatic skill in mediating strained Sino-British and Sino-Japanese relations. However, he showed little concern for the human rights of Chinese peasants or the economic sovereignty of China in his insistence on the right of American manufacturers to operate on Chinese soil, even when this meant the dislocation of traditional industries. Based on

Young's diplomatic dispatches at the National Archives, Washington, D.C., and the John Russell Young Papers in the Library of Congress; 38 notes.

J. Powell

495. Sizer, Nancy. THE FAILURE OF CHINESE EDUCATIONAL LEADERSHIP, 1919-1930. *Hist. of Educ. Q. 1979 19(3): 381-392.* Reviews Barry Keenan's *Dewey Experiment in China* (Cambridge, Mass.: Harvard U. Pr., 1977), which describes American philosopher John Dewey's influence on the New Education Reform movement in China resulting from his visit in 1919-21. Secondary sources; 9 notes.

J. Powell

496. Škvařil, Jaroslav. ČÍNA NA JEDNÉ LODI S AMERICKÝM IMPERIALISMEM [China in the same boat as American imperialism]. *Hist. a Vojenství [Czechoslovakia] 1980 29(5): 110-127, (6): 149-167.* Part I: NĚKTERE ASPEKTY VÝVOJE ČÍNSKO-AMERICKÝCH VZTAHŮ [aspects of the development of Chinese-American relations]. The ideology of the current Chinese leadership can be traced to traditional nationalism, which increasingly influences the Chinese Communist Party, and to the victory of popular revolution in China, which created the desire for ideological and political hegemony in the worker's movement and the world. The story of American-Chinese approaches is thus a tale about the common desire to pragmatically use the other partner for one's own imperialistic plans. What the United States reactivated in 1971 had already begun in 1942. Part II: CESTA PLNÁ ROZPORŮ [On the way to conflict]. After President Richard M. Nixon's visit in 1972, the Chinese leaders accepted the theory that an alliance with the United States was possible and desirable in the struggle against the USSR. However, normalization during 1973-76 raised questions about bilateral relations. President Jimmy Carter's "new China policy" increased these tensions. Based on published diplomatic accounts, newspapers, and secondary sources; 105 notes.

G. E. Pergl

497. Slonim, Shlomo. ISRAEL, THE U.S., AND CHINA. *Midstream 1979 25(6): 20-25.* Although the announcement 15 December 1978 that the United States was formally recognizing the People's Republic of China was at first interpreted as a possible threat to Israel (which was then being pressured by the United States to accept certain Egyptian proposals in the draft peace treaty), later reflection indicated that the move would undoubtedly redound to Israel's benefit because China was obviously looking favorably upon Israeli-Egyptian-American cooperation and resistance to Soviet influence in the strategic Middle East.

498. Snow, Edgar. RECOGNITION OF THE PEOPLE'S REPUBLIC OF CHINA. *Ann. of the Am. Acad. of Pol. and Social Sci. 1959 (323): 75-88.* Chronicles US nonrecognition of China, 1937-58, examining the origin of foreign policy attitudes toward China and its strategic and diplomatic implications.

499. Snyder, William P. DOCUMENTS: DEAN RUSK TO JOHN FOSTER DULLES, MAY-JUNE 1953: THE OFFICE, THE FIRST 100 DAYS, AND RED CHINA. *Diplomatic Hist. 1983 7(1): 79-86.* Reprints and

comments on two letters. In the first, Rusk indicated that a successful secretary of state needs the support of the president, Congress, his own department, and the press. He advised Dulles to get a showing of presidential support, beware the Republican Right in Congress, improve departmental morale, and be wary of the press. In the second letter, Rusk suggested conditions under which Communist China could gain UN membership. Dulles was amenable to the concept. Based on the papers of John Foster Dulles; 16 notes. T. J. Heston

500. Soglian, Franco. LA POLITICA AMERICANA E LE ORIGINI DELLO SCISMO CINO-SOVIETICO (1955-1958) [American policy and the origins of the Sino-Soviet schism, 1955-58]. *Comunità [Italy] 1974 28(172): 71-165.* The principal reason for the enmity between the USSR and China in the 1960's was the anti-China policy of the West, especially the United States, and the warmer relations with the USSR. 213 notes.

501. Solomon, Richard H. THINKING THROUGH THE CHINA PROBLEM. *Foreign Affairs 1978 56(2): 324-356.* Analyzes Sino-American relations. Despite dialogues and exchanges since Kissinger's visit to the People's Republic of China, "... domestic political momentum toward normalization has just about played itself out both in the United States and the PRC." Progress cannot continue until many difficult issues have been resolved, e.g., Taiwan's fate and the position of Mao's successors on human rights. 34 notes. M. R. Yerburgh

502. Spector, Ronald. "WHAT THE LOCAL ANNAMITES ARE THINKING": AMERICAN VIEWS OF VIETNAMESE IN CHINA, 1942-1945. *Southeast Asia 1974 3(2): 741-751.* Maintains that little attention has been paid either to the contacts American officials had with the Vietnamese prior to 1945 or to the attitudes that resulted from these contacts. American contacts with the Vietnamese, including Ho Chi Minh, occurred in southern China as early as 1942, when the Vietminh sought American help in securing the release of Ho from a Chinese prison. In 1943 and 1944, American consuls provided Washington with additional assessments of Ho and his followers. American officials consistently underestimated the strength and determination of the Vietnamese independence movement, and at the highest policymaking levels information about Vietnamese nationalism appears to have been ignored. Based largely on US government documents; 48 notes.
R. H. Detrick

503. Speicher, Jacob, ed. HISTORICAL NOTES OF THE SOUTH CHINA MISSION, SBC. *Baptist Hist. and Heritage 1973 8(2): 77-79.* Reprint of a 1917 article from *The New East* on the origins of Southern Baptists' first missionary efforts in south China. S

504. Stacey, John A. THE NORTH CHINA MARINES: 1931-1941: A PHOTOGRAPHIC REVIEW FROM THE PAGES OF THEIR OWN PUBLICATIONS. *Military Collector & Hist. 1983 35(1): 4-11.* Photographs from the *American Legation Guard News,* the *American Embassy Guard*

News, the *Tientsin U.S. Marine*, the *Peiping Marine*, and the *Tientsin Marine* document peculiarities in the uniforms of marines in North China.

505. Stanley, Peter W. THE MAKING OF AN AMERICAN SINOLOGIST: WILLIAM W. ROCKHILL AND THE OPEN DOOR. *Perspectives in Am. Hist.* 1977-78 11: 417-460. Not until the US government took Far Eastern affairs seriously did William W. Rockhill's star rise within the State Department during the William McKinley and Theodore Roosevelt administrations. By that time the government had learned to recognize Rockhill's expertise and to rely upon his advice. Even though he had obtained many of the ideas for the Open Door Note from Alfred Hippisley, Rockhill openly took credit for the move, and his influence remained evident in US Far Eastern foreign policy for years. W. A. Wiegand

506. Stuart, Angela. THE GREAT WIND SHIPS. *Mankind* 1975 5(2): 28-33. In the 1840's and 1850's, the graceful, swift clipper ships sailed the seas, trading with China and transporting men to the gold fields of California.

507. Sun Yü-t'ang. THE HISTORICAL DEVELOPMENT AND AGGRESSIVE NATURE OF AMERICAN IMPERIALIST INVESTMENT IN CHINA (1784-1914). *Chinese Studies in Hist.* 1975 8(3): 3-17. Translates an article which originally appeared in *Li-shih chiao-hsüeh* [History Teaching] and then in a collective work in 1953. Before the American Revolution, US trade with China was handled through the East India Company. Following the war, the United States lost any such assistance as well as trading partners. Consequently, American merchants began the "China trade." These merchants actively engaged in the opium trade and the United States supported British and French aggression. From about 1875 trade declined and American shipping interests and merchant houses went out of business. Following the Sino-Japanese War imperialist trade with China increased and firms such as Standard Oil flourished. The post-Boxer War period saw an increase in American economic exploitation, with railway and banking interests being particularly successful. Note, biblio. M. R. Underdown

508. Sutter, Robert G. THE EVOLUTION OF CHINA'S APPROACH TO THE SOVIET UNION AND THE UNITED STATES. *Korea and World Affairs [South Korea]* 1979 3(1): 27-45. Wary of an attack by the USSR after the Soviet invasion of Czechoslovakia in 1968, China used rapprochement with the United States to offset Soviet pressure along the Sino-Soviet frontier.

509. Telford, Ted A. CHINESE MATERIALS ON MICROFILM AT THE GENEALOGICAL SOCIETY OF UTAH. *Ch'ing-shih Wen-t'i* 1980 4(3): 106-113. A description of the work being done by the Mormons to "obtain a microfilm copy of any Chinese local gazetteer and genealogy wherever available." Currently the Genealogical Society of Utah has over 5,000 local gazetteers and over 45,000 genealogies and plans to copy sources available outside China. The files are readily available to scholars. Based on the author's work in these materials; table, 8 notes. J. R. Pavia, Jr.

510. Thode, Frieda Oehlschlaeger. THE REV. E. L. ARNDT. *Concordia Hist. Inst. Q. 1974 47(2): 90-95.* Chronicles the work of Reverend E. L. Arndt, father of the China mission of the Lutheran Church, 1913-29. S

511. Thornton, Richard C. SOVIET STRATEGY AND THE VIETNAM WAR. *Asian Affairs 1974 1(4): 205-228.*

512. Thornton, Richard C. TOWARD A NEW EQUILIBRIUM? TRIPOLAR POLITICS, 1964-1976. *Naval War Coll. Rev. 1977 29(3): 3-18.* Examines the change from the post-World War II structure of international relations to a new one. Uses US involvement in Southeast Asia as a focal point in describing the complexities of the tripolar relations among the United States, the Soviet Union, and China. The United States utilized the Chinese interest in a balkanized Indochina to extricate itself from the Vietnam War. Once the United States achieved this goal, it was in its national interest to have a strong, united and Soviet-oriented Vietnam on China's southern flank in order to reinforce the long-term adversary relationship between the USSR and China.
J/S

513. Thurston, Anne F. NEW OPPORTUNITIES FOR RESEARCH IN CHINA. *Soc. Sci. Res. Council Items 1979 33(2): 13-17.* Discusses the increase in the number of opportunities for social science research exchange programs between the United States and China beginning in 1972.

514. Tilford, Earl H., Jr. TWO SCORPIONS IN A CUP: AMERICA AND THE SOVIET AIRLIFT TO LAOS. *Aerospace Hist. 1980 27(3): 151-162.* A detailed history of Russian, American, Chinese, and North Vietnamese intervention in Laos between 1959 and 1962. The civil war which resulted from this intervention involved two Laotian prime ministers and three armed factions contending for control. A shaky truce was realized in December 1962, after which both American and Soviet support was removed. The USSR had become involved to demonstrate Soviet support for anticolonial wars and to limit China's dominance in Southeast Asia. Hanoi also supported the USSR's effort to counter Chinese participation. The United States became involved to counter Soviet successes in Berlin and Cuba. Secondary sources; 11 photos, 3 maps, 68 notes.
C. W. Ohrvall

515. Tow, William T. AMERICA'S AMBIVALENCE AND SOVIET STRATEGIC "HEGEMONY": CHINESE PERCEPTIONS. *Asian Forum 1981 10(3): 53-66.* Surveys possible Chinese strategic policy options and policy limitations through the 1980's. Chinese nuclear capabilities could present problems to Soviet strategic planners, especially if coupled with at least a tacit backing of US technological and military power. Likewise China's decision to establish any long-term policies of cooperation with US foreign policy objectives will be contingent on a greater US propensity to reassert US political and military power in East Asia. 42 notes.
R. B. Orr

516. Tow, William T. CHINA'S NUCLEAR STRATEGY AND US REACTIONS IN THE "POST-DÉTENTE" ERA. *Military Rev. 1976 56(6): 80-90.* Discusses the implications of China's nuclear strategy for arms control

agreements and foreign policy toward the United States in the 1970's; examines China's desire to weaken detente between the United States and the USSR.

517. Tozer, Warren W. LAST BRIDGE TO CHINA: THE SHANGHAI POWER COMPANY, THE TRUMAN ADMINISTRATION AND THE CHINESE COMMUNISTS. *Diplomatic Hist. 1977 1(1): 64-78.* A study of the American-owned Shanghai Power Company during 1949-50 indicates that the United States "was primarily responsible for closing the Open Door in China. The People's Republic of China (PRC) not only appeared willing to tolerate American firms for the short term but sought to establish some type of relationship with the United States.... The Truman administration, pursuing a policy of containment, refused to deal with the Chinese Communists, except on its own terms, and attempted to control trade with the PRC in order to force compliance with American demands." Based primarily on the Boise Cascade Corporation Archives; 55 notes. G. H. Curtis

518. Ts'ai, Shih-Shan H. CHINESE IMMIGRATION THROUGH COMMUNIST CHINESE EYES: AN INTRODUCTION TO THE HISTORIOGRAPHY. *Pacific Hist. Rev. 1974 43(3): 395-408.* A bibliographic and critical study of all Communist works available outside of mainland China on Chinese immigration to the United States. They focus on three aspects: "the motives and processes of Chinese immigration; the background of a series of treaties and laws by which the United States managed the immigration; and the reasons for the anti-Chinese movement.... Though we might not accept their Marxist analyses, we must recognize that the Communist Chinese researchers have added a considerable array of new data to the study of Chinese immigration." 43 notes. R. V. Ritter

519. Ts'ai, Shih-Shan H. REACTION TO EXCLUSION: THE BOYCOTT OF 1905 AND CHINESE NATIONAL AWAKENING. *Historian 1976 39(1): 95-110.* In May 1905 the Shanghai Chamber of Commerce passed a resolution urging Chinese citizens to boycott American goods. This boycott was to strike back at the 1894 Gresham Yang Treaty which recognized the legality of many anti-Chinese registrations. Yet the boycott against the treaty took place 11 years later. The answer is found in the steady growth of Chinese national pride after the 1894 Sino-Japanese War. The boycott represented political rather than economic nationalism and showed the extent of Chinese frustrations about discrimination and exclusion in American immigration policy. Notes. M. J. Wentworth

520. Tsai Wei-ping. MORALITY AND DIPLOMACY: PRESIDENT CARTER'S FOREIGN POLICY ORIENTATION. *Issues and Studies [Taiwan] 1977 13(4): 1-11.* Examines the general importance of the US in international affairs and then concentrates on the Carter administration's attitude toward foreign policy (incorporating human rights and moral values); touches on the US attitude toward China.

521. Tsai Wei-ping. WASHINGTON-PEIPING RELATIONS AFTER MAO. *Issues and Studies [Taiwan] 1978 14(6): 1-12.* America's post-World

War II policy of supporting noncommunist governments in Asia should not be supplanted by reliance on China.

522. Tsou, Tang. STATESMANSHIP AND SCHOLARSHIP. *World Pol. 1974 26(3): 428-451.* Several recent scholarly works on American and Chinese policies clarify the alternatives confronting the United States in 1971, and give us a glimpse of the Nixon Administration's objectives, strategies, tactics, considerations, and calculations in the opening to China. Together with these works, the processes and results of the negotiations with China constitute the fullest public record to date of Henry A. Kissinger's and Richard M. Nixon's general approach to international politics. But their policy toward China has a unique feature: the frank acknowledgment of the uncertainty of both the immediate and final outcome. This posture has bolstered their courage to take audacious initiatives, giving their policy the necessary flexibility and strengthening their bargaining position. The scholarly works built a consensus behind the new policy. Their findings point to the theoretical proposition that an accommodation may be achieved if the revolutionary state is given a fair stake in the system and if it cannot improve its position by revolutionary methods.
J

523. Tucker, Nancy Bernkopf. AN UNLIKELY PEACE: AMERICAN MISSIONARIES AND THE CHINESE COMMUNISTS, 1948-1950. *Pacific Hist. Rev. 1976 45(1): 97-116.* During 1948-50 the Chinese Communists pursued a policy of toleration of religion, including foreign missionaries. The outbreak of the Korean War ended the policy. The toleration policy was more fully observed in urban than in rural areas. Protestants were better treated than Catholics. American missionaries were divided in their response to Chinese Communists: Catholics and fundamentalist Protestants were hostile, but modernist Protestants were more likely to believe cooperation was possible. Other missionaries who decided to cooperate were motivated by the desires of Chinese Christians and by a concern to protect their churches' property holdings in China. Some missionaries also attempted to influence American policy. Many lobbied in 1949 for an end to American aid to the Kuomintang and for recognition of the Communists. Based on manuscripts in church archives, published primary sources, and published and unpublished secondary works; 66 notes.
W. K. Hobson

524. Uhalley, Stephen Jr. EDUCATION IN CHINA TODAY AND PROSPECTS FOR AMERICAN INVOLVEMENT. *South Atlantic Q. 1975 74(1): 12-20.* Before the Great Proletarian Cultural Revolution, China possessed two unequal systems of education. The first system, inherited from the Western Christian educational institutions, produced specialized technicians and professionals. It stressed academic performance and elitist class distinctions over socialist values of political education and respect for physical labor. The second system of mass education left the proletariat alienated and dissatisfied. A revitalized mass education system came to dominate China following the upheavals of 1966. Educational processes are now mostly local community concerns aimed at enriching the masses and imparting practical skills of immediate local needs. Bitter experiences with Western domination prevents Chinese educators from seeking foreign contacts, and prospects for

exchanges with the US appear negligible. Based on primary and secondary sources; 4 notes. W. L. Olbrich

525. Van Alstyne, Richard W. THE UNITED STATES AND THE CHINESE REVOLUTION: 1949-1972. *Current Hist. 1973 65(385): 97-101, 133.* Traces US-Chinese relations since 1949. S

526. Varg, Paul A. SINO-AMERICAN RELATIONS PAST AND PRESENT. *Diplomatic Hist. 1980 4(2): 101-111.* American relations with China have been both between governments and between peoples. Renewed relations have brought expectations that the old pre-World War II path can be resumed, but China has changed; the social, political, and economic undergirdings of the relationship have been altered greatly. 2 notes. T. L. Powers

527. Vidich, Arthur J. SOCIAL CONFLICT IN THE ERA OF DETENTE: NEW ROLES FOR IDEOLOGUES, REVOLUTIONARIES, AND YOUTH. *Social Res. 1975 42(1): 64-87.* Discusses the roles of the USSR, United States, and Communist China throughout the Cold War and after and notes how social conflict was caused and at the same time contained by these three powers (1950's-70's). S

528. Vigny, Georges. ONE MAN'S "CHINACARD" IS ANOTHER'S "AMERICA CARD." *Int. Perspectives [Canada] 1979 (Mar-Apr): 19-22.* The leaders of the People's Republic of China, who possess a sharp perception of reality, now are eagerly aspiring to achieve world power. The US view of Taiwan as a serious obstacle to normalization of relations was an illusion, deliberately created by the Chinese, who are quite conscious of the benefits of Sino-American rapprochement. These benefits include the checking of Soviet ambitions in Asia and the help of US technology in getting China's industrialization off the ground. E. S. Palais

529. Volokhova, A. A. MEZHDUNARODNYI IMPERIALIZM I KITAI: DISKUSSIIA V SOVREMENNOM AMERIKANSKOM KITAEVEDENII [International imperialism and China: polemic in contemporary American Sinology]. *Voprosy Istorii [USSR] 1974 (8): 173-178.* Reviews American works published since the mid-1960's on the Chinese agrarian economy in the late 19th-early 20th centuries and the influence of foreign capitalism and trade on China's economic development. American neo-liberals such as Rhoads Murphey, Ramon Hawley Myers, Jack M. Potter, Dwight Heald Perkins, and Albert Feuerwerker refute any detrimental influence of foreign capital on Chinese agricultural and industrial development. This point of view was attacked by James Peck "The Roots of Rhetoric: the Professional Ideology of America's China Watchers" *(Bulletin of Concerned Asian Scholars* 1969 2(1): 59-69) and followed by a polemic exchange between Peck, John K. Fairbank, Andrew J. Nathan, Joseph Esherick, and Marilyn Young in the same journal [1970 (2)3: 51-70; 1972 4(4): 3-8, 9-16; and 1973 5(2): 32-35]. 21 notes. N. Frenkley

530. Walsh, James P. THE DEATH OF JOHN BIRCH—DOCUMENTED. *Wisconsin Mag. of Hist. 1975 58(3): 209-218.* Because of limited access to

classified government documents, researchers have had to rely on some interviews, selected sources, and Robert H. W. Welch, Jr.'s *The Life of John Birch* to learn of the circumstances surrounding Birch's death at the hands of the Chinese Communists in 1945. The recent declassification of certain records allows a more complete picture, revealing that Captain John M. Birch, son of missionary parents, imbibed a zealous patriotism that he carried with him into his intelligence gathering work for the Air Force in China. In fact, Birch's hostile and threatening attitude in dealing with the Communists who were interrogating him accounted in part for his death. 7 illus., 25 notes.

N. C. Burckel

531. Wang, James C. F. COMPARATIVE STUDIES OF CHINESE POLITICS: PERSPECTIVES FROM THE US. *Issues and Studies [Taiwan] 1977 13(4): 34-48.* Examines research carried on in the United States pertaining to politics in China; divides the periods into 1950-65 and 1965-76, highlighting model designs, social science theories, and methodological sophistication; speculates on future trends in scholarship.

532. Wedemeyer, Albert C. RELATIONS WITH WARTIME CHINA: A REMINISCENCE. *Asian Affairs: An Am. Rev. 1977 4(3): 196-201.* Describes the author's experiences as an American emissary to China during and after World War II. Analyzes his motivations in the light of his military background. Based on the author's remarks at the 18th Annual Conference of the American Association for Chinese Studies held in St. Louis, Missouri. Note.

R. B. Mendel

533. Weiss, Ruth. LU XUN—HE SPEAKS TO US AND TO OUR DAY. *Eastern Horizon [Hong Kong] 1981 20(9): 29-33.* Discusses the life, literary and academic careers, and political views of Lu Xun (Lu Hsun, 1881-1936), whose real name was Zhou Shuren (Chou Shu-jen), a writer of short stories, and describes the numerous memorials and institutes created in his memory throughout China.

534. Welch, William. CONTAINMENT: AMERICAN AND SOVIET VERSIONS. *Studies in Comparative Communism 1973 6(3): 215-240.* Compares the American foreign policy of containment of the USSR with the Soviet policy of containment of China which since 1959 has aimed at restricting Chinese influence and opposing Chinese irredentism. The Russians see the Chinese threat as local rather than global, and they make use of fewer military alliances. They seek instead collective security agreements which include a potential aggressor. The Soviets make great use of propaganda and have at times been aggressive in opposing the Chinese. They generally take few risks, however, in furthering their great concern for military security. 83 notes.

D. Balmuth

535. Werking, Richard H. THE BOXER INDEMNITY REMISSION AND THE HUNT THESIS. *Diplomatic Hist. 1978 2(1): 103-106.* The indemnity received by the United States in the wake of the Boxer Rebellion was returned to China, which used it to educate Chinese youth in the United States. In 1972, historian Michael Hunt argued that American pressure forced

the reluctant Chinese to spend it in that manner. Further study supports Hunt's thesis. Examination of alternate proposals for use of the indemnity reveals that the remission, and all American policy in this incident, was motivated by self-interest rather than altruism. Based on State Department records; 8 notes.
T. L. Powers

536. Whetten, Lawrence L. SECURITY AND SOUTH-WEST ASIA: SECURITY IMPLICATIONS OF RECENT POLITICAL CHANGES. *Round Table [Great Britain] 1979 (273): 31-40.* In 1977 and 1978, efforts of Southwest Asian countries to negotiate defense alliances intensified because of the increased political, diplomatic, and economic activities in that area by the United States, the USSR, and China.

537. White, John Albert. AS THE RUSSIANS SAW OUR CHINA POLICY. *Pacific Hist. Rev. 1957 26(2): 147-160.* Soviet interpretation of US foreign policy in China, 1944-49, represented the United States as aggressor in an effort to cover up Soviet imperialism and to distort the US international image.

538. Whiting, Allen S. THE DRAGON'S TEETH: A REVIEW ARTICLE. *Armed Forces and Soc. 1977 3(2): 347-352.* Reviews four books on recent Chinese military developments: Yueh-yun Liu's *China As A Nuclear Power in World Politics* (New York: Taplinger, 1972) speculates in a journalistic fashion on the role of China after it acquires nuclear arms; J. H. Kalicki's *The Pattern of Sino-American Crises* (London: Cambridge U. Pr., 1975) bridges a gap seldom attempted through an excellent analysis of the interaction of Sino-American diplomatic and strategic policies; William W. Whitson's *The Military and Political Power in China In the 1970's* (New York: Praeger, 1972) presents a collection of essays that examine contemporary events within China against the perspective of Chinese military developments; and John Yin's *Sino-Soviet Dialogue on the Problem of War* (The Hague: Martinus Nijhoff, 1971) depicts Sino-Soviet arguments on the art of warmaking.
J. P. Harahan

539. Whiting, Allen S. SINO-AMERICAN DETENTE. *China Q. [Great Britain] 1980 (82): 334-341.* A review of H. R. Haldeman's *The Ends of Power,* Henry A. Kissinger's *White House Years,* and Richard M. Nixon's *The Memoirs of Richard M. Nixon.* Though critical of all three, the author does praise the Kissinger volume for its insights into high-level diplomacy.
J. R. Pavia, Jr.

540. Whiting, Allen S. SINO-AMERICAN RELATIONS: THE DECADE AHEAD. *Orbis 1982 26(3): 697-719.* Examines the role of US commitments to Taiwan since 1979 and analyzes the myths and realities of the assumptions that underlie present rhetoric concerning Sino-American relations as well as China's future. The previous decade had seen a much better relationship develop between the United States and China. Neither side has allowed the Taiwan issue to damage that relationship. Furthermore, each has communicated its views to the other on important matters, the essence of normalization. Note.
J. W. Thacker, Jr.

541. Wilson, David A.　PRINCIPLES AND PROFITS: STANDARD OIL RESPONDS TO CHINESE NATIONALISM, 1925-1927. *Pacific Hist. Rev. 1977 46(4): 625-647.* In March 1925 the Kuomintang (Nationalist) government in Kwangtung Province sought to solve its financial problems by imposing a tax on imported kerosene. The tax was resisted by the two major suppliers, Standard Oil Company of New York and the Asiatic Petroleum Company, Ltd., as contrary to treaty provisions. The oil companies imposed an embargo, to which the Nationalists responded by threatening to create a government monopoly to control kerosene prices. Support from workers in Kwangtung and Hong Kong and oil from the Soviet Union enabled the Kuomintang to resist the embargo. In March 1926, the companies agreed to accept a tax in return for dissolution of the government monopoly. The American government reluctantly accepted the agreement despite the encroachment on treaty rights. The foreign companies and governments had recognized the strength of the Nationalist government in South China, but had also strengthened the conservative elements in the Nationalist coalition, which were willing to compromise with foreign powers. Based on documents in the National Archives and Hoover Library and on published primary sources; 70 notes.
W. K. Hobson

542. Wilson, R. C.　THE PEKING MAN MYSTERY. *Mankind 1980 6(8): 29-32, 34.* The fossil remains of Peking Man were lost in the confusion of war in 1941. The inquiries of Harry F. Shapiro in 1971 and Christopher Janus in 1972-73 failed to solve the mystery of the whereabouts of the fossils. Significant questions remain open to serious investigation. 4 illus.
D. J. Maika

543. Wong, J. Y.　THE ROLE OF PETER PARKER IN THE OPENING OF CHINA. *China Q. [Great Britain] 1975 (63): 539-542.* A review article criticizing Edward Gulick's *Peter Parker and the Opening of China* (Cambridge: Harvard U. Pr., 1973), for concentrating more on Parker the man than on the events of the "opening" of China. 12 notes.

544. Wong, Leslie.　ROOTS IN CHINA, A FIRST ENCOUNTER. *Smithsonian 1977 8(1): 116-120.* The author recounts a trip to China in 1976 with his mother to visit relatives whom she had not seen in 30 years; discusses family life and the occupations, culture, and pastimes of his relatives.

545. Worden, Robert L.　A PERSPECTIVE ON U.S.-CHINA RELATIONS SINCE THE SHANGHAI COMMUNIQUE. *Asian Profile [Hong Kong] 1979 7(1): 1-16.* Discusses relations between the United States and China from the joint signing of the Shanghai Communique in 1972 until 1978. The years 1972-73 witnessed Richard M. Nixon's visit to China, the withdrawal of US troops from Vietnam, and the normalization of relations between China and the United States. The years 1974-75 witnessed a status quo in relations between the two countries. In 1976 Nixon visited China for the second time, although the Chinese were worried about the Soviet threat and the ability of the United States to withstand it. During the years 1977-78 the

Taiwan question and US weakness vis-à-vis the USSR were emphasized by the Chinese. Based on statements of the official Chinese media; 64 notes.

J. Powell

546. Wu Chen-tsai. THE NEW FACE OF THE COLD WAR. *Issues & Studies [Taiwan] 1973 9(12): 18-25.* Detente between the United States and the USSR and between the United States and China has not diminished the Cold War from 1971 to 1973.

547. Xiang Rong. ON THE "OPEN DOOR" POLICY. *Chinese Studies in Hist. 1982-83 16(1-2): 145-154.* The Open Door Policy was not established by US diplomats to insure the administrative and territorial integrity of China but rather to secure American interests in China on an equal level with the other powers involved there at the time. Secondary sources; 19 notes.

A. C. Migliazzo

548. Yahuda, Michael B. CHINESE FOREIGN POLICY AFTER THE VICTORIES IN INDOCHINA. *World Today [Great Britain] 1975 31(7): 291-298.* While hailed by the Chinese, revolutionary victories in Cambodia and South Vietnam in 1975 add ambiguity to US-China relations for the future.

549. Yang Chih-hung. WEI CHI HSIAO HSI CH'U PU KUO SAN CHIH YEN CHIU—YI "MEI KUO YÜ CHUNG KUNG CHIEN CHIAO" HSIAO HSI WEI LI [A study of the initial stage of news dissemination in a crisis—using the US diplomatic recognition of the Chinese Communists as an example]. *Ssu yü Yen (Thought and Word) [Taiwan] 1981 19(2): 35-65.* Evaluates the performance of the Taiwan communication system when the United States established diplomatic relations with Communist China. Data was gathered by telephone interview. Among the findings: word of mouth was the primary news source; nearly 67% of the population learned of the event within the first three and one-half hours; about half believed the news on first hearing. 34 tables, 2 charts, 24 notes.

J. A. Krompart

550. Yao Meng-hsüan. A STUDY OF PEIPING'S U.S. POLICY. *Issues and Studies [Taiwan] 1977 13(7): 76-85.* Since 1970, Communist China has seemed to have assumed a friendlier attitude toward the United States, but its policy is really its old one of "unity with struggle," which is used to oppose adversaries of superior strength.

551. Yee, Albert. EXPANDING AMERICAN HISTORY BEYOND CHAUVINISM. *Peace and Change 1980 6(1-2): 99-104.* Historians and textbook publishers promulgate a history of America that seems guided more by attitudes and biases than by accurate representation of the actual themes, events, persons, motivations, and circumstances that took place; gives as a primary example China's influence upon the formation of America.

552. Yen, Susan Morrison. THE RENOUF PAPERS: AN AMERICAN ACADEMIC IN CHINA, 1903-1910. *J. of the Rutgers U. Lib. 1977 39(2): 98-107.* Vincent Adams Renouf (1876-1910), an American, taught at the Imperial Peiyang University in Tientsin from 1905 to 1910. His papers, recently presented to the Rutgers University Library, provide a first-hand

account of the intellectual turmoil China experienced at this time. In addition to teaching and lecturing on China's population problem, Renouf wrote a textbook, *Outline of General History for Eastern Students,* used in several countries in the Far East and which went through 20 printings.

R. F. Van Benthuysen

553. Yin Ch'ing-yao. PEIPING-WASHINGTON RELATIONS: THEIR VARIOUS ASPECTS. *Issues and Studies [Taiwan] 1974 10(12): 2-16.* Discusses foreign relations between China and the United States in light of President Richard M. Nixon's 1972 China visit, emphasizing aspects of China's diplomatic strategy, 1969-70's.

554. Yin Ch'ing-yao. COMMUNIST CHINA'S ANTI-HEGEMONY POLICY: ITS RECENT DEVELOPMENT AND PROSPECTS. *Issues & Studies [Taiwan] 1982 18(5): 55-77.* Communist China's antihegemony attacks are currently more focused on the United States than on the USSR. But China will not return to the Russian camp, in spite of the present improvement in relations between the two Communist nations. Based on a paper presented at the 9th Sino-Japanese Conference on Mainland China, Taipei, 30 April-2 May 1982; 59 notes.

J. A. Krompart

555. Yin Ch'ing-yao. PEIPING'S STRATEGY AS SEEN FROM ITS POLICY TOWARD THE UNITED STATES. *Issues and Studies [Taiwan] 1975 11(1): 2-20.* Discusses Mao Tse-tung and China's diplomatic strategy and foreign policy toward the United States in the 1960's and 70's, including the implications of President Richard M. Nixon's visit to China in 1972.

556. Yin Ch'ing-yao. THE WASHINGTON-MOSCOW-PEIPING STRATEGIC TRIANGLE: AN OVERALL VIEW. *Issues and Studies [Taiwan] 1979 15(2): 11-35.* Reviews foreign relations between the United States, the USSR, and China since World War II in light of the establishment of US-Chinese diplomatic relations in the 1970's.

557. Yodfat, Aryeh. THE USA, USSR, CHINA AND THE ARAB-ISRAELI CONFLICT. *Int. Problems [Israel] 1981 20(2-4): 85-93.*

558. Yodfat, Aryeh Y. ARTSOT HA-BERIT, BERIT HA-MO'ATSOT VE-SIN VE-HA-SIKHSUKH HA-'ARAVI-YIŚRAELI [The United States, the USSR, the People's Republic of China, and the Arab-Israeli conflict]. *Int. Problems [Israel] 1979 18(3-4): 14-22.* Reviews the positions of the three powers in the Middle East: the United States plays a central role; the USSR has been forced into a more passive one; and China can still only watch from the distance.

559. Young, Kenneth Ray. THE STILWELL CONTROVERSY: A BIBLIOGRAPHICAL REVIEW. *Military Affairs 1975 39(2): 66-68.* Reviews General Joseph W. Stilwell's career in Asia and examines the controversy over Stilwell's effectiveness as the China-India-Burma Theater commander (1942-44). Summarizes the different viewpoints and concludes that Stilwell's mission to China was doomed from the start. 23 notes.

A. M. Osur

560. Yung Wei. PEIPING-WASHINGTON RELATIONS IN THE POST-MAO ERA. *Issues and Studies [Taiwan] 1976 12(11): 21-34.* Analyzes the immediate effect of the death of Mao Tse-tung in terms of China's foreign relations with the USSR and the United States, and speculates on possible changes in internal politics in China.

561. Zanegin, B. N. K VOPROSU OB OSNOVAKH AMERIKANO-KITAISKOGO SBLIZHENIIA [The basis for the Sino-American rapprochement]. *Narody Azii i Afriki [USSR] 1976 (4): 32-45.* Describes US political approaches to China beginning with World War II. The appearance of American athletes and journalists in China in April 1971 ended the almost 25-year state of confrontation between the two nations. The rapprochement process followed the 1968-69 period of sharp conflict. The present US policy, based on the amoral concept of the balance of power, determines Washington's position on any major international problem. Nationalist anti-Soviet motivation has determined China's foreign policy. 25 notes. L. Kalinowski

562. —. [ACHESON AND HIS ADVISORS]. Borg, Dorothy and Heinrichs, Waldo, ed. *Uncertain Years: Chinese-American Relations, 1947-1950* (New York: Columbia U. Pr., 1980): 13-59.
Cohen, Warren I. ACHESON, HIS ADVISERS, AND CHINA, 1949-1950. pp. 13-52. Dean Acheson as US Secretary of State, 1949-50, was willing to ignore the advice of Asia desk subordinates as well as the China Lobby when it violated his policy of salutary neglect of China, sought accommodation with the Chinese Communists and consistently resisted growing anti-Communist US public opinion until the final and fatal decision to cross the 38th parallel in Korea.
Heinrichs, Waldo. SUMMARY OF DISCUSSION, pp. 53-59. Response to Cohen's paper at the Conference on Chinese-American Relations, sponsored by the East Asian Institute of Columbia University at Mt. Kisco, New York.

563. —. [CHINA AND THE FOREIGN SERVICE]. *Foreign Service J. 1973 50(3): 17-24.*
—. INTRODUCTION, *p. 17.*
Tuchman, Barbara. WHY POLICY MAKERS DO NOT LISTEN, *pp. 18-21.*
Service, John S. FOREIGN SERVICE REPORTING, *pp. 22-24.* Discusses the gap between Foreign Service officers' reports and foreign policy, focusing on the dismissal of John S. Service in 1952 for disloyalty. S

564. —. [THE DEFENSIVE PERIMETER CONCEPT]. Borg, Dorothy and Heinrichs, Waldo, ed. *Uncertain Years: Chinese-American Relations, 1947-1950* (New York: Columbia U. Pr., 1980): 61-128.

Gaddis, John Lewis. THE STRATEGIC PERSPECTIVE: THE RISE AND FALL OF THE "DEFENSIVE PERIMETER" CONCEPT, 1947-1951, pp. 61-118. The idea that as a result of World War II the US strategic frontier had shifted from the West Coast to the Asian offshore islands, centered on Okinawa and excluding mainland Asia, had become common wisdom in 1949-50, only to be ignored with the decision to intervene in Korea.

Heinrichs, Waldo. SUMMARY OF DISCUSSIONS, pp. 119-128. Discussants at the Conference on Chinese-American Relations, Mt. Kisco, New York, 1978, "probed the nature and limits of the original strategy, explored its context, and debated when and why shifts away from the perimeter strategy occurred."

565. —. [GLOBAL POWERS' FOREIGN POLICY IN THE SEVENTIES]. *Survey [Great Britain] 1973 19(2): 101-131.*

Aspaturian, Vernon D. THE USSR, THE USA AND CHINA IN THE SEVENTIES, pp. 103-122. "The 1970s will see the emergence of a new world order with existing national ideological and social systems more or less intact, although considerably modified in extent and character." There will be an identity crisis in the US and USSR as both nations seek to redefine their global role, and this will lead to a reduction in world commitments. China's identity crisis will focus on whether to become a global power. There will be succession problems in the USSR and China. Moving beyond détente, the United States can "open up" the Soviet and perhaps Chinese systems by helping them to operate more efficiently.

Scalapino, Robert A. COMMENT, pp. 123-126. The American withdrawal in the world is a result of success more than failure, and the Soviets are increasing their commitments right now, particularly in Asia. The timing of superpower decisions may be as important as the decisions themselves. China will not be regarded as a global power for years to come. Rejects the idea that messianism has been a force in postwar US foreign policy.

Zook, Benjamin M. COMMENT, pp. 127-128. Ideology or messianism has not motivated postwar US foreign policy, but it is and will be important to the Soviets. Aspaturian seems overly optimistic on Communist-US cooperation and harmony in the 1970's. China will remain a regional power. The polycentric international system will raise more problems for Moscow.

Triska, Jan F. COMMENT, pp. 129-131. There will be deglobalization in security matters, but increased globalization in other international transactions—goods, services, messages. Western Europe will not become an area of Soviet opportunity. China will become a world power in the new deglobalized world, and this will force more compromise, negotiation, and bargaining. Part of a special issue on the future of Soviet foreign policy. R. B. Valliant

566. —. [INTRODUCTION TO AND JOURNAL OF CHESTER FRITZ'S TRAVELS IN WESTERN CHINA]. *North Dakota Q. 1981 49(2): 5-120.*

Rylance, Daniel F.   INTRODUCTION, PROVENANCE AND EDITORIAL NOTE, *pp. 5-8.* Outlines why Chester Fritz undertook his six-month journey through western China in 1917 and discusses how the log of that journey came to be published.

Vivian, James F., ed.   THE JOURNAL OF CHESTER FRITZ, *pp. 9-120.* Reproduces, in scholarly accurate form, the travel log which recorded the experiences of Chester Fritz during his six-month tour of western China in 1917.

567.   —.   [ISSACHAR J. ROBERTS]. *Pro. of the South Carolina Hist. Assoc. 1981: 28-55.*

Pruden, George B., Jr.   ISSACHAR J. ROBERTS: A SOUTHERN MISSIONARY PIONEER IN CHINA, *pp. 28-52.* Examines the early missionary career of Issachar Jacob Roberts in China during 1837-47. In the latter year his floating mission was sunk by a mob of angry Chinese. Roberts's success as a Baptist missionary was limited by his difficult personality. Based on the papers of the Southern Baptist Missionary Board and published works; 64 notes.

Gettys, James W., Jr.   COMMENTARY, *pp. 53-55.* Discussion of Roberts's earlier career as a farmer and his theology might help explain his differences with other missionaries.   J. W. Thacker, Jr.

568.   —.   LEGAL IMPLICATIONS OF RECOGNITION OF PEOPLE'S REPUBLIC OF CHINA. *Am. Soc. of Int. Law. Pro. 1978 72: 240-268.*

Surrey, Walter S.   INTRODUCTION, *p. 240.* The 1972 Shanghai Communique acknowledged the differences between the United States and the People's Republic of China and emphasized the need to address the Taiwan issue in order to promote US recognition of "one China."

Cohen, Jerome Alan.   REMARKS, *pp. 240-249.* Favors honoring the Shanghai Communique, asserting that normalization of relations with the People's Republic of China does not necessarily cut off Taiwan or abrogate former treaties.

Hungdah Chiu.   REMARKS, *pp. 250-255.* Contemplates domestic and international legal aspects of US termination of treaties with Taiwan, the impending international legal status of Taiwan, and the impact of the recognition of China on Taiwan's international status.

Theroux, Eugene A.   REMARKS, *pp. 255-263.* Examines legal problems associated with US recognition of China, the necessity of normalization as a precondition to increased trade relations between the two, and the legal obstacles to such trade.

Hyndman, Vance.   REMARKS, *pp. 263-264.* Reflects on strategic, legal, and political repercussions of normalization of relations with China.

Malloy, Michael P.   DISCUSSION, *pp. 264-268.* Responses to questions from the floor dealing with conduct of foreign policy by the executive branch; defense, strategic, and nuclear implications; Pacific politics and relations; and the binding or nonbinding nature of the Shanghai Communique.

569.   —.   SHANGHAI, 1937-1938: HOW BITTERSWEET IT WAS. *US Naval Inst. Pro. 1974 100(11): 79-91.* A pictorial essay, "the results of efforts

by Professor Robert M. Leventhal." Many of the photographs were taken by the late Sergeant Major Albert C. Marts, US Marine Corps, who served with the Fourth Marine Regiment in China during the 1920's and 1930's. For 10 years prior to the summer of 1937, with a brief interlude of fighting between the Chinese and Japanese in 1932, "reality ... was guard duty and liberty" for the Fourth Marines in Shanghai, and after "the daily drudgery of duty" they "entered a kind of oriental Valhalla." War came again to Shanghai in July 1937, and life for the Marines began to change seven months later when the Japanese occupied the city. From that time on, "it was the Japanese whose word was law in China's largest city." 28 photos. A. N. Garland

3

HONG KONG

570. Chan, Kit-cheng. THE UNITED STATES AND THE QUESTION OF HONG KONG, 1941-45. *J. of the Hong Kong Branch of the Royal Asiatic Soc. [Hong Kong] 1979 19: 1-20.* Discusses the US attitude to the conflict between Great Britain and China over Hong Kong during World War II. The United States did not view British claims to Hong Kong with sympathy. The reason was twofold: Franklin D. Roosevelt personally desired an end to colonialism and imperialism; secondly, the US government under Roosevelt and Truman feared that China and Chiang Kai-shek would cease fighting the Japanese and so weaken Allied efforts in the Asian theater if the United States was perceived as favoring the British. These two aspects of the US response become evident by examining letters and documents associated with the key figures involved. Based on the letters and papers of Stanley K. Hornbeck, Joseph W. Ballantine, and Henry Morgenthau; 72 notes.
G. V. Wasson

571. Chan, Steve and Bobrow, Davis B. HORSE RACES, SECURITY MARKETS, AND FOREIGN RELATIONS: SOME IMPLICATIONS AND EVIDENCE FOR CRISIS PREDICTION. *J. of Conflict Resolution 1981 25(2): 187-236.* Securities markets in Hong Kong and New York City, 1964-79, were more likely to react to, rather than predict, crises in foreign relations.

572. Lawrie, Gordon G. AMERICAN STUDIES IN HONG KONG. *Am. Studies Int. 1976 14(3): 31-36.* Although there are no formal programs in American Studies in the University of Hong Kong, the connection to the United States is strong. The university offers many undergraduate courses in the literature, history, and government of the United States.
L. L. Athey

4

JAPAN

573. Abegglen, James C. and Hout, Thomas M. FACING UP TO THE TRADE GAP WITH JAPAN. *Foreign Affairs 1978 57(1): 146-168.* Details the US trade deficit with Japan. It is simplistic to believe that Japanese protectionism is responsible for this imbalance; as a small yet densely populated island nation, Japan must import heavily. The fact of the matter is that in recent years, the United States has been losing its share of that market in almost every product category. If the United States is to have any chance at all of becoming more competitive in the world market, the government must create a more favorable environment for American industry; e.g., provide tax incentives and relax enforcement of the antitrust laws. 4 notes.
M. R. Yerburgh

574. Aigrain, Pierre. TECHNOLOGIE ET RAPPORTS DE FORCE [Technology and the profits of strength]. *Défense Natl. [France] 1979 35(Mar): 9-24.* Provides a comparative study of technological research and development in France, Great Britain, Japan, West Germany, the United States, and Italy between 1964 and 1976 and argues that France must continue to expand in the field of research and development in order to stimulate growth and to stabilize its balance of payments. 5 tables, diagram, 3 notes.

575. Aliev, R. IAPONIIA I ZAPADNAIA EVROPA: PARTNËRSTVO I SOPERNICHESTVO [Japan and Western Europe: partnership and rivalry]. *Mirovaia Ekonomika i Mezhdunarodnye Otnosheniia [USSR] 1981 9: 69-80.* The emergence in the early 1970's of three centers of imperialist competition—the United States, Western Europe, and Japan—qualitatively changed the relationships among capitalist states.

576. Alvarez, Donato and Cooper, Brian. PRODUCTIVITY TRENDS IN MANUFACTURING AT HOME AND ABROAD. *Monthly Labor Rev. 1984 107(1): 52-58.* Examines manufacturing output and labor productivity for the United States, Canada, Japan, and Western Europe.

577. Amakawa, Akira. SENRYŌ SHOKI NO SEIJI JŌKYŌ [The political situation in the initial stage of the occupation]. *Shakai Kagaku Kenkyū [Japan] 1975 26(2): 1-59.* Describes the political process that led to constitutional reform in Japan during the American military occupation. Shortly after the surrender, the US government decided to govern Japan indirectly. It thus instructed that the GHQ Government Section undertake revision of the Japanese constitution. The Japanese government confronted the indirect gov-

erning process by having the Ministry of Internal Affairs amend the election law. Based on letters and telegraphs exchanged between officals of the GHQ and the United States and secondary sources; 5 diagrams, notes. S. Davis

578. Anderson, Irvine H., Jr. THE 1941 *DE FACTO* EMBARGO ON OIL TO JAPAN: A BUREAUCRATIC REFLEX. *Pacific Hist. Rev. 1975 44(2): 201-231.* Heretofore unused documents reveal that President Franklin D. Roosevelt did not intend to terminate Japan's oil supply when he froze funds in July 1941. He correctly anticipated that Japan would attack the Netherlands East Indies if oil was cut off, but Roosevelt allowed the order to be written as all-inclusive so that policy could be changed day-to-day without issuing further orders. Neither the public nor the British, Dutch, or Japanese were given a clear idea of the American policy. This ambiguity allowed a bureaucracy biased against Japan, specifically the Foreign Funds Control Interdepartmental Committee, to establish a de facto oil embargo which Roosevelt and Cordell Hull supported by mid-September out of fear that a relaxation would be interpreted as a sign of weakness. Based on government documents at the Federal Records Center, Suitland, Maryland and the National Archives, private papers at Hoover Institution and Yale University, and other primary and secondary sources; 107 notes. W. K. Hobson

579. Ano, Masaharu. LOYAL LINGUISTS: NISEI OF WORLD WAR II LEARNED JAPANESE IN MINNESOTA. *Minnesota Hist. 1977 45(7): 273-287.* During and after World War II, the Military Intelligence Service Language School at Camp Savage and later at Fort Snelling, Minnesota, gave 5,500 Nisei men and women an opportunity to train for the war against Japan and the resultant American occupation. The school was commanded by, and owed its existence largely to, Kai E. Rasmussen. Captain (later Colonel) Rasmussen had had prewar experience with the US Army in Japan, and he had genuine empathy for the often-abused Nisei under his command. The students were intensely and extensively trained in Japanese language and culture, enabling them to decipher Japanese plans and military documents in combat situations. The graduates used their knowledge in combat situations in the Aleutians and later in the South Pacific and Okinawa. Off-duty contacts between the Nisei and native Minnesotans were generally free of tension. Based on primary sources. N. Lederer

580. Armstrong, David M. PEARL HARBOR! AN EYEWITNESS ACCOUNT. *Am. Hist. Illus. 1974 9(5): 4-11, 41-48.* The author, an ensign on the *USS Zane,* gives a personal account of the Japanese attack on Pearl Harbor, 1942.

581. Aruga, Tadashi. THE AMBIGUITY OF THE AMERICAN EMPIRE: A JAPANESE VIEW. *Rev. in Am. Hist. 1974 2(4): 592-597.* Review article prompted by *Creation of the American Empire: U.S. Diplomatic History,* by Lloyd C. Gardner, Walter F. LaFeber, and Thomas J. McCormick (Chicago: Rand McNally & Co., 1973); predicts and analyzes the book's reception in Japan, discusses the authors' ambiguous use of terms and concepts such as "empire of trade," outlines the book's emphasis on territorial and

economic expansion, and finds the explication of Cold War diplomacy and US involvement in Vietnam to be inadequate.

582. Auer, J. E. JAPANESE MILITARISM. *U. S. Naval Inst. Pro. 1973 99(9): 46-55.* Up to now Japan has had neither the means nor the motivation to be a militaristic nation. Militarism will assert itself only if Japan feels abandoned, alarmed, or threatened, with no readily apparent alternative, which is unlikely as long as change in the US-Japanese defense arrangement is gradual and results from frank discussions between the two governments. 9 illus.   J. K. Ohl

583. Baerwald, Hans H. LOCKHEED AND JAPANESE POLITICS. *Asian Survey 1976 16(9): 817-829.* Japanese politicians accepted bribes from Lockheed Corporation officials in 1976; the disclosures affected Lockheed and Japanese national politics.

584. Ballendorf, Dirk Anthony. EARL HANCOCK ELLIS: THE MAN AND HIS MISSION. *US Naval Inst. Pro. 1983 109(11): 53-60.* Marine Lieutenant Colonel Earl H. Ellis gained recognition as a brilliant military planner during 1911-21. He was also an alcoholic. In 1921-23 Ellis undertook a secret intelligence reconnaissance of Japanese bases in Micronesia. His nephritis grew worse as he traveled through the islands and he died in Palau on 12 May 1923. The Japanese then confiscated his notes, charts, and code books. Based on archival sources; biblio., 5 notes.   K. J. Bauer

585. Balsam, Jerome M. THE NEGATIVE COMMERCE CLAUSE—A STRICT TEST FOR STATE TAXATION OF FOREIGN COMMERCE: *JAPAN LINE, LTD. V. COUNTY OF LOS ANGELES. New York U. J. of Int. Law and Pol. 1980 13(1): 135-166.* Analyzes a recent Supreme Court ruling which invalidated a special tariff levied by Los Angeles County against foreign container cargo and criticizes the court's role.

586. Barbeau, Arthur E. THE JAPANESE AT BEDFORD. *Western Pennsylvania Hist. Mag. 1981 64(2): 151-172.* Discusses the internment of Japanese diplomats in Bedford, Pennsylvania, at the Bedford Springs Hotel in 1945.

587. Barbeiro, Heródoto S. O DIÁRIO DE VIAGEM DO TENENTE G. H. PREBLE (CONTRIBUCAŌ PARA O ESTUDO DO INÍCIO DAS RELAÇÕES DIPLOMATICAS ENTRE OS ESTADOS UNIDOS E O JAPAŌ) (I) [The diary of Lieutenant G. H. Preble: contribution to the study of the initiation of diplomatic relations between the United States and Japan. Part I]. *Rev. de Hist. [Brazil] 1974 4(99): 97-116.* The voyage of Commodore Matthew C. Perry to Japan marks the initiation of US-Japanese diplomatic relations. This was fundamental to US participation in Asian commercial relations. The diary of US Naval Lieutenant G. W. Preble, one of the junior officers accompanying Perry, is the source for both a narrative of the voyage and an analysis of its importance in the history of both countries. Primary and secondary sources; 5 tables, 40 notes. Article to be continued.
     C. A. Preece

588. Barnouw, Erik. THE HIROSHIMA-NAGASAKI FOOTAGE: A REPORT. *Hist. J. of Film, Radio and Television [Great Britain] 1982 2(1): 91-100.* Hiroshima-Nagasaki, August 1945, made by Erik Barnouw of the Center for Mass Communication of Columbia University in 1970 from a confiscated Japanese film in the US National Archives, has been much used by educational and nuclear disarmament organizations, both in the United States and in Japan. Illus., 25 ref. A. E. Standley

589. Bartlett, Merrill and Love, Robert William, Jr. ANGLO-AMERICAN NAVAL DIPLOMACY AND THE BRITISH PACIFIC FLEET, 1942-1945. *Am. Neptune 1982 42(3): 203-216.* In the spring of 1942, Great Britain pressed the United States to take offensive actions in the Pacific to force Japanese withdrawal from the Indian Ocean. American launched raids helped accomplish this and led Japan to plan an attack on Midway Island. When the United States asked Britain to make diversionary attacks to weaken the Japanese attacks on Midway and the Solomon Islands the British refused. In 1944, after the tide had turned, Britain demanded a role in a major naval operations in the Central Pacific. American naval leaders rightly saw that Britain was motivated by a wish to increase its postwar influence and objected, insisting Britain be limited to the Malaya area, but Franklin D. Roosevelt backed Britain, and it was given a role. Based on records in the Naval Historical Division and National Archives in Washington, in the FDR Library at Hyde Park, and elsewhere; 60 notes. J. C. Bradford

590. Bartlett, Merrill L. COMMODORE JAMES BIDDLE AND THE FIRST NAVAL MISSION TO JAPAN, 1845-1846. *Am. Neptune 1981 41(1): 25-35.* In July 1846 James Biddle (1783-1848) led the first US government-sponsored mission into Tokyo Bay. The author describes the week-long visit and Japan's rebuff of American requests for a treaty. James Glynn (1801-71), commander of a second naval expedition to Japan in 1849, believed that Biddle had variously acted too meekly or adopted a bellicose manner, and succeeded in obtaining the release of 15 shipwrecked American seamen. The perception of Biddle's mission as a failure and of Glynn's as a success influenced Matthew C. Perry's (1794-1858) conduct during his famous mission to "open" Japan. 34 notes. J. C. Bradford

591. Bayley, David H. LEARNING ABOUT CRIME—THE JAPANESE EXPERIENCE. *Public Interest 1976 (44): 55-68.* The per capita incidence of serious crime in the United States is four times the overall rate of crime in Japan. This dramatic contrast between two wealthy, modern nations exists not because of differences in modernity, population congestion, the criminal justice system, or violent traditions. The sources of social order in Japan are the informal controls over individuals exercised by small scale social groups, such as families, fellow workers, and neighbors. American society, with its belief in social mobility and its resulting impersonal environment, contrasts with Japanese society, with its "stable network of named people," which has a great capacity for social control. S. Harrow

592. Bearden, Russell. THE FALSE RUMOR OF TUESDAY: ARKANSAS'S INTERNMENT OF JAPANESE-AMERICANS. *Arkansas Hist. Q.*

1982 41(4): 327-339. Describes the background of the Japanese relocation program at Rowher Camp, Arkansas, and some of the specific incidents which occurred there during World War II. 2 photos, 31 notes. G. R. Schroeder

593. Beatty, Roger Dean and Yamaguchi, Yasuko. ORIGAMI FROM JAPANESE FOLK ART TO AMERICAN POPULAR ART. *J. of Popular Culture 1976 9(4): 808-815.* Origami, the art of ancient Japanese paper folding, has become a part of American popular culture. Originally, origami was used to make toys for Japanese children, but interest declined as manufactured toys became available. Discusses the literature of the art, types of paper used, current publications on the subject, and the aesthetics of origami. 21 notes.
D. L. Grant

594. Bedeski, Robert E. OPTIONS IN RELATIONS WITH JAPAN. *Int. J. [Canada] 1979 34(4): 680-698.* American attempts to normalize relations with China were carried out without consulting Japan, indicating to the Japanese that their special relationship with the United States was over. Japan immediately took steps to improve its relations with China, and succeeded with the Treaty of Peace and Friendship in 1978. Throughout its negotiations, Japan proceeded cautiously, attempting to upset neither the United States nor the USSR. Consultation with the United States and common interests allowed the Japanese to maintain friendly relations with the United States, but relations with the USSR have deteriorated. M. J. Wentworth/S

595. Behnam, M. Reza. DEVELOPMENT AND STRUCTURE OF THE GENERALIZED SYSTEM OF PREFERENCES. *J. of World Trade Law [Switzerland] 1975 9(4): 442-458.* Treats the development, organization, problems and prospects of the Generalized System of Preferences. A comparison between the implementation of the EEC and Japanese preference schemes is made and attention is drawn to the disparities extant in individual schemes offered by developed countries that have hindered the efficacy of preference-granting.
J

596. Bell, Charles. SHOOTOUT AT SAVO. *Am. Hist. Illus. 1975 9(9): 28-38.* A report on the World War II naval battle at Savo Island, off the coast of Guadalcanal. The Allied fleet protecting the invasion beachhead was large and well-armed. The small Japanese fleet took advantage of Allied blunders to enter the bay without alerting the guard ships. The battle was a one-sided Japanese victory. The defeat caused Allied commanders to remain alert thereafter, and never again did they underestimate the enemy. 2 maps, 14 photos. V. L. Human

597. Bell, Roger. AUSTRALIAN-AMERICAN DISAGREEMENT OVER THE PEACE SETTLEMENT WITH JAPAN, 1944-46. *Australian Outlook [Australia] 1976 30(2): 238-262.* The disagreement was a continuation of friction over Allied strategic priorities precipitated by rapid Japanese advances in 1942. Australia opposed the Anglo-American policy of defeating Germany first, and after 1943 Australian criticism of America became more pronounced. The reluctance of the USSR to sustain the temporary wartime alliance after 1945 and growing American suspicions of Soviet intentions in

occupied Germany and Eastern Europe increased the US determination to dominate the Far Eastern counteroffensive and monopolize control of defeated Japan. Australia's resistance to American policy was largely unsuccessful although it did obtain some powers of advisory consultation and led the British Commonwealth Occupation Force and the Allied Control Council in Japan. Primary and secondary sources; 88 notes. R. G. Neville

598. Benz, Wolfgang. AMERIKANISCHE BESATZUNGSPOLITIK IN JAPAN 1945-1947 [American occupation policies in Japan, 1945-47]. *Vierteljahrshefte für Zeitgeschichte [West Germany] 1978 26(2): 265-346.* An abridged reprint (of the English original) and summary analysis of three reports issued by the Public Information Office of General Headquarters, Supreme Commander for the Allied Powers in Japan, in 1947 under the general title of "Two Years of Occupation." The first report deals with reform of political institutions (constitution, government, parties, administration, elections), the second with social areas such as education, religion, health, the arts, and media, and the third with economic structures including communications transportation, finance, trade and industry, trusts, labor, and research. Based on reports found in the OMGUS (Military Government in Germany) Papers in the National Archives and on secondary sources; 49 notes.
D. Prowe

599. Ben-Zvi, Abraham. AMERICAN PRECONCEPTIONS AND POLICIES TOWARD JAPAN, 1940-1941: A CASE STUDY IN MISPERCEPTION. *Int. Studies Q. 1975 19(2): 228-248.* An attempt to develop a new typology of American policymakers involved in US-Japanese relations during 1940 and 1941. The typology consists of three major categories: 1) the globalist-realists, Henry Stimson, Henry Morgenthau, and Stanley Hornbeck, 2) the globalist-idealists like Cordell Hull, and 3) the nationalist-pragmatists, Franklin D. Roosevelt and Joseph Grew. 5 notes. G. J. Boughton

600. Ben-Zvi, Abraham. PERCEPTION, ACTION AND REACTION: A COMPARATIVE ANALYSIS OF DECISION-MAKING PROCESSES IN BILATERAL CONFLICTS. *J. of Pol. Sci. 1980 7(2): 95-111.* Decisionmakers in foreign policy act in accordance with their perceptions of reality, not in response to reality itself. Breaking away too sharply from misperceptions can prove as harmful as clinging to the original notions. Based on studies of the Arab-Israeli conflict, 1967-73, and the United States and Japan, 1941-45. 58 notes. T. P. Richardson

601. Bernos, Roger. LES RAPPORTS ÉTATS-UNIS EUROPE: UN CONFLIT POUR LA CROISSANCE [United States-Europe relations: a conflict over growth]. *Rev. Écon. [France] 1973 24(5): 867-878.* The relations between the major industrialized countries can be analyzed as the rivalry between a dominant power, the United States, and two secondary powers, Japan and Europe, which are attempting to escape US influence. Economic growth is a sine qua non for the power of these entities. The United States would like to preserve its position by moderating the growth rate of the two rivals. Recovering now from a severe recession, it has one weapon with which to cow Europe and Japan: the threat of a partial withdrawal of US military

protection, for nations such as Japan and West Germany have based their prosperity in part on a cheap American military umbrella.

J. C. Billigmeier

602. Bernstein, Barton J. THE DROPPING OF THE A-BOMB: HOW DECISIONS ARE MADE WHEN A NATION IS AT WAR. *Center Mag. 1983 16(2): 7-15.* In 1945, President Harry S. Truman and his advisors did not question the necessity of dropping atomic bombs over Hiroshima and Nagasaki, Japan, to destroy industrial plants, civilians, and the Japanese morale; to obtain the unconditional surrender of Japan without further loss of American troops, and to intimidate the Soviets.

603. Bernstein, Barton J. HIROSHIMA RECONSIDERED—THIRTY YEARS LATER. *Foreign Service J. 1975 52(8): 8-13, 32-33.* Reviews the decision to use atomic warfare against Japan in 1945. S

604. Bernstein, Barton J. THE PERILS AND POLITICS OF SURRENDER: ENDING THE WAR WITH JAPAN AND AVOIDING THE THIRD ATOMIC BOMB. *Pacific Hist. Rev. 1977 46(1): 1-27.* The ambiguous American response to Japan's 10 August 1945 surrender offer strengthened the militarists in Japan and nearly prolonged the war. President Truman and Secretary of State James F. Byrnes were reluctant to retain the Emperor. Byrnes and Truman were concerned about domestic political effects and feared a popular backlash if the surrender terms were not harsh enough. They were therefore willing to consider using a third atomic bomb or mounting a costly invasion of Japan. Secretary of War Henry L. Stimson and Admiral William Leahy urged acceptance of Japan's surrender terms in order to end the war quickly, keep Russia out of the peace settlement, and avoid world-wide horror at the use of a third atomic bomb. Based on documents in numerous manuscript collections; 92 notes.

W. K. Hobson

605. Bernstein, Barton J. SHATTERER OF WORLDS: HIROSHIMA AND NAGASAKI. *Bull. of the Atomic Scientists 1975 31(10): 12-22.* US policymakers in the Roosevelt and Truman administrations had little doubt about the desirability of using atomic weapons both for ending the war in the Pacific and for intimidating the USSR.

606. Best, Gary Dean. JACOB SCHIFF'S EARLY INTEREST IN JAPAN. *Am. Jewish Hist. 1980 69(3): 355-359.* Jacob Schiff's (1847-1920) relationship with Japan in 1904-05 is well known. He had, however, tried to involve himself in Japanese economic development as early as 1872. In that year, the Meiji government, advised by an American, George B. Williams, sought to float a bond issue of 12 million yen. Williams negotiated with H. L. Bischoffsheim, a prominent English banker. Schiff, working on behalf of his own company and his clients, James H. Wilson and Edward F. Winslow, tried to be included in this deal in the hope of obtaining advantages in the Japanese empire. In the end, however, to Schiff's annoyance, the Oriental Bank Corporation won the bond issue. Based largely on the James H. Wilson Papers, Library of Congress; 12 notes.

J. D. Sarna

607. Birdsall, Steve. TARGET: RABAUL! *Air Force Mag. 1975 58(9): 108-113.* General George Kenney's Fifth Air Force in the South Pacific destroyed Japan's air and naval power on New Britain Island in October 1943.

608. Blee, Ben W. WHODUNNIT? *US Naval Inst. Pro. 1982 108(7): 42-47.* Argues that the aircraft carrier *Wasp*, battleship *North Carolina*, and destroyer *O'Brien* were all struck by a single spread of six torpedoes fired by the Japanese submarine *I-19* on the afternoon of 15 September 1942 southeast of Guadalcanal. Based on action reports of American vessels involved.
K. J. Bauer

609. Blicksilver, Edith. THE JAPANESE-AMERICAN WOMAN, THE SECOND WORLD WAR, AND THE RELOCATION CAMP EXPERIENCE. *Women's Studies Int. Forum 1982 5(3-4): 351-353.* Discusses Janice Mirikitani's poem "Lullaby," in which this Japanese-American woman expressed the emotions of her experience in an American internment camp during World War II; the text of the poem is provided.

610. Boller, Paul F., Jr. HIROSHIMA AND THE AMERICAN LEFT: AUGUST 1945. *Int. Social Sci. Rev. 1982 57(1): 13-28.* Many Leftists insist today that Japan was thoroughly beaten in August 1945 and that the United States dropped atomic bombs mainly to intimidate the Soviet Union. Careful examination of American Leftist opinion in 1945, however, reveals that the strongest defenders of the atomic bombing of Hiroshima and Nagasaki were the groups friendliest to Stalinist Russia and that the bitterest critics were anti-Stalinist liberals and radicals. The former also supported and the latter condemned a harsh unconditional-surrender policy toward Japan. J

611. Borisova, K. KAPITALISTICHESKAIA AVTOPROMYSHLENNOST': IZ KRIZISA V KRIZIS [Capitalist auto industry; from crisis to crisis]. *Mirovaia Ekonomika i Mezhdunarodnye Otnosheniia [USSR] 1981 (3): 120-128.* Explores some aspects of the automobile industry in the United States and Western Europe and the role of Japan.

612. Boyd, Carl. ATTACKING THE *INDIANAPOLIS:* A REEXAMINATION. *Warship Int. 1976 13(1): 15-25.* Examines the sinking of the *USS Indianapolis* by the Japanese submarine *I-58*; includes histories of both vessels and analyses of why the 1945 attack took place, including the possibility of the use of kaitens, the submarine equivalent of kamikaze planes.

613. Britsch, R. Lanier. THE CLOSING OF THE EARLY JAPAN MISSION. *Brigham Young U. Studies 1975 15(2): 171-190.* On 7 August 1924, after 23 years of effort and sacrifice by missionaries and church members, the Mormon Church ended its first mission in Japan. The missionary effort of the Mormons, begun in 1901, was not notably successful. Analyzes the conditions in Japan that caused the leaders of the Church to abandon missionary activity there. 2 tables, 49 notes.
M. S. Legan

614. Bronfenbrenner, Martin. JAPANESE-AMERICAN ECONOMIC WAR? SOME FURTHER REFLECTIONS. *Q. R. of Econ. and Business*

1973 13(3): 33-42. "While reaffirming (almost) all the contents of the author's 1970 lecture and article on this subject, he now goes a little further. It appears that underlying the five issues given previously, there are two others meriting exploration. The first such issue is a theoretical one, relating to the standard economic problem of the gains from international trade. The second issue is less economic than psychological; it relates to 'ways of doing business' in the two countries, particularly ways of conducting negotiations." J

615. Brooke, George M., Jr. "A HIGH OLD CRUISE": JOHN MERCER BROOKE AND THE AMERICAN VOYAGE OF THE *KANRIN MARU*. *Virginia Cavalcade 1980 29(4): 174-183.* Discusses American naval officer John Mercer Brooke (1826-1906), focusing on his trip as a naval advisor on the Japanese steamer *Kanrin Maru,* which sailed from Japan to the United States in February 1860 to exchange ratifications of the 1858 Harris Treaty opening new trade ports in Japan, and his voyage as an escort to the Japanese mission that sailed to the United States in an American man-of-war.

616. Brune, Lester H. CONSIDERATIONS OF FORCE IN CORDELL HULL'S DIPLOMACY, JULY 26 TO NOVEMBER 26, 1941. *Diplomatic Hist. 1978 2(4): 389-405.* The Japanese occupation of much of Indochina in mid-1941 resulted in Secretary of State Cordell Hull's disillusionment with the prospects for successful negotiations, but resulted also in a decision—to defend the Philippines when hostilities commenced—which laid upon him the task of continuing negotiations solely for the military purpose of buying time. Hull, who never seemed to appreciate the practical connections between diplomatic and military considerations, was not the man for this job, and he bungled it rather badly. On 26 November Hull and Roosevelt, reversing a war council decision of the previous day, scrapped plans to offer the Japanese a few token concessions, and thus abandoned the effort to extend negotiations until American preparations were complete in February or March 1942. Published primary and secondary sources; 48 notes. L. W. Van Wyk

617. Buckley, Roger. THE BRITISH MODEL: INSTITUTIONAL REFORM AND OCCUPIED JAPAN. *Modern Asian Studies [Great Britain] 1982 16(2): 233-250.* The relevance of the British political and economic experience to postsurrender Japan has been overlooked by students of the occupation period, as reflected in the nationalistic interpretation of American historiography. The author seeks to redress the balance of the value of Allied diplomacy and examines the extent to which British and American officials considered the appropriateness of the British example when planning reform of Japan's monarchy, parliamentary system, economy, social services, and industrial relations. Based mainly on Public Record Office documents; 65 notes.
P. J. Durell

618. Bur, Lawrence J. THE SUCCESS OF JAPANESE CARS IN AMERICA. *Towson State J. of Int. Affairs 1982 16(2): 57-61.* Japan produces small, fuel-efficient cars that have been successful in the United States; unlike the US economy, "the Japanese economy survives for the sole purpose of long-term profits"; Japanese workers are more devoted and the problems between

labor and management do not exist as they do in America, and companies are efficiently managed.

619. Byrd, Martha H. BATTLE OF THE PHILIPPINE SEA. *Am. Hist. Illus. 1977 12(4): 20-35.* Chronicles the Battle of the Philippine Sea, a naval and air battle of World War II between US forces and Japan, June 1944.

620. Byrd, Martha H. "CAPTURED BY THE AMERICANS." *Am. Hist. Illus. 1977 11(10): 24-35.* Discusses life for German, Japanese, and Italian prisoners of war in POW camps across the US, 1942-45.

621. Byrd, Martha H. SIX MINUTES TO VICTORY: THE BATTLE OF MIDWAY. *Am. Hist. Illus. 1975 10(2): 33-43.* Discusses the battle between US and Japanese naval forces near the Pacific island of Midway in 1942.

622. Calder, Kent E. OPENING JAPAN. *Foreign Policy 1982 (47): 82-97.* Discusses the Japanese economy, imports needed, and tariffs and quotas established for international trade items. Despite a general perception that substantial barriers block foreign access to the Japanese market, there are significant elements in Japan's business, political, and government structure that are working for a freer trade economy. Analyzes US exports to Japan and their impact on the Japanese economy. M. K. Jones

623. Cameron, Allan W. THE STRATEGIC SIGNIFICANCE OF THE PACIFIC ISLANDS: A NEW DEBATE BEGINS. *Orbis 1975 19(3): 1012-1036.* Discusses naval strategy and economic policy regarding the significance of Micronesia for the United States and Japan, 1945-75.

624. Capdevielle, Patricia; Alvarez, Donato; and Cooper, Brian. INTERNATIONAL TRENDS IN PRODUCTIVITY AND LABOR COSTS. *Monthly Labor Rev. 1982 105(12): 3-14.* Indexes of relative trends in manufacturing productivity as related to hourly compensation in 1981 and in unit labor costs in the 1974-75 and 1980-81 recessions increased in most European countries, Canada, Japan, and the United States.

625. Carano, Paul. LIBERATION DAY, PRELUDE TO FREEDOM. *Guam Recorder 1973 3(3): 3-9.* Discusses World War II on Guam, February-August 1944, from Japanese control to liberation by US forces which turned Guam into an outpost of democracy in three months.

626. Carney, Robert B. "UNDER THE COLD GAZE OF THE VICTORIOUS." *US Naval Inst. Pro. 1983 109(12): 41-50.* Reproduces a 2 September 1945 account by Robert B. Carney, then chief of staff to Admiral William F. Halsey, of the initial American landings in Japan and the surrender ceremony on board the USS *Missouri*. K. J. Bauer

627. Caruso, Samuel T. AFTER PEARL HARBOR: ARIZONA'S RESPONSE TO THE GILA RIVER RELOCATION CENTER. *J. of Arizona Hist. 1973 14(4): 335-346.* Sixteen thousand Japanese Americans were imprisoned 1942-45 at Sacaton, a barbed-wire city better known as the Gila River

Relocation Center, in south central Arizona. Whites reacted to them as they had to their Apache predecessors—open hostility drowning out sympathetic understanding and concern. Whatever the racial slurs, the restrictive legislation, and other degradations they suffered, the Japanese produced millions of tons of vegetables and performed much labor on state roads. 2 illus., 46 notes.
D. L. Smith

628. Cary, Otis. THE SPARING OF KYOTO—MR. STIMSON'S "PET CITY." *Japan Q. [Japan] 1975 22(4): 337-347.* There have been a number of stories told about why the city of Kyoto was not heavily bombed by the US air forces during World War II or why the city was spared from nuclear attack even though its name had appeared high on the list of target cities prepared by various US air commanders. One story credits Florence Denton, a long-time teacher at Dōshisha Women's College, as the person responsible for having Kyoto removed from the target lists. Another credits Langdon Warner, from Harvard's Fogg Museum. A third gives credit to Professor Edwin O. Reischauer, also of Harvard University. It was really Henry L. Stimson, US Secretary of War in 1945, who caused Kyoto to be removed from the US target lists, and he did so with President Truman's knowledge and approval. 20 notes.
A. N. Garland

629. Chandler, Alfred. INSTITUTIONAL INTEGRATION: AN APPROACH TO COMPARATIVE STUDIES OF THE HISTORY OF LARGE-SCALE BUSINESS ENTERPRISE. *Rev. Econ. [France] 1976 27(2): 177-199.* The concept of institutional aggregation and integration in business history provides a more relevant approach to the study of the development of large-scale modern enterprise than does that of institutional specialization and disintegration. A focus on the division of labour is largely misleading in respect to the history of business enterprise. Many analysts fail to realize that large-scale enterprises never went through a stage of pure competition and that the first oligopolists were also the nation's first multinationals. Historical evidence comes from the main industrial and transportation sectors of the American economy. The author asserts the hypothesis that, despite important differences, the same analysis would fit the Western European cases or even the Japanese one.
J

630. Chevallier, François-Xavier. CRISE DE L'OFFRE AU JAPON [Japan's supply crisis]. *Rev. d'Econ. Pol. [France] 1982 92(5-6): 918-930.* Focuses on Japan's economic acceleration since 1975 and threats to the Japanese thrust by changes in US economic policies since 1980.

631. Christopher, Robert C. THE U.S. AND JAPAN: A TIME FOR HEALING. *Foreign Affairs 1978 56(4): 857-866.* The strains in US-Japanese relations are more perceptible now than they have been for two decades. By failing to brief Japan about important foreign policy departures, by holding Japan primarily responsible for an embarrassing trade deficit, and by denying Japan the latitude to develop breeder reactors, the United States has demonstrated somewhat crude and insensitive behavior.
M. R. Yerburgh

632. Ciccarelli, Orazio. PERU'S ANTI-JAPANESE CAMPAIGN IN THE 1930S: ECONOMIC DEPENDENCY AND ABORTIVE NATIONALISM. *Can. Rev. of Studies in Nationalism [Canada] 1982 9(1): 113-133.* The Peruvian government encouraged the settlement of Japanese merchants and agriculturists in the late 1800's. By the 1930's, they numbered over 16,000 and became victims of a virulent anti-Japanese campaign because of their role in the local economy. Japanese shops were looted and burned in the early 1930's, and in 1934 a Japanese-Peruvian trade agreement was revoked. In 1936 a law limited the number of Japanese residents, restricted their business activities, and set quotas on the numbers of foreigners in each profession. In 1942-43, 1,771 Japanese Peruvians were shipped to internment camps in the United States. Based on US Department of State records; 79 notes. R. Aldrich

633. Close, Winton R. B-29S IN THE CBI—A PILOT'S ACCOUNT. *Aerospace Hist. 1983 30(1): 6-14.* Describes Winton R. Close's experiences flying a US Army Air Force B-29 in the China-Burma-India Theater in 1944. Using bases near Calcutta as supply terminals and forward bases in China as operation centers, the B-29s struck strategic targets in Japan, returned to China, went to India for repair, and then repeated the cycle. Logistical deficiencies, mechanical problems, weather, uncertainty over tactics, and crude living conditions created serious difficulties for the crews; few were sorry to leave the CBI theater when they were transferred to the Marianas in 1945. 9 illus. J. K. Ohl

634. Cohen, Yehudi A. SHRINKING HOUSEHOLDS. *Society 1981 18(2): 48-52.* Discusses the role of technological innovations in agriculture in decreasing the average size of the American family (1689-1975); offers comparisons with Fiji, Japan, and the Israeli kibbutzim; and suggests that this decrease in family size may contribute to a feeling of loneliness prevalent in American society.

635. Cole, Robert E. FUNCTIONAL ALTERNATIVES AND ECONOMIC DEVELOPMENT: AN EMPIRICAL EXAMPLE OF PERMANENT EMPLOYMENT IN JAPAN. *Am. Sociol. Rev. 1973 38(4): 424-438.* "The presentation concerns the utility of conceptualizing the structural changes associated with modern economic development as functional alternatives. The concept is compared to other approaches represented as historicism, convergence, and structural modeling with environmental effects. The advantages of the functional alternative conceptualization are demonstrated through comparison of selected employment characteristics in Japan and the United States." J

636. Corsi, Matteo. TRILATERALISMO, GIAPPONE ED EUROPA [Trilateralism, Japan, and Europe]. *Affari Esteri [Italy] 1977 9(36): 608-620.* The Trilateral Commission, begun in 1973 by David Rockefeller, has united powerful representatives of Japan, the United States, and Western Europe around their common interests and offers one of the first opportunities for a political dialogue between Japan and the European Economic Community.

637. Crepeau, Richard C. PEARL HARBOR: A FAILURE OF BASEBALL? *J. of Popular Culture 1982 15(4): 67-74.* Reviews the extravagant claims made for baseball as a promoter of democracy and the "American way" during the 1920's and 30's, claims which were given temporary credence by the dramatic rise in the popularity of the sport in Japan after World War I, and the numerous tours undertaken by Japanese and American teams until 1940. Based on contemporary newspaper and sports magazine materials; 40 notes.
D. G. Nielson

638. Culley, John J. WORLD WAR II AND A WESTERN TOWN: THE INTERNMENT OF THE JAPANESE RAILROAD WORKERS OF CLOVIS, NEW MEXICO. *Western Hist. Q. 1982 13(1): 43-61.* Prior to the "relocation" of people of Japanese ancestry from the Pacific Coast area under the 1942 War Relocation Authority, the Justice Department carried out an earlier internment and detention camp program for aliens only. The 10 Japanese who worked for the railroad in Clovis, New Mexico, and their family members were interned. Their experiences were not satisfactory. None returned to Clovis after the war. Satisfactory prewar working conditions and Clovis acceptance of the Japanese were reversed by the war. Map, 50 notes.
D. L. Smith

639. Daniels, Gordon. BEFORE HIROSHIMA: THE BOMBING OF JAPAN, 1944-5. *Hist. Today [Great Britain] 1982 32(Jan): 14-18.* Describes the bombing of Nagoya, Osaka, Kobe, Okinawa, and Iwojima by American bombers, which resulted in the death of 200,000 and the razing of cities despite Japan's civil defense preparations, which began in 1937 with the Air Defense Law and with preparation training by the Greater Japan Air Defense Association, beginning in 1939.

640. Daniels, Roger. THE BUREAU OF THE CENSUS AND THE RELOCATION OF JAPANESE AMERICANS: A NOTE AND DOCUMENT. *Amerasia J. 1982 9(1): 101-106.* Provides a previously prepared, but unpublished, 1975 letter by Frederick G. Bohme that describes the US Census Bureau activities in regard to the relocation of Japanese Americans following the attack on Pearl Harbor. The Census Bureau provided more personnel and data than earlier known. 13 notes.
E. S. Johnson

641. Daniels, Roger. THE DECISIONS TO RELOCATE THE NORTH AMERICAN JAPANESE: ANOTHER LOOK. *Pacific Hist. Rev. 1982 51(1): 71-77.* In 1942 Canada and the United States relocated people of Japanese ancestry who lived in the coastal strip between the mountains and the Pacific Ocean. Evacuation was carried out by the Army in the United States and by the Mounted Police in Canada. Similarity of treatment of Japanese by Canada and the United States was the consequence of Canadian-American Joint Board of Defense discussions in 1941. It appears that preliminary discussion of the relocation of Japanese occurred between the US and Canadian governments in 1941. Ethnicity was the criterion involved in the decision to relocate the Japanese. Based on W. L. Mackenzie Papers, Jay Pierrepont Moffat Journals, and other primary sources; 12 notes.
R. N. Lokken

642. Daniels, Roger. JAPANESE RELOCATION AND REDRESS IN NORTH AMERICA: A COMPARATIVE VIEW. *Pacific Hist. 1982 26(1): 2-13.* Compares the treatment of Japanese by the governments of Canada and the United States before World War II, through the evacuation and relocation, and outlines developments in attitudes toward Japanese citizens since the war. 6 illus., table, 9 notes. H. M. Evans

643. Danovitch, Sylvia E. THE PAST RECAPTURED? THE PHOTOGRAPHIC RECORD OF THE INTERNMENT OF JAPANESE AMERICANS. *Prologue 1980 12(2): 91-103.* Discusses the value of photographs as historical documents while focusing on an analysis of the 12,500 photographs in the National Archives that the War Relocation Authority made in connection with the forced evacuation and internment of Japanese Americans after the bombing of Pearl Harbor. This study concentrates on preevacuation photographs, evacuation photographs, Manzanar and Tule Lake Camps photographs, and relocation or resettlement photographs. The purpose of the photographing of the War Relocation Authority Program set forth in Administrative Instruction no. 74 dated 2 January 1943 was to document the program as fully as possible. Based on National Archives photographs of the War Relocation Authority; 41 notes. M. A. Kascus

644. Davidson, Sue. AKI KATO KUROSE: PORTRAIT OF AN ACTIVIST. *Frontiers 1983 7(1): 91-97.* Discusses Aki Kato Kurose's experiences as a nisei growing up in Seattle, Washington, and later living in a relocation camp during World War II.

645. Davis, Frank. OPERATION OLYMPIC: THE INVASION OF JAPAN: NOVEMBER 1, 1945. *Strategy & Tactics 1974 (45): 4-20.*

646. Dayer, Roberta Allbert. THE BRITISH WAR DEBTS TO THE UNITED STATES AND THE ANGLO-JAPANESE ALLIANCE, 1920-1923. *Pacific Hist. Rev. 1976 45(4): 569-596.* A study of the influence of the British war debts on the United States in its decision to terminate the Anglo-Japanese alliance. The David Lloyd George government believed that cooperation with the United States on Far Eastern questions might, by fostering American goodwill, lead either to outright cancellation or, at least, to a scaling down of the debts. An examination of the communications between the two powers would suggest that these hopes were not without US encouragement. Ultimately Whitehall concurrently surrendered the alliance and accepted a harsh debt settlement, all through the influence of American bankers, simply because Britain did not hold the "financial cards." 113 notes.
R. V. Ritter

647. De Cecco, Marcello. THE PRESSURE OF ECONOMIC DIFFICULTIES. *Internat. Affairs [Great Britain] 1974 50(3): 394-403.* Considers the present position and the future outlook for the economies of the European Economic Community as well as for the world economy, with particular emphasis on the three "core areas"—the United States, Germany, and Japan. Analyzes trading patterns, especially the impact of the recent oil crisis. Based

partly on OECD statistics. Based on a paper read at Chatham House.

P. J. Beck

648. de la Sierra Fernández, Luis. PEARL HARBOR [Pearl Harbor]. *Rev. General de Marina [Spain] 1977 192(6): 645-651; 193 (8-9): 169-184; 193(12): 629-635; 1978 194(2): 137-150; 194(4): 403-424.* Part I. For thousands of years before the Spanish discovery of the Pacific, Micronesian, Melanesian, and especially Polynesian sailors had conquered that vast ocean. These sailors had learned accurate celestial navigation and were used to sailing thousands of miles. Their heroic exploits form a fitting perspective on the equally heroic naval struggle between the United States and Japan which began with the attack on Pearl Harbor in 1941. Part II. The rise of Japan as a Pacific Asian power, the clash of US and Japanese interests in China and the Pacific, and racial antagonism led to each considering the other as a potential enemy by 1909. The acquisition of mandated islands after World War I greatly expanded Japan's power into the Pacific, and thus readied the area for a future conflict. Japan built a modern fleet up to treaty limits. A US building program led Japan to withdraw from naval limitation in 1936 and begin construction of the *Yamato* super-battleships. The United States then entered a naval race with Japan. Part III. Discusses Roosevelt's concentration of the US fleet at Pearl Harbor in 1940, impositions of serious trade restrictions on Japan, and increased pressure on Japan to abandon imperial ambitions in Asia. The United States deliberately intensified tensions and rejected Japanese offers of compromise, yet never foresaw a Japanese attack on Pearl Harbor. Part IV. Admiral Isoroku Yamamoto's war Plan Z entailed use of carrier aircraft to destroy the US Pacific Fleet, after which the United States would sue for a compromise peace. The naval staff accepted the plan in October 1941. Yamamoto always hoped that a diplomatic breakthrough might allow a cancellation, but it never came. The overconfident US Admiral Husband E. Kimmel took inadequate precautions, but unfortunately for Japan, the US aircraft carriers were at sea. The Japanese naval staff decided that the moored battleships were sufficient targets. Part V. Despite US detection of Japanese aircraft and submarines, the surprise on 7 December 1941 was complete. The US vessels were either sunk or severely damaged, and only the US carriers remained at large. Fearing counter attack, Admiral Nagumo turned for home. Japan's tactical and strategic victory allowed Japanese consolidation of its position in China and the Pacific. The Japanese selection of the US battleships as the primary targets and the decision to withdraw were correct. Washington was responsible for the unpreparedness at Pearl Harbor. 8 notes.

W. C. Frank

649. Delpech, Jean Laurens. LA COMPÉTITION ENTRE L'INDUSTRIE EUROPÉENNE ET LE RESTE DU MONDE [Competition between European industry and the rest of the world]. *Défense Natl. [France] 1973 29(8-9): 101-116.* Compares industrial competition to a world war, complete with strategies directed toward dominating the industrial automobile market, as well as other world markets, using the United States, Japan, and Europe as examples, 1969-73.

650. Denicoff, Todd. AUTOMATION IN THE UNITED STATES AND JAPAN. *Towson State J. of Int. Affairs 1982 16(2): 63-67.* Compares high-technology automation in American and Japanese factories, finding that Japan has the edge because automation has been encouraged there since the 1960's while US automation in factories is a relatively new concept that has emerged only as a response to Japanese competition.

651. Denoon, David B. H. JAPAN AND THE U.S.—THE SECURITY AGENDA. *Current Hist. 1983 82(487): 353-356, 393-394.* Differences with the United States over trade relations, changing relations with China, and the Soviet threat have induced Japan to undertake a more self-reliant defense posture.

652. Dickson, W. David. NAVAL TACTICS: AN INTRODUCTION. *Warship Int. 1976 13(3): 168-176.* Discusses naval tactics in terms of maneuvering, gunnery formation, torpedo use, and naval communications pertaining to the US, British, and Japanese navies, during World War II, 1943-45.

653. Dingman, Roger V. THEORIES OF, AND APPROACHES TO, ALLIANCE POLITICS. Lauren, Paul Gordon, ed. *Diplomacy: New Approaches in History, Theory, and Policy* (New York: Free Pr., 1979): 245-266. Reflects on "the limitations of much of the existing literature on the theory of alliance; the historian's need for a working conceptual understanding of alliances; and the relative utility of various methods, new and old, for analyzing alliances." Examines particularly the unequal 1951 treaty of alliance negotiated by John Foster Dulles and Yoshida Shigeru between the United States and Japan which allowed US troops stationed in Japan to put down internal disturbances at Japan's request. Based on *Foreign Relations of the United States,* other primary and secondary sources; 52 notes. S

654. Dreisch, Andrew. THE IMPACT OF JAPAN'S ECONOMIC GROWTH ON THE SECURITY OF JAPAN. *Towson State J. of Int. Affairs 1982 16(2): 81-85.* Discusses the relatively small allocation to defense US military aid to Japan under their Mutual Security Treaty, and the future responsibility of Japan's Self-Defense Forces.

655. DuBoff, Richard. TRADE WAR EXERCISES. *Can. Dimension [Canada] 1973 9(6): 37-40.* Examines the implications of President Richard M. Nixon's devaluation of the dollar for economic relations and trade with Japan and the European Common Market, 1971-73.

656. Durden, Robert F. TAR HEEL TOBACCONIST IN TOKYO, 1899-1904. *North Carolina Hist. Rev. 1976 53(4): 347-363.* Edward James Parrish (1846-1920), of Durham, North Carolina, served as representative of James B. Duke's American Tobacco Company interests in Japan between 1899 and 1904. Appointed vice-president of the Murai Brothers Company, Ltd., Parrish worked closely with this Duke business affiliate to improve production, financing, and marketing techniques. When the Japanese Diet initiated government ownership of all tobacco manufacturing, Parrish was instrumental in

obtaining a reasonably good settlement for the company. Based on Parrish's personal papers; 8 illus., 32 notes.   T. L. Savitt

657. Ebel, Wilfred L. JAPAN-US RELATIONS. *Military Rev. 1977 57(5): 35-41.* The Asian balance of power rests on the foreign policy of Japan. The rapid increase of Japan's GNP has made her an economic superpower and the third largest industrial nation. She must insure a steady supply of oil to maintain her economy and might, therefore, have to deal with rivals of the United States. Japan, however, is pledged to peace and her foreign policy can be expected to do nothing to jeopardize her security or international peace if given US support in the Pacific. 3 illus., 4 notes.   D. J. Kommer

658. Eggleston, Noel C. ROLE PLAYING: THE ATOMIC BOMB AND THE END OF WORLD WAR II. *Teaching Hist. A J. of Methods 1978 3(2): 52-58.* Describes in detail the development of a historical role-playing exercise for classroom use revolving around the question, "Should the United States drop an atomic bomb on Japan?" Discusses setting in 1945, character participants, discussion questions, and the historical works used as well as the specific goals, results, and benefits of this exercise. Examines the value of role playing technique for history instructors. 8 notes.

659. Eismeier, Dana L. U.S. OIL POLICY, JAPAN, AND THE COMING OF WAR IN THE PACIFIC, 1940-1941. *Michigan Acad. 1982 14(4): 359-367.* The policy adopted by Great Britain and by President Franklin D. Roosevelt of continued oil shipments to Japan, combined with limited restrictions and threats, delayed possible war in 1940 until late 1941 when the United States was better prepared both materially and psychologically; oil diplomacy allowed Roosevelt to control US entry into the war until the United States could make a more viable military commitment to the Allied cause.

660. Emmerson, John K. JAPANESE AND AMERICANS IN PERU, 1942-1943. *Foreign Service J. 1977 54(5): 40-47, 56.* Reminisces about duties in the US embassy in Peru, 1942-43, and of the internment (in the USA) of Japanese Peruvians.

661. Emmerson, John K. TOKYO 1941. *Foreign Service J. 1976 53(4): 10-14, 25.* Describes life in the US embassy in Tokyo and US-Japanese diplomacy during 1941. Article to be continued.

662. Emmerson, John K. TOKYO 1941. *Foreign Service J. 1976 53(5): 5-9, 26.* Continued from a previous article (see abstract in this chapter). Part II. Discusses differing evaluations in the US State Department in Washington, D.C., and in the US embassy in Tokyo over diplomatic negotiations with Japan during 1941.

663. Estes, Donald H. ASAMA GUNKAN: THE REAPPRAISAL OF A WAR SCARE. *J. of San Diego Hist. 1978 24(3): 267-299.* A rebuttal of Barbara Tuchman's view (in *The Zimmerman Telegram,* 1958, 1965) that the *Asama,* a Japanese armored cruiser grounded in Baja, California in 1915, was on a secret mission for the Japanese government.

664. Etō, Juiz. JAPAN'S SHIFTING IMAGE: REFLECTIONS FROM THE LOCAL AMERICAN PRESS, 1969-1971. *Japan Interpreter [Japan] 1973 8(1): 63-75.* Argues that the already wide gulf of understanding between Japan and the United States continues to widen. In Japan the reversion of Okinawa has produced an emotional and nationalistic issue, involving self confidence and wounded pride. In the United States, as seen in local press articles, there is a growing anger and an undercurrent of antipathy toward Japan, as reflected in the Nixon shocks, the textile talks, and comments on the Japanese economy. F. W. Iklé

665. Feld, Werner J. TRADE WITH WEST EUROPE AND JAPAN. *Current Hist. 1979 76(447): 201-205, 223-226.* Discusses American interest in trade with Western Europe and Japan in the 1970's.

666. Ferretti, Valdo. RECENTI STUDI STORICI SUL GIAPPONE CONTEMPORÁNEO [Recent historical studies on contemporary Japan]. *Storia e Politica [Italy] 1977 16(3): 552-564.* A report of the international meeting on American-Japanese relations held in July 1969 in Japan. The proceedings of the meeting are now published by S. Okamoto and D. Borg, *Pearl Harbour as History: Japanese-American Relations 1931-1941,* (New York, 1973). 14 notes. A. Canavero

667. Finn, Dallas. JAPAN AT THE CENTENNIAL, 1876. *Foreign Service J. 1977 54(7): 12-15, 28-29.* Discusses the Japanese delegation which visited the United States during the 1876 Centennial celebration.

668. Flick, Alvin S. THE GREAT MARIANAS TURKEY SHOOT. *Aviation Q. 1979 5(3): 214-235.* The Japanese aerial-naval offensive of June 1944 failed to control the Marianas Islands; it was called the most lopsided air battle of World War II.

669. Frank, Larry J. THE UNITED STATES NAVY V. THE *CHICAGO TRIBUNE. Historian 1980 42(2): 284-303.* On 7 June 1942 an article, authored by Stanley Johnston, appeared in the *Chicago Tribune* relating the Navy's advance knowledge of the Japanese plans for an attack at Midway Island. Fearing that the Japanese would discover that the Navy had broken the Japanese Fleet Operations Code, the US Office of Censorship cited the *Tribune* for violation of the Voluntary Censorship Code. Unfortunately, for the government, a grand jury failed to indict the newspaper. Recently declassified US Navy documents and *Chicago Tribune* Archives provide a new story to this case. The *Tribune* had gone beyond criticism of the Roosevelt administration to dissemination of a story that was harmful to the war effort. The entire affair produced more censorship regulation and greater threats to the First Amendment and free press which were so passionately defended by the *Tribune* owner-publisher Robert McCormick. Primary sources; 97 notes.
R. S. Sliwoski

670. Franz, Margaret-Mary and Chiba, Motoko. ABORTION, CONTRACEPTION, AND MOTHERHOOD IN POST-WAR JAPAN AND THE UNITED STATES. *Int. J. of Women's Studies [Canada] 1980 3(1): 66-75.*

Analyzes the reduced fertility rates in Japan and the United States, comparing their methods for population control through abortion legislation, birth control, and abortion practices during the postwar years; 1940's-1979.

671. Freedman, Lawrence. THE STRATEGY OF HIROSHIMA. *J. of Strategic Studies [Great Britain] 1978 1(1): 76-97.* Follows the Roosevelt Administration's decisionmaking on the operational use of the first atomic bombs. Cities were attacked because of the lack of significant military targets and to increase the bomb's shock value over conventional strategic bombing, and not for experimental value or to intimidate the Soviet Union. The bombing of Nagasaki was the logical extension of the decision to use the bomb in the first place. Primary sources; 45 notes. A. M. Osur

672. Fyfield-Shayler, B. A. THE BRITISH TYPEWRITER MUSEUM: A HISTORY OF THE TYPEWRITER MANUFACTURING INDUSTRY AND AN INTRODUCTION TO THE BEECHING COLLECTION AT BOURNEMOUTH. *Industrial Archaeol. [Great Britain] 1979 14(3): 210-244.* Describes the history of typewriter manufacturing in the United States, Western Europe and Japan with particular reference to Wilfred Beeching's *Century of the Typewriter* (London: Heinemann, 1974) and to his collection of typewriters at the British Typewriter Museum, Bournemouth.

673. Gabriele, Mariano. IL PACIFICO: SCACCHIERE IN EVOLUZIONE [The Pacific chessboard]. *Riv. Marittima [Italy] 1979 (10): 15-24.* Discusses the US, Japanese, and Russian struggle for power in the Pacific since the early 1900's.

674. Geyer, Hans Martin. DIE WACHSENDE ROLLE JAPANS IN DER USA-MILITÄRSTRATEGIE IM ASIATISCH-PAZIFISCHEN RAUM [The growing role of Japan in US military strategy in the Asian-Pacific area]. *Militärgeschichte [East Germany] 1983 22(1): 50-65.* Sketches the policy of the United States toward Japan following World War II to the present and makes a comparison with US military strategy in the Asian-Pacific area during 1938-41. Emphasizes the importance of Japan as an air force base, as a naval support point, and as a repair and supply base for US forces. The United States has applied constant pressure to insure that Japan will develop into a significant regional military power. Map, 2 tables, graph, 27 notes.

J/T (H. D. Andrews)

675. Ginzberg, Eli and Brecher, Charles. THE ECONOMIC IMPACT OF JAPANESE INVESTMENT. *New York Affairs 1979 5(3): 97-110.* Examines the effects of foreign investments on the US economy, in particular, the enormous impact that Japanese investments have had on New York City since the mid-1960's.

676. Gordon, Bernard K. JAPAN, THE UNITED STATES, AND SOUTHEAST ASIA. *Foreign Affairs 1978 56(3): 579-600.* No longer confident in America's military and economic commitments in Southeast Asia, Japan has decided to extend unilaterally its influence. Prime Minister Takeo Fukuda, for example, recently pledged a $1 billion package for economic

development projects in Indonesia, Malaysia, the Philippines, Singapore, and Thailand. It is essential to the interests of Japan and the United States that their close and interdependent relationship continue "in the East Asian rim areas, whose continued involvement in the non-communist world structure is essential to both." 27 notes. M. R. Yerburgh

677. Gordon, Bernard K. LOOSE CANNON ON A ROLLING DECK? JAPAN'S CHANGING SECURITY POLICIES. *Orbis 1979 22(4): 967-1005.* Notes the Carter administration's steps in 1978 seeking "to convey its intention and capacity to remain very active, politically and militarily, in East Asia." Believes that the United States is no longer capable or willing to ensure Japan's long-term security. Japan will, therefore, increase significantly its defense capacity. It is a myth that America is "withdrawing from Asia" and that foreigners are subjecting Tokyo to economic pressure. Tokyo is committed to meet China's requirements. 68 notes. E. P. Stickney

678. Gordon, Robert J. WHY U.S. WAGE AND EMPLOYMENT BEHAVIOUR DIFFERS FROM THAT IN BRITAIN AND JAPAN. *Econ. J. [Great Britain] 1982 92(365): 13-44.* A comparative historico-theoretical analysis of wages and employment behavior in these three countries from the late 19th century to the present. The author considers the connection between wage stickiness and employment fluctuations; evidence on the responsiveness of wages, hours, and employment; the organization of labor markets; and the origins of labor market institutions in Japan, the United States, and Britain. Based on U.S., British and Japanese statistical data covering the period 1873-1981, available from the U.S. Department of Commerce, OECD Historical Statistics for Britain and Japan, and secondary sources; 5 tables, 22 notes, biblio. G. L. Neville

679. Goren, Dina. COMMUNICATION INTELLIGENCE AND THE FREEDOM OF THE PRESS: THE *CHICAGO TRIBUNE'S* BATTLE OF MIDWAY DISPATCH AND THE BREAKING OF THE JAPANESE NAVAL CODE. *J. of Contemporary Hist. [Great Britain] 1981 16(4): 663-690.* On 7 June 1942, during the Battle of Midway, a *Chicago Tribune* story revealed that the United States had broken the Japanese naval codes and had prior knowledge of the enemy attack. The next day the Bureau of Censorship notified the paper that it had been cited for violating the censorship code. Careful study of the legal aspects of this case discloses that fear of retaliation by the Japanese had prompted the citation, but actually the Japanese seemed unaware that the United States knew their code. The case against the *Tribune* was eventually dropped but the censorship code was changed to include news items describing advance knowledge about the movements of enemy troops, planes, and ships. Based on archival sources; 59 notes. M. P. Trauth

680. Grace, Richard J. WHITEHALL AND THE GHOST OF APPEASEMENT: NOVEMBER 1941. *Diplomatic Hist. 1979 3(2): 173-191.* Great Britain refused to support Cordell Hull's peace initiative with the Japanese in 1941. Ultimately the US position was that both the United States and Japan would disavow military action for three months, Japan would

reduce its presence in Indochina, the United States would remove the freeze on Japanese assets and would encourage the allies to do the same, and the Americans would encourage Japan and China to negotiate a peace. Britain could have used this period to strengthen its defenses in the Far East. Its refusal to support the US position was due in part to its desire to apply pressure on the Japanese to insure that they would not invade the USSR. Mainly, however, the refusal was due to its experience with appeasement in 1938. Based on archival and published primary sources; 52 notes. S

681. Grebennikova, E. THE WEST IN SEARCH OF A NEW CURRENCY SYSTEM. *Int. Affairs [USSR] 1973 (1): 35-42.* Discusses currency crises in the monetary systems of the United States, Japan, and Western Europe in the 1970's; examines disequilibrium in trade-and-payments relations and dissimilar rates of inflation growth.

682. Greenhut, M. L. SPATIAL PRICING IN THE UNITED STATES, WEST GERMANY AND JAPAN. *Economica [Great Britain] 1981 48(189): 79-86.* Investigates the spatial pricing policies of a sample of firms in the United States, West Germany, and Japan, and examines whether differences between countries in spatial discrimination can be explained by a theory of spatial pricing. Considerably greater use is made of discriminatory pricing policies in these countries, compared with nondiscriminatory pricing; theorems based on nondiscriminatory pricing may thus be comparatively unimportant. American firms discriminate less in price than West German and Japanese firms, whose other discriminatory practices differ significantly also. This may possibly be due to the influence of the Robinson-Patman Act, as a result of which many Americans believe all types of geographical price discrimination are illegal. Ref., appendix. D. H. Murdoch

683. Griffiths, William E. THE "WYOMING" IN THE STRAITS OF SHIMONOSÉKI. *By Valor and Arms 1975 2(1): 43-51.* Discusses the role of Captain David McDougal and the US battleship *Wyoming* in protecting the American Legation and American residents in Japan during the straits of Shimonoseki crisis in 1863.

684. Hadley, Eleanor M. IS THE U.S.-JAPAN TRADE IMBALANCE A PROBLEM? ECONOMISTS ANSWER "NO," POLITICIANS "YES." *J. of Northeast Asian Studies 1982 1(1): 35-56.* Debates the relative danger of the US-Japan trade imbalance, presenting a variety of views and fears voiced by professional and political factions.

685. Haga, Shōji. WASHIN JŌYAKU-KI NO BAKUFU GAIKŌ NI TSUITE [The Shogunate diplomacy of the Treaty of Peace and Amity, 1853-58]. *Rekishigaku Kenkyū [Japan] 1980 (482): 1-13, 52.* Identifies the features of Shogunate diplomacy at the time of the Treaty of Peace and Amity (1853-58). Focuses on the Shogunate's acceptance of the treaty in accordance with international diplomatic principles. The Shogunate government regarded the diplomatic idea of friendship as different from diplomatic relations with Korea and Ryūkū, trade relations with China, and friendship and commercial relations with Holland. 41 notes. R. Shibasaki/S

686. Haight, John McVickar, Jr. FDR'S "BIG STICK." *US Naval Inst. Pro. 1980 106(7): 68-73.* From late 1937 to early 1938, President Franklin D. Roosevelt tried to find some way to blunt Japan's aggression in China. As he intimated privately to close associates and publicly in the famous Quarantine Speech in Chicago in early October 1937, he wanted a naval blockade of Japan. He realized, though, that he needed American public opinion behind him before proceeding and that unless he could get Great Britain to commit the British fleet, a blockade of Japan would be unsuccessful and damage US interests in the Far East. Despite the Japanese attack on the USS *Panay* in China in December 1937, Roosevelt failed to rally the American people. When Prime Minister Neville Chamberlain rebuffed Roosevelt's suggestion about using the British fleet, the blockade idea died. A preliminary version of this article appeared in the *Pacific Historical Review,* May 1971. 5 photos, 14 notes. A. N. Garland

687. Haines, Gerald K. AMERICAN MYOPIA AND THE JAPANESE MONROE DOCTRINE, 1931-41. *Prologue 1981 13(2): 101-114.* Traces the development of the Japanese regional policy for the Far East, the reaction of the Roosevelt adminstration to this policy, and the reluctance of American policymakers to recognize the legitimacy of Japan's regional claims. The American myopia with regard to Japan's regional claims contributed to the inability to reach a compromise solution in the Pacific. Based on Public Papers and Addresses of Roosevelt, National Archives records, Foreign Relations Documents, and newspapers; 2 illus., 9 photos, 65 notes. M. A. Kascus

688. Halliday, Jon and McCormack, Gavan. JAPAN AND AMERICA: ANTAGONISTIC ALLIES. *New Left R. [Great Britain] 1973 (77): 59-74.* The "Nixon Shocks" of 1971—the establishment of relations between the United States and China, and of protection—exerted an important effect upon Japan, and accelerated Japan's political and diplomatic moves in Eastern and Southeast Asia. Japan's previous advances in this area had been mainly economic, contrasting with the pre-1945 period, during which Japan's expansion was mainly determined by political and military factors. Relations between the United States and Japan tend to be uneasy, characterized by both cooperation and rivalry. Basic components of this relationship include trade and investment. Existing contradictions eventually will overthrow Japanese imperialism. Adapted from the final chapter of the authors' forthcoming book (1973), *Japanese Imperialism Today.* Based mainly on the press and secondary sources; table, 42 notes. P. J. Beck

689. Hamilton, David Mike. SOME CHIN-CHIN AND TEA: JACK LONDON IN JAPAN. *Pacific Hist. 1979 23(2): 19-25.* In 1904, Jack London went to Japan to cover the Russo-Japanese War as a correspondent for William Randolph Hearst. Despite some bungling, London turned out to be an excellent reporter. Based largely on the Jack London Collection, Henry E. Huntington Library, San Marino, California; 3 photos, 22 notes.
H. M. Parker, Jr.

690. Hammond, James W., Jr. A FLEET FOR ALL SEASONS. *US Naval Inst. Pro. 1982 108(12): 66-72.* President Theodore Roosevelt feared the rising

influence in the Pacific of Japan. He viewed the cruise of the Atlantic Squadron's battleships to the Pacific in 1907 as a means of restraining Japanese jingoism. The successful cruise to the Pacific and the readiness to fight, which the force showed on its arrival, in the president's mind would convince Japan that it could not win a war with the United States. — K. J. Bauer

691. Hansen, Arthur A. and Hacker, David A. THE MANZANAR RIOT: AN ETHNIC PERSPECTIVE. *Amerasia J. 1974 2(2): 112-157.* Describes a riot at the Manzanar War Relocation Center, California, in 1942 following the arrest of Harry Ueno for assaulting a Nisei. The Project Director's decision to appoint only Nisei to the planned Self-Government Commission led to Kibei rejection. Based on archival and secondary sources; 126 notes. — M. R. Underdown

692. Harrington, Daniel F. A CARELESS HOPE: AMERICAN AIR POWER AND JAPAN, 1941. *Pacific Hist. Rev. 1979 48(2): 217-238.* Hope and rationalization shaped US military strategy in the Pacific during the months before the Japanese attack on Pearl Harbor. Before 1941, American military planners had considered the Philippines indefensible, and the War Department had been uninterested in developing military aviation. In the summer and fall of 1941, US military policy shifted to strategic air power in the Philippines with the intention of halting Japanese expansion without the risk of war. When the Japanese attacked Pearl Harbor, the Far Eastern Air Force in the Philippines was insufficient, unprepared, and quickly destroyed by Japanese air attacks. Based on military archives, records of Congressional hearings, diaries and personal papers of military officers, and secondary sources; 47 notes. — R. N. Lokken

693. Harris, Ruth R. THE "MAGIC" LEAK OF 1941 AND JAPANESE-AMERICAN RELATIONS. *Pacific Hist. Rev. 1981 50(1): 77-96.* As the result of a British communications lapse in April 1941 the German embassy in Washington knew that American cryptoanalysts had broken the Japanese diplomatic code. In May American naval intelligence learned of the leak from a decoded Japanese message from Berlin to Tokyo. Until 1 November, delivery of intercepted Japanese messages to the White House was curtailed, and, inadequately informed, President Franklin D. Roosevelt made diplomatic mistakes that worsened relations with Japan. In August American naval intelligence did not inform the president that the Japanese had decided not to transmit highly secret policy decisions because of the danger of interception. Decoded Japanese messages in the fall of 1941 contained information that misled American officials. Based on Japanese diplomatic messages in the US National Archives and other primary sources; 44 notes. — R. N. Lokken

694. Harvey, Thomas H., Jr. THE PORTENTS OF SIGNALS: U.S.-JAPAN RELATIONS. *Naval War Coll. Rev. 1979 32(2): 77-81.* Quoting a Japanese view of a "regrettable but understandable decline in American determination and willingness to take a direct role in preserving peace and maintaining the status quo" in Northeast Asia, this paper, originally prepared

as a Naval War College student elective requirement, considers the options available to Japan and their significance to U.S. national interests. J

695. Hata, Ikuhiko. JAPAN UNDER THE OCCUPATION. *Japan Interpreter [Japan] 1976 10(3-4): 361-380.* Elaborates on the American military occupation of Japan, 1946-51, focusing on its advantages and disadvantages from a Japanese perspective. The chief legacies are the Americanization of Japan, the introduction of Midwestern democracy, and the shaping of Japanese education. F. Iklé

696. Hatakeda, Shigeo. BETONAMU SENSŌ TO NIHON [Japan and the Vietnam War]. *Ajia Afurika Kenkyū [Japan] 1975 15(8): 64-72.* Discusses the offer of air bases and economic aid as the means by which the Japanese government and monopolistic capital supported the American war effort. The author criticizes this relationship with the United States and Japan's substantial assistance in the Vietnam War since 1960 under the Security Pact. Yet the movement to support the Vietnamese people developed by the Japanese people and labor is highly regarded. H. Kawanami

697. Havens, Thomas R. AMERICAN UNDERGRADUATE PROGRAMS IN JAPAN AND THE NEEDS OF JAPAN STUDIES IN THE UNITED STATES. *Asian Studies Professional R. 1973 2(2): 64-69.* Critiques programs for an undergraduate year in Japan, citing problems with the home institutions in providing adequate preparation. A liberal education will benefit the student whether or not he becomes a Japan specialist. An undergraduate year-in-Japan program should include language training, reading courses, visual, creative, and field-oriented work, independent study, residential life, and travel. R. H. Detrick

698. Heath, Laurel. EDUCATION FOR CONFUSION: A STUDY OF EDUCATION IN THE MARIANA ISLANDS 1688-1941. *J. of Pacific Hist. [Australia] 1975 10(1): 20-37.* Examines the educational policies of the successive governments of Spain, America, Germany and Japan in the Mariana Islands. Differing national aims and religions led to confusion. The schools suppressed the native language, imposed four foreign languages, 1886-1915, and followed curricula designed for children of foreign backgrounds. The failure of administrations to recognize and develop native culture have resulted in lack of integration between Micronesian immigrants and the natives, and loss of identity. Based on government documents and statistics, and newspapers; 57 notes. E. Spencer

699. Hellwig, David J. AFRO-AMERICAN REACTIONS TO THE JAPANESE AND THE ANTI-JAPANESE MOVEMENT, 1906-1924. *Phylon 1977 38(1): 93-104.* The Johnson Immigration Act (1924) included a provision to effectively deny Japanese entrance into the United States. This law culminated two decades of anti-Japanese agitation. The position of most black Americans was that some immigration restrictions or quotas were probably needed, but that the Japanese ought not to be singled out for unfair treatment. Blacks readily saw similarities with their own plight and viewed the matter as a racial one. They called for "a policy applied equally to all." An exception to

this general view was Howard University educator Kelly Miller, who argued that blacks would do better to identify with whites than with a group of newcomers. By the late 1920's, Miller's views seemed to dominate. Primary and secondary sources; 49 notes.　　　　　　　　　　　　　　B. A. Glasrud

700. Henrikson, Alan K. CALMING THE PACIFIC. *Reviews in Am. Hist. 1975 3(4): 489-493.* R. J. C. Butow's *The John Doe Associates: Backdoor Diplomacy for Peace, 1941* (Stanford, California: Stanford U. Pr., 1974) examines "private efforts for a Japanese-American peace settlement in 1940-41" and Stephen E. Pelz's *Race to Pearl Harbor: The Failure of the Second London Naval Conference and the Onset of World War II* (Cambridge: Harvard U. Pr.) concentrates on the naval arms race in the 1930's; both authors emphasize avoidable mistakes in diplomacy that led to the outbreak of war.

701. Hibel, Franklin. CHENNAULT: MAVERICK TO MARVEL. *Air Force Mag. 1974 57(11): 90-94.* General Claire Lee Chennault (1890-1958), the leader of the Flying Tigers, fought the Japanese in air warfare over China during World War II.

702. Hidagi, Yasushi. ATTACK AGAINST THE U.S. HEARTLAND. *Aerospace Hist. 1981 27(2): 87-93.* The translated and edited report for the record, written following World War II by an operations staff member of the Balloon Force of the Japanese Army Air Force, then Major Yasushi Hidagi (later a major general in the Japanese Self-Defense Force). Includes the planning for the balloon force, design matters, organization, attack orders, and results. 5 photos.　　　　　　　　　　　　　　　　　　C. W. Ohrvall

703. Hikins, James W. THE RHETORIC OF "UNCONDITIONAL SURRENDER" AND THE DECISION TO DROP THE ATOMIC BOMB. *Q. J. of Speech 1983 69(4): 379-400.* Analyzes the atomic attacks on Hiroshima and Nagasaki from a rhetorical purview, arguing that they were launched in large measure because of an American commitment to a particular rhetoric— the "rhetoric of unconditional surrender." First articulated by President Roosevelt at the Casablanca Conference in 1943, the slogan changed by 1945 into a political shibboleth which operated to constrain policymakers. By August 1945 the doctrine's calcifying effect on American decisionmaking precluded an earlier end to hostilities in the Pacific and resulted in atomic devastation for the two Japanese cities.　　　　　　　　　　　　　　J/S

704. Hilgenberg, James F., Jr. TO ENLIST AN ALLY: THE AMERICAN BUSINESS PRESS, JAPAN, AND THE COLD WAR, 1948-1952. *J. of the West Virginia Hist. Assoc. 1979 3(1): 17-29.* Discusses the relationship of the media and foreign policy, analyzing the interaction of the American business press, Japan and the United States at the beginning of the Cold War.

705. Hinckley, Ted C. and Hinckley, Caryl C., eds. THE 1870 MEETING BETWEEN WILLIAM H. SEWARD AND THE JAPANESE EMPEROR. *Pacific Historian 1975 19(3): 271-290.* Presents edited excerpts from William H. Seward's *Travels Around the World*, published in 1873. The book was a

product of Seward's 1870-71 world tour. The excerpts here deal primarily with Seward's meeting with Emperor Mutsuhito and with Seward's "acute insights" on Japan. Seward observed, "the great problem now is, whether the European civilization can be extended over Japan, without the destruction, not merely of the political institutions of the country, but of the Japanese nation itself. The Japanese are practically defenseless against the Western States." 19 notes.

G. L. Olson

706. Hoddeson, Lillian. ESTABLISHING KEK IN JAPAN AND FERMILAB IN THE US: INTERNATIONALISM, NATIONALISM AND HIGH ENERGY ACCELERATORS. *Social Studies of Sci. [Great Britain] 1983 13(1): 1-48.* Examines the background history and establishment of the Fermi National Accelerator Laboratory (Fermilab) in the United States, and the Kō Enerugii Butsurigaku Kenkyusho (KEK) in Japan, 1930's-60's, and reveals the working of both internationalism and nationalism in high energy physics.

707. Hollerman, Leon. JAPANESE DIRECT INVESTMENT IN CALIFORNIA. *Asian Survey 1981 21(10): 1080-1095.* The United States has recently attracted direct Japanese investment by means of the contrary principle of import substitution. Much of Japan's direct investment in the United States has come to California, which as a host region offers certain natural advantages and which has urged Japan to export employment rather than products. Because of problems created by excessive, capricious, and unpredictable administrative intervention and regulation by the state government, however, some major firms that might have entered California have chosen to go elsewhere. Based on documents and newspapers. M. A. Eide

708. Hollerman, Leon. JAPAN'S ECONOMIC IMPACT ON THE UNITED STATES. *Ann. of the Am. Acad. of Pol. and Social Sci. 1982 (460): 127-135.* Japan has become increasingly competitive rather than complementary in relations with the United States. Its impact on the US economy stems from its vertical anatomy of foreign trade, largely determined by its unbalanced physical endowment and its supply-side strategy, specifically linked to the doctrine of dynamic comparative advantage to achieve international competitive power in US markets, among others. The US response to its persistent trade deficits with Japan has tended to be bilateral and protectionist. The various "voluntary" export restraints Japan has adopted under US pressure have dark implications because of the cartel arrangements by which they are enforced. J/S

709. Hollerman, Leon. LOCOMOTIVE STRATEGY AND UNITED PROTECTIONISM: A JAPANESE VIEW. *Pacific Affairs [Canada] 1979 52(2): 193-209.* Examines the locomotive strategy of international economics adopted by the United States in 1976. The initial idea proposed by the OECD secretariat urged the leading industrial powers, the United States, West Germany, and Japan to adopt expansionary fiscal and monetary policies. These changes would activate unutilized production capabilities of the major industrial nations which would act as locomotives pulling other nations out of recession. In the United States, however, the real growth rate for the GNP

dropped more than 1% in the first year, in Japan it increased more than 5%, and in Germany it grew by 2.5%. In terms of inflation it became clear that the inflation rates were declining in Japan and Germany while rising in the United States. Concludes that Japan has made a genuine contribution of stable and noninflationary economic growth, but the United States has refused to complement and emulate this rational behavior. Secondary sources; 34 notes.

S. H. Frank

710. Homan, Gerlof D. THE UNITED STATES AND THE INDONESIAN QUESTION, DECEMBER 1941-DECEMBER 1946. *Tijdschrift voor Geschiedenis [Netherlands] 1980 93(1): 35-56.* The United States showed no concern about Dutch colonial policy in Asia before World War II. The Roosevelt administration was aware of the colony's economic significance and encouraged the Dutch to resist Japanese encroachments. During the war, various American officials urged the Dutch to make substantial reforms in their colonial administration and to prepare the Netherlands East Indies for independence. After the war the United States showed less concern and hoped that the Dutch, assisted by the British, would make important concessions to the Indonesian nationalists. Still most American officials preferred a strong Dutch presence. Primary materials; 112 notes.

A

711. Homma, Nagayo. HOW WE SEE EACH OTHER: JAPANESE AND AMERICANS. *Rev. in Am. Hist. 1977 5(1): 8-13.* Review article prompted by Akira Iriye, ed., *Mutual Images: Essays in American-Japanese Relations* (Cambridge, Mass.: Harvard U. Pr., 1975).

712. Homma, Nagayo. PORTRAIT OF THE INTELLECTUAL AS AN AMERICAN. *Am. Studies Int. 1979 18(1): 24-34.* Shows how Japanese intellectuals have viewed the United States and American intellectuals. Initially attracted by America, Japanese intellectuals became critical of its materialism after World War I. Defeat and occupation intensified the problem of judging American civilization. Japanese intellectuals studied closely the anti-Communist pragmatic liberals and the reconciliation of intellectuals with American society in the 1950's, the counterculture intellectuals of the 1960's, and those in power under John Kennedy. American intellectuals currently give the picture of a society in fragmentation and raise the fear that they will continue to be trans-Atlantic provincials rather than help build a trans-Pacific intellectual community. 2 illus., 23 notes.

R. E. Noble

713. Hooper, Paul F. A FOOTNOTE ON THE PACIFIC WAR. *Hawaiian J. of Hist. 1975 9: 121-127.* Describes the efforts of David L. Crawford, then president of the University of Hawaii, to bring about a peace pact between the United States and Japan in 1940-41. Crawford worked through the Institute of Pacific Relations, and the position paper was completed on 5 December 1941.

R. Alvis

714. Horder, Mervyn. IF NO ATOM BOMB? *Blackwood's Mag. [Great Britain] 1975 318(1918): 110-115.* Discusses the military strategy and circumstances of the release of two atom bombs over Japan in 1945.

S

715. Hosoya, Chihiro. JAPANESE-AMERICAN RELATIONS. *Pacific Hist. 1979 23(4): 9-27.* Japanese Prime Minister Konoe Fumimaro's idea of a summit conference with Franklin D. Roosevelt in October 1941 was intended to work out a settlement in the Pacific area. Some historians have placed the blame for Pearl Harbor on the State Department's cool reception to Konoe's proposal, but through his 1934 trip to the United States Konoe had so alienated important American businessmen and statesmen that his actions as prime minister were suspect, and this was what prevented Roosevelt from proceeding with the conference with Konoe. H. M. Parker, Jr.

716. Howell, Susan E. POLITICAL INFORMATION: THE EFFECTS OF SYSTEM AND INDIVIDUAL CHARACTERISTICS. *Comparative Pol. Studies 1976 8(4): 413-435.* Discusses voter sophistication and levels of political information in Australia, Netherlands, Italy, Japan, and the United States in the 1960's and 70's.

717. Ichioka, Yuji. JAPANESE ASSOCIATIONS AND THE JAPANESE GOVERNMENT: A SPECIAL RELATIONSHIP, 1909-1926. *Pacific Hist. Rev. 1977 46(3): 409-437.* The voluntary associations of the Japanese Americans in the United States, the Japanese associations, had a closer relationship with the Japanese government than did any other American immigrant associations with the governments of their countries of origin. The Gentlemen's Agreement of 1907-08 created this close relationship. However, the relationship was not as close or one-sided as exclusionists claimed. The associations could choose their own officers and were able to exercise some independence, often to the detriment of Japanese immigrants. Based on microfilmed government documents in the Japanese American Research Project Collection, newspapers, and other Japanese-language published primary and secondary sources; 2 tables, 62 notes. W. K. Hobson

718. Idéo, Rosella. OKINAWA NELLA POLITICA INTERNAZIONALE: DALLA PRIMA ALLA SECONDA OCCUPAZIONE AMERICANA: 1853-1972 [Okinawa in international politics: From the first to the second American occupation, 1853-1972]. *Politico [Italy] 1973 38(3): 513-545.* "The return of Okinawa under Japanese sovereignty after 27 years of American occupation did not diminish, according to the A., the strategic importance of the island either for the United States or for Japan whose military forces together with those still considerable of the ally are gradually taking its defence upon themselves. Occupied for the first time by Commodore Perry in 1853 for its nearness to China and particularly to Japan of which he wanted to force the opening, Okinawa was annexed a little later to the Meiji Japan, anxious about the interest shown by the Western nations for its extreme maritime border. Exploited by large Japanese trusts and far more undeveloped than the other prefectures, Okinawa acquired new international importance during the second world war (inter-allied conferences). Last defensive link around Japan, the island was occupied by the Americans in June 1945 after one of the most ruthless battles in the Pacific. The aggravation of the cold war with the advent of the Communists in China and the opening of hostilities in Korea determined the destiny of Okinawa which, in accordance with the much debated peace Treaty of S. Francisco, became also *de jure* a territory of the

U.S., although the so-called residual sovereignty of Japan was allowed over it. From 1951 onwards the problem of Okinawa has been one of the deadlocks in the Japanese-American relations of which the A. examines the most significant stages. The final arrangements for the restitution of Okinawa to Japan were those between Nixon and Sato in 1969 which, though constituting a turning point in the bilateral relations between the two Countries, did not solve the many problems attached to them. Above all, the terms of the agreement were welcomed neither in Japan nor in Okinawa, the latter having seen confirmed its status of military bulwark. The persistent flow of Japanese capital and investments steadily increasing since 1969, may very likely revive the same unhappy colonial situation of the past." J

719. Iiyama, Patty. AMERICAN CONCENTRATION CAMPS: RACISM AND JAPANESE-AMERICANS DURING WORLD WAR II. *Int. Socialist Rev. 1973 34(4): 24-33.*

720. Ingersoll, Robert S. TOWARD A BILATERAL PARTNERSHIP: IMPROVING ECONOMIC RELATIONS. *J. of Int. Affairs 1983 37(1): 21-28.* With Japan's economic growth dropping dramatically since the 1970's, protectionist measures are not likely to solve the problems of either the United States or Japan.

721. Ion, A. Hamish. EDWARD WARREN CLARK AND EARLY MEIJI JAPAN: A CASE STUDY OF CULTURAL CONTACT. *Modern Asian Studies [Great Britain] 1977 11(4): 557-572.* Studies Edward Warren Clark's (1849-1907) evangelistic work in Shizuoka and Tokyo and his influence on Japanese intellectuals. At the age of 22, he accepted a teaching position in Japan. He insisted on arrival that he be allowed to teach the Bible. He greatly influenced Nakamura Masanao (1832-91), who translated several works into Japanese, some with distortions attributable to Clark's utilitarian view of Christianity. After three years, Clark returned to the United States, becoming a clergyman in the Protestant Episcopal Church. 54 notes. J. Tull

722. Iriye, Akira. AMERICANOLOGY IN JAPAN. *R. in Am. Hist. 1975 3(2): 143-154.* K. Ōhashi, H. Katō, and M. Saitō, eds. *Amerika no bunka* [American civilization] (Tokyo: Nan'undo, 1969-71), 7 volumes, and M. Saitō, N. Homma, and S. Kamei, eds. *Nihon to Amerika* [Japan and America] (Tokyo: Nan'undo, 1973), 3 volumes, contain some of the few examples of Japanese historiography of American culture, social conditions, and national self-image in the 19th and 20th centuries.

723. Iriye, Akira. THE JOHN DOE ASSOCIATES: BACKDOOR DIPLOMACY FOR PEACE, 1941. *J. of Japanese Studies 1975 2(1): 127-131.* Reviews *The John Doe Associates: Backdoor Diplomacy for Peace, 1941*, (Stanford U. Pr., 1974), R. J. Butow's study of the "backdoor diplomacy" of private individuals, who sought to avert war in the months immediately preceding Pearl Harbor. Bishop Walsh and Father Drought established contacts with banker Paul Wikawa and Foreign Minister Yosuke Masuoka endeavoring to bring the leaders of both countries to a summit meeting. Agrees with the traditional interpretation presented by Stanley K. Hornbeck, Secretary

of State Cordell Hull's chief adviser. The John Doe Associates represent a case study of misunderstanding and confusion arising when private individuals undertake to mediate between the officials of two governments. Butow characterizes this episode of private diplomacy as damaging to the cause of peace in the Pacific in 1941, although this was certainly not the intention of the "John Does." S. H. Frank

724. Isby, David C. "CA": TACTICAL NAVAL WARFARE IN THE PACIFIC, 1941-43. *Strategy and Tactics 1973 (38): 5-19.* Discusses the development (from the 1920's to 1943) of US and Japanese tactics used in early naval battles in the Pacific during World War II.

725. Isby, David C. ISLAND WAR: THE U.S. AMPHIBIOUS OFFENSIVE AGAINST IMPERIAL JAPAN, 1942 TO 1945. *Strategy & Tactics 1975 (52): 21-36.* Describes American amphibious operations against Japanese-occupied Pacific islands during World War II.

726. Ishikawa, Hirotomo. THE HIDDEN HAND—MULTINATIONAL CORPORATIONS. *Japan Q. [Japan] 1976 23(3): 247-254.* The "military-industrial complex" now finds expression in the burgeoning of the multinational corporations. Their "money power" is so great as to be able to influence the fate of nations. This can be seen in relation to US politics during the Richard M. Nixon regime, but also around the world. A major tool in the transfer of huge sums of money are the numerous "tax-havens" they use around the world, secrecy being an important factor in the process, thereby wielding immense power in times of currency crisis. They were strongly behind the movement toward detente, having much to gain. The Japanese "general trading companies" are essentially a Japanese version of the multinational corporation.
R. V. Ritter

727. Ito, Hiroshi. THE U.S.-JAPAN AGREEMENT ON THE AUTOMOBILE EXPORT RESTRAINT. *Asian Thought & Soc. 1981 6(17-18): 222-230.* Traces the increased number of Japanese automobiles imported into the United States, 1970-81, and analyzes foreign policy on imports and exports, concentrating on the political process which resulted in controls on the Japanese automobile trade in 1981.

728. Itō, Tsuneo. SENGO NO ATARASHII DAIGAKU NO RINEN: UEHARA SENROKU SHI NO "DAIGAKURON" KENKYŪ MEMO [The new ideas of the university after World War II: a study of Senroku Uehara's *The University*]. *Matsuyama Shōdai Ronshū [Japan] 1973 24(1-2): 43-85.* From the US Education Mission to Japan, 1946.

729. Iwao, Sumiko; Pool, Ithiel de Sola; and Hagiwara, Shigeru. JAPANESE AND U.S. MEDIA: SOME CROSS-CULTURAL INSIGHTS INTO TV VIOLENCE. *J. of Communication 1981 31(2): 28-36.* Examines the difference in how violence is presented on Japanese and US television since 1972 and asks whether the relationship between TV viewing and behavior in any culture is a function of sheer quantity of televised violence or a function of the treatment of violence.

730. Jablon, Howard. CORDELL HULL, HIS "ASSOCIATES," AND RELATIONS WITH JAPAN, 1933-1936. *Mid-America 1974 56(3): 160-174.* Cordell Hull did not exercise the control over US foreign policy in the mid-1930's which he has claimed, but was a force in some areas, such as commercial matters. In Far Eastern policy he continued the programs of his predecessor, Henry L. Stimson, without substantial modification. Franklin D. Roosevelt's concern with domestic matters permitted Hull a freer rein in foreign policy. However, when Hull gained this freedom, it was often paradoxically surrendered to his Division heads. Since the Division heads were staunch Stimson men, Hull was advised to continue the policy toward Japan adopted by his predecessor. As a result, foreign policy of the mid-1930's remained inflexible and unimaginative. Based on manuscript and printed primary and secondary sources; 63 notes. T. D. Schoonover

731. Janke, Peter. NUCLEAR DENIAL: THE POLITICS OF DIRECT DEMOCRACY. *Contemporary Rev. [Great Britain] 1979 234(1359): 174-180.* Examines the hostility surrounding the nuclear issue in Europe, Japan, and the United States and assesses the extent to which it has been manipulated by politically orientated groups hostile to the survival of liberal democracy, suggesting that only the USSR has anything to gain by the slowing down of western nuclear technology.

732. Johnson, Paul W. THE JOURNALIST AS DIPLOMAT: E. J. DILLON AND THE PORTSMOUTH PEACE CONFERENCE. *Journalism Q. 1976 53(4): 689-693.* Dr. Emile Joseph Dillon (1854-1953), the St. Petersburg correspondent for the London *Daily Telegraph* during the Russo-Japanese War (1904-05), led the public relations campaign with the American press on behalf of Russian Minister of Finance Sergei Witte in a successful effort to influence public opinion regarding Russian desires for a favorable agreement at the Portsmouth Peace Conference.

733. Johnson, Randall A. JAPANESE BALLOONS BOMBED WEST. *Pacific Northwesterner 1976 20(3): 33-43.* During the final year of World War II, Japan sent balloon-carried bombs via wind currents to the United States, many of which landed in the Pacific Northwest.

734. Jorgenson, Dale W. and Nishimizu, Mieko. U. S. AND JAPANESE ECONOMIC GROWTH, 1952-1974: AN INTERNATIONAL COMPARISON. *Econ. J. [Great Britain] 1978 88(352): 707-726.* Compares aggregate economic growth in the United States and Japan, 1952-74, during which period the United States maintained its position as the world's largest economy, while Japan rose to third position. Japanese output grew rapidly, relative to the United States, due to an increase in the level of technology and labor input, 1952-60. The years 1960-74 saw substantial growth in the United States, but extremely rapid growth in Japan, the average rate of growth of capital input being more than double that in the United States, and the rate of return on business capital being approximately double that in the United States. Based on economic statistics and secondary works; 4 tables, 7 notes. D. J. Nicholls

735. Jorgenson, Dale W. and Nishimizu, Mieko. U.S. AND JAPANESE ECONOMIC GROWTH, 1952-1974: AN INTERNATIONAL COMPARISON. *Econ. J. [Great Britain] 1978 88(352): 707-726.* Provides an international comparison of aggregate economic growth between the United States and Japan for 1952-74, during which the United States maintained its position as the world's largest economy, while Japan rose to third position. During 1952-60 Japanese output grew rapidly relative to the United States due to an increase in the level of technology and labor input. Substantial growth occurred in the United States during 1960-74, but Japan doubled in capital input and the rate of return. Based on economic statistics and secondary works; 4 tables, 7 notes. D. J. Nicholls

736. Josephy, Alvin M., Jr. IWO JIMA. *Am. Heritage 1981 32(4): 92-101.* It took two months of air and naval bombardment, 26 days of intense fighting, and 6,318 American deaths to secure the island of Iwo Jima, vital to Japanese air defense plans. 6 illus. J. F. Paul

737. Junghans, Earl A. WAKE'S POWS. *US Naval Inst. Pro. 1983 109(2): 43-50.* Recounts the experience of Earl A. Junghans, as commander on Wake Island and the repatriation of the Japanese garrison there as well as the experiences of the American Marines and civilians captured by the Japanese in 1941. The American prisoners, except for 98 men, were transferred to a prison camp near Shanghai, China, in 1942. Two of the 98 were executed for theft and 95 were shot on 7 October 1943 when an American invasion was feared. One man escaped but was subsequently caught and executed. The Japanese officer responsible, Rear Admiral Shigematsu Sakaibara, was hung as a war criminal on 18 June 1947. Based on printed and archival sources; 12 notes.
K. J. Bauer

738. Kahn, B. Winston. THE DIPLOMACY OF MATSUOKA YOSUKE, 1940-1941. *Asian Forum 1979 10(1): 35-49.* Explains the diplomacy of Matsuoka Yōsuke, Japanese foreign minister, 1940-41, through the examination of his personality and thought in the light of the political and social environment. His approach to diplomacy was unconventional and provocative. His unique style of personal diplomacy and his strategy of brinkmanship proved ineffective in negotiating peace with the United States. Instead of forcing US recognition of Japan's position in Asia he further antagonized the American public. He misjudged American psychology despite his early years of education and work experience in the United States. 42 notes. R. B. Orr

739. Kamei Shunsuke. JAPANESE SEE AMERICA: A CENTURY OF FIRSTHAND IMPRESSIONS. *Japan Interpreter [Japan] 1976 11(1): 6-35.* Japanese travel accounts since the mid-19th century reveal much about the United States and its alternating positive and negative models. Japanese accounts of the United States display greater depths and wider vacillations as well as insatiable curiosity than do American accounts of Japan. The range between admiring approval and expressions of displeasure and disappointment starting with Fukuzawa Yukichi displays an awareness of the common problems found in the worldwide civilization of the 20th century.
F. W. Iklé

740. Kanda, Fumito. SHOHYŌ: NAKAMURA TAKAHIDE HEN, *SENRYŌKI NIPPON NO KEIZAI TO SEIJI* [Book review: Nakamura Takahide, ed., *Economy and Politics in Occupied Japan*]. *Shigaku Zasshi [Japan] 1981 90(4): 70-77.* Reviews *Senryōki Nippon no Keizai to Seiji* (1979), which contains 12 essays on politics and the economy during the occupation of Japan by the US Army. Based largely on US documents. M. Kawaguchi

741. Kanda, James. THE KANEKO CORRESPONDENCE. *Monumenta Nipponica [Japan] 1982 37(1): 41-76, (2): 223-256, (3): 289-316.* Kaneko Kentarō (1852-1942) was a recognized diplomat, scholar, statesman and Japanese jurist, and one of the foremost Japanese authorities on the United States. A graduate of the Harvard Law School in 1878, he was a close personal friend of Oliver Wendell Holmes, Jr., John Chipman Gray and James Bradley Thayer. His 130 personal letters to various American friends present a valuable legacy of a man of the Meiji era with close American connections. Topics of discussion included the law and US-Japanese relations. A number of his letters are included in the article. F. W. Iklé

742. Karashchuk, E. V. POSLEDSTVIIA PODDERZHKI IAPONIEI AMERIKANSKOI AGRESSII V INDOKITAE [The consequences of Japan's support of American aggression in Indochina]. *Narody Azii i Afriki [USSR] 1977 (3): 42-53.* During the entire Vietnam War, the ruling circles of Japan gave moral, political, diplomatic, economic, and military support to the American aggressor because they were just as interested as the Americans in defending the positions of imperialism and eliminating the national liberation movement in Southeast Asia. They were also interested in expanding their influence, making inflated wartime profits, and creating beneficial conditions for the return of the Ryukyus. The author describes the events of the Vietnam War which concerned the two powers, starting with the American provocation on 4 August 1965 at Tonkin Bay, and gives an account of Japan's economic gains and internal problems arising from its support of US aggression. 39 notes. L. Kalinowski

743. Kashima, Tetsuden. JAPANESE AMERICAN INTERNEES RETURN, 1945 TO 1955: READJUSTMENT AND SOCIAL AMNESIA. *Phylon 1980 41(2): 107-115.* The Japanese have experienced five epochs of crisis in their historical sojourn in the United States: immigration and adjustment (1869-1906), exclusion (1906-24), accommodation in a hostile social environment (1924-41), World War II internment (1941-45), and readjustment (1945-55). Understanding the model minority image of Japanese Americans must originate with the crisis of readjustment. 24 notes.
N. G. Sapper

744. Kaspi, André. CONTROVERSE: FALLAIT-IL BOMBARDER HIROSHIMA? [Debate: should the bomb have been dropped on Hiroshima?]. *Histoire [France] 1981 (32): 87-91.* Examines the significance of the use of the atomic bomb in the closing days of World War II after President Harry S. Truman returned from the Potsdam Conference. Its use was as a weapon of diplomacy, marking the beginning of the Cold War.

745. Kawahito, Kiyoshi. THE STEEL DUMPING ISSUE IN RECENT U.S.-JAPANESE RELATIONS. *Asian Survey 1980 20(10): 1038-1047.* By December 1977 the allegation that Japanese producers had engaged in massive steel dumping in the US market, particularly in 1976, had become widely accepted in the United States. But Japanese producers generally did not dump steel in the US market. Both general economic conditions and the steel industry's anti-import campaigns caused the misunderstanding. Japanese steel producers contributed to US misconceptions by responding ineffectively to the charges. 20 notes. M. A. Eide

746. Keene, Donald. JOURNEY WITH JAPANESE. *Am. Scholar 1982 51(2): 245-248.* Presents a personal reminiscence of the author's life-long fascination with all things Japanese, 1930's-80's. F. F. Harling/S

747. Kelley, Ronald R.; Stunkel, Kenneth R.; and Wescott, Richard R. THE POLITICS OF THE ENVIRONMENT: THE UNITED STATES, THE USSR, AND JAPAN. *Am. Behavioral Scientist 1974 17(5): 751-770.* Compares "the political and administrative aspects of pollution abatement in three widely varying political systems." S

748. Kesauan, K. V. THE ATTITUDE OF THE PHILIPPINES TOWARD THE JAPANESE PEACE TREATY. *Internat. Studies [India] 1973 12(2): 222-250.* During World War II, the Philippine Islands were devastated by Japan. Postwar Philippine President Elpidio Quirino requested two settlements from Japan: 1) just material reparations and 2) safety from possible remilitarization of Japan. Quirino expected American aid in realizing these objectives, and when the US began trying to rebuild Japan, the Philippine government voiced strong objections. Serious problems emerged when the US drafted a peace treaty asking for waiving of the reparations owed by Japan and an absence of restrictions on Japanese rearmament. Quirino refused to accept the treaty unless it was amended. Japan eventually paid reparations, and the US promised aid to the Philippines against attack from any source. The Philippines signed the peace treaty on 8 September 1951, but due to the objections of the Nationalist Party the treaty was not ratified in the Philippine senate until 1956. Based on Philippine and American government publications, secondary works; newspapers; 132 notes. G. R. Hess

749. Kesavan, K. V. JAPAN'S RESPONSE TO THE SWING IN US-SOVIET RELATIONS. *Int. Studies [India] 1974 13(4): 677-693.* Examines how US-Soviet detente has benefited Japan's trade relations and removed obstacles in its foreign policy in the years 1971-74. From a special issue on detente.

750. Kesavan, K. V. THE VIETNAM WAR AS AN ISSUE IN JAPAN'S RELATIONS WITH THE UNITED STATES. *Int. Studies [India] 1977 16(4): 501-519.* Although the Vietnam War irritated most segments of the Japanese population, it did not impair US-Japanese relations in a serious way. The government extended its moral support to the American position, while the Japanese people and mass media viewed the American venture in Southeast Asia as an "unnecessary intervention." For eight years (1964-73), the Vietnam

War "remained the main focus of the attention of the Japanese people in the realm of foreign affairs." 54 notes. T. P. Linkfield

751. Khlynov, V. OBOSTRENIE IAPONO-AMERIKANSKIKH PROTIVORECHII [The sharpening conflicts in US-Japanese relations]. *Mirovaia Ekonomika i Mezhdunarodnye Otnosheniia [USSR] 1981 (1): 98-103.* Examines increasing economic conflicts between the United States and Japan, 1978-80.

752. Kim, Hong N. THE SATO GOVERNMENT AND THE POLITICS OF OKINAWA REVERSION. *Asian Survey 1973 13(11): 1021-1035.*

753. Kim, Paul Sunik. AMERICAN REFORM OF JAPANESE LOCAL AUTONOMY. *Asian Forum 1974 6(1): 45-62.* Analyzes Japanese local government and its administration in the postwar period. S

754. Kimbara, Samon. ORIENTAMENTI E PROBLEMI DEGLI STUDI SULLA MODERNIZZAZIONE DEL GIAPPONE NEGLI STATI UNITI [Orientations and problems of studies on the modernization of Japan in the United States]. *Riv. Storica Italiana [Italy] 1977 89(2): 376-405.* The United States, represented by Commodore Matthew Perry, opened Japan to the West in the 1850's. Reviews recent US works dealing with Japan from the Meiji Restoration of 1867-68 to the present, mentioning among others the work of Edwin O. Reischauer. 32 notes. J. C. Billigmeier

755. Kishi, Masaaki. IMAGES OF AMERICANS IN JAPANESE POPULAR LITERATURE. *J. of Popular Culture 1975 9(1): 1-13.* Gives a chronological survey of the images of Americans in novels and short stories, 1934-73. Japanese popular literature, which dates from the early 1920's, has only rarely had foreign characters, but the impact of the United States on Japanese popular culture was noticeable in the 1920's and 1930's and increased considerably in the 1960's after the postwar reactions. Except for the wartime images, characterization of Americans has changed little and is generally favorable. They are stereotyped as aggressive but simple-hearted, vulgar but innocent, materialistic but generous. 3 tables, 18 notes. J. D. Falk

756. Kissinger, Henry A. CREATIVITY TOGETHER OR IRRELEVANCE APART. *Atlantic Community Q. 1973/74 11(4): 413-421.* "In his speech to the Pilgrims [in London, 12 December 1973] Secretary of State Kissinger analyzed the difficulties of 1973 and the possibilities of 1974 and beyond for Atlantic relationships. Our era of profound political, strategic, economic and psychological changes requires a revitalization of the relations between a unifying Europe and the US. Closer consultation, common vision and recognition of shared goals are essential to this wider 'special relationship.' Specifically, he proposed the creation of an Energy Action Group of Europe, North America and Japan to begin immediately formulating long-term cooperative measures." J

757. Klimes, Rudolf E. POWER STRUCTURE OF JAPANESE UNIVERSITIES. *Michigan Academician 1975 7(3): 335-345.* Identifies the power

structure of Japanese universities, and compares it with that of American universities. S

758. Korsunskii, A. PROMYSHLENNOST' IAPONII I SSHA: OPYT SOPOSTAVLENIIA [The industry of Japan and the United States: an experimental comparison]. *Mirovaia Ekonomika i Mezhdunarodnye Otnosheniia [USSR] 1975 (1): 77-88.* Compares quantitatively the industrial development of the United States and Japan since the 1960's, which suggests future Japanese rivalry with the United States.

759. Krammer, Arnold. JAPANESE PRISONERS OF WAR IN AMERICA. *Pacific Hist. Rev. 1983 52(1): 67-91.* Few Japanese were taken prisoner largely because they committed suicide rather than surrender. Prisoners of military-intelligence value were brought to interrogation centers for questioning. When prisoners had no further information to divulge, they were shipped to POW camps. Although the Japanese wished to die, once in the camps there were few self-inflicted injuries among them. In 1943 the War Department put prisoners to work, but some Japanese refused to work, suspecting that their labor would assist the American war effort. Very few Japanese attempted to escape. After Japan's surrender Japanese prisoners were indoctrinated in principles of American democracy. Their integration into postwar Japanese society was a long and difficult process. Based on Provost Marshal General's Office records and other primary sources; 62 notes. R. N. Lokken

760. Krauss, Ellis S. and Fendrich, James M. POLITICAL IDENTIFICATION AND BEHAVIOR OF FORMER STUDENT ACTIVISTS. *Japan Interpreter [Japan] 1977 11(3): 313-336.* An analysis of the relationship between the goals and the behavior of student activists and their political attitudes 10-15 years later. The majority of the former generation of student radicals tended, in the United States and elsewhere, to maintain their liberal and radical identification, and, in Japan, continue to participate in politics, engage in political demonstrations, and be employed in the knowledge and human service industries. F. W. Iklé

761. Krummel, John W. METHODIST MISSIONARY GRAVES IN JAPAN. *Methodist Hist. 1977 15(2): 122-130.* Through a study of American Methodist missionaries buried in Japan, the author relates the efforts of these men and women in Japan from 1876 to 1957. Includes biographical data as well as information on the nature of their missionary work. H. L. Calkin

762. Krummel, John W. OF MISSION BOARDS AND MISSIONARIES: THE ORGANIZATION OF AN ANNUAL CONFERENCE IN JAPAN. *Methodist Hist. 1981 19(2): 99-117.* The Methodist Protestant Church of the United States founded its mission in Japan in 1880. From the beginning there was misunderstanding between the missionaries and the Board of Foreign Missions and the Woman's Foreign Missionary Society as well as among the missionaries themselves. The controversy arose over differences about whether Yokohama or Nagoya should be the center of their work in Japan and whether emphasis should be placed on education or evangelism. The confrontation led to the establishment in 1892 of the Japan Mission Annual Conference in

Yokohama, the result of a mood for self-assertive nationalism. Based on the archives on the Methodist Protestant Church; 39 notes. H. L. Calkin

763. Krummel, John W. THE UNION SPIRIT IN JAPAN IN THE 1880'S. *Methodist Hist. 1978 16(3): 152-168.* The Methodist Protestant Church founded its mission in Yokohama in 1880; it was a blend of denominational pride and inter-denominational cooperation. Frederick C. Klein (1857-1926), the first ordained Methodist Protestant male missionary, changed his attitude toward union with other Methodist denominations in Japan from outright rejection in 1883 to active support in 1887 and continued to work for union until he left Japan in 1893. Based on records in the Archives of the United Methodist Church, Lake Junaluska, North Carolina, and the Wesley Theological Seminary, Washington, D.C. 62 notes. H. L. Calkin

764. Kuczewski, André G. [ADMIRAL YAMAMOTO AND THE IMPERIAL NAVY]. *Asian Profile [Hong Kong] 1982 10(5): 507-514.* Reviews Hiroyuki Agawa's *The Reluctant Admiral: Yamamoto and the Imperial Navy* (1979). Contrary to the picture painted by the American press of a boastful man full of hatred and desire for revenge, Yamamoto was a tragic figure, forced to fight a war that he did not want and knew he could not win. The top Japanese naval commander from Pearl Harbor to his death in 1943, Yamamoto was a man of great ability and great modesty. In death as in life he was used by a military clique to further its own ends. 4 notes. J. V. Coutinho

765. Kumamoto, Bob. THE SEARCH FOR SPIES: AMERICAN COUNTERINTELLIGENCE AND THE JAPANESE AMERICAN COMMUNITY 1931-1942. *Amerasia J. 1979 6(2): 45-75.* Counterintelligence activities of the Army and Navy and the Federal Bureau of Investigation (FBI) vis-à-vis Japanese living in the United States, during 1931-42 were marked by excessive paranoia, racism, and stupidity, and fired by the economic jealousy of white Americans. Every Japanese fraternal or business organization was suspected of subversion; old and poor fishermen were irresponsibly accused of having sophisticated espionage equipment aboard. Reliable counterreports have come to light, such as that of Curtis B. Munson of the State Department and FBI Special Agent in Charge N. J. L. Peiper showing no indictable evidence of subversive activities. In spite of this, after Pearl Harbor and US entry into World War II, Japanese citizens of the United States were herded en masse into relocation centers, despoiled of their property and civil rights. 63 notes.
H. F. Thomson

766. Kunadze, G. BANAL'NAIA ISTORIIA [A banal story]. *Aziia i Afrika Segodnia [USSR] 1981 (8): 38-39.* Discusses the role of corruption in Japanese political life, focusing on the Lockheed bribery scandal as a backdrop for an account of corruption involving a Japanese politician and the Liberal Democratic Party.

767. Kurihara, Akira. AMERICAN YOUTH: FROM POLITICS TO RELIGION. *Japan Interpreter [Japan] 1976 11(2): 216-218.* In America and Japan youth are moving away from political activism toward mysticism, reflective introspection, and religious movements such as Transcendental

Meditation, Zen, and Sufism. Institutionalized religion seems to be on the wane, but young people show mounting enthusiasm for popular religious movements, which stress ethical content, including an interest in the "emperor system" and "Japan worship." F. W. Iklé

768. Kyrychenko, V. P. ZAHOSTRENNIA MIZIMPERIALISTYCH-NYKH SUPERECHNOSTEI U LATYNS'KII AMERYTSI V 70-KH ROKAKH [Conflict among imperialists in Latin America in the 1970's]. *Ukrains'kyi Istorychnyi Zhurnal [USSR] 1981 (1): 89-96.* Notes the struggle among imperialist forces of the United States, Japan, and Western Europe in Latin America due to conflicting interests in industry, finance, and trade. Primary Soviet sources; 2 tables, 19 notes. I. Krushelnyckyj

769. Laidlaw, Lansing S. ALEUTIAN EXPERIENCE OF THE "MAD M." *Oregon Hist. Q. 1979 80(1): 30-49.* Although 47 years old, Lansing Laidlaw enlisted in the Coast Guard during World War II. Assigned to the USS *Arthur Middleton*, or "Mad M", Laidlaw saw action in the Aleutians and the South Pacific The *Arthur Middleton* was ordered to the Aleutians and arrived in Constantine Harbor on Amchitka Island 12 January 1943. Soon afterward a storm blew the *Middleton* onto the rocks. The ship was finally refloated three months later and towed to Bremerton, Washington, for repairs. While on the rocks the *Middleton* was attacked frequently by Japanese air forces. However, despite the fact that the ship was aground the air attacks inflicted no serious damage. 8 illus. D. R. McDonald

770. Larsen, Lawrence H. WAR BALLOONS OVER THE PRAIRIE: THE JAPANESE INVASION OF SOUTH DAKOTA. *South Dakota Hist. 1979 9(2): 103-115.* In project FUGO, the Japanese launched thousands of armed balloons between late 1944 and August 1945 which were intended to land and explode in the United States. Of the 300 balloon landings, at least nine dropped on South Dakota. Because of military censorship, nothing about the balloons appeared in South Dakota newspapers until after the war. This attack caused an additional expenditure of time and money for American defense measures, but did not affect the outcome of the war, even though it represented the only prolonged threat against the continental United States during World War II. Primary sources; illus., 5 photos, 20 notes.
P. L. McLaughlin

771. Larson, Sarah. EAST INDIA SQUADRON LETTERS: A PASSAGE OF ARMS. *Prologue 1981 13(1): 39-48.* Discusses the Navy Squadron Letters, 1846-49, focusing on the incident of the arrival on the coast of Japan of 16 shipwrecked survivors of the American whaler *Lagoda* which left Massachusetts in August of 1846. The survivors were detained for formal investigation and remained hostages of the Japanese government. Describes their day-to-day activities, including many attempts to escape captivity since they were unaware that the Navy sloop of war *Preble* had been delegated by the American government to rescue them. On 17 April 1849 Captain Glynn and the *Preble* arrived to collect the crew and on 11 June, after successfully negotiating with the Japanese, the captain sailed for America with the survivors. These records provide insight into the daily experience of the naval

crew, the overland migration from east to west, and vessel routes and destinations. Based on Navy Squadron Letters, 1841-86; 6 illus., photo, 33 notes.
M. A. Kascus

772. Lauren, Paul Gordon. HUMAN RIGHTS IN HISTORY: DIPLOMACY AND RACIAL EQUALITY AT THE PARIS PEACE CONFERENCE. *Diplomatic Hist. 1978 2(3): 257-278.* Describes the efforts of the Japanese delegation at the Paris Peace Conference (1919) to have a statement on racial equality included in the League of Nations Covenant. Japanese assurances that they would not use such a clause as a wedge for gaining admission of Japanese immigrants to other countries failed to impress Australian Prime Minister and White Australia advocate William Morris Hughes. In the end, Woodrow Wilson (a Southerner who introduced segregation into US federal departments) killed the Japanese proposal, which 11 of 17 League of Nations commission members supported, by means of a parliamentary ploy which involved palpable inconsistency. Based on archival and other primary sources, including the Japanese press as cited in contemporary issues of the English-language *Japan Times;* 143 notes.
L. W. Van Wyk

773. Lawcock, Larry. COMMODORE BIDDLE AND MR. TAGUCHI. *Guam Recorder 1978 8: 12-14.* Discusses three aspects of Japanese relations with neighbors in the Pacific Area: 1) a Japanese ballad written in 1846 describes the anticipated visit of Commodore James Biddle to Japan: 2) Taguchi Ukichi's commercial expedition to the Mariana Islands in 1890, which led to a crisis in Japanese-Spanish relations by 1897; and 3) the employment of Japanese valets and servants by US naval officers in Guam in 1899.

774. Lee, Sang-Chul. THE AMERICAN IMAGE OF RELATIONS WITH JAPAN PROJECTED IN THREE U.S. DAILIES. *Gazette [Netherlands] 1979 25(1): 31-45.* The image of Japan in American newspapers over the last 75 years has been inconsistent and dependent on current relations between the two countries. By content analysis of a random sampling of issues of the *New York Times,* the *Chicago Tribune,* and the *Los Angeles Times,* the biases of the American press and the image of Japan projected are evident. US officials were quoted more often than Japanese officials on issues which concerned both countries.
W. A. Wiegand

775. Leonard, Thomas M. STANLEY K. HORNBECK: MAJOR DETERRENT TO AMERICA-JAPANESE SUMMITRY, 1941. *Towson State J. of Internat. Affairs 1974 8(2): 113-121.*

776. Lester, Richard K. U.S.-JAPANESE NUCLEAR RELATIONS: STRUCTURAL CHANGE AND POLITICAL STRAIN. *Asian Survey 1982 22(5): 417-433.* Although attention has focused on US nonproliferation policy and its impact on the Japanese nuclear energy program, civil nuclear policy also has provided a serious point of contention in US-Japanese relations in recent years. Nuclear recession in the United States has contrasted with steadily increasing reliance on nuclear energy in Japan. These contradictory national trends will influence the future direction of the Japanese nuclear

energy program and the future course of US-Japanese nuclear relations. Based on newspapers, documents; 21 notes. M. A. Eide

777. Levy, Walter J. AN ATLANTIC-JAPANESE ENERGY POLICY. *Atlantic Community Q. 1973 11(2): 188-204.* "Outlines in startling detail the scope of the energy crises, both from the standpoint of the sources of energy and of the money to pay for it. He sees the need for an Atlantic-Japanese Energy Policy and presents an outline for such a policy." Shortened review of a paper to appear in *The Atlantic Challenge,* to be published by Charles Knight, London. J

778. Levy, Walter J. AN ATLANTIC-JAPANESE ENERGY POLICY. *Foreign Policy 1973 (11): 159-190.*

779. Libby, Justin H. THE AMERICAN-JAPANESE RELATIONS AND THE COMING WAR IN THE PACIFIC: A CONGRESSIONAL VIEW. *Pacific Hist. 1978 22(4): 379-390.* A study of congressional opinion regarding Japan during the final months of peace preceding the attack on Pearl Harbor. Earlier hesitancy to antagonize Japan was, by autumn, replaced by a climate of opinion favorable to belligerent measures. Four forces had effected the change: Japan's continuing threat to the status quo in Asia, sympathy for China's deteriorating plight, Tokyo's signing the Tripartite Pact, and American pressure groups lobbying for sanctioning legislation for action. An analysis of statements and calls to action by congressional leaders indicated a rapid shrinking of the influence of noninterventionists. Already, before Pearl Harbor, Congress had reversed itself, and was ready for confrontation. 50 notes.
R. V. Ritter

780. Libby, Justin H. ANTI-JAPANESE SENTIMENT IN THE PACIFIC NORTHWEST: SENATOR SCHELLENBACH AND CONGRESSMAN COFFEE ATTEMPT TO EMBARGO JAPAN. *Mid-America 1976 58(3): 167-174.* Analyzes the efforts in the 1930's of Senator Lewis B. Schellenbach and Congressman John M. Coffee, Democrats of Washington State, to enact an American embargo of Japan. Both were concerned with the fishing interests of their state, and this led to their anti-Japanese efforts. Both were noninterventionists and desired to keep the United States out of a war with Japan. A militarily weak Japan was also one of their objectives. Eventually, an anti-Japanese initiative was taken by Franklin D. Roosevelt in 1940, and it achieved what Schwellenbach and Coffee failed to do in Congress with outside support. Based on archival material, news accounts, and speeches; 22 notes.
J. M. Lee

781. Libby, Justin H. THE IRRECONCILABLE CONFLICT: KEY PITTMAN AND JAPAN DURING THE INTERWAR YEARS. *Nevada Hist. Soc. Q. 1975 18(3): 128-139.* Analyzes the anti-Japanese views of Key Pittman during the period between the two world wars. Pittman, Chairman of the Senate Committee on Foreign Relations during the 1930's, worked unsuccessfully for stronger American resistance to Japanese aggression in the Far East. Based on primary and secondary sources; photo, 53 notes.
H. T. Lovin

782. Libby, Justin H. SENATORS KING AND THOMAS AND THE COMING WAR WITH JAPAN. *Utah Hist. Q. 1974 42(4): 370-380.* Growing enmity toward Japan during the interwar years was mingled with hopes for renewed accord, and Utah's senators reflected these opposing views. Senator William King was fond of China and hostile toward Japan. Senator Elbert Thomas was a student of Japan, but as Japanese aggression intensified in the Orient, he moved gradually to an anti-Japanese position. By 1940 both men were in agreement. 3 photos, 42 notes. V. L. Human

783. Lindsey, David. PERRY IN JAPAN. *Am. Hist. Illus. 1978 13(5): 4-8, 44-49.* Describes the intricate diplomatic maneuvering by Matthew C. Perry, resulting in US initiation of trade and diplomatic relations with Japan, 1853.

784. Lord, Walter. ORDEAL AT VELLA LAVELLA. *Am. Heritage 1977 28(4): 30-43.* In 1943, American survivors of a naval battle in the Solomon Islands landed on Vella Lavella. After months of avoiding contact with Japanese forces occupying the island, the men were rescued by the US Navy. 12 illus., map. B. J. Paul

785. Lummis, C. Douglas. JAPANESE PACIFISM UNDER THE U.S. WAR MACHINE: THE LATENT FORCE. *Bull. of Peace Proposals [Norway] 1982 13(1): 43-48.* Although the American occupation of Japan has ended, the Japanese people have not gained full political sovereignty. Through the Japan-US Security Treaty, the United States maintains control over broad outlines of Japanese foreign policy. Moreover, Japan continues to harbor US strategic bases. Nevertheless, Japanese pacifism remains strong and the majority of the people still may opt for it. 4 notes. R. B. Orr

786. Lyon, Jessi Sanders. HUERTA AND ADACHI: AN INTERPRETATION OF JAPANESE-MEXICAN RELATIONS, 1913-1914. *Americas (Acad. of Am. Franciscan Hist.) 1978 34(4): 476-489.* Anti-Japanese legislation in California and the US refusal to recognize the government of Victoriano Huerta favored the development of closer relations between Huerta and Japan. The diplomatic encouragement that he received from Japanese minister to Mexico Adachi Minechiro strengthened Huerta's resistance to US pressure, which in turn forced the United States to take overt action against him. Based on US and Japanese diplomatic records, and published sources; 65 notes.
D. Bushnell

787. MacEachron, David. THE UNITED STATES AND JAPAN: THE BILATERAL POTENTIAL. *Foreign Affairs 1982-83 61(2): 400-415.* Maintaining the relationship between the United States and Japan is important; failure to do so would adversely affect world stability. Considers the economic relationship. Based on US government agencies' reports; 4 notes.
A. A. Englard

788. Maddox, Robert J. BANDITS OVER CLARK FIELD. *Am. Hist. Illus. 1974 9(3): 20-27.* In the Japanese attack on Clark Field, Philippines,

immediately after the attack on Pearl Harbor in December 1941, the loss of US men and materiel in the attack revealed basic unpreparedness for war.

789. Maeda, Laura. LIFE AT MINIDOKA: A PERSONAL HISTORY OF THE JAPANESE-AMERICAN RELOCATION. *Pacific Hist. 1976 20(4): 379-387.* During World War II Japanese American Tomeji Mukaida and his family were sent to a relocation camp at Minidoka, Idaho organized by military procedure. Hardships were numerous, and some stigma have remained to the present. 2 illus., biblio. G. L. Olson

790. Magdoff, Harry. EXPANSIÓN IMPERIALISTA: ACCIDENTE Y DESIGNIO [Imperialist expansion: accident and design]. *Investigación Econ. [Mexico] 1975 34(134): 225-238.* Analyzes US expansion and imperialism from the 19th century, with particular reference to the Far East since World War II.

791. Manchester, William. THE MAN WHO COULD SPEAK JAPANESE. *Am. Heritage 1975 27(1): 36-39, 91-95.* The story of Harold Dumas, a con-artist who convinced the Marines he could speak Japanese. Serving in the 29th Marine battalion in the Pacific, Dumas was exposed when he tried his line on a graduate of one of the military's Japanese language schools. 2 illus.
J. F. Paul

792. Manoff, Robert Karl. THE MEDIA: NUCLEAR SECRECY VS. DEMOCRACY. *Bull. of the Atomic Sci. 1984 40(1): 26-29.* US and Japanese journalists have been hindered by the secrecy surrounding nuclear arms; the values of the "nuclear regime" run counter to those of a free press and democracy.

793. Marumoto, Masaji. VIGNETTE OF EARLY HAWAII-JAPAN RELATIONS: HIGHLIGHTS OF KING KALAKAUA'S SOJOURN IN JAPAN ON HIS TRIP AROUND THE WORLD AS RECORDED IN HIS PERSONAL DIARY. *Hawaiian J. of Hist. 1976 10: 52-63.* In 1881 Kalakaua embarked upon a trip around the world which took nine months and nine days to complete. The author consulted a diary kept by the King relating to experiences in Japan. The 48-page narrative is in the Bishop Museum Library in Honolulu. Kalakaua intended to visit Japan incognito but changed his mind and allowed his royal standard to be hoisted on the masthead of the liner he was traveling on. He was given state honors, received by the Emperor, and conducted on tours of Tokyo. Provides extracts from the diary. R. Alvis

794. Mason, Robert. EYEWITNESS. *US Naval Inst. Pro. 1982 108(6): 40-45.* Credits Lieutenant Commander Robert E. Dixon with informing the Federal Bureau of Investigation that he saw Commander Morton Seligman show *Chicago Tribune* reporter Stanley Johnston the highly classified summary of Japanese plans for the June 1942 attack on Midway Island. Johnston's subsequent publication of the information, had it reached Japan, would have disclosed that the United States had broken the Japanese naval code. Based on an interview with Dixon. K. J. Bauer

795. Mattiace, John M. JOE FOSS AND GUADALCANAL. *Marine Corps Gazette 1973 57(6): 43-47.* Describes the actions of Captain Joseph J. Foss in the air battle for Guadalcanal, 13-25 October 1942, when he shot down 16 planes.

796. Matveev, V. "TREKHSTORONNIAIA STRATEGIIA" I EE EVOLIUTSIIA ["Trilateral strategy" and its evolution]. *Mirovaia Ekonomika i Mezhdunarodnye Otnosheniia [USSR] 1977 (3): 14-24.* The meager results of conferences among the United States, Western Europe, and Japan in 1974 and 1975 suggest that political and economic conflict results in closed blocks of capitalist forces.

797. McAlmon, George. AMERICAN MANUFACTURERS ARE LOSING WORLD MARKETS. *Center Mag. 1979 12(6): 8-12.* Discusses the decline in the quantity and quality of US products in the face of increased competition from superior technology and engineering from West Germany and Japan; 1970's.

798. McCandless, Bruce. INCIDENT IN THE NANPO SHOTO. *US Naval Inst. Pro. 1973 99(7): 67-77.* In February, 1945, the US Navy destroyer *Gregory* rescued three American airmen floating in the sea near the Japanese occupied island of Chichi Jima. Based on the reminiscences of the author, who was serving as commanding officer of the *Gregory*; 3 illus., map.

J. K. Ohl

799. McCoart, J. J. OKINAWA: PREFECTURE OF JAPAN. *Marine Corps Gazette 1974 58(4): 25-28.* Presents the history of the island, 1200-1975.

S

800. McDermott, Jeanne. ROBOTS ARE PLAYING NEW ROLES AS THEY TAKE A HAND IN OUR AFFAIRS. *Smithsonian 1983 14(8): 61-69.* Discusses US and Japanese progress in robotics.

801. McKinnon, Ronald I. DOLLAR STABILIZATION AND AMERICAN MONETARY POLICY. *Am. Econ. Rev. 1980 70(2): 382-386.* Industrial and nonindustrial economics make different demands on the dollar. Joint action by the United States, Japan, and West Germany would adjust their domestic money supplies to shifting international demands, and would reduce official intervention. Covers 1945-78. 10 ref. D. K. Pickens

802. McMorris, Penny. THE CRAZY QUILT: A FABRIC SCRAPBOOK. *Art & Antiques 1983 6(5): 42-49.* Chronicles, with photographs, the late 19th-century fad for handmade quilts of irregular design, citing especially Japanese motifs and influences.

803. McNeil, W. K. LAFCADIO HEARN, AMERICAN FOLKLORIST. *J. of Am. Folklore 1978 91(362): 947-967.* Lafcadio Hearn (1850-1904), an American amateur folklorist and professional literary artist, made major contributions in collecting exotic legends and folk beliefs from Creole New

Orleans, Martinique, and Japan. Based on Hearn's published work and secondary sources; 57 notes. W. D. Piersen

804. McNelly, Theodore. AMERICAN POLITICAL TRADITIONS AND JAPAN'S POSTWAR CONSTITUTION. *World Affairs 1977 140(1): 58-66.* General Douglas MacArthur demanded that the postwar Japanese government accept US-drafted Constitution which reflected the basic principles of popular sovereignty, civilian political control, judicial review, and universalism that are enumerated in America's fundamental law.

805. Mechling, Charles, Jr. JAPAN AND THE UNITED STATES: THE BRITTLE ALLIANCE. *Virginia Q. Rev. 1981 57(1): 15-31.* The so-called alliance imposed on Japan after World War II no longer fits world conditions. Moreover, it is being used, especially in the last five years, to force Japan to conform to the shifting political and economic needs of the United States. The alliance is brittle because the United States understands neither the Japanese ethnocentric outlook nor its consensus approach. Details US reaction to and meddling with Japan's extremely successful economy and its ignoring of Japan's legitimate defense concerns. The United States urgently needs to revise its policy toward Japan. O. H. Zabel

806. Meltzer, Ronald I. COLOR-TV SETS AND U.S.-JAPANESE RELATIONS: PROBLEMS OF TRADE-ADJUSTMENT POLICYMAKING. *Orbis 1979 23(2): 421-446.* A study of the problems in trade adjustment policy in the US-Japan color TV controversy. Analyzes the conditions which led to trade adjustment difficulties, noting the pressures, the constraints, and the concerns facing the US and Japanese governments in dealing with this situation. These governments' handling of the evolving difficulties and events in this controversy and their very limited results provide little basis for hope. 73 notes. R. V. Ritter

807. Mendel, Douglas H., Jr. OKINAWAN REVERSION IN RETROSPECT. *Pacific Affairs [Canada] 1975 48(3): 398-412.* Analyzes the impact of the reversion to Japanese control on native Okinawans after governance by the US military, 1945-72. Deals with the ambivalent cultural self-perceptions and Okinawan expectations of Japan, the economic costs of returning to Japanese control, and the issue of continuing US military bases and the presence of 5,500 Japan Self-Defense Forces on Okinawa. Based on interviews in Okinawa and Japan and poll data from Naha newspapers; table, 37 notes.
S. H. Frank

808. Mendl, Wolf. JAPAN: THE RELUCTANT GIANT. *World Survey [Great Britain] 1974 (71): 1-17.* Describes the influence of domestic politics and economic growth on Japan's foreign policy and trade since the end of the US occupation in 1952; also discusses US occupation.

809. Mérigot, J.-G. LES ÉTATS-UNIS, LE JAPON ET LA RÉPUBLIQUE FÉDÉRALE D'ALLEMAGNE SUR LE CHEMIN DE LA REPRISE [The United States, Japan, and West Germany on the road to recovery]. *Défense Natl. [France] 1976 32(7): 109-118.* Compares and contrasts

economic development in the United States, Japan, and West Germany, 1973-76, and its effect on international relations.

810. Merillat, Herbert Christian. THE "ULTRA WEAPON" AT GUADALCANAL. *Marine Corps Gazette 1982 66(9): 44-49.* Discusses the importance to the US Navy at the 1942 battle of Guadalcanal of information about Japanese movements and battle plans gathered from intercepted Japanese radio messages.

811. Mieczkowski, Bogdan and Mieczkowski, Seiko. HORACE CAPRON AND THE DEVELOPMENT OF HOKKAIDO: A REAPPRAISAL. *J. of the Illinois State Hist. Soc. 1974 67(5): 487-504.* The Meiji government hired Horace Capron in 1871 to develop the economic potential of Hokkaido island. Capron, who was agricultural commissioner under President Andrew Johnson, recommended controversial measures that ranged from importing new agricultural techniques to education and land reform. This program suited neither the Japanese psychology nor the island's state of development. After Capron left Japan in 1875, the government abandoned most of his programs. Yet the official Kuroda report praised his mission in order to "save face," and the Japanese, who came to esteem American advice, prospered from their subsequent modernizing efforts. Based on the Capron memoirs, Japanese documents, and secondary sources; 5 illus., 86 notes. W. R. Hively

812. Mikesh, Robert C. THE EMPEROR'S ENVOYS. *Air Force Mag. 1975 58(8): 62-67.* Two Japanese members of the delegation to General Douglas MacArthur's headquarters in Manila describe their part in the surrender arrangements at at the end of World War II.

813. Mikulín, Antonín. JAPONSKO V PLÁNECH USA A NATO [Japan in the plans of the United States and NATO]. *Hist. a Vojenství [Czechoslovakia] 1981 30(4): 139-166.* US encouragement of Japanese militarization in defiance of the Potsdam Agreement is a major part of NATO's military strategy to trap the USSR between two fronts in the event of a future global war. Secondary sources; 52 notes. G. E. Pergl/S

814. Miller, Alan. THE INFORMATION IMBALANCE. *Japan Interpreter [Japan] 1978 12(2): 254-259.* When 18-year-old Aoki Yasuteru began his year as an exchange student in a northeastern American high school, he was often asked about life in China. On one occasion he was approached by a classmate whose father had been to Tokyo. Aoki's smile quickly changed to a look of surprise when the boy then inquired, "Isn't that close to Japan?" The bright, personable, young Aoki handled these disconcerting encounters with circumspection. But inside he felt hurt. "While Japanese are so curious about the States, Americans don't know about Japan and knowing about Japan is not very important," he commented after his return to Tokyo. J

815. Minear, Richard H. CROSS-CULTURAL PERCEPTION AND WORLD WAR II: AMERICAN JAPANISTS OF THE 1940'S AND THEIR IMAGES OF JAPAN. *Int. Studies Q. 1980 24(4): 555-580.* An examination of the writings of six Americans who wrote about Japan in the 1940's suggests

that those authors who were most fully committed to the defense of the American way of life were least able to write objectively. The attitudes of Ruth Benedict, John M. Maki, and Edwin O. Reischauer were generally condescending and pejorative, in contrast to those of Charles B. Fahs, John F. Embree, and Helen Mears, who were sufficiently critical of the United States that they could take a sympathetic view of Japan. 58 notes. E. S. Palais

816. Mitson, Betty E. LOOKING BACK IN ANGUISH: ORAL HISTORY AND JAPANESE-AMERICAN EVACUATION. *Oral Hist. Rev. 1974: 24-51.* Discusses West Coast oral history projects on the evacuation and incarceration of Japanese Americans during World War II with details from the taped experiences of Togo Tanaka and Karl and Elaine Yoneda. Illus., 53 notes. D. A. Yanchisin

817. Miura, Yō-ichi. SENRYŌ-KA KEISATSU KAIKAKU NO ICHIDANMEN: 1947-NEN 9-GATSU 16-NICHI MACARTHUR SHOKAN NO SEIRITSU KATEI [One phase of the police reorganization under the Allied occupation: the background of MacArthur's letter of 16 September 1947]. *Rekishigaku Kenkyū [Japan] 1981 (498): 35-51.* Douglas MacArthur's long letter to Prime Minister Tetsu Katayama in September 1947, described how to reform the police system and urged immediate implementation of that plan. Focuses upon the decisionmaking process regarding military occupation polices prior to MacArthur's letter, and thereby clarifies that process in terms of both the opposition between the Government Section (GS) and the Second Staff (G II) and the compromise finally attained due to their shared anti-communist feelings. 11 notes. R. Shibasaki

818. Miyamoto, S. Frank. THE FORCED EVACUATION OF THE JAPANESE MINORITY DURING WORLD WAR II. *J. of Social Issues 1973 29(2): 11-32.* "Three general causes of the Japanese American evacuation are examined. *Collective disposition* considers the antagonism toward immigrants, special characteristics of California politics, economic competition, segregation and racial stereotypes, and Japanese American international relations as conditions which instituted a persistent anti-Japanese attitude on the West Coast. *Situational factors* include the tendency to suspect treachery of all Japanese following Pearl Harbor and the time pressures which curtailed deliberation by government officials on the evacuation question. *Collective interaction* considers the interaction among the main elements which produced the evacuation decision. A short section describes the relocation centers and the evacuees' reaction to detention." J

819. Moore, Jamie W. ECONOMIC INTERESTS AND AMERICAN-JAPANESE RELATIONS: THE PETROLEUM CONTROVERSY. *Historian 1973 35(4): 551-567.* In March 1934, the Japanese Diet enacted legislation taking the nation's oil industry out of the hands of foreigners. During three years of diplomatic controversy the United States followed a policy which avoided deference to a single corporate interest while defending the right of Americans to trade in the Far East. The incident reveals general aspects of contemporary US State Department policy. The United States believed that the Nationalist government would not be able to continue in power in China, and

820. Moore, Ray A. THE OCCUPATION OF JAPAN AS HISTORY: SOME RECENT RESEARCH. *Monumenta Nipponica [Japan] 1981 36(3): 317-328.* The occupation period has now become a point of departure for the study of postwar Japan, since it has clearly shaped present Japanese values and behavior. This article studies the major approaches, new perspectives, and Japanese conceptions of the American military occupation, discussing works dealing with such matters as general studies on occupation planning and policy, the occupation as seen as part of Japanese history rather than American, and the reversal of course taken by the United States in 1948.

F. W. Iklé

821. Morgan, William Michael. THE ANTI-JAPANESE ORIGINS OF THE HAWAIIAN ANNEXATION TREATY OF 1897. *Diplomatic Hist. 1982 6(1): 23-44.* Discusses the impact of the Japanese threat to Hawaii on the American decision to acquire the islands. Japanese nationals constituted a quarter of the archipelago's population by 1897. After Hawaii abridged the immigrants' civil rights and began to severely restrict immigration from Japan, Tokyo protested and sent a warship to Honolulu in May 1897. Washington then ordered the navy to prepare war plans, sent ships to Hawaii, and secretly drew up the annexation treaty. Japan significantly increased the pressure on Hawaii in June, thereby causing the United States to rapidly unveil the treaty as a warning against further Japanese action. Based on State and Navy department records, documents in the state archives of Hawaii, and other primary sources; 96 notes.

T. J. Heston

822. Morita, Akio. DO COMPANIES NEED LAWYERS? *Japan Q. [Japan] 1983 30(1): 2-8.* The Sony Company's experiences in the United States point out the different perceptions of contracts. In America, where there are 15 times as many lawyers as in Japan, the company endured legal harassment, and needed legal services all the time. In Japan, much greater harmony prevails. Lawyers are a handicap to business.

F. W. Iklé

823. Morrow, James. OPENING THE DOOR: THE MORROW JOURNAL. *Am. Hist. Illus. 1978 13(5): 40-42.* Excerpts from the travel diaries of Dr. James Morrow, an agriculturalist who accompanied the Matthew Perry expedition into Japan in 1854, offer impressions of Japan and relate Japanese reaction to a miniature steam locomotive and telegraph line and other inventions.

824. Mushakoji, Kinhide. LE JAPON DEVANT LES ÉTATS-UNIS: 1ère DU MALENTENDU [Japan confronts the United States: the first misunderstanding]. *Esprit [France] 1973 (2): 535-542.* A study of the modern relationship between Japan and the United States, stressing the growing need for a redefinition of politics to include the concept of multipolarity in negotiations. With the Nixon Doctrine, the United States adopted a new position toward

China and the Soviet Union, forcing US-Japanese relations to enter a new phase. The US image as "Big Brother" and previous strong ties are diminishing. S. Sevilla

825. Mushakōji, Kinhide. THE SOURCES OF THE IMAGE GAP. *Japan Interpreter [Japan] 1973 8(1): 88-95.* Notes need to transcend the particularistic approach by both Japan and the United States in their mutual relations. New images both in a multipolar and a multilateral context should be created by means of multichannel transmission to overcome the growing antagonism and disillusionment between the two countries. F. W. Iklé

826. Nagai, Yōnosuke. CONFLICTING PERCEPTIONS: JAPAN AND THE U.S. *Japan Interpreter [Japan] 1973 8(1): 76-87.* The perception gap between the United States and Japan is illustrated by the divergent reactions of both countries to the Nixon shocks, the overture to China, and the dollar defense measures. The sudden reentry of Japan into international society is seen as a danger and economic threat by Americans, while the Japanese are confused in regard to Japan's self-image. Both countries should develop a system of international cooperation balancing the economic policy with environmental disruptions and resource development. F. W. Iklé

827. Napierała, Jerzy. TRANSFER TECHNIKI I ORGANIZACJI POMIĘDZY CENTRAMI PRZEMYSŁOWYMI ŚWIATA KAPITALISTYCZNEGO [The transfer of organizational information and technology between capitalist countries]. *Przegląd Zachodni [Poland] 1976 32(4): 161-195.* Discusses forms of technological transfer between the United States, Western Europe, and Japan with special emphasis on licence agreements as the optimum form of cooperation. The United States is the main exporter of new technology and organizational information and it has the largest expenditure on development and research, while Japan is the main importer of licences. The high level of exchange is due to the lack of serious restrictive barriers between capitalist industrial centers, except in the fields of nuclear energy, armaments, and space research. 5 tables, 54 notes. M. K. Montgomery

828. Navarro, Vicente. THE CRISIS OF INTERNATIONAL CAPITALISM. *Social Policy 1980 11(2): 12-15.* Discusses the challenge since the 1960's to the strength of US capital and industry from the working class in Western capitalist countries, competition from Germany and Japan, "the appearance of forces in the peripheral countries that demanded a higher share of the plunder in those countries," the threat of revolutionary anti-imperialist and anti-capitalist movements in countries peripheral to world capitalism, and the growth of socialism as an alternative to the world capitalist system, and the US response to the challenge.

829. Neu, Charles E. AMERICAN FOREIGN POLICY BETWEEN THE WARS. *Reviews in Am. Hist. 1975 3(3): 376-379.* Reviews Arnold A. Offner's *The Origins of the Second World War: American Foreign Policy and World Politics, 1917-1941* (New York: Praeger, 1975). Notes the weaknesses in Offner's multinational approach, assesses his analysis of the making of US foreign policy in the 1920's and 1930's, and suggests that his is not so much an

examination of the origins of World War II as a study of US foreign policy and world politics, especially in Europe and Japan, 1917-41.

830. Ney, Virgil. TOWNSEND HARRIS: AMERICAN DIPLOMAT EXTRAORDINARY. *Daughters of the Am. Revolution Mag. 1974 108(5): 410-417.* Describes the efforts of Harris, first American Consul General to Japan, in 1856-58. S

831. Nezadorov, G. V. AN AMERICAN HISTORIAN ON SOVIET-JAPANESE RELATIONS IN THE 1920'S. *Soviet Studies in Hist. 1973 12(2): 90-98.* Discusses the American view of Soviet-Japanese relations as expressed by George Alexander Lensen in his *Japanese Recognition of the USSR: Soviet-Japanese Relations, 1921-1930* (Tallahassee, Tennessee, 1970).

832. Nickel, Herman. THE REDISCOVERY OF JAPAN. *Foreign Policy 1974 (14): 157-163.* The US and European foreign policy establishments' "discovery and acceptance of Japan as a major factor in world affairs" does not necessarily mean that the Japanese are equally ready to assume great power responsibility. S

833. Nikolayev, N. and Alexandrov, A. JAPANESE-AMERICAN RELATIONS: OLD PROBLEMS, NEW TENDENCIES. *Far Eastern Affairs [USSR] 1983 (1): 72-87.* Japanese-American situations of the 1980's with roots in the 1970's include trade problems and the US desire for stronger but circumscribed, Japanese military forces.

834. Niksch, Larry A. DEFENSE BURDEN-SHARING IN THE PACIFIC: U.S. EXPECTATIONS AND JAPANESE RESPONSES. *Asian Affairs: An Am. Rev. 1981 8(6): 331-345.* Compares and contrasts the approaches and content of US-Japanese dialogue on defense matters in the Carter and Reagan administrations. Discusses Japanese responsibilities (sea control, mining and port-blockading strategies, air defense screening) and US responsibilities (possible offensive operations toward eastern Siberia, defense of South Korea), Japanese political environment and pacificism, Pacific power equilibrium, and US and Japanese financial considerations. Based on press and government sources; 15 notes. R. B. Mendel

835. Nishihara, Masashi. WIE LANGE HÄLT DIE "YOSHIDA-DOKTRIN" NOCH? JAPAN VOR DER NOTWENDIGKEIT AUSSENPOLITISCHER ANPASSUNGEN [How long will the Yoshida doctrine hold? Japan and the necessity of foreign policy adaptations]. *Europa Archiv [West Germany] 1978 33(14): 441-452.* Prime Minister Shigeru Yoshida posited the policy of close cooperation with the United States in the immediate post-World War II period. This policy has required readjustment given the Chinese-American rapprochment and increasing Japanese domestic instability in the 1970's.

836. Nolley, Kenneth S. THE WESTERN AS JIDAI-GEKI. *Western Am. Literature 1976 11(3): 231-238.* Compares an American film and its reflection on our national experience with an example from the *jidai-geki*, a parallel

national genre of Japan. The two films were *The Magnificent Seven* and *Seven Samurai*.
M. Genung

837. Norquist, Ernest O. THREE YEARS IN PARADISE: A GI'S PRISONER-OF-WAR DIARY, 1942-1945. *Wisconsin Mag. of Hist. 1979 63(1): 2-35.* After the US Army surrendered during the siege of Bataan in the Philippines, the author was taken prisoner by the Japanese. His diary, partly reprinted here from his manuscripts at the State Historical Society of Wisconsin, reflects the prison life he led as a medic, on various work details, and in a foundry, first at Cabanatuan and then in Japan. 16 illus., 3 notes.
N. C. Burckel

838. Notehelfer, F. G. L. L. JANES IN JAPAN: CARRIER OF AMERICAN CULTURE AND CHRISTIANITY. *J. of Presbyterian Hist. 1975 53(4): 313-338.* Describes the assignment of Leroy Lansing Janes, former soldier and teacher, as a private educator in Kumamoto in the 1870's. Janes' personal integrity and self-discipline appealed greatly to the former samurai youth whom he taught in the Meiji Reformation. Permission was denied him to teach the Christian faith formally, but he was able to inculcate in his students great principles of Americanization and the Christian faith, which he identified as one and the same. At first his teaching embraced agriculture, science, technology, and literature, but later he was able to bring in the Bible and Christian teachings. Thirty-five of his students took the Hanaoka Oath which left an indelible mark on the Protestant movement of the Meiji period. Ultimately every student who took the oath went on to an important public career in the Church, publishing, education, business, or government. Primary and secondary sources; 95 notes.
H. M. Parker, Jr.

839. Ohira, Masayoshi. PROSPECTS FOR U.S.-JAPAN RELATIONS: THE DURABLE PARTNERSHIP. *Freedom at Issue 1974 (27): 10-12, 18.* Discusses foreign relations, trade and economic interdependence between Japan and the United States in the 1970's.

840. Ohrn, Karin Becker. WHAT YOU SEE IS WHAT YOU GET: DOROTHEA LANGE AND ANSEL ADAMS AT MANZANAR. *Journalism Hist. 1977 4(1): 15-22.* Discusses the photographic histories by Dorothea Lange and Ansel Adams of Japanese Americans interned at the Manzanar War Relocation Center in California during World War II and their different interpretations of the camps.

841. Okamura, Raymond Y. THE AMERICAN CONCENTRATION CAMPS: A COVER-UP THROUGH EUPHEMISTIC TERMINOLOGY. *J. of Ethnic Studies 1982 10(3): 95-109.* The use of euphemistic official language as a cover for the embarrassing truth of the concentration camp system for Japanese Americans during World War II was a deliberate linguistic deception fostered by the US government and institutionalized by numerous scholars thereafter. The process bears a striking resemblance to the propaganda techniques of the Third Reich. Calling the camps "evacuation" or "relocation" centers accomplished a number of objectives—sidetracking legal and constitutional challenges, allowing the government to maintain a decent public image,

leading the victims into willing cooperation, permitting white civilian employees to work without self-reproach, and keeping the historical record in the government's favor. To this day the story needs rewriting. Government archives, published documents, secondary works; 33 notes. G. J. Bobango

842. Okihiro, Gary Y. JAPANESE RESISTANCE IN AMERICA'S CONCENTRATION CAMPS: A REEVALUATION. *Amerasia J.* 1973 1(2): 20-34. "Proposes that the assumptions of the revisionist histories of slave and colonized groups provide a more realistic basis for an analysis of Japanese reaction to concentration camp authority than do the older notions of Japanese 'loyalty' and helplessness." S

843. Okihiro, Gary Y. TULE LAKE UNDER MARTIAL LAW: A STUDY IN JAPANESE RESISTANCE. *J. of Ethnic Studies* 1977 5(3): 71-85. Examines the "orthodox interpretation" of the wartime internment of American Japanese, and the simplistic categorizations of Issei, Kibei, and Nisei found at the base of most treatments of the topic. Also attacks the "myth of the model minority" relative to Japanese Americans, especially as seen in *The Spoilage* by Thomas and Nishimoto. Analyzes the period of military rule by the Army at the Tule Lake Camp for "segregees" or "disloyals" during November 1943-January 1944, with the arrest and detention of the democratically elected representative body for the internees, the *Daihyo Sha Kai,* and the substitution of Army-named "block managers" for maintaining order. The authorities manipulated the famous "Status Quo" ballot of 11 January 1944, but the basic unity of purpose among factions of the internees did not waver; various groupings among the prisoners simply held different approaches to the same goal, that of gaining respect for their basic human rights and bringing reforms into camp administration. Primary sources; 44 notes.

G. J. Bobango

844. Okita, Saburo. REDUCING JAPANESE-U.S. FRICTION. *Washington Q.* 1983 6(2): 115-119. The balance of payments is a multilateral rather than a bilateral problem, and, further, other activities can compensate for some imbalance.

845. Okun, Nathan. ARMOR AND ITS APPLICATION TO WARSHIPS. *Warship Int.* 1976 13(2): 113-122; 1977 14(2): 98-103; 1978 15(4): 284-293. Part 1. Discusses the use of German, Japanese, and American armor and armoring techniques on naval vessels, 1850-1900. Part 2. Discusses projectile and armor interaction and oblique impact effects; utilizes European and US studies mainly from the 20th century. Part 3. Provides examples of armor used on ships since the turn of the century.

846. Orange, Vincent. PEARL HARBOR, 7 DECEMBER 1941. *Hist. News [New Zealand]* 1980 (40): 1-8. Discusses the Japanese attack on the American Pacific fleet in December 1941, emphasizing the Japanese planning of the operation and the reasons why the American command was taken by surprise.

847. Osipov, B. PROBLEMY NEFTEKHIMII KAPITALISTICHESKIKH STRAN [Problems of petroleum industry in capitalist countries]. *Mirovaia Ekonomika i Mezhdunarodnye Otnosheniia [USSR] 1976 (3): 113-120.* Analyzes the growth, structure, technology, and prospects of the oil industry and trade in Western Europe, the United States and Japan.

848. Otis, Cary. ATOMIC BOMB TARGETING: MYTHS AND REALITIES. *Japan Q. [Japan] 1979 26(4): 506-516.* A Japanese myth holds that Kyoto was spared from destruction in the final months before Japan's surrender in 1945 because of the influence of Langdon Warner, the Harvard art historian. In truth, the interim Target Committee, meeting with Secretary of War Stimson and Chief of Staff General George Marshall in Washington, 31 May 1945, did not approve Kyoto as a target, contrary to its earlier recommendations.   F. W. Ikle

849. Ozaki, Robert S. UNITED STATES-JAPANESE ECONOMIC RELATIONS. *Current Hist. 1983 82(487): 357-361, 390.* Tensions in US-Japan trade relations stem from the efficacy of Japan's government-industry cooperation, disorder in the international monetary system, and Japan's need to limit its dependence on imports.

850. Packard, George R. A CRISIS IN UNDERSTANDING. *Foreign Service J. 1973 50(1): 8-11.* Condescension, competition, and poor communication are responsible for strained US-Japanese foreign relations.   S

851. Patokallio, Pasi. ENERGY IN JAPANESE-AMERICAN RELATIONS: A STRUCTURAL VIEW. *J. of Contemporary Asia [Sweden] 1975 5(1): 19-41.* Examines the role of US investments in Japan, particularly in the energy sector. Although there is no significant foreign control over the Japanese economy overall, US capital controls Japan's energy sources. This has led to a change in Japanese energy policy, but with limited success. In the future US control of energy in Japan may be used as a political weapon in American-Japanese relations.   F. D. Birch

852. Patrick, Stephen B. THE BATTLE FOR GUADALCANAL, 7 AUGUST 1942-7 FEBRUARY 1943. *Strategy & Tactics 1973 (39): 23-38.* Discusses the struggle waged by the United States and Japan for Guadalcanal.

853. Peatross, Oscar F. THE MAKIN RAID. *Marine Corps Gazette 1979 63(11): 96-103.* The author describes his participation with the 2d Raiders, US Marines, in their raid on the Japanese-held Makin Islands (in the Gilbert Islands), 17-18 August 1942; describes the reactions of the Japanese defenders, their eventual beheading of nine Marine prisoners, and the postwar execution and prison sentences visited upon their officers for that crime.

854. Perkins, Bradford. ALLIES OF THE USUAL KIND. *Rev. in Am. Hist. 1978 6(4): 537-543.* Review article prompted by William Roger Louis's *Imperialism at Bay: The United States and the Decolonization of the British Empire, 1941-1945* (New York: Oxford U. Pr., 1978) and Christopher

Thorne's *Allies of a Kind: The United States, Britain, and the War against Japan, 1941-1945* (New York: Oxford U. Pr., 1978).

855. Petras, James and Rhodes, Robert. THE RECONSOLIDATION OF US HEGEMONY. *New Left Rev. [Great Britain] 1976 (97): 37-53.* Discusses economic aspects of alleged US neocolonialism in its foreign policy toward Japan, Europe, and the Organization of Petroleum Exporting Countries (OPEC), 1969-70's.

856. Phillips, Elizabeth M. MINIATURE BOOKS: A HISTORY. *California Librarian 1978 39(3): 24-31.* Chronicles the publication of miniature books during the 15th-19th centuries in Europe and in the 20th century in the United States, Germany, Japan, and Hungary.

857. Potis, Michael J. AN ANALYSIS OF JAPAN'S AUTOMOBILE EXPORT RESTRAINTS. *Towson State J. of Int. Affairs 1982 16(2): 51-55.* Discusses congressional action since 1971 to curtail imports, especially from Japan, in the form of the Burke-Hartke Bill, which failed in 1973, and focuses on Japan's voluntary automobile export curbs to the United States.

858. Potter, E. B. THE CRYPT OF CRYPTANALYSTS. *US Naval Inst. Pro. 1983 109(8): 52-55.* Using fragmentary decoded radio intercepts, the Combat Information Unit at Pearl Harbor deduced the strength, direction, and date of approach of the Japanese force headed for Midway in June 1942.

K. J. Bauer

859. Powles, Cyril. E. H. NORMAN AS A HISTORIAN: A CANADIAN PERSPECTIVE: A REVIEW ARTICLE. *Pacific Affairs [Canada] 1977-78 50(4): 660-667.* Examines the debate among Japanese and Western historians regarding the scholarship of E. Herbert Norman. In the summer of 1977, George Akita, writing in the *Journal of Japanese Studies,* detailed the most serious negative criticisms of Norman's writings. Norman earned the respect of virtually all scholars and students of the history of Japan for his work, *Japan's Emergence as a Modern State.* Even 20 years after his death Norman the diplomat and scholar was the subject of considerable critical investigation. Charles Taylor believes that Norman's perspectives and writings were molded by his Canadian upbringing. Based on secondary sources; 30 notes.

S. H. Frank

860. Prados, John. THE WAR AGAINST JAPAN 1941-45. *Strategy and Tactics 1977 65: 27-32.* US industrial productivity, qualitatively superior aircraft, and naval advantages in radar and damage control decisively affected the Battle of the Pacific.

861. Prioli, Carmine A. THE FU-GO PROJECT. *Am. Heritage 1982 33(3): 88-92.* The Japanese Fu-Go Project, a plan to send balloon bombs to the United States, caused six deaths near Bly, Oregon, in 1945. Begun in November 1944, the project was an attempt to regain prestige by inflicting damage on US forests and other resources. Because of the potential for

biological warfare, the project caused fears among US officials, who attempted to keep it secret from the public for a time. 6 illus. J. F. Paul

862. Pronin, V. THE DEFEAT OF JAPANESE MILITARISM AND CHANGES IN THE FAR EAST. *Int. Affairs [USSR] 1975 (10): 24-32.* Discusses mistruths in US historiography of the USSR's role in the defeat of Japan in World War II, emphasizing the relationship to later revolutionary movements in China, Korea and Vietnam, 1930's-49.

863. Pugach, Noel H. AMERICAN FRIENDSHIP FOR CHINA AND THE SHANTUNG QUESTION AT THE WASHINGTON CONFERENCE. *J. of Am. Hist. 1977 64(1): 67-86.* Assesses the role of American diplomats in the Shantung dispute which resulted from the 1914 Japanese occupation of Shantung Province, China. Led by Secretary of State Charles Evans Hughes, US and British diplomats conducted informal negotiations that led to a compromise between Japan and China. Despite the intransigence of several US advisers who insisted on the absolute and unconditional right of China to Shantung, US friendship and sympathy were instrumental in persuading Japan to give up Shantung for certain concessions, and in persuading China to accept this compromise. 51 notes. J. B. Reed

864. Purka, Joseph W. LAUNCHING ACROSS THE PACIFIC. *Aerospace Hist. 1975 22(3): 135-138.* Describes briefly early attempts to fly across the Pacific Ocean and details the successful effort of Hugh Herndon and Clyde Pangborn to fly from Japan to the United States in 1931. The two had started a flight around the world from east New York. By the time they arrived in Khabarovsk, Siberia, they realized that they would not better the record. While there they heard of a prize of $25,000.00 offered by a Japanese newspaper to the first person to fly the Pacific. They flew to Japan and prepared to attempt the transpacific flight, but were detained by the Japanese authorities because they had flown over military installations. Finally they were released and given permission for one attempt. At 7:01 a.m., 4 October 1931, their aircraft, *Miss Veedol*, lifted off of the beach at Sabishiro. They had planned to land at Spokane but since it was fogged in they landed at Wenatchee, Washington 41 hours and 13 minutes after takeoff. On 4 November 1971, a 25-foot tall stone monument was dedicated at Sabishiro to the aviators. C. W. Ohrvall

865. Pushkin, A. BOEVYE DEISTVIIA AMERIKANSKIKH I IAPONSKIKH PODVODNYKH LODOK PROTIV AVIANOSTSEV V PERIOD VTOROI MIROVOI VOINY [The military activity of American and Japanese submarines against aircraft carriers during World War II]. *Morskoi Sbornik [USSR] 1979 (9): 11-26.* Aircraft carriers were the crucial factor in the Pacific in World War II. Analyzes the conflict between them and the submarines, evaluating such factors as noise levels, secrecy, air cover, anti-submarine defenses and the advantages of operating together with other vessels. The Japanese suffered heavier losses mainly because of their poor tactics and the Americans' superior technology. A table provides a detailed description of all major incidents. 2 tables, diagram, 25 notes. B. Holland

866. Puślecki, Zdzisław. PROTEKCJONIZM TRZECH CENTRÓW ŚWIATOWEJ GOSPODARKI KAPITALISTYCZNEJ: U.S.A., EUROPY ZACHODNIEJ, JAPONII [Protectionism in the three centers of the world capitalist economy: the United States, Western Europe and Japan]. *Przegląd Zachodni [Poland] 1980 36(1): 23-34.* From 1948 to 1973 annual world production grew 5% and the volume of international trade grew 7%. The US economy grew sluggishly, unlike the economies of Western Europe and Japan. Protectionist measures were demanded. Since 1971 these demands have been compounded by economic changes: an explosive rise in oil prices, inflation, breakdown of the international currency system, severe fluctuations in the balance of payments, and the failure to keep employment high. The solution was to come from the Tokyo Round of trade talks that ended in the 1979 Geneva Trade Agreement. The treaty lowered both tariff and nontariff barriers, but trade is still imperiled by inflation, currency instability, and disparity between the new leading capital-intensive computer technology and high interest rates due to inflation. The latter may restrict economic development.
M. Krzyzaniak

867. Ramsey, Norman F. AUGUST 1945: THE B-29 FLIGHT LOGS. *Bull. of the Atomic Sci. 1982 38(10): 33-35.* Presents a military account of the two atomic bombs over Hiroshima and Nagasaki, Japan, in 1945.

868. Rapp, William V. INDUSTRIAL STRUCTURE AND JAPANESE TRADE FRICTION: U.S. POLICY RESPONSES. *J. of Int. Affairs 1983 37(1): 67-79.* Discusses US approaches to ending the trade imbalance with Japan.

869. Reed, Steven R. PATTERNS OF DIFFUSION IN JAPAN AND AMERICA. *Comparative Pol. Studies 1983 16(2): 215-234.* Despite the fact that Japan is smaller, more homogeneous, and less diverse than the United States, information has not always diffused more rapidly there.

870. Richardson, John R. CAPTAIN LEROY DOW AND *CLARISSA B. CARVER. Am. Neptune 1980 40(2): 108-116.* Captain Leroy Dow (1842-1902) commanded the *Carver* when it collided with the *Glamorganshire* off Japan in 1885. During the incident he correctly held his course and afterward engaged an attorney, supervised sale of the sunken vessel and its cargo, and tenaciously fought a court battle to obtain compensation for the loss from the owners of the *Glamorganshire*. The entire incident is analyzed and the legal battle traced through the courts. Based on an interview and court testimony printed in the *Japan Gazette*.
J. C. Bradford

871. Rigin, Y. THE ENERGY FAMINE AND THE US MONOPOLIES. *Int. Affairs [USSR] 1974 (5): 52-60.* Discusses the role of oil industry monopolies in the energy shortages of the United States, Western Europe and Japan in the 1970's; considers the implications of the Organization of Petroleum Exporting Countries' (OPEC) raising prices.

872. Roberts, Brad. THE ENIGMATIC TRILATERAL COMMISSION: BOON OR BANE? *Millennium: J. of Int. Studies [Great Britain] 1982 11(3):*

185-202. Discusses the political and economic philosophies and goals of the Trilateral Commission, established in 1973 to promote shared problem-solving and understanding among Japan, Western Europe, and North America.

873. Roberts, John G. THE "JAPAN CROWD" AND THE ZAIBATSU RESTORATION. *Japan Interpreter [Japan] 1979 12(3-4): 384-415.* Details the postwar activities of the American Council on Japan (ACJ) and the personal interconnections of its principals in the United States and Japan. The ACJ and the broader Japan lobby originated in Joseph C. Grew's prewar State Department "Japan Crowd." In the years 1947-50, it managed to completely reverse the established US occupation government policy of breaking up Japan's zaibatsu and purging war-tainted businessmen from postwar economic leadership positions. The rising threat of communism, the anxiety of US businessmen to facilitate investment and economic recovery, and the intervention of powerful individuals, combined to reverse US democratizing policy and restore Japan's prewar economic and political elite, especially after the outbreak of the Korean War and the firing of General Douglas MacArthur. Based on interviews, US State Department and Japanese documents, contemporary press, and secondary sources; 64 notes. S

874. Roden, Donald. BASEBALL AND THE QUEST FOR NATIONAL DIGNITY IN MEIJI JAPAN. *Am. Hist. Rev. 1980 85(3): 511-534.* Explores the rise of baseball in late 19th-century Japan and assesses its immediate impact on American-Japanese relations and on conceptions of national honor and social status. First played by Americans living in the Treaty Port of Yokohama, baseball quickly spread, in the 1880's, among Japanese students for whom the sport provided an unusual opportunity to demonstrate manliness and honor to the foreign settlements. Discusses the fanfare and excitement that surrounded the first baseball series between American and Japanese teams in 1896. Baseball, a symbol of manliness and of the Social Darwinist spirit, contributed to inter-Pacific tensions and misunderstandings. It also greatly enhanced the public standing of Japan's student elite. Based on a variety of primary accounts, including the Japanese press and student newspapers; 5 illus., 81 notes. A

875. Roemer, John E. JAPANESE DIRECT FOREIGN INVESTMENT IN MANUFACTURES: SOME COMPARISONS WITH THE US PATTERN. *Q. Rev. of Econ. and Business 1976 16(2): 91-111.* Japanese direct investment in foreign manufacturing is a phenomenon mainly of the last decade. The author provides a brief review of the basic characteristics of this investment, and challenges the conventional notion that Japanese investment is fundamentally different from US foreign investment. In the coming period Japanese investment will take on more of the characteristics of US investment, and a review of recent Japanese investment is provided to lend support to this point. In particular, the international division of labor which Japan claims to have fostered with its foreign investment is ephemeral. J

876. Rogers, Everett M. and Larsen, Judith K. SILICON VALLEY CONFRONTS JAPAN. *Society 1982 19(5): 53-57.* Discusses the differences in technological information exchange between semiconductor firms in Japan and

the United States, as well as exchange of information between firms in the two countries.

877. Rosenstone, Robert A. LEARNING FROM THOSE "IMITATIVE" JAPANESE: ANOTHER SIDE OF THE AMERICAN EXPERIENCE IN THE MIKADO'S EMPIRE. *Am. Hist. Rev. 1980 85(3): 572-595.* Although the stereotype of the Japanese as an imitative people goes back at least as far as the Perry expedition, it has always been counterbalanced by the opposite view, that Japan was a nation from which the United States might learn. Examines that strong theme among American residents of 19th-century Japan and says that they—missionaries, scientists, journalists, diplomats, and artists—found much to admire in Japanese culture. Yet, when admiration became a desire for emulation, the Americans were confronted with a paradox. The potential lessons of Japan in the realms of art, manners, morals, and behavior were so human and personal, so culture-specific, that they could not be transported home. For this reason, the lessons always remained largely in the realm of discourse rather than behavior. Based on published and archival diaries, memoirs, and travel accounts of American residents in Japan; 5 illus., 63 notes.
A

878. Ryder, Richard C. YANKS DOWN UNDER: "GREAT WHITE FLEET" IN AUSTRALIA. *Am. Hist. Illus. 1981 16(5): 8-17.* Describes the arrival of the American "Great White Fleet" of 16 battleships in Sydney, Australia, on 20 August 1908 during the fleet's 14-month world cruise, which was ostensibly a training mission but was more a show of strength to Japan in light of worsening Japanese-American relations, a diversion away from domestic troubles in an election year, and a way to get Congress to appropriate more money to the nation's naval operations.

879. Saeki, Shōichi. THE AMERICAN CIVIL WAR AND THE MEIJI RESTORATION. *Japan Q. [Japan] 1982 29(3): 357-370.* Both historical events occurred at the same time, and both are usually estimated from the winner's point of view, resulting in a harsh treatment of the losers, the South and the shogunate. Both civil wars resulted in national unification, and subsequent expansionism. Both the North and the leaders of the Meiji Restoration also faced a dangerous international situation: the "Trent" affair with Great Britain and the possibility of Western interference in Japan. Both victors also had their share of luck. In both cases the urge to unify the nation and to achieve social changes were the motivating force, and the point of departure for rapid modernization and national expansion.
F. W. Iklé

880. Saitō, Makoto. WHAT EFFECT HAS THE OCCUPATION HAD ON JAPAN-US RELATIONS? *Japan Q. [Japan] 1981 28(4): 497-501.* The author comments on the 2d edition of *Japan Diary* by Mark Gayn, a *Chicago Sun* reporter who, in the period 1945-48, gave an inside view of SCAP and the relationship between the American military occupation and Japan's upper classes. In that period the United States was a protector of Japan, and the Japanese saw themselves as protegés of America. Today the same relationship exists; Japan is treated by America as if the occupation were still in effect.
F. W. Iklé

881. Sakata, Yasuo. IN MEMORIAM: T. SCOTT MIYAKAWA. *Amerasia J. 1981 8(2): v-viii.* Obituary of T. Scott Miyakawa, first director of the Japanese American Research Project. E. S. Johnson

882. Salaff, Stephen. THE LUCKY DRAGON. *Bull. of the Atomic Scientists 1978 34(5): 21-23.* The crew and catch of a Japanese fishing vessel, the *Lucky Dragon,* were exposed to radioactive ash from the 1 March 1954 hydrogen bomb detonation on Bikini Atoll. US officials refused to admit that deaths and contamination resulted from their exposure.

883. Sanders, Sol W. THE NEW, NEW JAPAN. *Asian Affairs 1974 1(6): 371-376.* Japan is entering an era that will probably determine its policies for the next half-century. Economic problems, erosion of Liberal Democratic Party stability, and the decline of America's role in East Asia are factors which have to be resolved. Notes the weakness of Prime Minister Kakuei Tanaka's government. S. Prisco

884. Santoni, Alberto. LA BATTAGLIA AERONAVALE DI LEYTE [The naval-air battle at Leyte]. *Riv. Marittima [Italy] 1973 106(11): 51-68.* Describes the phases of the naval battle of Leyte, October 1944, in Philippine waters, noting the significance of the suicide missions by Japanese pilots, and emphasizing that the US victory virtually destroyed the Japanese fleet.

885. Santoni, Alberto. PEARL HARBOR TRENTANOVE ANNI DOPO [Pearl Harbor—39 years after]. *Riv. Marittima [Italy] 1980 113(4): 41-50.* Describes the Japanese attack on Pearl Harbor on 7 December 1941.

886. Sato, Hideo. JAPANESE-AMERICAN RELATIONS. *Current Hist. 1978 75(441): 145-148, 180-181.* With the elections in 1976 of Jimmy Carter and Takeo Fukuda, a new era in Japanese-American relations began, strained initially because of disagreements over nuclear energy development and Carter's intention of withdrawing 32,000 American troops from South Korea.

887. Sato, Hideo. UNITED STATES-JAPANESE RELATIONS. *Current Hist. 1975 68(404): 154-157.* In the final analysis, whether the United States and Japan can maintain a viable relationship will depend on how much dialogue takes place between Americans and the Japanese opposition groups and on who controls the Japanese government.

888. Satō, Seizaburo. JAPAN-US RELATIONS: YESTERDAY AND TOMORROW. *Japan Interpreter [Japan] 1974 8(4): 432-449.* A comparison of the 1930's and the 1970's shows the differences between Japan and the United States to be greater than the similarities. Due to major structural achievements in international trade and cooperation, the 1970's are an era of reduced tensions and peaceful coexistence. Caution and close ties with the United States will best serve Japan's foreign policy. F. W. Iklé

889. Satoh, Yukio. WESTERN SECURITY: A JAPANESE POINT OF VIEW. *Naval War Coll. Rev. 1983 36(5): 75-90.* Reviews defense issues in Europe and East Asia in light of the erosion of US deterrent capability.

Western Europeans contribute too little to their own defense and impede US efforts to restrain the USSR, unlike the Japanese, who seem willing to contribute their share toward meeting any threat perceived by the Japanese, although they are reluctant to go beyond that. D. Powell

890. Savin, A. RAZGROM IAPONII V OSVESHCHENII BURZHUAZ-NOI ISTORIOGRAFII [The defeat of Japan in bourgeois historiography]. *Voenno-Istoricheskii Zhurnal [USSR] 1975 (9): 55-59.* Criticizes Western historians for their attempts to prove that Japan was defeated in World War II exclusively by the US armed forces; emphasizes the Soviet contribution to victory.

891. Scalapino, Robert A. THE AMERICAN OCCUPATION OF JAPAN—PERSPECTIVES AFTER THREE DECADES. *Ann. of the Am. Acad. of Pol. and Social Sci. 1976 428: 104-113.* The occupation of Japan provided an unusual opportunity for the United States to influence the patterns of political life in a country that was defeated both psychologically and physically. Under the personal leadership of General Douglas MacArthur, punishment was dealt to "war criminals," thus reducing severely Japan's military establishment; a series of economic and political reforms were instituted, resulting in the constitution of 1947, which has not been amended since. With the rise of the People's Republic of China (1949), the Korean War (1950), and the end of the occupation in the early 1950's, the circumstances of the Cold War led to an alliance between Japan and the United States that stressed the importance of Japan's regional defensive strength rather than the demilitarized posture of the occupation years. The occupation was a signal success for its time and purpose. It is likely that Japan will maintain most of the political changes made by the constitution of 1947 and will continue its special strategic and economic relationship with the United States, while at the same time making accommodations with China and other states in the world.
J

892. Schaller, Michael. SECURING THE GREAT CRESCENT: OCCUPIED JAPAN AND THE ORIGINS OF CONTAINMENT IN SOUTHEAST ASIA. *J. of Am. Hist. 1982 69(2): 392-414.* Concerned with charting Japan's future after 1945, American planners and policymakers viewed that nation as the key pivot in a crescent that stretched to Afghanistan. A strong Japan, linked to the West and economically dominant in Asia, could help contain any Communist threat in Asia. Communist control of Northeast Asia, however, would seriously impair Japanese recovery. Based on records and reports from the State Department and other government agencies plus private correspondence of officials like George Kennan and Dean Acheson; 57 notes.
T. P. Linkfield

893. Schonberger, Howard. AMERICAN LABOR'S COLD WAR IN OCCUPIED JAPAN. *Diplomatic Hist. 1979 3(3): 249-272.* American labor leaders participated actively in the administration of Occupied Japan, 1945-52. Their major goal was the creation of an American-style Japanese labor movement which could offset the economic dominance of the great Zaibatsu businesses, forcing them to attend more to domestic economic needs and less to

foreign trade in competition with American interests, and which could serve as a political bulwark against both supernationalism and communism. A large labor movement did arise in Japan, but its leaders, even the non-Communists, generally opposed American policies, considering them contrary to the interests of Japanese workers. Based on English-language primary sources; 67 notes.
T. L. Powers

894. Schonberger, Howard. THE JAPAN LOBBY IN AMERICAN DIPLOMACY, 1947-1952. *Pacific Hist. Rev. 1977 46(3): 327-359.* Explores the role of the American Council on Japan (ACJ), a loosely structured pressure group, in influencing the shift in American occupation policy away from that policy's original far-reaching reforms. The ACJ sought "to make Japan a bulwark against communism in Asia, and to rivet Japan onto an American-dominated world capitalist system." Harry F. Kern, foreign affairs editor of *Newsweek* from 1945 to 1954, was the principal organizer and leader of the ACJ. Based on documents in manuscript collections; 83 notes.
W. K. Hobson

895. Schonberger, Howard. U.S. POLICY IN POST-WAR JAPAN: THE RETREAT FROM LIBERALISM. *Sci. & Soc. 1982 46(1): 39-59.* US policy in occupied Japan greatly contributed to, not simply reflected, the bipolarization that occurred in the late 1940's. George F. Kennan of the State Department and Undersecretary of the Army William H. Draper, Jr., combined to force General Douglas MacArthur to retreat from the reformist policy of deconcentrating Japanese industry into a policy that sought to make Japan the Asian workshop of a global capitalist order dominated by the United States. Mainly primary sources; 54 notes.
L. V. Eid

896. Schwab, Susan C. JAPAN AND THE U.S. CONGRESS: PROBLEMS AND PROSPECTS. *J. of Int. Affairs 1983 37(1): 123-139.* Discusses sentiments in Congress to pass protectionist legislation.

897. Seidensticker, Edward. INTELLECTUALS, JAPANESE-STYLE. *Commentary 1975 60(5): 57-61.* Discusses Japanese intellectuals' attitudes toward the United States 1945-75.

898. Shapiro, Edward S. THE MILITARY OPTIONS TO HIROSHIMA: A CRITICAL EXAMINATION OF GAR ALPEROVITZ'S *ATOMIC DIPLOMACY*. *Amerikastudien/Am. Studies [West Germany] 1978 23(1): 60-72.* Gar Alperovitz's *Atomic Diplomacy* (1965) is a polemical revisionist tract. At no time was President Harry S. Truman advised by his military chiefs that Japan was on the verge of surrender or that Japanese capitulation would occur without use of the atomic bomb. Of little value in understanding the circumstances surrounding the dropping of the atomic bomb in 1945, *Atomic Diplomacy* reveals much about the outlook and methodology of one representative revisionist diplomatic historian.
J/S

899. Sharpston, Michael. INTERNATIONAL SUB-CONTRACTING. *Oxford Econ. Papers [Great Britain] 1975 27(1): 94-135.* Surveys the process of subcontracting manufacturing by developed countries such as Great Britain,

Japan, and the United States, to developing nations, 1966-76, and analyzes the reasons for its growth. Economic and political effects of this practice are widespread. Overall high profits to the contracting firms have not resulted. Protectionist lobbying against imported subcontracted goods is confined to unions and hence is less effective than combined lobbying against direct imports from developing countries. Unskilled labor tends to experience a net loss from international subcontracting, though the latter may be an alternative to legal or illegal immigration of workers. Labor's hostility to the practice is chiefly concerned with possible unemployment effects. International subcontracting by retailing interests creates adjustment problems for both labor and small, backward firms with the developed countries, where government assistance may be ill-organized. 7 tables. D. H. Murdoch

900. Shellenberger, Jack H. WILLIAM FAULKNER—STAG (SHORT TERM AMERICAN GRANTEE). *Foreign Service J. 1977 54(1): 10-11, 30.* Relates the author's experiences as a member of the US Information Service making a documentary film on novelist William Faulkner's impressions while travelling through Japan in 1955.

901. Sherrod, Robert. TARAWA: THE SECOND DAY. *Marine Corps Gazette 1973 57(11): 38-47.* A personal account of the second day of the battle of Tarawa, January 1944, as experienced by a journalist.

902. Shiozaki, Hiroaki. NICHI-BEI KAIDAN ZENSHI: "JOHN DOE ASSOCIATES" NO SEIRITSU TO SONO SEIJITEKI HAIKEI [The prehistory of the Japanese-American conversations: the formation and political background of John Doe Associates]. *Shigaku Zasshi [Japan] 1975 84(7): 39-63.* Covers 1936-41.

903. Shiozaki, Hiroaki. TAIHEIYŌ SENSŌ E-NO MICHI TO EIBEI KANKEI: W. WAIZUMAN NO YAKUWARI NI TSUITE [British-American relations before the Pacific War: the role of Sir William Wiseman]. *Shigaku Zasshi [Japan] 1981 90(2): 57-82.* Sir William Wiseman (1885-1962), a British intelligence agent (MI6) assigned to New York, played an important role together with Colonel Edward Mandell House (1858-1938) in organizing Anglo-American Allied activities during World War I. After World War I, Wiseman became an employee and later a partner of Kuhn, Loeb & Co. in New York City. When World War II broke out, Wiseman unofficially cooperated with Anglo-American activities. He planned attacks on Hitler, attempted to detach Japan from the war and to shorten the war with Japan. Wiseman's diplomatic involvement in World War II with Father James Drought has been little studied, although he contributed to building the Anglo-American alliance in both wars with his pro-Jewish thought. 207 notes.
M. Kawaguchi

904. Shunsuke, Tsurumi. JAPANESE DEMOCRACY AND THE AMERICAN OCCUPATION. *Democracy 1982 2(1): 75-88.* Examines the process of forced democratization of Japan during the postwar American occupation, which restructured Japanese social and political life and created a

complex legacy of relationships among the United States, Japan, and Japan's former vassal-state, Korea.

905. Sims, Jack A. THE DOOLITTLE RAID—A SURVIVOR'S DIARY. *Aerospace Hist. 1983 30(2): 92-100.* Describes the author's experiences during Lieutenant Colonel James H. Doolittle's bombing raid against Japan in April 1942, the first American raid against Japan in World War II. The planes took off from the carrier *Hornet,* dropped bombs on several Japanese cities, and then flew on to China. There most either crash-landed or the crews were forced to bail out. Many of the survivors returned to the United States by way of India, the Middle East, Africa, and South America. 7 illus. J. K. Ohl

906. Sinha, R. P. JAPAN AND THE OIL CRISIS. *World Today [Great Britain] 1974 30(8): 335-344.* "Extreme vulnerability to the oil crisis has led to an intensified search for other energy sources. Efforts to reduce dependence on the Middle East and the international oil companies are fraught with political implications—not least for the relationship with the United States." J

907. Sledge, Eugene B. PELELIEU: A NEGLECTED BATTLE. *Marine Corps Gazette 1979 63(11): 88-95, (12): 28-41; 1980 64(1): 32-42.* Part I. DEFENSE IN DEPTH. Although the battle of Pelelieu Island (in the Palau Islands) in September-November 1944 largely is overlooked by historians and the public, it was probably the toughest battle of World War II. Notes that Admiral William (Bull) Halsey argued that the entire Palau Islands operation, intended to shore up General Douglas MacArthur's right flank for his invasion of the Philippines, was not even necessary. The author describes the horror of his combat on Pelelieu during 15 September-15 October with Company K, 3d Battalion, 5th Marines, 1st Marine Division, most of them not yet 21 years old, against the *bushido*-inspired defense in depth practiced by Colonel Kunio Nakagawa, his 14th Infantry Division, and other Japanese units. Part II. ASSAULT INTO HELL. The author describes the landing on Pelelieu, the move inland, Japanese counterattacks, and more US attacks, including that on adjacent Ngesebus Island, 28 September. Part III. VICTORY AT HIGH COST. The author describes the close quarters and hand-to-hand combat, battle fatigue, the Marines' esprit de corps, their relief by the 81st Infantry on 15 October, the killing of the last Japanese by 27 November, casualty totals, and the effectiveness of Marine Corps training. D. J. Engler

908. Smyth, H. D. THE "SMYTH REPORT." *Princeton U. Lib. Chronicle 1976 37(3): 173-189.* Discusses the author's role in preparing a War Department report on the military feasibility of using atomic energy for strategic purposes against Japan during World War II.

909. Sodei, Rinjirō. WHAT THE VIETNAM WAR MEANS TO US. *Japan Q. [Japan] 1975 22(4): 314-317.* Although the Beheiren movement, headed by Mononobe Nagaoki, opposed the Vietnam War, most Japanese public opinion was indifferent. For many Japanese corporations, the war was profitable and stimulated the country's prosperity much as the Korean War had in the 1950's. For most Japanese, the Vietnam War is now completely

forgotten, despite the fact the results of that war will determine the course of Asian politics for years to come. A. N. Garland

910. Sommer, Theo; Kosaka, Masataka; and Bowie, Robert R. STRATEGIC FORUM: AMERICAN POLICY AFTER VIETNAM. *Survival [Great Britain] 1973 15(3): 106-110.* Discusses US foreign policy and military strategy in light of the ending of the Vietnam War in the 1970's, emphasizing economic implications for Japan and Europe.

911. Sorrentino, Constance and Moy, Joyanna. UNEMPLOYMENT IN THE UNITED STATES AND EIGHT FOREIGN COUNTRIES. *Monthly Labor Rev. 1974 97(1): 47-52.* Compares unemployment rates in 1972 and the first half of 1973 in the United States, Canada, Great Britain, Italy, France, Sweden, Australia, Japan, and Germany; rates declined in Canada and the United States, but remained high compared with most industrial countries.

912. Speer, R. T. LET PASS SAFELY THE AWA MARU. *U.S. Naval Inst. Pro. 1974 100(4): 69-76.* During the night of 1 April 1945 the US submarine *Queenfish* attacked and sank the Japanese steamship *Awa Maru*, even though the latter had been granted safe passage by the US government to carry relief supplies to prisoner of war camps in the East Indies. The sinking was the result of a series of unfortunate circumstances. The *Queenfish*'s commander was tried by general court martial and received a light sentence. The US government did express its formal apology to the Japanese government, but the war ended before discussions regarding a replacement ship could be concluded. 3 photos, 7 notes. A. N. Garland

913. Spickard, Paul R. THE NISEI ASSUME POWER: THE JAPANESE AMERICAN CITIZENS LEAGUE, 1941-1942. *Pacific Hist. Rev. 1983 52(2): 147-174.* Before Pearl Harbor the Issei dominated Japanese-American communities, but a minority of young Nisei belonging to the Japanese American Citizens League challenged Issei hegemony and proclaimed its Americanism. After the mass imprisonment of Japanese in 1941-42, the Japanese American Citizens League assumed power and tried to convince federal and state authorities that Japanese Americans were loyal. The league failed to oppose evacuation and thereby encountered opposition from Japanese Americans. The league lost power, but when the war ended Nisei replaced Issei in almost all positions of authority in Japanese-American communities. Although a failure, the league represented the Nisei desire to be identified with the American middle class. Based on the Japanese American Research Project Archives and other primary sources; 59 notes. R. N. Lokken

914. Sprague, Claire D. "TILL YOU COME BACK." *Pacific Hist. 1980 24(2): 192-195.* Personal account of forced relocation during World War II. The author relates experiences in the assembly centers for Japanese Americans as told to her in letters from her former pupils (French Camp Grammar School) and their families. The evacuees were held in assembly centers before being shipped to relocation centers. 5 photos. G. L. Lake

915. Stebbins, Robert A. FORMALIZATION: NOTES ON A THEORY OF THE RISE AND CHANGE OF SOCIAL NORMS. *Int. J. of Contemporary Sociol.* 1974 11(2-3): 105-119. Discusses behavioristic and sociological theory regarding the origin of social norms and values 1940's-70's, emphasizing the example of attitudes toward Japanese Americans during World War II.

916. Stokesbury, James. BATTLE OF ATTU. *Am. Hist. Illus.* 1979 14(1): 30-38. Chronicles the battle between US and Japanese forces for the island of Attu in the Aleutian Islands, 1942.

917. Strauss, William L. THE MILITARY ARMISTICE COMMISSION: DETERRENT OF CONFLICT? *J. of Korean Affairs* 1975 5(1): 24-46. Evaluates the effectiveness of the Military Armistice Commission established in Korea at the end of the Korean War to enforce boundary lines along the 38th Parallel, 1953-73.

918. Sugimoto, Yoshio. LABOR REFORM AND INDUSTRIAL TURBULENCE: THE CASE OF THE AMERICAN OCCUPATION OF JAPAN. *Pacific Sociol. Rev.* 1977 20(4): 492-514. Following the American occupation of Japan, the institution of American labor reform brought about the equalization of the relationship between employers and employees which led to labor disturbance; examines the impact of the American labor system on wages and working conditions, 1952-60.

919. Sullivan, Alfred B. and Deshazo, E. A. A NEW RISING SUN. *Asian Profile [Hong Kong]* 1973 1(1): 103-112. Expands on the theme of Herman Kahan's *The Emerging Japanese Super State* and similar studies of the 1970's. Examines the interplay of economics and politics in Japan during 1945-72, an era of unprecedented industrial productivity, export development, and government protection. Japan's Security Treaty with the United States, coupled with Article 9 of its constitution, which in effect outlaws offensive war and offensive armed forces, enabled Japan to restrict itself to a relatively modest self-defense force. Reviews American initiatives in the 1970's such as a gradual withdrawal of American armed forces from the periphery of China, the "recognition" of China, and a major revision of all external trading arrangements. Suggests adjustments in American foreign policy to improve the long-lived alliance between America and Japan. Based on a paper presented to the Western Conference of the Association for Asian Studies, November 1972. Secondary sources; 36 notes. S. H. Frank

920. Sullivan, Denis G. and Massey, Joseph A. POWER AND INDULGENCE: THE CHANGING JAPANESE-AMERICAN RELATIONSHIP, 1972-1978. *Korea & World Affairs [South Korea]* 1979 3(3): 409-420. Traces the economic relations between Japan and the United States.

921. Sumiya, Mikio. LE ORIGINI DEL SOCIALISMO IN GIAPPONE. SOCIALISMO E INTERNAZIONALISMO NEL PENSIERO E NELL'AZIONE DI KATAYAMA SEN [The origins of socialism in Japan: socialism and internationalism in the thought and actions of Sen Katayama]. *Riv. Storica Italiana [Italy]* 1977 69(2): 301-333. Sen Katayama, later to

become one of the founders of Japanese socialism and a member of the Comintern, came to the United States in 1884 at the age of 25. He worked as a cook until he saved enough money and learned enough English to attend a university. He eventually graduated from Yale with a divinity degree, having been converted to Christianity. On his return to Japan in 1896, he became an advocate of Christian Socialism and was a founder of the Japan Social Democratic Party in 1901. In exile in the United States, Katayama helped form a Communist Party in 1919. In 1921 he went to Moscow as an official of the Comintern and in 1924 was elected secretary of its executive committee. He followed the Stalinist line, and approved the purges of Leon Trotsky, Nikolai Bukharin, and Grigori Zinoviev, although all three had been his friends. 16 notes. J. C. Billigmeier

922. Sunahara, M. Ann. THE JAPANESE AMERICAN AND JAPANESE CANADIAN RELOCATION IN WORLD WAR II: HISTORICAL RECORDS AND COMPARISONS. *Can. Ethnic Studies [Canada] 1978 10(1): 126-128.* A critical review of the 4-5 May 1978, Bellingham, Washington, conference sponsored by the Canadian-American Studies Center of Western Washington University and the National Archives and Records Service of the United States, where both academics and evacuees discussed and compared the experiences of Japanese Canadians and Japanese Americans.

923. Suzuki, Zenji. GENETICISTS AND EUGENICS MOVEMENT IN JAPAN AND AMERICA: A COMPARATIVE STUDY. *XIVth International Congress of the History of Science, Proceedings No. 3* (Tokyo and Kyoto: Science Council of Japan, 1975): 68-70. Differing social organization and racial-ethnic constitutions in Japan and America led to the active reception of the eugenics movement in the United States, with experiments in transference of traits in humans, and only passing interest in Japan, where research was limited to plant and animal hybridization, 1920's-30's.

924. Sysoev, I. MEZHDUNARODNYE MONOPOLII I VALIUTNAIA SISTEMA ZAPADA [International monopolies and the monetary system of the West]. *Mirovaia Ekonomika: Mezhdunarodnye Otnosheniia [USSR] 1973 (9): 48-56.* Discusses international associations of monopolies, the currency tactics of international monopolies, maneuvers of American corporations, and the practices of European and Japanese monopolies. Concludes that currency and financial relations of capitalist states are conditioned increasingly by the interests of international monopolies, particularly American multinational corporations. To weaken the influence of American monopolies, the countries of the European Economic Community and Japan have undertaken separate measures to create currency groupings with currency regimes that respond to the level of development of their productive forces. Regional attempts at solving world currency problems have hindered attempts for more centralized currency reforms. Based on secondary sources; 17 notes. L. Kalinowski

925. Tabb, William. ZAPPING LABOR. *Marxist Perspectives 1980 3(1): 64-77.* The Trilateral Commission seeks to create space in which to transform the economy of the United States by forcing down real wages and cutting social services.

926. Takemae, Eiji. AMERIKA NO SHOKI TAINICHI RŌDŌ SEISAKU [The initial US labor policy for occupied Japan]. *Shakai Kagaku Kenkyū [Japan] 1973 25(1): 100-119.* Discusses the sources of the initial American labor policy for Japan and the influence of American labor unions on those of Japan. The initial policy, which was based on the Civil Affairs Guide issued by the Department of the Army, was progressive but essentially anti-communist. Irving Brown a representative of the AFL-CIO, was one of the policymakers who drafted the instructions for labor organizing activities, and introduced methods used by the CIO. 3 tables, notes.
S. Davis

927. Takeyman, Yasuo. THE OUTLOOK FOR U.S.-JAPAN ECONOMIC AND TRADE RELATIONS. *J. of Internat. Affairs 1974 28(1): 38-53.* The rise of "cross cutting coalitions" of political-economic relations, the decline of the US dollar, the unified free economy, and parallel economic and political security systems threaten to create hostile economic blocs. As the Japanese economy becomes fully internationalized and becomes more service-oriented, it must maintain high productivity, avert socio-political instability, and still integrate economic relations with all other aspects of foreign policy.
R. D. Frederick

928. Taylor, Sandra C. ABBY M. COLBY: THE CHRISTIAN RESPONSE TO SEXIST SOCIETY. *New England Q. 1979 52(1): 68-79.* Women, who comprised two-thirds of the missionaries to Japan in the late 19th century, received lower pay than men and were only allowed to vote on matters of "women's work" within their organization. Abby M. Colby (1848-1917) was a feminist who served as a Congregational missionary in Japan between 1879 and 1914 and opposed these practices as much as she did Japanese practices of male-dominated marriages, concubinage, and prostitution. Based on Colby's letters in the papers of the American Board of Commissioners for Foreign Missions at Houghton Library, Harvard University; 29 notes.
J. C. Bradford

929. Taylor, Sandra C. JAPAN'S MISSIONARY TO THE AMERICANS: SIDNEY L. GULICK AND AMERICA'S INTERWAR RELATIONSHIP WITH JAPAN. *Diplomatic Hist. 1980 4(4): 387-407.* The Reverend Sidney Lewis Gulick was a former missionary to Japan, an administrator with the Federal Council of Churches, a scholar, and a private diplomat who sought Japanese-American harmony, regulated immigration, fair treatment for Asians in America, and world peace. "Appearing to a few as a menace, a Japanese agent, and a threat to American values, Gulick was perceived by his supporters and friends as a compassionate Christian dedicated to justice, equity, and a peaceful world.... A study of his career illuminates the relationship between the Asian missionary community, Protestant church leaders, and American policy toward Japan in the interwar years." 85 notes.
T. L. Powers

930. Thompson, William R. and Zuk, Gary. AMERICAN ELECTIONS AND THE INTERNATIONAL ELECTORAL-ECONOMIC CYCLE: A TEST OF THE TUFTE HYPOTHESIS. *Am. J. of Pol. Sci. 1983 27(3): 464-484.* Tufte's hypothesis on the existence of an international electoral-

economic cycle specifies that government economic stimulation for reelection purposes tends to spill over and affect the economies of other industrialized democracies, but quarterly gross national product growth data provide little corroboration for the notion of systematic and diffused electoral impact on the economies of Canada, Japan, West Germany, Italy, and Great Britain. J/S

931. Thomson, Sandra Caruthers. MEIJI JAPAN THROUGH MISSIONARY EYES: THE AMERICAN PROTESTANT EXPERIENCE. *J. of Religious Hist. [Australia] 1973 7(3): 248-259.* An examination of several missionary memoirs and diaries about their works in Meiji Japan during the second half of the 19th century. The emphasis is on the success of Protestant missionaries and how their initial visions of Japan were altered when they encountered a highly complex and sophisticated society. The author explores the various difficulties which developed between the Japanese government and some of the Western churches. 55 notes. W. T. Walker

932. Tibbets, Paul W. TRAINING THE 509TH FOR HIROSHIMA. *Air Force Mag. 1973 56(8): 49-55.* The author, pilot of the B-29 that dropped an atomic bomb on Hiroshima in 1945, recalls the training of the 509th Composite Group, which performed the mission.

933. Tillman, Barrett. HELLCATS OVER TRUK. *US Naval Inst. Pro. 1977 103(3): 63-71.* In 1944, Truk Atoll was probably the most important Japanese anchorage outside the home islands, and the US Navy, at least until early that year, had been unable to gather much intelligence about the Japanese establishment at that location. Still, the Navy felt it had to attack Truk in some way in order to disrupt this major Japanese way station and supply base. An aerial reconnaissance mission flown in early February 1944 brought back some helpful photographs. Rear Admiral Marc A. Mitscher's Task Force 58 was ordered to knock out Truk by using air power. On 17 February 1944, five US aircraft carriers launched 70 Grumman F6F Hellcat fighters to gain air superiority. The next day was scheduled for attack on ground installations and shipping. Both attacks were spectacular successes. Truk was hit again and again during the ensuing months but none "exceeded the first for prolonged intensity of aerial combat." 10 photos, map, 2 tables. A. N. Garland

934. Tomabechi, Toshihiro. THE U.S.-JAPAN CONNECTION IN THE CHANGING WORLD MARKETPLACE: A TRADER'S PERSPECTIVE. *J. of Int. Affairs 1983 37(1): 43-48.* The artificially expensive dollar and cheap yen are culprits in the trade imbalance.

935. Toshitani, Nobuyoshi. NŌGYŌ SHISAN SŌZOKU TOKUREI HŌAN TO GHQ [The bill providing for exceptions to succession to agricultural property and the GHQ]. *Shakai Kagaku Kenkyū [Japan] 1975 26(3/4): 100-132.* Demonstrates the process of reconstruction and democratization in postwar Japan by elaborating on the disputes surrounding this bill, especially among American officials at GHQ who were in disagreement over the abolition of the *ie seido* (family system) and agricultural democratization. Based on memoranda of GHQ officials. Y. Ishihara

936. Tow, William T. ANZUS AND AMERICAN SECURITY. *Survival [Great Britain] 1981 23(6): 261-271.* Examines the role of the ANZUS Pact among Australia, New Zealand, and the United States in US security and foreign policy from 1951, when the treaty was initialed, to 1981, when discussion focused on the possibility of incorporating Japan into the pact.

937. Tow, William T. THE JANZUS OPTION: A KEY TO ASIAN/ PACIFIC SECURITY. *Asian Survey 1978 18(12): 1221-1234.* Considers three issue-areas related to the Australian-New Zealand-US Tripartite agreement (ANZUS): The Soviet military power thrust; measures which could upgrade Japan's defense role; and "what levels of commitments might be desired by Japan and the other ANZUS powers to attain a credible defense posture vis-à-vis the Soviet Union and/or China in the Asia/Pacific." Discusses threats justifying a "JANZUS" arrangement, noting that significant US backing must be included. Since 1945 Japan has depended on American military power "as the ultimate guarantee of its own security." "American awareness of Japan's revised status should be reflected in its willingness to incorporate Japan into a defense relationship that enhances such a recognition to both countries' mutual benefit." The JANZUS alliance seems to offer the best opportunity for both countries. 29 notes. E. P. Stickney

938. Trefousse, Hans L. PEARL HARBOR WITHOUT RANCOR: A GERMAN VIEW. *Rev. in Am. Hist. 1981 9(4): 526-530.* Review of Peter Herde's *Pearl Harbor, 7. Dezember 1941: Der Ausbruch des Krieges zwischen Japan und den Vereinigten Staaten und die Ausweitung des europäischen Krieges zum Zweiten Weltkrieg. Impulse der Forschung,* vol. 33 (1980), which presents a German view of the Japanese attack on Pearl Harbor.

939. Trofimenko, G. POLITIKA BEZ PERSPEKTIVY (O TAK NAZIVAIEMOI DOKTRINE KARTERA) [A policy without prospects, or, the so-called Carter doctrine]. *Mirovaia Ekonomika i Mezhdunarodnye Otnosheniia [USSR] 1980 (3): 17-27.* The freezing of relations with Moscow has become an integral part of the foreign policy of the Carter administration; the policy involves closer relations with the countries of Western Europe and with Japan, on the basis of anti-Sovietism and militarism, efforts to attract the support of developing nations, and the undermining of detente.

940. Tsuchimochi, Gary H. THE TREND OF RESEARCH ON EDUCATIONAL REFORM UNDER THE AMERICAN OCCUPATION OF JAPAN WITH PARTICULAR REFERENCE TO DOCTORAL DISSERTATIONS IN THE U.S. *Asian Profile [Hong Kong] 1982 10(2): 129-142.* Surveys US doctoral dissertations on educational reform in Japan under US occupation. Dissertations of the 1950's were often written by American officers having direct personal experience with their subject of research. During the 1960's interest in the subject waned but was stimulated in the late 1970's by the publication of Robert E. Ward and Frank J. Shulman's *The Allied Occupation of Japan, 1945-1952: An Annotated Bibliography of Western-Language Materials,* 1974. Table, 27 notes, biblio. J. Powell

941. Tsumoda, Jun and Uchida, Kazutomi. THE PEARL HARBOR ATTACK: ADMIRAL YAMAMOTO'S FUNDAMENTAL CONCEPT WITH REFERENCE TO PAUL S. DULL'S *A BATTLE HISTORY OF THE IMPERIAL JAPANESE NAVY (1941-1945)*. Naval War College Rev. 1978 31(2): 83-88.

942. Uchida, Yoshiko. TOPAZ, CITY OF DUST. *Utah Hist. Q. 1980 48(3): 234-243*. Interned with her family in 1942, the author spent eight months in Topaz, Utah, at a Sevier Desert concentration camp for Japanese Americans. Her home was an unfinished tar-paper barracks furnished only with four army cots without mattresses. Frustrated, despondent residents coped with waterless laundries, unlighted latrines, gaping holes in roofs, uninstalled stoves, and all-pervasive dust storms. Schools had no supplies, no equipment, no lights, no heat, no tables, no chairs. 2 illus., note.
J. L. Hazelton

943. Urwin, Gregory. THE ROAD BACK FROM WAKE ISLAND. *Am. Hist. Illus. 1980 15(8): 16-23; 1981 15(9): 43-49.* Part I. [JOHN KINNEY, PRISONER OF WAR]. Account of Japanese imprisonment in China of American troops defending Wake Island in December 1941, focusing on the ordeal of Marine 2d Lt. John F. Kinney from his capture until 1944. Part II. A BLIND LEAP TO FREEDOM TAKES JOHN KINNEY HOME. Account of Marine Lt. John F. Kinney's capture by the Imperial Japanese Navy at Wake Island on 23 December 1941, his subsequent imprisonment for four years, and his escape in May 1945.

944. Usoskin, V.; Khesin, E.; Shenaev, V.; and Idanov, I. POSLEVOENNAIA EVOLIUTSIIA FINANSOVOGO KAPITALA [The postwar evolution of finance capital]. *Mirovaia Ekonomika i Mezhdunarodnye Otnosheniia [USSR] 1974 (5): 45-62.* Discusses finance capital, with particular reference to the United States, Europe and Japan, as well as the lasting relevance of Marxist-Leninist theory to understanding the development of monopolies since 1950.

945. Utkin, A. "ATLANTIZM" I IAPONILA ["Atlantism" and Japan]. *Mirovaia Ekonomika i Mezhdunarodnye Otnosheniia [USSR] 1976 (6): 56-63.* Discusses attempts since World War II to extend the idea of "atlantism," i.e., the relationship between the United States and Western Europe, into "neo-atlantism" by including Japan.

946. Utley, Jonathan G. DIPLOMACY IN A DEMOCRACY: THE UNITED STATES AND JAPAN, 1937-1941. *World Affairs 1976 139(2): 130-140.* Discusses conflicts in US foreign policy and diplomacy regarding the issue of trade with Japan, 1937-41.

947. Utley, Jonathan G. JAPANESE EXCLUSION FROM AMERICAN FISHERIES, 1936-1939: THE DEPARTMENT OF STATE AND THE PUBLIC INTEREST. *Pacific Northwest Q. 1974 65(1): 8-16.* Reviews the pressures exerted by US fishing interests to exclude Japanese salmon fishing adjacent to American waters, and the careful diplomacy of the State Depart-

ment in this difficult situation. The department was determined to take no actions which would further strain Japanese-American relations. Analyzes the methods of Miller Freeman, publisher of the *Pacific Fisherman*, in espousing the cause of the fishing interests; of Senator Lewis B. Schwellenbach, of Washington; and of the State Department, whose moderation and temporization successfully settled both the domestic and diplomatic problems. 43 notes.

R. V. Ritter

948. Utley, Jonathan G. UPSTAIRS, DOWNSTAIRS AT FOGGY BOTTOM: OIL-EXPORTS AND JAPAN, 1940-41. *Prologue 1976 8(1): 17-28.* Historians have generally failed to investigate the manner in which the cautious foreign policy toward Japan, formulated by President Roosevelt and Secretary of State Cordell Hull, was implemented at lower levels of the foreign service bureaucracy. Lower echelon administrators such as Assistant Secretary of State Dean Acheson favored a stronger and more aggressive attitude toward Japan than did their superiors and they changed the whole character of their instructions to reflect their personal views. Acheson and independent agencies like the Foreign Funds Control Committee prevented Japan from obtaining the oil supplies to which it was entitled under the conditions laid down by the president and the secretary of state. Based on secondary sources and government archival records.

N. Lederer

949. Uyeda, Clifford I. THE PARDONING OF "TOKYO ROSE": A REPORT ON THE RESTORATION OF AMERICAN CITIZENSHIP TO IVA IKUKO TOGURI. *Amerasia J. 1978 5(2): 69-93.* The 1977 presidential pardon of Iva Ikuko Toguri d'Aquino, who, as "Tokyo Rose," had been convicted of treason after World War II, was the result of the work of many people, institutions, and organizations. A committee formed by John Hada and the author coordinated the massive campaign to reeducate the public about the facts of the case, the garnering of support from widespread sources, and the mechanics of filing the petition for pardon. The Japanese American Citizens League had done little or nothing for Toguri prior to the work of the committee and did not order the formation of the committee, but it tried to claim credit for the pardon.

T. L. Powers

950. Varma, Lalima. OKINAWA BEFORE AND SINCE REVERSION. *Int. Studies [India] 1980 19(1): 43-57.* Compares conditions in Okinawa during US military occupation, 1952-72, with conditions since its reversion to Japan in 1972. Okinawa acquired a strategic position after World War II because of American ambitions in the Pacific, and it proved indispensable as a military base during the Vietnam conflict. Since reversion to Japan, Okinawa's economy has remained dependent on American military presence. 40 notes.

T. P. Linkfield

951. Viksnins, George J. U.S.-JAPANESE TRADE: PERCEPTIONS AND REALITY. *Asian Survey 1979 19(3): 205-229.* Analyzes trends in US-Japanese economic relations, 1970-77, and the interface of American and Japanese interests in the Pacific Asia region. The United States is the major market for Japanese exports, and Japan ranks second only to Canada as a market for US goods. The attitudes and regulations of the two countries

regarding exports and imports differ substantially. Both play an important role in the maintenance of peace and stability, as markets and suppliers, and as providers of development assistance in East and Southeast Asia, where Japan's economic influence is predominant and US influence is expanding. Based on official statistics and secondary works; 10 tables, 43 notes. M. A. Eide

952. Villa, Brian L. THE U.S. ARMY, UNCONDITIONAL SURRENDER, AND THE POTSDAM PROCLAMATION. *J. of Am. Hist. 1976 63(1): 66-92.* Examines the critical factors affecting the timing of the Japanese surrender. Clarifies the politico-military position assumed by Roosevelt, the Congress, and the US Army. Conflicts arising from differing goals (Roosevelt desired "the rooting out of evil philosophies"; the Army wanted military supremacy) and semantic interpretations ("surrender" was unknown to the Japanese) delayed peace. 69 notes. V. P. Rilee

953. Vlahos, Michael. THE NAVAL WAR COLLEGE AND THE ORIGINS OF WAR-PLANNING AGAINST JAPAN. *Naval War College Rev. 1980 33(4): 23-41.* In the first decade of this century, the Naval War College played a leading role in the newly institutionalized war planning process. One of the first plans, and the first transoceanic plan, was the Orange Special Situation against Japan. The origins and development of War Plan Orange—"a grand strategy for a war of illusions"—are related here. J

954. Vorontsov, G. A. TREKHSTORONNIAIA KONTSEPTSIIA: TEORIIA I PRAKTIKA [The conception of trilateralism: theory and practice]. *Voprosy Istorii [USSR] 1979 (4): 94-109.* Examines the foreign policy conception of "trilateralism," which has gained wide currency in the West in recent years and has become especially popular in the United States. At the basis of this conception lies an appeal for the maximum unity of the three main centers of imperialism (the United States, Western Europe, and Japan), the elaboration by these centers of a single strategy and tactic in an attempt to stabilize the capitalist system and to counteract the revolutionary forces of our time. The author analyzes the theoretical sources and class essence of the conception, characterizing the practical attempts made by some of the capitalist states to put into effect individual elements of the concept of trilateralism. Secondary sources; 54 notes. J

955. Wabuda, Susan. ELIZABETH BACON CUSTER IN JAPAN: 1903. *Manuscripts 1983 35(1): 12-18.* Elizabeth Bacon Custer survived her husband, General George Armstrong Custer, by nearly 57 years. In 1903, she traveled to Japan, recording her experiences in a journal. Her attitude toward Japan and the Japanese was complex and contradictory, like that of many other early American visitors to Japan. Based on Elizabeth Bacon Custer's manuscript journal; illus., 5 notes. D. A. Yanchisin

956. Wagner, David H. THE DESTINY OF PETE ELLIS. *Marine Corps Gazette 1976 60(6): 50-55.* Discusses circumstances surrounding the mysterious death of Marine Corps Lieutenant Colonel Earl Ellis in the Japanese-mandated Caroline Islands, 1920-23, including aspects of naval strategy.

957. Wakatsuki, Yasno. JAPANESE EMIGRATION TO THE UNITED STATES, 1866-1924: A MONOGRAPH. *Perspectives in Am. Hist. 1979 12: 387-516.* Discusses the primary factors which motivated Japanese emigration to the United States and the social conditions in Japan which contributed to those motivations, and identifies the social and economic status of those who did emigrate. Analysis of the records on Japanese emigrants preserved in Japan reveals that the emigrants did better their social and financial status, often earning enough money in several years to return to Japan and buy land. While many returned, more stayed away and made new homelands for a variety of reasons: evading military conscription, attraction to the mythical paradise which the West represented, and a perception of Japan as a semi-feudalistic society which repressed basic freedoms. W. A. Wiegand

958. Waldner, George W. JAPAN, GEORGIA, AND THE JAPAN-AMERICAN SOCIETY OF GEORGIA: THE VIEWPOINT OF ITS EXECUTIVE DIRECTOR. *West Georgia Coll. Studies in the Social Sci. 1983 22: 95-99.* Because of the increasing Japanese population and Japanese involvement in commercial and scholastic affairs, a Georgia chapter of the Associated Japan-America Societies of the United States, Inc., was initiated in 1979.

959. Wallerstein, Immanuel. FRIENDS AS FOES. *Foreign Policy 1980 (40): 119-131.* America's steady decline from international economic preeminence parallels paths taken by Great Britain, 1873-96, and the United Provinces, 1650-72. The process is neither fortuitous, mysterious, nor reversible. By 1990, this change within the capitalist world economy will cause the dissolution of the US alliance with Western Europe, and Japan. Meanwhile, nationalism and socialism will threaten the existence of the system itself.
T. L. Powers

960. Warren, Shields. HIROSHIMA AND NAGASAKI THIRTY YEARS AFTER. *Pro. of the Am. Phil. Soc. 1977 121(2): 97-99.* Medical teams from the military and the Manhattan Project began studying the effects of radiation on Japanese civilian survivors five weeks after the atomic bombs fell. In 1946 President Truman ordered the National Academy of Sciences to form the Atomic Bomb Casualty Commission to care for the 100,000 severely affected survivors. The commission also studied death rates, chromosome anomalies, and cancer incidences. In 1975 the joint US-Japanese Radiation Effects Research Foundation took over from the commission.
W. L. Olbrich

961. Watanabe, Masao. AMERICAN SCIENCE TEACHERS IN THE EARLY MEIJI PERIOD. *Japanese Studies in the Hist. of Sci. [Japan] 1976 15: 127-144.* Investigates the selection, age, period of stay, and contribution of American college teachers employed by the University of Tokyo and Sapporo Agricultural College to teach western science, 1860-78, and considers their activities in the context of the history of cultural exchange between Japan and the West to 1900.

962. Watanabe, Toshio. BENJAMIN FRANKLIN AND THE YOUNGER GENERATION OF JAPAN. *Am. Studies Int. 1980 18(2): 35-49.* The

reactions of Japanese humanities students to the autobiographies of Benjamin Franklin and of Fukuzawa Yukichi (1835-1901), one of the forerunners of modern Japan. Most students rejected Franklin's utilitarianism, moralizing, and open self-advancement, prefering Fukuzawa's love of learning for its own sake, antipathy toward worldly success, and avoidance of political commitment. Despite their partiality for things Western, the students remain persistently Japanese in their traditional views and values. Illus., 2 photos.

R. E. Noble

963. Watkins, Floyd C. EVEN HIS NAME WILL DIE: THE LAST DAYS OF PAUL NOBUO TATSUGUCHI. *J. of Ethnic Studies 1976 3(4): 37-48.* Paul Nobuo Tatsuguchi, an American-educated physician, was sent back to Japan by the Seventh-Day Adventist Church, drafted into the Japanese army in 1941, and sent to the remote Attu Island in the Aleutians where he was killed in the final suicidal attack against American positions in May 1943. His diary, which he kept during the last two and one half weeks, is a moving picture of a man caught between two cultures, not fully trusted by the Japanese, and forced to fight people he did not consider enemies. Refutes by implication the question of whether he killed his wounded patients to prevent their capture. Details the reactions of his wife, children, and friends to the family tragedy and postwar efforts by Americans to help them. Transcription problems of the diary itself are numerous, but the dramatic picture of the final preparations for death of the remaining 1,000 Japanese on Attu is incomparable. Based on the author's own wartime experience and study of numerous copies of the diary.

G. J. Bobango

964. Webber, Bert. THE BOMBING OF NORTH AMERICA. *Am. Hist. Illus. 1976 11(8): 30-42.* Discusses the Japanese attempt to bomb North America via air balloons loaded with bombs during World War II.

965. Weiner, Charles. CYCLOTRONS AND INTERNATIONALISM: JAPAN, DENMARK AND THE UNITED STATES, 1935-1945. *XIVth International Congress of the History of Science, Proceedings No. 2 (Tokyo and Kyoto: Science Council of Japan, 1974): 353-368.* Examines the process, 1935-45, by which nuclear physics became a major field of research in Japan, Denmark and the United States following the invention of the cyclotron by Ernest Lawrence in the early 1930's.

966. Weintraub, Sidney. NORTH-SOUTH DIALOGUE AT THE UNITED NATIONS: HOW THE UN VOTES ON ECONOMIC ISSUES. *Int. Affairs [Great Britain] 1977 53(2): 188-201.* The major powers and the developing nations have adopted different attitudes toward voting in the UN General Assembly; especially, the developing countries tend to use their votes to force issues, even if the resulting majority decisions are usually unenforceable. Analyzes six UN economic meetings, 1972-76, in order to establish national voting patterns, with emphasis on the developing nations on the one hand, and the United States, Great Britain, France, Germany, and Japan on the other. The former act to promote confrontation in order to force unilateral concessions or negotiations elsewhere. The UN, in its economic sphere, is a "confrontational forum," stressing the solidarity of the developing nations

against the major powers. Based on UN and press sources; 20 notes.

P. J. Beck

967. White, G. Edward. THE UNACKNOWLEDGED LESSON: EARL WARREN AND THE JAPANESE RELOCATION CONTROVERSY. *Virginia Q. Rev. 1979 55(4): 613-629.* While attorney general and governor of California during World War II, Earl Warren strongly approved Japanese "relocation centers." Describes Warren's career and suggests that the Japanese position contrasted with his position on civil rights as chief justice. In stating in his memoirs that "it was wrong to react so impulsively," Warren was "settling acounts with himself" about a matter that "weighed on his conscience." The author was a Warren law clerk who had read drafts of his posthumously-published memoirs. O. H. Zabel

968. Wiegand, Wayne A. AMBASSADOR IN ABSENTIA: GEORGE MEYER, WILLIAM II AND THEODORE ROOSEVELT. *Mid-America 1974 56(1): 3-15.* George von Lengerke Meyer (1858-1918), US Ambassador to Italy and Russia before World War I, established a close personal relationship with the Emperor William II, not unlike the relationship which developed between German Ambassador Speck von Sternberg and Theodore Roosevelt. The relationship between Meyer and William II served to improve general relations between Germany and the United States and was a factor in prompting William to exert influence on the tsar to submit to US mediation of the Russo-Japanese War in 1905. Based on manuscript, and primary and secondary sources; 28 notes. T. D. Schoonover

969. Wilkins, Mira. AMERICAN-JAPANESE DIRECT FOREIGN INVESTMENT RELATIONSHIPS, 1930-1952. *Business Hist. Rev. 1982 56(4): 497-518.* American direct investment in Japan peaked in 1930 at $61 million and declined to $33 million by 1941. Though the amount of American investment in Japan was not great, the effect of the US presence was significant. The asset value of Japanese-controlled enterprises in America was $35 million in 1941, concentrated in finance, insurance, trading, and shipping. After World War II, American reinvestment in Japan was slow because of restrictive occupation policies designed to eliminate the old industrial concentrations. Based on public records and published sources with some business archival material; 6 tables, 82 notes. C. J. Pusateri

970. Williams, J. E. SIAM: A BONE OF CONTENTION BETWEEN BRITAIN AND THE UNITED STATES, 1942-46. *Rev. of Int. Studies [Great Britain] 1982 8(3): 187-202.* The declared war between Thailand and both Great Britain and the United States was seen as hostility by the British but merely as Thai subordination to the Japanese invaders by the United States.

971. Williams, Justin, Sr. FROM CHARLOTTESVILLE TO TOKYO: MILITARY GOVERNMENT TRAINING AND DEMOCRATIC REFORMS IN OCCUPIED JAPAN. *Pacific Hist. Rev. 1982 51(4): 407-422.* The School of Military Government (SMG) program at the University of Virginia in 1944 and 1945 had a significant impact on the Allied occupation of Japan.

After completing their studies at SMG, the student-officers studied Japanese civilization and language at one of six civil affairs training schools. In Tokyo on 26 September 1945, they were informed by General Douglas MacArthur's chief of staff that there would be no military government in Japan. Some of them were assigned nonmilitary tasks in Japan: economic, scientific, civil information, education, public health and welfare, natural resources, and government. Their objective was the democratization of Japan. MacArthur's success as proconsul of Japan owes much to them. Based on Justin Williams, Sr., Collection, McKeldin Library, University of Maryland, and other primary sources; 17 notes. R. N. Lokken

972. Williamson, John A. and Lanier, William D. THE TWELVE DAYS OF THE *ENGLAND*. *US Naval Inst. Pro. 1980 106(3): 76-83.* In May 1944, the USS *England* (DE-635) was a recently commissioned destroyer escort operating in the Pacific Ocean. As part of Escort Division 39, the *England*, between 19 May and 30 May 1944, sank six Japanese submarines, one of which, the *I-16*, was one of the largest submarines ever built in Japan. Author Williamson was the *England*'s executive officer during that time. 4 photos, map. A. N. Garland

973. Winiecki, Jan. DE FORENTE STATER IN VERDENSØKONOMIEN—AKTUELLE TENDENSER OG PERSPEKTIVER [The United States in the world economy—trends and perspectives]. *Internasjonal Politikk [Norway] 1975 (1): 89-108.* At the beginning of the 1970's many predicted, for a number of reasons, an American economic setback vis-à-vis Western Europe and Japan. Recently, however, world economic trends and various phenomena, together with a strengthening of the American national economic basis and measures undertaken by the government, tend to decelerate this tendency and to some extent re-establish the strong American position. J

974. Winiecki, Jan. ŹRÓDŁA INFLACJI W GOSPODARCE KAPITALISTYCZNEJ: CECHY CHARAKTERYSTYCZNE WSPÓŁCZESNEJ INFLACJI [Sources of inflation in the capitalist economy: contemporary characteristics of inflation]. *Ekonomista [Poland] 1979 (3): 691-711.* Analyzes inflation in the capitalist countries, particularly in Western Europe, the United States, and Japan, 1958-68.

975. Wittner, Lawrence S. FORUM: JAPANESE-AMERICAN MILITARY RELATIONS IN THE POSTWAR ERA. *Peace and Change 1976 4(1): 64-67.* Discusses US funding of military bases and of Japan's rearmament following World War II; questions the real strategic importance of Japan in US security and defense policy, 1946-70's.

976. Wolk, Herman S. THE B-29, THE A-BOMB, AND THE JAPANESE SURRENDER. *Air Force Mag. 1975 58(2): 55-61.* Discusses the role of air power in the war against Japan, 1941-45, relying on conversations between the author and General Curtis Lemay.

977. Wollenberg, Charles. SCHOOLS BEHIND BARBED WIRE. *California Hist. Q. 1976 55(3): 210-217.* A brief survey of the public school system set

up by the War Relocation Authority for the children of Japanese Americans sent to the relocation centers in World War II. Of 110,000 evacuees, 25,000 were school age children. The public schools sought to teach American ideals within the hypocritical framework of prison camps. Supplies, equipment, books, and teachers were characterized as second-rate. Yet school life offered continuity amid the shattering effect of relocation. The traditional emphasis on education continued through the war years. Despite imprisonment because of race and shortcomings in the schools, most Nisei remained committed to the ideals of assimilation and education. Based on contemporary and secondary published works; photos, 24 notes. A. Hoffman

978. Wright, Christopher C., comp. COMPARATIVE NOTES ON U.S. TREATY CRUISER DESIGN. *Warship Int. 1980 17(4): 311-332.* Presents selected data on design work by the US Navy on 10,000-ton cruisers, 1925-27, and compares it to some contemporary Japanese cruisers, focusing on protection and weight.

979. Yagisawa, Mitsuo. AMERICA'S FOUR UMBRELLAS—BOTH SIDES OF THE JAPAN-U.S. SECURITY SYSTEM. *Japan Q. [Japan] 1981 28(2): 161-174.* Japan is dependent on the United States for food, energy, natural resources, and for its nuclear umbrella. Japan is the world's largest food-importing country, getting 80% of its feed grains, soybeans, wheat, and corn from the United States. It is 99% dependent on foreign oil, most of which is controlled by American companies, and also depends for nuclear fuel supplies on the Anglo-Saxon nations. In terms of resources, it is the second largest resource-consuming country in the world, most of the scarce metals again being controlled by the United States. F. W. Iklé

980. Yamamura, Kozo. RECENT RESEARCH IN JAPANESE ECONOMIC HISTORY, 1600-1945. *Res. in Econ. Hist. 1977 (Supplement 1): 221-245.* Reviews English-language literature available to the US researcher on Japanese economic history, 1600-1945. Works on the Tokugawa period exist but are not plentiful; the post-Tokugawa period is thoroughly covered. Notes and describes the major works. Only one study is available on World War II. 9 notes. V. L. Human

981. Yang, Caroline A. THE CONTINUING IMPORTANCE OF EDUCATIONAL EXCHANGE. *Japan Q. [Japan] 1983 30(1): 72-75.* The only reliable long-term method of promoting greater understanding among nations is the exchange of people, and most effective are the long-term educational exchange programs. Of these, the Fulbright program is the oldest, best known, and most effective. It is now equally funded and managed by both the United States and Japan, and is the only program also receiving private sector support.
F. W. Iklé

982. Yao, Richard. JAPANESE CAR QUOTAS AND ANTITRUST—A REEXAMINATION. *New York U. J. of Int. Law and Pol. 1983 15(3): 697-730.* Political pressure on Japan's automobile industry, which in 1981 forced the Japanese to impose quotas on imports to the United States, is a form of price-fixing and is illegal under the Sherman Antitrust Act.

983. Yasukawa, Takeshi. JAPAN AND AMERICA LOOKING AHEAD. *Atlantic Community Q. 1975 13(2): 189-192.* In an address to a trade symposium in Miami in early 1975 the Japanese Ambassador surveys the major political-economic issues of concern to the United States and Japan in the years ahead. J

984. Yavenditti, Michael J. THE AMERICAN PEOPLE AND THE USE OF ATOMIC BOMBS ON JAPAN: THE 1940S. *Historian 1974 36(2): 224-247.* A study of American public opinion in the 1940's on the use of atomic bombs on Japan. The immediate response was largely favorable since it undoubtedly shortened World War II, with little sense of personal responsibility or guilt, especially in view of the secrecy surrounding its development and use. There was adept use of a double standard in evaluation of the conduct of the war, including matters related to the bombs. The controversy which developed was significant but limited in participation. The vocal minority of critics "could not even persuade many members of the intelligentsia to condemn the atomic bombings." 82 notes. R. V. Ritter

985. Yavenditti, Michael J. THE HIROSHIMA MAIDENS AND AMERICAN BENEVOLENCE IN THE 1950'S. *Mid-America 1982 64(2): 21-39.* Recounts the experiences of participants in the 1955-56 attempts to provide reconstructive surgery to 25 young Japanese women, victims of the 1945 atomic bombing of Hiroshima, Japan. Private impetus in the United States generated most of the necessary funds, and the US Air Force furnished transportation to a New York hospital. American motivation for the effort seemed to be sympathy rather than guilt. The patients' demeanor, known nationally through heavy media coverage, favorably disposed American public opinion to the maidens. Medically, the operations were largely successful; politically, they fostered good relations between Japan and the United States. Mainly secondary sources, with some reference to the Norman Cousins Papers; 80 notes. P. J. Woehrmann

986. Yeats, A. J. EFFECTIVE TARIFF PROTECTION IN THE UNITED STATES, THE EUROPEAN ECONOMIC COMMUNITY, AND JAPAN. *Q. R. of Econ. and Business 1974 14(2): 41-50.* "Adoption of measures to expand developing-country exports is being increasingly advocated as a form of economic aid. Since the reduction of tariff barriers presents one of the most effective means of achieving this objective, this article estimates current rates of effective protection against developing-country products in major industrial markets. The study shows that seemingly low, nominal tariffs frequently mask effective rates which are several times higher. Further, nominal and effective protection is shown to be graduated by stage of processing, which results in a strong disincentive for the development of manufacturing industries in developing nations." J

987. Yonekawa, Shin'ichi. SAIRON BŌSEKI KIGYŌ SEICHŌ NO KOKUSAI HIKAKU [The growth of cotton spinning firms—a comparative study]. *Shakaikeizaishigaku (Socio-Economic Hist.) [Japan] 1982 47(5): 1-32.* Compares the growth of cotton spinning firms in Great Britain, the United States, India, and Japan during the years 1870-1939.

988. Yonge, C. M. THE SEA-OTTER AND HISTORY. *Hist. Today [Great Britain] 1978 28(3): 171-177.* Gives a history of human interaction with sea otters, 18th-20th centuries, throughout Pacific coastal areas in the United States, Canada, and Japan; highlights present endangered status of the animals and their former importance in the fur trade.

989. Yoshitsu, Michael M. IRAN AND AFGHANISTAN IN JAPANESE PERSPECTIVE. *Asian Survey 1981 21(5): 501-514.* The Iranian situation severely strained Japan's relations with America by sparking sharp differences over strategic, economic, and energy policy. Japanese leaders employed a series of approaches designed to strike a balance between their Middle East interests and US friendship. With regard to the Soviet invasion of Afghanistan, the Japanese leaders wanted to react decisively. Prime Minister Ohira and his advisers adopted a forceful tone, but the policies employed were more symbolic than substantive. Differences between Tokyo and Washington, highlighted during recent Middle East crises, may resurface in the future. Based on interviews and newspapers; 51 notes. M. A. Eide

990. Young, Dana B. THE VOYAGE OF THE *KANRIN MARU* TO SAN FRANCISCO, 1860. *California History 1983 61(4): 264-275.* Describes the welcome given by San Franciscans to the *Kanrin Maru,* the ship bearing the vanguard of the official ambassadorial party that would ratify the Treaty of Amity and Commerce between the United States and Japan. The ship arrived on 17 March 1860, and its crew received considerable attention from local politicians and newspapers. Despite the great cultural differences in customs and language, a general atmosphere of friendliness prevailed. The Japanese officials attended several receptions, stayed at the International Hotel, and visited local tradesmen. The US Navy put the *Kanrin Maru* in drydock for repairs, at no charge. On 8 May the ship returned to Japan, having set a historical precedent for Japanese visits to the United States. Photos, 23 notes. A. Hoffman

991. Yü, Yüh-chao. SHIH-T'ING-SHENG PU CH'ENG-JÊN CHU-I CHIH YAN-CHIU [A study of Henry Stimson's doctrine of "Non-Recognition"]. *Shih-ta Hsüeh-pao (Bull. of National Taiwan Normal U.) [Taiwan] 1981 26: 353-380.* Henry L. Stimson's doctrine of nonrecognition for the Japanese puppet-state of Manchukuo developed from an initially conciliatory approach to Japanese aggression in Manchuria in September 1931 to a sternly worded nonrecognition principle in January 1932. Unfortunately, this doctrine had little effect on Japanese aggression in China, largely because it did not receive the support of the European powers and because President Herbert Hoover refused to back the doctrine with military force. Nevertheless, Stimson's doctrine did help to bar the Japanese puppet-state of Manchukuo from receiving international recognition, thus giving China indirectly legal as well as moral support in her efforts to recover Manchuria. Based on Stimson's *Diary* and *The Far Eastern Crisis,* the Lytton Report, and secondary sources; 64 notes, biblio. R. C. Houston

992. Zancardi, Pietro and Merlo, Vittorio. LA BATTAGLIA DI MIDWAY [World War II in the Pacific: the battle of Midway]. *Riv. Marittima*

[Italy] 1974 107(6): 28-40, (7/8): 63-76. Part I. Emphasizes the strategical importance of the battle of Midway which was the turning point of the war in the Pacific. Outlines the Japanese and American planning of the complex MI operation; describes the development of operations; and critically examines the various stages, stressing the new aspect of the war in the Pacific based on the employment of aircraft carriers. Part II. Explains the errors of Japanese planning, the rigidity of which, together with the non-massing of their forces on sea, favored the success of Nimitz's operative concept of calculated risk and the attainment of surprise and air control by the American forces. The actions of the most important protagonists of the battle are described in detail.   J

993. Zimmerman, E. C.   HENRY SIGNARO MIDSUNO: A JAPAN MISSION IN 1895? *Concordia Hist. Inst. Q. 1981 54(3): 102-112.* Biography of Henry Signaro Midsuno (1870-1933); born in Japan and educated at Concordia College in Ft. Wayne, Indiana, he returned to Japan in 1895 as a Lutheran missionary and eventually converted to Catholicism.

994. Zobrist, Benedict K.   RESOURCES OF PRESIDENTIAL LIBRARIES FOR THE HISTORY OF POST-WORLD WAR II AMERICAN MILITARY GOVERNMENT IN GERMANY AND JAPAN. *Military Affairs 1978 42(1): 17-19.* Presidential libraries present to the scholar almost boundless research resources on the major aspects of the history of American military government in Germany and Japan. The Franklin D. Roosevelt Library contains much material, especially the papers of Henry M. Morgenthau. The Truman and Eisenhower libraries contain relatively little material, while the John F. Kennedy Library has significant holdings. The Hoover Library has material on his views. A systematic study of the post-World War II occupation of Germany and Japan is still to be written. 2 notes.

A. M. Osur

995. Zorgbibe, Charles.   TRILATÉRALISME [Trilateralism]. *Défense Natl. [France] 1978 34(7): 41-53.* Considers the origins and aims of the Trilateral Commission set up by the Rockefellers in 1973, indicating the preponderance of American interest in this strategic triangle which also includes Japan and Western Europe.

996. —.   EKONOMICHESKII SPAD V KAPITALISTICHESKOM MIRE [Decline of the capitalist economy]. *Mirovaia Ekonomika i Mezhdunarodnye Otnosheniia [USSR] 1981 (7): 106-130.*
Grigor'ev, L.   NEKOTORYE PROBLEMY MIROVOGO EKONOMICHESKOGO KRIZISA 1980 G. [Some problems of the world economic crisis of 1980], *pp. 106-109.*
Entov, R.   SPAD V SSHA [Decline in the United States], *pp. 109-112.*
Shenaev, Viacheslav.   EKONOMIKA ZAPADNOI EVROPY [The economy of Western Europe], *pp. 112-115.*
Pevzner, Ia.   IAPONIIA: PROTIVORECHIIA "REINDUSTRIALIZATSIIA" [Japan: the contradictions of reindustrialization], *pp. 115-117.*
Khesin, E.   UGLUBLENIE EKONOMICHESKOGO KRIZISA V VELIKOBRITANII [The deepening economic crisis in Great Britain], *pp. 117-119.*

Bel'chuk, A.   MIROVOI KRIZIS 1980-1981 GG.: OBSHCHAIA OTSEN-KA POLOZHENIIA [World crisis, 1980-81: general evaluation of the situation], *pp. 121-122.*

Acharkan, V.   OSOBENNOSTI SOVREMENNOGO MEKHANIZMA FORMIROVANIIA VALIUTNYKH KURSOV [Features of the contemporary mechanism for establishing currency exchange rates], *pp. 123-124.*

Nikolaenko, S.   POTREBLENIE I EKONOMICHESKII TSIKL V SSHA [Consumption and the economic cycle in the United States], *pp. 124-125.* Conference reports from the Academy of Sciences of the USSR on economic conditions in capitalist countries, 1970-80.

997. —.   [THE FUTURE OF THE DOLLAR]. *Foreign Policy 1973 (11): 3-32.*
Cooper, Richard N.   THE FUTURE OF THE DOLLAR, pp. 3-23.
Oppenheimer, Peter M.   A BRITISH VIEW, pp. 23-28.
Salin, Pascal.   A FRENCH VIEW, pp. 28-31.
Koji, Motoo.   A JAPANESE VIEW, pp. 31-32. Discusses the strengths and weakness of the dollar in the international monetary system.   S

998. —.   INTERVIEW WITH ROBERT W. TUCKER. *SAIS Rev. 1981 (1): 83-91.* Interview with Robert W. Tucker, professor of political science at the Johns Hopkins University on his various writings of 1968-80 on American power in the Persian Gulf, American ties with Japan and Europe, America's role in Eastern Europe, and the agenda for the Reagan administration.

999. —.   THE JAPAN/UNITED STATES TEXTBOOK STUDY PROJECT: PERCEPTIONS IN THE TEXTBOOKS OF EACH COUNTRY ABOUT THE HISTORY OF THE OTHER. *Hist. Teacher 1983 16(4): 541-567.*
Goodman, Grant K.   THE PROJECT, *pp. 541-543.* Describes the Japan/United States Textbook Study Project, which evaluated the treatment accorded to each country in the other nation's leading history, geography, and social studies textbooks.
Homma, Nagayo.   THE AMERICAN TEXTBOOK, *pp. 543-552.* Evaluates 28 US textbooks from a Japanese perspective, for their treatment of Japan and Japanese people.
Najita, Tetsuo.   TEXTBOOKS AND POLITICS IN CONTEMPORARY JAPAN, *pp. 553-562.* Describes the role of textbooks in Japanese education, and discusses their treatment of Americans and American history.
Becker, James M.   COMMENTARY: IN SEARCH OF BETTER TEXTBOOKS, *pp. 563-567.* Gives a general comparison of textbooks used in the United States and Japan.   L. K. Blaser

1000. —.   [PEARL HARBOR AND THE *COLORADO, NEVADA, TANEY,* AND *UTAH*]. *US Naval Inst. Pro. 1976 102(12): 46-54.*

Shrader, Grahame F. USS COLORADO: THE "OTHER" BATTLESHIP, *pp. 46-47.* The *Colorado* (BB45), on 7 December 1941, was at the Puget Sound Navy Yard in Bremerton, Washington; she had arrived there for overhaul on 3 August 1941, and was due to return to Pearl Harbor in late November 1941 to relieve the *West Virginia.* She was delayed because of blower trouble, and was spared the fate of her sister ships at Pearl Harbor. Although the crew of the *Colorado* spent a number of tense days after 7 December, 1941, expecting a Japanese attack on the west coast of the United States, nothing happened. She left Bremerton in February 1942 but did not get into actual combat until November, 1943, at Tarawa. Unfortunately, because she had not gone through the Pearl Harbor experience, "the *Colorado* continued throughout the war with an antiquated secondary battery that was virtually useless against enemy aircraft." 2 photos.

Merdinger, Charles J. UNDER WATER AT PEARL HARBOR, *pp. 48-49.* The author was serving on the battleship *Nevada* on 7 December 1941 when that ship, the only battleship at Pearl Harbor to get underway that day, received one torpedo and five bomb hits and was beached. When the *Nevada* sank later in the day, the author was stationed in the ship's plotting room, which was then actually lower than the surface of the water. He and his men stayed in position until 3:00 p.m., when water began to enter the room. They climbed topside through an adjacent communications tube. This article is based on the author's recollections which have been recorded as part of the Naval Institute's Oral History Program. 2 photos.

Kraft, Carl and Kraft, Nell. USCGC TANEY: STILL IN SERVICE 35 YEARS LATER, *pp. 50-51.* Of the 101 US military vessels in the vicinity of Pearl Harbor on 7 December 1941, only one, the US Coast Guard cutter *Taney* (WHEC-37) is still in active service. Because of certain fortuitous happenings, she was ready for combat that Sunday morning, but most of the action took place beyond the range of her guns. For the next week she patrolled the harbor entrance; she served with distinction throughout the war, suffered no major damage, and survived "to fight in two more wars." She now operates from the Coast Guard station at Portsmouth, Virginia. 4 photos.

Eldredge, Michael S. THE OTHER SIDE OF THE ISLAND: USS UTAH AT PEARL HARBOR, *pp. 52-54.* Not many of the US Navy's ships were older than the USS *Utah* on 7 December 1941. She had been commissioned in 1911 and had "served for 19 years as BB-31." In July 1931 she had been redesignated AG-16 and was "destined to serve out her final years as a target ship." At the time of the Japanese attack she was berthed at Fox-11, on the northwest side of Ford Island, which was usually assigned to an aircraft carrier. Struck by two torpedoes, the *Utah* eventually capsized. Two attempts to salvage her failed and Fox-11 remains her final resting place; 54 of her crew are still entombed in her hull. In 1970 Congress authorized construction of a memorial over the ship, and she is now "one of the two remaining hulks that remind us of the tragedy of Pearl Harbor." 5 photos. A. N. Garland

1001. —. RITE OF PASSAGE: THE COMMISSION HEARINGS 1981. Amerasia J. 1981 8(2): 53-100. Selected transcripts of testimonies by first, second, and third generation Japanese Americans before the Commission on Wartime Relocation and Internment of Civilians, held in August 1981 in Los Angeles and San Francisco. The testimonies relate the immediate and delayed impact of the internment on Japanese Americans during World War II.
E. S. Johnson

1002. —. SALT AND MBFR: THE NEXT PHASE—REPORT OF A TRILATERAL CONFERENCE. Survival [Great Britain] 1975 17(1): 14-24. Discusses topics covered at a 1974 conference on Strategic Arms Limitation Talks between the United States and the USSR, including the military objectives of Western Europe and Japan.

1003. —. SEKAI SHIHONSHUGI TO AJIA NO IMIN—19-SEIKI KŌHAN KARA 20-SEIKI SHOTŌ [World capitalism and emigration in Asia, 1834-1930]. Shakaikeizaishigaku (Socio-Economic Hist.) [Japan] 1981 47(4): 1-117.
Tsunoyama, Sakae. MONDAI TEIKI [Introduction], pp. 1-7. The vast migration movements in Asia, 1834-1930, took place mainly in response to the demands of the international market. There were two kinds of emigrants: emigrants as coolies in the plantations and mines, and emigrant groups engaged in the service sector and commercial activities in Southeast Asia.
Sugihara, Kaoru. INDO-JIN IMIN TO PURANTĒSHON-KEIZAI— 19-SEKIMATSU DAIICHIJITAISENKO NO TŌ, NAN AJIA O CHŪSHIN NI [Indian emigration and the export economies of South and Southeast Asia, 1890-1920], pp. 8-25. Shows the basic pattern of Indian emigration and the role it played in the process of integration of South and Southeast Asia into the world economy, 1890-1920. Firstly, compares the nature of the *kangany* and *maistry* recruited emigration of Burma, Ceylon, and Malaya with that of the indentured emigration; and secondly, looks at the economic basis of the *kangany* and *maistry* systems.
Yasuba, Yasukichi. KOMENTO I: TŌNAN AJIA NI OKERU RŌDŌ IDŌ [Comment: labor migration in Southeast Asia], pp. 26-32. Describes and analyzes the Chinese migrants, estimated at two million, to Siam in the period between the middle of the 19th century and World War I. The reason for high migration was that Siam needed Chinese immigrants for male, unskilled labor, while life in South China was so difficult as to push Chinese to migrate.
Itō, Toshikatsu. KOMENTO II: SHIMO-BIRUMA NO KAIHATSU TO IMIN—UE-BIRUMA KARA NO IMIN O MEGUTTE [Comment: development of the delta in lower Burma and immigration—the "pull-push" approach to migration from upper Burma], pp. 33-56. Traces the trends of immigration to the delta and discusses the "pull-push" factors of migration, concentrating on the "push" factor of migration from upper Burma. Examines the relationship between "push" factors and colonial policies, 1881-1931.

Shiba, Yoshinobu. MEIJIKI NIHON RAIJŪ KAKYŌ NI TSUITE [The Chinese merchants in Hakodate, 1854-1910], pp. 57-72. Describes the activities of Chinese merchants who settled in the city of Hakodate, a treaty port of Japan, with its opening for international trade in 1854. This port would soon be a very important center of Sino-Japanese trade.

Kodama, Masaaki. MEIJIKI AMERIKA GASSHŪKOKU E NO NIHONJIN IMIN [Japanese emigration to the United States in the Meiji era], pp. 73-99. Analyzes the social and economic base of Japanese emigration to the United States from 1885 until the conclusion of the Gentleman's Agreement between Japan and the United States in 1908. Concentrates on the period of industrialization in Japan and on emigration policy in Japan and the United States.

Kimura, Kenji. MEIJIKI CHŌSEN SHINSHUTSU NIHONJIN NI TSUITE [Japanese residents in Korea in the Meiji era], pp. 100-117. Japanese residents in Korea, 1880-1910, mainly consisted of foreign traders, brokers, and retail dealers who obtained a base of penetration, settling there with the help of the Japanese government's policy on behalf of the residents and with the support of privileged big *seishō* (businessmen with political affiliations).

1004. —. [ULYSSES S. GRANT VISITS JAPAN, 1879]. *Am. Hist. Illus.* 1981 16(3): 36-45.
Finn, Dallas. GRANT IN JAPAN, pp. 36-37, 40-45.
Grant, Julia Dent. MRS. GRANT REMEMBERS JAPAN, pp. 38-39. Accounts of General Ulysses S. Grant and Mrs. Grant's 1879 trip to Japan for both private and official reasons after Grant had served two terms as President.

1005. —. THE WASHINGTON ENERGY CONFERENCE. *Atlantic Community Q.* 1974 12(1): 22-54.
Kissinger, Henry A. THE AMERICAN CHALLENGE, pp. 22-30.
Jobert, Michel. THE FRENCH RESPONSE, pp. 31-34.
Douglas-Home, Alex. THE BRITISH VIEW, pp. 35-37.
Schmidt, Helmut. THE GERMAN VIEW, pp. 37-42.
Ohira, Masayoshi. THE JAPANESE VIEW, pp. 43-47.
Evensen, Jens. THE NORWEGIAN VIEW, pp. 47-50.
Scheel, Walter. THE VIEW OF THE EUROPEAN COMMUNITIES, pp. 51-54. "The world's most developed nations met in Washington to assess the damages of the oil crises—both from the standpoint of supply and the overriding burden of cost. The meeting was seen as a prelude to others that will follow, involving both the underdeveloped and producing nations. The meeting was called by the United states and ... Secretary of State Henry Kissinger outlines the dimensions of the problem and the necessity for cooperative action among all nations of the world to solve it. France's Michel Jobert has a largely negative reaction to the United States initiative ... More positive are the British View, ... the German View, ... the Japanese View, ... the Norwegian View, ... and the View of the European Communities as presented by its President, Walter Scheel. The meeting adopted a program ... from which France dissented in many major respects. The other nations were unanimous." J

1006. —. THE WORLD CAR: WHO'S BEHIND THE WHEEL? AN INTERVIEW WITH SAM GINDON, RESEARCH DIRECTOR OF THE CANADIAN UAW. *Can. Dimension [Canada] 1981 15(5): 20-23.* Gindon traces the history of the auto industry in Western Europe, Japan, and the United States during the postwar period, describes the concept of the world car, "a (fuel-efficient) car produced not just for a single market but for numerous markets around the world," and discusses the possibility of public ownership of a country's auto industries and what all of the above means for Canadian auto workers.

1007. —. THE 35TH ANNIVERSARY OF THE DEFEAT OF IMPERIALIST JAPAN. *Far Eastern Affairs [USSR] 1980 (4): 3-14.* Blames World War II on the anti-Communist strategy of US imperialism, designed to encourage Japanese aggression.

5

KOREA

(including North Korea, South Korea, and the Korean War)

1008. Amody, Francis J. THE SABRE TOOTH CHEETAHS OF OSAN. *Am. Aviation Hist. Soc. J.* 1980 25(1): 42-44. Discusses the flights of the F-86F Sabres, converted from F-51D Mustangs, ships of the UN Command (UNC) during the Korean War, the first jet-equipped ships of the South African Air Force and the first to be flown by foreign airmen under their own flag, which operated from Osan Air Base near Seoul; 1950-53.

1009. Bacchus, Wilfred A. THE RELATIONSHIP BETWEEN COMBAT AND PEACE NEGOTIATIONS: FIGHTING WHILE TALKING IN KOREA, 1951-1953. *Orbis* 1973 17(2): 545-574.

1010. Baker, Edward J. POLITICS IN SOUTH KOREA. *Current Hist.* 1982 81(474): 173-174, 177-178. Discusses the assassination of South Korean President Park Chung-hee in 1979, his replacement by General Chun Doo-hwan, and US-Korean relations since the incident.

1011. Benson, Larry. THE USAF'S KOREAN WAR RECRUITING RUSH... AND THE GREAT TENT CITY AT LACKLAND AIR FORCE BASE. *Aerospace Hist.* 1978 25(2): 61-73. As a result of the Communist invasion of South Korea in June, 1950, the United States was compelled to rebuild its armed forces to a wartime level. The Air Force, always a volunteer service, lifted enlistment quotas and a stampede of youth joined. The only basic training center was Lackland Air Force Base near San Antonio, Texas. Its population soon rose to more than 70,000 airmen. Recounts the resulting problems in preparing civilians to man the Air Force and the investigations of the situation by Congressional committees. Based on official sources; Unit histories, Senate Reports and the Congressional Record, interviews with USAF personnel, newspaper and magazine articles, and secondary sources; 13 photos, table, 76 notes. C. W. Ohrvall

1012. Bernstein, Barton J. THE ORIGINS OF AMERICA'S COMMITMENT IN KOREA. *Foreign Service J.* 1978 55(3): 10-13, 34. Recently declassified documents concerning events in Korea, 1950-60, demonstrate that US presence in Korea has stabilized the area and held it firm against continued Communist expansion; Syngman Rhee had to be restrained in his insistence that US military presence continue until Korea could be united.

1013. Bernstein, Barton J. THE POLICY OF RISK: CROSSING THE 38TH PARALLEL AND MARCHING TO THE YALU. *Foreign Service J. 1977 54(3): 16-22, 29.* Discusses foreign policy and military strategy in the Korean War, 1950-52, concentrating on the actions of Harry S. Truman, Dean Acheson, and Douglas MacArthur.

1014. Bernstein, Barton J. THE WEEK WE WENT TO WAR: AMERICAN INTERVENTION IN THE KOREAN CIVIL WAR. *Foreign Service J. 1977 54(1): 6-9, 33-35.* Discusses President Harry S. Truman and Secretary of State Dean Acheson's appraisals of the USSR's military aims in Korea as a major factor in the US decision to intervene in the Korean War in June 1950. Article to be continued.

1015. Bishop, Donald M. NAVY BLUE IN OLD KOREA: THE ASIATIC SQUADRON AND THE AMERICAN LEGATION, 1892-1897. *J. of Social Sciences and Humanities [South Korea] 1975 (42): 49-63.* Describes the naval dimension of American policy in Korea following the signing of the Korean-American Treaty of 1882. The Asiatic Squadron routinely surveyed the coast, showed the flag, and protected lives and commerce against overt threats. A coaling station was proposed; "good offices" were extended after the Soldier's Revolt of 1882. Naval officers were generally reluctant to involve the US Navy in Korean affairs, but the Korean king desired an American presence to help stabilize his senescent dynasty. The Navy therefore played an occasional role in Korean internal affairs. Nonetheless, the Navy more faithfully reflected the official American policy of noninvolvement than did the legation. Based on legation and naval correspondence files, contemporary reports, and on English-language secondary sources; 51 notes. A

1016. Brooks, James L. THAT DAY (OVER THE YALU). *Aerospace Historian 1975 22(2): 65-69.* The author flew F-86 Sabre jet fighters during the Korean War. A World War II fighter ace, he was in the first group of F-86 pilots and aircraft transferred to Korea in November, 1950, and was in one of the first encounters between United Nations and North Korean jet fighters. 5 photos. C. W. Ohrvall

1017. Brun, Ellen and Hersh, Jacques. THE KOREAN WAR: 20 YEARS LATER. *Monthly R. 1973 25(2): 44-53.* American imperialist-motivated interference in Korean politics was the key factor in the origins of the Korean War.

1018. Chung, Yong Hwan. REPATRIATION UNDER THE UNITED STATES ARMY MILITARY GOVERNMENT IN KOREA, 1945-1948. *Asian Forum 1976 8(2): 25-44.* Examines the impact of the repatriation of Koreans from Manchuria, China, Japan, and other areas of the world and of the refugees from North Korea from 1945 to 1948, and the impact of the repatriation of Japanese and other foreigners from South Korea to their homelands during the same period. Based on an interview with Dr. John Wook Moon, former member of the US Army Military Government in Korea, and published sources; 77 notes. R. B. Orr

1019. Cigliani, Carlo. POLITICA E GUERRA [Politics and war]. *Riv. Militare [Italy] 1978 101(5): 97-108.* Describes military operations in Korea, 1950-51, and maintains that General Douglas MacArthur's analysis of the political situation was correct.

1020. Cole, James L., Jr. LAMPLIGHTERS & GYPSIES. *Aerospace Historian 1973 20(1): 30-35.* Describes various missions flown by the C-47 "Gooney Bird" during the Korean War. S

1021. Colebrook, Joan. PRISONERS OF WAR. *Commentary 1974 57(1): 30-37.* Discusses American public opinion and Communist propaganda about treatment of prisoners of war in the Korean War and the Vietnam War. S

1022. Coolidge, T. Jefferson, Jr. KOREA: THE CASE AGAINST WITHDRAWAL. *Asian Affairs: An Am. Rev. 1976 4(2): 71-84.* Analyzes the consequences of US withdrawal for the Republic of Korea as a nation (military security, political stability, humanitarian concerns); US-Asian relations; and Soviet, Communist Chinese, and North Korean reactions. Primary sources; 3 notes. R. B. Mendel

1023. Cooling, B. Franklin. ALLIED INTEROPERABILITY IN THE KOREAN WAR. *Military Rev. 1983 63(6): 26-52.* The Korean War is an excellent example of interoperability of allied combat forces in action. The US Army quickly learned the two basic points necessary for efficient allied interoperability—the standardization of weapons and ammunition, and the need for language commonality as a means of communication. Beyond this, Americans learned that cultural and moral understandings of allied troop's native beliefs greatly improved the integration of these units into the allied chain of command. 5 pictures, 2 charts, 36 notes. D. H. Cline

1024. Delmas, Claude. IL Y A VINGT-CINQ ANS: LA GUERRE DE CORÉE OU LE PAROXYSME DE LA GUERRE FROIDE [Twenty-five years ago: the Korean War or the culminating point of the Cold War]. *Défense Natl. [France] 1975 31(7): 45-56.* Examines the role of the Korean War in the evolution of foreign relations between the USSR, the United States, and China, indicating its significance as the culminating point of the Cold War.

1025. Delmas, Claude. IL Y A VINGT-CINQ ANS: LE CONFLICT TRUMAN-MAC ARTHUR [Twenty-five years ago: the Truman-MacArthur conflict]. *Défense Natl. [France] 1976 32(6): 83-98.* The conflict between President Harry S. Truman and General Douglas MacArthur over US foreign policy toward China during the Korean War demonstrates the need for the soldier's subordination to the politician, and their common adherence to clearly defined objectives.

1026. Delmas, J. STRATÉGIE ET TACTIQUE: CORÉE 1950 [Strategy and tactics: Korea 1950]. *Rev. Hist. des Armées [France] 1975 2(4): 85-104.* Describes in detail the beginning of the Korean War from the North Korean attack on South Korea on 24 June 1950, to the period in December 1950 when Chinese troops intervened against the UN Expeditionary Force led by General

Douglas MacArthur. Examines the political questions raised by the Chinese passage of the Yalu River, and the personal relationships among MacArthur, General Walton L. Walker, Commander of the US 8th Army, and President Harry S. Truman. Based largely on the memoirs of Truman and MacArthur, the US Army's published account of the war, and secondary sources; 4 illus., 3 maps, 6 notes. A. Blumberg

1027. Dill, James. WINTER OF THE YALU. *Am. Heritage 1982 34(1): 33-48.* First Lieutenant James Dill recounts the march to the Yalu River and back by Battery B, 31st Field Artillery Battalion, 7th Division, following the Inchon landing in September of 1950. After marching to Pusan, they sailed for Iwon, where they went ashore and began their march toward the Yalu. Halting at Kapsan in November, they were quickly ordered to retreat back to Hungnam and eventual evacuation by sea when the waves of Chinese troops intervened. Many of those positioned so far to the north did not make it out in time. 8 photos, illus. J. F. Paul

1028. Dorwart, Jeffery M. THE INDEPENDENT MINISTER: JOHN M. B. SILL AND THE STRUGGLE AGAINST JAPANESE EXPANSION IN KOREA, 1894-1897. *Pacific Hist. Rev. 1975 44(4): 485-502.* John M. B. Sill, US minister and consul general to Korea 1894-97, used his position to resist Japanese expansionism a decade before such a position became official American policy. He obtained an American-named legation guard in Seoul during the Sino-Japanese War, rather than relying on a Japanese guard, as US Navy officers suggested. After the war, Sill constantly cabled Secretary of State Walter Q. Gresham warnings about Japan's threat to American interests in Korea. He enunciated in 1895 a clear statement of what would later become known as the Open Door policy. He also gave aid and asylum to Korean officials opposed to Japan, violating an explicit State Department directive to avoid involvement in Korea's internal politics. Based on documents in the National Archives, the Horace Allen Papers (New York Public Library) and the W. W. Rockhill Papers (Harvard). 62 notes. W. K. Hobson

1029. Doyle, James H. and Mayer, Arthur J. DECEMBER 1950 AT HUNGNAM. *US Naval Inst. Pro. 1979 105(4): 44-55.* In December 1950, a US naval force assembled off the port of Hungnam, North Korea, to evacuate the US Army's X Corps and its fighting and support units. In addition, the naval force had to evacuate tons of supplies and thousands of Korean refugees. Despite the evacuation's eventual success, it was fraught with danger, and only the dedicated work and outstanding support rendered by many persons and units permitted it to succeed. 15 photos, map. A. N. Garland

1030. Elowitz, Larry and Spanier, John W. KOREA AND VIETNAM: LIMITED WAR AND THE AMERICAN POLITICAL SYSTEM. *Orbis 1974 18(2): 510-534.*

1031. Endicott, Stephen L. GERM WARFARE AND "PLAUSIBLE DENIAL": THE KOREAN WAR, 1952-1953. *Modern China 1979 5(1): 79-104.* The Chinese and North Korean governments' charges of 1952 that the United States used bacteriological warfare during the Korean War have never been accepted by most Western authorities. Testimony before the 1976 Senate Select Committee to Study Governmental Operations with Respect to Intelligence Activities suggests two points that may lend credence to the charges: bacteriological agents and delivery systems were being developed in Maryland, and a "doctrine of plausible denial" was an accepted part of US diplomacy. Furthermore, several US military leaders favored bacteriological warfare. Confessions, later repudiated, of American airmen released by the North Koreans were supported by statements of Chinese leaders and extensive physical evidence. 13 notes, ref.

K. W. Berger

1032. Farmer, James H. THE MAKING OF THE BATTLE HYMN. *Am. Aviation Hist. Soc. J. 1978 23(1): 37-48.* Dean Elmer Hess was a technical director during 1956 on the film *Battle Hymn,* which was about his career as a fighter pilot in the Korean War and his saving 900 South Korean war orphans.

1033. Foot, Rosemary. THE SINO-AMERICAN CONFLICT IN KOREA: THE US ASSESSMENT OF CHINA'S ABILITY TO INTERVENE IN THE WAR. *Asian Affairs [Great Britain] 1983 14(2): 160-166.* Analyzes the thinking in Washington between July and October 1950 regarding the willingness or ability of the Peoples Republic of China to enter the Korean War. No response from China was expected when troops were sent north of the 38th Parallel. The Pentagon thought that China was too weak politically and militarily, and wholly dependent on the Soviet Union. These errors in judgment contributed to a much enlarged and protracted conflict. Secondary sources; 21 notes.

S. H. Frank

1034. Frisbee, John L. KOREA: LINCHPIN OF US ASIAN POLICY. *Air Force Mag. 1975 58(12): 36-42.* Strategic, economic, political, and military considerations have made US relations with South Korea crucial to US policy in Southeast Asia.

1035. Gittings, John. TALKS, BOMBS AND GERMS: ANOTHER LOOK AT THE KOREAN WAR. *J. of Contemporary Asia [Sweden] 1975 5(2): 205-217.* Criticizes three accepted myths of the Korean War. Americans acted in bad faith at the Panmunjom negotiations because they preferred military victory against the Chinese. They used the issue of prisoners of war in an inflammatory manner and displayed double standards in their own treatment of POW's. Thirdly, they did not practice military restraint against North Korean cities and civilians. Plans were made to use nerve gas, and perhaps also germ warfare.

F. D. Birch

1036. Gross, Charles J. A DIFFERENT BREED OF CATS: THE AIR NATIONAL GUARD AND THE 1968 RESERVE MOBILIZATIONS. *Air U. Rev. 1983 34(2): 92-99.* The mixed success of the Air National Guard mobilization and subsequent service in Vietnam and South Korea during 1968-69 illustrates both the weaknesses and the many strong points of air reserve forces.

1037. Habib, Philip C. US POLICY TOWARD KOREA. *Asian Affairs 1974 1(5): 302-305.*

1038. Halliday, Jon. WHO STARTED THE KOREAN WAR? *Monthly Rev. 1983 34(10): 43-53.* Reviews Bruce Cumings's *The Origins of the Korean War: Liberation and the Emergence of Separate Regimes 1945-1947* (1981), which examines imperialism and class conflict as root causes of the Korean War.

1039. Hamm, Michael J. THE *PUEBLO* AND *MAYAGUEZ* INCIDENTS: A STUDY OF FLEXIBLE RESPONSE AND DECISION-MAKING. *Asian Survey 1977 17(6): 545-555.* The US policy of flexible response was conceived to meet small, limited crises by reacting in graduated and ever-increasing persuasion. Discusses this policy within the framework of the seizure of the *Pueblo* by the North Koreans in 1969 and the capture of the *Mayaguez* by Cambodia in 1975, and points out the reason for its failure in 1969 but its success in 1975. Examines why the US government did not resort to force in the *Pueblo* incident but did employ force in the *Mayaguez* incident. The *Pueblo* incident was a political setback for the United States, but the *Mayaguez* incident was a political victory for President Gerald Ford. Based on newspaper reports and secondary sources; 22 notes. M. Feingold/S

1040. Han, Sungjoo. SOUTH KOREA AND THE UNITED STATES: THE ALLIANCE SURVIVES. *Asian Survey 1980 20(11): 1075-1086.* The Korean-American relationship has been the foremost foreign policy concern of successive governments of the Republic of Korea (ROK) since its establishment in 1948. The United States has provided extensive military and economic assistance to the ROK, needed until well into the 1960's. In the past decade, however, certain changes in international and South Korean conditions both enable and require the ROK's foreign policy to gradually become less dependent on the United States. Based on economic and political documents and newspapers; 14 notes. M. A. Eide

1041. Han, Sungjoo. SOUTH KOREA: THE POLITICAL ECONOMY OF DEPENDENCY. *Asian Survey 1974 14(1): 43-51.* Dependence of South Korea on Japan and the United States in political, economic, and international affairs caused domestic problems for President Park. One of ten articles in A Survey of Asia in 1973: Part I. S

1042. Han, Sungjoo. SOUTH KOREA 1977: PREPARING FOR SELF-RELIANCE. *Asian Survey 1978 18(1): 45-57.* President Carter's decision to withdraw all US ground forces from South Korea by 1982 caused the ROK government to seek military and economic self-reliance. The Park Tong-sun lobbying scandal strained relations with the United States. In spite of these foreign policy difficulties, South Korea has enjoyed economic growth. 4 tables, 21 notes. M. Feingold

1043. Han, Sungjoo. SOUTH KOREA'S PARTICIPATION IN THE VIETNAM CONFLICT: AN ANALYSIS OF THE U.S.-KOREAN ALLIANCE. *Orbis 1978 21(4): 893-912.* Examines the military participation of South Korea in the Vietnam War from October 1965 to March 1973.

1044. Han, Yung-Chul. THE CARTER ADMINISTRATION'S POLICY TOWARD EAST ASIA: WITH FOCUS ON KOREA. *Am. Studies Int. 1979 18(1): 35-48.* Traces the background of US involvement in Korea, emphasizing initial fear of monolithic communism and the change in attitude caused by Vietnam, detente, and the new China policy. Carter's decision to pull American ground troops out of South Korea had two major motives: normalize relations with North Korea and avoid involvement in another Asian land war. Carter may reconsider: the troops virtually guarantee no North Korean invasion, Japan sees them as an essential part of its US protection, China sees them as a check on Soviet expansion, and even the Soviet view is probably ambivalent. 2 illus., 13 notes. R. E. Noble

1045. Harrison, Selig S. ONE KOREA? *Foreign Policy 1974/75 (17): 35-62.* Proposes a new US policy for Korea based on Korean reunification. Suggests several steps in formulating a new policy: 1) after 1977, instead of giving military equipment to South Korea, the United States should sell supplies on a cash basis; 2) the United States should gradually withdraw its military forces by 1980; 3) while maintaining the US-Korean Security Treaty, the United States should renegotiate it at a later date, provided that North Korea has demonstrated its independence of its Communist allies; and 4) take other steps leading to de facto neutralization of Korea. Based partly on primary sources; 10 notes. R. F. Kugler

1046. Herzon, Frederick D.; Kincaid, John; and Dalton, Verne. PERSONALITY & PUBLIC OPINION: THE CASE OF AUTHORITARIANISM, PREJUDICE, & SUPPORT FOR THE KOREAN & VIETNAM WARS. *Polity 1978 11(1): 92-113.* Relates the authoritarianism theory developed after World War II, and racial prejudice, to US public support for the Korean War and Vietnam War; personality traits influence public opinion only under "conducive conditions."

1047. Hetzel, Frederick A. and Hitchens, Harold L. AN INTERVIEW WITH GENERAL MATTHEW B. RIDGWAY. *Western Pennsylvania Hist. Mag. 1982 65(4): 279-307.* Recounts General Matthew B. Ridgway's military career from 1917, stressing the years 1950-51 when he commanded the American 8th Army in Korea.

1048. Houchins, Lee and Houchins, Chang-su. THE KOREAN EXPERIENCE IN AMERICA, 1903-1924. *Pacific Hist. R. 1974 43(4): 548-575.* Like most Asian emigrants the Koreans, though few in number, were motivated by the hope of improving their economic situation. They preserved their identity "by means of their increasingly politicized community organizations and their generally deep involvement in the Korean independence movement abroad." The political history of Koreans in America is emphasized as well as the basic patterns of the immigration process itself. Significant leadership was given to these political activities by Syngman Rhee (1875-1965). After 1923 the Korean community and its political leadership fell into a disarray which lasted until the 1940's. 96 notes. R. V. Ritter

1049. James, D. Clayton. THE WAR THAT FADED AWAY. *Rev. in Am. Hist. 1978 6(4): 544-547.* Review article prompted by *The Korean War: A 25-Year Perspective,* edited by Francis H. Heller (Lawrence: The Regents Pr. of Kansas, 1977).

1050. Jervis, Robert. THE IMPACT OF THE KOREAN WAR ON THE COLD WAR. *J. of Conflict Resolution 1980 24(4): 563-592.* US foreign policy, 1946-50, was not coherent, viewing Soviet expansionism as a serious threat, but minimizing military expenditures. The fall of China and Soviet nuclear tests led to the US National Security Council's policy paper NSC-68, which advocated a new policy of high defense budgets and the globalization of commitments, a policy that was implemented, as it might not otherwise have been, as a direct result of the Korean War.

1051. Jessup, Philip C. THE RECORD OF WAKE ISLAND: A CORRECTION. *J. of Am. Hist. 1981 67(4): 866-870.* Takes issue with William Manchester, who claims in *American Caesar: Douglas MacArthur, 1880-1964* that a secretary took secret notes of the meeting between President Harry S. Truman and General Douglas MacArthur on Wake Island in October 1950. Had Manchester consulted the official record of the meeting, he would not have made the error. 11 notes. T. P. Linkfield

1052. Johnson, Ronald W. THE KOREAN WAR RED SCARE IN MISSOURI. *Red River Valley Hist. Rev. 1979 4(2): 72-86.* Missourians formed groups such as the Crusade for Freedom and enacted anti-Communist city ordinances.

1053. Kaspi, André. L'EUROPE A-T-ELLE ÉTÉ SAUVÉE PAR LA GUERRE DE CORÉE? [Was Europe saved by the Korean War?]. *Histoire [France] 1982 (48): 100-103.* Europe may have been saved from nuclear war due to the resolute US reaction to Russian and North Korean aggression in Korea.

1054. Kawagoe, Keizō. FUTATSU NO CHŌSEN SEISAKU O MEGURU KŌSŌ [Struggles resulting from the two Koreas policy]. *Ajia Afurika Kenkyū [Japan] 1973 13(12): 46-50.* Strongly criticizes the two Koreas policy of the Nixon administration. The year 1973 was eventful for Korea, and US policy was the cause of much of the unrest there. Discusses future policy options for the countries involved. H. Kawanami

1055. Kim, Ok-Yul. EARLY KOREAN-AMERICAN RELATIONS. *J. of Social Sci. and Humanities [South Korea] 1976 (43): 55-79.* Describes the diplomatic relations of the kingdom of Korea and the United States, 1883-94. The dominant diplomatic challenge concerned Korea's independence from China and Japan. A series of American representatives—Lucius Foote (1826-1915), George C. Foulk (1857-93), and Hugh A. Dinsmore (1850-1930)—and an American foreign affairs advisor, Owen N. Denny (1838-1900), worked to keep Korea free from Chinese influence. The replacement of Foulk by Secretary of State Thomas Bayard (1828-98), however, indicated Washington's desire for noninvolvement in Korea. Denny's replacement by Li Hung-chang (1823-1901) marked the assertion of Chinese hegemony. Based on English-language secondary sources; 41 notes. D. M. Bishop

1056. Kim, Won Mo. AMERICAN "GOOD OFFICES" IN KOREA, 1882-1905. *J. of Social Sci. and Humanities [South Korea] 1975 (41): 93-139.* The Korean-American Treaty of 1882 contained a good offices clause on the model of the American-Chinese Treaty of 1858. With the ratification of the treaty, the United States recognized Korea's independence, but a review of American foreign policy decisions on Korea demonstrates a pattern of nonfulfillment of its obligations. The United States lent Korea no meaningful support during either the Sino- or the Russo-Japanese wars and failed to recognize the pleas of various royal envoys after the Japanese established the protectorate in 1905. The flagrant breach of faith abandoned Korea to brutal Japanese overlordship. 170 notes. D. M. Bishop

1057. Kim, Won Mo. THEODORE ROOSEVELT'S KOREAN POLICY IN THE FAR EAST, 1901-1905. *J. of Social Sci. and Humanities [South Korea] 1976 (43): 99-116.* Describes Theodore Roosevelt's view of Asian power politics and his policy toward the independence of Korea in the aftermath of the Russo-Japanese War. Roosevelt regarded Russia as America's foremost rival in Asia, but he could not directly confront Russian attempts at Asian hegemony. He thus backed Japanese efforts to control the strategic Korean peninsula; the Taft-Katsura agreement of 1905 reflected the policy. With the withdrawal of the American legation from Seoul and the refusal of the Secretary of State to receive a Korean protest mission, Korea's fate was sealed. English-language sources; 144 notes. D. M. Bishop

1058. Kim, Young C. NORTH KOREA'S REUNIFICATION POLICY: A MAGNIFICENT OBSESSION? *J. of Korean Affairs 1974 3(4): 15-24.* The obstacle to reunification in North Korea is US military presence in South Korea. S

1059. Klimp, Jack W. THE BATTLE FOR SEOUL: MARINES AND MOUT. *Marine Corps Gazette 1981 65(11): 79-82.* Describes military operations on urbanized terrain (MOUT) which "encompasses not only fighting within cities and villages but also combat operations conducted on the surrounding rural terrain," focusing on the Marine Corps' fight to seize Seoul, South Korea during 20-28 September 1950.

1060. Knight, Charlotte. KOREA: A TWENTY-FIFTH ANNIVERSARY. *Air Force Mag. 1975 58(6): 59-63.* Reprints a field report from the August 1950 issue of *Air Force Magazine* regarding the performance of the US Air Force in the first month of the Korean War.

1061. Kobak, Cantius J. DON GASPAR DE GUEVARA OF BILIRAN ISLAND, LEYTE: A LEGENDARY FIGURE OR A HISTORICAL PERSONALITY? *Leyte-Samar Studies [Philippines] 1979 13(2): 150-153.* Don Gaspar, a figure still revered as a hero—and even as a saint—by the older people of the island of Biliran, as well as parts of Leyte and Samar, is described in the writings of contemporary Franciscans as a local heresiarch and troublemaker. Don Gaspar Ignacio de Guevara was appointed curate of San Juan Nepomuceno in Biliran in 1765 and during the next 10 years earned a reputation for doctrinal deviations, being accused by the canonical visitor Fray Joachin Jose Martinez (writing in 1775) of having enthroned himself at one point in a "chair of Peter." He was killed by the Moros. Based on documents in the Archivo de Pastrana (Guadalajara, Spain) and the Philippine National Archives; 8 notes. L. Van Wyk

1062. Kotch, John Barry. AMERICA IN KOREA: THE END OR A NEW BEGINNING? *Foreign Service J. 1978 55(3): 14-16, 32-33.* Reviewing diplomatic, military, and political events in Korea, 1945-78, concludes that the United States must support stability in the area so that some reconciliation between the two Koreas can take place.

1063. Lee, Chong-Sik. HUMAN RIGHTS IN SOUTH KOREA AND UNITED STATES POLICY. *J. of Korean Affairs 1975 5(3): 26-32.* Examines the relationship between the repression of civil rights in South Korea by President Park Chung Hee and American foreign policy there since 1969 when the United States sought to lessen its military responsibility in Southeast Asia.

1064. Lee, Chong-Sik. KOREA IN DER SACKGASSE [Korea in a cul-de-sac]. *Europa Archiv [West Germany] 1976 31(20): 663-672.* Neither North nor South Korea has the strength to conquer the other; both are dependent on their respective patrons (the USSR and US) for military aid, so the situation should remain frozen, just as it has since 1953.

1065. Lee, Raymond S. H. EARLY KOREAN WAR COVERAGE. *Journalism Q. 1978 55(4): 789-792.* Surveys news from the war front carried by the *New York Times,* the *Washington Post,* and four South Korean newspapers in 1950. The US papers, unaffected by official censorship, were consistently more accurate than were the censored South Korean papers in describing the imminent danger of an invasion of the South by North Korea. 3 tables, 15 notes. R. P. Sindermann, Jr.

1066. Lee, Young-Ho. U.S. POLICY AND KOREAN SECURITY. *Korea and World Affairs [South Korea] 1979 3(2): 183-196.* Reviews American foreign policy toward Korea and the military capability of North and South Korea during the 1970's.

1067. Lee, Young-Woo. BIRTH OF THE KOREAN ARMY, 1945-50: EVALUATION OF THE ROLE OF THE U.S. OCCUPATION FORCES. *Korea & World Affairs [South Korea] 1980 4(4): 639-656.* Examines attempts to create a modern army in Korea since 1880, focusing on the US role from 1945 to 1950 in laying the groundwork for the South Korean Army. Compares the American experience with that of the USSR in North Korea.

1068. Linden, W. H. van der. DE POGING TOT LIQUIDATIE VAN DE NOORD-KOREAANSE STAAT IN DE HERFST VAN 1950; DE ROL VAN MAC ARTHUR, WASHINGTON EN DE VERENIGDE NATIES [The attempt to liquidate the North Korean state in the autumn of 1950; the role of MacArthur, Washington, and the United Nations]. *Tijdschrift voor Geschiedenis [Netherlands] 1973 86(1): 51-83*. Attempts to show that the UN Security Council's June 1950 resolution to halt North Korean aggression at the 38th parallel were broadened by the US government to include the unification of the Koreas by the military occupation of the North and imposition of a democratic government controlled by UN forces under American command. This American aim, until thwarted by Chinese intervention, became the prevailing one at the United Nations and determined General Douglas MacArthur's action in crossing the 38th parallel. Based on UN and US official documents of the period, including the congressional hearings on MacArthur's dismissal, on newspapers and press releases, memoirs, and secondary works; 108 notes. G. Herritt

1069. Lo, Clarence Y. H. CIVILIAN POLICY MAKERS AND MILITARY OBJECTIVES: A CASE STUDY OF THE U.S. OFFENSIVE TO WIN THE KOREAN WAR. *J. of Pol. and Military Sociol. 1979 7(2): 229-242*. The civilians who directed the Truman administration's foreign policy formulated the "pragmatic doctrine" (Janowitz, 1960), which emphasized alliances and limited war for political objectives. Nevertheless, civilian policy makers during the Korean War supported some of the "absolutist" positions of General MacArthur. These included rolling back Communism in Korea, seeking a decisive military victory, ignoring allies' calls for restraint, and valuing displays of military strength. This article utilizes recently declassified government documents to argue that civilian policy makers favored and directly approved MacArthur's offensive to the Chinese border, which brought on a Chinese counterattack, with disastrous results for the U.N. forces. The evidence does not support the standard interpretation that attributes the offensive to MacArthur's insubordination and a breakdown of civilian control of the military. J

1070. Lovell, John P. FROM DEFENSE POLICY TO NATIONAL SECURITY POLICY: THE TORTUOUS ADJUSTMENT FOR AMERICAN MILITARY PROFESSIONALS. *Air. U. Rev. 1981 32(4): 42-54*. Discusses the reaction of American military professionals to the growing emphasis on national security policy from 1946 to 1981, focusing on the impact of military and political developments caused by the Korean and Vietnam Wars, the concept of limited wars, counterterrorism, and the trend toward a technology-intensive military organization.

1071. Lumley, Frederick. THE HERMIT WITH THE DIVIDED HEART: NOTES ON THE DEVELOPMENT OF EURO-KOREAN RELATIONS. *Korea and World Affairs [South Korea] 1978 2(2): 198-217*. Discusses South Korea's foreign relations, particularly with the United States, during the 1950's-70's.

1072. Lyu, Kingsley K. KOREAN NATIONALIST ACTIVITIES IN HAWAII AND THE CONTINENTAL UNITED STATES, 1900-1945: PART I: 1900-1919. *Amerasia J. 1977 4(1): 23-90*. The Korean immigrant community in Hawaii and the United States became a center of nationalist activity after coming under the control of American-educated Korean intellectuals in the early 1900's. Differences of approach to the liberation of Korea from Japanese control split the movement: Pak Yong-man favored military training of Korean immigrants in preparation for a war of liberation; An Ch'ang-ho placed faith in "the cultivation of Korean national spirit through education"; and Yi Sung-man (Syngman Rhee) advocated diplomatic persuasion of friendly powers to fight for the cause. Through unscrupulous and undemocratic tactics, Rhee gained control of the movement. Primary documents and personal interviews; 124 notes. Article to be continued.

T. L. Powers

1073. Lyu, Kingsley K. KOREAN NATIONALIST ACTIVITIES IN HAWAII AND THE CONTINENTAL UNITED STATES, 1900-1945: PART II: 1919-1945. *Amerasia J.* 1977 4(2): 53-100. Continued from the preceding article. Koreans living in the United States provided great support for the Korean Provisional Government-in-exile, which had been formed in 1919 to promote Korea's independence from Japanese suzerainty. Severe schisms developed over the attempts of Syngman Rhee, head of the Provisional Government and a dweller in America, to exert absolute authority over the independence movement and its finances. This factionalism badly weakened the movement, and prevented Korean nationalists from dealing effectively with those foreign powers concerned with the restoration of an independent Korea. 72 notes.

T. L. Powers

1074. Macdonald, Donald. THE 1946 ELECTIONS AND LEGISLATIVE ASSEMBLY IN SOUTH KOREA: AMERICA'S BUMBLING TUTELAGE. *J. of Northeast Asian Studies* 1982 1(3): 53-69. Discusses the October 1946 Korean election which was managed by the American Military Government, the consequent interim legislative assembly which was formed, and the consequences of both the election and the assembly on Korea.

1075. Macdonald, Donald S. AMERICAN INFLUENCE ON KOREAN CULTURE: IMPACT OF A CENTURY OF RELATIONS. *Korea & World Affairs [South Korea]* 1982 6(3): 470-486. Describes US educational and economic aid to Korea since the days of the missionaries in the 1880's; shows that since 1960 the United States has had a significant effect on Korean politics and culture.

1076. Macdonald, Donald S. WELLSPRINGS OF INTERVENTION: THE UNITED STATES AND KOREA. *Asian Affairs: An Am. Rev.* 1981 9(2): 104-128. Surveys the relationship between the United States and Korea from the mid-1800's to the present. Attempts to assess the causes, means, and results of "external influence" (defined as positive "intervention" rather than as "interference"). Based on memoirs and government documents; 71 notes.

R. B. Mendel

1077. MacIsaac, David and Wells, Samuel F., Jr. THE AMERICAN MILITARY: A "MINUTEMAN" TRADITION. *Wilson Q.* 1979 3(2): 109-124. From ca. 1784 until 1945, the United States, out of distrust, cost-consciousness, and isolationism, relied on an army of amateur minutemen; military unpreparedness during the Korean War provided the impetus for

American rearmament and an increasing emphasis on nuclear weaponry, but the reaction against the Vietnam War led to a decline in US defense spending and a partial return to the old minuteman tradition.

1078. Maddox, Robert. WAR IN KOREA: THE DESPERATE TIMES. *Am. Hist. Illus.* 1978 13(4): 26-38. Describes the early months of the Korean War, from 25 June 1950, when North Korean troops crossed the 38th parallel, to the stabilizing of the Pusan Perimeter in early August. Americans suffered at this time from a severe shortage of effective antitank weapons. Lack of sufficient communications equipment caused disproportionate casualties among American officers. Focuses on the experience of "Task Force Smith," which suffered nearly 50% casualties in the first Korean action involving Americans, on the attempt of the 24th Infantry Division to hold at the Kum River, and on the latter's subsequent costly success in delaying the Communist advance in the area of Taejon. 10 illus., map. L. W. Van Wyk

1079. Marinov, V. SOUTH KOREA IN THE VICE OF NEO-COLONIALISM. *Int. Affairs [USSR]* 1978 (7): 70-75. Exposes the South Korean regime as an extension of US neocolonialist strategy, 1960-76.

1080. Marks, John D. FROM KOREA WITH LOVE. *Washington Monthly* 1974 5(12): 55-61. Examines Korean prophet Sun Myung Moon and his Unification Church, with adherents in over 40 countries. S

1081. Matray, James I. AMERICA'S RELUCTANT CRUSADE: TRUMAN'S COMMITMENT OF COMBAT TROOPS IN THE KOREAN WAR. *Historian* 1980 42(3): 437-455. US intervention in the Korean War in June 1950 was a pivotal event in postwar history, but President Harry S. Truman's decision was not a major reversal of US foreign policy. A more accurate appraisal of Truman's response finds it consistent with past policy. Before the attack the United States had devoted its efforts in South Korea to supporting self-defense and military protection. The North Korean attack destroyed the intellectual foundations of Truman's policy, which had rested on the conviction that the USSR would not engage in open military aggression. Truman committed US troops only after South Korea demonstrated its inability to defend itself. Truman's decision to use combat troops marked the beginning of US dependence on military intervention rather than nationalism and indigenous hostility to Soviet domination as the best method for combating international communism. Primary sources; 62 notes. R. S. Sliwoski

1082. Matray, James I. CAPTIVE OF THE COLD WAR: THE DECISION TO DIVIDE KOREA AT THE 38TH PARALLEL. *Pacific Hist. Rev.* 1981 50(2): 145-168. The partition of Korea at the 38th parallel was the consequence of deteriorating Soviet-American relations in 1945, President Truman's desire to prevent the Soviet occupation of all Korea, and Stalin's efforts to protect Russian national security interests in northeastern Asia. Truman accepted American military leaders' recommendation that Soviet forces enter Korea and Manchuria to accept the Japanese surrender, but during the Potsdam Conference America's Korea policy was transformed, as American military leaders shifted to an anti-Soviet position. The early Soviet entry into the Pacific War and Japan's surrender were followed by the American military and State Department agreement to divide Korea at the 38th parallel into US and Soviet occupation zones. Based on US Department of State papers, US Army Staff records, and other primary sources; 84 notes.

R. N. Lokken

1083. Matray, James I. AN END TO INDIFFERENCE: AMERICA'S KOREAN POLICY DURING WORLD WAR II. *Diplomatic Hist. 1978 2(2): 181-196.* After Pearl Harbor, it became evident to American policymakers that future peace in Asia would depend on postwar stability in Korea. Thanks to 40 years of Japanese domination of the country, an independent government of inexperienced and unprepared Koreans would probably have been unable to maintain stability in the face of British imperialism, Chinese expansionism, and Soviet Communism. President Franklin D. Roosevelt advocated an international trusteeship for postwar Korea, believing that such an arrangement would bring stability without encouraging imperialism while preparing Koreans for eventual independence. 67 notes.

T. L. Powers

1084. Matray, James I. TRUMAN'S PLAN FOR VICTORY: NATIONAL SELF-DETERMINATION AND THE THIRTY-EIGHTH PARALLEL DECISION IN KOREA. *J. of Am. Hist. 1979 66(2): 314-333.* President Harry S. Truman's decision in 1950 to send General Douglas MacArthur across the Korean 38th Parallel was the culmination of US policy since World War II. Such a move would guarantee for all Koreans the right of national self-determination and would allow them to choose the US model, not the Soviet, for their future development. Because Truman interpreted the Korean War as part of a global, Soviet-US competition, a decisive victory in Korea would also be a great defeat for the Soviet policy of expansion. 84 notes.

T. P. Linkfield

1085. Matsulenko, V. O NEKOTORYKH VOPROSAKH UPRAVLENIIA VOISKAMI V LOKAL'NYKH VOINAKH (PO MATERIALAM INOSTRANNOI PECHATI) [Administering troops in local wars (using material from the foreign press)]. *Voenno-Istoricheskii Zhurnal [USSR] 1980 (3): 52-63.* The Korean and Vietnam Wars indicate the importance of centralization and a highly qualified command to secure efficiency and flexibility of leadership. The growth of technology has considerably complicated the task of troop commmand. Secondary sources; 29 notes.

G. Dombrovski

1086. Mazuzan, George T. AMERICA'S U.N. COMMITMENT, 1945-1953. *Historian 1978 40(2): 309-330.* Traces the career of Warren R. Austin, of Vermont, as America's first ambassador to the United Nations. Appointed by President Truman in June, 1946, Austin discovered that his internationalism had to be reconciled with the unilateral policy that the United States often followed. Concludes that Austin was capable of rationalizing the conflicting national versus international policies by viewing the growth of the UN as evolutionary. Major attention is devoted to Austin's role at the UN in justifying the Truman Doctrine and America's foreign policy in Korea.

M. S. Legan

1087. McLain, Glenn A. SOUTH KOREA: CARTER'S DILEMMA. *Contemporary Rev. [Great Britain] 1978 232(1349): 300-305.* Discusses changes in the American attitude toward South Korea under President Jimmy Carter during 1977-78.

1088. Modelski, George. UNITED STATES ALLIANCES: OBSOLESCENCE OF THE "KOREAN" SYSTEM? *World Affairs 1976 139(2): 75-86.* Questions the relevance of the alliance system in US foreign policy in light of international political change 1945-70's, emphasizing the role of NATO and issues in defense and military strategy.

1089. Moon, Chang Joo. THE INFLUENCE OF U.S. FOREIGN POLICY AND PUBLIC OPINION ON KOREA-U.S. RELATIONS. *Korea & World Affairs [South Korea] 1982 6(2): 241-270.* Surveys economic and foreign policy issues between the United States and Korea during 1952-80; examines US public opinion and South Korea's courting of it, in addition to Korea's unification and oil in the East China Sea.

1090. Niksch, Larry A. U.S. TROOP WITHDRAWAL FROM SOUTH KOREA: PAST SHORTCOMINGS AND FUTURE PROSPECTS. *Asian Survey 1981 21(3): 325-341.* On 20 July 1979 Zbigniew Brzezinski, President Carter's National Security Adviser, announced that plans had been abandoned to withdraw US ground forces from South Korea by 1982. This was done because neither the US Congress or the public supported the withdrawal plans, nor did the Japanese government or public. The issue of US troops in Korea may be reassessed by the Reagan administration, but a renewal of troop withdrawals is not expected, barring a more satisfactory military balance between North and South Korea and improvement in their diplomatic relations. Based on newspapers and US government documents; 26 notes.
M. A. Eide

1091. Ogburn, Robert W. IMPLEMENTING THE CARTER HUMAN RIGHTS POLICY IN SOUTH KOREA: HISTORIC MILIEU. *Towson State J. of Int. Affairs 1980 14(2): 75-91.* Examines US-Korean relations since 1945, describing the regime of Park Chung-hee and US human rights policy.

1092. O'Neill, Robert. CONSTRAINT WITH HONOUR. *Internat. J. [Canada] 1974 29(3): 350-355.* Reviews Denis Stairs' *The Diplomacy of Constraint: Canada, the Korean War, and the United States* (Toronto: University of Toronto Press, 1973). R. V. Kubicek

1093. Owen, Joseph R. CHOSIN RESERVOIR REMEMBERED. *Marine Corps Gazette 1980 64(12): 52-58.* Account of the Chosin Reservoir Campaign of the Korean War on the 30th anniversary of that victory by the US Marines in 1950.

1094. Park, Bong-Shik. KOREA AND THE U.S. FROM THE KOREAN VIEWPOINT. *Korea & World Affairs [South Korea] 1979 3(4): 463-470.* Reviews US policies toward Korea, Korean perspectives on US-Korean relations, and prospects; covers 1882-1979.

1095. Park, Chang Jin. AMERICAN FOREIGN POLICY IN KOREA AND VIETNAM: COMPARATIVE CASE STUDIES. *R. of Pol. 1975 37(1): 20-47.* In both the Korean War and the Vietnam War, the United States pursued a gradualistic policy of intervention to repel communist expansion. "The desire to help protect the territorial and political integrity of South Korea and South Vietnam, the politics of prestige and the moralistic approach to foreign affairs all influenced American decisions to fight in Korea and Vietnam." The Nixon-Kissinger team succeeded in ending the Vietnam War because they saw it as a conflict of nation-states rather than of moral forces. Primary and secondary sources; 57 notes. L. E. Ziewacz

1096. Park, Chang Jin. THE INFLUENCE OF SMALL STATES UPON THE SUPERPOWERS: UNITED STATES-SOUTH KOREAN RELATIONS AS A CASE STUDY, 1950-53. *World Pol. 1975 28(1): 97-117.* One of the important developments in world politics during the Cold War era was the relationship between the superpowers and small nation states. In contrast to the period before the Cold War, small nation states had considerable latitude for maneuvering in pursuit of their own interests. This phenomenon was largely rooted in the imperatives of the Cold War. The relationship between the United States and the Republic of Korea during the period of the Korean War is critically analyzed in light of the new reality in international relations. South Korea tried to influence the conduct of the United States in Korea by employing five techniques: 1) a public call for assistance; 2) a public call for mutual cooperation against the common enemy; 3) a calculated policy proposal for bargaining advantage; 4) refusal to cooperate; and 5) moral suasion. These techniques are examined, with the conclusion that of the five, (1) and (2) were effective; (3) and (4) were least effective; and (5) was most effective. J

1097. Park, Hong-Kyu. AMERICAN INVOLVEMENT IN THE KOREAN WAR. *Hist. Teacher 1983 16(2): 249-264.* A review essay on the historiography of the Korean War. Major issues discussed include the origins of the war, the US decision to intervene, the Truman-MacArthur controversy, and the conclusion of the war. 55 notes. L. K. Blaser

1098. Park, Hong-Kyu. U.S.-KOREAN RELATIONS, 1945-1947. *Asian Profile [Hong Kong] 1980 8(1): 45-52.* Examines US attempts to repeal the division of Korea along the 38th Parallel through bilateral negotiations with the USSR 1945-47, followed by an analysis of the reasons for failure. Based on US Department of State documents, newspaper reports, and other sources; 44 notes. J. Cushnie

1099. Park, Kyoung-Suh. ROK-U.S. RELATIONS IN THE 1980S. *Korea & World Affairs [South Korea] 1981 5(1): 5-17.* Scrutinizes US policies and US-South Korean relations and praises President Reagan for a return to "realistic power politics" in a US foreign policy that affirms the importance of close cooperation between Korea and the United States.

1100. Park, Tong-jin. KOREA AND THE UNITED STATES: AN ENDURING PARTNERSHIP. *Asian Affairs 1979 6(3): 139-147.* A brief review of Korean-American friendship and cooperation during the past century. Touches on mutual economic, strategic, and security considerations. Adapted by *Asian Affairs'* editor William Henderson from an address given by Republic of Korea Minister of Foreign Affairs Park in New York on 23 February 1979. R. B. Mendel

1101. Patterson, Wayne. SUGAR-COATED DIPLOMACY: HORACE ALLEN AND KOREAN IMMIGRATION TO HAWAII, 1902-1905. *Diplomatic Hist. 1979 3(1): 19-38.* Horace Allen used his position as US Minister to Korea to help sugar planters import Korean laborers into Hawaii in violation of American law. This involved violation of his official instructions against interfering in Korean internal affairs. His actions illustrate the two-tiered nature of US-Korean relations at the turn of the century: an official policy of goodwill and noninterference, and a submerged dedication to intervention and the advancement of private interests over public policy. 80 notes.
T. L. Powers

1102. Payer, Cheryl. PUSHED INTO THE DEBT TRAP: SOUTH KOREA'S EXPORT "MIRACLE." *J. of Contemporary Asia [Sweden] 1975 5(2): 153-164.* South Korea has achieved a fast growth rate through US-sponsored export expansion. Rapid growth depended upon cheap labor and government subsidization in Korea and overseas. However, a rise in imports, financed by foreign borrowing, has increased indebtedness. The domestic manufacturing and agricultural sectors are suffering. Severe stabilization programs are necessary; incomes and the rate of growth may be reduced.
F. D. Birch

1103. Peake, Louis A. THE UNITED STATES "WEEKEND WAR" WITH KOREA. *Military Collector and Hist. 1981 33(1): 13-17.* Relates the circumstances, military leaders, and actions of the so-called Weekend War between the United States and Korea in 1871, intended to open up Korea to the western world and to gather information about the destruction of the American schooner, *General Sherman,* in 1866 by the Koreans.

1104. Pelz, Stephen E. WHEN THE KITCHEN GETS HOT, PASS THE BUCK: TRUMAN AND KOREA IN 1950. *Rev. in Am. Hist. 1978 6(4): 548-555.* Review article prompted by US Department of State's *Foreign Relations of the United States, 1950, vol. 7, Korea* (Washington, D.C.: US Government Printing Office, 1976).

1105. Poll, F. G. van der. DE KOREAANSE OORLOG [The Korean War]. *Kleio [Netherlands] 1978 19(10): 871-873.* Views the Korean War (1950-53) as the first experiment with a "limited war," begun unexpectedly and ending in an armistice, made possible by Eisenhower's election and Stalin's death. Biblio. H. P. Waalwijk

1106. Poropat, Liviana. LA GUERRA DI COREA: PRIMA FASE DEL CONFRONTO CINO-AMERICANO [The Korean War: first phase of the Sino-American confrontation]. *La Seconda Guerra Mondiale nella Prospettiva Storica a Trent'Anni dall'Epilogo* (Como: Casa Editrice Pietro Cairoli, 1977): 509-514. A brief analysis of the Korean War, concluding that this conflict aided in China's advent as a super power and signaled the beginning of a multipolar balance of power. Biblio. M. T. Wilson

1107. Porter, Gareth. TIME TO TALK WITH NORTH KOREA. *Foreign Policy 1979 (34): 52-73.* The stalemate in Korea persists, despite the altered "strategic realities" in northeast Asia wrought by the shuffling of relationships among the United States, the Soviet Union, China, and Japan. The rigidity of American foreign policy is a major reason for the continued tension. Washington must now move to initiate negotiations among the two Koreas and itself, aimed at reducing military pressures. The negotiations should also lead to the withdrawal from South Korea of American forces, whose presence has been rendered unnecessary by changed conditions in Korea and the world. Note. T. L. Powers

1108. Potapov, I. MORSKIE DESANTNYE SILY SSHA V POSLEVOENNYI PERIOD [American marine landing capabilities in the postwar period]. *Voenno-Istoricheskii Zhurnal [USSR] 1973 (1): 39-46.* Traces the development and use of the US Marine Corps and amphibious warfare vessels, stating that from its founding in 1776 to the beginning of World War II the Marine Corps rose from 268 men to 66,000 men, that during World War II its numbers increased seven times, and that by 1945 it comprised 468,000 soldiers and officers; also examines the use of the marines in Korea and Vietnam, the development of various troop carriers, and states that marine landing forces are the basis of America's power against national freedom movements.

1109. Price, Thomas J. CONSTRAINTS ON FOREIGN POLICY DECISION MAKING: STABILITY AND FLEXIBILITY IN THREE CRISES. *Int. Studies Q. 1978 22(3): 357-376.* Because leaders must choose from a range of alternatives, single-factor explanations of foreign policy decisionmaking are unsatisfactory. The two major causes of constraints on political choices are stability (a multifactor variable) and flexibility. Analyses of three crises indicate that these two factors offer adequate explanations of the ultimate policy decisions. The three crises, all of which exhibit a limited and sequential range of choices, are the German decision to declare war in 1914, and the US decisions to enter the Korean War and to establish a blockade of Cuba. 8 tables, 37 ref. E. S. Palais

1110. Ranard, Donald L. THE KOREAN CIA IN THE USA. *Worldview 1976 19(11): 19-21.* The author, the former Director of the Office of Korean Affairs in the Department of State, gives an account of Korean CIA activities in the United States between 1970 and 1974.

1111. Ranard, Donald L. THE U.S. IN KOREA: WHAT PRICE SECURITY? *Worldview 1977 20(1-2): 23-26, 35-38.* Provides an overview of Korean affairs following the coup of Park Chung Hee, 1961-77, examines Korean-American foreign relations, 1950-77, and questions continued American support of repressive and corrupt government.

1112. Risedorph, Gene. "MOSQUITO." *Am. Aviation Hist. Soc. J. 1979 24(1): 45-51.* The author reminisces about his experience as a fighter pilot out of Ch'unch'on, South Korea, during the Korean War, 1952.

1113. Sakamoto, Yoshikazu. KOREA AS A WORLD ORDER ISSUE. *Alternatives 1978 3(3): 385-413.* Views the Korean problem, not as an aspect of the East-West conflict but as a world-order problem. Briefly traces Korea's history up to 1945, when the USA and the Soviets, engaged in fierce maneuvers to carve out and extend their respective spheres of domination, divided Korea arbitrarily and almost casually into two countries which became hostile and even went to war. In the process, both halves have been robbed of their autonomy, had their economies skewed, and become prey to repressive regimes. Makes constructive suggestions for reducing tension between the two to pave the way for an eventual solution acceptable to the Korean people. Initiatives must emanate from the two center states, which are responsible for Korea's tragic plight, but some will have to be taken by the Korean people themselves. J

1114. Sandler, Shmuel. THE IMPACT OF PROTRACTED PERIPHERAL WARS ON THE AMERICAN DOMESTIC SYSTEM. *Jerusalem J. of Int. Relations [Israel] 1978 3(4): 27-53.* Public opinion polls indicate that the American public's growing objections to intervention in the costly and protracted wars in Korea, 1950-53, and Vietnam, 1965-73, had profound political implications on the domestic front.

1115. Scholin, Allan R. ON THE GRAVEYARD SHIFT. *Air Force Mag. 1973 56(9): 102-106.* On night bombing missions, the US Air Force's B-26 bombers in the Korean War pounded convoys, supply dumps, and the North Korean railroad system in a campaign to prevent the Communists from assembling the material to launch new ground assaults, 1950-52.

1116. Shulman, Frank Joseph. AMERICAN DOCTORAL RESEARCH ON KOREA, 1970-1974: A BRIEF STATISTICAL ANALYSIS AND BIBLIOGRAPHICAL LISTING. *J. of Korean Affairs 1976 6(2): 59-83.* Continued from a previous article (see following abstract). Lists 302 doctoral dissertations on Korea written at American universities between 1970 and 1974. Institutional index. D. M. Bishop

1117. Shulman, Frank Joseph. AMERICAN DOCTORAL RESEARCH ON KOREA, 1970-1974: A BRIEF STATISTICAL ANALYSIS AND BIBLIOGRAPHICAL LISTING. *J. of Korean Affairs 1976 6(1): 61-80.* Categorizes 302 doctoral dissertations written between 1970 and 1974 on topics relating to Korea by institution, year, academic field, and by sex and national background of the author. Korean area studies are underdeveloped. Comparatively few dissertations have been written by Americans concentrated at Asian area studies centers. More have been written by scholars of Korean background spread throughout the American university system who choose to apply their disciplinary training to Korean subjects. Based on the author's compilation, *Doctoral Dissertations on Japan and Korea, 1969-1974* (Ann Arbor: University Microfilms, 1976); 8 tables, 10 notes. D. M. Bishop

1118. Skaggs, David Curtis. THE KATUSA EXPERIMENT: THE INTEGRATION OF KOREAN NATIONALS INTO THE U.S. ARMY. *Military Affairs 1974 38(2): 53-58.* KATUSA (Korean Augmentation to the U.S. Army) troops were envisioned as a means of providing filler for the undermanned American units sent to Korea in 1950. Initially the program failed because the men had little training; but as they acquired experience the Koreans became excellent troops. Problems developed after the close of fighting in 1953, and the program ceased in 1965. Based on special studies and general works; 11 notes. K. J. Bauer

1119. Stalbo, K. VOENNO-MORSKIE SILY V LOKAL'NYKH VOINAKH [Naval forces in local wars]. *Morskoi Sbornik [USSR] 1976 (9): 23-29.* Discusses the important roles of the US Navy in the Korean and Vietnam wars, and the Anglo-French naval forces in the Suez conflict.

1120. Steigleder, Horst. ZUR ROLLE UND FUNKTION DER USA-SEESTREITKRÄFTE IN DEN AGGRESSIONSKRIEGEN GEGEN KOREA UND VIETNAM [On the role and function of American naval forces in the wars of aggression against Korea and Vietnam]. *Militärgeschichte [East Germany] 1976 15(5): 557-569.* Since World War II the US Navy has functioned as a strategic deterrent to nuclear war, as an arm of intervention in conventional conflicts, and as a means of "rolling back" socialism without a direct conflict with the Soviet Union. The aggressive wars in Korea and Vietnam were stages in the development of these capacities. In these conflicts the US Navy had four specific functions: 1) blockading, 2) sea landings, 3) direct support of land forces, and 4) security of military sea transport. In Korea and Vietnam the worldwide strategy and tactics of US naval forces were formulated. Secondary works; map, table, chart, 33 notes. J. B. Street

1121. Stewart, Roy P. RAYMOND S. MCLAIN: AMERICA'S GREATEST CITIZEN SOLDIER. *Chronicles of Oklahoma 1981 59(1): 4-29.* Raymond Stallings McLain emerged from a childhood of poverty to achieve a successful career as business executive and general during World War II. He joined the Oklahoma National Guard in 1912 and four years later participated in Pershing's Punitive Expedition against Pancho Villa. Following service in World War I, McLain returned to private business but was reactivated to the regular army as a general in 1941. Throughout the war, he distinguished himself for always being in the forefront of major battles, from the Sicily invasion, to the Italian operations, to the D-Day landings at Normandy. McLain briefly served as military governor over the occupied area around Frankfurt, Germany, and during the Korean War acted as Army Comptroller. 8 photos. M. L. Tate

1122. Stilwell, Richard G. KOREA: THE IMPLICATIONS OF WITHDRAWAL. *Asian Affairs: An Am. Rev. 1977 4(5): 279-289.* Discusses development of post-World War II geopolitical problems facing the regional and Great Powers and the UN in the Korean peninsula. Analyzes the military imbalance between the two Koreas, the personal ambitions of North Korea's Kim Il Sung and South Korea's Park Chung Hee, Soviet ambivalence toward the US presence as a balancing force, American credibility as an ally, Korean-

Japanese relations, and East Asian political and military security. Adaptation of General Stilwell's address to a Defense Strategy Forum, Washington, D.C., 20 April 1977.
R. B. Mendel

1123. Suffrin, Mark. INCIDENT AT CHOSIN RESERVOIR. *Mankind 1973 4(1): 52-59.* Navy Lieutenant Thomas Hudner received the Congressional Medal of Honor for his unsuccessful rescue attempt of Ensign Jesse Brown, the only black naval officer commissioned as a pilot during the Korean War.
S

1124. Suhrke, Astri and Morrison, Charles E. CARTER AND KOREA: THE DIFFICULTIES OF DISENGAGEMENT. *World Today [Great Britain] 1977 33(10): 366-375.* Discusses current Carter administration aims to withdraw all US ground troops in South Korea, 1977-81; southern strength may cause North Korea to go to desperate lengths, which may spur the arms race and cause closer connections between North Korea and either Communist China or the USSR.

1125. Swartout, Robert, Jr. AMERICAN HISTORIANS AND THE OUTBREAK OF THE KOREAN WAR: AN HISTORIOGRAPHICAL ESSAY. *Asia Q. [Belgium] 1979 (1): 65-77.* There are two interpretations concerning the outbreak of the Korean War, 25 June 1950 to 27 July 1953. The first led by Allen S. Whiting, Adam B. Ulam, John W. Spanier, and Walter LaFeber is that the Soviet Union planned and ordered the initial North Korean strike southward. The second led by I. F. Stone, D. Frank Fleming, David Horowitz, Joyce and Gabriel Kolko, is that South Korea under Syngman Rhee and the United States under Douglas MacArthur were responsible. The author presents a third theory that North Korea under Kim Il-song planned and carried out the 25 June invasion. No definitive conclusions can be made, however, until the Soviet, North Korean, and Chinese documents are made public. Based on Government documents; 32 notes.
G. M. White

1126. Swartout, Robert, Jr. CULTURAL CONFLICT AND GUNBOAT DIPLOMACY: THE DEVELOPMENT OF THE 1871 KOREAN-AMERICAN INCIDENT. *J. of Social Sci. and Humanities [South Korea] 1976 (43): 117-169.* The Low-Rodgers US naval expedition of 1871 was an East-West cultural conflict; it demonstrates the basic distinctions between American and Korean concepts of diplomacy in the 19th century. In 1871 the US Navy deployed off Korea to demand a shipwreck treaty. Experiences in the Mediterranean had conditioned Americans to regard force as legitimate and necessary to obtain commercial and diplomatic ends with "uncivilized" peoples. Adhering to Confucian norms, the Koreans did not understand the demands of Western diplomacy, and they expected "social behavior" as the prelude to any intercourse. The Americans perceived Korean delay and reluctance as a calculated insult, provoked an incident, and landed Marines and sailors to attack Korean garrisons. The result of mutual misunderstanding was conflict. Based on Korean and American primary sources; 180 notes.
D. M. Bishop

1127. Swartout, Robert R., Jr. and Bohm, Fred C. AN AMERICAN NAVAL OFFICER IN 19TH CENTURY KOREA: THE JOURNAL OF GEORGE W. WOODS. *J. of Social Sci. and Humanities [South Korea] 1980 (52): 18-30.* A review of the experiences of American naval officer George W. Woods in the Korea of 1884. Includes background material concerned with the coming of the West, Woods's observations on cities, towns, the countryside, the diplomatic community, and Korean customs. The journal is valuable because it shows Korea before Western contacts changed it and because Woods, though patronizing, did not hesitate to praise when he perceived that praise was deserved. 41 notes. V. L. Human

1128. Tarpey, John F. KOREA: 25 YEARS LATER. *US Naval Inst. Pro. 1978 104(8): 50-57.* One of the least recognized results of the Korean War has been 25 years of regional stability in northeast Asia. Although the stalemate that resulted from the war is probably not considered a totally satisfactory solution to all countries with an interest in Korea, it is undoubtedly the best thing that could have happened given the circumstances. The Korean peninsula is still a highly volatile area, and the political stability of northeast Asia is still delicate. Our statesmen, and those of all the other countries in the area, will have to respect that stability. 5 photos, 3 notes. A. N. Garland

1129. Temple, Harry. DEAF CAPTAINS: INTELLIGENCE, POLICY, AND THE ORIGINS OF THE KOREAN WAR. *Int. Studies Notes 1981-82 8(3-4): 19-23.* Describes the world view expressed in National Security Council report NSC-68, *Report to the National Security Council by the Executive Secretary on the United States Objectives and Programs for National Security*, in 1950 and how this view caused the United States to ignore the explosive situation in Korea, 1948-50.

1130. Thach, John S. "RIGHT ON THE BUTTON": MARINE CLOSE AIR SUPPORT IN KOREA. *US Naval Inst. Pro. 1975 101(11): 54-56.* The author, a Navy fighter pilot in World War II, commanded the escort carrier *Sicily* (CVE-118) during the early months of the Korean War. "As an unofficial Marine carrier, her entire 'air wing' consisted of 24 F4U Corsairs of VMF-214, the 'Black Sheep' squadron." The aircraft started flying close air support missions on 3 August 1950 along the west coast of Korea, and the author tells of some of the early missions and of some of the men who flew those missions. The Marine pilots "really were the top pros in the business... in the whole world." Based on recollections from the Naval Institute's Oral History Program; 3 photos. A. N. Garland

1131. Thomas, James A. LIMITED WAR: THE THEORY AND THE PRACTICE. *Military Rev. 1973 53(2): 75-82.* In Korea and Vietnam the United States chose to fight limited wars in which universality of expectation clashed with finitude of goals. In each case the result has been a lingering, enervating dissatisfaction within the Army. To prepare psychologically for the next limited war the Army should arrange a desensitizing program based on formal instruction in the nature of limited war and appropriate field or post exercises. Primary and secondary sources; 13 notes. J. K. Ohl

1132. Thompson, Mark E. THE TRUMAN-MAC ARTHUR CONTROVERSY: A BIBLIOGRAPHICAL ESSAY. *Studies in Hist. and Soc. 1974 5(2): 66-73.* Reviews the reasons President Harry S. Truman removed General Douglas MacArthur from his post as United Nations Commander during the Korean War. Supporters of the president generally argue that he had to remove the general in order to carry on the war as he saw fit. MacArthur's supporters claim that the general was either a victim of poor communications or a scapegoat for failure to win the war. The controversy clearly shows the political problems inherent in limited warfare. V. L. Human

1133. Tilford, Earl H., Jr. SEARCH AND RESCUE IN SOUTHEAST ASIA, 1961-1975. *Air U. Rev. 1980 31(2): 60-74.* Discusses the development of the Air Rescue Service, now called the Aerospace Rescue and Recovery Service (ARRS), from a peacetime search and rescue force in the continental United States to an overseas search and rescue force in Southeast Asia during the Korean and Vietnam Wars.

1134. Toinet, Marie-France. MACARTHUR OU LA PROSPÉRITÉ DE L'INCOMPÉTENCE [MacArthur, or the prosperity of incompetence]. *Histoire [France] 1982 (46): 16-26.* Recounts the life and career of General Douglas MacArthur, emphasizing his military role from the outbreak of World War II to his dismissal as director of operations in Korea by President Harry Truman, in 1951.

1135. Toner, James H. AMERICAN SOCIETY AND THE AMERICAN WAY OF WAR: KOREA AND BEYOND. *Parameters 1981 11(1): 79-90.* The US military during the Korean War tended to reflect the values of American civilian society. For instance, due to societal constraints against losing lives during training, US combat training was limited in severity even though this increased the level of casualties in the field. The American concern for individual lives also resulted in the expenditure of equipment and ammunition instead of lives, although this often caused devastation to Korean towns and villages. A rotation system insured that men were in combat a fixed and equal amount of time, although this often meant there was a shortage of experienced combat soldiers. All of these and other similar factors were determined by the values of US civilian society which colors the American way of waging war. Government documents, newspaper accounts, and secondary sources; 63 notes. L. R. Maxted

1136. Toner, James H. EXCEPTIONAL WAR, EXCEPTIONAL PEACE: THE 1953 CEASE-FIRE IN KOREA. *Military Rev. 1976 56(7): 3-13.* Examines President-elect Dwight D. Eisenhower and the UN's role in diplomacy and peace negotiations to end the Korean War in 1952-53.

1137. Toner, James H. THE MAKING OF A MORASS. *Military Rev. 1977 57(10): 3-16.* Chronicles the US presence in South Korea, 1945-50.

1138. Warner, Geoffrey. THE KOREAN WAR. *Int. Affairs [Great Britain] 1980 56(1): 98-107.* Discusses the Korean War, focusing on Sino-Soviet-US involvement. A. Ladyzhensky

1139. Weems, John E. BLACK WINGS OF GOLD. *US Naval Inst. Pro. 1983 109(7): 35-39.* Ensign Jesse L. Brown was the first black designated an aviator in the US Navy. In October 1950 he was shot down over North Korea and died as a result of his injuries while rescuers attempted to free him from his plane. Based on reminiscences and newspaper accounts; 12 notes.
K. J. Bauer

1140. Westerfield, H. Bradford. U.S. FOREIGN POLICY PRIORITIES AND A PEACEFUL UNIFICATION OF KOREA. *Korea & World Affairs [South Korea] 1983 7(1): 40-56.* A strong United States campaign for Korean reunification is not evident based on activities since the 1960's; it is hoped that Korea is not included in the Japanese defense perimeter.

1141. Wiltz, John Edward. THE MACARTHUR HEARINGS OF 1951: THE SECRET TESTIMONY. *Military Affairs 1975 39(4): 167-173.* Examines the May and June 1951 Senate inquiry into the relief of General Douglas MacArthur and the Far Eastern military situation. The testimony, previously classified, contains material useful to historians of the Korean War, Cold War, and America's Far Eastern policies, and reveals that military leaders in Washington disagreed with MacArthur's views. Had the testimony been released in 1951, American understanding of the Korean conflict and Cold War might have been enhanced. Based on primary and secondary sources; 80 notes.
A. M. Osur

1142. Wiltz, John Edward. TRUMAN AND MACARTHUR: THE WAKE ISLAND MEETING. *Military Affairs 1978 42(4): 169-176.* Summarizes historical evaluations of the October 1950 meeting between President Harry S. Truman and General of the Army Douglas MacArthur at Wake Island, giving the background to and a detailed account of the meeting. Many accounts contain inaccuracies and mistaken assumptions. Truman's purpose in calling the meeting was "public relations" for the upcoming election, and historians should be careful not to assume exalted motives for exalted personages. Based on the *Log of President Truman's Trip,* interviews, and secondary sources; 34 notes.
A. M. Osur

1143. Witze, Claude. PANMUNJOM TO PARIS. *Air Force Mag. 1973 56(2): 11-13.* American preparations for the Paris peace talks with Vietnam should be made while recalling similar peace talks with North Korea in Panmunjom, 1951-53.

1144. Yim, Yong Soon. KOREA IN THE AMERICAN MILITARY STRATEGY. *Asian Thought and Soc. 1979 4(12): 313-325.* Continued from a previous article (see abstract in this chapter). Part II. Evaluates the place of South Korea in American military thinking.

1145. Yim, Yong Soon. SOUTH KOREA IN AMERICAN MILITARY STRATEGY. *Asian Thought and Soc. 1979 4(10): 60-72.* Explores the position of South Korea in US military strategy from the Truman administration to the Carter administration.

1146. Yu, Suk-Ryul. AMERICAN FOREIGN POLICY TOWARD THE KOREAN PENINSULA: PEACE OR UNIFICATION. *Korea and World Affairs [South Korea] 1978 2(3): 380-394.* Reviews US policy in Korea since 1949; US interests are generally related to the containment of Communism, which can be achieved through defense of South Korea from attack by North Korea at the present borders, but Korean interests throughout the entire peninsula are for reunification, which is the responsibility of the Koreans themselves.

1147. —. AN EXCHANGE OF OPINION [THE KOLKO THESIS OF COLD WAR REVISIONISM AND THE OUTBREAK OF THE KOREAN WAR]. *Pacific Hist. Rev. 1973 42(4): 537-575.*
Stueck, William.   COLD WAR REVISIONISM AND THE ORIGINS OF THE KOREAN CONFLICT: THE KOLKO THESIS, *pp. 537-560.*
Kolko, Joyce and Kolko, Gabriel.   "TO ROOT OUT THOSE AMONG THEM"—A RESPONSE. *560-566.*
Stueck, William.   REJOINDER BY WILLIAM STUECK, *pp. 566-573.*
Kolko, Joyce and Kolko, Gabriel.   REJOINDER BY JOYCE AND GABRIEL KOLKO, *pp. 573-575.* A criticism and defense of Cold War revisionism based on Joyce and Gabriel Kolko's *The Limits of Power: The World and United States Foreign Policy, 1945-1954* (New York: Harper & Row, 1972). The USSR merely looked after its interests while the US took the offensive. As here applied to the outbreak of the Korean War in June 1950, South Korea's aggressive President Syngman Rhee provoked the attack by North Korea. General Douglas MacArthur supported Rhee and Washington accepted his recommendations. Stueck concludes that the Kolko thesis "does not stand up well in the face of either the available evidence or rational speculation." 84 notes.
C. W. Olson

1148. —. [INTERPRETATION OF AMERICAN FOREIGN POLICY]. *J. of Peace Res. [Norway] 1981 18(3): 299-301.*
Simon, Jeffrey D.   A RESPONSE TO STEN SPARRE NILSON'S REJOINDER, *pp. 299-300.* A criticism of Nilson's complaint (see Journal of Peace Research (Norway) 1980 17(1): 9-28 and 17(4): 357-359) that Simon's use of different variables colors his conclusions about public access to communications, but quotes a source presenting the same conclusion. Nilson's contention that US lessons from the Korean War resulted in the policy of stationing US troops in friendly nations is a simple interpretation of a very complex problem.
Nilson, Sten Sparre.   A SHORT REPLY, *p. 301.* Simon is not entirely incorrect, but doubt remains as to the validity of his assumption that the withdrawal of US troops from Korea in 1949 was not very influential in the future direction of related foreign policy. The question indeed is very complex. 12 notes.
V. L. Human

6

TAIWAN

1149. Auw, David C. L. COMMITMENT, POLICY LEGACY, AND POLICY OPTIONS: THE U.S.-R.O.C. RELATIONS UNDER REAGAN. *Issues & Studies [Taiwan] 1982 18(3): 8-26.* President Reagan's "quiet approach" to restoration of mutual trust between Washington and Taiwan is too limited. US policy toward the Republic of China should not be restricted to the Taiwan Relations Act or interest in playing the "China card" but must recognize wider economic and strategic factors that make Taiwan a valuable ally. 30 notes.   J. A. Krompart

1150. Bellows, Thomas J. NORMALIZATION: A TAIWAN PERSPECTIVE. *Asian Affairs: An Am. Rev. 1979 6(6): 339-358.* Discusses the factors which led to the establishment of foreign relations between the United States and China, the events immediately preceding and following President Jimmy Carter's announcement on 15 December 1978, the reactions of Taiwan and the USSR, and the problems facing Taiwan. Based on media, primary, and secondary sources; 16 notes.   R. B. Mendel

1151. Bourne, Peter G. THE CHINESE STUDENT—ACCULTURATION AND MENTAL ILLNESS. *Psychiatry 1975 38(3): 269-277.* Reviews the history of the Chinese student in America, examining the conflicts which the special role of the Chinese on campus has created.   S

1152. Chang, David W. A CASE STUDY ON UNCONVENTIONAL DIPLOMACY: THE REPUBLIC OF CHINA'S RELATIONS WITH THE U.S. AND OTHER WESTERN NATIONS. *Asian Forum 1981 10(3): 1-26.* Discusses the Republic of China's economic relations with the United States and other Western European nations. Taiwan considers formal diplomatic relations with the United States as the most important factor, which in turn affects and influences its economic and political relations with other nations. Given the current strategic power relations among the four major nations of East Asia, and in view of the existing Sino-Soviet conflict, Taiwan will be able to defend itself militarily against invasion from China. The United States seems to realize its moral obligation and that strategically it has little to gain and much to lose in abandoning its ally. 54 notes.   R. B. Orr

1153. Chang, King-yuh. PARTNERSHIP IN TRANSITION: A REVIEW OF RECENT TAIPEI-WASHINGTON RELATIONS. *Asian Survey 1981 21(6): 603-621.* Surveys the relations between the United States and Taiwan since 1949, especially since the Taiwan Relations Act adopted by congress on 29 March 1979 to establish ties between the two countries in the wake of President Carter's decision to establish diplomatic relations with China and sever official relations with Taiwan. Outlines the difficulties for Taiwan that have arisen in the area of economics and defense as a result of Carter's action. Secondary sources; 56 notes. J. Powell

1154. Chen, Robert P. LIBRARY RESOURCES FOR AMERICAN STUDIES IN TAIWAN. *Int. Lib. Rev. [Great Britain] 1977 9(4): 441-454.* Since its foundation in 1969, the Center for American Studies has accumulated many library materials to support graduate American Studies, but the material in individual universities and throughout the island as a whole is not yet adequate to support a quality program.

1155. Copper, John Franklin. TAIWAN'S OPTIONS. *Asian Affairs: An Am. Rev. 1979 6(5): 282-294.* Traces the Taiwan predicament from the 1972 Shanghai Communique to the unilateral US abrogation of its treaty obligations in 1979 and analyzes Taiwanese options. Based on government documents; other primary and secondary sources. R. B. Mendel

1156. Cox, Thomas R. HARBINGERS OF CHANGE: AMERICAN MERCHANTS AND THE FORMOSA ANNEXATION SCHEME. *Pacific Hist. Rev. 1973 42(2): 163-184.* Studies changing attitudes and the development of American interests in Taiwan. Some have evaluated Peter Parker's (Commissioner of the United States to China) 1857 proposal of annexation of Taiwan as an expression of nationalist expansionism. Reassesses this judgment in the light of burgeoning mercantile interests in the direction of this island. In an analysis of the mercantile enterprises launched and promoted in the years immediately preceding 1857 it is evident that there were other motives, especially fear of British control that would spoil an increasingly lucrative trade. However, these small-time entrepreneurs never had the political influence that historians have sometimes assumed. 69 notes. R. V. Ritter

1157. Fairbank, John K. TAIWAN: OUR HARDY PERENNIAL PROBLEM. *Foreign Service J. 1974 51(9): 16-20.* Continued US expansion of economic relations with Taiwan may generate support for Taiwan's independence movement from China.

1158. Fraser, A. M. FUTURE OF TAIWAN. *Marine Corps Gazette 1973 57(2): 39-45.* Outlines the history of Taiwan since World War II, focusing on the role of the United States and relations between Taiwan and China.

1159. Gregor, A. James. THE UNITED STATES, THE REPUBLIC OF CHINA, AND THE TAIWAN RELATIONS ACT. *Orbis 1980 24(3): 609-623.* Analyzes the policy of the Carter administration toward Taiwan and the Republic of China from 1978 to 1980. Despite promises made to Taiwan and the American people, the Carter administration was either unable or unwilling to carry out the Taiwan Relations Act. "Accommodation of the People's Republic seems to have had so high a place in the Carter Administration's priority list that the Taiwan Relations Act was to be gutted... The Republic of China or Taiwan, regardless of all administration assurances, has been, in fact, largely abandoned in the fevered courtship of the People's Republic." Based on published sources and government documents; 30 notes.

J. W. Thacker, Jr.

1160. Hauptman, Laurence M. and Knapp, Ronald G. DUTCH-ABORIGINAL INTERACTION IN NEW NETHERLAND AND FORMOSA: AN HISTORICAL GEOGRAPHY OF EMPIRE. *Pro. of the Am. Phil. Soc. 1977 121(2): 166-182.* The 17th-century Dutch colonial empire depended on commerce and profit, not social interaction. Resulting policies towards nonwhites were neither uniform nor consistent. Religious conversion efforts and cultural diffusion in both colonies remained minimal. The Dutch imported Chinese laborers to supplant the native Formosans; the coastal Algonkins of New Netherland were simply eradicated by diseases, alcohol, and the ample weapons provided to their enemies, the Five Nations. 2 maps, table, 83 notes.

W. L. Olbrich

1161. Hoxie, R. Gordon. PRESIDENTIAL LEADERSHIP AND AMERICAN FOREIGN POLICY: SOME REFLECTIONS ON THE TAIWAN ISSUE, WITH PARTICULAR CONSIDERATIONS ON ALEXANDER HAMILTON, DWIGHT EISENHOWER, AND JIMMY CARTER. *Presidential Studies Q. 1979 9(2): 131-143.* Discusses American foreign policy toward Taiwan during the presidencies of Dwight D. Eisenhower and Jimmy Carter, based on Alexander Hamilton's doctrine of presidential power set forth in 1793.

1162. Javits, Jacob K. CONGRESS AND FOREIGN RELATIONS: THE TAIWAN RELATIONS ACT. *Foreign Affairs 1981 60(1): 54-62.* Discusses Congress's importance in helping to shape foreign policy, using the Taiwan Relations Act (US, 1979) as an example. In writing the act, Congress solved the problems posed to US-Taiwan relations after official recognition of China. The legislation enabled the United States both to maintain friendly relations with Taiwan and to develop relations with China. Senate Foreign Relations Committee hearings and reports; 3 notes.

A. A. England

1163. Kao, Charles H. C. and Lee, Jae Won. AN EMPIRICAL ANALYSIS OF CHINA'S BRAIN DRAIN INTO THE UNITED STATES. *Econ. Development and Cultural Change 1973 21(3): 500-513.* The authors examine the economic, political, social, demographic, and professional factors in the United States and the Republic of China which may explain Chinese scholars' decisions to stay in the United States upon completing their education rather than to return to Taiwan. Data from 1905 to 1968 indicate that the causes are multifaceted and that the brain drain will continue but probably not become worse. Based on secondary sources and a questionnaire; 4 tables, 15 notes.

J. W. Thacker, Jr.

1164. Langley, Harold D. GIDEON NYE AND THE FORMOSA ANNEXATION SCHEME. *Pacific Hist. R. 1965 34(4): 397-420.* Gideon Nye, Jr. (1833-88) made a fortune in the China trade. As a merchant in Canton, he was one of the principal participants in the 1857 conspiracy to influence the United States to seize the island of Formosa, working through personal contacts to convince high US officials. He justified annexation on the basis of advancing civilization, spreading Christianity, and expanding commercial and US national interests. 56 notes. D. L. Smith

1165. Lasater, Martin L. THUNDER AND LIGHTNING OVER TAIWAN. *Naval War Coll. Rev. 1983 36(4): 73-82.* China claims that a basic contradiction exists between the 1979 Taiwan Relations Act and the 1982 joint Sino-American communique on future arms sales to Taiwan. Although the United States denies any contradiction, it is clear that the 1979 act permits arms sales to Taiwan, which the Chinese consider to be intervention in their internal affairs. These policy statements would be strained if China became militarily aggressive against Taiwan or if it achieves closer relations with the USSR. 12 notes. D. Powell

1166. Lei, Joanna C. and Cheng Yu-p'ing. LUN MEI KUO KUO HUI CHIH LI FA CHIEN TU CHUNG MEI KUAN HSI CHUNG CHÜN SHIH SHOU YÜ CHIH KO AN YEN CHIU [American congressional oversight: the case of American arms sales to Taiwan]. *Ssu yü Yen (Thought and Word) [Taiwan] 1982 19(5): 13-38.* The US Congress should make increased use of its powers of oversight to induce the State Department to fully effect the Taiwan Relations Act of 1979, which provides for arms sales to meet Taiwan's defense needs. Additional hearings, with expanded use of the testimony of representatives from the citizenry (including American businessmen) and from Taiwan, is one congressional option that should be employed. Based on the Taiwan Relations Act; 70 notes, biblio. J. A. Krompart

1167. Li, Wen L. and Yu, Linda. INTERPERSONAL CONTACT AND RACIAL PREJUDICE: A COMPARATIVE STUDY OF AMERICAN AND CHINESE STUDENTS. *Sociol. Q. 1974 15(4): 559-566.* "The extent of the causal relation between interpersonal contact and racial prejudice is examined with emphasis on how this relation is intervened by the effects of family socioeconomic status. A cross-cultural, comparative study of American and [Taiwanese] Chinese students is attempted using a stereotype questionnaire adapted, with some modifications, from Katz and Braly's adjective list. The data indicate that a) family socioeconomic status is significantly related to cross-national contact among both the Americans and Chinese, b) increased contact does not linearly reduce prejudice for both the Americans and Chinese and c) family socioeconomic status is, relatively speaking, more important than interpersonal contact in its relation to prejudice and significantly so in the American sample." J

1168. Liu, Ben-Chieh. ECONOMIC GROWTH AND QUALITY OF LIFE: A COMPARATIVE INDICATOR ANALYSIS BETWEEN CHINA (TAIWAN), U.S.A. AND OTHER DEVELOPED COUNTRIES. *Am. J. of Econ. and Sociol. 1980 39(1): 1-21.* Using a composite Quality of Life (QOL) indicator model based on social economic, energy and environmental, health and education, and national vitality and security components, ranks 32 developed countries and Taiwan according to their component and overall QOL measures. The influence of income and other variables was not as significantly related to the composite QOL indexes as were other variables and

Taiwan's QOL rankings far exceed its per capita income ranking in the international comparison. The United States surpassed all the countries studied in providing its citizens with basic human needs and the highest material standard of living. The national vitality and security component indicated, however, that the United States may have lost, militarily and strategically, some of its influence and perceived power to the USSR. Table, 7 notes, biblio., appendix. J

1169. Miller, Milton H. et al. THE AMERICAN STUDENT IN TAIWAN. *Internat. Studies Q. 1973 17(3): 359-372.* Discusses the cultural experiences of American college students in Taiwan in 1969. S

1170. Myers, Ramon H. and Schroder, Norma. AMERICA'S ECONOMIC STAKE IN TAIWAN. *Asian Affairs: An Am. Rev. 1975 3(2): 99-106.* Statistics for 1974 show that the United States was Taiwan's largest foreign market, absorbing 36.82 percent of the exports. Agricultural products have declined precipitously from a 49.2 percent share to 17.1 percent of exports in the decade from 1962-72. In 1973, Taiwan was the 15th largest purchaser of US exports, outranking Switzerland and Israel; by 1974 it had jumped to 10th place among our export markets. Observers foresee a decline in Japan's comparative share of the Taiwan market, and an increase in the US share. The industries on Taiwan that have attracted the most foreign capital are (in descending order) electronics and appliances, chemicals, and machinery and instruments. 10 notes. E. P. Stickney

1171. Pappas, Anna Mamalakis. THE CONSTITUTIONAL ALLOCATION OF COMPETENCE IN THE TERMINATION OF TREATIES. *New York U. J. of Int. Law and Pol. 1981 13(3): 473-523.* Considers international legal norms of treaty termination with reference to the Vienna Convention of 1969, and with special attention to the termination by the United States of the Mutual Defense Treaty between the United States and the Republic of China, signed in 1954 and terminated in 1980.

1172. Petukhov, V. "TAIVAN'SKAIA KARTA" [The "Taiwanese card"]. *Aziia i Afrika Segodnia [USSR] 1981 (9): 17-21.* Examines the apparent paradoxes involved in the US rapprochement with China in 1978 and its continued ties with Taiwan, and discusses the motives for China's reconciliation to a US "two-China" policy.

1173. Sutter, Robert. U.S. ARMS SALES TO TAIWAN: IMPLICATIONS FOR AMERICAN INTERESTS. *J. of Northeast Asian Studies 1982 1(3): 27-40.* Examines arguments for and against US sales of arms to Taiwan, the changing policies of the Reagan administration, and implications for future US-Taiwan relations.

1174. Unger, Leonard. TAIWAN: THE PROSPEROUS PARIAH: DERECOGNITION WORKED. *Foreign Policy 1979 (36): 105-121.* The baleful prophecies which accompanied President Jimmy Carter's derecognition of the Nationalist Chinese government on Taiwan have not come true. United States safeguarded its interests in Taiwan while improving its relations with China. 2 notes. T. L. Powers

1175. Yee, Herbert S. THIRD PARTY RESPONSE IN FOREIGN POLICY: TAIWAN'S RESPONSE TO CANADIAN AND JAPANESE CHINA POLICIES. *Asia Q. [Belgium] 1979 (4): 309-325.* Canada, on 13 October 1970, announced its establishment of diplomatic relations with the People's Republic of China. Tokyo did the same on 29 September 1972. Taipei has made effective use of nondiplomatic channels to maintain economic, cultural, and other relations with countries which have not had diplomatic relations with it. Foreign policy since 1970 has been innovative and adaptive. Emphasis on economic development has helped to establish a viable and healthy economy. Peking's strategy of diplomatic isolation resulted in political determination and self-confidence. Based on newspapers and other sources; 40 notes. G. M. White

1176. —. [THE UNITED STATES AND THE DECLINE OF NATIONALIST CHINA]. Borg, Dorothy and Heinrichs, Waldo, ed. *Uncertain Years: Chinese-American Relations, 1947-1950* (New York: Columbia U. Pr., 1980): 131-177.
Tucker, Nancy Bernkopf. NATIONALIST CHINA'S DECLINE AND ITS IMPACT ON SINO-AMERICAN RELATIONS, 1949-1950, pp. 131-171. After the military disasters of late 1948, the Jiang Jieshi (Chiang Kai-shek) government fell into a panic; internal factional strife exacerbated military weakness and made the longed-for US military aid that much more difficult to secure.
Borg, Dorothy. SUMMARY OF DISCUSSION, pp. 172-177. Participants at the Conference on Chinese-American Relations, Mt. Kisco, New York, 1978, pointed out other reasons for Jiang's decline and for his difficulty in securing the desired US aid.

SUBJECT INDEX

Subject Profile Index (ABC-SPIndex) carries both generic and specific index terms. Begin a search at the general term but also look under more specific or related terms. This index includes selective cross-references.

Each string of index descriptors is intended to present a profile of a given article; however, no particular relationship between any two terms in the profile is implied. Terms within the profile are listed alphabetically after the leading term. The variety of punctuation and capitalization reflects production methods and has no intrinsic meaning; e.g., there is no difference in meaning between "Intervention, military" and "Intervention (military)."

Cities, towns, and counties are listed following their respective states or provinces for US and Canadian place names, and following their country for non-US and non-Canadian place names, e.g., China (Beijing).

Note that, because the United States is the implicit subject of this bibliography, "United States" is not used as a leading index term. When an entry refers to both Canada and the United States, both "Canada" and "USA" appear in the string of index descriptors, but "USA" is not a leading term. When an entry refers to any other country or region and the United States, only the other country or region is indexed.

Acronyms and initialisms are generally not found in this index; notable exceptions include GNP, UN, and NATO.

The Pinyin system of Romanizing Chinese names has been used wherever possible, except in the case of Taiwanese and Hong Kong Chinese names.

The chronology of the bibliographic entry follows the subject index descriptors. In the chronology, "c" stands for "century," e.g., "19c" means "19th century."

The last number in the index string, in italics, refers to the abstract number.

A

Abortion. Birth control. Japan. 1940's-79. *670*
Academia Sinica (Tsungli Yamen Archive). China. Foreign Relations. Public Administration. 1868-94. *220*
Acculturation. Chinese. Colleges and Universities. Mental illness. Students. Taiwan. 1854-1973. *1151*
—. Internment. Japanese Americans. Social Conditions. 1945-55. *743*
Acheson, Dean. China. Foreign Relations. 1944-50. *562*
—. Intervention. Korean War. Truman, Harry S. USSR. 1950. *1014*
Adachi Minechiro. Foreign Relations. Huerta, Victoriano. Japan. Mexico. 1913-14. *786*
Adams, Ansel. California. Internment. Japanese Americans. Lange, Dorothea. Manzanar War Relocation Center. Photography, Journalistic. World War II. 1941-45. *840*
Adventist Medical Cadet Corps. Armies. Dick, Everett N. (account). Korean War. Military service. World War II. 1934-53. *29*
Afghanistan. China. Foreign Relations. Invasions. Military cooperation. USSR. Vietnam. 1965-80. *232*
—. China. Government. Pakistan. 1979-81. *146*
—. Foreign Relations. Iran. Japan. 1979-81. *989*
—. Invasions. Korean War. Limited war (concept). USSR. Vietnam War. War Powers Act (US, 1973). 1945-79. *104*
Africa. China. Foreign Relations. USA. USSR. ca 1949-70's. *327*
—. China. USSR. 1976. *6*

Agawa, Hiroyuki. Japan. Military officers. Navies. World War II. Yamamoto, Isoroku (review article). 1930's-43. *764*
Agricultural Development. China. Regional studies. 1900-20. *193*
Agricultural Policy. China. Famine. Mao Zedong. 1960-76. *371*
Agricultural property. Democratization. Inheritance. Japan. Military Occupation. 1945-52. *935*
Agricultural Technology and Research. Family. Fiji. Israel. Japan. Social Change. 1689-1975. *634*
Agriculture (comparative study). Boserup, Ester. China. North America. Russia. South. 18c-19c. *465*
Air Forces. *See also* Army Air Forces; Naval Air Forces; Pilots.
—. Atomic bomb. Japan (Hiroshima). Military training. Personal narratives. Tibbets, Paul W. World War II. 1945. *932*
—. Balloon Force. Documents. Japan. World War II. 1942-45. *702*
—. *Battle Hymn* (film). Hess, Dean Elmer. Korean War. Orphans. 1950-56. *1032*
—. China. World War II. 1943-45. *402*
—. F-13 (aircraft). Korean War. World War II. 1944-54. *82*
—. F-86F (aircraft). Korean War. Osan Air Base. South Africa. UN Command. 1950-53. *1008*
—. Japan. Kenney, George. Rabaul (battle). World War II. 1943. *607*
—. Japan. Military Capability. Philippines. World War II. 1941. *692*
—. Knight, Charlotte (field report). Korean War. 1950. *1060*
—. Korean War. Lackland Air Force Base. Legislative Investigations. Military Training. Texas (San Antonio). 1950-66. *1011*

230 Air National

Air National Guard. Korea, South. Military Reserves. Mobilization. Vietnam War. 1968-69. *1036*
Air Rescue Service. Korean War. Vietnam War. 1961-75. *1133*
Air Transport Command. Burma Road. China. Convoys. Frost, Edwin C. Personal Narratives. Transportation, Military. 1945. *259*
Air Warfare. American Volunteer Group. China. Flying Tigers. Shoulder patches. World War II. 23d Fighter Group. 1930's-45. *25*
—. Army Air Force. China. Flying Tigers. Holloway, Bruce K. (account). P-40 (aircraft). World War II. 1942-43. *297*
—. Balloons. Bombing. Japan. North America. World War II. 1940-45. *964*
—. Bombing. China (Gailan). Coal Mines and Mining. Combs, Cecil E. Personal narratives. World War II. 1942. *213*
—. Bombing. Japan. Personal Narratives. Sims, Jack A. World War II. 1942. *905*
—. Bombing, night. B-26 (aircraft). Korean War. 1950-52. *1115*
—. Chennault, Claire Lee. China. Flying Tigers. Japan. World War II. 1941-45. *701*
—. Chennault, Claire Lee. China. Japan. World War II. 1937-45. *98*
—. C-47 (aircraft). Korean War. 1950-53. *1020*
—. Foss, Joseph J. Guadalcanal (battle). Japan. World War II. 1942. *795*
—. Hellcats. Japan. Task Force 58. Truk (battle). World War II. 1944. *933*
—. Japan. Lemay, Curtis. World War II. 1940-45. *976*
—. Japan. Mariana Islands (battle). World War II. 1944. *668*
—. Korea, South (Ch'unch'on). Korean War. Risedorph, Gene (reminiscences). 1952. *1112*
—. Korean War. Military Strategy. Vietnam War. World War II. 1940-72. *52*
Air warfare, clandestine. China. Japan. 1940-41. *474*
Aircraft carriers. Japan. Submarine Warfare. World War II. 1941-45. *865*
Airplane Industry and Trade. China. Embargoes. Great Britain. Vickers Ltd. 1919-21. *448*
Airplanes. *See also* names of specific aircraft, e.g., F-13 (aircraft); P-40 (aircraft).
—. China (Kunming). Ghana (Accra). Laughlin, C. H. (reminiscences). World War II. 1942. *347*
Airplanes, Military. Japan. Navies. Productivity. World War II. 1941-45. *860*
Alabama (Mobile). China. Missions and Missionaries. Presbyterian Church. Stuart, Mary Horton. 1840's-1947. *284*
Alaska. British Columbia. China (Macao). Cook, James. Fur trade. Pacific Area. 1778-79. *49*
Alaska (Aleutian Islands). *Arthur Middleton* (vessel). Coast Guard. Japan. Laidlaw, Lansing. World War II. 1942-43. *769*
—. Attu (battle). Japan. World War II. 1942. *916*
Alienation. China. Cuba. Intellectuals, western. Pilgrimages. USSR. Vietnam, North. 1930's. 1970's. *296*
Allen, Horace. Diplomacy. Hawaii. Immigration. Korea. Sugar. 1902-05. *1101*
Alliances. Asia, Southwest. China. National Security. USSR. 1977-78. *536*
—. Boxer Rebellion. China, East. Great Britain. Russia. 1900. *138*
—. Carter, Jimmy. Korea, South. Military Aid. Taiwan. 1970's. *30*
—. China. Multipolarity. USSR. 1970's. *436*
—. Defense. Military strategy. NATO. Political change, international. 1945-70's. *1088*
—. Dulles, John Foster. Japan. Political Theory. Treaties. Yoshida, Shigeru. 5c BC-20c. 1951. *653*

—. Economic Growth. Ethnocentrism. Japan. 1945-80. *805*
—. Korea, South. Military. Vietnam War. 1965-73. *1043*
Alliances (review article). British Empire. Japan. Louis, William Roger. Thorne, Christopher. World War II. 1941-45. *854*
Alperovitz, Gar (review article). Atomic Warfare. Decisionmaking. Historiography. Japan (Hiroshima). World War II. 1945-65. *898*
Amerasia (periodical). China. Communist Party. Espionage. Foreign policy. Nationalists. Service, John Stewart (reports). ca 1937-45. *343*
American Board of Commissioners for Foreign Missions. Attitudes. China. Missions and Missionaries. 1830-60. *467*
American Council on Japan. Economic Policy. Foreign Policy. Japan. Lobbying. Military Occupation. 1945-50's. *873*
—. Foreign Policy. Japan. Lobbying. 1947-52. *894*
American history. China. History Teaching. Textbooks. 18c-20c. *551*
American International Corporation. China. Vanderlip, Frank A. 1915-19. *386*
American Revolution. China. Ideology. Nationalism. Revolutionary Movements. Sun Zhongshan. 1776-83. 1905-25. *187*
American Studies. China. Literature. 1950-80. *298*
—. Hong Kong, University of. 1945-76. *572*
—. Libraries. Taiwan. 1969-75. *1154*
American Tobacco Company. Government ownership. Japan (Tokyo). Parrish, Edward James. Tobacco. 1899-1904. *656*
American Volunteer Group. Air Warfare. China. Flying Tigers. Shoulder patches. World War II. 23d Fighter Group. 1930's-45. *25*
Americanology. Historiography (review article). Japan. National self-image. Social conditions. 19c-20c. 1969-73. *722*
Americans. Baptists. China. Fielde, Adele M. Siam. 1865-90. *60*
—. Japan. Literature, popular. 1934-73. *755*
Americans (protected). Japan (Shimonoseki Strait). McDougal, David. Naval battles. *Wyoming* (vessel). 1863. *683*
Amphibious operations. Japan. World War II. 1942-45. *725*
Anderson, Irvine H., Jr. (review article). Asia, East. Foreign Investments. Foreign policy. Oil Industry and Trade. Standard-Vacuum Oil Company. 1933-41. 1975. *97*
Angell, James B. China. Immigration. Trade. Treaties. 1880-81. *185*
Annexation. Business. Taiwan. 1850-60. *1156*
—. Hawaii. Japan. Treaties. 1897. *821*
—. Nye, Gideon, Jr. Taiwan. 1857. *1164*
Anticolonialism. Asia. Roosevelt, Franklin D. USA. World War II. 1941-45. *51*
Anti-Communist Movements. Asia. Foreign Policy. Reagan, Ronald (administration). Taiwan. 1981. *64*
—. China. Foreign Policy. May, Gary. McCarthy, Joseph R. Vincent, John Carter. 1942-51. *279*
—. China. USSR. 1917-50. *267*
—. Korean War. Missouri. 1950-53. *1052*
Antitrust. Automobile Industry and Trade. Federal Policy. Imports. Japan. Protectionism. 1981-83. *982*
ANZUS. Australia. Japan. National Security. New Zealand. Treaties. 1951-81. *936*
—. Defense Policy. Foreign Relations. Japan. 1945-78. *937*
Apathy. Colonization. Death and Dying. Korean War. Malnutrition. Prisoners of war. Virginia (Jamestown). World War II. 1607-24. 1941-53. *74*
Appeasement (proposal). Diplomacy. Great Britain. Japan. World War II. 1941. *680*

Asia   231

Arab States. Japan. Oil Industry and Trade. 1970's. *778*
Arab-Israeli conflict. China. USSR. 1977-79. *558*
—. China. USSR. 1979-80. *557*
—. Conflict and Conflict Resolution. Decisionmaking. Foreign Policy. Japan. World War II. 1941-45. 1967-73. *600*
Archaeology. China. Janus, Christopher. Peking Man. Shapiro, Harry F. 1941-73. *542*
Archival Catalogs and Inventories. China. Genealogical Society of Utah. Utah (Salt Lake City). 15c-20c. *509*
Archives. China. Japan. Korea. Missions and Missionaries. Presbyterian Historical Society. 1829-1911. *39*
—. China. Missions and Missionaries. Protestantism. Yale University Library (collection). Yale-in-China Association. 1901-51. *237*
Archives, National. Asia, East. Asian Americans. Georgia (Atlanta). 18c-20c. *100*
Arizona. Gila River Relocation Center. Japanese Americans. Public Opinion. Race Relations. World War II. 1942-45. *627*
Arkansas (Rowher Camp). Internment. Japanese Americans. World War II. 1942-45. *592*
Armies. See also terms beginning with "Army"; Air Forces; Military; Navies.
—. Adventist Medical Cadet Corps. Dick, Everett N. (account). Korean War. Military service. World War II. 1934-53. *29*
—. China. Cope, Jesse D. (article). 1898-1902. 1931. *214*
—. Dill, James. Korean War. Personal narratives. 7th Infantry Division, US (31st Field Artillery Battalion). 1950-51. *1027*
—. Japan. Marines. Peleliu (battle). Sledge, Eugene B. (account). World War II. 1944. *907*
—. Korea, South. Military Occupation. 1880-1950. *1067*
—. Korean Augmentation to the U.S. Army. 1950-65. *1118*
Arms control. Canada. China. India. Nuclear Arms. Nuclear power. Regionalism. USA. 1951-78. *493*
Arms control agreements. China. Detente. Nuclear strategy. USSR. 1970's. *516*
Arms race. China. Korean War. Rostow, Eugene V. USSR. 1953-82. *8*
Arms trade. Asia, East. Association of South East Asian Nations. Foreign policy. 1982. *48*
—. China. Foreign Relations. Taiwan. 1979-82. *1165*
—. Foreign Relations. Taiwan. 1978-82. *1173*
—. Taiwan Relations Act (US, 1979). 1979-81. *1166*
Arms Trade (prohibited). China. Civil war. Japan. Western Nations. 1919-29. *17*
Armstrong, David M. (personal account). Hawaii. Japan. Pearl Harbor (attack). World War II. 1942. *580*
Army Air Force. Air Warfare. China. Flying Tigers. Holloway, Bruce K. (account). P-40 (aircraft). World War II. 1942-43. *297*
—. China. Communist Party. 1946-47. *438*
Arndt, E. L. China. Lutheran Church. Missions and Missionaries. 1913-29. *510*
Arnhold & Company. China (Chang River). Hawley, Edwin C. Propaganda. Theater. Tretiakov, Sergei *(Roar China!)*. 1924-75. *394*
Art. China. Chinnery, George. Ports. Sailors. 18c-19c. *423*
Arthur Middleton (vessel). Alaska (Aleutian Islands). Coast Guard. Japan. Laidlaw, Lansing. World War II. 1942-43. *769*
Arts and crafts. China. Exhibits and Expositions. Missouri (St. Louis). World's fair. 1904. *216*

Asama (vessel). Japan. Mexico (Baja California, Turtle Bay). Tuchman, Barbara. 1915. *663*
Asia. Anticolonialism. Roosevelt, Franklin D. USA. World War II. 1941-45. *51*
—. Anti-Communist Movements. Foreign Policy. Reagan, Ronald (administration). Taiwan. 1981. *64*
—. Association of South East Asian Nations. China. Foreign Relations. 1970's. *260*
—. Balance of power. China. Foreign Policy. Japan. 1950's-74. *112*
—. Balance of power. China. Japan. USSR. 1970-73. *80*
—. China. Foreign Policy. 1945-78. *521*
—. China. Foreign policy. 1950's-78. *190*
—. Defensive perimeter concept. Military Strategy. 1947-51. *564*
—. Economic Conditions. Emigration. Labor. 1834-1930. *1003*
—. Foreign Relations. Japan. 1945-72. *110*
—. Historiography, US. Japan. Revolutionary movements. USSR. World War II. 1930's-49. *862*
Asia American Studies Center. Bibliographies. California, University of, Los Angeles. Chinese. Chinese Americans. 1854-1978. *344*
Asia, East. Anderson, Irvine H., Jr. (review article). Foreign Investments. Foreign policy. Oil Industry and Trade. Standard-Vacuum Oil Company. 1933-41. 1975. *97*
—. Archives, National. Asian Americans. Georgia (Atlanta). 18c-20c. *100*
—. Arms trade. Association of South East Asian Nations. Foreign policy. 1982. *48*
—. Balance of Power. China. Foreign policy. Japan. 1968-73. *133*
—. Barnett, A. Doak. China. Foreign Relations. USSR. 1944-78. *123*
—. Blum, Robert M. Buhite, Russell D. Foreign Relations (review article). McMahon, Robert J. 1945-60's. *24*
—. China. Cold War (review article). Truman, Harry S. 1940's-71. *210*
—. China. Development. Foreign Relations. Political Attitudes. Wilson, James H. 1885-1910. *169*
—. China. Foreign Relations. 1945-82. *160*
—. China. Foreign Relations. 1979. *114*
—. Collection building. Libraries (US). 15c-20c. 1960's-70's. *127*
—. Defense Policy. Military Strategy. War. 1945-50. *32*
—. Diplomacy. Four-Power Treaty. Karnebeek, Hermann Adriaan van. Netherlands. Washington Conference. 1921-22. *9*
—. Economic Conditions. Foreign Relations. 1982. *66*
—. Economic problems. Foreign Relations. Japan. Political Leadership. Tanaka, Kakuei. 1971-74. *883*
—. Education. Public Opinion. USA. 1973. *5*
—. Foreign policy. 1981. *119*
—. Foreign Policy. Japan. 1948-78. *694*
—. Foreign Policy. Japan. Korea. Nixon Doctrine. Vietnam. 1969-73. *90*
—. Foreign Policy. Japan. World War II (antecedents). 1931-41. *687*
—. Foreign policy. Lansing, Robert. World War I (antecedents). 1914-17. *54*
—. Foreign Policy. Navies. Sino-Japanese War. 1894-95. *37*
—. Foreign Policy. USSR. 1945-80. *113*
—. Foreign Policy (review article). 1945-77. *121*
—. Foreign Relations. 1776-1976. *27*
—. Foreign Relations. USSR. 1948-81. *88*
—. Georgia. 1865-1983. *47*
—. Georgia (Atlanta). International Trade. 1945-82. *86*

232 Asia

—. Imperialism. 19c-1975. *790*
—. Middle East. Naval Tactics. 1945-79. *42*
Asia (East, Southeast). Foreign policy. 1951-70's. *132*
Asia, North. Documents. Geography. Geology. Japan. 1848-83. *99*
Asia, northeast. Foreign Policy. Korean War. Political conditions. 1953-78. *1128*
Asia, South. China. Foreign Policy. USSR. 1970's. *426*
Asia, Southeast. Balance of power. China. Communism. USSR. War. 1920-79. *31*
—. Brezhnev, Leonid. China. Foreign policy. Military aid. 1968-79. *488*
—. China. Detente. 1970's. *376*
—. China. Foreign Relations. Vietnam War. 1973-75. *256*
—. Economic development. Foreign Policy. Fukuda, Takeo. Japan. 1978. *676*
—. Foreign Policy. Japan. 1945-73. *688*
—. Foreign Policy. Korea, South. Military Strategy. 1960's-70's. *1034*
—. Great Powers. 1960-76. *452*
Asia, Southwest. Alliances. China. National Security. USSR. 1977-78. *536*
Asian Americans. See also Chinese Americans; Japanese Americans; Korean Americans.
—. Archives, National. Asia, East. Georgia (Atlanta). 18c-20c. *100*
Asian studies. China. Secondary Education (curriculum reform). USA. 1972-73. *373*
Asiatic Squadron. Diplomacy. Korea. Navies. 1882-97. *1015*
Assassination. Foreign Relations. Korea, South. Park Chung-hee. Politics. 1979-82. *1010*
Associated Japan-America Societies of the United States. Cultural relations. Georgia. International Trade. Japan. 1979-82. *958*
Association of South East Asian Nations. Arms trade. Asia, East. Foreign policy. 1982. *48*
—. Asia. China. Foreign Relations. 1970's. *260*
Associations. Gentlemen's Agreement. Immigrants. Japan. Japanese Americans. 1907-26. *717*
Atlantic Community. Energy policy. Japan. 1972-73. *777*
Atomic Bomb. See also Nuclear Arms and other terms at the heading "Nuclear."
—. Air Forces. Japan (Hiroshima). Military training. Personal narratives. Tibbets, Paul W. World War II. 1945. *932*
—. Barnouw, Erik. *Hiroshima-Nagasaki, August 1945* (film). Japan. 1945-70. *588*
—. Charities. Japan (Hiroshima). Surgery. Women. World War II. 1945-57. *985*
—. Documents. Japan (Hiroshima, Nagasaki). World War II. 1945. *867*
—. Japan. Military Strategy. Truman, Harry S. World War II. 1945. *602*
—. Japan. Public opinion. World War II. 1945-49. *984*
—. Japan (Hiroshima, Nagasaki). Truman, Harry S. World War II. 1942-47. *605*
Atomic Bomb Casualty Commission. Civilians. Japan (Hiroshima, Nagasaki). Medical Research. Radiation Effects Research Foundation. 1945-75. *960*
Atomic energy. Japan. Military Strategy. Smyth Report, 1945. USA. World War II. 1940-45. *908*
Atomic Warfare. Alperovitz, Gar (review article). Decisionmaking. Historiography. Japan (Hiroshima). World War II. 1945-65. *898*
—. Cold War. Japan (Hiroshima). World War II. 1945. *744*
—. Decisionmaking. Japan (Hiroshima, Nagasaki). Military Strategy. World War II. 1944-45. *671*
—. History Teaching. Japan. Simulation and Games. World War II. 1945. 1978. *658*

—. Japan. Leftists. USSR. World War II. 1945. *610*
—. Japan. Military strategy. World War II. 1945. *714*
—. Japan. Politics. Surrender. Truman, Harry S. (administration). World War II. 1945. *604*
—. Japan (Hiroshima, Nagasaki). Military Strategy. Surrender, unconditional. World War II. 1943-45. *703*
—. Japan (Hiroshima, Nagasaki). Military Strategy. World War II. 1945. *603*
—. Japan (Kyoto). World War II. 1945. *848*
Attitudes. See also Political Attitudes.
—. American Board of Commissioners for Foreign Missions. China. Missions and Missionaries. 1830-60. *467*
—. Authoritarianism. Chinese. Students. 1949-70. *191*
—. Authors. Japan. USA. World War II. 1940-49. *815*
—. Canada. Internment. Japanese Americans. Japanese Canadians. World War II. 1940-80. *642*
—. Carter, Jimmy (administration). Korea, South. 1977-78. *1087*
—. China. 1970-82. *281*
—. China. Foreign policy. 1970-80. *280*
—. China. Missions and Missionaries. Presbyterian Church. 1837-1900. *212*
—. Custer, Elizabeth Bacon. Japan. Travel accounts. 1903. *955*
—. Democracy. Europe. Interest Groups. Japan. Nuclear Science and Technology. USSR. 1970's. *731*
—. High Schools. Japan. Yasuteru, Aoki. 1970's. *814*
—. History. Japan/United States Textbook Study Project. Textbooks. 1981. *999*
—. Intellectuals. Japan. ca 1945-75. *897*
—. Japanese Americans. Sociology. Values. World War II. 1940's-70's. *915*
Attu (battle). Alaska (Aleutian Islands). Japan. World War II. 1942. *916*
—. Japan. Tatsuguchi, Paul Nobuo (diary). USA. World War II. 1941-43. *963*
Austin, Warren R. Foreign policy. Korean War. Truman Doctrine. UN. 1945-53. *1086*
Australia. ANZUS. Japan. National Security. New Zealand. Treaties. 1951-81. *936*
—. Canada. Europe. Japan. Unemployment. USA. 1972-73. *911*
—. Circumnavigations. Foreign Relations. Japan. Warships. 1908. *878*
—. Foreign policy. International Trade. Japan. New Zealand. 1968-70's. *41*
—. Italy. Japan. Netherlands. Political information. Voting and Voting Behavior. 1960's-70's. *716*
—. Japan. Peace settlement. World War II. 1942-46. *597*
Australia-New Zealand-US Security Council. See ANZUS.
Authoritarianism. Attitudes. Chinese. Students. 1949-70. *191*
Authoritarianism (theory). Korean War. Personality. Public opinion. Racism. Vietnam War. 1950-78. *1046*
Authors. Attitudes. Japan. USA. World War II. 1940-49. *815*
Autobiography. Franklin, Benjamin. Fukuzawa, Yukichi. Japan. 1980. *962*
Automation. Japan. 1970-81. *650*
Automobile Industry and Trade. Antitrust. Federal Policy. Imports. Japan. Protectionism. 1981-83. *982*
—. Canada. Europe, Western. Gindon, Sam (interview). Japan. Labor. World car (concept). 1945-80. *1006*

—. Competition. Europe. Industry. Japan. 1969-73. *649*
—. Europe, Western. Japan. 1973-80. *611*
—. Imports. Japan. 1975-81. *618*
—. Japan. Trade Regulations. 1971-81. *857*
Automobiles. Foreign Policy. Imports. Japan. Trade Regulations. 1970-81. *727*
Aviation. China. Fraser, Douglas. Military training. Nationalists. Saskatchewan (Saskatoon). 1919-22. *217*
Awa Maru (vessel). Japan. Navies. *Queenfish* (submarine). World War II. 1945. *912*

B

Balance of Payments. International Trade. Japan. 1977-81. *844*
Balance of power. Asia. China. Foreign Policy. Japan. 1950's-74. *112*
—. Asia. China. Japan. USSR. 1970-73. *80*
—. Asia, East. China. Foreign policy. Japan. 1968-73. *133*
—. Asia, Southeast. China. Communism. USSR. War. 1920-79. *31*
—. Bowles, Chester. China. Foreign Relations. India. Nehru, Jawaharlal. 1949-54. *16*
—. China. Coffey, Joseph I. Military capability. USA. USSR. ca 1965-73. *158*
—. China. Cold War. USSR. 1956-80. *325*
—. China. Europe. Foreign Relations. USSR. 1970's. *229*
—. China. Europe. USSR. 1945-73. *242*
—. China. Foreign policy. 1970's. *456*
—. China. Foreign policy. Nixon, Richard M. (administration). USSR. 1969-72. *462*
—. China. Foreign Policy. USSR. Vietnam War. 1964-76. *512*
—. China. Foreign Relations. Japan. 1970's. *1*
—. China. Korean War. 1948-51. *1106*
—. China. USSR. 1974. *241*
—. Cold War. Foreign policy. Korean War. USSR. 1946-50. *1050*
—. Foreign Aid. Korea. 1945-74. *1037*
—. Foreign policy. Japan. Military Aid. 1945-77. *657*
Balloon Force. Air Forces. Documents. Japan. World War II. 1942-45. *702*
Balloons. Air Warfare. Bombing. Japan. North America. World War II. 1940-45. *964*
Balloons, armed. Japan. Project FUGO. South Dakota. World War II. 1944-45. *770*
Bank of England. China. Economic crises. International Trade. Magniac and Co. Yrissari and Co. 1823-27. *18*
Banking. See also names of specific banks, e.g., Oriental Bank Corporation.
—. China. Chinese-American Bank of Commerce. 1910-20. *450*
—. China. Foreign Investments. Foreign Policy. Great Britain. 1908-20. *219*
—. Europe. Japan. Monopolies. ca 1950's-70's. *944*
Baptist Church. China. Missions and Missionaries. Shuck, Eliza G. Sexton. 1846-63. *322*
Baptists. Americans. China. Fielde, Adele M. Siam. 1865-90. *60*
Baptists (Southern). China. Missions and Missionaries. Roberts, Issachar Jacob. 1837-47. *567*
—. China, south. Missions and Missionaries. 1845-76. *503*
Barefoot doctor movement. China. Medicine, Western. Political systems. Public Health. 1973. *411*
Barnett, A. Doak. Asia, East. China. Foreign Relations. USSR. 1944-78. *123*
Barnett, A. Doak (review article). China. Foreign Relations. USSR. 1950-76. *401*

Barnouw, Erik. Atomic Bomb. *Hiroshima-Nagasaki, August 1945* (film). Japan. 1945-70. *588*
Barrett, John. China. Foreign policy. Open Door Policy. 1898-99. *445*
Barton, Fred. China (Shansi). Cowboys. Horse breeding. Montana. Politics. 1912-32. *400*
Baseball. Democracy. Japan. Values. 1920-41. *637*
—. Foreign Relations. Japan. 1875-1900. *874*
Bashford, James W. China. Methodist Episcopal Church. Missions and Missionaries. Social gospel. 1889-1919. *320*
Battle Hymn (film). Air Forces. Hess, Dean Elmer. Korean War. Orphans. 1950-56. *1032*
Battle of the Bulge. China. Cuban Missile Crisis. Korean War. Military intelligence. 1944-80. *3*
Behavior. Communications. Japan. Television. 1972-81. *729*
Berry, Mary (speech). China. Communism. Education. Shanker, Albert (views). 1977. *167*
Bethune, Angus. China (Canton). International Trade. North America. North West Company. 1812-17. *469*
Bibliographies. Asia American Studies Center. California, University of, Los Angeles. Chinese. Chinese Americans. 1854-1978. *344*
—. China. Foreign Policy. Taiwan. 1949-82. *12*
—. China. Foreign Relations. 1844-1974. *292*
—. Dissertations. Korea. 1970-74. *1116*
—. Dissertations. Korea. 1970-74. *1117*
—. Historiography (review article). Korean War. 1950-55. *1097*
Biddle, James. Japan. Naval missions. Negotiations. 1845-54. *590*
—. Japan. Pacific Area. Spain. Taguchi Ukichi. 1846-90's. *773*
Bikini Atoll. Hydrogen bomb. Japan. *Lucky Dragon* (vessel). Pacific Dependencies (US). 1954-75. *882*
Biography. China. Ming dynasty. 1368-1644. *227*
Birch, John (death). China. Communists. Military Intelligence. 1945. *530*
Birth control. Abortion. Japan. 1940's-79. *670*
Blacks. Brown, Jesse. Hudner, Thomas. Korean War. Military officers. Navies. 1950. *1123*
—. Brown, Jesse. Korean War. Naval Air Forces. Pilots. 1948-50. *1139*
—. China. Discrimination. Foreign Policy. Political Attitudes. 1971. *492*
—. Immigration restriction. Japanese. Miller, Kelly. Race Relations. 1906-24. *699*
Blockades. Chamberlain, Neville. China. Great Britain. Japan. Roosevelt, Franklin D. World War II (antecedents). 1937-38. *686*
Blum, Robert M. Asia, East. Buhite, Russell D. Foreign Relations (review article). McMahon, Robert J. 1945-60's. *24*
Bohme, Frederick G. Census Bureau. Japanese Americans. Letters. Relocation. World War II. 1942-45. *640*
Bombing. See also Atomic Bomb; Hydrogen Bomb; Nuclear Arms.
—. Air Warfare. Balloons. Japan. North America. World War II. 1940-45. *964*
—. Air Warfare. China (Gailan). Coal Mines and Mining. Combs, Cecil E. Personal narratives. World War II. 1942. *213*
—. Air Warfare. Japan. Personal Narratives. Sims, Jack A. World War II. 1942. *905*
—. B-29 (aircraft). China-Burma-India Theater. Close, Winton R. Japan. Personal narratives. World War II. 1944. *633*
—. Japan. World War II. 1937-45. *639*
Bombing exemption. Japan (Kyoto). Stimson, Henry L. World War II. 1940-45. *628*
Bombing, night. Air Warfare. B-26 (aircraft). Korean War. 1950-52. *1115*
Bombs, balloon-carried. Japan. Pacific Northwest. World War II. 1945. *733*

234 Bombs

Bombs (glide, smart). Korean War. Tactics. Vietnam War. World War II. 1919-74. *4*
Books, miniature. Europe. Japan. Publishers and Publishing. 15c-20c. *856*
Boserup, Ester. Agriculture (comparative study). China. North America. Russia. South. 18c-19c. *465*
Boundaries. Korea (38th Parallel). Korean War. Military Armistice Commission. 1953-73. *917*
Bowles, Chester. Balance of power. China. Foreign Relations. India. Nehru, Jawaharlal. 1949-54. *16*
Boxer Rebellion. Alliances. China, East. Great Britain. Russia. 1900. *138*
—. China. Education. Foreign Policy. Historiography. Hunt, Michael (thesis). Reparations. 1900-06. 1972. *535*
—. China (Beijing). Military occupation. 1900-01. *314*
—. China (Beijing, Taku, Tianjin). Marines. 1900. *295*
Boycott. Chamber of Commerce. China (Shanghai). Immigration policy. Nationalism. 1905. *519*
Brain drain. Immigration. Scholars. Taiwan. 1905-73. *1163*
Brezhnev, Leonid. Asia, Southeast. China. Foreign policy. Military aid. 1968-79. *488*
Bribery. Japan. Liberal Democratic Party. Lockheed Aircraft Corporation. 1975-81. *766*
British Columbia. Alaska. China (Macao). Cook, James. Fur trade. Pacific Area. 1778-79. *49*
British Empire. Alliances (review article). Japan. Louis, William Roger. Thorne, Christopher. World War II. 1941-45. *854*
British Typewriter Museum (Wilfred Beeching collection). Europe, Western. Japan. Typewriter. 1711-1970's. *672*
Broadcasts. China. USSR. Vietnam War. 1968-73. *152*
Brooke, John Mercer. Japan. *Kanrin Maru* (vessel). Navies. Trade. Treaties. Voyages. 1860. *615*
Brooks, James L. (personal account). F-86 (aircraft). Korean War. Pilots. 1950. *1016*
Brown, Irving. Japan. Labor policy. Military Occupation. 1945-72. *926*
Brown, Jesse. Blacks. Hudner, Thomas. Korean War. Military officers. Navies. 1950. *1123*
—. Blacks. Korean War. Naval Air Forces. Pilots. 1948-50. *1139*
Brownson, Willard H. China (Nanking). Diplomacy. Gelm, George E. (journal). International Trade. Tuan Fang. 1907. *265*
Bruce, Frederick William. Burlingame, Anson. China. Cooperative Policy. Diplomacy. 1860-65. *334*
Brussels Conference. Diplomacy. Roosevelt, Franklin D. Sino-Japanese War. 1937. *117*
Bueler, William H. China. Cohen, Warren I. (review article). Davies, John Paton, Jr. Foreign Relations. 1830-1955. *392*
Buhite, Russell D. Asia, East. Blum, Robert M. Foreign Relations (review article). McMahon, Robert J. 1945-60's. *24*
Burlingame, Anson. Bruce, Frederick William. China. Cooperative Policy. Diplomacy. 1860-65. *334*
—. China. Diplomacy. 1861-71. *149*
—. China. Diplomacy. House of Representatives. Republican Party. 1854-69. *148*
—. China. Foreign Relations. 1861-67. *333*
Burma. *See also* China-Burma-India Theater.
—. China. Foreign Relations. Indonesia. 1950's-75. *168*
Burma Road. Air Transport Command. China. Convoys. Frost, Edwin C. Personal Narratives. Transportation, Military. 1945. *259*
Business. Annexation. Taiwan. 1850-60. *1156*

—. China (Shanghai). Race Relations. Rea, George Bronson. 1920's. *301*
—. Cold War. Foreign policy. Japan. Press. 1948-52. *704*
—. Germany, West. Japan. Prices. 1980. *682*
—. Japan. Lawyers. Sony Company. 1982. *822*
Business Cycles. Canada. Elections. Europe, Western. Federal Policy. Japan. 1955-80. *930*
—. Economic Structure. Europe, Western. Great Britain. Japan. 1967-80. *959*
Business History. Comparative analysis. Enterprises, large-scale. Europe, Western. Japan. 19c-20c. *629*
Buss, Claude A. China. Fairbank, John K. Foreign Relations (review article). Whiting, Allen S. 1949-76. *234*
Butler, Smedley D. China, North. Marines. Pilots. Williams, Clarence S. 1927-28. *410*
Butow, R. J. Diplomacy, private. Japan. John Doe Associates. Peace (review article). World War II (antecedents). 1940-41. *723*
B-26 (aircraft). Air Warfare. Bombing, night. Korean War. 1950-52. *1115*
B-29 (aircraft). Bombing. China-Burma-India Theater. Close, Winton R. Japan. Personal narratives. World War II. 1944. *633*

C

California. Adams, Ansel. Internment. Japanese Americans. Lange, Dorothea. Manzanar War Relocation Center. Photography, Journalistic. World War II. 1941-45. *840*
—. China. Clipper ships. International Trade. USA. 1840's-50's. *506*
—. China (Guangdong). Emigration. Social Conditions. 1850-82. *390*
—. Chinese Americans. Metropolitan areas. Tong societies. 1850-1972. *204*
—. Concentration Camps. Japanese Americans. Manzanar War Relocation Center. Riots. Ueno, Harry (arrest). World War II. 1942. *691*
—. Detention. Japanese Americans. Racism. World War II. 1941-45. *818*
—. Foreign Investments. Japan. 1975-80. *707*
—. Japanese Americans. Relocation. Warren, Earl. World War II. 1941-45. *967*
California (Los Angeles). Containerization. *Japanese Lines, Ltd.* v. *County of Los Angeles.* Supreme Court. Tariff. 1970-79. *585*
California (Pasadena). China (Shanghai). Daughters of the American Revolution. Young Men's Christian Association. 1916-57. *422*
California (San Francisco). China. Huang Tsun-hsien. Reform. 1882-85. *328*
—. Japan. *Kanrin Maru* (vessel). Treaties. 1860. *990*
California, University of, Los Angeles. Asia American Studies Center. Bibliographies. Chinese. Chinese Americans. 1854-1978. *344*
Cambodia. China. Foreign aid. 1955-74. *257*
—. China. Foreign Policy. Vietnam, South. 1975. *548*
—. China. Foreign Relations. USSR. Vietnam. 1978-80. *105*
—. Decisionmaking. Flexible response. Korea, North. *Mayaguez* incident. *Pueblo* incident. 1969-75. *1039*
Canada. Arms control. China. India. Nuclear Arms. Nuclear power. Regionalism. USA. 1951-78. *493*
—. Attitudes. Internment. Japanese Americans. Japanese Canadians. World War II. 1940-80. *642*
—. Australia. Europe. Japan. Unemployment. USA. 1972-73. *911*

China

—. Automobile Industry and Trade. Europe, Western. Gindon, Sam (interview). Japan. Labor. World car (concept). 1945-80. *1006*

—. Business Cycles. Elections. Europe, Western. Federal Policy. Japan. 1955-80. *930*

—. China. Developing nations. Foreign relations. USSR. 1950-75. *318*

—. China. Diplomacy. Odlum, Victor Wentworth. 1943-46. *418*

—. China. Diplomatic relations. Economic development. Foreign policy. Japan. Taiwan. 1949-72. *1175*

—. China. Foreign Relations. International Trade. USSR. 1969-72. *367*

—. Chinese. Pao-huang Hui Party. Political Factions. 1899-1904. *153*

—. Diplomacy. Korean War. Stairs, Denis (review article). 1950-53. *1092*

—. Ethnicity. Internment. Japanese Americans. Japanese Canadians. Joint Board of Defense. World War II. 1941-42. *641*

—. Europe. Japan. Labor costs. Manufacturing. Productivity. 1974-81. *624*

—. Europe, Western. Japan. Labor. Manufacturing. Productivity. 1960-82. *576*

—. Fur trade. Japan. Sea otters. Wildlife Conservation. 18c-20c. *988*

—. Historians. Japan. Norman, E. Herbert (review article). 1940-77. *859*

—. Internment (conference). Japanese. World War II. 1941-45. 1978. *922*

Canton Christian College. China. Church Schools. Revolution. Yale-in-China Association. 1925-27. *300*

Capitalism. Competition. Japan. 1968-80. *828*

—. Economic conditions. Europe, Western. Great Britain. Japan. 1970-80. *996*

Capron, Horace. Economic Development. Japan (Hokkaido). Modernization. 1871-75. *811*

Carlson, Evans. China. Intelligence mission. Japan. Roosevelt, Franklin D. 1937-38. *40*

—. China. Intelligence mission. Japan. Roosevelt, Franklin D. 1937-38. *128*

Carney, Robert B. Japan. Personal Narratives. Surrender. World War II. 1945. *626*

Caroline Islands. Ellis, Earl. Japan. Marines. Naval strategy. 1920-23. *956*

Carter, Jimmy. Alliances. Korea, South. Military Aid. Taiwan. 1970's. *30*

—. China. Foreign relations. Normalization. Taiwan. USSR. 1978-79. *1150*

—. Eisenhower, Dwight D. Executive Power. Foreign policy. Hamilton, Alexander. Taiwan. 1793-1979. *1161*

Carter, Jimmy (administration). Attitudes. Korea, South. 1977-78. *1087*

—. China. Foreign policy. Human rights. Morality. 1976-77. *520*

—. China. Foreign Policy. Korea. Taiwan. 1970's. *137*

—. China. Foreign policy. Public opinion. 1967-78. *340*

—. Defense Policy. Japan. 1978-79. *677*

—. Detente. Developing nations. Europe, Western. Foreign policy. Japan. USSR. 1977-80. *939*

—. Foreign Policy. Human rights. Korea, South. 1945-79. *1091*

—. Foreign Policy. Japan. Korea, South. Military Ground Forces (withdrawal). 1950's-78. *131*

—. Foreign Policy. Korea. 1950-79. *1044*

—. Foreign Policy. Korea. Military Ground Forces (withdrawal). 1977. *1124*

Catholic Church. China. Christians. Communists. Missions and Missionaries. Protestant Churches. 1948-50. *523*

—. China (Hunan). Missions and Missionaries. Passionists. 1921-29. *186*

—. China (Kanchow). Foreign policy. Missions and Missionaries. 1929-32. *303*

—. Clergy. Guevara, Gaspar Ignacio de. Heresy. Philippines (Biliran). 1765-75. *1061*

Cease-fire. Eisenhower, Dwight D. Korean War. Peace negotiations. UN. 1952-53. *1136*

Censorship. Chicago Tribune. Cryptography. Japan. Midway (battle). Reporters and Reporting. World War II. 1942. *679*

—. Chicago Tribune. Grand Juries. Japan. Midway (battle). Navies. World War II. 1942. *669*

—. Korea, South. Korean War. Newspapers. 1950. *1065*

Census Bureau. Bohme, Frederick G. Japanese Americans. Letters. Relocation. World War II. 1942-45. *640*

Centennial. Japan. 1876. *667*

Chamber of Commerce. Boycott. China (Shanghai). Immigration policy. Nationalism. 1905. *519*

Chamberlain, Neville. Blockades. China. Great Britain. Japan. Roosevelt, Franklin D. World War II (antecedents). 1937-38. *686*

Charities. Atomic bomb. Japan (Hiroshima). Surgery. Women. World War II. 1945-57. *985*

Chemical and Biological Warfare. Korean War. 1940-75. *46*

—. Korean War. 1952-53. *1031*

Chennault, Claire Lee. Air warfare. China. Flying Tigers. Japan. World War II. 1941-45. *701*

—. Air Warfare. China. Japan. World War II. 1937-45. *98*

Chiang Kai-shek. *See* Jiang Jieshi.

Chicago Tribune. Censorship. Cryptography. Japan. Midway (battle). Reporters and Reporting. World War II. 1942. *679*

—. Censorship. Grand Juries. Japan. Midway (battle). Navies. World War II. 1942. *669*

China. 1970-72. *451*

—. Academia Sinica (Tsungli Yamen Archive). Foreign Relations. Public Administration. 1868-94. *220*

—. Acheson, Dean. Foreign Relations. 1944-50. *562*

—. Afghanistan. Foreign Relations. Invasions. Military cooperation. USSR. Vietnam. 1965-80. *232*

—. Afghanistan. Government. Pakistan. 1979-81. *146*

—. Africa. Foreign Relations. USA. USSR. ca 1949-70's. *327*

—. Africa. USSR. 1976. *6*

—. Agricultural Development. Regional studies. 1900-20. *193*

—. Agricultural Policy. Famine. Mao Zedong. 1960-76. *371*

—. Agriculture (comparative study). Boserup, Ester. North America. Russia. South. 18c-19c. *465*

—. Air Forces. World War II. 1943-45. *402*

—. Air Transport Command. Burma Road. Convoys. Frost, Edwin C. Personal Narratives. Transportation, Military. 1945. *259*

—. Air Warfare. American Volunteer Group. Flying Tigers. Shoulder patches. World War II. 23d Fighter Group. 1930's-45. *25*

—. Air Warfare. Army Air Force. Flying Tigers. Holloway, Bruce K. (account). P-40 (aircraft). World War II. 1942-43. *297*

—. Air warfare. Chennault, Claire Lee. Flying Tigers. Japan. World War II. 1941-45. *701*

—. Air Warfare. Chennault, Claire Lee. Japan. World War II. 1937-45. *98*

—. Air warfare, clandestine. Japan. 1940-41. *474*

—. Airplane Industry and Trade. Embargoes. Great Britain. Vickers Ltd. 1919-21. *448*

—. Alabama (Mobile). Missions and Missionaries. Presbyterian Church. Stuart, Mary Horton. 1840's-1947. *284*

236   China

—. Alienation. Cuba. Intellectuals, western. Pilgrimages. USSR. Vietnam, North. 1930's. 1970's. *296*
—. Alliances. Asia, Southwest. National Security. USSR. 1977-78. *536*
—. Alliances. Multipolarity. USSR. 1970's. *436*
—. *Amerasia* (periodical). Communist Party. Espionage. Foreign policy. Nationalists. Service, John Stewart (reports). ca 1937-45. *343*
—. American Board of Commissioners for Foreign Missions. Attitudes. Missions and Missionaries. 1830-60. *467*
—. American history. History Teaching. Textbooks. 18c-20c. *551*
—. American International Corporation. Vanderlip, Frank A. 1915-19. *386*
—. American Revolution. Ideology. Nationalism. Revolutionary Movements. Sun Zhongshan. 1776-83. 1905-25. *187*
—. American Studies. Literature. 1950-80. *298*
—. Americans. Baptists. Fielde, Adele M. Siam. 1865-90. *60*
—. Angell, James B. Immigration. Trade. Treaties. 1880-81. *185*
—. Anti-Communist Movements. Foreign Policy. May, Gary. McCarthy, Joseph R. Vincent, John Carter. 1942-51. *279*
—. Anti-Communist Movements. USSR. 1917-50. *267*
—. Arab-Israeli conflict. USSR. 1977-79. *558*
—. Arab-Israeli Conflict. USSR. 1979-80. *557*
—. Archaeology. Janus, Christopher. Peking Man. Shapiro, Harry F. 1941-73. *542*
—. Archival Catalogs and Inventories. Genealogical Society of Utah. Utah (Salt Lake City). 15c-20c. *509*
—. Archives. Japan. Korea. Missions and Missionaries. Presbyterian Historical Society. 1829-1911. *39*
—. Archives. Missions and Missionaries. Protestantism. Yale University Library (collection). Yale-in-China Association. 1901-51. *237*
—. Armies. Cope, Jesse D. (article). 1898-1902. 1931. *214*
—. Arms control. Canada. India. Nuclear Arms. Nuclear power. Regionalism. USA. 1951-78. *493*
—. Arms control agreements. Detente. Nuclear strategy. USSR. 1970's. *516*
—. Arms race. Korean War. Rostow, Eugene V. USSR. 1953-82. *8*
—. Arms Trade. Foreign Relations. Taiwan. 1979-82. *1165*
—. Arms Trade (prohibited). Civil war. Japan. Western Nations. 1919-29. *17*
—. Army Air Force. Communist Party. 1946-47. *438*
—. Arndt, E. L. Lutheran Church. Missions and Missionaries. 1913-29. *510*
—. Art. Chinnery, George. Ports. Sailors. 18c-19c. *423*
—. Arts and crafts. Exhibits and Expositions. Missouri (St. Louis). World's fair. 1904. *216*
—. Asia. Association of South East Asian Nations. Foreign Relations. 1970's. *260*
—. Asia. Balance of power. Foreign Policy. Japan. 1950's-74. *112*
—. Asia. Balance of power. Japan. USSR. 1970-73. *80*
—. Asia. Foreign Policy. 1945-78. *521*
—. Asia. Foreign policy. 1950's-78. *190*
—. Asia, East. Balance of Power. Foreign policy. Japan. 1968-73. *133*
—. Asia, East. Barnett, A. Doak. Foreign Relations. USSR. 1944-78. *123*
—. Asia, East. Cold War (review article). Truman, Harry S. 1940's-71. *210*
—. Asia, East. Development. Foreign Relations. Political Attitudes. Wilson, James H. 1885-1910. *169*
—. Asia, East. Foreign Relations. 1945-82. *160*
—. Asia, East. Foreign Relations. 1979. *114*
—. Asia, South. Foreign Policy. USSR. 1970's. *426*
—. Asia, Southeast. Balance of power. Communism. USSR. War. 1920-79. *31*
—. Asia, Southeast. Brezhnev, Leonid. Foreign policy. Military aid. 1968-79. *488*
—. Asia, Southeast. Detente. 1970's. *376*
—. Asia, Southeast. Foreign Relations. Vietnam War. 1973-75. *256*
—. Asian studies. Secondary Education (curriculum reform). USA. 1972-73. *373*
—. Attitudes. 1970-82. *281*
—. Attitudes. Foreign policy. 1970-80. *280*
—. Attitudes. Missions and Missionaries. Presbyterian Church. 1837-1900. *212*
—. Aviation. Fraser, Douglas. Military training. Nationalists. Saskatchewan (Saskatoon). 1919-22. *217*
—. Balance of power. Bowles, Chester. Foreign Relations. India. Nehru, Jawaharlal. 1949-54. *16*
—. Balance of Power. Coffey, Joseph I. Military capability. USA. USSR. ca 1965-73. *158*
—. Balance of power. Cold War. USSR. 1956-80. *325*
—. Balance of Power. Europe. Foreign Relations. USSR. 1970's. *229*
—. Balance of power. Europe. USSR. 1945-73. *242*
—. Balance of power. Foreign policy. 1970's. *456*
—. Balance of power. Foreign policy. Nixon, Richard M. (administration). USSR. 1969-72. *462*
—. Balance of Power. Foreign Policy. USSR. Vietnam War. 1964-76. *512*
—. Balance of power. Foreign Relations. Japan. 1970's. *1*
—. Balance of power. Korean War. 1948-51. *1106*
—. Balance of Power. USSR. 1974. *241*
—. Bank of England. Economic crises. International Trade. Magniac and Co. Yrissari and Co. 1823-27. *18*
—. Banking. Chinese-American Bank of Commerce. 1910-20. *450*
—. Banking. Foreign Investments. Foreign Policy. Great Britain. 1908-20. *219*
—. Baptist Church. Missions and Missionaries. Shuck, Eliza G. Sexton. 1846-63. *322*
—. Baptists (Southern). Missions and Missionaries. Roberts, Issachar Jacob. 1837-47. *567*
—. Barefoot doctor movement. Medicine, Western. Political systems. Public Health. 1973. *411*
—. Barnett, A. Doak (review article). Foreign Relations. USSR. 1950-76. *401*
—. Barrett, John. Foreign policy. Open Door Policy. 1898-99. *445*
—. Bashford, James W. Methodist Episcopal Church. Missions and Missionaries. Social gospel. 1889-1919. *320*
—. Battle of the Bulge. Cuban Missile Crisis. Korean War. Military intelligence. 1944-80. *3*
—. Berry, Mary (speech). Communism. Education. Shanker, Albert (views). 1977. *167*
—. Bibliographies. Foreign Policy. Taiwan. 1949-82. *12*
—. Bibliographies. Foreign Relations. 1844-1974. *292*
—. Biography. Ming dynasty. 1368-1644. *227*
—. Birch, John (death). Communists. Military Intelligence. 1945. *530*
—. Blacks. Discrimination. Foreign Policy. Political Attitudes. 1971. *492*
—. Blockades. Chamberlain, Neville. Great Britain. Japan. Roosevelt, Franklin D. World War II (antecedents). 1937-38. *686*

China   237

—. Boxer Rebellion. Education. Foreign Policy. Historiography. Hunt, Michael (thesis). Reparations. 1900-06. 1972. *535*
—. Broadcasts. USSR. Vietnam War. 1968-73. *152*
—. Bruce, Frederick William. Burlingame, Anson. Cooperative Policy. Diplomacy. 1860-65. *334*
—. Bueler, William H. Cohen, Warren I. (review article). Davies, John Paton, Jr. Foreign Relations. 1830-1955. *392*
—. Burlingame, Anson. Diplomacy. 1861-71. *149*
—. Burlingame, Anson. Diplomacy. House of Representatives. Republican Party. 1854-69. *148*
—. Burlingame, Anson. Foreign Relations. 1861-67. *333*
—. Burma. Foreign Relations. Indonesia. 1950's-75. *68*
—. Buss, Claude A. Fairbank, John K. Foreign Relations (review article). Whiting, Allen S. 1949-76. *234*
—. California. Clipper ships. International Trade. USA. 1840's-50's. *506*
—. California (San Francisco). Huang Tsun-hsien. Reform. 1882-85. *328*
—. Cambodia. Foreign aid. 1955-74. *257*
—. Cambodia. Foreign Policy. Vietnam, South. 1975. *548*
—. Cambodia. Foreign Relations. USSR. Vietnam. 1978-80. *105*
—. Canada. Developing nations. Foreign relations. USSR. 1950-75. *318*
—. Canada. Diplomacy. Odlum, Victor Wentworth. 1943-46. *418*
—. Canada. Diplomatic relations. Economic development. Foreign policy. Japan. Taiwan. 1949-72. *1175*
—. Canada. Foreign Relations. International Trade. USSR. 1969-72. *367*
—. Canton Christian College. Church Schools. Revolution. Yale-in-China Association. 1925-27. *300*
—. Carlson, Evans. Intelligence mission. Japan. Roosevelt, Franklin D. 1937-38. *40*
—. Carlson, Evans. Intelligence mission. Japan. Roosevelt, Franklin D. 1937-38. *128*
—. Carter, Jimmy. Foreign relations. Normalization. Taiwan. USSR. 1978-79. *1150*
—. Carter, Jimmy (administration). Foreign policy. Human rights. Morality. 1976-77. *520*
—. Carter, Jimmy (administration). Foreign Policy. Korea. Taiwan. 1970's. *137*
—. Carter, Jimmy (administration). Foreign policy. Public opinion. 1967-78. *340*
—. Catholic Church. Christians. Communists. Missions and Missionaries. Protestant Churches. 1948-50. *523*
—. Christianity. Democracy. Foreign Policy. Japan. Missions and Missionaries. Socialism. 1830-1979. *125*
—. Chu Teh. Communism. Smedley, Agnes. Sorge, Richard. 1893-1950. *323*
—. Church Historical Society archives. Episcopal Church, Protestant. Missions and Missionaries (papers). 1835-1951. *223*
—. Churchill, Winston. Colonies. deGaulle, Charles. Foreign Policy. Indochina. Roosevelt, Franklin D. 1942-45. *75*
—. Civil War. Hurley, Patrick J. (resignation). Newspapers. Reporters and Reporting. 1945-46. *282*
—. Civil war. Intervention. 1945-49. *287*
—. Civil war. Intervention. Laos. USSR. 1959-62. *514*
—. Claims-assets issue. Foreign Investments. Nationalization. 1950-78. *233*
—. Clark, Grenville. Foreign Relations. Letters. Snow, Edgar. 1963-67. *489*
—. Clubb, O. Edmund. Foreign Relations. 1949-50. *208*

—. Cohen, Warren I. (review article). Foreign policy. Japan. Leadership. Public opinion. ca 1900-50. 1978. *26*
—. Cold War. Communism. Smedley, Agnes. Strong, Anna Louise. USSR. 1920-70. *246*
—. Cold War. Detente. USSR. 1971-73. *546*
—. Cold war. Foreign Relations. Korean War. Taiwan. USSR. 1947-79. *211*
—. Cold War. Foreign relations. Korean War. USSR. 1945-72. *1024*
—. Cold War. Social conflict. USSR. 1950's-70's. *527*
—. Cold War (origins). Communism. Foreign policy. 1945. *198*
—. Colleges and Universities. Communism. Grading, peer group. Political Science. 1964-72. *453*
—. Communications. Diplomatic recognition. Taiwan. 1978. *549*
—. Communism. Containment. Foreign policy. Korea. Taiwan. 1945-50. *10*
—. Communism. Economic reform. Social Reform. 1949-72. *421*
—. Communism. Equal opportunity. Social Organization. Talent selection. 1973. *203*
—. Communism. Foreign Policy. 1930. *304*
—. Communism. Foreign Policy. Marshall, George C. Sprouse, Philip D. (report). 1945-47. 1970's. *391*
—. Communism. Ho Chi Minh. Independence movements. Vietnamese. 1942-45. *502*
—. Communism. India. Lu Xun. Revolutionary Movements. Smedley, Agnes. 1910-50. *375*
—. Communism. Marines. 1944-49. *151*
—. Communism. Marshall, George C. Mediation. Nationalists. USSR. 1946. *356*
—. Communist Party. Diplomacy. Stuart, John Leighton. 1949. *486*
—. Communist Party. Diplomacy. World War II. 1944. *244*
—. Communist Party. Diplomacy (secret). Mao Zedong. Revolution. 1949. *350*
—. Communist Party. Foreign policy. 1949-50. *355*
—. Communist Party. Foreign Policy. Manchuria. Taiwan. Wedemeyer, Albert C. (report). 1946-49. *351*
—. Communist Party. Foreign policy. Mao Zedong. Speeches. 1944-50. *274*
—. Communist Party. Foreign Policy. State Department. Stuart, John Leighton. 1949. *181*
—. Communist Party. Foreign Relations. 1936-80. *348*
—. Communist Party. Foreign relations. USSR. 1948-49. *317*
—. Communists. Foreign Policy. Liberals. Scholars. 1944-71. *380*
—. Communists. Foreign Policy. Shanghai Power Company. Truman, Harry S. (administration). 1948-50. *517*
—. Conference on Chinese-American Relations. Foreign Policy. Roosevelt, Franklin D. Truman, Harry S. 1944-48. 1978. *289*
—. Congregationalism. Missions and Missionaries. Nationalism. 1910-48. *288*
—. Congress. International Trade. Lobbying. Roosevelt, Franklin D. (administration). Silver Purchase Act (1934). 1934. *268*
—. Constitutional development. Goodnow, Frank Johnson. Yuan Shikai. 1913-15. *449*
—. Containment. Europe. 1947-49. *428*
—. Containment. USSR. 1945-73. *534*
—. Credit. Depressions. Great Britain. International Trade (agencies). Tea. 1883-37. *197*
—. Cuba. Imperialism. Military Occupation. Native races. Philippines. 1898-1903. *316*
—. Cultural attitudes. Great Britain. Social status. Women. 1840-1927. *243*
—. Cultural exchange. 1971-75. *405*

China

—. Cultural relations. 1970-76. *165*
—. Cultural relations. Diplomacy. 1950-72. *362*
—. Cultural relations. Foreign Aid. 1942-45. *416*
—. Cultural Revolution. Education. 1949-75. *524*
—. Cushing, Caleb. Diplomacy. Trade. 1784-1840's. *239*
—. Decisionmaking. Eisenhower, Dwight D. Taiwan Strait crisis. 1954-55. *468*
—. Defense Department. Military Capability. 1974. *258*
—. Defense Policy. Economics. Foreign Relations. Taiwan. 1949-81. *1153*
—. Defense Policy. Foreign policy. Military Strategy. USSR. 1975-79. *335*
—. Defense Policy. Foreign Relations. USSR. 1970-83. *182*
—. Defense Policy. Strategic Arms Limitation Talks (SALT II). USSR. 1968-79. *262*
—. Denby, Charles. Foreign Policy. Indemnity. 1889. *222*
—. Detente. Foreign policy. 1966-72. 1976. *196*
—. Detente. Foreign policy. USSR. 1945-79. *173*
—. Detente. Foreign Relations. India. 1974. *278*
—. Detente. Japan. Nixon, Richard M. (visit). 1971. *79*
—. Detente. Nixon, Richard M. 1970's. *247*
—. Detente. USSR. 1970-75. *471*
—. Detente. USSR. 1977. *283*
—. Detente (review article). Nixon, Richard M. USSR. 1971-73. *443*
—. Dewey, John. Educational Reform (review article). Keenan, Barry. Leadership. 1919-30. 1977. *495*
—. Diaries. Diplomacy. Zhang Yinhuan. 1886-89. *159*
—. Diaries. Diplomats. Jones, William Patterson. 1862-68. *331*
—. Diego Garcia. Indian Ocean and Area. Naval Strategy. USSR. 20c. *364*
—. Diplomacy. Foreign Investments. Great Britain. Japan. World War I. 1915-17. *28*
—. Diplomacy. Foreign policy. Japan. Nixon, Richard M. 1971-72. *91*
—. Diplomacy. Foreign Policy (review article). Imperialism. Philippines. Reinsch, Paul S. 1899-1945. *57*
—. Diplomacy. Great Britain. 1920-46. *425*
—. Diplomacy. Great Britain. Hong Kong. World War II. 1941-45. *570*
—. Diplomacy. Hurley, Patrick J. Jiang Jieshi. Mao Zedong. State Department. Vincent, John Carter. 1944-45. *358*
—. Diplomacy. Japan. Stuart, John Leighton. USA. 1937-41. *118*
—. Diplomacy. Korea. Low, Frederick F. 1869-74. *2*
—. Diplomacy. Li Hungzhang. New York City. Public Opinion. 1896. *226*
—. Diplomacy. Li Hungzhang. Russia. Travel. 1896. *250*
—. Diplomacy. Manufacturing. Young, John Russell. 1882-83. *221*
—. Diplomacy. Marshall, Humphrey. Taiping Rebellion. 1853-54. *310*
—. Diplomacy. Reinsch, Paul S. 1913-19. *444*
—. Diplomacy. Service, John Stewart (dismissal). State Department (Foreign Service). 1932-73. *563*
—. Diplomacy. Vatican. World War I. 1918. *145*
—. Diplomacy. Vietnam. 1975-80. *442*
—. Diplomacy. Vietnam War. 1964-66. *460*
—. Diplomacy. Young, John Russell. 1882-85. *494*
—. Diplomatic recognition. Foreign policy. 1937-58. *498*
—. Diplomatic recognition. Great Britain. 1949-50. *424*

—. Diplomatic recognition. International Trade. Shanghai Communique. Taiwan. Treaties. 1972-78. *568*
—. Diplomatic recognition. Missions and Missionaries. Revolution. Sun Zhongshan. 1911-13. *395*
—. Diplomatic recognition. Sprouse, Philip D. Truman, Harry S. (administration). 1949-50. *209*
—. Diplomatic relations. Japan. 1972-77. *81*
—. Diplomatic relations. Taiwan. 1978. *22*
—. Disarmament. Nuclear arms. USSR. 1945-79. *377*
—. Disciples of Christ. Missions and Missionaries. Williams, Edward Thomas. 1887-1918. *349*
—. Dissertations. Graduate study. 1962-74. *464*
—. Domestic Policy. Foreign Policy. USSR. 1949-70's. *141*
—. Domestic problems. Foreign policy. Sino-Soviet conflict. USA. 1970's. *177*
—. Dulles, John Foster. Eisenhower, Dwight D. Foreign policy. USSR. 1953-56. *385*
—. Dulles, John Foster. Letters. Politics. Rusk, Dean. State Department. 1953. *499*
—. Economic aid. Trade. 1928-41. *269*
—. Economic Conditions. Foreign Policy. Political Attitudes. Taiwan. 1949-82. *473*
—. Economic Conditions. Rhode Island (Providence). Sino-Japanese War. Weapons. 1894. *36*
—. Economic policy. Foreign Relations. International Trade. 1949-75. *248*
—. Economic relations. 1776-1940's. *270*
—. Economic relations. Foreign Relations. Taiwan. 1840's-1974. *1157*
—. Education. Foreign Relations. 20c. *482*
—. Educational Exchange Programs. Research. Social Sciences. 1972-79. *513*
—. Educational exchange programs. Students. 1911-36. *199*
—. Educational Policy. Higher education. Labor experience. 1976. *330*
—. Egypt. Foreign Policy. Israel. Middle East. USSR. 1978. *497*
—. Elections (presidential). Foreign Policy. Korean War. 1949-52. *150*
—. Episcopal Church, Protestant. Long, Charles H. Missions and Missionaries. Revolution. 1946-49. *372*
—. Episcopal Church, Protestant. Missions and Missionaries. Roots, Eliza McCook. Roots, Logan H. 1900-34. *477*
—. Europe. Foreign Relations. International Trade. Urban concessions. 1876-85. *404*
—. Europe. Foreign Relations. Nuclear Arms. Strategic Arms Limitation Talks. Trilateralism. USSR. 1970's-83. *381*
—. Europe, Eastern. Nixon, Richard M. (visit). Press. 1971-72. *253*
—. Europe, Western. Foreign Relations. International Security. NATO. 1970's-82. *407*
—. Exports. Trade Regulations. 1969-80. *218*
—. Extraterritoriality. Great Britain. Treaties. 1929-43. *188*
—. Fairbank, John K. Foreign Policy. 1941-72. *252*
—. Fairbank, John K. (review article). Missions and Missionaries. ca 1860-1949. 1974. *336*
—. Family. Occupations. Social Customs. Travel (accounts). 1976. *544*
—. *Far Eastern Review* (newspaper). Foreign Policy. Japan. Rea, George Bronson. 1904-36. *59*
—. Feminism. Haygood, Laura A. Methodist Episcopal Church (South). Missions and Missionaries. 1884-1900. *427*
—. Foreign aid. UN (membership). Voting and Voting Behavior. 1961-68. *144*

—. Foreign Investments. Nationalism. 1890-1931. *313*
—. Foreign Policy. 1940's-70's. *365*
—. Foreign Policy. 1940-73. *140*
—. Foreign policy. 1942-76. *561*
—. Foreign Policy. 1949-78. *472*
—. Foreign Policy. 1949-79. *184*
—. Foreign Policy. 1950's-70's. *231*
—. Foreign Policy. 1964-76. *484*
—. Foreign Policy. 1970's. *550*
—. Foreign policy. 1971-77. *393*
—. Foreign Policy. 1978-79. *528*
—. Foreign policy. Gandhi, Indira. India. USSR. 1946-71. *93*
—. Foreign Policy. Globalization. Great Powers (role definition). USSR. 1970's. *565*
—. Foreign Policy. History Teaching. Legislative Investigations. Senate. Simulation and Games. 1949. 1978. *378*
—. Foreign policy. Hostages. USA. 1923. *225*
—. Foreign Policy. India. Pakistan. USSR. 1945-75. *409*
—. Foreign policy. International Trade. Pacific Area. Vietnam War. 1960's-70's. *166*
—. Foreign Policy. International trade. USSR. 1950's-74. *72*
—. Foreign policy. Intervention. Shipping. Yangtze Rapid Steamship Company. 1924-36. *302*
—. Foreign Policy. Isolationism. Militarism. 1969-76. *179*
—. Foreign Policy. Japan. Nixon, Richard M. 1971-73. *135*
—. Foreign Policy. Japan. Public opinion. World War II. 1937-45. *65*
—. Foreign Policy. Jiang Jieshi. Vandenberg, Arthur Hendricks, Sr. 1945-50. *255*
—. Foreign Policy. Kissinger, Henry A. Nixon, Richard M. 1960's-70's. *522*
—. Foreign policy. Kissinger, Henry A. USSR. 1969-76. *276*
—. Foreign policy. Korea. 1950-79. *94*
—. Foreign Policy. Korea. Stueck, William Whitney, Jr. (review article). 1947-50. *134*
—. Foreign policy. Korea (38th Parallel). Korean War. Military strategy. 1950-52. *1013*
—. Foreign policy. Korean War. MacArthur, Douglas. Politics and the Military. Truman, Harry S. 1949-52. *1025*
—. Foreign Policy. League of Nations. Paris Peace Conference. Treaties, unequal. Wilson, Woodrow. 1919. *19*
—. Foreign policy. Mao Zedong. Nixon, Richard M. 1960's-70's. *555*
—. Foreign policy. Maoism. ca 1960's-70's. *360*
—. Foreign Policy. Marshall, Humphrey. Taiping Rebellion. 1853-54. *312*
—. Foreign Policy. Military. 1970-80. *415*
—. Foreign policy. Military. Political Factions. USSR. Zhou Enlai. 1970-71. *263*
—. Foreign policy. Military strategy. USSR. 1969-70's. *293*
—. Foreign Policy. Modernization. USSR. 1950-79. *412*
—. Foreign Policy. Navies. 1974-80. *163*
—. Foreign Policy. Pacific area. USSR. 1950-83. *157*
—. Foreign Policy. Peace. USSR. 1970's. *305*
—. Foreign policy. Press. USSR. 1979-80. *398*
—. Foreign policy. Rhetoric. 1899-. *413*
—. Foreign Policy. Service, John Stewart. World War II. 1945-49. *342*
—. Foreign policy. Service, John Stewart (*Lost Chance in China*, excerpts). State Department (Foreign Service). World War II. 1945-50's. *483*
—. Foreign policy. Sino-Soviet conflict. 1960's-76. *139*
—. Foreign Policy. Sun Zhongshan. 1920-24. *266*

—. Foreign Policy. Taiwan. 1947-81. *23*
—. Foreign Policy. Taiwan. 1949-76. *15*
—. Foreign policy. Taiwan. 1950's-70's. *61*
—. Foreign Policy. Taiwan. 1972-79. *77*
—. Foreign Policy. Taiwan. USSR. 1972-78. *62*
—. Foreign Policy. Thailand. 1950-76. *271*
—. Foreign policy. Tripolarity. USSR. 1970's. *417*
—. Foreign policy. USSR. 1944-49. *537*
—. Foreign policy. USSR. 1954. *388*
—. Foreign Policy. USSR. 1955-58. *500*
—. Foreign Policy. USSR. 1961-79. *481*
—. Foreign Policy. USSR. 1968-69. *235*
—. Foreign Policy. USSR. 1968-70's. *508*
—. Foreign Policy. USSR. 1971-81. *346*
—. Foreign Policy. USSR. 1972-79. *435*
—. Foreign Policy. USSR. 1976-82. *554*
—. Foreign policy. USSR. 1980-81. *515*
—. Foreign policy. USSR. 20c. *306*
—. Foreign Policy. USSR. Vietnam. 1973. *45*
—. Foreign Policy (review article). 1944-50. *236*
—. Foreign Relations. 1793-1974. *366*
—. Foreign Relations. 1844-1982. *374*
—. Foreign Relations. 1897-1979. *526*
—. Foreign Relations. 1942-80. *496*
—. Foreign Relations. 1944-78. *290*
—. Foreign Relations. 1947-50. *162*
—. Foreign Relations. 1949-71. *441*
—. Foreign Relations. 1949-72. *525*
—. Foreign Relations. 1960's-70's. *286*
—. Foreign Relations. 1969-72. *142*
—. Foreign Relations. 1969-79. *171*
—. Foreign Relations. 1969-82. *420*
—. Foreign Relations. 1970-81. *369*
—. Foreign Relations. 1977-81. *459*
—. Foreign Relations. 1980-81. *309*
—. Foreign Relations. 20c. *353*
—. Foreign Relations. Georgia (Atlanta). Students. US-China People's Friendship Association. 1972-83. *339*
—. Foreign Relations. Girard College (Stephen Girard Collection). Historical Society of Pennsylvania. International Trade. Pennsylvania (Philadelphia). 1775-1840. 1980. *273*
—. Foreign Relations. Historiography. 1928-37. 1970's. *338*
—. Foreign Relations. Human rights. 1970's. *501*
—. Foreign Relations. Indian Ocean and Area. Persian Gulf and Area. 1946-80. *103*
—. Foreign Relations. Industry. Japan. Korea. USSR. 1970-76. *95*
—. Foreign relations. International trade. 1977. *354*
—. Foreign Relations. International Trade. Japan. 1979. *87*
—. Foreign Relations. International Trade. Navies. Taiping Rebellion. 1850-61. *291*
—. Foreign Relations. International Trade. Taiwan. 1949-82. *379*
—. Foreign Relations. Japan. 1978-81. *68*
—. Foreign Relations. Japan. 1978. *106*
—. Foreign Relations. Japan. Korea, North. Korea, South. Unification. USSR. 1970's-. *20*
—. Foreign Relations. Japan. Korea, South. Military. Taiwan. 1960-80. *56*
—. Foreign relations. Japan. Taiwan. USSR. 1972. *78*
—. Foreign Relations. Japan. USSR. 1970's. *107*
—. Foreign Relations. Japan. USSR. 1970's. *594*
—. Foreign Relations. Japan. USSR. 1981-84. *111*
—. Foreign Relations. Jiang Jieshi. Military aid. 1948-50. *1176*
—. Foreign Relations. Kahn, E. J., Jr. (review article). Politics. State Department (Foreign Service). 1940's-50's. 1975. *384*
—. Foreign relations. Korea. Taiwan. 1971-77. *115*
—. Foreign Relations. Korea. USSR. 1960's-82. *122*
—. Foreign Relations. Loans (consortium). Wilson, Woodrow. 1910-13. *383*

China

—. Foreign relations. Mao Zedong (death). 1976. *560*
—. Foreign Relations. Military aid. National Security. USSR. 1970-75. *440*
—. Foreign relations. Nixon, Richard M. 1969-70's. *553*
—. Foreign Relations. Nixon, Richard M. 1972-78. *545*
—. Foreign Relations. Political Commentary. Vietnam War. 1960's-70's. *419*
—. Foreign relations. Political conditions. 1969-70's. *307*
—. Foreign Relations. Press. Public information. 1970's. *368*
—. Foreign Relations. Publishers and Publishing. 1978-81. *359*
—. Foreign Relations. Research. 19c-20c. *399*
—. Foreign Relations. State Department (report). 1944-49. *414*
—. Foreign Relations. Taiwan. 1940-72. *1158*
—. Foreign Relations. Taiwan. 1970's-82. *130*
—. Foreign Relations. Taiwan. 1972-80. *120*
—. Foreign Relations. Taiwan. 1972-82. *92*
—. Foreign Relations. Taiwan. 1978-81. *1172*
—. Foreign Relations. Taiwan. 1979. *73*
—. Foreign Relations. Taiwan. USSR. 1972-82. *215*
—. Foreign Relations. Terranova, Francis. Trade. Trials. 1821-44. *240*
—. Foreign Relations. Thailand. USSR. 1974. *143*
—. Foreign Relations. USA. USSR. 1970's. *294*
—. Foreign relations. USSR. 1943-79. *556*
—. Foreign Relations. USSR. 1949-57. *176*
—. Foreign Relations. USSR. 1949-80. *192*
—. Foreign relations. USSR. 1949-83. *389*
—. Foreign Relations. USSR. 1950's-82. *308*
—. Foreign Relations. USSR. 1950-83. *332*
—. Foreign Relations. USSR. 1966-72. *457*
—. Foreign Relations. USSR. 1970's-82. *370*
—. Foreign relations. USSR. 1970's. *206*
—. Foreign Relations. USSR. 1970's. *382*
—. Foreign Relations. USSR. 1970's. *434*
—. Foreign Relations. USSR. 1970-74. *341*
—. Foreign Relations. USSR. 1972-. *207*
—. Foreign Relations. USSR. 1972-82. *540*
—. Foreign Relations. USSR. 1974. *480*
—. Foreign Relations. USSR. Vietnam War. 1949-74. *511*
—. Foreign Relations. Varg, Paul A. (review article). 1936-46. *490*
—. Foreign Relations. Vietnam, North. Vietnam War. 1970-80. *264*
—. Foreign relations. Vietnam War. 1960's-73. *454*
—. Foreign relations. Vietnam War. 1973. *228*
—. Foreign Relations. Ward, John Elliot. 1858-60. *261*
—. Foreign Relations. Wedemeyer, Albert C. (reminiscences). World War II. 1920-48. *532*
—. Foreign Relations (review article). Haldeman, H. R. Kissinger, Henry A. Nixon, Richard M. 1968-76. *539*
—. Foreign Relations (review article). Military. USSR. 1970-77. *538*
—. Fur Trade. North West Company. Oregon (Astoria). 1760's-1821. *275*
—. Fur trade. South Africa (Cape Colony). Voyages. 1800-02. *479*
—. George, Henry. Land ownership. Sun Zhongshan. Taxation. 1866-1973. *361*
—. Great Britain. International Relations (discipline). Japan. USSR. 1937-49. *437*
—. Great Britain. Intervention. Sovereignty. 1557-1949. *491*
—. Great Britain. Loan negotiations. World War II. 1941-44. *189*
—. Great Britain. Presidency. Yuan Shikai. 1911-12. *263*
—. Gulick, Edward V. (review article). Parker, Peter. 1840's-50's. *543*
—. Harkness, Ruth. Pandas. Tangier Smith, Floyd. 1936. *175*
—. Hay, John. Historiography (revisionist). International Trade. Open Door policy. 1899-1901. *170*
—. Historiography. Imperialism (economic). 19c-20c. 1965-73. *529*
—. Historiography. Open Door policy. 1899-1922. *403*
—. Historiography. Stilwell, Joseph W. World War II. 1942-44. *559*
—. Historiography (Chinese). Jefferson, Thomas. Liu Zuochang. Virginia, University of. 1770-1826. 1976-81. *321*
—. Historiography (Communist). Immigration. 19c-20c. 1949-73. *518*
—. Historiography (US). 19c-20c. 1950's-70's. *406*
—. Ideology. Women's liberation movement. 1960's-70's. *455*
—. Immigration policy (US). 1850-1974. *487*
—. Imperialism. International Trade. 1784-1914. *507*
—. Indochina. International crises. Korea. Laos. 1949-62. *345*
—. Intellectuals (Chinese). Political attitudes. Taiwan. 1970. *14*
—. International Security. Japan. Treaties. 1977-78. *84*
—. International trade. Pacific & Eastern Steamship Company. Ships. USA. World War I. 1914-16. *447*
—. International Trade. Pittman, Key. Senate. Silver Purchase Act (1934). USA. 1933-40. *485*
—. International Trade. Politics. 1789-1819. *277*
—. Japan. Kinney, John F. Marines. Prisoners of War. Wake Island. World War II. 1941-45. *943*
—. Japan. Korea, South. Public Opinion. Taiwan. Treaties, mutual defense. 1950's-77. *126*
—. Japan. League of Nations. Paris Peace Conference. Wilson, Woodrow. 1919. *85*
—. Japan. Press. Public opinion. Sino-Japanese war. USA. 1894-95. *53*
—. Jiang Jieshi. Marshall, George C. Military General Staff. Stilwell, Joseph W. World War II. 1944. *475*
—. Jiang Jieshi. Military strategy. Stilwell, Joseph W. World War II. 1942-44. *397*
—. Kerosene. Nationalism. Oil. Standard Oil Company of New York. Taxation. 1925-27. *541*
—. *Keys of the Kingdom* (film). Office of War Information. Propaganda. Stereotypes. World War II. 1940-45. *172*
—. Korean War. 1950. *1033*
—. Korean War. MacArthur, Douglas. Truman, Harry S. Walker, Walton L. 1950. *1026*
—. Korean War. USSR. 1950. *1138*
—. Law (study of). -1973. *200*
—. Leftism. Smedley, Agnes (review article). Women. 1930's-50. 1973-76. *329*
—. Literature. Lu Xun. 1920's-30's. *533*
—. Maoism. Strong, Anna Louise. USSR. 1919-70. *245*
—. Marshall, George C. Military Strategy. ca 1900-47. *463*
—. McGiffin, Philo Norton. Navies. Sino-Japanese War. 1885-95. *174*
—. Medical technology. Mortality. Social Organization. 19c. 1949-59. *470*
—. Methodology. Science. 20c. *180*
—. Military. Trade. 1970-80. *205*
—. Military relations. 1972-81. *202*
—. Military Strategy. USSR. 1950-76. *195*
—. Missions and Missionaries. Protestantism. Revivals. 1830-50. *466*
—. Missions and Missionaries. Religious toleration. Tianjin, Treaty of (Article XXIX). Translating. 1858-59. *429*

—. Navies. Sino-American Cooperation Association (SACO). World War II. 1942-45. *476*
—. Normalization. Taiwan. 1943-77. *63*
—. Nuclear stalemate. Peace. USSR. 1970's. *156*
—. Open Door Policy. 1899-1937. *547*
—. Open Door Policy. Rockhill, William W. State Department. 1886-1920. *505*
—. *People's Daily.* Reporters and Reporting. 1971-80. *352*
—. Political Theory. Progressivism. Sun Zhongshan. 1880-1912. *194*
—. Politics. Research. 1950-76. *531*
—. Porcelain. Trade. 18c-1825. *387*
—. Religion, popular. Sects, Religious. 1800-60. *164*
—. Shaw, Samuel. Trade. Voyages. 1784-85. *154*
—. Snow, Edgar. 1927-45. *319*
—. Social organization. USSR. 20c. *147*
—. Taiwan. Vance, Cyrus. 1972-77. *129*
—. Trade. 1943-50. *155*
—. Trade. 1950-70's. *201*
—. Trade. 1952-73. *249*
—. Trade. 1970-80. *357*
—. Trade. 1972-73. *337*
—. Trade. 1972. *183*
—. Trade. 19c-1970's. *446*
—. Trade Regulations. USSR. 1966-72. *299*
—. Travel accounts. 1966-73. *324*
China Aid Bill (US, 1948). Cold War. Foreign Aid. 1948. *254*
China (Beijing). Boxer Rebellion. Military occupation. 1900-01. *314*
—. Colleges and Universities. Missions and Missionaries. West, Philip. Yanjing University (review article). 1916-52. *161*
—. Cuba. Military occupation. Native races. Philippines. 1898-1903. *238*
China (Beijing, Taku, Tianjin). Boxer Rebellion. Marines. 1900. *295*
China (Canton). Bethune, Angus. International Trade. North America. North West Company. 1812-17. *469*
—. Europe. Trade. 3c-20c. *396*
China (Caoxian, Kai Chow). Mennonites. Missions and Missionaries. 1901-31. *326*
China (Chang River). Arnhold & Company. Hawley, Edwin C. Propaganda. Theater. Tretiakov, Sergei (*Roar China!*). 1924-75. *394*
China, East. Alliances. Boxer Rebellion. Great Britain. Russia. 1900. *138*
China (Gailan). Air Warfare. Bombing. Coal Mines and Mining. Combs, Cecil E. Personal Narratives. World War II. 1942. *213*
—. Chinese Engineering and Mining Company. Fraud. Great Britain. Hoover, Herbert. 1900-28. *224*
China (Guangdong). California. Emigration. Social Conditions. 1850-82. *390*
China (Hankow). Foreign Relations. *Petrel* (vessel). 1895. *431*
China (Harbin). Personal narratives. Russian language. Tolley, Kemp. 1935. *124*
China (Hubei). Ohio. Trade. 1979-82. *478*
China (Hunan). Catholic Church. Missions and Missionaries. Passionists. 1921-29. *186*
China (Inner Mongolia). Press. Rosholt, Malcolm (account). Travel. 1935. *461*
China (Kanchow). Catholic Church. Foreign policy. Missions and Missionaries. 1929-32. *303*
China (Kunming). Airplanes. Ghana (Accra). Laughlin, C. H. (reminiscences). World War II. 1942. *347*
China Lobby. Institute of Pacific Relations. McCarran Committee. Public opinion. Thomas, John N. (review article). Watergate trials. 1945-75. *58*
China (Macao). Alaska. British Columbia. Cook, James. Fur trade. Pacific Area. 1778-79. *49*

China (Nanking). Brownson, Willard H. Diplomacy. Gelm, George E. (journal). International Trade. Tuan Fang. 1907. *265*
China, North. Butler, Smedley D. Marines. Pilots. Williams, Clarence S. 1927-28. *410*
—. Civil war. Marines. Military Occupation. World War II. 1945-47. *33*
—. Marines. Photographs. Uniforms, Military. 1931-41. *504*
China (Shandong). Diplomacy. Hughes, Charles Evans. Japan. Washington Conference. 1919-22. *863*
China (Shanghai). Boycott. Chamber of Commerce. Immigration policy. Nationalism. 1905. *519*
—. Business. Race Relations. Rea, George Bronson. 1920's. *301*
—. California (Pasadena). Daughters of the American Revolution. Young Men's Christian Association. 1916-57. *422*
—. Episcopal Church, Protestant. Missions and Missionaries. Pott, Francis L. H. St. John's University. 1888-1941. *285*
—. Japan. Marines. Photographs. 1920's-30's. *569*
—. Marines. Personal Narratives. *Pittsburgh* (vessel). Smith, Wiley H. 1927. *408*
—. Methodist Episcopal Church, South. Missions and Missionaries. Publishers and Publishing. 1898-1920. *439*
China (Shansi). Barton, Fred. Cowboys. Horse breeding. Montana. Politics. 1912-32. *400*
China, south. Baptists, Southern. Missions and Missionaries. 1845-76. *503*
China studies (conference). High Schools. Wisconsin (Wingspread). 1972. *230*
China (Tianjin). Renouf, Vincent Adams (papers). Teaching. 1903-10. *552*
China, west. Fritz, Chester. Travel (accounts). 1917. *566*
China (Yangzi River). Diplomacy. Great Britain. International trade. Taiping Rebellion. 1850-61. *430*
—. Great Britain. Hope, James. Imperialism. Taiping Rebellion. Trade. 1850-61. *432*
China (Zhenjiang). Diplomats. Scruggs, William L. 1879-81. *433*
China-Burma-India Theater. Bombing. B-29 (aircraft). Close, Winton R. Japan. Personal narratives. World War II. 1944. *633*
—. Emmerson, John K. Memoirs. State Department (Foreign Service). World War II. 1941-44. *251*
Chinese. Acculturation. Colleges and Universities. Mental Illness. Students. Taiwan. 1854-1973. *1151*
Chinese. Asia American Studies Center. Bibliographies. California, University of, Los Angeles. Chinese Americans. 1854-1978. *344*
—. Attitudes. Authoritarianism. Students. 1949-70. *191*
—. Canada. Pao-huang Hui Party. Political Factions. 1899-1904. *153*
Chinese Americans. Asia American Studies Center. Bibliographies. California, University of, Los Angeles. Chinese. 1854-1978. *344*
—. California. Metropolitan areas. Tong societies. 1850-1972. *204*
—. Japanese Americans. Literature. 1850-1980. *13*
—. Nativism. Pacific Northwest. Racism. Religious sectarianism. ca 1840-1945. *21*
Chinese Engineering and Mining Company. China (Gailan). Fraud. Great Britain. Hoover, Herbert. 1900-28. *224*
Chinese-American Bank of Commerce. Banking. China. 1910-20. *450*
Chinnery, George. Art. China. Ports. Sailors. 18c-19c. *423*
Chosin Reservoir Campaign. Korean War. Marines. 1950. *1093*

Chou Enlai

Chou Enlai. *See* Zhou Enlai.
Christian Century (periodical). Foreign policy. Japan. Manchurian crisis. Morrison, Charles C. 1931-33. *96*
Christianity. China. Democracy. Foreign Policy. Japan. Missions and Missionaries. Socialism. 1830-1979. *125*
—. Janes, Leroy Lansing. Japan (Kumamoto). 1838-76. *838*
Christians. Catholic Church. China. Communists. Missions and Missionaries. Protestant Churches. 1948-50. *523*
Chu Teh. China. Communism. Smedley, Agnes. Sorge, Richard. 1893-1950. *323*
Church Historical Society archives. China. Episcopal Church, Protestant. Missions and Missionaries (papers). 1835-1951. *223*
Church Schools. Canton Christian College. China. Revolution. Yale-in-China Association. 1925-27. *300*
Churchill, Winston. China. Colonies. deGaulle, Charles. Foreign Policy. Indochina. Roosevelt, Franklin D. 1942-45. *75*
Circumnavigations. Australia. Foreign Relations. Japan. Warships. 1908. *878*
Citizenship. Ford, Gerald R. Hada, John. Japanese American Citizens League. Pardon. Tokyo Rose (Iva Toguri d'Aquino). Uyeda, Clifford I. (account). 1973-77. *949*
Civil rights. Counterintelligence. Internment. Japanese Americans. Munson, Curtis B. Peiper, N. J. L. World War II. 1931-42. *765*
—. Foreign policy. Korea, South. 1969-74. *1063*
Civil war. Arms Trade (prohibited). China. Japan. Western Nations. 1919-29. *17*
—. China. Hurley, Patrick J. (resignation). Newspapers. Reporters and Reporting. 1945-46. *282*
—. China. Intervention. 1945-49. *287*
—. China. Intervention. Laos. USSR. 1959-62. *514*
—. China, north. Marines. Military Occupation. World War II. 1945-47. *33*
—. Japan. Meiji Restoration. 1860-70. *879*
Civilians. Atomic Bomb Casualty Commission. Japan (Hiroshima, Nagasaki). Medical Research. Radiation Effects Research Foundation. 1945-75. *960*
—. Korean War. Policymaking. 1945-54. *1069*
Civil-Military Relations. Combat. Korean War. Values. 1950-53. *1135*
Claims-assets issue. China. Foreign Investments. Nationalization. 1950-78. *233*
Clarissa B. Carver (vessel). Courts. Dow, Leroy. *Glamorganshire* (vessel). Japan. Lawsuits. Ships. 1885-86. *870*
Clark, Edward Warren. Cultural relations. Japan (Shizuoka, Tokyo). Missions and Missionaries. Nakamura Masanao. ca1870-1907. *721*
Clark Field. Japan. Philippines. World War II. 1941-42. *788*
Clark, Grenville. China. Foreign Relations. Letters. Snow, Edgar. 1963-67. *489*
Class Struggle. Cumings, Bruce. Imperialism. Korean War (review article). 1945-47. *1038*
Clergy. Catholic Church. Guevara, Gaspar Ignacio de. Heresy. Philippines (Biliran). 1765-75. *1061*
Clipper ships. California. China. International Trade. USA. 1840's-50's. *506*
Close, Winton R. Bombing. B-29 (aircraft). China-Burma-India Theater. Japan. Personal narratives. World War II. 1944. *633*
Clubb, O. Edmund. China. Foreign Relations. 1949-50. *208*
Coal Mines and Mining. Air Warfare. Bombing. China (Gailan). Combs, Cecil E. Personal narratives. World War II. 1942. *213*

Coast Guard. Alaska (Aleutian Islands). *Arthur Middleton* (vessel). Japan. Laidlaw, Lansing. World War II. 1942-43. *769*
Coffee, John M. Congress. Embargoes. Japan. Schellenbach, Lewis B. Washington. 1930's-40. *780*
Coffey, Joseph I. Balance of Power. China. Military capability. USA. USSR. ca 1965-73. *158*
Cohen, Warren I. (review article). Bueler, William H. China. Davies, John Paton, Jr. Foreign Relations. 1830-1955. *392*
—. China. Foreign policy. Japan. Leadership. Public opinion. ca 1900-50. 1978. *26*
Colby, Abby M. Congregationalism. Feminism. Japan. Missions and Missionaries. 1879-1914. *928*
Cold War. *See also* Detente.
—. Atomic Warfare. Japan (Hiroshima). World War II. 1945. *744*
—. Balance of power. China. USSR. 1956-80. *325*
—. Balance of Power. Foreign policy. Korean War. USSR. 1946-50. *1050*
—. Business. Foreign policy. Japan. Press. 1948-52. *704*
—. China. Communism. Smedley, Agnes. Strong, Anna Louise. USSR. 1920-70. *246*
—. China. Detente. USSR. 1971-73. *546*
—. China. Foreign Relations. Korean War. Taiwan. USSR. 1947-79. *211*
—. China. Foreign relations. Korean War. USSR. 1945-72. *1024*
—. China. Social conflict. USSR. 1950's-70's. *527*
—. China Aid Bill (US, 1948). Foreign Aid. 1948. *254*
—. Foreign Relations. Korea, South. 1950-53. *1096*
—. Korean War. MacArthur, Douglas. Senate inquiry. Testimony, secret. 1951. *1141*
Cold War (origins). China. Communism. Foreign policy. 1945. *198*
Cold War (review article). Asia, East. China. Truman, Harry S. 1940's-71. *210*
Cold War revisionism. Foreign Policy. Kolko thesis (review article). Korean War. 1949-50. *1147*
Collection building. Asia, East. Libraries (US). 15c-20c. 1960's-70's. *127*
Colleges and Universities. Acculturation. Chinese. Mental illness. Students. Taiwan. 1854-1973. *1151*
—. China. Communism. Grading, peer group. Political Science. 1964-72. *453*
—. China (Beijing). Missions and Missionaries. West, Philip. Yanjing University (review article). 1916-52. *161*
—. Democracy. Japan. Military government. Virginia, University of (School of Military Government). 1944-45. *971*
—. Educational Exchange Programs. Japan studies. 1973. *697*
—. Educational Theory. Japan. Military Occupation. Senroku Uehara *(University)*. US Education Mission to Japan. 1945-62. *728*
—. Japan. Sapporo Agricultural College. Science. Teachers. Tokyo, University of. 1860-1900. *961*
Colonialism. Educational Policy. Germany. Japan. Mariana Islands. Spain. ca 1688-1940. *698*
Colonies. China. Churchill, Winston. deGaulle, Charles. Foreign Policy. Indochina. Roosevelt, Franklin D. 1942-45. *75*
Colonization. Apathy. Death and Dying. Korean War. Malnutrition. Prisoners of war. Virginia (Jamestown). World War II. 1607-24. 1941-53. *74*
—. Commerce. Indian-White Relations. Netherlands. New Netherland. Taiwan. 17c. *1160*
Combat. Civil-Military Relations. Korean War. Values. 1950-53. *1135*

Combat Information Unit. Cryptography. Japan. Midway (battle). Navies. World War II. 1942. *858*

Combs, Cecil E. Air Warfare. Bombing. China (Gailan). Coal Mines and Mining. Personal narratives. World War II. 1942. *213*

Commerce. Colonization. Indian-White Relations. Netherlands. New Netherland. Taiwan. 17c. *1160*

Communications. Behavior. Japan. Television. 1972-81. *729*

—. China. Diplomatic recognition. Taiwan. 1978. *549*

—. Great Britain. Japan. Naval Strategy. World War II. 1943-45. *652*

Communism. Asia, Southeast. Balance of power. China. USSR. War. 1920-79. *31*

—. Berry, Mary (speech). China. Education. Shanker, Albert (views). 1977. *167*

—. China. Chu Teh. Smedley, Agnes. Sorge, Richard. 1893-1950. *323*

—. China. Cold War. Smedley, Agnes. Strong, Anna Louise. USSR. 1920-70. *246*

—. China. Cold War (origins). Foreign policy. 1945. *198*

—. China. Colleges and Universities. Grading, peer group. Political Science. 1964-72. *453*

—. China. Containment. Foreign policy. Korea. Taiwan. 1945-50. *10*

—. China. Economic reform. Social Reform. 1949-72. *421*

—. China. Equal opportunity. Social Organization. Talent selection. 1973. *203*

—. China. Foreign Policy. 1930. *304*

—. China. Foreign Policy. Marshall, George C. Sprouse, Philip D. (report). 1945-47. 1970's. *391*

—. China. Ho Chi Minh. Independence movements. Vietnamese. 1942-45. *502*

—. China. India. Lu Xun. Revolutionary Movements. Smedley, Agnes. 1910-50. *375*

—. China. Marines. 1944-49. *151*

—. China. Marshall, George C. Mediation. Nationalists. USSR. 1946. *356*

—. Containment. Foreign Policy. Japan. 1945-50. *892*

—. Documents. Foreign Relations. State Department *(Relations with China).* 1944-81. *109*

—. Foreign policy. Intervention. Korean War. Truman, Harry S. USSR. 1950. *1081*

—. Foreign policy. Korea. Truman Doctrine. 1945-50. *43*

—. Korean War. Prisoners of war. Propaganda. Public opinion. Vietnam War. 1950-74. *1021*

Communist Countries. Foreign Policy. Korea, South. Military Ground Forces (withdrawal). 1950-78. *1022*

Communist Party. *Amerasia* (periodical). China. Espionage. Foreign policy. Nationalists. Service, John Stewart (reports). ca 1937-45. *343*

—. Army Air Force. China. 1946-47. *438*

—. China. Diplomacy. Stuart, John Leighton. 1949. *486*

—. China. Diplomacy. World War II. 1944. *244*

—. China. Diplomacy (secret). Mao Zedong. Revolution. 1949. *350*

—. China. Foreign policy. 1949-50. *355*

—. China. Foreign Policy. Manchuria. Taiwan. Wedemeyer, Albert C. (report). 1946-49. *351*

—. China. Foreign policy. Mao Zedong. Speeches. 1944-50. *274*

—. China. Foreign Policy. State Department. Stuart, John Leighton. 1949. *181*

—. China. Foreign Relations. 1936-80. *348*

—. China. Foreign relations. USSR. 1948-49. *317*

Communists. Birch, John (death). China. Military Intelligence. 1945. *530*

—. Catholic Church. China. Christians. Missions and Missionaries. Protestant Churches. 1948-50. *523*

—. China. Foreign Policy. Liberals. Scholars. 1944-71. *380*

—. China. Foreign Policy. Shanghai Power Company. Truman, Harry S. (administration). 1948-50. *517*

Comparative analysis. Business History. Enterprises, large-scale. Europe, Western. Japan. 19c-20c. *629*

Competition. Automobile Industry and Trade. Europe. Industry. Japan. 1969-73. *649*

—. Capitalism. Japan. 1968-80. *828*

—. Europe, Western. Japan. 1960's-70's. *575*

—. Germany, West. International Trade. Japan. Manufactures. 1970's. *797*

Concentration Camps. *See also* Internment; Prisoners of War; Relocation.

—. California. Japanese Americans. Manzanar War Relocation Center. Riots. Ueno, Harry (arrest). World War II. 1942. *691*

—. Japanese Americans. Public schools. World War II. 1942-45. *977*

—. Japanese Americans. Racism. World War II. 1940-45. *719*

—. Japanese Americans. World War II. 1942-46. *842*

Conference on Chinese-American Relations. China. Foreign Policy. Roosevelt, Franklin D. Truman, Harry S. 1944-48. 1978. *289*

Conflict and Conflict Resolution. Arab-Israeli Conflict. Decisionmaking. Foreign Policy. Japan. World War II. 1941-45. 1967-73. *600*

Congregationalism. China. Missions and Missionaries. Nationalism. 1910-48. *288*

—. Colby, Abby M. Feminism. Japan. Missions and Missionaries. 1879-1914. *928*

Congress. China. International Trade. Lobbying. Roosevelt, Franklin D. (administration). Silver Purchase Act (1934). 1934. *268*

—. Coffee, John M. Embargoes. Japan. Schellenbach, Lewis B. Washington. 1930's-40. *780*

—. Foreign policy. International Security. Taiwan. 1950-55. *178*

—. Foreign relations. Taiwan Relations Act (US, 1979). 1978-79. *1162*

—. Japan. Manchurian crisis. Public opinion. 1931-33. *83*

—. Japan. Protectionism. 1981-82. *896*

—. Japan. World War II (antecedents). 1940-41. *779*

Constitutional development. China. Goodnow, Frank Johnson. Yuan Shikai. 1913-15. *449*

Constitutional reform. Japan. Military occupation. Politics. 1945-52. *577*

Constitutions. Japan. MacArthur, Douglas. Military Occupation. Political tradition. 1945-76. *804*

Containerization. California (Los Angeles). *Japanese Lines, Ltd.* v. *County of Los Angeles.* Supreme Court. Tariff. 1970-79. *585*

Containment. China. Communism. Foreign policy. Korea. Taiwan. 1945-50. *10*

—. China. Europe. 1947-49. *428*

—. China. USSR. 1945-73. *534*

—. Communism. Foreign Policy. Japan. 1945-50. *892*

Convoys. Air Transport Command. Burma Road. China. Frost, Edwin C. Personal Narratives. Transportation, Military. 1945. *259*

Cook, James. Alaska. British Columbia. China (Macao). Fur trade. Pacific Area. 1778-79. *49*

Cooperative Policy. Bruce, Frederick William. Burlingame, Anson. China. Diplomacy. 1860-65. *334*

Cope, Jesse D. (article). Armies. China. 1898-1902. 1931. *214*

Cotton. Great Britain. India. Japan. Textile Industry. 1870-1939. *987*
Councils and Synods. Japan. Methodist Protestant Church. Missions and Missionaries. 1880-92. *762*
Counterintelligence. Civil rights. Internment. Japanese Americans. Munson, Curtis B. Peiper, N. J. L. World War II. 1931-42. *765*
Courts. *Clarissa B. Carver* (vessel). Dow, Leroy. *Glamorganshire* (vessel). Japan. Lawsuits. Ships. 1885-86. *870*
Cowboys. Barton, Fred. China (Shansi). Horse breeding. Montana. Politics. 1912-32. *400*
Crawford, David L. Hawaii, University of. Japan. Peace pact (proposed). USA. 1940-41. *713*
Credit. China. Depressions. Great Britain. International Trade (agencies). Tea. 1834-37. *197*
Creelman, James. New York *World* (newspaper). Port Arthur massacre. Press. Sino-Japanese War. 1894-95. *35*
Creighton, John Marie. Intervention. Japan. Military Intelligence. USSR (Eastern Siberia). 1922. *44*
Creoles. Folklore. Hearn, Lafcadio. Japan. Louisiana (New Orleans). Martinique. 1850-1904. *803*
Crime. Japan. Social Organization. 1948-70's. *591*
Cruisers. Design. Japan. Navies. 1925-27. *978*
Cryptography. Censorship. *Chicago Tribune.* Japan. Midway (battle). Reporters and Reporting. World War II. 1942. *679*
——. Combat Information Unit. Japan. Midway (battle). Navies. World War II. 1942. *858*
——. Guadalcanal (battle). Japan. Military Intelligence. Radio. World War II. 1942. *810*
Cuba. Alienation. China. Intellectuals, western. Pilgrimages. USSR. Vietnam, North. 1930's. 1970's. *296*
——. China. Imperialism. Military Occupation. Native races. Philippines. 1898-1903. *316*
——. China (Beijing). Military occupation. Native races. Philippines. 1898-1903. *238*
——. Decisionmaking. Foreign Policy. Germany. Korean War. World War I. 1914-62. *1109*
Cuban Missile Crisis. Battle of the Bulge. China. Korean War. Military intelligence. 1944-80. *3*
Cultural attitudes. China. Great Britain. Social status. Women. 1840-1927. *243*
Cultural exchange. China. 1971-75. *405*
Cultural Imperialism. Foreign Relations. Japan. Mutsuhito, Emperor. Seward, William H. 1870-71. *705*
Cultural relations. Associated Japan-America Societies of the United States. Georgia. International Trade. Japan. 1979-82. *958*
——. China. 1970-76. *165*
——. China. Diplomacy. 1950-72. *362*
——. China. Foreign Aid. 1942-45. *416*
——. Clark, Edward Warren. Japan (Shizuoka, Tokyo). Missions and Missionaries. Nakamura Masanao. ca1870-1907. *721*
——. Foreign Aid. Korea. 1882-1982. *1075*
——. Japan. 1856-1900. *877*
Cultural Revolution. China. Education. 1949-75. *524*
Cumings, Bruce. Class Struggle. Imperialism. Korean War (review article). 1945-47. *1038*
Cushing, Caleb. China. Diplomacy. Trade. 1784-1840's. *239*
Custer, Elizabeth Bacon. Attitudes. Japan. Travel accounts. 1903. *955*
Cyclotrons. Denmark. Japan. Nuclear physics. Scientific Experiments and Research. 1935-45. *965*
C-47 (aircraft). Air Warfare. Korean War. 1950-53. *1020*

D

Daily Life. Hostages. Japan. Letters. Navies. Rescues. 1846-49. *771*
——. Internment. Japanese Americans. Kurose, Aki Kato. Washington (Seattle). World War II. 1930's-50's. *644*
——. Internment. Japanese Americans. Personal narratives. Uchida, Yoshiko. Utah (Topaz). World War II. 1942-43. *942*
——. Korean War. Public Opinion. Vietnam War. 1950-73. *1114*
Daughters of the American Revolution. California (Pasadena). China (Shanghai). Young Men's Christian Association. 1916-57. *422*
Davies, John Paton, Jr. Bueler, William H. China. Cohen, Warren I. (review article). Foreign Relations. 1830-1955. *392*
Death and Dying. Apathy. Colonization. Korean War. Malnutrition. Prisoners of war. Virginia (Jamestown). World War II. 1607-24. 1941-53. *74*
Decisionmaking. Alperovitz, Gar (review article). Atomic Warfare. Historiography. Japan (Hiroshima). World War II. 1945-65. *898*
——. Arab-Israeli Conflict. Conflict and Conflict Resolution. Foreign Policy. Japan. World War II. 1941-45. 1967-73. *600*
——. Atomic Warfare. Japan (Hiroshima, Nagasaki). Military Strategy. World War II. 1944-45. *671*
——. Cambodia. Flexible response. Korea, North. *Mayaguez* incident. *Pueblo* incident. 1969-75. *1039*
——. China. Eisenhower, Dwight D. Taiwan Strait crisis. 1954-55. *468*
——. Cuba. Foreign Policy. Germany. Korean War. World War I. 1914-62. *1109*
Defense. Alliances. Military strategy. NATO. Political change, international. 1945-70's. *1088*
Defense Department. China. Military Capability. 1974. *258*
Defense Policy. ANZUS. Foreign Relations. Japan. 1945-78. *937*
——. Asia, East. Military Strategy. War. 1945-50. *32*
——. Carter, Jimmy (administration). Japan. 1978-79. *677*
——. China. Economics. Foreign Relations. Taiwan. 1949-81. *1153*
——. China. Foreign policy. Military Strategy. USSR. 1975-79. *335*
——. China. Foreign Relations. USSR. 1970-83. *182*
——. China. Strategic Arms Limitation Talks (SALT II). USSR. 1968-79. *262*
——. Foreign Relations. Japan. 1979-81. *834*
——. Foreign Relations. Japan. 1980-83. *651*
Defense spending. Korean War. Military. Minutemen. Political Attitudes. Vietnam War. 1784-1979. *1077*
Defensive perimeter concept. Asia. Military Strategy. 1947-51. *564*
deGaulle, Charles. China. Churchill, Winston. Colonies. Foreign Policy. Indochina. Roosevelt, Franklin D. 1942-45. *75*
Democracy. Attitudes. Europe. Interest Groups. Japan. Nuclear Science and Technology. USSR. 1970's. *731*
——. Baseball. Japan. Values. 1920-41. *637*
——. China. Christianity. Foreign Policy. Japan. Missions and Missionaries. Socialism. 1830-1979. *125*
——. Colleges and Universities. Japan. Military government. Virginia, University of (School of Military Government). 1944-45. *971*
Democratic People's Republic of Korea. *See* Korea, North.
Democratization. Agricultural property. Inheritance. Japan. Military Occupation. 1945-52. *935*

Denby, Charles. China. Foreign Policy. Indemnity. 1889. *222*
Denmark. Cyclotrons. Japan. Nuclear physics. Scientific Experiments and Research. 1935-45. *965*
Dependency. Japan. Korea, South. Political economy. 1973. *1041*
Depressions. China. Credit. Great Britain. International Trade (agencies). Tea. 1834-37. *197*
Design. Cruisers. Japan. Navies. 1925-27. *978*
Destroyer escorts. *England* (vessel). Japan. Submarine Warfare. Williamson, John A. (account). World War II. 1944. *972*
Detente. *See also* Cold War.
—. Arms control agreements. China. Nuclear strategy. USSR. 1970's. *516*
—. Asia, Southeast. China. 1970's. *376*
—. Carter, Jimmy (administration). Developing nations. Europe, Western. Foreign policy. Japan. USSR. 1977-80. *939*
—. China. Cold War. USSR. 1971-73. *546*
—. China. Foreign policy. 1966-72. 1976. *196*
—. China. Foreign policy. USSR. 1945-79. *173*
—. China. Foreign Relations. India. 1974. *278*
—. China. Japan. Nixon, Richard M. (visit). 1971. *79*
—. China. Nixon, Richard M. 1970's. *247*
—. China. USSR. 1970-75. *471*
—. China. USSR. 1977. *283*
—. Foreign policy. Japan. Trade. USSR. 1971-74. *749*
Detente (review article). China. Nixon, Richard M. USSR. 1971-73. *443*
Detention. California. Japanese Americans. Racism. World War II. 1941-45. *818*
Developing nations. Canada. China. Foreign relations. USSR. 1950-75. *318*
—. Carter, Jimmy (administration). Detente. Europe, Western. Foreign policy. Japan. USSR. 1977-80. *939*
—. Economic issues. Japan. Roll-call voting. UN General Assembly. Western Nations. 1970-76. *966*
—. European Economic Community. Japan. Tariff protection. 1960's-70's. *986*
—. Great Britain. Japan. Manufacturing. Subcontracting. 1966-76. *899*
Development. *See also* Economic Development.
—. Asia, East. China. Foreign Relations. Political Attitudes. Wilson, James H. 1885-1910. *169*
Dewey, John. China. Educational Reform (review article). Keenan, Barry. Leadership. 1919-30. 1977. *495*
Diaries. China. Diplomacy. Zhang Yinhuan. 1886-89. *159*
—. China. Diplomats. Jones, William Patterson. 1862-68. *331*
—. Japan. Norquist, Ernest O. Philippines. Prisoners of War. World War II. 1942-45. *837*
—. Korea. Naval officers. Woods, George W. 1884. *1127*
Dick, Everett N. (account). Adventist Medical Cadet Corps. Armies. Korean War. Military service. World War II. 1934-53. *29*
Diego Garcia. China. Indian Ocean and Area. Naval Strategy. USSR. 20c. *364*
Diffusion. Information. Japan. 1830's-1970's. *869*
—. Japan. Semiconductors. Technology. 1982. *876*
Dill, James. Armies. Korean War. Personal narratives. 7th Infantry Division, US (31st Field Artillery Battalion). 1950-51. *1027*
Dillon, Emile Joseph. Portsmouth Peace Conference. Press. Public opinion. Russo-Japanese War. Witte, Sergei. 1904-05. *732*
Diplomacy. *See also* Negotiations; Peace Negotiations; Treaties.

—. Allen, Horace. Hawaii. Immigration. Korea. Sugar. 1902-05. *1101*
—. Appeasement (proposal). Great Britain. Japan. World War II. 1941. *680*
—. Asia, East. Four-Power Treaty. Karnebeek, Hermann Adriaan van. Netherlands. Washington Conference. 1921-22. *9*
—. Asiatic Squadron. Korea. Navies. 1882-97. *1015*
—. Brownson, Willard H. China (Nanking). Gelm, George E. (journal). International Trade. Tuan Fang. 1907. *265*
—. Bruce, Frederick William. Burlingame, Anson. China. Cooperative Policy. 1860-65. *334*
—. Brussels Conference. Roosevelt, Franklin D. Sino-Japanese War. 1937. *117*
—. Burlingame, Anson. China. 1861-71. *149*
—. Burlingame, Anson. China. House of Representatives. Republican Party. 1854-69. *148*
—. Canada. China. Odlum, Victor Wentworth. 1943-46. *418*
—. Canada. Korean War. Stairs, Denis (review article). 1950-53. *1092*
—. China. Communist Party. Stuart, John Leighton. 1949. *486*
—. China. Communist Party. World War II. 1944. *244*
—. China. Cultural relations. 1950-72. *362*
—. China. Cushing, Caleb. Trade. 1784-1840's. *239*
—. China. Diaries. Zhang Yinhuan. 1886-89. *159*
—. China. Foreign Investments. Great Britain. Japan. World War I. 1915-17. *28*
—. China. Foreign policy. Japan. Nixon, Richard M. 1971-72. *91*
—. China. Foreign Policy (review article). Imperialism. Philippines. Reinsch, Paul S. 1899-1945. *57*
—. China. Great Britain. 1920-46. *425*
—. China. Great Britain. Hong Kong. World War II. 1941-45. *570*
—. China. Hurley, Patrick J. Jiang Jieshi. Mao Zedong. State Department. Vincent, John Carter. 1944-45. *358*
—. China. Japan. Stuart, John Leighton. USA. 1937-41. *118*
—. China. Korea. Low, Frederick F. 1869-74. *2*
—. China. Li Hungzhang. New York City. Public Opinion. 1896. *226*
—. China. Li Hungzhang. Russia. Travel. 1896. *250*
—. China. Manufacturing. Young, John Russell. 1882-83. *221*
—. China. Marshall, Humphrey. Taiping Rebellion. 1853-54. *310*
—. China. Reinsch, Paul S. 1913-19. *444*
—. China. Service, John Stewart (dismissal). State Department (Foreign Service). 1932-73. *563*
—. China. Vatican. World War I. 1918. *145*
—. China. Vietnam. 1975-80. *442*
—. China. Vietnam War. 1964-66. *460*
—. China. Young, John Russell. 1882-85. *494*
—. China (Shandong). Hughes, Charles Evans. Japan. Washington Conference. 1919-22. *863*
—. China (Yangzi River). Great Britain. International trade. Taiping Rebellion. 1850-61. *430*
—. Embassy, US. Japan (Tokyo). 1941. *661*
—. Emmerson, John K. Internment. Japanese Peruvians. Memoirs. Peru. World War II. 1942-43. *660*
—. Emmerson, John K. Japan (Tokyo). Memoirs. State Department. World War II (antecedents). 1941. *662*
—. Europe. Japan. World War II (antecedents; review article). 1930's-41. *700*
—. Fishing. Japan. State Department. 1936-39. *947*
—. Foreign policy. International Trade. Japan. World War II (antecedents). 1937-41. *946*

246   Diplomacy

—. France (Paris). Korea, South (Panmunjom). Peace. Vietnam. 1951-73. *1143*
—. Hornbeck, Stanley K. Japan. World War II (antecedents). 1937-41. *775*
—. Hull, Cordell. Indochina. Japan. Philippines. World War II (antecedents). 1941. *616*
—. International Trade. Japan. Perry, Matthew C. 1853. *783*
—. Japan. Konoe Fumimaro. 1934-41. *715*
—. Japan. MacArthur, Douglas. Philippines (Manila). Surrender. World War II. 1945. *812*
—. Japan. Military Intelligence. Roosevelt, Franklin D. World War II (antecedents). 1940-41. *693*
—. Japan. Yōsuke, Matsuoka. 1940-41. *738*
—. Korea. Naval expedition. 1840-71. *1126*
Diplomacy (personal). Germany. Meyer, George von Lengerke. Roosevelt, Theodore. Russo-Japanese War. William II. 1902-14. *968*
Diplomacy, private. Butow, R. J. Japan. John Doe Associates. Peace (review article). World War II (antecedents). 1940-41. *572*
Diplomacy (secret). China. Communist Party. Mao Zedong. Revolution. 1949. *350*
Diplomatic recognition. China. Communications. Taiwan. 1978. *549*
—. China. Foreign policy. 1937-58. *498*
—. China. Great Britain. 1949-50. *424*
—. China. International Trade. Shanghai Communique. Taiwan. Treaties. 1972-78. *568*
—. China. Missions and Missionaries. Revolution. Sun Zhongshan. 1911-13. *395*
—. China. Sprouse, Philip D. Truman, Harry S. (administration). 1949-50. *209*
—. Japan. Manchuria. Stimson, Henry L. 1931-34. *991*
Diplomatic Relations. *See also* Foreign Relations.
—. Canada. China. Economic development. Foreign policy. Japan. Taiwan. 1949-72. *1175*
—. China. Japan. 1972-77. *81*
—. China. Taiwan. 1978. *22*
Diplomats. China. Diaries. Jones, William Patterson. 1862-68. *331*
—. China (Zhenjiang). Scruggs, William L. 1879-81. *433*
—. Japanese. Pennsylvania (Bedford). Prisoners of War. World War II. 1945. *586*
Disarmament. China. Nuclear arms. USSR. 1945-79. *377*
Disciples of Christ. China. Missions and Missionaries. Williams, Edward Thomas. 1887-1918. *349*
Discrimination. Blacks. China. Foreign Policy. Political Attitudes. 1971. *492*
—. Japanese. Peru. 1931-43. *632*
Dissertations. Bibliographies. Korea. 1970-74. *1116*
—. Bibliographies. Korea. 1970-74. *1117*
—. China. Graduate study. 1962-74. *464*
—. Educational reform. Historiography. Japan. Military Occupation. 1950-80. *940*
District of Columbia. Energy Conference (report). Europe, Western. Foreign Policy. Japan. 1974. *1005*
Dixon, Robert E. Japan. Johnston, Stanley. Midway (battle). Military Strategy. Personal narratives. Reporters and Reporting. World War II. 1942. *794*
Documentation. Evacuations. Internment. Japanese Americans. Photographs. War Relocation Authority. World War II. 1941-43. *643*
Documents. Air Forces. Balloon Force. Japan. World War II. 1942-45. *702*
—. Asia, North. Geography. Geology. Japan. 1848-83. *99*
—. Atomic bomb. Japan (Hiroshima, Nagasaki). World War II. 1945. *867*
—. Communism. Foreign Relations. State Department *(Relations with China)*. 1944-81. *109*

—. Japan. Military Occupation. 1945-47. *598*
Dollar. Economic Regulations. Monetary system, international. Smithsonian Agreement (1971). 1971-72. *997*
Dollar stabilization. Economic Policy. Germany, West. Japan. 1945-78. *801*
Domestic Policy. China. Foreign Policy. USSR. 1949-70's. *141*
Domestic problems. China. Foreign policy. Sino-Soviet conflict. USA. 1970's. *177*
Dow, Leroy. *Clarissa B. Carver* (vessel). Courts. *Glamorganshire* (vessel). Japan. Lawsuits. Ships. 1885-86. *870*
Dull, Paul S. (review article). Japan. Naval Strategy. Pearl Harbor. World War II. Yamamoto, Isoroku. 1941-45. *941*
Dulles, John Foster. Alliances. Japan. Political Theory. Treaties. Yoshida Shigeru. 5c BC-20c. 1951. *653*
—. China. Eisenhower, Dwight D. Foreign policy. USSR. 1953-56. *385*
—. China. Letters. Politics. Rusk, Dean. State Department. 1953. *499*
Dumas, Harold. Japanese language. Marines. World War II. 1944-45. *791*
Dumping. International Trade. Japan. Public Opinion. Steel. 1974-78. *745*

E

Economic aid. China. Trade. 1928-41. *269*
—. Japan. Vietnam War. 1960-75. *696*
Economic Conditions. Asia. Emigration. Labor. 1834-1930. *1003*
—. Asia, East. Foreign Relations. 1982. *66*
—. Capitalism. Europe, Western. Great Britain. Japan. 1970-80. *996*
—. China. Foreign Policy. Political Attitudes. Taiwan. 1949-82. *473*
—. China. Rhode Island (Providence). Sino-Japanese War. Weapons. 1894. *36*
—. Federal Policy. International Trade. Japan. 1945-83. *868*
—. Foreign policy. International Trade (relations). Japan. 1945-74. *927*
—. Foreign relations. Hong Kong. New York City. Securities. 1964-79. *571*
—. Foreign Relations. Japan. 1982. *787*
—. Foreign Relations. Japan. Pacific free trade area. 1945-74. *71*
—. Foreign Relations. Korea, South. 1977. *1042*
—. Great Britain. Japan. Military Occupation. Political Systems. 1945-49. *617*
—. International Trade. Japan. 1970-81. *684*
—. Japan. Military occupation. Ryukyu Islands (Okinawa). 1952-79. *950*
—. Japan (review article). Nakamura Takahide. Politics. 1945-49. *740*
Economic crises. Bank of England. China. International Trade. Magniac and Co. Yrissari and Co. 1823-27. *18*
Economic development. Asia, Southeast. Foreign Policy. Fukuda, Takeo. Japan. 1978. *676*
—. Canada. China. Diplomatic relations. Foreign policy. Japan. Taiwan. 1949-72. *1175*
—. Capron, Horace. Japan (Hokkaido). Modernization. 1871-75. *811*
—. Employment, permanent. Japan. Social Theory. 1973. *635*
—. Europe, Western. Japan. Protectionism. Trade. 1948-80. *866*
—. Exports. Foreign loans. Korea, South. 1950's-70's. *1102*
—. Foreign Relations. Germany, West. Japan. 1973-76. *809*
—. Great Britain. Japan. Thailand. 1926-80. *102*

—. Japan. Oriental Bank Corporation. Schiff, Jacob. Williams, George B. Wilson, James H. Winslow, Edward F. 1872-73. *606*
—. Japan. Supply. 1975-82. *630*
Economic Growth. Alliances. Ethnocentrism. Japan. 1945-80. *805*
—. Europe. Foreign Relations. Japan. Military Aid. 1970's. *601*
—. Japan. 1952-74. *734*
—. Japan. 1952-74. *735*
—. Japan. National Security. 1950's-82. *654*
—. Standard of living. Taiwan. 1973-75. *1168*
Economic History. Historiography. Japan. 1600-1945. ca 1970-77. *980*
Economic issues. Developing nations. Japan. Roll-call voting. UN General Assembly. Western Nations. 1970-76. *966*
Economic Policy. American Council on Japan. Foreign Policy. Japan. Lobbying. Military Occupation. 1945-50's. *873*
—. China. Foreign Relations. International Trade. 1949-75. *248*
—. Dollar stabilization. Germany, West. Japan. 1945-78. *801*
—. Foreign policy. Japan. Military. Politics. 1945-72. *919*
—. Foreign Policy. Japan. Military Occupation. 1945-49. *895*
—. Foreign Relations. Japan. 1970's-80. *708*
—. Foreign Relations. Japan. 1978-80. *751*
—. Foreign Relations. Natural Resources (development). USSR. 1950's-70's. *50*
—. Germany, West. GNP. Inflation. Japan. Protectionism. 1976-78. *709*
—. Japan. Naval strategy. Pacific Dependencies (US). USA. 1945-75. *623*
Economic problems. Asia, East. Foreign Relations. Japan. Political Leadership. Tanaka, Kakuei. 1971-74. *883*
Economic reform. China. Communism. Social Reform. 1949-72. *421*
Economic Regulations. Dollar. Monetary system, international. Smithsonian Agreement (1971). 1971-72. *997*
Economic Relations. *See also* International Trade; Trade.
—. China. 1776-1940's. *270*
—. China. Foreign Relations. Taiwan. 1840's-1974. *1157*
—. Japan. 1972-78. *920*
Economic Structure. Business Cycles. Europe, Western. Great Britain. Japan. 1967-80. *959*
—. Foreign investments. Japan. New York City. 1960's-70's. *675*
Economic trends, world. Europe, Western. Japan. 1970-75. *973*
Economic war. International trade. Japan. 1970's. *614*
Economics. China. Defense Policy. Foreign Relations. Taiwan. 1949-81. *1153*
Education. Asia, East. Public Opinion. USA. 1973. *5*
—. Berry, Mary (speech). China. Communism. Shanker, Albert (views). 1977. *167*
—. Boxer Rebellion. China. Foreign Policy. Historiography. Hunt, Michael (thesis). Reparations. 1900-06. 1972. *535*
—. China. Cultural Revolution. 1949-75. *524*
—. China. Foreign Relations. 20c. *482*
Educational Exchange Programs. China. Research. Social Sciences. 1972-79. *513*
—. China. Students. 1911-36. *199*
—. Colleges and Universities. Japan studies. 1973. *697*
—. Fulbright program. Japan. 1982. *981*
Educational Policy. China. Higher education. Labor experience. 1976. *330*

—. Colonialism. Germany. Japan. Mariana Islands. Spain. ca 1688-1940. *698*
Educational reform. Dissertations. Historiography. Japan. Military Occupation. 1950-80. *940*
Educational Reform (review article). China. Dewey, John. Keenan, Barry. Leadership. 1919-30. 1977. *495*
Educational Theory. Colleges and Universities. Japan. Military Occupation. Senroku Uehara (*University*). US Education Mission to Japan. 1945-62. *728*
Egypt. China. Foreign Policy. Israel. Middle East. USSR. 1978. *497*
Eisenhower, Dwight D. Carter, Jimmy. Executive Power. Foreign policy. Hamilton, Alexander. Taiwan. 1793-1979. *1161*
—. Cease-fire. Korean War. Peace negotiations. UN. 1952-53. *1136*
—. China. Decisionmaking. Taiwan Strait crisis. 1954-55. *468*
—. China. Dulles, John Foster. Foreign policy. USSR. 1953-56. *385*
Elections. Business Cycles. Canada. Europe, Western. Federal Policy. Japan. 1955-80. *930*
—. Korea, South. Legislative assembly. Military Occupation. 1945-48. *1074*
Elections (presidential). China. Foreign Policy. Korean War. 1949-52. *150*
Ellis, Earl. Caroline Islands. Japan. Marines. Naval strategy. 1920-23. *956*
—. Japan. Marines. Micronesia. Military Intelligence. 1911-23. *584*
Embargoes. Airplane Industry and Trade. China. Great Britain. Vickers Ltd. 1919-21. *448*
—. Coffee, John M. Congress. Japan. Schellenbach, Lewis B. Washington. 1930's-40. *780*
—. Foreign Policy. Japan. Oil. Roosevelt, Franklin D. 1941. *578*
Embassy, US. Diplomacy. Japan (Tokyo). 1941. *661*
Emigration. *See also* Immigration.
—. Asia. Economic Conditions. Labor. 1834-1930. *1003*
—. California. China (Guangdong). Social Conditions. 1850-82. *390*
—. Japan. Social conditions. 1866-1924. *957*
Emmerson, John K. China-Burma-India Theater. Memoirs. State Department (Foreign Service). World War II. 1941-44. *251*
—. Diplomacy. Internment. Japanese Peruvians. Memoirs. Peru. World War II. 1942-43. *660*
—. Diplomacy. Japan (Tokyo). Memoirs. State Department. World War II (antecedents). 1941. *662*
Employment, permanent. Economic development. Japan. Social Theory. 1973. *635*
Energy. *See also* Atomic Energy (for the splitting of atoms); Nuclear Power (for energy as a public power source).
—. Food. International Security. Japan. Natural resources. Nuclear Power. 1970's-80. *979*
—. Foreign Relations. Investments. Japan. 1970's. *851*
Energy Action Group. Europe. Foreign Relations. Japan. North America. 1973-. *756*
Energy Conference (report). District of Columbia. Europe, Western. Foreign Policy. Japan. 1974. *1005*
Energy policy. Atlantic Community. Japan. 1972-73. *777*
England (vessel). Destroyer escorts. Japan. Submarine Warfare. Williamson, John A. (account). World War II. 1944. *972*
Enterprises, large-scale. Business History. Comparative analysis. Europe, Western. Japan. 19c-20c. *629*

248 Episcopal Church

Episcopal Church, Protestant. China. Church Historical Society archives. Missions and Missionaries (papers). 1835-1951. *223*
—. China. Long, Charles H. Missions and Missionaries. Revolution. 1946-49. *372*
—. China. Missions and Missionaries. Roots, Eliza McCook. Roots, Logan H. 1900-34. *477*
—. China (Shanghai). Missions and Missionaries. Pott, Francis L. H. St. John's University. 1888-1941. *285*
Equal opportunity. China. Communism. Social Organization. Talent selection. 1973. *203*
Equality (proposed). Hughes, William Morris. Japan. League of Nations Covenant. Paris Peace Conference. Race Relations. Wilson, Woodrow. 1919. *772*
Espionage. *Amerasia* (periodical). China. Communist Party. Foreign policy. Nationalists. Service, John Stewart (reports). ca 1937-45. *343*
Ethnicity. Canada. Internment. Japanese Americans. Japanese Canadians. Joint Board of Defense. World War II. 1941-42. *641*
Ethnocentrism. Alliances. Economic Growth. Japan. 1945-80. *805*
Eugenics. Genetics. Japan. Social organization. 1920's-30's. *923*
Europe. Attitudes. Democracy. Interest Groups. Japan. Nuclear Science and Technology. USSR. 1970's. *731*
—. Australia. Canada. Japan. Unemployment. USA. 1972-73. *911*
—. Automobile Industry and Trade. Competition. Industry. Japan. 1969-73. *649*
—. Balance of Power. China. Foreign Relations. USSR. 1970's. *229*
—. Balance of power. China. USSR. 1945-73. *242*
—. Banking. Japan. Monopolies. ca 1950's-70's. *944*
—. Books, miniature. Japan. Publishers and Publishing. 15c-20c. *856*
—. Canada. Japan. Labor costs. Manufacturing. Productivity. 1974-81. *624*
—. China. Containment. 1947-49. *428*
—. China. Foreign Relations. International Trade. Urban concessions. 1876-85. *404*
—. China. Foreign Relations. Nuclear Arms. Strategic Arms Limitation Talks. Trilateralism. USSR. 1970's-83. *381*
—. China (Canton). Trade. 3c-20c. *396*
—. Diplomacy. Japan. World War II (antecedents; review article). 1930's-41. *700*
—. Economic growth. Foreign Relations. Japan. Military Aid. 1970's. *601*
—. Energy Action Group. Foreign Relations. Japan. North America. 1973-. *756*
—. Foreign policy. Japan. 1970's. *832*
—. Foreign policy. Japan. Military strategy. Vietnam War. 1970's. *910*
—. Foreign policy. Japan. Neocolonialism. Organization of Petroleum Exporting Countries. 1969-70's. *855*
—. Foreign policy. Japan. Offner, Arnold A. World War II (antecedents; review article). 1917-41. *829*
—. Foreign Relations. Japan. 1974. *116*
—. Foreign Relations. Japan. Persian Gulf and Area. Tucker, Robert W. (interview). 1968-80. *998*
—. Foreign relations. Korea, South. 1950's-70's. *1071*
—. Japan. Monetary Systems. Multinational corporations. USA. 1967-73. *924*
—. Japan. Research and development. Technology. ca 1964-76. *574*
—. Japan. Warships. 1850-1930's. *845*
—. Korean War. 1945-50. *1053*
Europe, Eastern. China. Nixon, Richard M. (visit). Press. 1971-72. *253*

Europe, Western. Automobile Industry and Trade. Canada. Gindon, Sam (interview). Japan. Labor. World car (concept). 1945-80. *1006*
—. Automobile Industry and Trade. Japan. 1973-80. *611*
—. British Typewriter Museum (Wilfred Beeching collection). Japan. Typewriter. 1711-1970's. *672*
—. Business Cycles. Canada. Elections. Federal Policy. Japan. 1955-80. *930*
—. Business Cycles. Economic Structure. Great Britain. Japan. 1967-80. *959*
—. Business History. Comparative analysis. Enterprises, large-scale. Japan. 19c-20c. *629*
—. Canada. Japan. Labor. Manufacturing. Productivity. 1960-82. *576*
—. Capitalism. Economic conditions. Great Britain. Japan. 1970-80. *996*
—. Carter, Jimmy (administration). Detente. Developing nations. Foreign policy. Japan. USSR. 1977-80. *939*
—. China. Foreign Relations. International Security. NATO. 1970's-82. *407*
—. Competition. Japan. 1960's-70's. *575*
—. District of Columbia. Energy Conference (report). Foreign Policy. Japan. 1974. *1005*
—. Economic development. Japan. Protectionism. Trade. 1948-80. *866*
—. Economic trends, world. Japan. 1970-75. *973*
—. Finance. Imperialism. Industry. Japan. Latin America. Trade. 1970's. *768*
—. Foreign Policy. International Security. Japan. Military Capability. 1980-82. *889*
—. Foreign Policy. International Trade. Japan. Rockefeller family. Trilateral Commission. 1973-78. *995*
—. Foreign Policy. Japan. Trilateralism. 1950's-70's. *945*
—. Foreign Relations. Japan. Trilateral Commission. 1973-82. *872*
—. Inflation. Japan. 1958-68. *974*
—. International Trade. Japan. Monetary systems. 1970's. *681*
—. Japan. Monopolies. Oil industry and Trade. Organization of Petroleum Exporting Countries. 1970's. *871*
—. Japan. Mutual Balanced Force Reductions. Strategic Arms Limitation Talks. USSR. 1974. *1002*
—. Japan. Oil industry and trade. 1960's-70's. *847*
—. Japan. Political Theory. Trilateralism. 1970's. *954*
—. Japan. Public services. Trilateral Commission. Wages. 1973-79. *925*
—. Japan. Technology. 1960-75. *827*
—. Japan. Trade. 1970's. *665*
—. Japan. Trilateralism. 1970's. *796*
European Economic Community. Developing nations. Japan. Tariff protection. 1960's-70's. *986*
—. Generalized System of Preferences. Japan. Tariff. 1966-75. *595*
—. Germany, West. Japan. Oil crisis. Trade. 1974. *647*
—. International Trade. Japan. Monetary policy (devaluation). Nixon, Richard M. 1971-73. *655*
—. Japan. Trilateral Commission. 1973-77. *636*
Evacuations. Documentation. Internment. Japanese Americans. Photographs. War Relocation Authority. World War II. 1941-43. *643*
—. Korea, North (Hungnam). Navies. 1950. *1029*
Exchange Programs. *See* Educational Exchange Programs.
Executive Power. Carter, Jimmy. Eisenhower, Dwight D. Foreign policy. Hamilton, Alexander. Taiwan. 1793-1979. *1161*
Exhibits and Expositions. Arts and crafts. China. Missouri (St. Louis). World's fair. 1904. *216*

Expansionism, Japanese. Japan. Korea. Sill, John M. B. 1894-97. *1028*
Exports. China. Trade Regulations. 1969-80. *218*
—. Economic Development. Foreign loans. Korea, South. 1950's-70's. *1102*
—. Foreign policy. Japan. Oil. State Department. 1940-41. *948*
—. Great Britain. Japan. Oil Industry and Trade. Roosevelt, Franklin D. World War II. 1940-41. *659*
Extraterritoriality. China. Great Britain. Treaties. 1929-43. *188*

F

Fairbank, John K. Buss, Claude A. China. Foreign Relations (review article). Whiting, Allen S. 1949-76. *234*
—. China. Foreign Policy. 1941-72. *252*
Fairbank, John K. (review article). China. Missions and Missionaries. ca 1860-1949. 1974. *336*
Family. Agricultural Technology and Research. Fiji. Israel. Japan. Social Change. 1689-1975. *634*
—. China. Occupations. Social Customs. Travel (accounts). 1976. *544*
Famine. Agricultural Policy. China. Mao Zedong. 1960-76. *371*
Far Eastern Review (newspaper). China. Foreign Policy. Japan. Rea, George Bronson. 1904-36. *59*
Faulkner, William. Japan. Shellenberger, Jack H. (account). Travel. US Information Agency. 1955. *900*
Federal Policy. Antitrust. Automobile Industry and Trade. Imports. Japan. Protectionism. 1981-83. *982*
—. Business Cycles. Canada. Elections. Europe, Western. Japan. 1955-80. *930*
—. Economic Conditions. International Trade. Japan. 1945-83. *868*
—. Frontier and Pioneer Life. Indians. Japan. Military Strategy. Taiwan. 18c-1915. *70*
—. Japan. Journalism. Nuclear arms. Secrecy. 1983. *792*
Feminism. China. Haygood, Laura A. Methodist Episcopal Church (South). Missions and Missionaries. 1884-1900. *427*
—. Colby, Abby M. Congregationalism. Japan. Missions and Missionaries. 1879-1914. *928*
Fermi National Accelerator Laboratory. Japan. Kō Enerugii Butsurigaku Kenkyusho. Nationalism. Physics. 1930-69. *706*
Fielde, Adele M. Americans. Baptists. China. Siam. 1865-90. *60*
Fiji. Agricultural Technology and Research. Family. Israel. Japan. Social Change. 1689-1975. *634*
Films. Japan. *The Magnificent Seven* (film). National Characteristics. *Seven Samurai* (film). 1960's. *836*
Finance. Europe, Western. Imperialism. Industry. Japan. Latin America. Trade. 1970's. *768*
Fishing. Diplomacy. Japan. State Department. 1936-39. *947*
Flexible response. Cambodia. Decisionmaking. Korea, North. *Mayaguez* incident. *Pueblo* incident. 1969-75. *1039*
Flying Tigers. Air Warfare. American Volunteer Group. China. Shoulder patches. World War II. 23d Fighter Group. 1930's-45. *25*
—. Air Warfare. Army Air Force. China. Holloway, Bruce K. (account). P-40 (aircraft). World War II. 1942-43. *297*
—. Air warfare. Chennault, Claire Lee. China. Japan. World War II. 1941-45. *701*

Folk art. Japan. Origami. Popular Culture. 1900-76. *593*
Folklore. Creoles. Hearn, Lafcadio. Japan. Louisiana (New Orleans). Martinique. 1850-1904. *803*
Food. Energy. International Security. Japan. Natural resources. Nuclear Power. 1970's-80. *979*
Ford, Gerald R. Citizenship. Hada, John. Japanese American Citizens League. Pardon. Tokyo Rose (Iva Toguri d'Aquino). Uyeda, Clifford I. (account). 1973-77. *949*
Foreign Aid. *See also* Economic Aid; Military Aid.
—. Balance of Power. Korea. 1945-74. *1037*
—. Cambodia. China. 1955-74. *257*
—. China. Cultural relations. 1942-45. *416*
—. China. UN (membership). Voting and Voting Behavior. 1961-68. *144*
—. China Aid Bill (US, 1948). Cold War. 1948. *254*
—. Cultural relations. Korea. 1882-1982. *1075*
Foreign Investments. Anderson, Irvine H., Jr. (review article). Asia, East. Foreign policy. Oil Industry and Trade. Standard-Vacuum Oil Company. 1933-41. 1975. *97*
—. Banking. China. Foreign Policy. Great Britain. 1908-20. *219*
—. California. Japan. 1975-80. *707*
—. China. Claims-assets issue. Nationalization. 1950-78. *233*
—. China. Diplomacy. Great Britain. Japan. World War I. 1915-17. *28*
—. China. Nationalism. 1890-1931. *313*
—. Economic Structure. Japan. New York City. 1960's-70's. *675*
—. Japan. 1930-52. *969*
—. Japan. Manufactures. 1950's-70's. *875*
Foreign loans. Economic Development. Exports. Korea, South. 1950's-70's. *1102*
Foreign Policy. *See also* specific terms that imply a policy, e.g., Containment, Normalization; names of specific policies, e.g., Open Door Policy; Policymaking.
—. *Amerasia* (periodical). China. Communist Party. Espionage. Nationalists. Service, John Stewart (reports). ca 1937-45. *343*
—. American Council on Japan. Economic Policy. Japan. Lobbying. Military Occupation. 1945-50's. *873*
—. American Council on Japan. Japan. Lobbying. 1947-52. *894*
—. Anderson, Irvine H., Jr. (review article). Asia, East. Foreign Investments. Oil Industry and Trade. Standard-Vacuum Oil Company. 1933-41. 1975. *97*
—. Anti-Communist Movements. Asia. Reagan, Ronald (administration). Taiwan. 1981. *64*
—. Anti-Communist Movements. China. May, Gary. McCarthy, Joseph R. Vincent, John Carter. 1942-51. *279*
—. Arab-Israeli Conflict. Conflict and Conflict Resolution. Decisionmaking. Japan. World War II. 1941-45. 1967-73. *600*
—. Arms trade. Asia, East. Association of South East Asian Nations. 1982. *48*
—. Asia. Balance of power. China. Japan. 1950's-74. *112*
—. Asia. China. 1945-78. *521*
—. Asia. China. 1950's-78. *190*
—. Asia, East. 1981. *119*
—. Asia, East. Balance of Power. China. Japan. 1968-73. *133*
—. Asia, East. Japan. 1948-78. *694*
—. Asia, East. Japan. Korea. Nixon Doctrine. Vietnam. 1969-73. *90*
—. Asia, East. Japan. World War II (antecedents). 1931-41. *687*

Foreign Policy

——. Asia, East. Lansing, Robert. World War I (antecedents). 1914-17. *54*
——. Asia, East. Navies. Sino-Japanese War. 1894-95. *37*
——. Asia, East. USSR. 1945-80. *113*
——. Asia (East, Southeast). 1951-70's. *132*
——. Asia, northeast. Korean War. Political conditions. 1953-78. *1128*
——. Asia, South. China. USSR. 1970's. *426*
——. Asia, Southeast. Brezhnev, Leonid. China. Military aid. 1968-79. *488*
——. Asia, Southeast. Economic development. Fukuda, Takeo. Japan. 1978. *676*
——. Asia, Southeast. Japan. 1945-73. *688*
——. Asia, Southeast. Korea, South. Military Strategy. 1960's-70's. *1034*
——. Attitudes. China. 1970-80. *280*
——. Austin, Warren R. Korean War. Truman Doctrine. UN. 1945-53. *1086*
——. Australia. International Trade. Japan. New Zealand. 1968-70's. *41*
——. Automobiles. Imports. Japan. Trade Regulations. 1970-81. *727*
——. Balance of power. China. 1970's. *456*
——. Balance of power. China. Nixon, Richard M. (administration). USSR. 1969-72. *462*
——. Balance of Power. China. USSR. Vietnam War. 1964-76. *512*
——. Balance of Power. Cold War. Korean War. USSR. 1946-50. *1050*
——. Balance of power. Japan. Military Aid. 1945-77. *657*
——. Banking. China. Foreign Investments. Great Britain. 1908-20. *219*
——. Barrett, John. China. Open Door Policy. 1898-99. *445*
——. Bibliographies. China. Taiwan. 1949-82. *12*
——. Blacks. China. Discrimination. Political Attitudes. 1971. *492*
——. Boxer Rebellion. China. Education. Historiography. Hunt, Michael (thesis). Reparations. 1900-06. 1972. *535*
——. Business. Cold War. Japan. Press. 1948-52. *704*
——. Cambodia. China. Vietnam. South. 1975. *548*
——. Canada. China. Diplomatic relations. Economic development. Japan. Taiwan. 1949-72. *1175*
——. Carter, Jimmy. Eisenhower, Dwight D. Executive Power. Hamilton, Alexander. Taiwan. 1793-1979. *1161*
——. Carter, Jimmy (administration). China. Human rights. Morality. 1976-77. *520*
——. Carter, Jimmy (administration). China. Korea. Taiwan. 1970's. *137*
——. Carter, Jimmy (administration). China. Public opinion. 1967-78. *340*
——. Carter, Jimmy (administration). Detente. Developing nations. Europe, Western. Japan. USSR. 1977-80. *939*
——. Carter, Jimmy (administration). Human rights. Korea, South. 1945-79. *1091*
——. Carter, Jimmy (administration). Japan. Korea, South. Military Ground Forces (withdrawal). 1950's-78. *131*
——. Carter, Jimmy (administration). Korea. 1950-79. *1044*
——. Carter, Jimmy (administration). Korea. Military Ground Forces (withdrawal). 1977. *1124*
——. Catholic Church. China (Kanchow). Missions and Missionaries. 1929-32. *303*
——. China. 1940's-70's. *365*
——. China. 1940-73. *140*
——. China. 1942-76. *561*
——. China. 1949-78. *472*
——. China. 1949-79. *184*
——. China. 1950's-70's. *231*
——. China. 1964-76. *484*
——. China. 1970's. *550*
——. China. 1971-77. *393*
——. China. 1978-79. *528*
——. China. Christianity. Democracy. Japan. Missions and Missionaries. Socialism. 1830-1979. *125*
——. China. Churchill, Winston. Colonies. deGaulle, Charles. Indochina. Roosevelt, Franklin D. 1942-45. *75*
——. China. Cohen, Warren I. (review article). Japan. Leadership. Public opinion. ca 1900-50. 1978. *26*
——. China. Cold War (origins). Communism. 1945. *198*
——. China. Communism. 1930. *304*
——. China. Communism. Containment. Korea. Taiwan. 1945-50. *10*
——. China. Communism. Marshall, George C. Sprouse, Philip D. (report). 1945-47. 1970's. *391*
——. China. Communist Party. 1949-50. *355*
——. China. Communist Party. Manchuria. Taiwan. Wedemeyer, Albert C. (report). 1946-49. *351*
——. China. Communist Party. Mao Zedong. Speeches. 1944-50. *274*
——. China. Communist Party. State Department. Stuart, John Leighton. 1949. *181*
——. China. Communists. Liberals. Scholars. 1944-71. *380*
——. China. Communists. Shanghai Power Company. Truman, Harry S. (administration). 1948-50. *517*
——. China. Conference on Chinese-American Relations. Roosevelt, Franklin D. Truman, Harry S. 1944-48. 1978. *289*
——. China. Defense Policy. Military Strategy. USSR. 1975-79. *335*
——. China. Denby, Charles. Indemnity. 1889. *222*
——. China. Detente. 1966-72. 1976. *196*
——. China. Detente. USSR. 1945-79. *173*
——. China. Diplomacy. Japan. Nixon, Richard M. 1971-72. *91*
——. China. Diplomatic recognition. 1937-58. *498*
——. China. Domestic Policy. USSR. 1949-70's. *141*
——. China. Domestic problems. Sino-Soviet conflict. USA. 1970's. *177*
——. China. Dulles, John Foster. Eisenhower, Dwight D. USSR. 1953-56. *385*
——. China. Economic Conditions. Political Attitudes. Taiwan. 1949-82. *473*
——. China. Egypt. Israel. Middle East. USSR. 1978. *497*
——. China. Elections (presidential). Korean War. 1949-52. *150*
——. China. Fairbank, John K. 1941-72. *252*
——. China. *Far Eastern Review* (newspaper). Japan. Rea, George Bronson. 1904-36. *59*
——. China. Gandhi, Indira. India. USSR. 1946-71. *93*
——. China. Globalization. Great Powers (role definition). USSR. 1970's. *565*
——. China. History Teaching. Legislative Investigations. Senate. Simulation and Games. 1949. 1978. *378*
——. China. Hostages. USA. 1923. *225*
——. China. India. Pakistan. USSR. 1945-75. *409*
——. China. International Trade. Pacific Area. Vietnam War. 1960's-70's. *166*
——. China. International trade. USSR. 1950's-74. *72*
——. China. Intervention. Shipping. Yangtze Rapid Steamship Company. 1924-36. *302*
——. China. Isolationism. Militarism. 1969-76. *179*
——. China. Japan. Nixon, Richard M. 1971-73. *135*
——. China. Japan. Public opinion. World War II. 1937-45. *65*
——. China. Jiang Jieshi. Vandenberg, Arthur Hendrick, Sr. 1945-50. *255*
——. China. Kissinger, Henry A. Nixon, Richard M. 1960's-70's. *522*

Foreign Policy   251

—. China. Kissinger, Henry A. USSR. 1969-76. *276*
—. China. Korea. 1950-79. *94*
—. China. Korea. Stueck, William Whitney, Jr. (review article). 1947-50. *134*
—. China. Korea (38th Parallel). Korean War. Military strategy. 1950-52. *1013*
—. China. Korean War. MacArthur, Douglas. Politics and the Military. Truman, Harry S. 1949-52. *1025*
—. China. League of Nations. Paris Peace Conference. Treaties, unequal. Wilson, Woodrow. 1919. *19*
—. China. Mao Zedong. Nixon, Richard M. 1960's-70's. *555*
—. China. Maoism. ca 1960's-70's. *360*
—. China. Marshall, Humphrey. Taiping Rebellion. 1853-54. *312*
—. China. Military. 1970-80. *415*
—. China. Military. Political Factions. USSR. Zhou Enlai. 1970-71. *263*
—. China. Military strategy. USSR. 1969-70's. *293*
—. China. Modernization. USSR. 1950-79. *412*
—. China. Navies. 1974-80. *163*
—. China. Pacific area. USSR. 1950-83. *157*
—. China. Peace. USSR. 1970's. *305*
—. China. Press. USSR. 1979-80. *398*
—. China. Rhetoric. 1899-. *413*
—. China. Service, John Stewart. World War II. 1945-49. *342*
—. China. Service, John Stewart (*Lost Chance in China*, excerpts). State Department (Foreign Service). World War II. 1945-50's. *483*
—. China. Sino-Soviet conflict. 1960's-76. *139*
—. China. Sun Zhongshan. 1920-24. *266*
—. China. Taiwan. 1947-81. *23*
—. China. Taiwan. 1949-76. *15*
—. China. Taiwan. 1950's-70's. *61*
—. China. Taiwan. 1972-79. *77*
—. China. Taiwan. USSR. 1972-78. *62*
—. China. Thailand. 1950-76. *271*
—. China. Tripolarity. USSR. 1970's. *417*
—. China. USSR. 1944-49. *537*
—. China. USSR. 1954. *388*
—. China. USSR. 1955-58. *500*
—. China. USSR. 1961-79. *481*
—. China. USSR. 1968-69. *235*
—. China. USSR. 1968-70's. *508*
—. China. USSR. 1971-81. *346*
—. China. USSR. 1972-79. *435*
—. China. USSR. 1976-82. *554*
—. China. USSR. 1980-81. *515*
—. China. USSR. 20c. *306*
—. China. USSR. Vietnam. 1973. *45*
—. *Christian Century* (periodical). Japan. Manchurian crisis. Morrison, Charles C. 1931-33. *96*
—. Civil rights. Korea, South. 1969-74. *1063*
—. Cold War revisionism. Kolko thesis (review article). Korean War. 1949-50. *1147*
—. Communism. Containment. Japan. 1945-50. *892*
—. Communism. Intervention. Korean War. Truman, Harry S. USSR. 1950. *1081*
—. Communism. Korea. Truman Doctrine. 1945-50. *43*
—. Communist Countries. Korea, South. Military Ground Forces (withdrawal). 1950-78. *1022*
—. Congress. International Security. Taiwan. 1950-55. *178*
—. Cuba. Decisionmaking. Germany. Korean War. World War I. 1914-62. *1109*
—. Detente. Japan. Trade. USSR. 1971-74. *749*
—. Diplomacy. International Trade. Japan. World War II (antecedents). 1937-41. *946*
—. District of Columbia. Energy Conference (report). Europe, Western. Japan. 1974. *1005*
—. Economic Conditions. International Trade (relations). Japan. 1945-74. *927*
—. Economic Policy. Japan. Military. Politics. 1945-72. *919*
—. Economic Policy. Japan. Military Occupation. 1945-49. *895*
—. Embargoes. Japan. Oil. Roosevelt, Franklin D. 1941. *578*
—. Europe. Japan. 1970's. *832*
—. Europe. Japan. Military strategy. Vietnam War. 1970's. *910*
—. Europe. Japan. Neocolonialism. Organization of Petroleum Exporting Countries. 1969-70's. *855*
—. Europe. Japan. Offner, Arnold A. World War II (antecedents; review article). 1917-41. *829*
—. Europe, Western. International Security. Japan. Military Capability. 1980-82. *889*
—. Europe, Western. International Trade. Japan. Rockefeller family. Trilateral Commission. 1973-78. *995*
—. Europe, Western. Japan. Trilateralism. 1950's-70's. *945*
—. Exports. Japan. Oil. State Department. 1940-41. *948*
—. Gresham, Walter Quintin. Korea. Sino-Japanese War. 1894-95. *38*
—. Gulick, Sidney Lewis. Japan. Missions and Missionaries. 1914-45. *929*
—. Hull, Cordell. Japan. Roosevelt, Franklin D. Stimson, Henry L. 1933-36. *730*
—. International politics. Japan. Okinawa. 1853-1972. *718*
—. International Security. Korea. 1944-77. *1122*
—. International Trade. Japan. Military Occupation. 1945-74. *808*
—. Japan. 1970's. *631*
—. Japan. 1977-78. *101*
—. Japan. Kim Dae Jung case. Korea. 1973. *136*
—. Japan. Korea. 1960's-82. *1140*
—. Japan. Korea. Roosevelt, Theodore. Russia. 1901-05. *1057*
—. Japan. Korea. Sino-Japanese War. 1894-95. *76*
—. Japan. Netherlands East Indies. World War II. 1941-46. *710*
—. Japan. Oil exports. State Department. 1940-41. *948*
—. Japan. Oil industry and Trade. 1934-37. *819*
—. Japan. Treaties. 1853-58. *685*
—. Japan. Vietnam War. 1965-73. *742*
—. Japan. World War II (antecedents). 1940-41. *599*
—. Japan. Yoshida Shigeru. 1945-78. *835*
—. Korea. 1945-78. *1062*
—. Korea. 1949-78. *1146*
—. Korea. 1973. *1054*
—. Korea. 1979. *1107*
—. Korea. Military Aid. 1950's. *1012*
—. Korea. Partition. World War II. 1945. *1082*
—. Korea. Treaties. 1882-1905. *69*
—. Korea. Treaties. 1882-1905. *1056*
—. Korea. Unification. 1950's-75. *1045*
—. Korea. World War II. 1941-45. *1083*
—. Korea, North. Korea, South. Military capability. 1970's. *1066*
—. Korea, South. Military Ground Forces. 1976-80. *1090*
—. Korea, South. Public opinion. 1952-80. *1089*
—. Korea (38th Parallel). Korean War. MacArthur, Douglas. Self-determination. Truman, Harry S. USSR. 1943-50. *1084*
—. Korean War. Military Bases. 1950-80. *1148*
—. Korean War. Vietnam War. 1950-53. 1961-73. *1095*
—. Mao Zedong. 1948-50. *315*
—. Sino-Soviet conflict. Taiwan. 1966-75. *311*
—. Taiwan. 1981-82. *1149*
Foreign Policy (review article). Asia, East. 1945-77. *121*
—. China. 1944-50. *236*

Foreign Policy

—. China. Diplomacy. Imperialism. Philippines. Reinsch, Paul S. 1899-1945. *57*
—. Gardner, Lloyd C. Japan. LaFeber, Walter F. McCormick, Thomas J. USA. 1776-1973. *581*
Foreign Relations. *See also* Alliances; Balance of Power; Boundaries; Cultural Relations; Detente; Diplomacy; Disarmament; Economic Relations; International Trade; Intervention; Rearmament; Tariff; Trade; Treaties.
—. Academia Sinica (Tsungli Yamen Archive). China. Public Administration. 1868-94. *220*
—. Acheson, Dean. China. 1944-50. *562*
—. Adachi Minechiro. Huerta, Victoriano. Japan. Mexico. 1913-14. *786*
—. Afghanistan. China. Invasions. Military cooperation. USSR. Vietnam. 1965-80. *232*
—. Afghanistan. Iran. Japan. 1979-81. *989*
—. Africa. China. USA. USSR. ca 1949-70's. *327*
—. ANZUS. Defense Policy. Japan. 1945-78. *937*
—. Arms Trade. China. Taiwan. 1979-82. *1165*
—. Arms Trade. Taiwan. 1978-82. *1173*
—. Asia. Association of South East Asian Nations. China. 1970's. *260*
—. Asia. Japan. 1945-72. *110*
—. Asia, East. 1776-1976. *27*
—. Asia, East. Barnett, A. Doak. China. USSR. 1944-78. *123*
—. Asia, East. China. 1945-82. *160*
—. Asia, East. China. 1979. *114*
—. Asia, East. China. Development. Political Attitudes. Wilson, James H. 1885-1910. *169*
—. Asia, East. Economic Conditions. 1982. *66*
—. Asia, East. Economic problems. Japan. Political Leadership. Tanaka, Kakuei. 1971-74. *883*
—. Asia, East. USSR. 1948-81. *88*
—. Asia, Southeast. China. Vietnam War. 1973-75. *256*
—. Assassination. Korea, South. Park Chung-hee. Politics. 1979-82. *1010*
—. Australia. Circumnavigations. Japan. Warships. 1908. *878*
—. Balance of power. Bowles, Chester. China. India. Nehru, Jawaharlal. 1949-54. *16*
—. Balance of Power. China. Europe. USSR. 1970's. *229*
—. Balance of power. China. Japan. 1970's. *1*
—. Barnett, A. Doak (review article). China. USSR. 1950-76. *401*
—. Baseball. Japan. 1875-1900. *874*
—. Bibliographies. China. 1844-1974. *292*
—. Bueler, William H. China. Cohen, Warren I. (review article). Davies, John Paton, Jr. 1830-1955. *392*
—. Burlingame, Anson. China. 1861-67. *333*
—. Burma. China. Indonesia. 1950's-75. *168*
—. Cambodia. China. USSR. Vietnam. 1978-80. *105*
—. Canada. China. Developing nations. USSR. 1950-75. *318*
—. Canada. China. International Trade. USSR. 1969-72. *367*
—. Carter, Jimmy. China. Normalization. Taiwan. USSR. 1978-79. *1150*
—. China. 1793-1974. *366*
—. China. 1844-1982. *374*
—. China. 1897-1979. *526*
—. China. 1942-80. *496*
—. China. 1944-78. *290*
—. China. 1947-50. *162*
—. China. 1949-71. *441*
—. China. 1949-72. *525*
—. China. 1960's-70's. *286*
—. China. 1969-72. *142*
—. China. 1969-79. *171*
—. China. 1969-82. *420*
—. China. 1970-81. *369*
—. China. 1977-81. *459*
—. China. 1980-81. *309*

—. China. 20c. *353*
—. China. Clark, Grenville. Letters. Snow, Edgar. 1963-67. *489*
—. China. Clubb, O. Edmund. 1949-50. *208*
—. China. Cold war. Korean War. Taiwan. USSR. 1947-79. *211*
—. China. Cold War. Korean War. USSR. 1945-72. *1024*
—. China. Communist Party. 1936-80. *348*
—. China. Communist Party. USSR. 1948-49. *317*
—. China. Defense Policy. Economics. Taiwan. 1949-81. *1153*
—. China. Defense Policy. USSR. 1970-83. *182*
—. China. Detente. India. 1974. *278*
—. China. Economic policy. International Trade. 1949-75. *248*
—. China. Economic relations. Taiwan. 1840's-1974. *1157*
—. China. Education. 20c. *482*
—. China. Europe. International Trade. Urban concessions. 1876-85. *404*
—. China. Europe. Nuclear Arms. Strategic Arms Limitation Talks. Trilateralism. USSR. 1970's-83. *381*
—. China. Europe, Western. International Security. NATO. 1970's-82. *407*
—. China. Georgia (Atlanta). Students. US-China People's Friendship Association. 1972-83. *339*
—. China. Girard College (Stephen Girard Collection). Historical Society of Pennsylvania. International Trade. Pennsylvania (Philadelphia). 1775-1840. 1980. *273*
—. China. Historiography. 1928-37. 1970's. *338*
—. China. Human rights. 1970's. *501*
—. China. Indian Ocean and Area. Persian Gulf and Area. 1946-80. *103*
—. China. Industry. Japan. Korea. USSR. 1970-76. *95*
—. China. International trade. 1977. *354*
—. China. International Trade. Japan. 1979. *87*
—. China. International Trade. Navies. Taiping Rebellion. 1850-61. *291*
—. China. International Trade. Taiwan. 1949-82. *379*
—. China. Japan. 1978-81. *68*
—. China. Japan. 1978. *106*
—. China. Japan. Korea, North. Korea, South. Unification. USSR. 1970's-. *20*
—. China. Japan. Korea, South. Military. Taiwan. 1960-80. *56*
—. China. Japan. Taiwan. USSR. 1972. *78*
—. China. Japan. USSR. 1970's. *107*
—. China. Japan. USSR. 1970's. *594*
—. China. Japan. USSR. 1981-84. *111*
—. China. Jiang Jieshi. Military aid. 1948-50. *1176*
—. China. Kahn, E. J., Jr. (review article). Politics. State Department (Foreign Service). 1940's-50's. 1975. *384*
—. China. Korea. Taiwan. 1971-77. *115*
—. China. Korea. USSR. 1960's-82. *122*
—. China. Loans (consortium). Wilson, Woodrow. 1910-13. *383*
—. China. Mao Zedong (death). 1976. *560*
—. China. Military aid. National Security. USSR. 1970-75. *440*
—. China. Nixon, Richard M. 1969-70's. *553*
—. China. Nixon, Richard M. 1972-78. *545*
—. China. Political Commentary. Vietnam War. 1960's-70's. *419*
—. China. Political conditions. 1969-70's. *307*
—. China. Press. Public information. 1970's. *368*
—. China. Publishers and Publishing. 1978-81. *359*
—. China. Research. 19c-20c. *399*
—. China. State Department (report). 1944-49. *414*
—. China. Taiwan. 1940-72. *1158*
—. China. Taiwan. 1970's-82. *130*
—. China. Taiwan. 1972-80. *120*
—. China. Taiwan. 1972-82. *92*

Frontier   253

—. China. Taiwan. 1978-81. *1172*
—. China. Taiwan. 1979. *73*
—. China. Taiwan. USSR. 1972-82. *215*
—. China. Terranova, Francis. Trade. Trials. 1821-44. *240*
—. China. Thailand. USSR. 1974. *143*
—. China. USA. USSR. 1970's. *294*
—. China. USSR. 1943-79. *556*
—. China. USSR. 1949-57. *176*
—. China. USSR. 1949-80. *192*
—. China. USSR. 1949-83. *389*
—. China. USSR. 1950's-82. *308*
—. China. USSR. 1950-83. *332*
—. China. USSR. 1966-72. *457*
—. China. USSR. 1970's-82. *370*
—. China. USSR. 1970's. *206*
—. China. USSR. 1970's. *382*
—. China. USSR. 1970's. *434*
—. China. USSR. 1970-74. *341*
—. China. USSR. 1972-. *207*
—. China. USSR. 1972-82. *540*
—. China. USSR. 1974. *480*
—. China. USSR. Vietnam War. 1949-74. *511*
—. China. Varg, Paul A. (review article). 1936-46. *490*
—. China. Vietnam, North. Vietnam War. 1970-80. *264*
—. China. Vietnam War. 1960's-73. *454*
—. China. Vietnam War. 1973. *228*
—. China. Ward, John Elliot. 1858-60. *261*
—. China. Wedemeyer, Albert C. (reminiscences). World War II. 1920-48. *532*
—. China (Hankow). *Petrel* (vessel). 1895. *431*
—. Cold War. Korea, South. 1950-53. *1096*
—. Communism. Documents. State Department *(Relations with China)*. 1944-81. *109*
—. Congress. Taiwan Relations Act (US, 1979). 1978-79. *1162*
—. Cultural Imperialism. Japan. Mutsuhito, Emperor. Seward, William H. 1870-71. *705*
—. Defense Policy. Japan. 1979-81. *834*
—. Defense Policy. Japan. 1980-83. *651*
—. Economic Conditions. Hong Kong. New York City. Securities. 1964-79. *571*
—. Economic Conditions. Japan. 1982. *787*
—. Economic Conditions. Japan. Pacific free trade area. 1945-74. *71*
—. Economic Conditions. Korea, South. 1977. *1042*
—. Economic development. Germany, West. Japan. 1973-76. *809*
—. Economic growth. Europe. Japan. Military Aid. 1970's. *601*
—. Economic Policy. Japan. 1970's-80. *708*
—. Economic Policy. Japan. 1978-80. *751*
—. Economic policy. Natural Resources (development). USSR. 1950's-70's. *50*
—. Energy. Investments. Japan. 1970's. *851*
—. Energy Action Group. Europe. Japan. North America. 1973-. *756*
—. Europe. Japan. 1974. *116*
—. Europe. Japan. Persian Gulf and Area. Tucker, Robert W. (interview). 1968-80. *998*
—. Europe. Korea, South. 1950's-70's. *1071*
—. Europe, Western. Japan. Trilateral Commission. 1973-82. *872*
—. Gayn, Mark *(Japan Diary)*. Japan. Military occupation. 1945-81. *880*
—. Gray, John Chipman. Holmes, Oliver Wendell. Japan. Kaneko Kentarō. Law. Letters. Thayer, James Bradley. 1878-1924. *741*
—. Great Britain. Japan. Thailand. World War II. 1942-46. *970*
—. Great Britain. Japan. War debts. 1920-23. *646*
—. Harris, Townsend. Japan. 1856-58. *830*
—. International trade. Japan. 1930's-70's. *888*
—. International Trade. Japan. 1970's-83. *720*
—. International Trade. Japan. 1970's-83. *849*

—. International Trade. Japan. Military Capability. Trade. 1970's-82. *833*
—. International Trade. Korea. Military Strategy. 1905-79. *1100*
—. Japan. 1900-72. *850*
—. Japan. 1931-41. *666*
—. Japan. 1945-75. *887*
—. Japan. 1960's-73. *825*
—. Japan. 1965-74. *108*
—. Japan. 1968-72. *826*
—. Japan. 1976-78. *886*
—. Japan. John Doe Associates. 1936-41. *902*
—. Japan. King, William. Thomas, Elbert. Utah. ca 1922-40. *782*
—. Japan. Korea. 1945-74. *67*
—. Japan. Korea, South. 1950-80. *89*
—. Japan. Lensen, George Alexander (review article). USSR. 1921-30. *831*
—. Japan. Militarism. 1945-73. *582*
—. Japan. Newspapers. 1900-78. *774*
—. Japan. Nixon Doctrine. 1945-72. *824*
—. Japan. Nuclear energy. 1974-82. *776*
—. Japan. Oil crisis. 1974. *906*
—. Japan. Okinawa. Public Opinion. Sato, Eisaku. 1969. *752*
—. Japan. Perry, Matthew C. Preble, G. W. (diary). 1852-54. *587*
—. Japan. Philippines. Quirino, Elpidio. Treaties. World War II. 1945-56. *748*
—. Japan. Pittman, Key. 1920-40. *781*
—. Japan. Press. 1969-71. *664*
—. Japan. Trade. 1970's. *839*
—. Japan. Vietnam War. 1964-73. *750*
—. Japan. Yasukawa, Takeshi (speech). 1975. *983*
—. Korea. 1845-1980. *1076*
—. Korea. 1882-1979. *1094*
—. Korea. 1883-94. *1055*
—. Korea. 1950-77. *1111*
—. Korea. Unification. USSR. 1945-47. *1098*
—. Korea, South. 1945-79. *1040*
—. Korea, South. 1950-81. *1099*
—. Taiwan. 1960-79. *1155*
—. Taiwan. 1978-79. *1174*
—. Taiwan. 1980-81. *1152*
—. Taiwan Relations Act (US, 1979). 1978-80. *1159*

Foreign Relations (review article). Asia, East. Blum, Robert M. Buhite, Russell D. McMahon, Robert J. 1945-60's. *24*
—. Buss, Claude A. China. Fairbank, John K. Whiting, Allen S. 1949-76. *234*
—. China. Haldeman, H. R. Kissinger, Henry A. Nixon, Richard M. 1968-76. *539*
—. China. Military. USSR. 1970-77. *538*
—. Japan. 1876-1976. *711*
—. Korean War. Truman, Harry S. 1950. 1976. *1104*
Foss, Joseph J. Air Warfare. Guadalcanal (battle). Japan. World War II. 1942. *795*
Four-Power Treaty. Asia, East. Diplomacy. Karnebeek, Hermann Adriaan van. Netherlands. Washington Conference. 1921-22. *9*
France (Paris). Diplomacy. Korea, South (Panmunjom). Peace. Vietnam. 1951-73. *1143*
Franklin, Benjamin. Autobiography. Fukuzawa, Yukichi. Japan. 1980. *962*
Fraser, Douglas. Aviation. China. Military training. Nationalists. Saskatchewan (Saskatoon). 1919-22. *217*
Fraud. China (Gailan). Chinese Engineering and Mining Company. Great Britain. Hoover, Herbert. 1900-28. *224*
Fritz, Chester. China, west. Travel (accounts). 1917. *566*
Frontier and Pioneer Life. Federal Policy. Indians. Japan. Military Strategy. Taiwan. 18c-1915. *70*

254   Frost

Frost, Edwin C. Air Transport Command. Burma Road. China. Convoys. Personal Narratives. Transportation, Military. 1945. *259*
Fukuda, Takeo. Asia, Southeast. Economic development. Foreign Policy. Japan. 1978. *676*
Fukuzawa, Yukichi. Autobiography. Franklin, Benjamin. Japan. 1980. *962*
Fulbright program. Educational exchange programs. Japan. 1982. *981*
Fur trade. Alaska. British Columbia. China (Macao). Cook, James. Pacific Area. 1778-79. *49*
—. Canada. Japan. Sea otters. Wildlife Conservation. 18c-20c. *988*
—. China. North West Company. Oregon (Astoria). 1760's-1821. *275*
—. China. South Africa (Cape Colony). Voyages. 1800-02. *479*
F-13 (aircraft). Air Forces. Korean War. World War II. 1944-54. *82*
F-86 (aircraft). Brooks, James L. (personal account). Korean War. Pilots. 1950. *1016*
F-86F (aircraft). Air Forces. Korean War. Osan Air Base. South Africa. UN Command. 1950-53. *1008*

G

Gandhi, Indira. China. Foreign policy. India. USSR. 1946-71. *93*
Gardner, Lloyd C. Foreign Policy (review article). Japan. LaFeber, Walter F. McCormick, Thomas J. USA. 1776-1973. *581*
Gayn, Mark *(Japan Diary)*. Foreign Relations. Japan. Military occupation. 1945-81. *880*
Gelm, George E. (journal). Brownson, Willard H. China (Nanking). Diplomacy. International Trade. Tuan Fang. 1907. *265*
Genealogical Society of Utah. Archival Catalogs and Inventories. China. Utah (Salt Lake City). 15c-20c. *509*
General Sherman (vessel). Korea. War. 1871. *1103*
Generalized System of Preferences. European Economic Community. Japan. Tariff. 1966-75. *595*
Generations. Internment. Japanese American Citizens League. Patriotism. World War II. 1941-42. *913*
Genetics. Eugenics. Japan. Social organization. 1920's-30's. *923*
Gentlemen's Agreement. Associations. Immigrants. Japan. Japanese Americans. 1907-26. *717*
Geography. Asia, North. Documents. Geology. Japan. 1848-83. *99*
Geology. Asia, North. Documents. Geography. Japan. 1848-83. *99*
George, Henry. China. Land ownership. Sun Zhongshan. Taxation. 1866-1973. *361*
Georgia. Asia, East. 1865-1983. *47*
—. Associated Japan-America Societies of the United States. Cultural relations. International Trade. Japan. 1979-82. *958*
Georgia (Atlanta). Archives, National. Asia, East. Asian Americans. 18c-20c. *100*
—. Asia, East. International Trade. 1945-82. *86*
—. China. Foreign Relations. Students. US-China People's Friendship Association. 1972-83. *339*
Germany. Colonialism. Educational Policy. Japan. Mariana Islands. Spain. ca 1688-1940. *698*
—. Cuba. Decisionmaking. Foreign Policy. Korean War. World War I. 1914-62. *1109*
—. Diplomacy (personal). Meyer, George von Lengerke. Roosevelt, Theodore. Russo-Japanese War. William II. 1902-14. *968*
—. Japan. Libraries, Presidential. Military government. Research. 1945-78. *994*
Germany, West. Business. Japan. Prices. 1980. *682*

—. Competition. International Trade. Japan. Manufactures. 1970's. *797*
—. Dollar stabilization. Economic Policy. Japan. 1945-78. *801*
—. Economic development. Foreign Relations. Japan. 1973-76. *809*
—. Economic Policy. GNP. Inflation. Japan. Protectionism. 1976-78. *709*
—. European Economic Community. Japan. Oil crisis. Trade. 1974. *647*
Ghana (Accra). Airplanes. China (Kunming). Laughlin, C. H. (reminiscences). World War II. 1942. *347*
Gila River Relocation Center. Arizona. Japanese Americans. Public Opinion. Race Relations. World War II. 1942-45. *627*
Gilbert, Prentiss B. Japan. Kellogg-Briand Pact. League of Nations. Manchuria. Military Occupation. Stimson, Henry L. 1931. *34*
Gindon, Sam (interview). Automobile Industry and Trade. Canada. Europe, Western. Japan. Labor. World car (concept). 1945-80. *1006*
Girard College (Stephen Girard Collection). China. Foreign Relations. Historical Society of Pennsylvania. International Trade. Pennsylvania (Philadelphia). 1775-1840. 1980. *273*
Glamorganshire (vessel). *Clarissa B. Carver* (vessel). Courts. Dow, Leroy. Japan. Lawsuits. Ships. 1885-86. *870*
Globalization. China. Foreign Policy. Great Powers (role definition). USSR. 1970's. *565*
GNP. Economic Policy. Germany, West. Inflation. Japan. Protectionism. 1976-78. *709*
Goodnow, Frank Johnson. China. Constitutional development. Yuan Shikai. 1913-15. *449*
Government. Afghanistan. China. Pakistan. 1979-81. *146*
Government ownership. American Tobacco Company. Japan (Tokyo). Parrish, Edward James. Tobacco. 1899-1904. *656*
Grading, peer group. China. Colleges and Universities. Communism. Political Science. 1964-72. *453*
Graduate study. China. Dissertations. 1962-74. *464*
Grand Juries. Censorship. *Chicago Tribune*. Japan. Midway (battle). Navies. World War II. 1942. *669*
Grant, Julia Dent. Grant, Ulysses S. (visit). Japan. 1879. *1004*
Grant, Ulysses S. (visit). Grant, Julia Dent. Japan. 1879. *1004*
Graves. Japan. Methodism. Missions and Missionaries. 1876-1957. *761*
Gray, John Chipman. Foreign Relations. Holmes, Oliver Wendell. Japan. Kaneko Kentarō. Law. Letters. Thayer, James Bradley. 1878-1924. *741*
Great Britain. Airplane Industry and Trade. China. Embargoes. Vickers Ltd. 1919-21. *448*
—. Alliances. Boxer Rebellion. China, East. Russia. 1900. *138*
—. Appeasement (proposal). Diplomacy. Japan. World War II. 1941. *680*
—. Banking. China. Foreign Investments. Foreign Policy. 1908-20. *219*
—. Blockades. Chamberlain, Neville. China. Japan. Roosevelt, Franklin D. World War II (antecedents). 1937-38. *686*
—. Business Cycles. Economic Structure. Europe, Western. Japan. 1967-80. *959*
—. Capitalism. Economic conditions. Europe, Western. Japan. 1970-80. *996*
—. China. Credit. Depressions. International Trade (agencies). Tea. 1834-37. *197*
—. China. Cultural attitudes. Social status. Women. 1840-1927. *243*
—. China. Diplomacy. 1920-46. *425*
—. China. Diplomacy. Foreign Investments. Japan. World War I. 1915-17. *28*

—. China. Diplomacy. Hong Kong. World War II. 1941-45. *570*
—. China. Diplomatic recognition. 1949-50. *424*
—. China. Extraterritoriality. Treaties. 1929-43. *188*
—. China. International Relations (discipline). Japan. USSR. 1937-49. *437*
—. China. Intervention. Sovereignty. 1557-1949. *491*
—. China. Loan negotiations. World War II. 1941-44. *189*
—. China. Presidency. Yuan Shikai. 1911-12. *363*
—. China (Gailan). Chinese Engineering and Mining Company. Fraud. Hoover, Herbert. 1900-28. *224*
—. China (Yangzi River). Diplomacy. International trade. Taiping Rebellion. 1850-61. *430*
—. China (Yangzi River). Hope, James. Imperialism. Taiping Rebellion. Trade. 1850-61. *432*
—. Communications. Japan. Naval Strategy. World War II. 1943-45. *652*
—. Cotton. India. Japan. Textile Industry. 1870-1939. *987*
—. Developing nations. Japan. Manufacturing. Subcontracting. 1966-76. *899*
—. Economic Conditions. Japan. Military Occupation. Political Systems. 1945-49. *617*
—. Economic development. Japan. Thailand. 1926-80. *102*
—. Exports. Japan. Oil Industry and Trade. Roosevelt, Franklin D. World War II. 1940-41. *659*
—. Foreign Relations. Japan. Thailand. World War II. 1942-46. *970*
—. Foreign Relations. Japan. War debts. 1920-23. *646*
—. Japan. Military Intelligence. Wiseman, William. World War I. World War II. 1914-45. *903*
—. Japan. Naval Strategy. Pacific Area. World War II. 1941-45. *589*
—. Japan. Wages. ca 1873-1981. *678*
—. Korean War. Navies. Suez Crisis. USA. Vietnam War. 1950-76. *1119*
Great Powers. *See also* China; USA; USSR.
—. Asia, Southeast. 1960-76. *452*
Great Powers (role definition). China. Foreign Policy. Globalization. USSR. 1970's. *565*
Gregory (vessel). Japan (Bonin Islands). McCandless, Bruce (reminiscences). Navies. World War II. 1945. *798*
Gresham, Walter Quintin. Foreign policy. Korea. Sino-Japanese War. 1894-95. *38*
Gross National Product. *See* GNP.
Guadalcanal (battle). Air Warfare. Foss, Joseph J. Japan. World War II. 1942. *795*
—. Cryptography. Japan. Military Intelligence. Radio. World War II. Japan. 1942. *800*
—. *I-19* (submarine). Japan. *North Carolina* (vessel). *O'Brien* (vessel). *Wasp* (vessel). World War II. 1942. *608*
—. Japan. World War II. 1942-43. *852*
Guam (liberation). Japan. World War II. 1944. *625*
Guevara, Gaspar Ignacio de. Catholic Church. Clergy. Heresy. Philippines (Biliran). 1765-75. *1061*
Gulick, Edward V. (review article). China. Parker, Peter. 1840's-50's. *543*
Gulick, Sidney Lewis. Foreign Policy. Japan. Missions and Missionaries. 1914-45. *929*

H

Hada, John. Citizenship. Ford, Gerald R. Japanese American Citizens League. Pardon. Tokyo Rose (Iva Toguri d'Aquino). Uyeda, Clifford I. (account). 1973-77. *949*
Haldeman, H. R. China. Foreign Relations (review article). Kissinger, Henry A. Nixon, Richard M. 1968-76. *539*
Hamilton, Alexander. Carter, Jimmy. Eisenhower, Dwight D. Executive Power. Foreign policy. Taiwan. 1793-1979. *1161*
Harkness, Ruth. China. Pandas. Tangier Smith, Floyd. 1936. *175*
Harris, Townsend. Foreign Relations. Japan. 1856-58. *830*
Hawaii. Allen, Horace. Diplomacy. Immigration. Korea. Sugar. 1902-05. *1101*
—. Annexation. Japan. Treaties. 1897. *821*
—. Armstrong, David M. (personal account). Japan. Pearl Harbor (attack). World War II. 1942. *580*
—. Immigrants. Independence Movements. Korea. 1900-19. *1072*
—. Japan. Kalakaua, David (travel diary). 1881. *793*
—. Japan. Naval Vessels. Pearl Harbor. World War II. 1941. *1000*
—. Japan. Pearl Harbor. World War II. 1941. *885*
Hawaii, University of. Crawford, David L. Japan. Peace pact (proposed). USA. 1940-41. *713*
Hawley, Francis H. Arnhold & Company. China (Chang River). Propaganda. Theater. Tretiakov, Sergei (*Roar China!*). 1924-75. *394*
Hay, John. China. Historiography (revisionist). International Trade. Open Door policy. 1899-1901. *170*
Haygood, Laura A. China. Feminism. Methodist Episcopal Church (South). Missions and Missionaries. 1884-1900. *427*
Hearn, Lafcadio. Creoles. Folklore. Japan. Louisiana (New Orleans). Martinique. 1850-1904. *803*
Hellcats. Air Warfare. Japan. Task Force 58. Truk (battle). World War II. 1944. *933*
Heller, Francis H. (review article). Korean War. 1950-53. 1977. *1049*
Herde, Peter (review article). Japan. Pearl Harbor. World War II. 1941. *938*
Heresy. Catholic Church. Clergy. Guevara, Gaspar Ignacio de. Philippines (Biliran). 1765-75. *1061*
Herndon, Hugh. Japan. Pangborn, Clyde. Transpacific flight. USA. 1930-71. *864*
Hess, Dean Elmer. Air Forces. *Battle Hymn* (film). Korean War. Orphans. 1950-56. *1032*
High Schools. Attitudes. Japan. Yasuteru, Aoki. 1970's. *814*
—. China studies (conference). Wisconsin (Wingspread). 1972. *230*
Higher education. China. Educational Policy. Labor experience. 1976. *330*
Higher Education (power structure). Japan. 1968-73. *757*
Hiroshima-Nagasaki, August 1945 (film). Atomic Bomb. Barnouw, Erik. Japan. 1945-70. *588*
Historians. Canada. Japan. Norman, E. Herbert (review article). Foreign policy. 1940-77. *859*
Historians, Western. Japan. Military defeat. USSR. World War II. 1942-45. *890*
Historical Society of Pennsylvania. China. Foreign Relations. Girard College (Stephen Girard Collection). International Trade. Pennsylvania (Philadelphia). 1775-1840. 1980. *273*
Historiography. Alperovitz, Gar (review article). Atomic Warfare. Decisionmaking. Japan (Hiroshima). World War II. 1945-65. *898*

—. Boxer Rebellion. China. Education. Foreign Policy. Hunt, Michael (thesis). Reparations. 1900-06. 1972. *535*
—. China. Foreign Relations. 1928-37. 1970's. *338*
—. China. Imperialism (economic). 19c-20c. 1965-73. *529*
—. China. Open Door policy. 1899-1922. *403*
—. China. Stilwell, Joseph W. World War II. 1942-44. *559*
—. Dissertations. Educational reform. Japan. Military Occupation. 1950-80. *940*
—. Economic History. Japan. 1600-1945. ca 1970-77. *980*
—. Japan. Military occupation. 1945-52. *820*
—. Japan. Modernization (review article). 1867-1977. *754*
—. Korean War. MacArthur, Douglas. Politics. Public relations. Truman, Harry S. Wake Island. 1950. *1142*
—. Korean War (antecedents). 1950-53. *1125*
Historiography (Chinese). China. Jefferson, Thomas. Liu Zuochang. Virginia, University of. 1770-1826. 1976-81. *321*
Historiography (Communist). China. Immigration. 19c-20c. 1949-73. *518*
Historiography (review article). Americanology. Japan. National self-image. Social conditions. 19c-20c. 1969-73. *722*
—. Bibliographies. Korean War. 1950-55. *1097*
Historiography (revisionist). China. Hay, John. International Trade. Open Door policy. 1899-1901. *170*
Historiography, US. Asia. Japan. Revolutionary movements. USSR. World War II. 1930's-49. *862*
—. China. 19c-20c. 1950's-70's. *406*
History. Attitudes. Japan/United States Textbook Study Project. Textbooks. 1981. *999*
History Teaching. American history. China. Textbooks. 18c-20c. *551*
—. Atomic Warfare. Japan. Simulation and Games. World War II. 1945. 1978. *658*
—. China. Foreign Policy. Legislative Investigations. Senate. Simulation and Games. 1949. 1978. *378*
Ho Chi Minh. China. Communism. Independence movements. Vietnamese. 1942-45. *502*
Holloway, Bruce K. (account). Air Warfare. Army Air Force. China. Flying Tigers. P-40 (aircraft). World War II. 1942-43. *297*
Holmes, Oliver Wendell. Foreign Relations. Gray, John Chipman. Japan. Kaneko Kentarō. Law. Letters. Thayer, James Bradley. 1878-1924. *741*
Hong Kong. China. Diplomacy. Great Britain. World War II. 1941-45. *570*
—. Economic Conditions. Foreign relations. New York City. Securities. 1964-79. *571*
Hong Kong, University of. American Studies. 1945-76. *572*
Hoover, Herbert. China (Gailan). Chinese Engineering and Mining Company. Fraud. Great Britain. 1900-28. *224*
Hope, James. China (Yangzi River). Great Britain. Imperialism. Taiping Rebellion. Trade. 1850-61. *432*
Hornbeck, Stanley K. Diplomacy. Japan. World War II (antecedents). 1937-41. *775*
Horse breeding. Barton, Fred. China (Shansi). Cowboys. Montana. Politics. 1912-32. *400*
Hostages. China. Foreign Policy. USA. 1923. *225*
—. Daily Life. Japan. Letters. Navies. Rescues. 1846-49. *771*
House of Representatives. Burlingame, Anson. China. Diplomacy. Republican Party. 1854-69. *148*
Huang Tsun-hsien. California (San Francisco). China. Reform. 1882-85. *328*

Hudner, Thomas. Blacks. Brown, Jesse. Korean War. Military officers. Navies. 1950. *1123*
Huerta, Victoriano. Adachi Minechiro. Foreign Relations. Japan. Mexico. 1913-14. *786*
Hughes, Charles Evans. China (Shandong). Diplomacy. Japan. Washington Conference. 1919-22. *863*
Hughes, William Morris. Equality (proposed). Japan. League of Nations Covenant. Paris Peace Conference. Race Relations. Wilson, Woodrow. 1919. *772*
Hull, Cordell. Diplomacy. Indochina. Japan. Philippines. World War II (antecedents). 1941. *616*
—. Foreign policy. Japan. Roosevelt, Franklin D. Stimson, Henry L. 1933-36. *730*
Human rights. Carter, Jimmy (administration). China. Foreign policy. Morality. 1976-77. *520*
—. Carter, Jimmy (administration). Foreign Policy. Korea, South. 1945-79. *1091*
—. China. Foreign Relations. 1970's. *501*
Hunt, Michael (thesis). Boxer Rebellion. China. Education. Foreign Policy. Historiography. Reparations. 1900-06. 1972. *535*
Hurley, Patrick J. China. Diplomacy. Jiang Jieshi. Mao Zedong. State Department. Vincent, John Carter. 1944-45. *358*
Hurley, Patrick J. (resignation). China. Civil War. Newspapers. Reporters and Reporting. 1945-46. *282*
Hydrogen bomb. Bikini Atoll. Japan. *Lucky Dragon* (vessel). Pacific Dependencies (US). 1954-75. *882*

I

Idaho (Minidoka). Japanese Americans. Mukaida, Tomeji (reminiscences). Relocation. World War II. 1940's. *789*
Ideology. American Revolution. China. Nationalism. Revolutionary Movements. Sun Zhongshan. 1776-83. 1905-25. *187*
—. China. Women's liberation movement. 1960's-70's. *455*
Immigrants. Associations. Gentlemen's Agreement. Japan. Japanese Americans. 1907-26. *717*
—. Hawaii. Independence Movements. Korea. 1900-19. *1072*
Immigration. *See also* Emigration.
—. Allen, Horace. Diplomacy. Hawaii. Korea. Sugar. 1902-05. *1101*
—. Angell, James B. China. Trade. Treaties. 1880-81. *185*
—. Brain drain. Scholars. Taiwan. 1905-73. *1163*
—. China. Historiography (Communist). 19c-20c. 1949-73. *518*
—. Korean Americans. Political leadership. Rhee, Syngman. 1903-24. *1048*
Immigration policy. Boycott. Chamber of Commerce. China (Shanghai). Nationalism. 1905. *519*
Immigration policy (US). China. 1850-1974. *487*
Immigration restriction. Blacks. Japanese. Miller, Kelly. Race Relations. 1906-24. *699*
Imperialism. Asia, East. 19c-1975. *790*
—. China. Cuba. Military Occupation. Native races. Philippines. 1898-1903. *316*
—. China. Diplomacy. Foreign Policy (review article). Philippines. Reinsch, Paul S. 1899-1945. *57*
—. China. International Trade. 1784-1914. *507*
—. China (Yangzi River). Great Britain. Hope, James. Taiping Rebellion. Trade. 1850-61. *432*
—. Class Struggle. Cumings, Bruce. Korean War (review article). 1945-47. *1038*
—. Europe, Western. Finance. Industry. Japan. Latin America. Trade. 1970's. *768*

—. Japan. Navigation. Pacific Area. Pearl Harbor. World War II (antecedents). Prehistory-1941. *648*
Imperialism (economic). China. Historiography. 19c-20c. 1965-73. *529*
Imports. Antitrust. Automobile Industry and Trade. Federal Policy. Japan. Protectionism. 1981-83. *982*
—. Automobile Industry and Trade. Japan. 1975-81. *618*
—. Automobiles. Foreign Policy. Japan. Trade Regulations. 1970-81. *727*
Indemnity. China. Denby, Charles. Foreign Policy. 1889. *222*
Independence movements. China. Communism. Ho Chi Minh. Vietnamese. 1942-45. *502*
—. Hawaii. Immigrants. Korea. 1900-19. *1072*
—. Korea. Political Factions. Rhee, Syngman. 1919-45. *1073*
India. Arms control. Canada. China. Nuclear Arms. Nuclear power. Regionalism. USA. 1951-78. *493*
—. Balance of power. Bowles, Chester. China. Foreign Relations. Nehru, Jawaharlal. 1949-54. *16*
—. China. Communism. Lu Xun. Revolutionary Movements. Smedley, Agnes. 1910-50. *375*
—. China. Detente. Foreign Relations. 1974. *278*
—. China. Foreign policy. Gandhi, Indira. USSR. 1946-71. *93*
—. China. Foreign Policy. Pakistan. USSR. 1945-75. *409*
—. Cotton. Great Britain. Japan. Textile Industry. 1870-1939. *987*
Indian Ocean and Area. China. Diego Garcia. Naval Strategy. USSR. 20c. *364*
—. China. Foreign Relations. Persian Gulf and Area. 1946-80. *103*
Indianapolis (vessel). *I-58* (vessel). Japan. Submarine Warfare. World War II. 1945. *612*
Indians. Federal Policy. Frontier and Pioneer Life. Japan. Military Strategy. Taiwan. 18c-1915. *70*
Indian-White Relations. Colonization. Commerce. Netherlands. New Netherland. Taiwan. 17c. *1160*
Indochina. China. Churchill, Winston. Colonies. deGaulle, Charles. Foreign Policy. Roosevelt, Franklin D. 1942-45. *75*
—. China. International crises. Korea. Laos. 1949-62. *345*
—. Diplomacy. Hull, Cordell. Japan. Philippines. World War II (antecedents). 1941. *616*
Indonesia. Burma. China. Foreign Relations. 1950's-75. *168*
Industrial development. Japan. 1960's-70's. *758*
Industry. Automobile Industry and Trade. Competition. Europe. Japan. 1969-73. *649*
—. China. Foreign Relations. Japan. Korea. USSR. 1970-76. *95*
—. Europe, Western. Finance. Imperialism. Japan. Latin America. Trade. 1970's. *768*
—. International Trade (deficit). Japan. 1970's. *573*
Inflation. Economic Policy. Germany, West. GNP. Japan. Protectionism. 1976-79. *571*
—. Europe, Western. Japan. 1958-68. *974*
Information. Diffusion. Japan. 1830's-1970's. *869*
Inheritance. Agricultural property. Democratization. Japan. Military Occupation. 1945-52. *935*
Institute of Pacific Relations. China Lobby. McCarran Committee. Public opinion. Thomas, John N. (review article). Watergate trials. 1945-75. *58*
Intellectuals. Attitudes. Japan. ca 1945-75. *897*
—. Japan. 1890-1979. *712*
Intellectuals (Chinese). China. Political attitudes. Taiwan. 1970. *14*

Intellectuals, western. Alienation. China. Cuba. Pilgrimages. USSR. Vietnam, North. 1930's. 1970's. *296*
Intelligence mission. Carlson, Evans. China. Japan. Roosevelt, Franklin D. 1937-38. *40*
—. Carlson, Evans. China. Japan. Roosevelt, Franklin D. 1937-38. *128*
Intelligence Service. *See also* Counterintelligence; Military Intelligence.
—. Korea, South. Ranard, Donald L. (account). 1970-74. *1110*
Interest Groups. Attitudes. Democracy. Europe. Japan. Nuclear Science and Technology. USSR. 1970's. *731*
International crises. China. Indochina. Korea. Laos. 1949-62. *345*
International Law. Taiwan. Treaties. 1980. *1171*
International politics. Foreign Policy. Japan. Okinawa. 1853-1972. *718*
International Relations (discipline). China. Great Britain. Japan. USSR. 1937-49. *437*
International Security. China. Europe, Western. Foreign Relations. NATO. 1970's-82. *407*
—. China. Japan. Treaties. 1977-78. *84*
—. Congress. Foreign policy. Taiwan. 1950-55. *178*
—. Energy. Food. Japan. Natural resources. Nuclear Power. 1970's-80. *979*
—. Europe, Western. Foreign Policy. Japan. Military Capability. 1980-82. *889*
—. Foreign Policy. Korea. 1944-77. *1122*
International System. Korea. USSR. 1945-78. *1113*
International Trade. *See also* Trade.
—. Asia, East. Georgia (Atlanta). 1945-82. *86*
—. Associated Japan-America Societies of the United States. Cultural relations. Georgia. Japan. 1979-82. *958*
—. Australia. Foreign policy. Japan. New Zealand. 1968-70's. *41*
—. Balance of Payments. Japan. 1977-81. *844*
—. Bank of England. China. Economic crises. Magniac and Co. Yrissari and Co. 1823-27. *18*
—. Bethune, Angus. China (Canton). North America. North West Company. 1812-17. *469*
—. Brownson, Willard H. China (Nanking). Diplomacy. Gelm, George E. (journal). Tuan Fang. 1907. *265*
—. California. China. Clipper ships. USA. 1840's-50's. *506*
—. Canada. China. Foreign Relations. USSR. 1969-72. *367*
—. China. Congress. Lobbying. Roosevelt, Franklin D. (administration). Silver Purchase Act (1934). 1934. *268*
—. China. Diplomatic recognition. Shanghai Communique. Taiwan. Treaties. 1972-78. *568*
—. China. Economic policy. Foreign Relations. 1949-75. *248*
—. China. Europe. Foreign Relations. Urban concessions. 1876-85. *404*
—. China. Foreign policy. Pacific Area. Vietnam War. 1960's-70's. *166*
—. China. Foreign Policy. USSR. 1950's-74. *72*
—. China. Foreign relations. 1977. *354*
—. China. Foreign Relations. Girard College (Stephen Girard Collection). Historical Society of Pennsylvania. Pennsylvania (Philadelphia). 1775-1840. 1980. *273*
—. China. Foreign Relations. Japan. 1979. *87*
—. China. Foreign Relations. Navies. Taiping Rebellion. 1850-61. *291*
—. China. Foreign Relations. Taiwan. 1949-82. *379*
—. China. Hay, John. Historiography (revisionist). Open Door policy. 1899-1901. *170*
—. China. Imperialism. 1784-1914. *507*
—. China. Pacific & Eastern Steamship Company. Ships. USA. World War I. 1914-16. *447*
—. China. Pittman, Key. Senate. Silver Purchase Act (1934). USA. 1933-40. *485*

International Trade

—. China. Politics. 1789-1819. *277*
—. China (Yangzi River). Diplomacy. Great Britain. Taiping Rebellion. 1850-61. *430*
—. Competition. Germany, West. Japan. Manufactures. 1970's. *797*
—. Diplomacy. Foreign policy. Japan. World War II (antecedents). 1937-41. *946*
—. Diplomacy. Japan. Perry, Matthew C. 1853. *783*
—. Dumping. Japan. Public Opinion. Steel. 1974-78. *745*
—. Economic Conditions. Federal Policy. Japan. 1945-83. *868*
—. Economic Conditions. Japan. 1970-81. *684*
—. Economic war. Japan. 1970's. *614*
—. Europe, Western. Foreign Policy. Japan. Rockefeller family. Trilateral Commission. 1973-78. *995*
—. Europe, Western. Japan. Monetary systems. 1970's. *681*
—. European Economic Community. Japan. Monetary policy (devaluation). Nixon, Richard M. 1971-73. *655*
—. Foreign policy. Japan. Military Occupation. 1945-74. *808*
—. Foreign Relations. Japan. 1930's-70's. *888*
—. Foreign Relations. Japan. 1970's-83. *720*
—. Foreign Relations. Japan. 1970's-83. *849*
—. Foreign Relations. Japan. Military Capability. Trade. 1970's-82. *833*
—. Foreign Relations. Korea. Military Strategy. 1905-79. *1100*
—. Japan. 1980-82. *934*
—. Japan. 1981-82. *622*
—. Marketing. Taiwan. 1962-74. *1170*
International Trade (agencies). China. Credit. Depressions. Great Britain. Tea. 1834-37. *197*
International Trade (deficit). Industry. Japan. 1970's. *573*
International Trade (relations). Economic Conditions. Foreign policy. Japan. 1945-74. *927*
Internment. *See also* Concentration Camps; Prisoners of War; Relocation.
—. Acculturation. Japanese Americans. Social Conditions. 1945-55. *743*
—. Adams, Ansel. California. Japanese Americans. Lange, Dorothea. Manzanar War Relocation Center. Photography, Journalistic. World War II. 1941-45. *840*
—. Arkansas (Rowher Camp). Japanese Americans. World War II. 1942-45. *592*
—. Attitudes. Canada. Japanese Americans. Japanese Canadians. World War II. 1940-80. *642*
—. Canada. Ethnicity. Japanese Americans. Japanese Canadians. Joint Board of Defense. World War II. 1941-42. *641*
—. Civil rights. Counterintelligence. Japanese Americans. Munson, Curtis B. Peiper, N. J. L. World War II. 1931-42. *765*
—. Daily Life. Japanese Americans. Kurose, Aki Kato. Washington (Seattle). World War II. 1930's-50's. *644*
—. Daily Life. Japanese Americans. Personal narratives. Uchida, Yoshiko. Utah (Topaz). World War II. 1942-43. *942*
—. Diplomacy. Emmerson, John K. Japanese Peruvians. Memoirs. Peru. World War II. 1942-43. *660*
—. Documentation. Evacuations. Japanese Americans. Photographs. War Relocation Authority. World War II. 1941-43. *643*
—. Generations. Japanese American Citizens League. Patriotism. World War II. 1941-42. *913*
—. Japanese Americans. Letters. World War II. 1942. *914*
—. Japanese Americans. Martial law. Tule Lake Camp. World War II. 1941-44. *843*
—. Japanese Americans. Mirikitani, Janice ("Lullaby"). Poetry. World War II. 1941-45. *609*
—. Japanese Americans. New Mexico (Clovis). World War II. 1942-45. *638*
—. Japanese Americans. Oral history. Tanaka, Togo. World War II. Yoneda, Elaine. Yoneda, Karl. 1941-45. *816*
—. Japanese Americans. Personal narratives. World War II. 1942-81. *1001*
—. Japanese Americans. Propaganda. World War II. 1942-45. *841*
Internment (conference). Canada. Japanese. World War II. 1941-45. 1978. *922*
Interpersonal contact. Race Relations. Students. Taiwan. USA. 1933-73. *1167*
Intervention. Acheson, Dean. Korean War. Truman, Harry S. USSR. 1950. *1014*
—. China. Civil war. 1945-49. *287*
—. China. Civil war. Laos. USSR. 1959-62. *514*
—. China. Foreign policy. Shipping. Yangtze Rapid Steamship Company. 1924-36. *302*
—. China. Great Britain. Sovereignty. 1557-1949. *491*
—. Communism. Foreign policy. Korean War. Truman, Harry S. USSR. 1950. *1081*
—. Creighton, John Marie. Japan. Military Intelligence. USSR (Eastern Siberia). 1922. *44*
Intervention (military). Japan. Russia. 1918-20. *55*
Invasions. Afghanistan. China. Foreign Relations. Military cooperation. USSR. Vietnam. 1965-80. *232*
—. Afghanistan. Korean War. Limited war (concept). USSR. Vietnam War. War Powers Act (US, 1973). 1945-79. *104*
—. Japan. Military Strategy. Operation Olympic. World War II. 1945. *645*
Inventions. Japan. Morrow, James. Travel (accounts). 1854. *823*
Investments. Energy. Foreign Relations. Japan. 1970's. *851*
Iran. Afghanistan. Foreign Relations. Japan. 1979-81. *989*
Isolationism. China. Foreign Policy. Militarism. 1969-76. *179*
Israel. Agricultural Technology and Research. Family. Fiji. Japan. Social Change. 1689-1975. *634*
—. China. Egypt. Foreign Policy. Middle East. USSR. 1978. *497*
Italy. Australia. Japan. Netherlands. Political information. Voting and Voting Behavior. 1960's-70's. *716*
Iwo Jima. Japan. World War II. 1944-45. *736*
I-19 (submarine). Guadalcanal (battle). Japan. *North Carolina* (vessel). *O'Brien* (vessel). *Wasp* (vessel). World War II. 1942. *608*
I-58 (vessel). *Indianapolis* (vessel). Japan. Submarine Warfare. World War II. 1945. *612*

J

Janes, Leroy Lansing. Christianity. Japan (Kumamoto). 1838-76. *838*
Janus, Christopher. Archaeology. China. Peking Man. Shapiro, Harry F. 1941-73. *542*
Japan. Abortion. Birth control. 1940's-79. *670*
—. Adachi Minechiro. Foreign Relations. Huerta, Victoriano. Mexico. 1913-14. *786*
—. Afghanistan. Foreign Relations. Iran. 1979-81. *989*
—. Agawa, Hiroyuki. Military officers. Navies. World War II. Yamamoto, Isoroku (review article). 1930's-43. *764*

—. Agricultural property. Democratization. Inheritance. Military Occupation. 1945-52. *935*
—. Agricultural Technology and Research. Family. Fiji. Israel. Social Change. 1689-1975. *634*
—. Air Forces. Balloon Force. Documents. World War II. 1942-45. *702*
—. Air Forces. Kenney, George. Rabaul (battle). World War II. 1943. *607*
—. Air Forces. Military Capability. Philippines. World War II. 1941. *692*
—. Air Warfare. Balloons. Bombing. North America. World War II. 1940-45. *964*
—. Air Warfare. Bombing. Personal Narratives. Sims, Jack A. World War II. 1942. *905*
—. Air warfare. Chennault, Claire Lee. China. Flying Tigers. World War II. 1941-45. *701*
—. Air Warfare. Chennault, Claire Lee. China. World War II. 1937-45. *98*
—. Air Warfare. Foss, Joseph J. Guadalcanal (battle). World War II. 1942. *795*
—. Air Warfare. Hellcats. Task Force 58. Truk (battle). World War II. 1944. *933*
—. Air Warfare. Lemay, Curtis. World War II. 1940-45. *976*
—. Air Warfare. Mariana Islands (battle). World War II. 1944. *668*
—. Air warfare, clandestine. China. 1940-41. *474*
—. Aircraft carriers. Submarine Warfare. World War II. 1941-45. *865*
—. Airplanes, Military. Navies. Productivity. World War II. 1941-45. *860*
—. Alaska (Aleutian Islands). *Arthur Middleton* (vessel). Coast Guard. Laidlaw, Lansing. World War II. 1942-43. *769*
—. Alaska (Aleutian Islands). Attu (battle). World War II. 1942. *916*
—. Alliances. Dulles, John Foster. Political Theory. Treaties. Yoshida Shigeru. 5c BC-20c. 1951. *653*
—. Alliances. Economic Growth. Ethnocentrism. 1945-80. *805*
—. Alliances (review article). British Empire. Louis, William Roger. Thorne, Christopher. World War II. 1941-45. *854*
—. American Council on Japan. Economic Policy. Foreign Policy. Lobbying. Military Occupation. 1945-50's. *873*
—. American Council on Japan. Foreign Policy. Lobbying. 1947-52. *894*
—. Americanology. Historiography (review article). National self-image. Social conditions. 19c-20c. 1969-73. *722*
—. Americans. Literature, popular. 1934-73. *755*
—. Amphibious operations. World War II. 1942-45. *725*
—. Annexation. Hawaii. Treaties. 1897. *821*
—. Antitrust. Automobile Industry and Trade. Federal Policy. Imports. Protectionism. 1981-83. *982*
—. ANZUS. Australia. National Security. New Zealand. Treaties. 1951-81. *936*
—. ANZUS. Defense Policy. Foreign Relations. 1945-78. *937*
—. Appeasement (proposal). Diplomacy. Great Britain. World War II. 1941. *680*
—. Arab States. Oil Industry and Trade. 1970's. *778*
—. Arab-Israeli Conflict. Conflict and Conflict Resolution. Decisionmaking. Foreign Policy. World War II. 1941-45. 1967-73. *600*
—. Archives. China. Korea. Missions and Missionaries. Presbyterian Historical Society. 1829-1911. *39*
—. Armies. Marines. Peleliu (battle). Sledge, Eugene B. (account). World War II. 1944. *907*
—. Arms Trade (prohibited). China. Civil war. Western Nations. 1919-29. *17*

—. Armstrong, David M. (personal account). Hawaii. Pearl Harbor (attack). World War II. 1942. *580*
—. *Asama* (vessel). Mexico (Baja California, Turtle Bay). Tuchman, Barbara. 1915. *663*
—. Asia. Balance of power. China. Foreign Policy. 1950's-74. *112*
—. Asia. Balance of power. China. USSR. 1970-73. *80*
—. Asia. Foreign Relations. 1945-72. *110*
—. Asia. Historiography, US. Revolutionary movements. USSR. World War II. 1930's-49. *862*
—. Asia, East. Balance of Power. China. Foreign policy. 1968-73. *133*
—. Asia, East. Economic problems. Foreign Relations. Political Leadership. Tanaka, Kakuei. 1971-74. *883*
—. Asia, East. Foreign Policy. 1948-78. *694*
—. Asia, East. Foreign Policy. Korea. Nixon Doctrine. Vietnam. 1969-73. *90*
—. Asia, East. Foreign Policy. World War II (antecedents). 1931-41. *687*
—. Asia, North. Documents. Geography. Geology. 1848-83. *99*
—. Asia, Southeast. Economic development. Foreign Policy. Fukuda, Takeo. 1978. *676*
—. Asia, Southeast. Foreign Policy. 1945-73. *688*
—. Associated Japan-America Societies of the United States. Cultural relations. Georgia. International Trade. 1979-82. *958*
—. Associations. Gentlemen's Agreement. Immigrants. Japanese Americans. 1907-26. *717*
—. Atlantic Community. Energy policy. 1972-73. *777*
—. Atomic Bomb. Barnouw, Erik. *Hiroshima-Nagasaki, August 1945* (film). 1945-70. *588*
—. Atomic bomb. Military Strategy. Truman, Harry S. World War II. 1945. *602*
—. Atomic bomb. Public opinion. World War II. 1945-49. *984*
—. Atomic energy. Military Strategy. Smyth Report, 1945. USA. World War II. 1940-45. *908*
—. Atomic Warfare. History Teaching. Simulation and Games. World War II. 1945. 1978. *658*
—. Atomic Warfare. Leftists. USSR. World War II. 1945. *610*
—. Atomic Warfare. Military strategy. World War II. 1945. *714*
—. Atomic Warfare. Politics. Surrender. Truman, Harry S. (administration). World War II. 1945. *604*
—. Attitudes. Authors. USA. World War II. 1940-49. *815*
—. Attitudes. Custer, Elizabeth Bacon. Travel accounts. 1903. *955*
—. Attitudes. Democracy. Europe. Interest Groups. Nuclear Science and Technology. USSR. 1970's. *731*
—. Attitudes. High Schools. Yasuteru, Aoki. 1970's. *814*
—. Attitudes. Intellectuals. ca 1945-75. *897*
—. Attu (battle). Tatsuguchi, Paul Nobuo (diary). USA. World War II. 1941-43. *963*
—. Australia. Canada. Europe. Unemployment. USA. 1972-73. *911*
—. Australia. Circumnavigations. Foreign Relations. Warships. 1908. *878*
—. Australia. Foreign policy. International Trade. New Zealand. 1968-70's. *41*
—. Australia. Italy. Netherlands. Political information. Voting and Voting Behavior. 1960's-70's. *716*
—. Australia. Peace settlement. World War II. 1942-46. *597*
—. Autobiography. Franklin, Benjamin. Fukuzawa, Yukichi. 1980. *962*

260 Japan

—. Automation. 1970-81. *650*
—. Automobile Industry and Trade. Canada. Europe, Western. Gindon, Sam (interview). Labor. World car (concept). 1945-80. *1006*
—. Automobile Industry and Trade. Competition. Europe. Industry. 1969-73. *649*
—. Automobile Industry and Trade. Europe, Western. 1973-80. *611*
—. Automobile Industry and Trade. Imports. 1975-81. *618*
—. Automobile Industry and Trade. Trade Regulations. 1971-81. *857*
—. Automobiles. Foreign Policy. Imports. Trade Regulations. 1970-81. *727*
—. *Awa Maru* (vessel). Navies. *Queenfish* (submarine). World War II. 1945. *912*
—. Balance of Payments. International Trade. 1977-81. *844*
—. Balance of power. China. Foreign Relations. 1970's. *1*
—. Balance of power. Foreign policy. Military Aid. 1945-77. *657*
—. Balloons, armed. Project FUGO. South Dakota. World War II. 1944-45. *770*
—. Banking. Europe. Monopolies. ca 1950's-70's. *944*
—. Baseball. Democracy. Values. 1920-41. *637*
—. Baseball. Foreign Relations. 1875-1900. *874*
—. Behavior. Communications. Television. 1972-81. *729*
—. Biddle, James. Naval missions. Negotiations. 1845-54. *590*
—. Biddle, James. Pacific Area. Spain. Taguchi Ukichi. 1846-90's. *773*
—. Bikini Atoll. Hydrogen bomb. *Lucky Dragon* (vessel). Pacific Dependencies (US). 1954-75. *882*
—. Blockades. Chamberlain, Neville. China. Great Britain. Roosevelt, Franklin D. World War II (antecedents). 1937-38. *686*
—. Bombing. B-29 (aircraft). China-Burma-India Theater. Close, Winton R. Personal narratives. World War II. 1944. *633*
—. Bombing. World War II. 1937-45. *639*
—. Bombs, balloon-carried. Pacific Northwest. World War II. 1945. *733*
—. Books, miniature. Europe. Publishers and Publishing. 15c-20c. *856*
—. Bribery. Liberal Democratic Party. Lockheed Aircraft Corporation. 1975-81. *766*
—. British Typewriter Museum (Wilfred Beeching collection). Europe, Western. Typewriter. 1711-1970's. *672*
—. Brooke, John Mercer. *Kanrin Maru* (vessel). Navies. Trade. Treaties. Voyages. 1860. *615*
—. Brown, Irving. Labor policy. Military Occupation. 1945-72. *926*
—. Business. Cold War. Foreign policy. Press. 1948-52. *704*
—. Business. Germany, West. Prices. 1980. *682*
—. Business. Lawyers. Sony Company. 1982. *822*
—. Business Cycles. Canada. Elections. Europe, Western. Federal Policy. 1955-80. *930*
—. Business Cycles. Economic Structure. Europe, Western. Great Britain. 1967-80. *959*
—. Business History. Comparative analysis. Enterprises, large-scale. Europe, Western. 19c-20c. *629*
—. Butow, R. J. Diplomacy, private. John Doe Associates. Peace (review article). World War II (antecedents). 1940-41. *723*
—. California. Foreign Investments. 1975-80. *707*
—. California (San Francisco). *Kanrin Maru* (vessel). Treaties. 1860. *990*
—. Canada. China. Diplomatic relations. Economic development. Foreign policy. Taiwan. 1949-72. *1175*

—. Canada. Europe. Labor costs. Manufacturing. Productivity. 1974-81. *624*
—. Canada. Europe, Western. Labor. Manufacturing. Productivity. 1960-82. *576*
—. Canada. Fur trade. Sea otters. Wildlife Conservation. 18c-20c. *988*
—. Canada. Historians. Norman, E. Herbert (review article). 1940-77. *859*
—. Capitalism. Competition. 1968-80. *828*
—. Capitalism. Economic conditions. Europe, Western. Great Britain. 1970-80. *996*
—. Carlson, Evans. China. Intelligence mission. Roosevelt, Franklin D. 1937-38. *40*
—. Carlson, Evans. China. Intelligence mission. Roosevelt, Franklin D. 1937-38. *128*
—. Carney, Robert B. Personal Narratives. Surrender. World War II. 1945. *626*
—. Caroline Islands. Ellis, Earl. Marines. Naval strategy. 1920-23. *956*
—. Carter, Jimmy (administration). Defense Policy. 1978-79. *677*
—. Carter, Jimmy (administration). Detente. Developing nations. Europe, Western. Foreign policy. USSR. 1977-80. *939*
—. Carter, Jimmy (administration). Foreign Policy. Korea, South. Military Ground Forces (withdrawal). 1950's-78. *131*
—. Censorship. *Chicago Tribune.* Cryptography. Midway (battle). Reporters and Reporting. World War II. 1942. *679*
—. Censorship. *Chicago Tribune.* Grand Juries. Midway (battle). Navies. World War II. 1942. *669*
—. Centennial. 1876. *667*
—. China. Christianity. Democracy. Foreign Policy. Missions and Missionaries. Socialism. 1830-1979. *125*
—. China. Cohen, Warren I. (review article). Foreign policy. Leadership. Public opinion. ca 1900-50. 1978. *26*
—. China. Detente. Nixon, Richard M. (visit). 1971. *79*
—. China. Diplomacy. Foreign Investments. Great Britain. World War I. 1915-17. *28*
—. China. Diplomacy. Foreign policy. Nixon, Richard M. 1971-72. *91*
—. China. Diplomacy. Stuart, John Leighton. USA. 1937-41. *118*
—. China. Diplomatic relations. 1972-77. *81*
—. China. *Far Eastern Review* (newspaper). Foreign Policy. Rea, George Bronson. 1904-36. *59*
—. China. Foreign Policy. Nixon, Richard M. 1971-73. *135*
—. China. Foreign Policy. Public opinion. World War II. 1937-45. *65*
—. China. Foreign Relations. 1978-81. *68*
—. China. Foreign Relations. 1978. *106*
—. China. Foreign Relations. Industry. Korea. USSR. 1970-76. *95*
—. China. Foreign Relations. International Trade. 1979. *87*
—. China. Foreign Relations. Korea, North. Korea, South. Unification. USSR. 1970's-. *20*
—. China. Foreign Relations. Korea, South. Military. Taiwan. 1960-80. *56*
—. China. Foreign relations. Taiwan. USSR. 1972. *78*
—. China. Foreign Relations. USSR. 1970's. *107*
—. China. Foreign Relations. USSR. 1970's. *594*
—. China. Foreign Relations. USSR. 1981-84. *111*
—. China. Great Britain. International Relations (discipline). USSR. 1937-49. *437*
—. China. International Security. Treaties. 1977-78. *84*
—. China. Kinney, John F. Marines. Prisoners of War. Wake Island. World War II. 1941-45. *943*

Japan

—. China. Korea, South. Public Opinion. Taiwan. Treaties, mutual defense. 1950's-77. *126*
—. China. League of Nations. Paris Peace Conference. Wilson, Woodrow. 1919. *85*
—. China. Press. Public opinion. Sino-Japanese war. USA. 1894-95. *53*
—. China (Shandong). Diplomacy. Hughes, Charles Evans. Washington Conference. 1919-22. *863*
—. China (Shanghai). Marines. Photographs. 1920's-30's. *569*
—. *Christian Century* (periodical). Foreign policy. Manchurian crisis. Morrison, Charles C. 1931-33. *96*
—. Civil war. Meiji Restoration. 1860-70. *879*
—. *Clarissa B. Carver* (vessel). Courts. Dow, Leroy. *Glamorganshire* (vessel). Lawsuits. Ships. 1885-86. *870*
—. Clark Field. Philippines. World War II. 1941-42. *788*
—. Coffee, John M. Congress. Embargoes. Schellenbach, Lewis B. Washington. 1930's-40. *780*
—. Colby, Abby M. Congregationalism. Feminism. Missions and Missionaries. 1879-1914. *928*
—. Colleges and Universities. Democracy. Military government. Virginia, University of (School of Military Government). 1944-45. *971*
—. Colleges and Universities. Educational Theory. Military Occupation. Senroku Uehara *(University)*. US Education Mission to Japan. 1945-62. *728*
—. Colleges and Universities. Sapporo Agricultural College. Science. Teachers. Tokyo, University of. 1860-1900. *961*
—. Colonialism. Educational Policy. Germany. Mariana Islands. Spain. ca 1688-1940. *698*
—. Combat Information Unit. Cryptography. Midway (battle). Navies. World War II. 1942. *858*
—. Communications. Great Britain. Naval Strategy. World War II. 1943-45. *652*
—. Communism. Containment. Foreign Policy. 1945-50. *892*
—. Competition. Europe, Western. 1960's-70's. *575*
—. Competition. Germany, West. International Trade. Manufactures. 1970's. *797*
—. Congress. Manchurian crisis. Public opinion. 1931-33. *83*
—. Congress. Protectionism. 1981-82. *896*
—. Congress. World War II (antecedents). 1940-41. *779*
—. Constitutional reform. Military occupation. Politics. 1945-52. *577*
—. Constitutions. MacArthur, Douglas. Military Occupation. Political tradition. 1945-76. *804*
—. Cotton. Great Britain. India. Textile Industry. 1870-1939. *987*
—. Councils and Synods. Methodist Protestant Church. Missions and Missionaries. 1880-92. *762*
—. Crawford, David L. Hawaii, University of. Peace pact (proposed). USA. 1940-41. *713*
—. Creighton, John Marie. Intervention. Military Intelligence. USSR (Eastern Siberia). 1922. *44*
—. Creoles. Folklore. Hearn, Lafcadio. Louisiana (New Orleans). Martinique. 1850-1904. *803*
—. Crime. Social Organization. 1948-70's. *591*
—. Cruisers. Design. Navies. 1925-27. *978*
—. Cryptography. Guadalcanal (battle). Military Intelligence. Radio. World War II. 1942. *810*
—. Cultural Imperialism. Foreign Relations. Mutsuhito, Emperor. Seward, William H. 1870-71. *705*
—. Cultural relations. 1856-1900. *877*
—. Cyclotrons. Denmark. Nuclear physics. Scientific Experiments and Research. 1935-45. *965*

—. Daily Life. Hostages. Letters. Navies. Rescues. 1846-49. *771*
—. Defense Policy. Foreign Relations. 1979-81. *834*
—. Defense Policy. Foreign Relations. 1980-83. *651*
—. Dependency. Korea, South. Political economy. 1973. *1041*
—. Destroyer escorts. *England* (vessel). Submarine Warfare. Williamson, John A. (account). World War II. 1944. *972*
—. Detente. Foreign policy. Trade. USSR. 1971-74. *749*
—. Developing nations. Economic issues. Roll-call voting. UN General Assembly. Western Nations. 1970-76. *966*
—. Developing nations. European Economic Community. Tariff protection. 1960's-70's. *986*
—. Developing nations. Great Britain. Manufacturing. Subcontracting. 1966-76. *899*
—. Diaries. Norquist, Ernest O. Prisoners. Prisoners of War. World War II. 1942-45. *837*
—. Diffusion. Information. 1830's-1970's. *869*
—. Diffusion. Semiconductors. Technology. 1982. *876*
—. Diplomacy. Europe. World War II (antecedents; review article). 1930's-41. *700*
—. Diplomacy. Fishing. State Department. 1936-39. *947*
—. Diplomacy. Foreign policy. International Trade. World War II (antecedents). 1937-41. *946*
—. Diplomacy. Hornbeck, Stanley K. World War II (antecedents). 1937-41. *775*
—. Diplomacy. Hull, Cordell. Indochina. Philippines. World War II (antecedents). 1941. *616*
—. Diplomacy. International Trade. Perry, Matthew C. 1853. *783*
—. Diplomacy. Konoe Fumimaro. 1934-41. *715*
—. Diplomacy. MacArthur, Douglas. Philippines (Manila). Surrender. World War II. 1945. *812*
—. Diplomacy. Military Intelligence. Roosevelt, Franklin D. World War II (antecedents). 1940-41. *693*
—. Diplomacy. Yōsuke, Matsuoka. 1940-41. *738*
—. Diplomatic recognition. Manchuria. Stimson, Henry L. 1931-34. *991*
—. Dissertations. Educational reform. Historiography. Military Occupation. 1950-80. *940*
—. District of Columbia. Energy Conference (report). Europe, Western. Foreign Policy. 1974. *1005*
—. Dixon, Robert E. Johnston, Stanley. Midway (battle). Military Strategy. Personal narratives. Reporters and Reporting. World War II. 1942. *794*
—. Documents. Military Occupation. 1945-47. *598*
—. Dollar stabilization. Economic Policy. Germany, West. 1945-78. *801*
—. Dull, Paul S. (review article). Naval Strategy. Pearl Harbor. World War II. Yamamoto, Isoroku. 1941-45. *941*
—. Dumping. International Trade. Public Opinion. Steel. 1974-78. *745*
—. Economic aid. Vietnam War. 1960-75. *696*
—. Economic Conditions. Federal Policy. International Trade. 1945-83. *868*
—. Economic Conditions. Foreign policy. International Trade (relations). 1945-74. *927*
—. Economic Conditions. Foreign Relations. 1982. *787*
—. Economic Conditions. Foreign Relations. Pacific free trade area. 1945-74. *71*
—. Economic Conditions. Great Britain. Military Occupation. Political Systems. 1945-49. *617*
—. Economic Conditions. International Trade. 1970-81. *684*
—. Economic Conditions. Military occupation. Ryukyu Islands (Okinawa). 1952-79. *950*

262   Japan

—. Economic development. Employment, permanent. Social Theory. 1973. *635*
—. Economic development. Europe, Western. Protectionism. Trade. 1948-80. *866*
—. Economic development. Foreign Relations. Germany, West. 1973-76. *809*
—. Economic development. Great Britain. Thailand. 1926-80. *102*
—. Economic development. Oriental Bank Corporation. Schiff, Jacob. Williams, George B. Wilson, James H. Winslow, Edward F. 1872-73. *606*
—. Economic Development. Supply. 1975-82. *630*
—. Economic Growth. 1952-74. *734*
—. Economic growth. 1952-74. *735*
—. Economic growth. Europe. Foreign Relations. Military Aid. 1970's. *601*
—. Economic growth. National Security. 1950's-82. *654*
—. Economic History. Historiography. 1600-1945. ca 1970-77. *980*
—. Economic Policy. Foreign policy. Military. Politics. 1945-72. *919*
—. Economic Policy. Foreign Policy. Military Occupation. 1945-49. *895*
—. Economic Policy. Foreign Relations. 1970's-80. *708*
—. Economic Policy. Foreign Relations. 1978-80. *751*
—. Economic Policy. Germany, West. GNP. Inflation. Protectionism. 1976-78. *709*
—. Economic policy. Naval strategy. Pacific Dependencies (US). USA. 1945-75. *623*
—. Economic relations. 1972-78. *920*
—. Economic Structure. Foreign investments. New York City. 1960's-70's. *675*
—. Economic trends, world. Europe, Western. 1970-75. *973*
—. Economic war. International trade. 1970's. *614*
—. Educational exchange programs. Fulbright program. 1982. *981*
—. Ellis, Earl. Marines. Micronesia. Military Intelligence. 1911-23. *584*
—. Embargoes. Foreign Policy. Oil. Roosevelt, Franklin D. 1941. *578*
—. Emigration. Social conditions. 1866-1924. *957*
—. Energy. Food. International Security. Natural resources. Nuclear Power. 1970's-80. *979*
—. Energy. Foreign Relations. Investments. 1970's. *851*
—. Energy Action Group. Europe. Foreign Relations. North America. 1973-. *756*
—. Equality (proposed). Hughes, William Morris. League of Nations Covenant. Paris Peace Conference. Race Relations. Wilson, Woodrow. 1919. *772*
—. Eugenics. Genetics. Social organization. 1920's-30's. *923*
—. Europe. Foreign policy. 1970's. *832*
—. Europe. Foreign policy. Military strategy. Vietnam War. 1970's. *910*
—. Europe. Foreign policy. Neocolonialism. Organization of Petroleum Exporting Countries. 1969-70's. *855*
—. Europe. Foreign policy. Offner, Arnold A. World War II (antecedents; review article). 1917-41. *829*
—. Europe. Foreign Relations. 1974. *116*
—. Europe. Foreign Relations. Persian Gulf and Area. Tucker, Robert W. (interview). 1968-80. *998*
—. Europe. Monetary Systems. Multinational corporations. USA. 1967-73. *924*
—. Europe. Research and development. Technology. ca 1964-76. *574*
—. Europe. Warships. 1850-1930's. *845*
—. Europe, Western. Finance. Imperialism. Industry. Latin America. Trade. 1970's. *768*

—. Europe, Western. Foreign Policy. International Security. Military Capability. 1980-82. *889*
—. Europe, Western. Foreign Policy. International Trade. Rockefeller family. Trilateral Commission. 1973-78. *995*
—. Europe, Western. Foreign Policy. Trilateralism. 1950's-70's. *945*
—. Europe, Western. Foreign Relations. Trilateral Commission. 1973-82. *872*
—. Europe, Western. Inflation. 1958-68. *974*
—. Europe, Western. International Trade. Monetary systems. 1970's. *681*
—. Europe, Western. Monopolies. Oil industry and Trade. Organization of Petroleum Exporting Countries. 1970's. *871*
—. Europe, Western. Mutual Balanced Force Reductions. Strategic Arms Limitation Talks. USSR. 1974. *1002*
—. Europe, Western. Oil industry and trade. 1960's-70's. *847*
—. Europe, Western. Political Theory. Trilateralism. 1970's. *954*
—. Europe, Western. Public services. Trilateral Commission. Wages. 1973-79. *925*
—. Europe, Western. Technology. 1960-75. *827*
—. Europe, Western. Trade. 1970's. *665*
—. Europe, Western. Trilateralism. 1970's. *796*
—. European Economic Community. Generalized System of Preferences. Tariff. 1966-75. *595*
—. European Economic Community. Germany, West. Oil crisis. Trade. 1974. *647*
—. European Economic Community. International Trade. Monetary policy (devaluation). Nixon, Richard M. 1971-73. *655*
—. European Economic Community. Trilateral Commission. 1973-77. *636*
—. Expansionism, Japanese. Korea. Sill, John M. B. 1894-97. *1028*
—. Exports. Foreign policy. Oil. State Department. 1940-41. *948*
—. Exports. Great Britain. Oil Industry and Trade. Roosevelt, Franklin D. World War II. 1940-41. *659*
—. Faulkner, William. Shellenberger, Jack H. (account). Travel. US Information Agency. 1955. *900*
—. Federal Policy. Frontier and Pioneer Life. Indians. Military Strategy. Taiwan. 18c-1915. *70*
—. Federal Policy. Journalism. Nuclear arms. Secrecy. 1983. *792*
—. Fermi National Accelerator Laboratory. Kō Enerugii Butsurigaku Kenkyusho. Nationalism. Physics. 1930-69. *706*
—. Films. *The Magnificent Seven* (film). National Characteristics. *Seven Samurai* (film). 1960's. *836*
—. Folk art. Origami. Popular Culture. 1900-76. *593*
—. Foreign Investments. 1930-52. *969*
—. Foreign investments. Manufactures. 1950's-70's. *875*
—. Foreign policy. 1970's. *631*
—. Foreign Policy. 1977-78. *101*
—. Foreign Policy. Gulick, Sidney Lewis. Missions and Missionaries. 1914-45. *929*
—. Foreign policy. Hull, Cordell. Roosevelt, Franklin D. Stimson, Henry L. 1933-36. *730*
—. Foreign Policy. International politics. Okinawa. 1853-1972. *718*
—. Foreign policy. International Trade. Military Occupation. 1945-74. *808*
—. Foreign Policy. Kim Dae Jung case. Korea. 1973. *136*
—. Foreign policy. Korea. 1960's-82. *1140*
—. Foreign Policy. Korea. Roosevelt, Theodore. Russia. 1901-05. *1057*

Japan

—. Foreign Policy. Korea. Sino-Japanese War. 1894-95. *76*
—. Foreign Policy. Netherlands East Indies. World War II. 1941-46. *710*
—. Foreign Policy. Oil industry and Trade. 1934-37. *819*
—. Foreign Policy. Treaties. 1853-58. *685*
—. Foreign Policy. Vietnam War. 1965-73. *742*
—. Foreign Policy. World War II (antecedents). 1940-41. *599*
—. Foreign policy. Yoshida Shigeru. 1945-78. *835*
—. Foreign Policy (review article). Gardner, Lloyd C. LaFeber, Walter F. McCormick, Thomas J. USA. 1776-1973. *581*
—. Foreign relations. 1900-72. *850*
—. Foreign Relations. 1931-41. *666*
—. Foreign Relations. 1945-75. *887*
—. Foreign Relations. 1960's-73. *825*
—. Foreign Relations. 1965-74. *108*
—. Foreign Relations. 1968-72. *826*
—. Foreign Relations. 1976-78. *886*
—. Foreign Relations. Gayn, Mark *(Japan Diary)*. Military occupation. 1945-81. *880*
—. Foreign Relations. Gray, John Chipman. Holmes, Oliver Wendell. Kaneko Kentarō. Law. Letters. Thayer, James Bradley. 1878-1924. *741*
—. Foreign Relations. Great Britain. Thailand. World War II. 1942-46. *970*
—. Foreign Relations. Great Britain. War debts. 1920-23. *646*
—. Foreign Relations. Harris, Townsend. 1856-58. *830*
—. Foreign Relations. International trade. 1930's-70's. *888*
—. Foreign Relations. International Trade. 1970's-83. *720*
—. Foreign Relations. International Trade. 1970's-83. *849*
—. Foreign Relations. International Trade. Military Capability. Trade. 1970's-82. *833*
—. Foreign Relations. John Doe Associates. 1936-41. *902*
—. Foreign Relations. King, William. Thomas, Elbert. Utah. ca 1922-40. *782*
—. Foreign relations. Korea. 1945-74. *67*
—. Foreign Relations. Korea, South. 1950-80. *89*
—. Foreign Relations. Lensen, George Alexander (review article). USSR. 1921-30. *831*
—. Foreign Relations. Militarism. 1945-73. *582*
—. Foreign Relations. Newspapers. 1900-78. *774*
—. Foreign Relations. Nixon Doctrine. 1945-72. *824*
—. Foreign Relations. Nuclear energy. 1974-82. *776*
—. Foreign Relations. Oil crisis. 1974. *906*
—. Foreign Relations. Okinawa. Public Opinion. Sato, Eisaku. 1969. *752*
—. Foreign Relations. Perry, Matthew C. Preble, G. W. (diary). 1852-54. *587*
—. Foreign Relations. Philippines. Quirino, Elpidio. Treaties. World War II. 1945-56. *748*
—. Foreign Relations. Pittman, Key. 1920-40. *781*
—. Foreign Relations. Press. 1969-71. *664*
—. Foreign relations. Trade. 1970's. *839*
—. Foreign Relations. Vietnam War. 1964-73. *750*
—. Foreign Relations. Yasukawa, Takeshi (speech). 1975. *983*
—. Foreign Relations (review article). 1876-1976. *711*
—. Germany. Libraries, Presidential. Military government. Research. 1945-78. *994*
—. Gilbert, Prentiss B. Kellogg-Briand Pact. League of Nations. Manchuria. Military Occupation. Stimson, Henry L. 1931. *34*
—. Grant, Julia Dent. Grant, Ulysses S. (visit). 1879. *1004*
—. Graves. Methodism. Missions and Missionaries. 1876-1957. *761*
—. Great Britain. Military Intelligence. Wiseman, William. World War I. World War II. 1914-45. *903*
—. Great Britain. Naval Strategy. Pacific Area. World War II. 1941-45. *589*
—. Great Britain. Wages. ca 1873-1981. *678*
—. Guadalcanal (battle). *I-19* (submarine). *North Carolina* (vessel). *O'Brien* (vessel). *Wasp* (vessel). World War II. 1942. *608*
—. Guadalcanal (battle). World War II. 1942-43. *852*
—. Guam (liberation). World War II. 1944. *625*
—. Hawaii. Kalakaua, David (travel diary). 1881. *793*
—. Hawaii. Naval Vessels. Pearl Harbor. World War II. 1941. *1000*
—. Hawaii. Pearl Harbor. World War II. 1941. *885*
—. Herde, Peter (review article). Pearl Harbor. World War II. 1941. *938*
—. Herndon, Hugh. Pangborn, Clyde. Transpacific flight. USA. 1930-71. *864*
—. Higher Education (power structure). 1968-73. *757*
—. Historians, Western. Military defeat. USSR. World War II. 1942-45. *890*
—. Historiography. Military occupation. 1945-52. *820*
—. Historiography. Modernization (review article). 1867-1977. *754*
—. Imperialism. Navigation. Pacific Area. Pearl Harbor. World War II (antecedents). Prehistory-1941. *648*
—. *Indianapolis* (vessel). *I-58* (vessel). Submarine Warfare. World War II. 1945. *612*
—. Industrial development. 1960's-70's. *758*
—. Industry. International Trade (deficit). 1970's. *573*
—. Intellectuals. 1890-1979. *712*
—. International Trade. 1980-82. *934*
—. International trade. 1981-82. *622*
—. Intervention (military). Russia. 1918-20. *55*
—. Invasions. Military Strategy. Operation Olympic. World War II. 1945. *645*
—. Inventions. Morrow, James. Travel (accounts). 1854. *823*
—. Iwo Jima. World War II. 1944-45. *736*
—. Junghans, Earl A. Marines. Personal narratives. Prisoners of War. Wake Island. War crimes. World War II. 1941-47. *737*
—. Katayama, Sen. Socialism. 1884-1932. *921*
—. Keene, Donald. Personal narratives. Scholarship. Social Customs. 1930's-80's. *746*
—. Korea. Military Occupation. Social Change. 1945-53. *904*
—. Labor movement. Military Occupation. 1945-52. *893*
—. Labor reform. Military Occupation. Wages. Working conditions. 1945-60. *918*
—. Letters. MacArthur, Douglas. Military occupation. 1947. *817*
—. Leyte (battle). Naval Warfare. World War II. 1944. *884*
—. Local government. Public Administration. Reform. 1940-69. *753*
—. Lockheed Aircraft Corporation. Political Corruption. 1976. *583*
—. London, Jack. Reporters and Reporting. Russo-Japanese War. 1904. *689*
—. Lutheran Church. Midsuno, Henry Signaro. Missions and Missionaries. 1870-1933. *993*
—. Makin Islands (raid). Marines (2d Raiders). Peatross, Oscar F. (account). Prisoners of War. World War II. 1942-47. *853*
—. Midway (battle). Military Strategy. World War II. 1942. *992*

Japan

—. Midway (battle). Navies. World War II. 1942. *621*
—. Military Occupation. 1945-60's. *891*
—. Military occupation. 1946-51. *695*
—. Military operations. Natural Resources. Oregon (Bly). Project FUGO. World War II. 1942-45. *861*
—. Military relations. Rearmament. 1946-70's. *975*
—. Military strategy. 1970-80. *674*
—. Military strategy. NATO. USSR. 1945-54. *813*
—. Military Strategy. Naval War College. War Plan Orange. 1900-12. *953*
—. Missions and Missionaries. Mormons. 1901-24. *613*
—. Missions and Missionaries. Personal Narratives. Protestantism. 1860-1905. *931*
—. Multinational corporations. Nixon, Richard M. Politics. ca 1948-76. *726*
—. Mysticism. Religion. Youth. 1976. *767*
—. National Security. Pacifism. 1945-82. *785*
—. Naval Tactics. Savo Island (battle). World War II. 1942. *596*
—. Naval Tactics. World War II. World War II. 1920's-43. *724*
—. Navies. 1907-08. *690*
—. Navies. Philippine Sea (battle). World War II. 1944. *619*
—. Navies. Shanghai crisis. Western nations. 1931-32. *458*
—. Navies. Solomon Islands (Vella Lavella). World War II. 1943. *784*
—. Okinawa. 1200-1975. *799*
—. Pacific Area. Russia. 1900's-79. *673*
—. Peace. Potsdam Conference. Surrender, unconditional. World War II. 1945. *952*
—. Pearl Harbor (attack). World War II. 1940-41. *846*
—. Political attitudes. Radicals and Radicalism. Students. 1960's-70's. *760*
—. Political systems. Pollution abatement. USSR. 1950's-74. *747*
—. Public opinion. Vietnam War. 1960's-70's. *909*
—. Quilts. 1876-1900. *802*
—. Robots. Technology. 1965-83. *800*
—. Sherrod, Robert (memoirs). Tarawa (battle). World War II. 1944. *901*
—. Television sets. Trade adjustment policy. 1970-78. *806*
—. Trade. 1970-77. *951*
—. Travel accounts. ca 1850-1975. *739*
—. World War II (antecedents). 1930's. *1007*
Japan (Bonin Islands). *Gregory* (vessel). McCandless, Bruce (reminiscences). Navies. World War II. 1945. *798*
Japan (Hiroshima). Air Forces. Atomic bomb. Military training. Personal narratives. Tibbets, Paul W. World War II. 1945. *932*
—. Alperovitz, Gar (review article). Atomic Warfare. Decisionmaking. Historiography. World War II. 1945-65. *898*
—. Atomic bomb. Charities. Surgery. Women. World War II. 1945-57. *985*
—. Atomic Warfare. Cold War. World War II. 1945. *744*
Japan (Hiroshima, Nagasaki). Atomic bomb. Documents. World War II. 1945. *867*
—. Atomic bomb. Truman, Harry S. World War II. 1942-47. *605*
—. Atomic Bomb Casualty Commission. Civilians. Medical Research. Radiation Effects Research Foundation. 1945-75. *960*
—. Atomic Warfare. Decisionmaking. Military Strategy. World War II. 1944-45. *671*
—. Atomic Warfare. Military Strategy. Surrender, unconditional. World War II. 1943-45. *703*
—. Atomic warfare. Military Strategy. World War II. 1945. *603*

Japan (Hokkaido). Capron, Horace. Economic Development. Modernization. 1871-75. *811*
Japan (Kumamoto). Christianity. Janes, Leroy Lansing. 1838-76. *838*
Japan (Kyoto). Atomic Warfare. World War II. 1945. *848*
—. Bombing exemption. Stimson, Henry L. World War II. 1940-45. *628*
Japan (review article). Economic Conditions. Nakamura Takahide. Politics. 1945-49. *740*
Japan (Shimonoseki Strait). Americans (protected). McDougal, David. Naval battles. *Wyoming* (vessel). 1863. *683*
Japan (Shizuoka, Tokyo). Clark, Edward Warren. Cultural relations. Missions and Missionaries. Nakamura Masanao. ca1870-1907. *721*
Japan studies. Colleges and Universities. Educational Exchange Programs. 1973. *697*
Japan (Tokyo). American Tobacco Company. Government ownership. Parrish, Edward James. Tobacco. 1899-1904. *656*
—. Diplomacy. Embassy, US. 1941. *661*
—. Diplomacy. Emmerson, John K. Memoirs. State Department. World War II (antecedents). 1941. *662*
Japan (Yokohama). Klein, Frederick C. Methodist Protestant Church. Missions and Missionaries. 1880-93. *763*
Japanese. Blacks. Immigration restriction. Miller, Kelly. Race Relations. 1906-24. *699*
—. Canada. Internment (conference). World War II. 1941-45. 1978. *922*
—. Diplomats. Pennsylvania (Bedford). Prisoners of War. World War II. 1945. *586*
—. Discrimination. Peru. 1931-43. *632*
—. Korea. Koreans. Military government. Repatriation. 1945-48. *1018*
—. Prisoners of war. World War II. 1941-45. *759*
Japanese American Citizens League. Citizenship. Ford, Gerald R. Hada, John. Pardon. Tokyo Rose (Iva Toguri d'Aquino). Uyeda, Clifford I. (account). 1973-77. *949*
—. Generations. Internment. Patriotism. World War II. 1941-42. *913*
Japanese American Research Project. Miyakawa, T. Scott. 1906-81. *881*
Japanese Americans. Acculturation. Internment. Social Conditions. 1945-55. *743*
—. Adams, Ansel. California. Internment. Lange, Dorothea. Manzanar War Relocation Center. Photography, Journalistic. World War II. 1941-45. *840*
—. Arizona. Gila River Relocation Center. Public Opinion. Race Relations. World War II. 1942-45. *627*
—. Arkansas (Rowher Camp). Internment. World War II. 1942-45. *592*
—. Associations. Gentlemen's Agreement. Immigrants. Japan. 1907-26. *717*
—. Attitudes. Canada. Internment. Japanese Canadians. World War II. 1940-80. *642*
—. Attitudes. Sociology. Values. World War II. 1940's-70's. *915*
—. Bohme, Frederick G. Census Bureau. Letters. Relocation. World War II. 1942-45. *640*
—. California. Concentration Camps. Manzanar War Relocation Center. Riots. Ueno, Harry (arrest). World War II. 1942. *691*
—. California. Detention. Racism. World War II. 1941-45. *818*
—. California. Relocation. Warren, Earl. World War II. 1941-45. *967*
—. Canada. Ethnicity. Internment. Japanese Canadians. Joint Board of Defense. World War II. 1941-42. *641*
—. Chinese Americans. Literature. 1850-1980. *13*

Korea   265

—. Civil rights. Counterintelligence. Internment. Munson, Curtis B. Peiper, N. J. L. World War II. 1931-42. *765*
—. Concentration Camps. Public schools. World War II. 1942-45. *977*
—. Concentration camps. Racism. World War II. 1940-45. *719*
—. Concentration Camps. World War II. 1942-46. *842*
—. Daily Life. Internment. Kurose, Aki Kato. Washington (Seattle). World War II. 1930's-50's. *644*
—. Daily Life. Internment. Personal narratives. Uchida, Yoshiko. Utah (Topaz). World War II. 1942-43. *942*
—. Documentation. Evacuations. Internment. Photographs. War Relocation Authority. World War II. 1941-43. *643*
—. Idaho (Minidoka). Mukaida, Tomeji (reminiscences). Relocation. World War II. 1940's. *789*
—. Internment. Letters. World War II. 1942. *914*
—. Internment. Martial law. Tule Lake Camp. World War II. 1941-44. *843*
—. Internment. Mirikitani, Janice ("Lullaby"). Poetry. World War II. 1941-45. *609*
—. Internment. New Mexico (Clovis). World War II. 1942-45. *638*
—. Internment. Oral history. Tanaka, Togo. World War II. Yoneda, Elaine. Yoneda, Karl. 1941-45. *816*
—. Internment. Personal narratives. World War II. 1942-81. *1001*
—. Internment. Propaganda. World War II. 1942-45. *841*
Japanese Americans (Nisei). Language School. Military Intelligence. Minnesota. Rasmussen, Kai E. World War II. 1941-46. *579*
Japanese Canadians. Attitudes. Canada. Internment. Japanese Americans. World War II. 1940-80. *642*
—. Canada. Ethnicity. Internment. Japanese Americans. Joint Board of Defense. World War II. 1941-42. *641*
Japanese control. Military Government. Okinawa. 1945-72. *807*
Japanese language. Dumas, Harold. Marines. World War II. 1944-45. *791*
Japanese Lines, Ltd. v. County of Los Angeles. California (Los Angeles). Containerization. Supreme Court. Tariff. 1970-79. *585*
Japanese Peruvians. Diplomacy. Emmerson, John K. Internment. Memoirs. Peru. World War II. 1942-43. *660*
Japan/United States Textbook Study Project. Attitudes. History. Textbooks. 1981. *999*
Jefferson, Thomas. China. Historiography (Chinese). Liu Zuochang. Virginia, University of. 1770-1826. 1976-81. *321*
Jiang Jieshi. China. Diplomacy. Hurley, Patrick J. Mao Zedong. State Department. Vincent, John Carter. 1944-45. *358*
—. China. Foreign Policy. Vandenberg, Arthur Hendrick, Sr. 1945-50. *255*
—. China. Foreign Relations. Military aid. 1948-50. *1176*
—. China. Marshall, George C. Military General Staff. Stilwell, Joseph W. World War II. 1944. *475*
—. China. Military strategy. Stilwell, Joseph W. World War II. 1942-44. *397*
John Doe Associates. Butow, R. J. Diplomacy, private. Japan. Peace (review article). World War II (antecedents). 1940-41. *723*
—. Foreign Relations. Japan. 1936-41. *902*

Johnston, Stanley. Dixon, Robert E. Japan. Midway (battle). Military Strategy. Personal narratives. Reporters and Reporting. World War II. 1942. *794*
Joint Board of Defense. Canada. Ethnicity. Internment. Japanese Americans. Japanese Canadians. World War II. 1941-42. *641*
Jones, William Patterson. China. Diaries. Diplomats. 1862-68. *331*
Journalism. Federal Policy. Japan. Nuclear arms. Secrecy. 1983. *792*
Junghans, Earl A. Japan. Marines. Personal narratives. Prisoners of War. Wake Island. War crimes. World War II. 1941-47. *737*

K

Kahn, E. J., Jr. (review article). China. Foreign Relations. Politics. State Department (Foreign Service). 1940's-50's. 1975. *384*
Kalakaua, David (travel diary). Hawaii. Japan. 1881. *793*
Kaneko Kentarō. Foreign Relations. Gray, John Chipman. Holmes, Oliver Wendell. Japan. Law. Letters. Thayer, James Bradley. 1878-1924. *741*
Kanrin Maru (vessel). Brooke, John Mercer. Japan. Navies. Trade. Treaties. Voyages. 1860. *615*
—. California (San Francisco). Japan. Treaties. 1860. *990*
Karnebeek, Hermann Adriaan van. Asia, East. Diplomacy. Four-Power Treaty. Netherlands. Washington Conference. 1921-22. *9*
Karns, A. P. Locke, Robert D. (interview). Oil well. Taiwan. 1877-78. *272*
Katayama, Sen. Japan. Socialism. 1884-1932. *921*
Keenan, Barry. China. Dewey, John. Educational Reform (review article). Leadership. 1919-30. 1977. *495*
Keene, Donald. Japan. Personal narratives. Scholarship. Social Customs. 1930's-80's. *746*
Kellogg-Briand Pact. Gilbert, Prentiss B. Japan. League of Nations. Manchuria. Military Occupation. Stimson, Henry L. 1931. *34*
Kenney, George. Air Forces. Japan. Rabaul (battle). World War II. 1943. *607*
Kerosene. China. Nationalism. Oil. Standard Oil Company of New York. Taxation. 1925-27. *541*
Keys of the Kingdom (film). China. Office of War Information. Propaganda. Stereotypes. World War II. 1940-45. *172*
Kim Dae Jung case. Foreign Policy. Japan. Korea. 1973. *136*
King, William. Foreign Relations. Japan. Thomas, Elbert. Utah. ca 1922-40. *782*
Kinney, John F. China. Japan. Marines. Prisoners of War. Wake Island. World War II. 1941-45. *943*
Kissinger, Henry A. China. Foreign Policy. Nixon, Richard M. 1960's-70's. *522*
—. China. Foreign policy. USSR. 1969-76. *276*
—. China. Foreign Relations (review article). Haldeman, H. R. Nixon, Richard M. 1968-76. *539*
Klein, Frederick C. Japan (Yokohama). Methodist Protestant Church. Missions and Missionaries. 1880-93. *763*
Knight, Charlotte (field report). Air Forces. Korean War. 1950. *1060*
Kō Enerugii Butsurigaku Kenkyusho. Fermi National Accelerator Laboratory. Japan. Nationalism. Physics. 1930-69. *706*
Kolko thesis (review article). Cold War revisionism. Foreign Policy. Korean War. 1949-50. *1147*
Konoe Fumimaro. Diplomacy. Japan. 1934-41. *715*
Korea. Allen, Horace. Diplomacy. Hawaii. Immigration. Sugar. 1902-05. *1101*

266 Korea

—. Archives. China. Japan. Missions and Missionaries. Presbyterian Historical Society. 1829-1911. *39*
—. Asia, East. Foreign Policy. Japan. Nixon Doctrine. Vietnam. 1969-73. *90*
—. Asiatic Squadron. Diplomacy. Navies. 1882-97. *1015*
—. Balance of Power. Foreign Aid. 1945-74. *1037*
—. Bibliographies. Dissertations. 1970-74. *1116*
—. Bibliographies. Dissertations. 1970-74. *1117*
—. Carter, Jimmy (administration). China. Foreign Policy. Taiwan. 1970's. *137*
—. Carter, Jimmy (administration). Foreign Policy. 1950-79. *1044*
—. Carter, Jimmy (administration). Foreign Policy. Military Ground Forces (withdrawal). 1977. *1124*
—. China. Communism. Containment. Foreign policy. Taiwan. 1945-50. *10*
—. China. Diplomacy. Low, Frederick F. 1869-74. *2*
—. China. Foreign policy. 1950-79. *94*
—. China. Foreign Policy. Stueck, William Whitney, Jr. (review article). 1947-50. *134*
—. China. Foreign Relations. Industry. Japan. USSR. 1970-76. *95*
—. China. Foreign relations. Taiwan. 1971-77. *115*
—. China. Foreign Relations. USSR. 1960's-82. *122*
—. China. Indochina. International crises. Laos. 1949-62. *345*
—. Communism. Foreign policy. Truman Doctrine. 1945-50. *43*
—. Cultural relations. Foreign Aid. 1882-1982. *1075*
—. Diaries. Naval officers. Woods, George W. 1884. *1127*
—. Diplomacy. Naval expedition. 1840-71. *1126*
—. Expansionism, Japanese. Japan. Sill, John M. B. 1894-97. *1028*
—. Foreign Policy. 1945-78. *1062*
—. Foreign policy. 1949-78. *1146*
—. Foreign Policy. 1973. *1054*
—. Foreign policy. 1979. *1107*
—. Foreign policy. Gresham, Walter Quintin. Sino-Japanese War. 1894-95. *38*
—. Foreign Policy. International Security. 1944-77. *1122*
—. Foreign policy. Japan. 1960's-82. *1140*
—. Foreign Policy. Japan. Kim Dae Jung case. 1973. *136*
—. Foreign Policy. Japan. Roosevelt, Theodore. Russia. 1901-05. *1057*
—. Foreign Policy. Japan. Sino-Japanese War. 1894-95. *76*
—. Foreign Policy. Military Aid. 1950's. *1012*
—. Foreign Policy. Partition. World War II. 1945. *1082*
—. Foreign policy. Treaties. 1882-1905. *69*
—. Foreign policy. Treaties. 1882-1905. *1056*
—. Foreign Policy. Unification. 1950's-70's. *1045*
—. Foreign Policy. World War II. 1941-45. *1083*
—. Foreign Relations. 1845-1980. *1076*
—. Foreign Relations. 1882-1979. *1094*
—. Foreign Relations. 1883-94. *1055*
—. Foreign relations. 1950-77. *1111*
—. Foreign Relations. International Trade. Military Strategy. 1905-79. *1100*
—. Foreign relations. Japan. 1945-74. *67*
—. Foreign Relations. Unification. USSR. 1945-47. *1098*
—. *General Sherman* (vessel). War. 1871. *1103*
—. Hawaii. Immigrants. Independence Movements. 1900-19. *1072*
—. Independence Movements. Political Factions. Rhee, Syngman. 1919-45. *1073*
—. International System. USSR. 1945-78. *1113*
—. Japan. Military Occupation. Social Change. 1945-53. *904*
—. Japanese. Koreans. Military government. Repatriation. 1945-48. *1018*
—. Military Service, Professional. Personal narratives. Ridgway, Matthew B. 8th Army, US. 1917-52. *1047*
Korea, North. Cambodia. Decisionmaking. Flexible response. *Mayaguez* incident. *Pueblo* incident. 1969-75. *1039*
—. China. Foreign Relations. Japan. Korea, South. Unification. USSR. 1970's-. *20*
—. Foreign policy. Korea, South. Military capability. 1970's. *1066*
—. Korea, South. Military aid. USSR. 1953-70's. *1064*
—. Korean War. MacArthur, Douglas. Military Offenses. UN. Unification. 1950. *1068*
—. Unification policy. 1973. *1058*
Korea, North (Hungnam). Evacuations. Navies. 1950. *1029*
Korea, South. Air National Guard. Military Reserves. Mobilization. Vietnam War. 1968-69. *1036*
—. Alliances. Carter, Jimmy. Military Aid. Taiwan. 1970's. *30*
—. Alliances. Military. Vietnam War. 1965-73. *1043*
—. Armies. Military Occupation. 1880-1950. *1067*
—. Asia, Southeast. Foreign Policy. Military Strategy. 1960's-70's. *1034*
—. Assassination. Foreign Relations. Park Chung-hee. Politics. 1979-82. *1010*
—. Attitudes. Carter, Jimmy (administration). 1977-78. *1087*
—. Carter, Jimmy (administration). Foreign Policy. Human rights. 1945-79. *1091*
—. Carter, Jimmy (administration). Foreign Policy. Japan. Military Ground Forces (withdrawal). 1950's-78. *131*
—. Censorship. Korean War. Newspapers. 1950. *1065*
—. China. Foreign Relations. Japan. Korea, North. Unification. USSR. 1970's-. *20*
—. China. Foreign Relations. Japan. Military. Taiwan. 1960-80. *56*
—. China. Japan. Public Opinion. Taiwan. Treaties, mutual defense. 1950's-77. *126*
—. Civil rights. Foreign policy. 1969-74. *1063*
—. Cold War. Foreign Relations. 1950-53. *1096*
—. Communist Countries. Foreign Policy. Military Ground Forces (withdrawal). 1950-78. *1022*
—. Dependency. Japan. Political economy. 1973. *1041*
—. Economic Conditions. Foreign Relations. 1977. *1042*
—. Economic Development. Exports. Foreign loans. 1950's-70's. *1102*
—. Elections. Legislative assembly. Military Occupation. 1945-48. *1074*
—. Europe. Foreign relations. 1950's-70's. *1071*
—. Foreign policy. Korea, North. Military capability. 1970's. *1066*
—. Foreign Policy. Military Ground Forces. 1976-80. *1090*
—. Foreign policy. Public opinion. 1952-80. *1089*
—. Foreign Relations. 1945-79. *1040*
—. Foreign Relations. 1950-81. *1099*
—. Foreign Relations. Japan. 1950-80. *89*
—. Intelligence Service. Ranard, Donald L. (account). 1970-74. *1110*
—. Korea, North. Military aid. USSR. 1953-70's. *1064*
—. Korean War (antecedents). Military. 1945-50. *1137*
—. Military strategy. 1947-78. *1145*
—. Military strategy. 1960's-70's. *1144*
—. Neocolonialism. 1960-76. *1079*

Korean War 267

Korea, South (Ch'unch'on). Air Warfare. Korean War. Risedorph, Gene (reminiscences). 1952. *1112*
Korea, South (Panmunjom). Diplomacy. France (Paris). Peace. Vietnam. 1951-73. *1143*
Korea (38th Parallel). Boundaries. Korean War. Military Armistice Commission. 1953-73. *917*
—. China. Foreign policy. Korean War. Military strategy. 1950-52. *1013*
—. Foreign Policy. Korean War. MacArthur, Douglas. Self-determination. Truman, Harry S. USSR. 1943-50. *1084*
Korean Americans. Immigration. Political leadership. Rhee, Syngman. 1903-24. *1048*
Korean Augmentation to the U.S. Army. Armies. 1950-65. *1118*
Korean War. 1950-53. *1035*
—. 1950-53. *1105*
—. Acheson, Dean. Intervention. Truman, Harry S. USSR. 1950. *1014*
—. Adventist Medical Cadet Corps. Armies. Dick, Everett N. (account). Military service. World War II. 1934-53. *29*
—. Afghanistan. Invasions. Limited war (concept). USSR. Vietnam War. War Powers Act (US, 1973). 1945-79. *104*
—. Air Forces. *Battle Hymn* (film). Hess, Dean Elmer. Orphans. 1950-56. *1032*
—. Air Forces. F-13 (aircraft). World War II. 1944-54. *82*
—. Air Forces. F-86F (aircraft). Osan Air Base. South Africa. UN Command. 1950-53. *1008*
—. Air Forces. Knight, Charlotte (field report). 1950. *1060*
—. Air Forces. Lackland Air Force Base. Legislative Investigations. Military Training. Texas (San Antonio). 1950-66. *1011*
—. Air Rescue Service. Vietnam War. 1961-75. *1133*
—. Air Warfare. Bombing, night. B-26 (aircraft). 1950-52. *1115*
—. Air Warfare. C-47 (aircraft). 1950-53. *1020*
—. Air Warfare. Korea, South (Ch'unch'on). Risedorph, Gene (reminiscences). 1952. *1112*
—. Air warfare. Military Strategy. Vietnam War. World War II. 1940-72. *52*
—. Anti-Communist Movements. Missouri. 1950-53. *1052*
—. Apathy. Colonization. Death and Dying. Malnutrition. Prisoners of war. Virginia (Jamestown). World War II. 1607-24. 1941-53. *74*
—. Armies. Dill, James. Personal narratives. 7th Infantry Division, US (31st Field Artillery Battalion). 1950-51. *1027*
—. Arms race. China. Rostow, Eugene V. USSR. 1953-82. *8*
—. Asia, northeast. Foreign Policy. Political conditions. 1953-78. *1128*
—. Austin, Warren R. Foreign policy. Truman Doctrine. UN. 1945-53. *1086*
—. Authoritarianism (theory). Personality. Public opinion. Racism. Vietnam War. 1950-78. *1046*
—. Balance of power. China. 1948-51. *1106*
—. Balance of Power. Cold War. Foreign policy. USSR. 1946-50. *1050*
—. Battle of the Bulge. China. Cuban Missile Crisis. Military intelligence. 1944-80. *3*
—. Bibliographies. Historiography (review article). 1950-55. *1097*
—. Blacks. Brown, Jesse. Hudner, Thomas. Military officers. Navies. 1950. *1123*
—. Blacks. Brown, Jesse. Naval Air Forces. Pilots. 1948-50. *1139*
—. Bombs (glide, smart). Tactics. Vietnam War. World War II. 1919-74. *4*
—. Boundaries. Korea (38th Parallel). Military Armistice Commission. 1953-73. *917*

—. Brooks, James L. (personal account). F-86 (aircraft). Pilots. 1950. *1016*
—. Canada. Diplomacy. Stairs, Denis (review article). 1950-53. *1092*
—. Cease-fire. Eisenhower, Dwight D. Peace negotiations. UN. 1952-53. *1136*
—. Censorship. Korea, South. Newspapers. 1950. *1065*
—. Chemical and Biological Warfare. 1940-75. *46*
—. Chemical and Biological Warfare. 1952-53. *1031*
—. China. 1950. *1033*
—. China. Cold war. Foreign Relations. Taiwan. USSR. 1947-79. *211*
—. China. Cold War. Foreign relations. USSR. 1945-72. *1024*
—. China. Elections (presidential). Foreign Policy. 1949-52. *150*
—. China. Foreign policy. Korea (38th Parallel). Military strategy. 1950-52. *1013*
—. China. Foreign policy. MacArthur, Douglas. Politics and the Military. Truman, Harry S. 1949-52. *1025*
—. China. MacArthur, Douglas. Truman, Harry S. Walker, Walton L. 1950. *1026*
—. China. USSR. 1950. *1138*
—. Chosin Reservoir Campaign. Marines. 1950. *1093*
—. Civilians. Policymaking. 1945-54. *1069*
—. Civil-Military Relations. Combat. Values. 1950-53. *1135*
—. Cold War. MacArthur, Douglas. Senate inquiry. Testimony, secret. 1951. *1141*
—. Cold War revisionism. Foreign Policy. Kolko thesis (review article). 1949-50. *1147*
—. Communism. Foreign policy. Intervention. Truman, Harry S. USSR. 1950. *1081*
—. Communism. Prisoners of war. Propaganda. Public opinion. Vietnam War. 1950-74. *1021*
—. Cuba. Decisionmaking. Foreign Policy. Germany. World War I. 1914-62. *1109*
—. Daily Life. Public Opinion. Vietnam War. 1950-73. *1114*
—. Defense spending. Military. Minutemen. Political Attitudes. Vietnam War. 1784-1979. *1077*
—. Europe. 1945-50. *1053*
—. Foreign Policy. Korea (38th Parallel). MacArthur, Douglas. Self-determination. Truman, Harry S. USSR. 1943-50. *1084*
—. Foreign policy. Military Bases. 1950-80. *1148*
—. Foreign policy. Vietnam War. 1950-53. 1961-73. *1095*
—. Foreign Relations (review article). Truman, Harry S. 1950. 1976. *1104*
—. Great Britain. Navies. Suez Crisis. USA. Vietnam War. 1950-76. *1119*
—. Heller, Francis H. (review article). 1950-53. 1977. *1049*
—. Historiography. MacArthur, Douglas. Politics. Public relations. Truman, Harry S. Wake Island. 1950. *1142*
—. Korea, North. MacArthur, Douglas. Military Offenses. UN. Unification. 1950. *1068*
—. Leadership. Military General Staff. Technology. Vietnam War. 1950-73. *1085*
—. Limited war. MacArthur, Douglas. Politics and the Military. Truman, Harry S. 1950-51. *1132*
—. Limited war. Military training. Vietnam War. 1945-73. *1131*
—. MacArthur, Douglas. Manchester, William. Military Strategy. Truman, Harry S. Wake Island. 1950. 1980. *1051*
—. MacArthur, Douglas. Military General Staff. World War II. ca 1939-51. *1134*
—. MacArthur, Douglas. Politics. 1950-51. *1019*
—. Marines. Naval Air Forces. Pilots. *Sicily* (vessel). 1950. *1130*

268   Korean War

—. Marines. Seoul (battle). 1950. *1059*
—. Marines. Transportation, Military. Vietnam War. 1945-73. *1108*
—. McLain, Raymond Stallings. Military General Staff. Oklahoma. Villa, Pancho. World War I. World War II. 1912-54. *1121*
—. Military. 1950-53. *1023*
—. Military Ground Forces. 1950. *1078*
—. Military Intelligence. National Security Council. 1948-50. *1129*
—. Military rescue concepts. Vietnam War. World War II. 1941-74. *11*
—. Military Service. National security. Vietnam War. 1946-81. *1070*
—. Military Strategy. October War. Pearl Harbor (attack). Surprise attacks. World War II. 1941-73. *7*
—. Navies. Vietnam War. 1945-75. *1120*
—. Peace negotiations. 1951-53. *1009*
—. Political Systems. Vietnam War. War, limited. 1950-75. *1030*
Korean War (antecedents). 1945-50. *1017*
—. Historiography. 1950-53. *1125*
—. Korea, South. Military. 1945-50. *1137*
Korean War (review article). Class Struggle. Cumings, Bruce. Imperialism. 1945-47. *1038*
Koreans. Japanese. Korea. Military government. Repatriation. 1945-48. *1018*
Kurose, Aki Kato. Daily Life. Internment. Japanese Americans. Washington (Seattle). World War II. 1930's-50's. *644*

L

Labor. Asia. Economic Conditions. Emigration. 1834-1930. *1003*
—. Automobile Industry and Trade. Canada. Europe, Western. Gindon, Sam (interview). Japan. World car (concept). 1945-80. *1006*
—. Canada. Europe, Western. Japan. Manufacturing. Productivity. 1960-82. *576*
Labor costs. Canada. Europe. Japan. Manufacturing. Productivity. 1974-81. *624*
Labor experience. China. Educational Policy. Higher education. 1976. *330*
Labor movement. Japan. Military Occupation. 1945-52. *893*
Labor policy. Brown, Irving. Japan. Military Occupation. 1945-72. *926*
Labor reform. Japan. Military Occupation. Wages. Working conditions. 1945-60. *918*
Lackland Air Force Base. Air Forces. Korean War. Legislative Investigations. Military Training. Texas (San Antonio). 1950-66. *1011*
LaFeber, Walter F. Foreign Policy (review article). Gardner, Lloyd C. Japan. McCormick, Thomas J. USA. 1776-1973. *581*
Laidlaw, Lansing. Alaska (Aleutian Islands). *Arthur Middleton* (vessel). Coast Guard. Japan. World War II. 1942-43. *769*
Land Tenure. China. George, Henry. Sun Zhongshan. Taxation. 1866-1973. *361*
Lange, Dorothea. Adams, Ansel. California. Internment. Japanese Americans. Manzanar War Relocation Center. Photography, Journalistic. World War II. 1941-45. *840*
Language School. Japanese Americans (Nisei). Military Intelligence. Minnesota. Rasmussen, Kai E. World War II. 1941-46. *579*
Lansing, Robert. Asia, East. Foreign policy. World War I (antecedents). 1914-17. *54*
Laos. China. Civil war. Intervention. USSR. 1959-62. *514*
—. China. Indochina. International crises. Korea. 1949-62. *345*

Latin America. Europe, Western. Finance. Imperialism. Industry. Japan. Trade. 1970's. *768*
Laughlin, C. H. (reminiscences). Airplanes. China (Kunming). Ghana (Accra). World War II. 1942. *347*
Law. Foreign Relations. Gray, John Chipman. Holmes, Oliver Wendell. Japan. Kaneko Kentarō. Letters. Thayer, James Bradley. 1878-1924. *741*
Law (study of). China. -1973. *200*
Lawsuits. *Clarissa B. Carver* (vessel). Courts. Dow, Leroy. *Glamorganshire* (vessel). Japan. Ships. 1885-86. *870*
Lawyers. Business. Japan. Sony Company. 1982. *822*
Leadership. China. Cohen, Warren I. (review article). Foreign policy. Japan. Public opinion. ca 1900-50. 1978. *26*
—. China. Dewey, John. Educational Reform (review article). Keenan, Barry. 1919-30. 1977. *495*
—. Korean War. Military General Staff. Technology. Vietnam War. 1950-73. *1085*
League of Nations. China. Foreign Policy. Paris Peace Conference. Treaties, unequal. Wilson, Woodrow. 1919. *19*
—. China. Japan. Paris Peace Conference. Wilson, Woodrow. 1919. *85*
—. Gilbert, Prentiss B. Japan. Kellogg-Briand Pact. Manchuria. Military Occupation. Stimson, Henry L. 1931. *34*
League of Nations Covenant. Equality (proposed). Hughes, William Morris. Japan. Paris Peace Conference. Race Relations. Wilson, Woodrow. 1919. *772*
Leftism. China. Smedley, Agnes (review article). Women. 1930's-50. 1973-76. *329*
Leftists. Atomic Warfare. Japan. USSR. World War II. 1945. *610*
Legislative assembly. Elections. Korea, South. Military Occupation. 1945-48. *1074*
Legislative Investigations. Air Forces. Korean War. Lackland Air Force Base. Military Training. Texas (San Antonio). 1950-66. *1011*
—. China. Foreign Policy. History Teaching. Senate. Simulation and Games. 1949. 1978. *378*
Lemay, Curtis. Air Warfare. Japan. World War II. 1940-45. *976*
Lensen, George Alexander (review article). Foreign Relations. Japan. USSR. 1921-30. *831*
Letters. Bohme, Frederick G. Census Bureau. Japanese Americans. Relocation. World War II. 1942-45. *640*
—. China. Clark, Grenville. Foreign Relations. Snow, Edgar. 1963-67. *489*
—. China. Dulles, John Foster. Politics. Rusk, Dean. State Department. 1953. *499*
—. Daily Life. Hostages. Japan. Navies. Rescues. 1846-49. *771*
—. Foreign Relations. Gray, John Chipman. Holmes, Oliver Wendell. Japan. Kaneko Kentarō. Law. Thayer, James Bradley. 1878-1924. *741*
—. Internment. Japanese Americans. World War II. 1942. *914*
—. Japan. MacArthur, Douglas. Military occupation. 1947. *817*
Leyte (battle). Japan. Naval Warfare. World War II. 1944. *884*
Li Hungzhang. China. Diplomacy. New York City. Public Opinion. 1896. *226*
—. China. Diplomacy. Russia. Travel. 1896. *250*
Liberal Democratic Party. Bribery. Japan. Lockheed Aircraft Corporation. 1975-81. *766*
Liberals. China. Communists. Foreign Policy. Scholars. 1944-71. *380*
Libraries. American Studies. Taiwan. 1969-75. *1154*

Libraries, Presidential. Germany. Japan. Military government. Research. 1945-78. *994*
Libraries (US). Asia, East. Collection building. 15c-20c. 1960's-70's. *127*
Limited war. Korean War. MacArthur, Douglas. Politics and the Military. Truman, Harry S. 1950-51. *1132*
—. Korean War. Military training. Vietnam War. 1945-73. *1131*
Limited war (concept). Afghanistan. Invasions. Korean War. USSR. Vietnam War. War Powers Act (US, 1973). 1945-79. *104*
Literature. American Studies. China. 1950-80. *298*
—. China. Lu Xun. 1920's-30's. *533*
—. Chinese Americans. Japanese Americans. 1850-1980. *13*
Literature, popular. Americans. Japan. 1934-73. *755*
Liu Zuochang. China. Historiography (Chinese). Jefferson, Thomas. Virginia, University of. 1770-1826. 1976-81. *321*
Loan negotiations. China. Great Britain. World War II. 1941-44. *189*
Loans (consortium). China. Foreign Relations. Wilson, Woodrow. 1910-13. *383*
Lobbying. American Council on Japan. Economic Policy. Foreign Policy. Japan. Military Occupation. 1945-50's. *873*
—. American Council on Japan. Foreign Policy. Japan. 1947-52. *894*
—. China. Congress. International Trade. Roosevelt, Franklin D. (administration). Silver Purchase Act (1934). 1934. *268*
Local government. Japan. Public Administration. Reform. 1940-69. *753*
Locke, Robert D. (interview). Karns, A. P. Oil well. Taiwan. 1877-78. *272*
Lockheed Aircraft Corporation. Bribery. Japan. Liberal Democratic Party. 1975-81. *766*
—. Japan. Political Corruption. 1976. *583*
London, Jack. Japan. Reporters and Reporting. Russo-Japanese War. 1904. *689*
Long, Charles H. China. Episcopal Church, Protestant. Missions and Missionaries. Revolution. 1946-49. *372*
Louis, William Roger. Alliances (review article). British Empire. Japan. Thorne, Christopher. World War II. 1941-45. *854*
Louisiana (New Orleans). Creoles. Folklore. Hearn, Lafcadio. Japan. Martinique. 1850-1904. *803*
Low, Frederick F. China. Diplomacy. Korea. 1869-74. *2*
Lu Xun. China. Communism. India. Revolutionary Movements. Smedley, Agnes. 1910-50. *375*
—. China. Literature. 1920's-30's. *533*
Lucky Dragon (vessel). Bikini Atoll. Hydrogen bomb. Japan. Pacific Dependencies (US). 1954-75. *882*
Lutheran Church. Arndt, E. L. China. Missions and Missionaries. 1913-29. *510*
—. Japan. Midsuno, Henry Signaro. Missions and Missionaries. 1870-1933. *993*

M

MacArthur, Douglas. China. Foreign policy. Korean War. Politics and the Military. Truman, Harry S. 1949-52. *1025*
—. China. Korean War. Truman, Harry S. Walker, Walton L. 1950. *1026*
—. Cold War. Korean War. Senate inquiry. Testimony, secret. 1951. *1141*
—. Constitutions. Japan. Military Occupation. Political tradition. 1945-76. *804*
—. Diplomacy. Japan. Philippines (Manila). Surrender. World War II. 1945. *812*

—. Foreign Policy. Korea (38th Parallel). Korean War. Self-determination. Truman, Harry S. USSR. 1943-50. *1084*
—. Historiography. Korean War. Politics. Public relations. Truman, Harry S. Wake Island. 1950. *1142*
—. Japan. Letters. Military occupation. 1947. *817*
—. Korea, North. Korean War. Military Offenses. UN. Unification. 1950. *1068*
—. Korean War. Limited war. Politics and the Military. Truman, Harry S. 1950-51. *1132*
—. Korean War. Manchester, William. Military Strategy. Truman, Harry S. Wake Island. 1950. *1051*
—. Korean War. Military General Staff. World War II. ca 1939-51. *1134*
—. Korean War. Politics. 1950-51. *1019*
Magniac and Co. Bank of England. China. Economic crises. International Trade. Yrissari and Co. 1823-27. *18*
The Magnificent Seven (film). Films. Japan. National Characteristics. *Seven Samurai* (film). 1960's. *836*
Makin Islands (raid). Japan. Marines (2d Raiders). Peatross, Oscar F. (account). Prisoners of War. World War II. 1942-47. *853*
Malnutrition. Apathy. Colonization. Death and Dying. Korean War. Prisoners of war. Virginia (Jamestown). World War II. 1607-24. 1941-53. *74*
Manchester, William. Korean War. MacArthur, Douglas. Military Strategy. Truman, Harry S. Wake Island. 1950. 1980. *1051*
Manchuria. China. Communist Party. Foreign Policy. Taiwan. Wedemeyer, Albert C. (report). 1946-49. *351*
—. Diplomatic recognition. Japan. Stimson, Henry L. 1931-34. *991*
—. Gilbert, Prentiss B. Japan. Kellogg-Briand Pact. League of Nations. Military Occupation. Stimson, Henry L. 1931. *34*
Manchurian crisis. *Christian Century* (periodical). Foreign policy. Japan. Morrison, Charles C. 1931-33. *96*
—. Congress. Japan. Public opinion. 1931-33. *83*
Manufactures. Competition. Germany, West. International Trade. Japan. 1970's. *797*
—. Foreign investments. Japan. 1950's-70's. *875*
Manufacturing. Canada. Europe. Japan. Labor costs. Productivity. 1974-81. *624*
—. Canada. Europe, Western. Japan. Labor. Productivity. 1960-82. *576*
—. China. Diplomacy. Young, John Russell. 1882-83. *221*
—. Developing nations. Great Britain. Japan. Subcontracting. 1966-76. *899*
Manzanar War Relocation Center. Adams, Ansel. California. Internment. Japanese Americans. Lange, Dorothea. Photography, Journalistic. World War II. 1941-45. *840*
—. California. Concentration Camps. Japanese Americans. Riots. Ueno, Harry (arrest). World War II. 1942. *691*
Mao Zedong. Agricultural Policy. China. Famine. 1960-76. *371*
—. China. Communist Party. Diplomacy (secret). Revolution. 1949. *350*
—. China. Communist Party. Foreign policy. Speeches. 1944-50. *274*
—. China. Diplomacy. Hurley, Patrick J. Jiang Jieshi. State Department. Vincent, John Carter. 1944-45. *358*
—. China. Foreign policy. Nixon, Richard M. 1960's-70's. *555*
—. Foreign policy. 1948-50. *315*
Mao Zedong (death). China. Foreign relations. 1976. *560*
Maoism. China. Foreign policy. ca 1960's-70's. *360*

—. China. Strong, Anna Louise. USSR. 1919-70. *245*
Mariana Islands. Colonialism. Educational Policy. Germany. Japan. Spain. ca 1688-1940. *698*
Mariana Islands (battle). Air Warfare. Japan. World War II. 1944. *668*
Marines. Armies. Japan. Peleliu (battle). Sledge, Eugene B. (account). World War II. 1944. *907*
—. Boxer Rebellion. China (Beijing, Taku, Tianjin). 1900. *295*
—. Butler, Smedley D. China, North. Pilots. Williams, Clarence S. 1927-28. *410*
—. Caroline Islands. Ellis, Earl. Japan. Naval strategy. 1920-23. *956*
—. China. Communism. 1944-49. *151*
—. China. Japan. Kinney, John F. Prisoners of War. Wake Island. World War II. 1941-45. *943*
—. China, north. Civil war. Military Occupation. World War II. 1945-47. *33*
—. China, north. Photographs. Uniforms, Military. 1931-41. *504*
—. China (Shanghai). Japan. Photographs. 1920's-30's. *569*
—. China (Shanghai). Personal Narratives. *Pittsburgh* (vessel). Smith, Wiley H. 1927. *408*
—. Chosin Reservoir Campaign. Korean War. 1950. *1093*
—. Dumas, Harold. Japanese language. World War II. 1944-45. *791*
—. Ellis, Earl. Japan. Micronesia. Military Intelligence. 1911-23. *584*
—. Japan. Junghans, Earl A. Personal narratives. Prisoners of War. Wake Island. War crimes. World War II. 1941-47. *737*
—. Korean War. Naval Air Forces. Pilots. *Sicily* (vessel). 1950. *1130*
—. Korean War. Seoul (battle). 1950. *1059*
—. Korean War. Transportation, Military. Vietnam War. 1945-73. *1108*
Marines (2d Raiders). Japan. Makin Islands (raid). Peatross, Oscar F. (account). Prisoners of War. World War II. 1942-47. *853*
Marketing. International Trade. Taiwan. 1962-74. *1170*
Marshall, George C. China. Communism. Foreign Policy. Sprouse, Philip D. (report). 1945-47. 1970's. *391*
—. China. Communism. Mediation. Nationalists. USSR. 1946. *356*
—. China. Jiang Jieshi. Military General Staff. Stilwell, Joseph W. World War II. 1944. *475*
—. China. Military Strategy. ca 1900-47. *463*
Marshall, Humphrey. China. Diplomacy. Taiping Rebellion. 1853-54. *310*
—. China. Foreign Policy. Taiping Rebellion. 1853-54. *312*
Martial law. Internment. Japanese Americans. Tule Lake Camp. World War II. 1941-44. *843*
Martinique. Creoles. Folklore. Hearn, Lafcadio. Japan. Louisiana (New Orleans). 1850-1904. *803*
May, Gary. Anti-Communist Movements. China. Foreign Policy. McCarthy, Joseph R. Vincent, John Carter. 1942-51. *279*
Mayaguez incident. Cambodia. Decisionmaking. Flexible response. Korea, North. *Pueblo* incident. 1969-75. *1039*
McCandless, Bruce (reminiscences). *Gregory* (vessel). Japan (Bonin Islands). Navies. World War II. 1945. *798*
McCarran Committee. China Lobby. Institute of Pacific Relations. Public opinion. Thomas, John N. (review article). Watergate trials. 1945-75. *58*
McCarthy, Joseph R. Anti-Communist Movements. China. Foreign Policy. May, Gary. Vincent, John Carter. 1942-51. *279*

McCormick, Thomas J. Foreign Policy (review article). Gardner, Lloyd C. Japan. LaFeber, Walter F. USA. 1776-1973. *581*
McDougal, David. Americans (protected). Japan (Shimonoseki Strait). Naval battles. *Wyoming* (vessel). 1863. *683*
McGiffin, Philo Norton. China. Navies. Sino-Japanese War. 1885-95. *174*
McLain, Raymond Stallings. Korean War. Military General Staff. Oklahoma. Villa, Pancho. World War I. World War II. 1912-54. *1121*
McMahon, Robert J. Asia, East. Blum, Robert M. Buhite, Russell D. Foreign Relations (review article). 1945-60's. *24*
Mediation. China. Communism. Marshall, George C. Nationalists. USSR. 1946. *356*
Medical Research. Atomic Bomb Casualty Commission. Civilians. Japan (Hiroshima, Nagasaki). Radiation Effects Research Foundation. 1945-75. *960*
Medical technology. China. Mortality. Social Organization. 19c. 1949-59. *470*
Medicine, Western. Barefoot doctor movement. China. Political systems. Public Health. 1973. *411*
Meiji Restoration. Civil war. Japan. 1860-70. *879*
Memoirs. China-Burma-India Theater. Emmerson, John K. State Department (Foreign Service). World War II. 1941-44. *251*
—. Diplomacy. Emmerson, John K. Internment. Japanese Peruvians. Peru. World War II. 1942-43. *660*
—. Diplomacy. Emmerson, John K. Japan (Tokyo). State Department. World War II (antecedents). 1941. *662*
Mennonites. China (Caoxian, Kai Chow). Missions and Missionaries. 1901-31. *326*
Mental illness. Acculturation. Chinese. Colleges and Universities. Students. Taiwan. 1854-1973. *1151*
Methodism. Graves. Japan. Missions and Missionaries. 1876-1957. *761*
Methodist Episcopal Church. Bashford, James W. China. Missions and Missionaries. Social gospel. 1889-1919. *320*
Methodist Episcopal Church (South). China. Feminism. Haygood, Laura A. Missions and Missionaries. 1884-1900. *427*
—. China (Shanghai). Missions and Missionaries. Publishers and Publishing. 1898-1920. *439*
Methodist Protestant Church. Councils and Synods. Japan. Missions and Missionaries. 1880-92. *762*
—. Japan (Yokohama). Klein, Frederick C. Missions and Missionaries. 1880-93. *763*
Methodology. China. Science. 20c. *180*
Metropolitan areas. California. Chinese Americans. Tong societies. 1850-1972. *204*
Mexico. Adachi Minechiro. Foreign Relations. Huerta, Victoriano. Japan. 1913-14. *786*
Mexico (Baja California, Turtle Bay). *Asama* (vessel). Japan. Tuchman, Barbara. 1915. *663*
Meyer, George von Lengerke. Diplomacy (personal). Germany. Roosevelt, Theodore. Russo-Japanese War. William II. 1902-14. *968*
Micronesia. Ellis, Earl. Japan. Marines. Military Intelligence. 1911-23. *584*
Middle East. Asia, East. Naval Tactics. 1945-79. *42*
—. China. Egypt. Foreign Policy. Israel. USSR. 1978. *497*
Midsuno, Henry Signaro. Japan. Lutheran Church. Missions and Missionaries. 1870-1933. *993*
Midway (battle). Censorship. *Chicago Tribune*. Cryptography. Japan. Reporters and Reporting. World War II. 1942. *679*
—. Censorship. *Chicago Tribune*. Grand Juries. Japan. Navies. World War II. 1942. *669*
—. Combat Information Unit. Cryptography. Japan. Navies. World War II. 1942. *858*

Military Occupation   271

—. Dixon, Robert E. Japan. Johnston, Stanley. Military Strategy. Personal narratives. Reporters and Reporting. World War II. 1942. *794*
—. Japan. Military Strategy. World War II. 1942. *992*
—. Japan. Navies. World War II. 1942. *621*
Militarism. China. Foreign Policy. Isolationism. 1969-76. *179*
—. Foreign Relations. Japan. 1945-73. *582*
Military. See also specific branches of the armed forces, e.g., Air Forces, Navies, Marines, etc.
—. Alliances. Korea, South. Vietnam War. 1965-73. *1043*
—. China. Foreign Policy. 1970-80. *415*
—. China. Foreign policy. Political Factions. USSR. Zhou Enlai. 1970-71. *263*
—. China. Foreign Relations. Japan. Korea, South. Taiwan. 1960-80. *56*
—. China. Foreign Relations (review article). USSR. 1970-77. *538*
—. China. Trade. 1970-80. *205*
—. Defense spending. Korean War. Minutemen. Political Attitudes. Vietnam War. 1784-1979. *1077*
—. Economic Policy. Foreign policy. Japan. Politics. 1945-72. *919*
—. Korea, South. Korean War (antecedents). 1945-50. *1137*
—. Korean War. 1950-53. *1023*
Military Aid. See also Economic Aid; Foreign Aid.
—. Alliances. Carter, Jimmy. Korea, South. Taiwan. 1970's. *30*
—. Asia, Southeast. Brezhnev, Leonid. China. Foreign policy. 1968-79. *488*
—. Balance of power. Foreign policy. Japan. 1945-77. *657*
—. China. Foreign Relations. Jiang Jieshi. 1948-50. *1176*
—. China. Foreign Relations. National Security. USSR. 1970-75. *440*
—. Economic growth. Europe. Foreign Relations. Japan. 1970's. *601*
—. Foreign Policy. Korea. 1950's. *1012*
—. Korea, North. Korea, South. USSR. 1953-70's. *1064*
Military Armistice Commission. Boundaries. Korea (38th Parallel). Korean War. 1953-73. *917*
Military Bases. Foreign policy. Korean War. 1950-80. *1148*
Military Capability. Air Forces. Japan. Philippines. World War II. 1941. *692*
—. Balance of Power. China. Coffey, Joseph I. USA. USSR. ca 1965-73. *158*
—. China. Defense Department. 1974. *258*
—. Europe, Western. Foreign Policy. International Security. Japan. 1980-82. *889*
—. Foreign policy. Korea, North. Korea, South. 1970's. *1066*
—. Foreign Relations. International Trade. Japan. Trade. 1970's-82. *833*
Military cooperation. Afghanistan. China. Foreign Relations. Invasions. USSR. Vietnam. 1965-80. *232*
Military defeat. Historians, Western. Japan. USSR. World War II. 1942-45. *890*
Military General Staff. China. Jiang Jieshi. Marshall, George C. Stilwell, Joseph W. World War II. 1944. *475*
—. Korean War. Leadership. Technology. Vietnam War. 1950-73. *1085*
—. Korean War. MacArthur, Douglas. World War II. ca 1939-51. *1134*
—. Korean War. McLain, Raymond Stallings. Oklahoma. Villa, Pancho. World War I. World War II. 1912-54. *1121*
Military government. Colleges and Universities. Democracy. Japan. Virginia, University of (School of Military Government). 1944-45. *971*

—. Germany. Japan. Libraries, Presidential Research. 1945-78. *994*
—. Japanese. Korea. Koreans. Repatriation. 1945-48. *1018*
—. Japanese control. Okinawa. 1945-72. *807*
Military Ground Forces. Foreign Policy. Korea, South. 1976-80. *1090*
—. Korean War. 1950. *1078*
Military Ground Forces (withdrawal). Carter, Jimmy (administration). Foreign Policy. Japan. Korea, South. 1950's-78. *131*
—. Carter, Jimmy (administration). Foreign Policy. Korea. 1977. *1124*
—. Communist Countries. Foreign Policy. Korea, South. 1950-78. *1022*
Military Intelligence. See also Intelligence Service.
—. Battle of the Bulge. China. Cuban Missile Crisis. Korean War. 1944-80. *3*
—. Birch, John (death). China. Communists. 1945. *530*
—. Creighton, John Marie. Intervention. Japan. USSR (Eastern Siberia). 1922. *44*
—. Cryptography. Guadalcanal (battle). Japan. Radio. World War II. 1942. *810*
—. Diplomacy. Japan. Roosevelt, Franklin D. World War II (antecedents). 1940-41. *693*
—. Ellis, Earl. Japan. Marines. Micronesia. 1911-23. *584*
—. Great Britain. Japan. Wiseman, William. World War I. World War II. 1914-45. *903*
—. Japanese Americans (Nisei). Language School. Minnesota. Rasmussen, Kai E. World War II. 1941-46. *579*
—. Korean War. National Security Council. 1948-50. *1129*
Military Occupation. Agricultural property. Democratization. Inheritance. Japan. 1945-52. *935*
—. American Council on Japan. Economic Policy. Foreign Policy. Japan. Lobbying. 1945-50's. *873*
—. Armies. Korea, South. 1880-1950. *1067*
—. Boxer Rebellion. China (Beijing). 1900-01. *314*
—. Brown, Irving. Japan. Labor policy. 1945-72. *926*
—. China. Cuba. Imperialism. Native races. Philippines. 1898-1903. *316*
—. China (Beijing). Cuba. Native races. Philippines. 1898-1903. *238*
—. China, north. Civil war. Marines. World War II. 1945-47. *33*
—. Colleges and Universities. Educational Theory. Japan. Senroku Uehara (*University*). US Education Mission to Japan. 1945-62. *728*
—. Constitutional reform. Japan. Politics. 1945-52. *577*
—. Constitutions. Japan. MacArthur, Douglas. Political tradition. 1945-76. *804*
—. Dissertations. Educational reform. Historiography. Japan. 1950-80. *940*
—. Documents. Japan. 1945-47. *598*
—. Economic Conditions. Great Britain. Japan. Political Systems. 1945-49. *617*
—. Economic Conditions. Japan. Ryukyu Islands (Okinawa). 1952-79. *950*
—. Economic Policy. Foreign Policy. Japan. 1945-49. *895*
—. Elections. Korea, South. Legislative assembly. 1945-48. *1074*
—. Foreign policy. International Trade. Japan. 1945-74. *808*
—. Foreign Relations. Gayn, Mark (*Japan Diary*). Japan. 1945-81. *880*
—. Gilbert, Prentiss B. Japan. Kellogg-Briand Pact. League of Nations. Manchuria. Stimson, Henry L. 1931. *34*
—. Historiography. Japan. 1945-52. *820*
—. Japan. 1945-60's. *891*
—. Japan. 1946-51. *695*

272 Military Occupation

—. Japan. Korea. Social Change. 1945-53. *904*
—. Japan. Labor movement. 1945-52. *893*
—. Japan. Labor reform. Wages. Working conditions. 1945-60. *918*
—. Japan. Letters. MacArthur, Douglas. 1947. *817*
Military Offenses. Korea, North. Korean War. MacArthur, Douglas. UN. Unification. 1950. *1068*
Military officers. Agawa, Hiroyuki. Japan. Navies. World War II. Yamamoto, Isoroku (review article). 1930's-43. *764*
—. Blacks. Brown, Jesse. Hudner, Thomas. Korean War. Navies. 1950. *1123*
Military operations. Japan. Natural Resources. Oregon (Bly). Project FUGO. World War II. 1942-45. *861*
Military relations. China. 1972-81. *202*
—. Japan. Rearmament. 1946-70's. *975*
Military rescue concepts. Korean War. Vietnam War. World War II. 1941-74. *11*
Military Reserves. Air National Guard. Korea, South. Mobilization. Vietnam War. 1968-69. *1036*
Military service. Adventist Medical Cadet Corps. Armies. Dick, Everett N. (account). Korean War. World War II. 1934-53. *29*
—. Korean War. National security. Vietnam War. 1946-81. *1070*
Military Service, Professional. Korea. Personal narratives. Ridgway, Matthew B. 8th Army, US. 1917-52. *1047*
Military Strategy. Air warfare. Korean War. Vietnam War. World War II. 1940-72. *52*
—. Alliances. Defense. NATO. Political change, international. 1945-70's. *1088*
—. Asia. Defensive perimeter concept. 1947-51. *564*
—. Asia, East. Defense Policy. War. 1945-50. *32*
—. Asia, Southeast. Foreign Policy. Korea, South. 1960's-70's. *1034*
—. Atomic bomb. Japan. Truman, Harry S. World War II. 1945. *602*
—. Atomic energy. Japan. Smyth Report, 1945. USA. World War II. 1940-45. *908*
—. Atomic Warfare. Decisionmaking. Japan (Hiroshima, Nagasaki). World War II. 1944-45. *671*
—. Atomic Warfare. Japan. World War II. 1945. *714*
—. Atomic Warfare. Japan (Hiroshima, Nagasaki). Surrender, unconditional. World War II. 1943-45. *703*
—. Atomic warfare. Japan (Hiroshima, Nagasaki). World War II. 1945. *603*
—. China. Defense Policy. Foreign policy. USSR. 1975-79. *335*
—. China. Foreign policy. Korea (38th Parallel). Korean War. 1950-52. *1013*
—. China. Foreign policy. USSR. 1969-70's. *293*
—. China. Jiang Jieshi. Stilwell, Joseph W. World War II. 1942-44. *397*
—. China. Marshall, George C. ca 1900-47. *463*
—. China. USSR. 1950-76. *195*
—. Dixon, Robert E. Japan. Johnston, Stanley. Midway (battle). Personal narratives. Reporters and Reporting. World War II. 1942. *794*
—. Europe. Foreign policy. Japan. Vietnam War. 1970's. *910*
—. Federal Policy. Frontier and Pioneer Life. Indians. Japan. Taiwan. 18c-1915. *70*
—. Foreign Relations. International Trade. Korea. 1905-79. *1100*
—. Invasions. Japan. Operation Olympic. World War II. 1945. *645*
—. Japan. 1970-80. *674*
—. Japan. Midway (battle). World War II. 1942. *992*
—. Japan. NATO. USSR. 1945-54. *813*
—. Japan. Naval War College. War Plan Orange. 1900-12. *953*
—. Korea, South. 1947-78. *1145*
—. Korea, South. 1960's-70's. *1144*
—. Korean War. MacArthur, Douglas. Manchester, William. Truman, Harry S. Wake Island. 1950. *1051*
—. Korean War. October War. Pearl Harbor (attack). Surprise attacks. World War II. 1941-73. *7*
Military training. Air Forces. Atomic bomb. Japan (Hiroshima). Personal narratives. Tibbets, Paul W. World War II. 1945. *932*
—. Air Forces. Korean War. Lackland Air Force Base. Legislative Investigations. Texas (San Antonio). 1950-66. *1011*
—. Aviation. China. Fraser, Douglas. Nationalists. Saskatchewan (Saskatoon). 1919-22. *217*
—. Korean War. Limited war. Vietnam War. 1945-73. *1131*
Miller, Kelly. Blacks. Immigration restriction. Japanese. Race Relations. 1906-24. *699*
Ming dynasty. Biography. China. 1368-1644. *227*
Minnesota. Japanese Americans (Nisei). Language School. Military Intelligence. Rasmussen, Kai E. World War II. 1941-46. *579*
Minutemen. Defense spending. Korean War. Military. Political Attitudes. Vietnam War. 1784-1979. *1077*
Mirikitani, Janice ("Lullaby"). Internment. Japanese Americans. Poetry. World War II. 1941-45. *609*
Missions and Missionaries. Alabama (Mobile). China. Presbyterian Church. Stuart, Mary Horton. 1840's-1947. *284*
—. American Board of Commissioners for Foreign Missions. Attitudes. China. 1830-60. *467*
—. Archives. China. Japan. Korea. Presbyterian Historical Society. 1829-1911. *39*
—. Archives. China. Protestantism. Yale University Library (collection). Yale-in-China Association. 1901-51. *237*
—. Arndt, E. L. China. Lutheran Church. 1913-29. *510*
—. Attitudes. China. Presbyterian Church. 1837-1900. *212*
—. Baptist Church. China. Shuck, Eliza G. Sexton. 1846-63. *322*
—. Baptists (Southern). China. Roberts, Issachar Jacob. 1837-47. *567*
—. Baptists, Southern. China, south. 1845-76. *503*
—. Bashford, James W. China. Methodist Episcopal Church. Social gospel. 1889-1919. *320*
—. Catholic Church. China. Christians. Communists. Protestant Churches. 1948-50. *523*
—. Catholic Church. China (Hunan). Passionists. 1921-79. *186*
—. Catholic Church. China (Kanchow). Foreign policy. 1929-32. *303*
—. China. Christianity. Democracy. Foreign Policy. Japan. Socialism. 1830-1979. *125*
—. China. Congregationalism. Nationalism. 1910-48. *288*
—. China. Diplomatic recognition. Revolution. Sun Zhongshan. 1911-13. *395*
—. China. Disciples of Christ. Williams, Edward Thomas. 1887-1918. *349*
—. China. Episcopal Church, Protestant. Long, Charles H. Revolution. 1946-49. *372*
—. China. Episcopal Church, Protestant. Roots, Eliza McCook. Roots, Logan H. 1900-34. *477*
—. China. Fairbank, John K. (review article). ca 1860-1949. 1974. *336*
—. China. Feminism. Haygood, Laura A. Methodist Episcopal Church (South). 1884-1900. *427*
—. China. Protestantism. Revivals. 1830-50. *466*

—. China. Religious toleration. Tianjin, Treaty of (Article XXIX). Translating. 1858-59. *429*
—. China (Beijing). Colleges and Universities. West, Philip. Yanjing University (review article). 1916-52. *161*
—. China (Caoxian, Kai Chow). Mennonites. 1901-31. *326*
—. China (Shanghai). Episcopal Church, Protestant. Pott, Francis L. H. St. John's University. 1888-1941. *285*
—. China (Shanghai). Methodist Episcopal Church, South. Publishers and Publishing. 1898-1920. *439*
—. Clark, Edward Warren. Cultural relations. Japan (Shizuoka, Tokyo). Nakamura Masanao. ca1870-1907. *721*
—. Colby, Abby M. Congregationalism. Feminism. Japan. 1879-1914. *928*
—. Councils and Synods. Japan. Methodist Protestant Church. 1880-92. *762*
—. Foreign Policy. Gulick, Sidney Lewis. Japan. 1914-45. *929*
—. Graves. Japan. Methodism. 1876-1957. *761*
—. Japan. Lutheran Church. Midsuno, Henry Signaro. 1870-1933. *993*
—. Japan. Mormons. 1901-24. *613*
—. Japan. Personal Narratives. Protestantism. 1860-1905. *931*
—. Japan (Yokohama). Klein, Frederick C. Methodist Protestant Church. 1880-93. *763*
Missions and Missionaries (papers). China. Church Historical Society archives. Episcopal Church, Protestant. 1835-1951. *223*
Missouri. Anti-Communist Movements. Korean War. 1950-53. *1052*
Missouri (St. Louis). Arts and crafts. China. Exhibits and Expositions. World's fair. 1904. *216*
Miyakawa, T. Scott. Japanese American Research Project. 1906-81. *881*
Mobilization. Air National Guard. Korea, South. Military Reserves. Vietnam War. 1968-69. *1036*
Modernization. Capron, Horace. Economic Development. Japan (Hokkaido). 1871-75. *811*
—. China. Foreign Policy. USSR. 1950-79. *412*
Modernization (review article). Historiography. Japan. 1867-1977. *754*
Monetary policy (devaluation). European Economic Community. International Trade. Japan. Nixon, Richard M. 1971-73. *655*
Monetary system, international. Dollar. Economic Regulations. Smithsonian Agreement (1971). 1971-72. *997*
Monetary Systems. Europe. Japan. Multinational corporations. USA. 1967-73. *924*
—. Europe, Western. International Trade. Japan. 1970's. *681*
Monopolies. Banking. Europe. Japan. ca 1950's-70's. *944*
—. Europe, Western. Japan. Oil industry and Trade. Organization of Petroleum Exporting Countries. 1970's. *871*
Montana. Barton, Fred. China (Shansi). Cowboys. Horse breeding. Politics. 1912-32. *400*
Moon, Sun Myung. Religion. Unification Church. 1970's. *1080*
Morality. Carter, Jimmy (administration). China. Foreign policy. Human rights. 1976-77. *520*
Mormons. Japan. Missions and Missionaries. 1901-24. *613*
Morrison, Charles C. *Christian Century* (periodical). Foreign policy. Japan. Manchurian crisis. 1931-33. *96*
Morrow, James. Inventions. Japan. Travel (accounts). 1854. *823*
Mortality. China. Medical technology. Social Organization. 19c. 1949-59. *470*

Mukaida, Tomeji (reminiscences). Idaho (Minidoka). Japanese Americans. Relocation. World War II. 1940's. *789*
Multinational corporations. Europe. Japan. Monetary Systems. USA. 1967-73. *924*
—. Japan. Nixon, Richard M. Politics. ca 1948-76. *726*
Multipolarity. *See also* Balance of Power; Tripolarity.
—. Alliances. China. USSR. 1970's. *436*
Munson, Curtis B. Civil rights. Counterintelligence. Internment. Japanese Americans. Peiper, N. J. L. World War II. 1931-42. *765*
Mutsuhito, Emperor. Cultural Imperialism. Foreign Relations. Japan. Seward, William H. 1870-71. *705*
Mutual Balanced Force Reductions. Europe, Western. Japan. Strategic Arms Limitation Talks. USSR. 1974. *1002*
Mysticism. Japan. Religion. Youth. 1976. *767*

N

Nakamura Masanao. Clark, Edward Warren. Cultural relations. Japan (Shizuoka, Tokyo). Missions and Missionaries. ca1870-1907. *721*
Nakamura Takahide. Economic Conditions. Japan (review article). Politics. 1945-49. *740*
National Characteristics. Films. Japan. *The Magnificent Seven* (film). *Seven Samurai* (film). 1960's. *836*
National Security. Alliances. Asia, Southwest. China. USSR. 1977-78. *536*
—. ANZUS. Australia. Japan. New Zealand. Treaties. 1951-81. *936*
—. China. Foreign Relations. Military aid. USSR. 1970-75. *440*
—. Economic growth. Japan. 1950's-82. *654*
—. Japan. Pacifism. 1945-82. *785*
—. Korean War. Military Service. Vietnam War. 1946-81. *1070*
National Security Council. Korean War. Military Intelligence. 1948-50. *1129*
National self-image. Americanology. Historiography (review article). Japan. Social conditions. 19c-20c. 1969-73. *722*
Nationalism. American Revolution. China. Ideology. Revolutionary Movements. Sun Zhongshan. 1776-83. 1905-25. *187*
—. Boycott. Chamber of Commerce. China (Shanghai). Immigration policy. 1905. *519*
—. China. Congregationalism. Missions and Missionaries. 1910-48. *288*
—. China. Foreign Investments. 1890-1931. *313*
—. China. Kerosene. Oil. Standard Oil Company of New York. Taxation. 1925-27. *541*
—. Fermi National Accelerator Laboratory. Japan. Kō Enerugii Butsurigaku Kenkyusho. Physics. 1930-69. *706*
Nationalists. *Amerasia* (periodical). China. Communist Party. Espionage. Foreign policy. Service, John Stewart (reports). ca 1937-45. *343*
—. Aviation. China. Fraser, Douglas. Military training. Saskatchewan (Saskatoon). 1919-22. *217*
—. China. Communism. Marshall, George C. Mediation. USSR. 1946. *356*
Nationalization. China. Claims-assets issue. Foreign Investments. 1950-78. *233*
Native races. China. Cuba. Imperialism. Military Occupation. Philippines. 1898-1903. *316*
—. China (Beijing). Cuba. Military occupation. Philippines. 1898-1903. *238*
Nativism. Chinese Americans. Pacific Northwest. Racism. Religious sectarianism. ca 1840-1945. *21*
NATO. *See also* Atlantic Community.

274 NATO

—. Alliances. Defense. Military strategy. Political change, international. 1945-70's. *1088*
—. China. Europe, Western. Foreign Relations. International Security. 1970's-82. *407*
—. Japan. Military strategy. USSR. 1945-54. *813*
Natural resources. Energy. Food. International Security. Japan. Nuclear Power. 1970's-80. *979*
—. Japan. Military operations. Oregon (Bly). Project FUGO. World War II. 1942-45. *861*
Natural Resources (development). Economic policy. Foreign Relations. USSR. 1950's-70's. *50*
Naval Air Forces. Blacks. Brown, Jesse. Korean War. Pilots. 1948-50. *1139*
—. Korean War. Marines. Pilots. *Sicily* (vessel). 1950. *1130*
Naval battles. Americans (protected). Japan (Shimonoseki Strait). McDougal, David. *Wyoming* (vessel). 1863. *683*
Naval expedition. Diplomacy. Korea. 1840-71. *1126*
Naval missions. Biddle, James. Japan. Negotiations. 1845-54. *590*
Naval officers. Diaries. Korea. Woods, George W. 1884. *1127*
Naval strategy. Caroline Islands. Ellis, Earl. Japan. Marines. 1920-23. *956*
—. China. Diego Garcia. Indian Ocean and Area. USSR. 20c. *364*
—. Communications. Great Britain. Japan. World War II. 1943-45. *652*
—. Dull, Paul S. (review article). Japan. Pearl Harbor. World War II. Yamamoto, Isoroku. 1941-45. *941*
—. Economic policy. Japan. Pacific Dependencies (US). USA. 1945-75. *623*
—. Great Britain. Japan. Pacific Area. World War II. 1941-45. *589*
Naval Tactics. Asia, East. Middle East. 1945-79. *42*
—. Japan. Savo Island (battle). World War II. 1942. *596*
—. Japan. World War II. World War II. 1920's-43. *724*
Naval Vessels. Hawaii. Japan. Pearl Harbor. World War II. 1941. *1000*
Naval War College. Japan. Military Strategy. War Plan Orange. 1900-12. *953*
Naval Warfare. Japan. Leyte (battle). World War II. 1944. *884*
Navies. Agawa, Hiroyuki. Japan. Military officers. World War II. Yamamoto, Isoroku (review article). 1930's-43. *764*
—. Airplanes, Military. Japan. Productivity. World War II. 1941-45. *860*
—. Asia, East. Foreign Policy. Sino-Japanese War. 1894-95. *37*
—. Asiatic Squadron. Diplomacy. Korea. 1882-97. *1015*
—. *Awa Maru* (vessel). Japan. *Queenfish* (submarine). World War II. 1945. *912*
—. Blacks. Brown, Jesse. Hudner, Thomas. Korean War. Military officers. 1950. *1123*
—. Brooke, John Mercer. Japan. *Kanrin Maru* (vessel). Trade. Treaties. Voyages. 1860. *615*
—. Censorship. *Chicago Tribune*. Grand Juries. Japan. Midway (battle). World War II. 1942. *669*
—. China. Foreign Policy. 1974-80. *163*
—. China. Foreign Relations. International Trade. Taiping Rebellion. 1850-61. *291*
—. China. McGiffin, Philo Norton. Sino-Japanese War. 1885-95. *174*
—. China. Sino-American Cooperation Association (SACO). World War II. 1942-45. *476*
—. Combat Information Unit. Cryptography. Japan. Midway (battle). World War II. 1942. *858*
—. Cruisers. Design. Japan. 1925-27. *978*

—. Daily Life. Hostages. Japan. Letters. Rescues. 1846-49. *771*
—. Evacuations. Korea, North (Hungnam). 1950. *1029*
—. Great Britain. Korean War. Suez Crisis. USA. Vietnam War. 1950-76. *1119*
—. *Gregory* (vessel). Japan (Bonin Islands). McCandless, Bruce (reminiscences). World War II. 1945. *798*
—. Japan. 1907-08. *690*
—. Japan. Midway (battle). World War II. 1942. *621*
—. Japan. Philippine Sea (battle). World War II. 1944. *619*
—. Japan. Shanghai crisis. Western nations. 1931-32. *458*
—. Japan. Solomon Islands (Vella Lavella). World War II. 1943. *784*
—. Korean War. Vietnam War. 1945-75. *1120*
Navigation. Imperialism. Japan. Pacific Area. Pearl Harbor. World War II (antecedents). Prehistory-1941. *648*
Negotiations. Biddle, James. Japan. Naval missions. 1845-54. *590*
Nehru, Jawaharlal. Balance of power. Bowles, Chester. China. Foreign Relations. India. 1949-54. *16*
Neocolonialism. Europe. Foreign policy. Japan. Organization of Petroleum Exporting Countries. 1969-70's. *855*
—. Korea, South. 1960-76. *1079*
Netherlands. Asia, East. Diplomacy. Four-Power Treaty. Karnebeek, Hermann Adriaan van. Washington Conference. 1921-22. *9*
—. Australia. Italy. Japan. Political information. Voting and Voting Behavior. 1960's-70's. *716*
—. Colonization. Commerce. Indian-White Relations. New Netherland. Taiwan. 17c. *1160*
Netherlands East Indies. Foreign Policy. Japan. World War II. 1941-46. *710*
New Mexico (Clovis). Internment. Japanese Americans. World War II. 1942-45. *638*
New Netherland. Colonization. Commerce. Indian-White Relations. Netherlands. Taiwan. 17c. *1160*
New York City. China. Diplomacy. Li Hungzhang. Public Opinion. 1896. *226*
—. Economic Conditions. Foreign relations. Hong Kong. Securities. 1964-79. *571*
—. Economic Structure. Foreign investments. Japan. 1960's-70's. *675*
New York *World* (newspaper). Creelman, James. Port Arthur massacre. Press. Sino-Japanese War. 1894-95. *35*
New Zealand. ANZUS. Australia. Japan. National Security. Treaties. 1951-81. *936*
—. Australia. Foreign policy. International Trade. Japan. 1968-70's. *41*
Newspapers. Censorship. Korea, South. Korean War. 1950. *1065*
—. China. Civil War. Hurley, Patrick J. (resignation). Reporters and Reporting. 1945-46. *282*
—. Foreign Relations. Japan. 1900-78. *774*
Nixon Doctrine. Asia, East. Foreign Policy. Japan. Korea. Vietnam. 1969-73. *90*
—. Foreign Relations. Japan. 1945-72. *824*
Nixon, Richard M. China. Detente. 1970's. *247*
—. China. Detente (review article). USSR. 1971-73. *443*
—. China. Diplomacy. Foreign policy. Japan. 1971-72. *91*
—. China. Foreign Policy. Japan. 1971-73. *135*
—. China. Foreign Policy. Kissinger, Henry A. 1960's-70's. *522*
—. China. Foreign policy. Mao Zedong. 1960's-70's. *555*
—. China. Foreign relations. 1969-70's. *553*

Organization 275

—. China. Foreign Relations. 1972-78. *545*
—. China. Foreign Relations (review article). Haldeman, H. R. Kissinger, Henry A. 1968-76. *539*
—. European Economic Community. International Trade. Japan. Monetary policy (devaluation). 1971-73. *655*
—. Japan. Multinational corporations. Politics. ca 1948-76. *726*
Nixon, Richard M. (administration). Balance of power. China. Foreign policy. USSR. 1969-72. *462*
Nixon, Richard M. (visit). China. Detente. Japan. 1971. *79*
—. China. Europe, Eastern. Press. 1971-72. *253*
Normalization. Carter, Jimmy. China. Foreign relations. Taiwan. USSR. 1978-79. *1150*
—. China. Taiwan. 1943-77. *63*
Norman, E. Herbert (review article). Canada. Historians. Japan. 1940-77. *859*
Norquist, Ernest O. Diaries. Japan. Philippines. Prisoners of War. World War II. 1942-45. *837*
North America. Agriculture (comparative study). Boserup, Ester. China. Russia. South. 18c-19c. *465*
—. Air Warfare. Balloons. Bombing. Japan. World War II. 1940-45. *964*
—. Bethune, Angus. China (Canton). International Trade. North West Company. 1812-17. *469*
—. Energy Action Group. Europe. Foreign Relations. Japan. 1973-. *756*
North Atlantic Treaty Organization. See NATO.
North Carolina (vessel). Guadalcanal (battle). *I-19* (submarine). Japan. *O'Brien* (vessel). *Wasp* (vessel). World War II. 1942. *608*
North Korea. See Korea, North.
North West Company. Bethune, Angus. China (Canton). International Trade. North America. 1812-17. *469*
—. China. Fur Trade. Oregon (Astoria). 1760's-1821. *275*
Nuclear Arms. See also Atomic Bomb.
—. Arms control. Canada. China. India. Nuclear power. Regionalism. USA. 1951-78. *493*
—. China. Disarmament. USSR. 1945-79. *377*
—. China. Europe. Foreign Relations. Strategic Arms Limitation Talks. Trilateralism. USSR. 1970's-83. *381*
—. Federal Policy. Japan. Journalism. Secrecy. 1983. *792*
Nuclear physics. Cyclotrons. Denmark. Japan. Scientific Experiments and Research. 1935-45. *965*
Nuclear power. Arms control. Canada. China. India. Nuclear Arms. Regionalism. USA. 1951-78. *493*
—. Energy. Food. International Security. Japan. Natural resources. 1970's-80. *979*
—. Foreign Relations. Japan. 1974-82. *776*
Nuclear Science and Technology. Attitudes. Democracy. Europe. Interest Groups. Japan. USSR. 1970's. *731*
Nuclear stalemate. China. Peace. USSR. 1970's. *156*
Nuclear strategy. Arms control agreements. China. Detente. USSR. 1970's. *516*
Nye, Gideon, Jr. Annexation. Taiwan. 1857. *1164*

O

O'Brien (vessel). Guadalcanal (battle). *I-19* (submarine). Japan. *North Carolina* (vessel). *Wasp* (vessel). World War II. 1942. *608*
Occupations. China. Family. Social Customs. Travel (accounts). 1976. *544*
October War. Korean War. Military Strategy. Pearl Harbor (attack). Surprise attacks. World War II. 1941-73. *7*
Odlum, Victor Wentworth. Canada. China. Diplomacy. 1943-46. *418*
Office of War Information. China. *Keys of the Kingdom* (film). Propaganda. Stereotypes. World War II. 1940-45. *172*
Offner, Arnold A. Europe. Foreign policy. Japan. World War II (antecedents; review article). 1917-41. *829*
Ohio. China (Hubei). Trade. 1979-82. *478*
Oil. China. Kerosene. Nationalism. Standard Oil Company of New York. Taxation. 1925-27. *541*
—. Embargoes. Foreign Policy. Japan. Roosevelt, Franklin D. 1941. *578*
—. Exports. Foreign Policy. Japan. State Department. 1940-41. *948*
Oil crisis. European Economic Community. Germany, West. Japan. Trade. 1974. *647*
—. Foreign Relations. Japan. 1974. *906*
Oil Industry and Trade. Anderson, Irvine H., Jr. (review article). Asia, East. Foreign Investments. Foreign policy. Standard-Vacuum Oil Company. 1933-41. 1975. *97*
—. Arab States. Japan. 1970's. *778*
—. Europe, Western. Japan. 1960's-70's. *847*
—. Europe, Western. Japan. Monopolies. Organization of Petroleum Exporting Countries. 1970's. *871*
—. Exports. Great Britain. Japan. Roosevelt, Franklin D. World War II. 1940-41. *659*
—. Foreign Policy. Japan. 1934-37. *819*
Oil well. Karns, A. P. Locke, Robert D. (interview). Taiwan. 1877-78. *272*
Okinawa. Foreign Policy. International politics. Japan. 1853-1972. *718*
—. Foreign Relations. Japan. Public Opinion. Sato, Eisaku. 1969. *752*
—. Japan. 1200-1975. *799*
—. Japanese control. Military Government. 1945-72. *807*
Oklahoma. Korean War. McLain, Raymond Stallings. Military General Staff. Villa, Pancho. World War I. World War II. 1912-54. *1121*
Open Door Policy. Barrett, John. China. Foreign policy. 1898-99. *445*
—. China. 1899-1937. *547*
—. China. Hay, John. Historiography (revisionist). International Trade. 1899-1901. *170*
—. China. Historiography. 1899-1922. *403*
—. China. Rockhill, William W. State Department. 1886-1920. *505*
Operation Olympic. Invasions. Japan. Military Strategy. World War II. 1945. *645*
Oral history. Internment. Japanese Americans. Tanaka, Togo. World War II. Yoneda, Elaine. Yoneda, Karl. 1941-45. *816*
Oregon (Astoria). China. Fur Trade. North West Company. 1760's-1821. *275*
Oregon (Bly). Japan. Military operations. Natural Resources. Project FUGO. World War II. 1942-45. *861*
Organization of Petroleum Exporting Countries. Europe. Foreign policy. Japan. Neocolonialism. 1969-70's. *855*
—. Europe, Western. Japan. Monopolies. Oil industry and Trade. 1970's. *871*

276 Oriental Bank

Oriental Bank Corporation. Economic development. Japan. Schiff, Jacob. Williams, George B. Wilson, James H. Winslow, Edward F. 1872-73. *606*
Origami. Folk art. Japan. Popular Culture. 1900-76. *593*
Orphans. Air Forces. *Battle Hymn* (film). Hess, Dean Elmer. Korean War. 1950-56. *1032*
Osan Air Base. Air Forces. F-86F (aircraft). Korean War. South Africa. UN Command. 1950-53. *1008*

P

Pacific & Eastern Steamship Company. China. International trade. Ships. USA. World War I. 1914-16. *447*
Pacific Area. Alaska. British Columbia. China (Macao). Cook, James. Fur trade. 1778-79. *49*
—. Biddle, James. Japan. Spain. Taguchi Ukichi. 1846-90's. *773*
—. China. Foreign policy. International Trade. Vietnam War. 1960's-70's. *166*
—. China. Foreign Policy. USSR. 1950-83. *157*
—. Great Britain. Japan. Naval Strategy. World War II. 1941-45. *589*
—. Imperialism. Japan. Navigation. Pearl Harbor. World War II (antecedents). Prehistory-1941. *648*
—. Japan. Russia. 1900's-79. *673*
Pacific Dependencies (US). Bikini Atoll. Hydrogen bomb. Japan. *Lucky Dragon* (vessel). 1954-75. *882*
—. Economic policy. Japan. Naval strategy. USA. 1945-75. *623*
Pacific free trade area. Economic Conditions. Foreign Relations. Japan. 1945-74. *71*
Pacific Northwest. Bombs, balloon-carried. Japan. World War II. 1945. *733*
—. Chinese Americans. Nativism. Racism. Religious sectarianism. ca 1840-1945. *21*
Pacifism. Japan. National Security. 1945-82. *785*
Pakistan. Afghanistan. China. Government. 1979-81. *146*
—. China. Foreign Policy. India. USSR. 1945-75. *409*
Pandas. China. Harkness, Ruth. Tangier Smith, Floyd. 1936. *175*
Pangborn, Clyde. Herndon, Hugh. Japan. Transpacific flight. USA. 1930-71. *864*
Pao-huang Hui Party. Canada. Chinese. Political Factions. 1899-1904. *153*
Pardon. Citizenship. Ford, Gerald R. Hada, John. Japanese American Citizens League. Tokyo Rose (Iva Toguri d'Aquino). Uyeda, Clifford I. (account). 1973-77. *949*
Paris Peace Conference. China. Foreign Policy. League of Nations. Treaties, unequal. Wilson, Woodrow. 1919. *19*
—. China. Japan. League of Nations. Wilson, Woodrow. 1919. *85*
—. Equality (proposed). Hughes, William Morris. Japan. League of Nations Covenant. Race Relations. Wilson, Woodrow. 1919. *772*
Park Chung-hee. Assassination. Foreign Relations. Korea, South. Politics. 1979-82. *1010*
Parker, Peter. China. Gulick, Edward V. (review article). 1840's-50's. *543*
Parrish, Edward James. American Tobacco Company. Government ownership. Japan (Tokyo). Tobacco. 1899-1904. *656*
Partition. Foreign Policy. Korea. World War II. 1945. *1082*
Passionists. Catholic Church. China (Hunan). Missions and Missionaries. 1921-29. *186*

Patriotism. Generations. Internment. Japanese American Citizens League. World War II. 1941-42. *913*
Peace. China. Foreign Policy. USSR. 1970's. *305*
—. China. Nuclear stalemate. USSR. 1970's. *156*
—. Diplomacy. France (Paris). Korea, South (Panmunjom). Vietnam. 1951-73. *1143*
—. Japan. Potsdam Conference. Surrender, unconditional. World War II. 1945. *952*
Peace negotiations. Cease-fire. Eisenhower, Dwight D. Korean War. UN. 1952-53. *1136*
—. Korean War. 1951-53. *1009*
Peace pact (proposed). Crawford, David L. Hawaii, University of. Japan. USA. 1940-41. *713*
Peace (review article). Butow, R. J. Diplomacy, private. Japan. John Doe Associates. World War II (antecedents). 1940-41. *723*
Peace settlement. Australia. Japan. World War II. 1942-46. *597*
Pearl Harbor. Dull, Paul S. (review article). Japan. Naval Strategy. World War II. Yamamoto, Isoroku. 1941-45. *941*
—. Hawaii. Japan. Naval Vessels. World War II. 1941. *1000*
—. Hawaii. Japan. World War II. 1941. *885*
—. Herde, Peter (review article). Japan. World War II. 1941. *938*
—. Imperialism. Japan. Navigation. Pacific Area. World War II (antecedents). Prehistory-1941. *648*
Pearl Harbor (attack). Armstrong, David M. (personal account). Hawaii. Japan. World War II. 1942. *580*
—. Japan. World War II. 1940-41. *846*
—. Korean War. Military Strategy. October War. Surprise attacks. World War II. 1941-73. *7*
Peatross, Oscar F. (account). Japan. Makin Islands (raid). Marines (2d Raiders). Prisoners of War. World War II. 1942-47. *853*
Peiper, N. J. L. Civil rights. Counterintelligence. Internment. Japanese Americans. Munson, Curtis B. World War II. 1931-42. *765*
Peking Man. Archaeology. China. Janus, Christopher. Shapiro, Harry F. 1941-73. *542*
Peleliu (battle). Armies. Japan. Marines. Sledge, Eugene B. (account). World War II. 1944. *907*
Pennsylvania (Bedford). Diplomats. Japanese. Prisoners of War. World War II. 1945. *586*
Pennsylvania (Philadelphia). China. Foreign Relations. Girard College (Stephen Girard Collection). Historical Society of Pennsylvania. International Trade. 1775-1840. 1980. *273*
People's Daily. China. Reporters and Reporting. 1971-80. *352*
People's Republic of China. See China.
Perry, Matthew C. Diplomacy. International Trade. Japan. 1853. *783*
—. Foreign Relations. Japan. Preble, G. W. (diary). 1852-54. *587*
Persian Gulf and Area. China. Foreign Relations. Indian Ocean and Area. 1946-80. *103*
—. Europe. Foreign Relations. Japan. Tucker, Robert W. (interview). 1968-80. *998*
Personal narratives. Air Forces. Atomic bomb. Japan (Hiroshima). Military training. Tibbets, Paul W. World War II. 1945. *932*
—. Air Transport Command. Burma Road. China. Convoys. Frost, Edwin C. Transportation, Military. 1945. *259*
—. Air Warfare. Bombing. China (Gailan). Coal Mines and Mining. Combs, Cecil E. World War II. 1942. *213*
—. Air Warfare. Bombing. Japan. Sims, Jack A. World War II. 1942. *905*
—. Armies. Dill, James. Korean War. 7th Infantry Division, US (31st Field Artillery Battalion). 1950-51. *1027*

Politics   277

—. Bombing. B-29 (aircraft). China-Burma-India Theater. Close, Winton R. Japan. World War II. 1944. *633*
—. Carney, Robert B. Japan. Surrender. World War II. 1945. *626*
—. China (Harbin). Russian language. Tolley, Kemp. 1935. *124*
—. China (Shanghai). Marines. *Pittsburgh* (vessel). Smith, Wiley H. 1927. *408*
—. Daily Life. Internment. Japanese Americans. Uchida, Yoshiko. Utah (Topaz). World War II. 1942-43. *942*
—. Dixon, Robert E. Japan. Johnston, Stanley. Midway (battle). Military Strategy. Reporters and Reporting. World War II. 1942. *794*
—. Internment. Japanese Americans. World War II. 1942-81. *1001*
—. Japan. Junghans, Earl A. Marines. Prisoners of War. Wake Island. War crimes. World War II. 1941-47. *737*
—. Japan. Keene, Donald. Scholarship. Social Customs. 1930's-80's. *746*
—. Japan. Missions and Missionaries. Protestantism. 1860-1905. *931*
—. Korea. Military Service, Professional. Ridgway, Matthew B. 8th Army, US. 1917-52. *1047*
Personality. Authoritarianism (theory). Korean War. Public opinion. Racism. Vietnam War. 1950-78. *1046*
Peru. Diplomacy. Emmerson, John K. Internment. Japanese Peruvians. Memoirs. World War II. 1942-43. *660*
—. Discrimination. Japanese. 1931-43. *632*
Petrel (vessel). China (Hankow). Foreign Relations. 1895. *431*
Philippine Sea (battle). Japan. Navies. World War II. 1944. *619*
Philippines. Air Forces. Japan. Military Capability. World War II. 1941. *692*
—. China. Cuba. Imperialism. Military Occupation. Native races. 1898-1903. *316*
—. China. Diplomacy. Foreign Policy (review article). Imperialism. Reinsch, Paul S. 1899-1945. *57*
—. China (Beijing). Cuba. Military occupation. Native races. 1898-1903. *238*
—. Clark Field. Japan. World War II. 1941-42. *788*
—. Diaries. Japan. Norquist, Ernest O. Prisoners of War. World War II. 1942-45. *837*
—. Diplomacy. Hull, Cordell. Indochina. Japan. World War II (antecedents). 1941. *616*
—. Foreign Relations. Japan. Quirino, Elpidio. Treaties. World War II. 1945-56. *748*
Philippines (Biliran). Catholic Church. Clergy. Guevara, Gaspar Ignacio de. Heresy. 1765-75. *1061*
Philippines (Manila). Diplomacy. Japan. MacArthur, Douglas. Surrender. World War II. 1945. *812*
Photographs. China, north. Marines. Uniforms, Military. 1931-41. *504*
—. China (Shanghai). Japan. Marines. 1920's-30's. *569*
—. Documentation. Evacuations. Internment. Japanese Americans. War Relocation Authority. World War II. 1941-43. *643*
Photography, Journalistic. Adams, Ansel. California. Internment. Japanese Americans. Lange, Dorothea. Manzanar War Relocation Center. World War II. 1941-45. *840*
Physics. Fermi National Accelerator Laboratory. Japan. Kō Enerugii Butsurigaku Kenkyusho. Nationalism. 1930-69. *706*
Pilgrimages. Alienation. China. Cuba. Intellectuals, western. USSR. Vietnam, North. 1930's. 1970's. *296*

Pilots. Blacks. Brown, Jesse. Korean War. Naval Air Forces. 1948-50. *1139*
—. Brooks, James L. (personal account). F-86 (aircraft). Korean War. 1950. *1016*
—. Butler, Smedley D. China, North. Marines. Williams, Clarence S. 1927-28. *410*
—. Korean War. Marines. Naval Air Forces. *Sicily* (vessel). 1950. *1130*
Pittman, Key. China. International Trade. Senate. Silver Purchase Act (1934). USA. 1933-40. *485*
—. Foreign Relations. Japan. 1920-40. *781*
Pittsburgh (vessel). China (Shanghai). Marines. Personal Narratives. Smith, Wiley H. 1927. *408*
Poetry. Internment. Japanese Americans. Mirikitani, Janice ("Lullaby"). World War II. 1941-45. *609*
Policymaking. Civilians. Korean War. 1945-54. *1069*
Political Attitudes. Asia, East. China. Development. Foreign Relations. Wilson, James H. 1885-1910. *169*
—. Blacks. China. Discrimination. Foreign Policy. 1971. *492*
—. China. Economic Conditions. Foreign Policy. Taiwan. 1949-82. *473*
—. China. Intellectuals (Chinese). Taiwan. 1970. *14*
—. Defense spending. Korean War. Military. Minutemen. Vietnam War. 1784-1979. *1077*
—. Japan. Radicals and Radicalism. Students. 1960's-70's. *760*
Political change, international. Alliances. Defense. Military strategy. NATO. 1945-70's. *1088*
Political Commentary. China. Foreign Relations. Vietnam War. 1960's-70's. *419*
Political conditions. Asia, northeast. Foreign Policy. Korean War. 1953-78. *1128*
—. China. Foreign relations. 1969-70's. *307*
Political Corruption. Japan. Lockheed Aircraft Corporation. 1976. *583*
Political economy. Dependency. Japan. Korea, South. 1973. *1041*
Political Factions. Canada. Chinese. Pao-huang Hui Party. 1899-1904. *153*
—. China. Foreign policy. Military. USSR. Zhou Enlai. 1970-71. *263*
—. Independence Movements. Korea. Rhee, Syngman. 1919-45. *1073*
Political information. Australia. Italy. Japan. Netherlands. Voting and Voting Behavior. 1960's-70's. *716*
Political Leadership. Asia, East. Economic problems. Foreign Relations. Japan. Tanaka, Kakuei. 1971-74. *883*
—. Immigration. Korean Americans. Rhee, Syngman. 1903-24. *1048*
Political Science. China. Colleges and Universities. Communism. Grading, peer group. 1964-72. *453*
Political systems. Barefoot doctor movement. China. Medicine, Western. Public Health. 1973. *411*
—. Economic Conditions. Great Britain. Japan. Military Occupation. 1945-49. *617*
—. Japan. Pollution abatement. USSR. 1950's-74. *747*
—. Korean War. Vietnam War. War, limited. 1950-75. *1030*
Political Theory. Alliances. Dulles, John Foster. Japan. Treaties. Yoshida Shigeru. 5c BC-20c. 1951. *653*
—. China. Progressivism. Sun Zhongshan. 1880-1912. *194*
—. Europe, Western. Japan. Trilateralism. 1970's. *954*
Political tradition. Constitutions. Japan. MacArthur, Douglas. Military Occupation. 1945-76. *804*
Politics. Assassination. Foreign Relations. Korea, South. Park Chung-hee. 1979-82. *1010*

278　Politics

—. Atomic Warfare. Japan. Surrender. Truman, Harry S. (administration). World War II. 1945. *604*
—. Barton, Fred. China (Shansi). Cowboys. Horse breeding. Montana. 1912-32. *400*
—. China. Dulles, John Foster. Letters. Rusk, Dean. State Department. 1953. *499*
—. China. Foreign Relations. Kahn, E. J., Jr. (review article). State Department (Foreign Service). 1940's-50's. 1975. *384*
—. China. International Trade. 1789-1819. *277*
—. China. Research. 1950-76. *531*
—. Constitutional reform. Japan. Military occupation. 1945-52. *577*
—. Economic Conditions. Japan (review article). Nakamura Takahide. 1945-49. *740*
—. Economic Policy. Foreign policy. Japan. Military. 1945-72. *919*
—. Historiography. Korean War. MacArthur, Douglas. Public relations. Truman, Harry S. Wake Island. 1950. *1142*
—. Japan. Multinational corporations. Nixon, Richard M. ca 1948-76. *726*
—. Korean War. MacArthur, Douglas. 1950-51. *1019*
Politics and the Military. China. Foreign policy. Korean War. MacArthur, Douglas. Truman, Harry S. 1949-52. *1025*
—. Korean War. Limited war. MacArthur, Douglas. Truman, Harry S. 1950-51. *1132*
Pollution abatement. Japan. Political systems. USSR. 1950's-74. *747*
Popular Culture. Folk art. Japan. Origami. 1900-76. *593*
Porcelain. China. Trade. 18c-1825. *387*
Port Arthur massacre. Creelman, James. New York *World* (newspaper). Press. Sino-Japanese War. 1894-95. *35*
Ports. Art. China. Chinnery, George. Sailors. 18c-19c. *423*
Portsmouth Peace Conference. Dillon, Emile Joseph. Press. Public opinion. Russo-Japanese War. Witte, Sergei. 1904-05. *732*
Potsdam Conference. Japan. Peace. Surrender, unconditional. World War II. 1945. *952*
Pott, Francis L. H. China (Shanghai). Episcopal Church, Protestant. Missions and Missionaries. St. John's University. 1888-1941. *285*
Preble, G. W. (diary). Foreign Relations. Japan. Perry, Matthew C. 1852-54. *587*
Presbyterian Church. Alabama (Mobile). China. Missions and Missionaries. Stuart, Mary Horton. 1840's-1947. *284*
—. Attitudes. China. Missions and Missionaries. 1837-1900. *212*
Presbyterian Historical Society. Archives. China. Japan. Korea. Missions and Missionaries. 1829-1911. *39*
Presidency. China. Great Britain. Yuan Shikai. 1911-12. *363*
Press. Business. Cold War. Foreign policy. Japan. 1948-52. *704*
—. China. Europe, Eastern. Nixon, Richard M. (visit). 1971-72. *253*
—. China. Foreign policy. USSR. 1979-80. *398*
—. China. Foreign Relations. Public information. 1970's. *368*
—. China. Japan. Public opinion. Sino-Japanese war. USA. 1894-95. *53*
—. China (Inner Mongolia). Rosholt, Malcolm (account). Travel. 1935. *461*
—. Creelman, James. New York *World* (newspaper). Port Arthur massacre. Sino-Japanese War. 1894-95. *35*
—. Dillon, Emile Joseph. Portsmouth Peace Conference. Public opinion. Russo-Japanese War. Witte, Sergei. 1904-05. *732*
—. Foreign Relations. Japan. 1969-71. *664*

Prices. Business. Germany, West. Japan. 1980. *682*
Prisoners of War. *See also* Concentration Camps; Internment; Relocation.
—. Apathy. Colonization. Death and Dying. Korean War. Malnutrition. Virginia (Jamestown). World War II. 1607-24. 1941-53. *74*
—. China. Japan. Kinney, John F. Marines. Wake Island. World War II. 1941-45. *943*
—. Communism. Korean War. Propaganda. Public opinion. Vietnam War. 1950-74. *1021*
—. Diaries. Japan. Norquist, Ernest O. Philippines. World War II. 1942-45. *837*
—. Diplomats. Japanese. Pennsylvania (Bedford). World War II. 1945. *586*
—. Japan. Junghans, Earl A. Marines. Personal narratives. Wake Island. War crimes. World War II. 1941-47. *737*
—. Japan. Makin Islands (raid). Marines (2d Raiders). Peatross, Oscar F. (account). World War II. 1942-47. *853*
—. Japanese. World War II. 1941-45. *759*
Prisoners of War (German, Japanese, Italian). World War II. 1942-45. *620*
Productivity. Airplanes, Military. Japan. Navies. World War II. 1941-45. *860*
—. Canada. Europe. Japan. Labor costs. Manufacturing. 1974-81. *624*
—. Canada. Europe, Western. Japan. Labor. Manufacturing. 1960-82. *576*
Progressivism. China. Political Theory. Sun Zhongshan. 1880-1912. *194*
Project FUGO. Balloons, armed. Japan. South Dakota. World War II. 1944-45. *770*
—. Japan. Military operations. Natural Resources. Oregon (Bly). World War II. 1942-45. *861*
Propaganda. Arnhold & Company. China (Chang River). Hawley, Edwin C. Theater. Tretiakov, Sergei (*Roar China!*). 1924-75. *394*
—. China. *Keys of the Kingdom* (film). Office of War Information. Stereotypes. World War II. 1940-45. *172*
—. Communism. Korean War. Prisoners of war. Public opinion. Vietnam War. 1950-74. *1021*
—. Internment. Japanese Americans. World War II. 1942-45. *841*
Protectionism. Antitrust. Automobile Industry and Trade. Federal Policy. Imports. Japan. 1981-83. *982*
—. Congress. Japan. 1981-82. *896*
—. Economic development. Europe, Western. Japan. Trade. 1948-80. *866*
—. Economic Policy. Germany, West. GNP. Inflation. Japan. 1976-78. *709*
Protestant Churches. Catholic Church. China. Christians. Communists. Missions and Missionaries. 1948-50. *523*
Protestantism. Archives. China. Missions and Missionaries. Yale University Library (collection). Yale-in-China Association. 1901-51. *237*
—. China. Missions and Missionaries. Revivals. 1830-50. *466*
—. Japan. Missions and Missionaries. Personal Narratives. 1860-1905. *931*
Public Administration. Academia Sinica (Tsungli Yamen Archive). China. Foreign Relations. 1868-94. *220*
—. Japan. Local government. Reform. 1940-69. *753*
Public Health. Barefoot doctor movement. China. Medicine, Western. Political systems. 1973. *411*
Public information. China. Foreign Relations. Press. 1970's. *368*
Public Opinion. Arizona. Gila River Relocation Center. Japanese Americans. Race Relations. World War II. 1942-45. *627*
—. Asia, East. Education. USA. 1973. *5*

—. Atomic bomb. Japan. World War II. 1945-49. *984*
—. Authoritarianism (theory). Korean War. Personality. Racism. Vietnam War. 1950-78. *1046*
—. Carter, Jimmy (administration). China. Foreign policy. 1967-78. *340*
—. China. Cohen, Warren I. (review article). Foreign policy. Japan. Leadership. ca 1900-50. 1978. *26*
—. China. Diplomacy. Li Hungzhang. New York City. 1896. *226*
—. China. Foreign Policy. Japan. World War II. 1937-45. *65*
—. China. Japan. Korea, South. Taiwan. Treaties, mutual defense. 1950's-77. *126*
—. China. Japan. Press. Sino-Japanese war. USA. 1894-95. *53*
—. China Lobby. Institute of Pacific Relations. McCarran Committee. Thomas, John N. (review article). Watergate trials. 1945-75. *58*
—. Communism. Korean War. Prisoners of war. Propaganda. Vietnam War. 1950-74. *1021*
—. Congress. Japan. Manchurian crisis. 1931-33. *83*
—. Daily Life. Korean War. Vietnam War. 1950-73. *1114*
—. Dillon, Emile Joseph. Portsmouth Peace Conference. Press. Russo-Japanese War. Witte, Sergei. 1904-05. *732*
—. Dumping. International Trade. Japan. Steel. 1974-78. *745*
—. Foreign policy. Korea, South. 1952-80. *1089*
—. Foreign Relations. Japan. Okinawa. Sato, Eisaku. 1969. *752*
—. Japan. Vietnam War. 1960's-70's. *909*
Public relations. Historiography. Korean War. MacArthur, Douglas. Politics. Truman, Harry S. Wake Island. 1950. *1142*
Public schools. Concentration Camps. Japanese Americans. World War II. 1942-45. *977*
Public services. Europe, Western. Japan. Trilateral Commission. Wages. 1973-79. *925*
Publishers and Publishing. Books, miniature. Europe. Japan. 15c-20c. *856*
—. China. Foreign Relations. 1978-81. *359*
—. China (Shanghai). Methodist Episcopal Church, South. Missions and Missionaries. 1898-1920. *439*
Pueblo incident. Cambodia. Decisionmaking. Flexible response. Korea, North. *Mayaguez* incident. 1969-75. *1039*
P-40 (aircraft). Air Warfare. Army Air Force. China. Flying Tigers. Holloway, Bruce K. (account). World War II. 1942-43. *297*

Q

Queenfish (submarine). *Awa Maru* (vessel). Japan. Navies. World War II. 1945. *912*
Quilts. Japan. 1876-1900. *802*
Quirino, Elpidio. Foreign Relations. Japan. Philippines. Treaties. World War II. 1945-56. *748*

R

Rabaul (battle). Air Forces. Japan. Kenney, George. World War II. 1943. *607*
Race Relations. Arizona. Gila River Relocation Center. Japanese Americans. Public Opinion. World War II. 1942-45. *627*
—. Blacks. Immigration restriction. Japanese. Miller, Kelly. 1906-24. *699*
—. Business. China (Shanghai). Rea, George Bronson. 1920's. *301*

—. Equality (proposed). Hughes, William Morris. Japan. League of Nations Covenant. Paris Peace Conference. Wilson, Woodrow. 1919. *772*
—. Interpersonal contact. Students. Taiwan. USA. 1933-73. *1167*
Racism. Authoritarianism (theory). Korean War. Personality. Public opinion. Vietnam War. 1950-78. *1046*
—. California. Detention. Japanese Americans. World War II. 1941-45. *818*
—. Chinese Americans. Nativism. Pacific Northwest. Religious sectarianism. ca 1840-1945. *21*
—. Concentration camps. Japanese Americans. World War II. 1940-45. *719*
Radiation Effects Research Foundation. Atomic Bomb Casualty Commission. Civilians. Japan (Hiroshima, Nagasaki). Medical Research. 1945-75. *960*
Radicals and Radicalism. Japan. Political attitudes. Students. 1960's-70's. *760*
Radio. Cryptography. Guadalcanal (battle). Japan. Military Intelligence. World War II. 1942. *810*
Ranard, Donald L. (account). Intelligence Service. Korea, South. 1970-74. *1110*
Rasmussen, Kai E. Japanese Americans (Nisei). Language School. Military Intelligence. Minnesota. World War II. 1941-46. *579*
Rea, George Bronson. Business. China (Shanghai). Race Relations. 1920's. *301*
—. China. *Far Eastern Review* (newspaper). Foreign Policy. Japan. 1904-36. *59*
Reagan, Ronald (administration). Anti-Communist Movements. Asia. Foreign Policy. Taiwan. 1981. *64*
Rearmament. Japan. Military relations. 1946-70's. *975*
Reform. *See also* Economic Reform; Educational Reform; Labor Reform; Social Reform.
—. California (San Francisco). China. Huang Tsunhsien. 1882-85. *328*
—. Japan. Local government. Public Administration. 1940-69. *753*
Regional studies. Agricultural Development. China. 1900-20. *193*
Regionalism. Arms control. Canada. China. India. Nuclear Arms. Nuclear power. USA. 1951-78. *493*
Reinsch, Paul S. China. Diplomacy. 1913-19. *444*
—. China. Diplomacy. Foreign Policy (review article). Imperialism. Philippines. 1899-1945. *57*
Religion. *See also* names of specific churches and denominations, e.g., Baptists, Lutherans, etc.; Missions and Missionaries.
—. Japan. Mysticism. Youth. 1976. *767*
—. Moon, Sun Myung. Unification Church. 1970's. *1080*
Religion, popular. China. Sects, Religious. 1800-60. *164*
Religious Sectarianism. *See also* Sects, Religious.
—. Chinese Americans. Nativism. Pacific Northwest. Racism. ca 1840-1945. *21*
Religious toleration. China. Missions and Missionaries. Tianjin, Treaty of (Article XXIX). Translating. 1858-59. *429*
Relocation. *See also* Concentration Camps; Internment.
—. Bohme, Frederick G. Census Bureau. Japanese Americans. Letters. World War II. 1942-45. *640*
—. California. Japanese Americans. Warren, Earl. World War II. 1941-45. *967*
—. Idaho (Minidoka). Japanese Americans. Mukaida, Tomeji (reminiscences). World War II. 1940's. *789*
Renouf, Vincent Adams (papers). China (Tianjin). Teaching. 1903-10. *552*

Reparations. Boxer Rebellion. China. Education. Foreign Policy. Historiography. Hunt, Michael (thesis). 1900-06. 1972. *535*
Repatriation. Japanese. Korea. Koreans. Military government. 1945-48. *1018*
Reporters and Reporting. Censorship. *Chicago Tribune.* Cryptography. Japan. Midway (battle). World War II. 1942. *679*
—. China. Civil War. Hurley, Patrick J. (resignation). Newspapers. 1945-46. *282*
—. China. *People's Daily.* 1971-80. *352*
—. Dixon, Robert E. Japan. Johnston, Stanley. Midway (battle). Military Strategy. Personal narratives. World War II. 1942. *794*
—. Japan. London, Jack. Russo-Japanese War. 1904. *689*
Republic of China. *See* Taiwan.
Republic of Korea. *See* Korea, South.
Republican Party. Burlingame, Anson. China. Diplomacy. House of Representatives. 1854-69. *148*
Rescues. Daily Life. Hostages. Japan. Letters. Navies. 1846-49. *771*
Research. China. Educational Exchange Programs. Social Sciences. 1972-79. *513*
—. China. Foreign Relations. 19c-20c. *399*
—. China. Politics. 1950-76. *531*
—. Germany. Japan. Libraries, Presidential. Military government. 1945-78. *994*
Research and development. Europe. Japan. Technology. ca 1964-76. *574*
Revivals. China. Missions and Missionaries. Protestantism. 1830-50. *466*
Revolution. Canton Christian College. China. Church Schools. Yale-in-China Association. 1925-27. *300*
—. China. Communist Party. Diplomacy (secret). Mao Zedong. 1949. *350*
—. China. Diplomatic recognition. Missions and Missionaries. Sun Zhongshan. 1911-13. *395*
—. China. Episcopal Church, Protestant. Long, Charles H. Missions and Missionaries. 1946-49. *372*
Revolutionary Movements. American Revolution. China. Ideology. Nationalism. Sun Zhongshan. 1776-83. 1905-25. *187*
—. Asia. Historiography, US. Japan. USSR. World War II. 1930's-49. *862*
—. China. Communism. India. Lu Xun. Smedley, Agnes. 1910-50. *375*
Rhee, Syngman. Immigration. Korean Americans. Political leadership. 1903-24. *1048*
—. Independence Movements. Korea. Political Factions. 1919-45. *1073*
Rhetoric. China. Foreign policy. 1899-. *413*
Rhode Island (Providence). China. Economic Conditions. Sino-Japanese War. Weapons. 1894. *36*
Ridgway, Matthew B. Korea. Military Service, Professional. Personal narratives. 8th Army, US. 1917-52. *1047*
Riots. California. Concentration Camps. Japanese Americans. Manzanar War Relocation Center. Ueno, Harry (arrest). World War II. 1942. *691*
Risedorph, Gene (reminiscences). Air Warfare. Korea, South (Ch'unch'on). Korean War. 1952. *1112*
Roberts, Issachar Jacob. Baptists (Southern). China. Missions and Missionaries. 1837-47. *567*
Robots. Japan. Technology. 1965-83. *800*
Rockefeller family. Europe, Western. Foreign Policy. International Trade. Japan. Trilateral Commission. 1973-78. *995*
Rockhill, William W. China. Open Door Policy. State Department. 1886-1920. *505*
Roll-call voting. Developing nations. Economic issues. Japan. UN General Assembly. Western Nations. 1970-76. *966*

Roosevelt, Franklin D. Anticolonialism. Asia. USA. World War II. 1941-45. *51*
—. Blockades. Chamberlain, Neville. China. Great Britain. Japan. World War II (antecedents). 1937-38. *686*
—. Brussels Conference. Diplomacy. Sino-Japanese War. 1937. *117*
—. Carlson, Evans. China. Intelligence mission. Japan. 1937-38. *40*
—. Carlson, Evans. China. Intelligence mission. Japan. 1937-38. *128*
—. China. Churchill, Winston. Colonies. deGaulle, Charles. Foreign Policy. Indochina. 1942-45. *75*
—. China. Conference on Chinese-American Relations. Foreign Policy. Truman, Harry S. 1944-48. 1978. *289*
—. Diplomacy. Japan. Military Intelligence. World War II (antecedents). 1940-41. *693*
—. Embargoes. Foreign Policy. Japan. Oil. 1941. *578*
—. Exports. Great Britain. Japan. Oil Industry and Trade. World War II. 1940-41. *659*
—. Foreign policy. Hull, Cordell. Japan. Stimson, Henry L. 1933-36. *730*
Roosevelt, Franklin D. (administration). China. Congress. International Trade. Lobbying. Silver Purchase Act (1934). 1934. *268*
Roosevelt, Theodore. Diplomacy (personal). Germany. Meyer, George von Lengerke. Russo-Japanese War. William II. 1902-14. *968*
—. Foreign Policy. Japan. Korea. Russia. 1901-05. *1057*
Roots, Eliza McCook. China. Episcopal Church, Protestant. Missions and Missionaries. Roots, Logan H. 1900-34. *477*
Roots, Logan H. China. Episcopal Church, Protestant. Missions and Missionaries. Roots, Eliza McCook. 1900-34. *477*
Rosholt, Malcolm (account). China (Inner Mongolia). Press. Travel. 1935. *461*
Rostow, Eugene V. Arms race. China. Korean War. USSR. 1953-82. *8*
Rusk, Dean. China. Dulles, John Foster. Letters. Politics. State Department. 1953. *499*
Russia. *See also* USSR.
—. Agriculture (comparative study). Boserup, Ester. China. North America. South. 18c-19c. *465*
—. China. Diplomacy. Li Hungzhang. Travel. 1896. *250*
—. Foreign Policy. Japan. Korea. Roosevelt, Theodore. 1901-05. *1057*
—. Intervention (military). Japan. 1918-20. *55*
—. Japan. Pacific Area. 1900's-79. *673*
Russian language. China (Harbin). Personal narratives. Tolley, Kemp. 1935. *124*
Russo-Japanese War. Dillon, Emile Joseph. Portsmouth Peace Conference. Press. Public opinion. Witte, Sergei, 1904-05. *732*
—. Diplomacy (personal). Germany. Meyer, George von Lengerke. Roosevelt, Theodore. William II. 1902-14. *968*
—. Japan. London, Jack. Reporters and Reporting. 1904. *689*
Ryukyu Islands (Okinawa). Economic Conditions. Japan. Military occupation. 1952-79. *950*

S

Sailors. Art. China. Chinnery, George. Ports. 18c-19c. *423*
St. John's University. China (Shanghai). Episcopal Church, Protestant. Missions and Missionaries. Pott, Francis L. H. 1888-1941. *285*
Sapporo Agricultural College. Colleges and Universities. Japan. Science. Teachers. Tokyo, University of. 1860-1900. *961*

Saskatchewan (Saskatoon). Aviation. China. Fraser, Douglas. Military training. Nationalists. 1919-22. *217*
Sato, Eisaku. Foreign Relations. Japan. Okinawa. Public Opinion. 1969. *752*
Savo Island (battle). Japan. Naval Tactics. World War II. 1942. *596*
Schellenbach, Lewis B. Coffee, John M. Congress. Embargoes. Japan. Washington. 1930's-40. *780*
Schiff, Jacob. Economic development. Japan. Oriental Bank Corporation. Williams, George B. Wilson, James H. Winslow, Edward F. 1872-73. *606*
Scholars. Brain drain. Immigration. Taiwan. 1905-73. *1163*
—. China. Communists. Foreign Policy. Liberals. 1944-71. *380*
Scholarship. Japan. Keene, Donald. Personal narratives. Social Customs. 1930's-80's. *746*
Science. China. Methodology. 20c. *180*
—. Colleges and Universities. Japan. Sapporo Agricultural College. Teachers. Tokyo, University of. 1860-1900. *961*
Scientific Experiments and Research. Cyclotrons. Denmark. Japan. Nuclear physics. 1935-45. *965*
Scruggs, William L. China (Zhenjiang). Diplomats. 1879-81. *433*
Sea otters. Canada. Fur trade. Japan. Wildlife Conservation. 18c-20c. *988*
Secondary Education (curriculum reform). Asian studies. China. USA. 1972-73. *373*
Secrecy. Federal Policy. Japan. Journalism. Nuclear arms. 1983. *792*
Sects, Religious. China. Religion, popular. 1800-60. *164*
Securities. Economic Conditions. Foreign relations. Hong Kong. New York City. 1964-79. *571*
Self-determination. Foreign Policy. Korea (38th Parallel). Korean War. MacArthur, Douglas. Truman, Harry S. USSR. 1943-50. *1084*
Semiconductors. Diffusion. Japan. Technology. 1982. *876*
Senate. China. Foreign Policy. History Teaching. Legislative Investigations. Simulation and Games. 1949. 1978. *378*
—. China. International Trade. Pittman, Key. Silver Purchase Act (1934). USA. 1933-40. *485*
Senate inquiry. Cold War. Korean War. MacArthur, Douglas. Testimony, secret. 1951. *1141*
Senroku Uehara *(University)*. Colleges and Universities. Educational Theory. Japan. Military Occupation. US Education Mission to Japan. 1945-62. *728*
Seoul (battle). Korean War. Marines. 1950. *1059*
Service, John Stewart. China. Foreign Policy. World War II. 1945-49. *342*
Service, John Stewart (dismissal). China. Diplomacy. State Department (Foreign Service). 1932-73. *563*
Service, John Stewart (*Lost Chance in China*, excerpts). China. Foreign policy. State Department (Foreign Service). World War II. 1945-50's. *483*
Service, John Stewart (reports). *Amerasia* (periodical). China. Communist Party. Espionage. Foreign policy. Nationalists. ca 1937-45. *343*
Seven Samurai (film). Films. Japan. *The Magnificent Seven* (film). National Characteristics. 1960's. *836*
Seward, William H. Cultural Imperialism. Foreign Relations. Japan. Mutsuhito, Emperor. 1870-71. *705*
Shanghai Communique. China. Diplomatic recognition. International Trade. Taiwan. Treaties. 1972-78. *568*

Shanghai crisis. Japan. Navies. Western nations. 1931-32. *458*
Shanghai Power Company. China. Communists. Foreign Policy. Truman, Harry S. (administration). 1948-50. *517*
Shanker, Albert (views). Berry, Mary (speech). China. Communism. Education. 1977. *167*
Shapiro, Harry F. Archaeology. China. Janus, Christopher. Peking Man. 1941-73. *542*
Shaw, Samuel. China. Trade. Voyages. 1784-85. *154*
Shellenberger, Jack H. (account). Faulkner, William. Japan. Travel. US Information Agency. 1955. *900*
Sherrod, Robert (memoirs). Japan. Tarawa (battle). World War II. 1944. *901*
Shipping. China. Foreign policy. Intervention. Yangtze Rapid Steamship Company. 1924-36. *302*
Ships. China. International trade. Pacific & Eastern Steamship Company. USA. World War I. 1914-16. *447*
—. *Clarissa B. Carver* (vessel). Courts. Dow, Leroy. *Glamorganshire* (vessel). Japan. Lawsuits. 1885-86. *870*
Shoulder patches. Air Warfare. American Volunteer Group. China. Flying Tigers. World War II. 23d Fighter Group. 1930's-45. *25*
Shuck, Eliza G. Sexton. Baptist Church. China. Missions and Missionaries. 1846-63. *322*
Siam. Americans. Baptists. China. Fielde, Adele M. 1865-90. *60*
Sicily (vessel). Korean War. Marines. Naval Air Forces. Pilots. 1950. *1130*
Sill, John M. B. Expansionism, Japanese. Japan. Korea. 1894-97. *1028*
Silver Purchase Act (1934). China. Congress. International Trade. Lobbying. Roosevelt, Franklin D. (administration). 1934. *268*
—. China. International Trade. Pittman, Key. Senate. USA. 1933-40. *485*
Sims, Jack A. Air Warfare. Bombing. Japan. Personal Narratives. World War II. 1942. *905*
Simulation and Games. Atomic Warfare. History Teaching. Japan. World War II. 1945. 1978. *658*
—. China. Foreign Policy. History Teaching. Legislative Investigations. Senate. 1949. 1978. *378*
Sino-American Cooperation Association (SACO). China. Navies. World War II. 1942-45. *476*
Sino-Japanese War. Asia, East. Foreign Policy. Navies. 1894-95. *37*
—. Brussels Conference. Diplomacy. Roosevelt, Franklin D. 1937. *117*
—. China. Economic Conditions. Rhode Island (Providence). Weapons. 1894. *36*
—. China. Japan. Press. Public opinion. USA. 1894-95. *53*
—. China. McGiffin, Philo Norton. Navies. 1885-95. *174*
—. Creelman, James. New York *World* (newspaper). Port Arthur massacre. Press. 1894-95. *35*
—. Foreign policy. Gresham, Walter Quintin. Korea. 1894-95. *38*
—. Foreign Policy. Japan. Korea. 1894-95. *76*
Sino-Soviet conflict. China. Domestic problems. Foreign policy. USA. 1970's. *139*
—. China. Foreign policy. 1960's-76. *139*
—. Foreign Policy. Taiwan. 1966-75. *311*
Sledge, Eugene B. (account). Armies. Japan. Marines. Peleliu (battle). World War II. 1944. *907*
Smedley, Agnes. China. Chu Teh. Communism. Sorge, Richard. 1893-1950. *323*
—. China. Cold War. Communism. Strong, Anna Louise. USSR. 1920-70. *246*

—. China. Communism. India. Lu Xun. Revolutionary Movements. 1910-50. *375*
Smedley, Agnes (review article). China. Leftism. Women. 1930's-50. 1973-76. *329*
Smith, Wiley H. China (Shanghai). Marines. Personal Narratives. *Pittsburgh* (vessel). 1927. *408*
Smithsonian Agreement (1971). Dollar. Economic Regulations. Monetary system, international. 1971-72. *997*
Smyth Report, 1945. Atomic energy. Japan. Military Strategy. USA. World War II. 1940-45. *908*
Snow, Edgar. China. 1927-45. *319*
—. China. Clark, Grenville. Foreign Relations. Letters. 1963-67. *489*
Social Change. Agricultural Technology and Research. Family. Fiji. Israel. Japan. 1689-1975. *634*
—. Japan. Korea. Military Occupation. 1945-53. *904*
Social Conditions. Acculturation. Internment. Japanese Americans. 1945-55. *743*
—. Americanology. Historiography (review article). Japan. National self-image. 19c-20c. 1969-73. *722*
—. California. China (Guangdong). Emigration. 1850-82. *390*
—. Emigration. Japan. 1866-1924. *957*
Social conflict. China. Cold War. USSR. 1950's-70's. *527*
Social Customs. China. Family. Occupations. Travel (accounts). 1976. *544*
—. Japan. Keene, Donald. Personal narratives. Scholarship. 1930's-80's. *746*
Social gospel. Bashford, James W. China. Methodist Episcopal Church. Missions and Missionaries. 1889-1919. *320*
Social Organization. China. Communism. Equal opportunity. Talent selection. 1973. *203*
—. China. Medical technology. Mortality. 19c. 1949-59. *470*
—. China. USSR. 20c. *147*
—. Crime. Japan. 1948-70's. *591*
—. Eugenics. Genetics. Japan. 1920's-30's. *923*
Social Reform. China. Communism. Economic reform. 1949-72. *421*
Social Sciences. China. Educational Exchange Programs. Research. 1972-79. *513*
Social status. China. Cultural attitudes. Great Britain. Women. 1840-1927. *243*
Social Theory. Economic development. Employment, permanent. Japan. 1973. *635*
Socialism. China. Christianity. Democracy. Foreign Policy. Japan. Missions and Missionaries. 1830-1979. *125*
—. Japan. Katayama, Sen. 1884-1932. *921*
Sociology. Attitudes. Japanese Americans. Values. World War II. 1940's-70's. *915*
Solomon Islands (Vella Lavella). Japan. Navies. World War II. 1943. *784*
Sony Company. Business. Japan. Lawyers. 1982. *822*
Sorge, Richard. China. Chu Teh. Communism. Smedley, Agnes. 1893-1950. *323*
South. Agriculture (comparative study). Boserup, Ester. China. North America. Russia. 18c-19c. *465*
South Africa. Air Forces. F-86F (aircraft). Korean War. Osan Air Base. UN Command. 1950-53. *1008*
South Africa (Cape Colony). China. Fur trade. Voyages. 1800-02. *479*
South Dakota. Balloons, armed. Japan. Project FUGO. World War II. 1944-45. *770*
South Korea. *See* Korea, South.
Sovereignty. China. Great Britain. Intervention. 1557-1949. *491*

Spain. Biddle, James. Japan. Pacific Area. Taguchi Ukichi. 1846-90's. *773*
—. Colonialism. Educational Policy. Germany. Japan. Mariana Islands. ca 1688-1940. *698*
Speeches. China. Communist Party. Foreign policy. Mao Zedong. 1944-50. *274*
Sprouse, Philip D. China. Diplomatic recognition. Truman, Harry S. (administration). 1949-50. *209*
Sprouse, Philip D. (report). China. Communism. Foreign Policy. Marshall, George C. 1945-47. 1970's. *391*
Stairs, Denis (review article). Canada. Diplomacy. Korean War. 1950-53. *1092*
Standard of living. Economic growth. Taiwan. 1973-75. *1168*
Standard Oil Company of New York. China. Kerosene. Nationalism. Oil. Taxation. 1925-27. *541*
Standard-Vacuum Oil Company. Anderson, Irvine H., Jr. (review article). Asia, East. Foreign Investments. Foreign policy. Oil Industry and Trade. 1933-41. 1975. *97*
State Department. China. Communist Party. Foreign Policy. Stuart, John Leighton. 1949. *181*
—. China. Diplomacy. Hurley, Patrick J. Jiang Jieshi. Mao Zedong. Vincent, John Carter. 1944-45. *358*
—. China. Dulles, John Foster. Letters. Politics. Rusk, Dean. 1953. *499*
—. China. Open Door Policy. Rockhill, William W. 1886-1920. *505*
—. Diplomacy. Emmerson, John K. Japan (Tokyo). Memoirs. World War II (antecedents). 1941. *662*
—. Diplomacy. Fishing. Japan. 1936-39. *947*
—. Exports. Foreign policy. Japan. Oil. 1940-41. *948*
State Department (Foreign Service). China. Diplomacy. Service, John Stewart (dismissal). 1932-73. *563*
—. China. Foreign policy. Service, John Stewart (*Lost Chance in China*, excerpts). World War II. 1945-50's. *483*
—. China. Foreign Relations. Kahn, E. J., Jr. (review article). Politics. 1940's-50's. 1975. *384*
—. China-Burma-India Theater. Emmerson, John K. Memoirs. World War II. 1941-44. *251*
State Department (*Relations with China*). Communism. Documents. Foreign Relations. 1944-81. *109*
State Department (report). China. Foreign Relations. 1944-49. *414*
Steel. Dumping. International Trade. Japan. Public Opinion. 1974-78. *745*
Stereotypes. China. *Keys of the Kingdom* (film). Office of War Information. Propaganda. World War II. 1940-45. *172*
Stilwell, Joseph W. China. Historiography. World War II. 1942-44. *559*
—. China. Jiang Jieshi. Marshall, George C. Military General Staff. World War II. 1944. *475*
—. China. Jiang Jieshi. Military strategy. World War II. 1942-44. *397*
Stimson, Henry L. Bombing exemption. Japan (Kyoto). World War II. 1940-45. *628*
—. Diplomatic recognition. Japan. Manchuria. 1931-34. *991*
—. Foreign policy. Hull, Cordell. Japan. Roosevelt, Franklin D. 1933-36. *730*
—. Gilbert, Prentiss B. Japan. Kellogg-Briand Pact. League of Nations. Manchuria. Military Occupation. 1931. *34*
Strategic Arms Limitation Talks. China. Europe. Foreign Relations. Nuclear Arms. Trilateralism. USSR. 1970's-83. *381*

Taiwan   283

—. Europe, Western. Japan. Mutual Balanced Force Reductions. USSR. 1974. *1002*
Strategic Arms Limitation Talks (SALT II). China. Defense Policy. USSR. 1968-79. *262*
Strong, Anna Louise. China. Cold War. Communism. Smedley, Agnes. USSR. 1920-70. *246*
—. China. Maoism. USSR. 1919-70. *245*
Stuart, John Leighton. China. Communist Party. Diplomacy. 1949. *486*
—. China. Communist Party. Foreign Policy. State Department. 1949. *181*
—. China. Diplomacy. Japan. USA. 1937-41. *118*
Stuart, Mary Horton. Alabama (Mobile). China. Missions and Missionaries. Presbyterian Church. 1840's-1947. *284*
Students. Acculturation. Chinese. Colleges and Universities. Mental Illness. Taiwan. 1854-1973. *1151*
—. Attitudes. Authoritarianism. Chinese. 1949-70. *191*
—. China. Educational exchange programs. 1911-36. *199*
—. China. Foreign Relations. Georgia (Atlanta). US-China People's Friendship Association. 1972-83. *339*
—. Interpersonal contact. Race Relations. Taiwan. USA. 1933-73. *1167*
—. Japan. Political attitudes. Radicals and Radicalism. 1960's-70's. *760*
—. Taiwan. 1969. *1169*
Study Abroad. See Educational Exchange Programs.
Stueck, William Whitney, Jr. (review article). China. Foreign Policy. Korea. 1947-50. *134*
Subcontracting. Developing nations. Great Britain. Japan. Manufacturing. 1966-76. *899*
Submarine Warfare. Aircraft carriers. Japan. World War II. 1941-45. *865*
—. Destroyer escorts. *England* (vessel). Japan. Williamson, John A. (account). World War II. 1944. *972*
—. *Indianapolis* (vessel). *I-58* (vessel). Japan. World War II. 1945. *612*
Suez Crisis. Great Britain. Korean War. Navies. USA. Vietnam War. 1950-76. *1119*
Sugar. Allen, Horace. Diplomacy. Hawaii. Immigration. Korea. 1902-05. *1101*
Sun Zhongshan. American Revolution. China. Ideology. Nationalism. Revolutionary Movements. 1776-83. 1905-25. *187*
—. China. Diplomatic recognition. Missions and Missionaries. Revolution. 1911-13. *395*
—. China. Foreign Policy. 1920-24. *266*
—. China. George, Henry. Land Tenure. Taxation. 1866-1973. *361*
—. China. Political Theory. Progressivism. 1880-1912. *194*
Supply. Economic Development. Japan. 1975-82. *630*
Supreme Court. California (Los Angeles). Containerization. *Japanese Lines, Ltd.* v. *County of Los Angeles.* Tariff. 1970-79. *585*
Surgery. Atomic bomb. Charities. Japan (Hiroshima). Women. World War II. 1945-57. *985*
Surprise attacks. Korean War. Military Strategy. October War. Pearl Harbor (attack). World War II. 1941-73. *7*
Surrender. Atomic Warfare. Japan. Politics. Truman, Harry S. (administration). World War II. 1945. *604*
—. Carney, Robert B. Japan. Personal Narratives. World War II. 1945. *626*

—. Diplomacy. Japan. MacArthur, Douglas. Philippines (Manila). World War II. 1945. *812*
Surrender, unconditional. Atomic Warfare. Japan (Hiroshima, Nagasaki). Military Strategy. World War II. 1943-45. *703*
—. Japan. Peace. Potsdam Conference. World War II. 1945. *952*

T

Tactics. Bombs (glide, smart). Korean War. Vietnam War. World War II. 1919-74. *4*
Taguchi Ukichi. Biddle, James. Japan. Pacific Area. Spain. 1846-90's. *773*
Taiping Rebellion. China. Diplomacy. Marshall, Humphrey. 1853-54. *310*
—. China. Foreign Policy. Marshall, Humphrey. 1853-54. *312*
—. China. Foreign Relations. International Trade. Navies. 1850-61. *291*
—. China (Yangzi River). Diplomacy. Great Britain. International trade. 1850-61. *430*
—. China (Yangzi River). Great Britain. Hope, James. Imperialism. Trade. 1850-61. *432*
Taiwan. Acculturation. Chinese. Colleges and Universities. Mental illness. Students. 1854-1973. *1151*
—. Alliances. Carter, Jimmy. Korea, South. Military Aid. 1970's. *30*
—. American Studies. Libraries. 1969-75. *1154*
—. Annexation. Business. 1850-60. *1156*
—. Annexation. Nye, Gideon, Jr. 1857. *1164*
—. Anti-Communist Movements. Asia. Foreign Policy. Reagan, Ronald (administration). 1981. *64*
—. Arms Trade. China. Foreign Relations. 1979-82. *1165*
—. Arms Trade. Foreign Relations. 1978-82. *1173*
—. Bibliographies. China. Foreign Policy. 1949-82. *12*
—. Brain drain. Immigration. Scholars. 1905-73. *1163*
—. Canada. China. Diplomatic relations. Economic development. Foreign policy. Japan. 1949-72. *1175*
—. Carter, Jimmy. China. Foreign relations. Normalization. USSR. 1978-79. *1150*
—. Carter, Jimmy. Eisenhower, Dwight D. Executive Power. Foreign policy. Hamilton, Alexander. 1793-1979. *1161*
—. Carter, Jimmy (administration). China. Foreign Policy. Korea. 1970's. *137*
—. China. Cold war. Foreign Relations. Korean War. USSR. 1947-79. *211*
—. China. Communications. Diplomatic recognition. 1978. *549*
—. China. Communism. Containment. Foreign policy. Korea. 1945-50. *10*
—. China. Communist Party. Foreign Policy. Manchuria. Wedemeyer, Albert C. (report). 1946-49. *351*
—. China. Defense Policy. Economics. Foreign Relations. 1949-81. *1153*
—. China. Diplomatic recognition. International Trade. Shanghai Communique. Treaties. 1972-78. *568*
—. China. Diplomatic relations. 1978. *22*
—. China. Economic Conditions. Foreign Policy. Political Attitudes. 1949-82. *473*
—. China. Economic relations. Foreign Relations. 1840's-1974. *1157*
—. China. Foreign Policy. 1947-81. *23*
—. China. Foreign Policy. 1949-76. *15*
—. China. Foreign policy. 1950's-70's. *61*
—. China. Foreign Policy. 1972-79. *77*
—. China. Foreign Policy. USSR. 1972-78. *62*
—. China. Foreign Relations. 1940-72. *1158*

284 Taiwan

—. China. Foreign Relations. 1970's-82. *130*
—. China. Foreign Relations. 1972-80. *120*
—. China. Foreign Relations. 1972-82. *92*
—. China. Foreign Relations. 1978-81. *1172*
—. China. Foreign Relations. 1979. *73*
—. China. Foreign Relations. International Trade. 1949-82. *379*
—. China. Foreign Relations. Japan. Korea, South. Military. 1960-80. *56*
—. China. Foreign relations. Japan. USSR. 1972. *78*
—. China. Foreign relations. Korea. 1971-77. *115*
—. China. Foreign Relations. USSR. 1972-82. *215*
—. China. Intellectuals (Chinese). Political attitudes. 1970. *14*
—. China. Japan. Korea, South. Public Opinion. Treaties, mutual defense. 1950's-77. *126*
—. China. Normalization. 1943-77. *63*
—. China. Vance, Cyrus. 1972-77. *129*
—. Colonization. Commerce. Indian-White Relations. Netherlands. New Netherland. 17c. *1160*
—. Congress. Foreign policy. International Security. 1950-55. *178*
—. Economic growth. Standard of living. 1973-75. *1168*
—. Federal Policy. Frontier and Pioneer Life. Indians. Japan. Military Strategy. 18c-1915. *70*
—. Foreign Policy. 1981-82. *1149*
—. Foreign Policy. Sino-Soviet conflict. 1966-75. *311*
—. Foreign Relations. 1960-79. *1155*
—. Foreign Relations. 1978-79. *1174*
—. Foreign Relations. 1980-81. *1152*
—. International Law. Treaties. 1980. *1171*
—. International Trade. Marketing. 1962-74. *1170*
—. Interpersonal contact. Race Relations. Students. USA. 1933-73. *1167*
—. Karns, A. P. Locke, Robert D. (interview). Oil well. 1877-78. *272*
—. Students. 1969. *1169*
Taiwan Relations Act (US, 1979). Arms Trade. 1979-81. *1166*
—. Congress. Foreign relations. 1978-79. *1162*
—. Foreign Relations. 1978-80. *1159*
Taiwan Strait crisis. China. Decisionmaking. Eisenhower, Dwight D. 1954-55. *468*
Talent selection. China. Communism. Equal opportunity. Social Organization. 1973. *203*
Tanaka, Kakuei. Asia, East. Economic problems. Foreign Relations. Japan. Political Leadership. 1971-74. *883*
Tanaka, Togo. Internment. Japanese Americans. Oral history. World War II. Yoneda, Elaine. Yoneda, Karl. 1941-45. *816*
Tangier Smith, Floyd. China. Harkness, Ruth. Pandas. 1936. *175*
Tarawa (battle). Japan. Sherrod, Robert (memoirs). World War II. 1944. *901*
Tariff. California (Los Angeles). Containerization. *Japanese Lines, Ltd.* v. *County of Los Angeles.* Supreme Court. 1970-79. *585*
—. European Economic Community. Generalized System of Preferences. Japan. 1966-75. *595*
Tariff protection. Developing nations. European Economic Community. Japan. 1960's-70's. *986*
Task Force 58. Air Warfare. Hellcats. Japan. Truk (battle). World War II. 1944. *933*
Tatsuguchi, Paul Nobuo (diary). Attu (battle). Japan. USA. World War II. 1941-43. *963*
Taxation. China. George, Henry. Land Tenure. Sun Zhongshan. 1866-1973. *361*
—. China. Kerosene. Nationalism. Oil. Standard Oil Company of New York. 1925-27. *541*
Tea. China. Credit. Depressions. Great Britain. International Trade (agencies). 1834-37. *197*

Teachers. Colleges and Universities. Japan. Sapporo Agricultural College. Science. Tokyo, University of. 1860-1900. *961*
Teaching. China (Tianjin). Renouf, Vincent Adams (papers). 1903-10. *552*
Technology. Diffusion. Japan. Semiconductors. 1982. *876*
—. Europe. Japan. Research and development. ca 1964-76. *574*
—. Europe, Western. Japan. 1960-75. *827*
—. Japan. Robots. 1965-83. *800*
—. Korean War. Leadership. Military General Staff. Vietnam War. 1950-73. *1085*
Television. Behavior. Communications. Japan. 1972-81. *729*
Television sets. Japan. Trade adjustment policy. 1970-78. *806*
Terranova, Francis. China. Foreign Relations. Trade. Trials. 1821-44. *240*
Testimony, secret. Cold War. Korean War. MacArthur, Douglas. Senate inquiry. 1951. *1141*
Texas (San Antonio). Air Forces. Korean War. Lackland Air Force Base. Legislative Investigations. Military Training. 1950-66. *1011*
Textbooks. American history. China. History Teaching. 18c-20c. *551*
—. Attitudes. History. Japan/United States Textbook Study Project. 1981. *999*
Textile Industry. Cotton. Great Britain. India. Japan. 1870-1939. *987*
Thailand. China. Foreign Policy. 1950-76. *271*
—. China. Foreign Relations. USSR. 1974. *143*
—. Economic development. Great Britain. Japan. 1926-80. *102*
—. Foreign Relations. Great Britain. Japan. World War II. 1942-46. *970*
Thayer, James Bradley. Foreign Relations. Gray, John Chipman. Holmes, Oliver Wendell. Japan. Kaneko Kentarō. Law. Letters. 1878-1924. *741*
Theater. Arnhold & Company. China (Chang River). Hawley, Edwin C. Propaganda. Tretiakov, Sergei (*Roar China!*). 1924-75. *394*
Thomas, Elbert. Foreign Relations. Japan. King, William. Utah. ca 1922-40. *782*
Thomas, John N. (review article). China Lobby. Institute of Pacific Relations. McCarran Committee. Public opinion. Watergate trials. 1945-75. *58*
Thorne, Christopher. Alliances (review article). British Empire. Japan. Louis, William Roger. World War II. 1941-45. *74*
Tianjin, Treaty of (Article XXIX). China. Missions and Missionaries. Religious toleration. Translating. 1858-59. *429*
Tibbets, Paul W. Air Forces. Atomic bomb. Japan (Hiroshima). Military training. Personal narratives. World War II. 1945. *932*
Tobacco. American Tobacco Company. Government ownership. Japan (Tokyo). Parrish, Edward James. 1899-1904. *656*
Tokyo Rose (Iva Toguri d'Aquino). Citizenship. Ford, Gerald R. Hada, John. Japanese American Citizens League. Pardon. Uyeda, Clifford I. (account). 1973-77. *949*
Tokyo, University of. Colleges and Universities. Japan. Sapporo Agricultural College. Science. Teachers. 1860-1900. *961*
Tolley, Kemp. China (Harbin). Personal narratives. Russian language. 1935. *124*
Tong societies. California. Chinese Americans. Metropolitan areas. 1850-1972. *204*
Trade. Angell, James B. China. Immigration. Treaties. 1880-81. *185*
—. Brooke, John Mercer. Japan. *Kanrin Maru* (vessel). Navies. Treaties. Voyages. 1860. *615*
—. China. 1943-50. *155*
—. China. 1950-70's. *201*

—. China. 1952-73. *249*
—. China. 1970-80. *357*
—. China. 1972-73. *337*
—. China. 1972. *183*
—. China. 19c-1970's. *446*
—. China. Cushing, Caleb. Diplomacy. 1784-1840's. *239*
—. China. Economic aid. 1928-41. *269*
—. China. Foreign Relations. Terranova, Francis. Trials. 1821-44. *240*
—. China. Military. 1970-80. *205*
—. China. Porcelain. 18c-1825. *387*
—. China. Shaw, Samuel. Voyages. 1784-85. *154*
—. China (Canton). Europe. 3c-20c. *396*
—. China (Hubei). Ohio. 1979-82. *478*
—. China (Yangzi River). Great Britain. Hope, James. Imperialism. Taiping Rebellion. 1850-61. *432*
—. Detente. Foreign policy. Japan. USSR. 1971-74. *749*
—. Economic development. Europe, Western. Japan. Protectionism. 1948-80. *866*
—. Europe, Western. Finance. Imperialism. Industry. Japan. Latin America. 1970's. *768*
—. Europe, Western. Japan. 1970's. *665*
—. European Economic Community. Germany, West. Japan. Oil crisis. 1974. *647*
—. Foreign Relations. International Trade. Japan. Military Capability. 1970's-82. *833*
—. Foreign relations. Japan. 1970's. *839*
—. Japan. 1970-77. *951*
Trade adjustment policy. Japan. Television sets. 1970-78. *806*
Trade Regulations. Automobile Industry and Trade. Japan. 1971-81. *857*
—. Automobiles. Foreign Policy. Imports. Japan. 1970-81. *727*
—. China. Exports. 1969-80. *218*
—. China. USSR. 1966-72. *299*
Translating. China. Missions and Missionaries. Religious toleration. Tianjin, Treaty of (Article XXIX). 1858-59. *429*
Transpacific flight. Herndon, Hugh. Japan. Pangborn, Clyde. USA. 1930-71. *864*
Transportation, Military. Air Transport Command. Burma Road. China. Convoys. Frost, Edwin C. Personal Narratives. 1945. *259*
—. Korean War. Marines. Vietnam War. 1945-73. *1108*
Travel. China. Diplomacy. Li Hungzhang. Russia. 1896. *250*
—. China (Inner Mongolia). Press. Rosholt, Malcolm (account). 1935. *461*
—. Faulkner, William. Japan. Shellenberger, Jack H. (account). US Information Agency. 1955. *900*
Travel accounts. Attitudes. Custer, Elizabeth Bacon. Japan. 1903. *955*
—. China. 1966-73. *324*
—. China. Family. Occupations. Social Customs. 1976. *544*
—. China, west. Fritz, Chester. 1917. *566*
—. Inventions. Japan. Morrow, James. 1854. *823*
—. Japan. ca 1850-1975. *739*
Treaties. *See also* names of specific treaties, e.g., Four-Power Treaty; Diplomacy; Peace.
—. Alliances. Dulles, John Foster. Japan. Political Theory. Yoshida Shigeru. 5c BC-20c. 1951. *653*
—. Angell, James B. China. Immigration. Trade. 1880-81. *185*
—. Annexation. Hawaii. Japan. 1897. *821*
—. ANZUS. Australia. Japan. National Security. New Zealand. 1951-81. *936*
—. Brooke, John Mercer. Japan. *Kanrin Maru* (vessel). Navies. Trade. Voyages. 1860. *615*
—. California (San Francisco). Japan. *Kanrin Maru* (vessel). 1860. *990*

—. China. Diplomatic recognition. International Trade. Shanghai Communique. Taiwan. 1972-78. *568*
—. China. Extraterritoriality. Great Britain. 1929-43. *188*
—. China. International Security. Japan. 1977-78. *84*
—. Foreign Policy. Japan. 1853-58. *685*
—. Foreign policy. Korea. 1882-1905. *69*
—. Foreign policy. Korea. 1882-1905. *1056*
—. Foreign Relations. Japan. Philippines. Quirino, Elpidio. World War II. 1945-56. *748*
—. International Law. Taiwan. 1980. *1171*
Treaties, mutual defense. China. Japan. Korea, South. Public Opinion. Taiwan. 1950's-77. *126*
Treaties, unequal. China. Foreign Policy. League of Nations. Paris Peace Conference. Wilson, Woodrow. 1919. *19*
Tretiakov, Sergei *(Roar China!)*. Arnhold & Company. China (Chang River). Hawley, Edwin C. Propaganda. Theater. 1924-75. *394*
Trials. China. Foreign Relations. Terranova, Francis. Trade. 1821-44. *240*
Trilateral Commission. Europe, Western. Foreign Policy. International Trade. Japan. Rockefeller family. 1973-78. *995*
—. Europe, Western. Foreign Relations. Japan. 1973-82. *872*
—. Europe, Western. Japan. Public services. Wages. 1973-79. *925*
—. European Economic Community. Japan. 1973-77. *636*
Trilateralism. China. Europe. Foreign Relations. Nuclear Arms. Strategic Arms Limitation Talks. USSR. 1970's-83. *381*
—. Europe, Western. Foreign Policy. Japan. 1950's-70's. *945*
—. Europe, Western. Japan. 1970's. *796*
—. Europe, Western. Japan. Political Theory. 1970's. *954*
Tripolarity. China. Foreign policy. USSR. 1970's. *417*
Truk (battle). Air Warfare. Hellcats. Japan. Task Force 58. World War II. 1944. *933*
Truman Doctrine. Austin, Warren R. Foreign policy. Korean War. UN. 1945-53. *1086*
—. Communism. Foreign policy. Korea. 1945-50. *43*
Truman, Harry S. Acheson, Dean. Intervention. Korean War. USSR. 1950. *1014*
—. Asia, East. China. Cold War (review article). 1940's-71. *210*
—. Atomic bomb. Japan. Military Strategy. World War II. 1945. *602*
—. Atomic bomb. Japan (Hiroshima, Nagasaki). World War II. 1942-47. *605*
—. China. Conference on Chinese-American Relations. Foreign Policy. Roosevelt, Franklin D. 1944-48. 1978. *289*
—. China. Foreign policy. Korean War. MacArthur, Douglas. Politics and the Military. 1949-52. *1025*
—. China. Korean War. MacArthur, Douglas. Walker, Walton L. 1950. *1026*
—. Communism. Foreign policy. Intervention. Korean War. USSR. 1950. *1081*
—. Foreign Policy. Korea (38th Parallel). Korean War. MacArthur, Douglas. Self-determination. USSR. 1943-50. *1084*
—. Foreign Relations (review article). Korean War. 1950. 1976. *1104*
—. Historiography. Korean War. MacArthur, Douglas. Politics. Public relations. Wake Island. 1950. *1142*
—. Korean War. Limited war. MacArthur, Douglas. Politics and the Military. 1950-51. *1132*

286 Truman

—. Korean War. MacArthur, Douglas. Manchester, William. Military Strategy. Wake Island. 1950. 1980. *1051*
Truman, Harry S. (administration). Atomic Warfare. Japan. Politics. Surrender. World War II. 1945. *604*
—. China. Communists. Foreign Policy. Shanghai Power Company. 1948-50. *517*
—. China. Diplomatic recognition. Sprouse, Philip D. 1949-50. *209*
Tuan Fang. Brownson, Willard H. China (Nanking). Diplomacy. Gelm, George E. (journal). International Trade. 1907. *265*
Tuchman, Barbara. *Asama* (vessel). Japan. Mexico (Baja California, Turtle Bay). 1915. *663*
Tucker, Robert W. (interview). Europe. Foreign Relations. Japan. Persian Gulf and Area. 1968-80. *998*
Tule Lake Camp. Internment. Japanese Americans. Martial law. World War II. 1941-44. *843*
Typewriter. British Typewriter Museum (Wilfred Beeching collection). Europe, Western. Japan. 1711-1970's. *672*

U

Uchida, Yoshiko. Daily Life. Internment. Japanese Americans. Personal narratives. Utah (Topaz). World War II. 1942-43. *942*
Ueno, Harry (arrest). California. Concentration Camps. Japanese Americans. Manzanar War Relocation Center. Riots. World War II. 1942. *691*
UN. Austin, Warren R. Foreign policy. Korean War. Truman Doctrine. 1945-53. *1086*
—. Cease-fire. Eisenhower, Dwight D. Korean War. Peace negotiations. 1952-53. *1136*
—. Korea, North. Korean War. MacArthur, Douglas. Military Offenses. Unification. 1950. *1068*
UN Command. Air Forces. F-86F (aircraft). Korean War. Osan Air Base. South Africa. 1950-53. *1008*
UN General Assembly. Developing nations. Economic issues. Japan. Roll-call voting. Western Nations. 1970-76. *966*
UN (membership). China. Foreign aid. Voting and Voting Behavior. 1961-68. *144*
Unemployment. Australia. Canada. Europe. Japan. USA. 1972-73. *911*
Unification. China. Foreign Relations. Japan. Korea, North. Korea, South. USSR. 1970's-. *20*
—. Foreign Policy. Korea. 1950's-70's. *1045*
—. Foreign Relations. Korea. USSR. 1945-47. *1098*
—. Korea, North. Korean War. MacArthur, Douglas. Military Offenses. UN. 1950. *1068*
Unification Church. Moon, Sun Myung. Religion. 1970's. *1080*
Unification policy. Korea, North. 1973. *1058*
Uniforms, Military. China, north. Marines. Photographs. 1931-41. *504*
Urban concessions. China. Europe. Foreign Relations. International Trade. 1876-85. *404*
US Education Mission to Japan. Colleges and Universities. Educational Theory. Japan. Military Occupation. Senroku Uehara (University). 1945-62. *728*
US Information Agency. Faulkner, William. Japan. Shellenberger, Jack H. (account). Travel. 1955. *900*
US-China People's Friendship Association. China. Foreign Relations. Georgia (Atlanta). Students. 1972-83. *339*
USSR. *See also* Russia.
—. Acheson, Dean. Intervention. Korean War. Truman, Harry S. 1950. *1014*

—. Afghanistan. China. Foreign Relations. Invasions. Military cooperation. Vietnam. 1965-80. *232*
—. Afghanistan. Invasions. Korean War. Limited war (concept). Vietnam War. War Powers Act (US, 1973). 1945-79. *104*
—. Africa. China. 1976. *6*
—. Africa. China. Foreign Relations. USA. ca 1949-70's. *327*
—. Alienation. China. Cuba. Intellectuals, western. Pilgrimages. Vietnam, North. 1930's. 1970's. *296*
—. Alliances. Asia, Southwest. China. National Security. 1977-78. *536*
—. Alliances. China. Multipolarity. 1970's. *436*
—. Anti-Communist Movements. China. 1917-50. *267*
—. Arab-Israeli conflict. China. 1977-79. *558*
—. Arab-Israeli Conflict. China. 1979-80. *557*
—. Arms control agreements. China. Detente. Nuclear strategy. 1970's. *516*
—. Arms race. China. Korean War. Rostow, Eugene V. 1953-82. *8*
—. Asia. Balance of power. China. Japan. 1970-73. *80*
—. Asia. Historiography, US. Japan. Revolutionary movements. World War II. 1930's-49. *862*
—. Asia, East. Barnett, A. Doak. China. Foreign Relations. 1944-78. *123*
—. Asia, East. Foreign Policy. 1945-80. *113*
—. Asia, East. Foreign Relations. 1948-81. *88*
—. Asia, South. China. Foreign Policy. 1970's. *426*
—. Asia, Southeast. Balance of power. China. Communism. War. 1920-79. *31*
—. Atomic Warfare. Japan. Leftists. World War II. 1945. *610*
—. Attitudes. Democracy. Europe. Interest Groups. Japan. Nuclear Science and Technology. 1970's. *731*
—. Balance of Power. China. 1974. *241*
—. Balance of Power. China. Coffey, Joseph I. Military capability. USA. ca 1965-73. *158*
—. Balance of power. China. Cold War. 1956-80. *325*
—. Balance of power. China. Europe. 1945-73. *242*
—. Balance of Power. China. Europe. Foreign Relations. 1970's. *229*
—. Balance of power. China. Foreign policy. Nixon, Richard M. (administration). 1969-72. *462*
—. Balance of Power. China. Foreign Policy. Vietnam War. 1964-76. *512*
—. Balance of Power. Cold War. Foreign policy. Korean War. 1946-50. *1050*
—. Barnett, A. Doak (review article). China. Foreign Relations. 1950-76. *401*
—. Broadcasts. China. Vietnam War. 1968-73. *152*
—. Cambodia. China. Foreign Relations. Vietnam. 1978-80. *105*
—. Canada. China. Developing nations. Foreign relations. 1950-75. *318*
—. Canada. China. Foreign Relations. International Trade. 1969-72. *367*
—. Carter, Jimmy. China. Foreign relations. Normalization. Taiwan. 1978-79. *1150*
—. Carter, Jimmy (administration). Detente. Developing nations. Europe, Western. Foreign policy. Japan. 1977-80. *939*
—. China. Civil war. Intervention. Laos. 1959-62. *514*
—. China. Cold War. Communism. Smedley, Agnes. Strong, Anna Louise. 1920-70. *246*
—. China. Cold War. Detente. 1971-73. *546*
—. China. Cold War. Foreign relations. Korean War. 1945-72. *1024*
—. China. Cold war. Foreign Relations. Korean War. Taiwan. 1947-79. *211*

—. China. Cold War. Social conflict. 1950's-70's. 527
—. China. Communism. Marshall, George C. Mediation. Nationalists. 1946. 356
—. China. Communist Party. Foreign relations. 1948-49. 317
—. China. Containment. 1945-73. 534
—. China. Defense Policy. Foreign policy. Military Strategy. 1975-79. 335
—. China. Defense Policy. Foreign Relations. 1970-83. 182
—. China. Defense Policy. Strategic Arms Limitation Talks (SALT II). 1968-79. 262
—. China. Detente. 1970-75. 471
—. China. Detente. 1977. 283
—. China. Detente. Foreign policy. 1945-79. 173
—. China. Detente (review article). Nixon, Richard M. 1971-73. 443
—. China. Diego Garcia. Indian Ocean and Area. Naval Strategy. 20c. 364
—. China. Disarmament. Nuclear arms. 1945-79. 377
—. China. Domestic Policy. Foreign Policy. 1949-70's. 141
—. China. Dulles, John Foster. Eisenhower, Dwight D. Foreign policy. 1953-56. 385
—. China. Egypt. Foreign Policy. Israel. Middle East. 1978. 497
—. China. Europe. Foreign Relations. Nuclear Arms. Strategic Arms Limitation Talks. Trilateralism. 1970's-83. 381
—. China. Foreign policy. 1944-49. 537
—. China. Foreign policy. 1954. 388
—. China. Foreign Policy. 1955-58. 500
—. China. Foreign policy. 1961-79. 481
—. China. Foreign Policy. 1968-69. 235
—. China. Foreign Policy. 1968-70's. 508
—. China. Foreign Policy. 1971-81. 346
—. China. Foreign Policy. 1972-79. 435
—. China. Foreign Policy. 1976-82. 554
—. China. Foreign policy. 1980-81. 515
—. China. Foreign policy. 20c. 306
—. China. Foreign policy. Gandhi, Indira. India. 1946-71. 93
—. China. Foreign Policy. Globalization. Great Powers (role definition). 1970's. 565
—. China. Foreign Policy. India. Pakistan. 1945-75. 409
—. China. Foreign Policy. International trade. 1950's-74. 72
—. China. Foreign policy. Kissinger, Henry A. 1969-76. 276
—. China. Foreign policy. Military. Political Factions. Zhou Enlai. 1970-71. 263
—. China. Foreign policy. Military strategy. 1969-70's. 293
—. China. Foreign Policy. Modernization. 1950-79. 412
—. China. Foreign Policy. Pacific area. 1950-83. 157
—. China. Foreign Policy. Peace. 1970's. 305
—. China. Foreign policy. Press. 1979-80. 398
—. China. Foreign Policy. Taiwan. 1972-78. 62
—. China. Foreign policy. Tripolarity. 1970's. 417
—. China. Foreign Policy. Vietnam. 1973. 45
—. China. Foreign relations. 1943-79. 556
—. China. Foreign Relations. 1949-57. 176
—. China. Foreign Relations. 1949-80. 192
—. China. Foreign relations. 1949-83. 389
—. China. Foreign Relations. 1950's-82. 308
—. China. Foreign Relations. 1950-83. 332
—. China. Foreign Relations. 1966-72. 457
—. China. Foreign Relations. 1970's-82. 370
—. China. Foreign relations. 1970's. 206
—. China. Foreign Relations. 1970's. 382
—. China. Foreign Relations. 1970's. 434
—. China. Foreign Relations. 1970-74. 341
—. China. Foreign Relations. 1972-. 207
—. China. Foreign Relations. 1972-82. 540
—. China. Foreign Relations. 1974. 480
—. China. Foreign Relations. Industry. Japan. Korea. 1970-76. 95
—. China. Foreign Relations. Japan. 1970's. 107
—. China. Foreign Relations. Japan. 1970's. 594
—. China. Foreign Relations. Japan. 1981-84. 111
—. China. Foreign Relations. Japan. Korea, North. Korea, South. Unification. 1970's-. 20
—. China. Foreign relations. Japan. Taiwan. 1972. 78
—. China. Foreign Relations. Korea. 1960's-82. 122
—. China. Foreign Relations. Military aid. National Security. 1970-75. 440
—. China. Foreign Relations. Taiwan. 1972-82. 215
—. China. Foreign Relations. Thailand. 1974. 143
—. China. Foreign Relations. USA. 1970's. 294
—. China. Foreign Relations. Vietnam War. 1949-74. 511
—. China. Foreign Relations (review article). Military. 1970-77. 538
—. China. Great Britain. International Relations (discipline). Japan. 1937-49. 437
—. China. Korean War. 1950. 1138
—. China. Maoism. Strong, Anna Louise. 1919-70. 245
—. China. Military Strategy. 1950-76. 195
—. China. Nuclear stalemate. Peace. 1970's. 156
—. China. Social organization. 20c. 147
—. China. Trade Regulations. 1966-72. 299
—. Communism. Foreign policy. Intervention. Korean War. Truman, Harry S. 1950. 1081
—. Detente. Foreign policy. Japan. Trade. 1971-74. 749
—. Economic policy. Foreign Relations. Natural Resources (development). 1950's-70's. 50
—. Europe, Western. Japan. Mutual Balanced Force Reductions. Strategic Arms Limitation Talks. 1974. 1002
—. Foreign Policy. Korea (38th Parallel). Korean War. MacArthur, Douglas. Self-determination. Truman, Harry S. 1943-50. 1084
—. Foreign Relations. Japan. Lensen, George Alexander (review article). 1921-30. 831
—. Foreign Relations. Korea. Unification. 1945-47. 1098
—. Historians, Western. Japan. Military defeat. World War II. 1942-45. 890
—. International System. Korea. 1945-78. 1113
—. Japan. Military strategy. NATO. 1945-54. 813
—. Japan. Political systems. Pollution abatement. 1950's-74. 747
—. Korea, North. Korea, South. Military aid. 1953-70's. 1064
USSR (Eastern Siberia). Creighton, John Marie. Intervention. Japan. Military Intelligence. 1922. 44
Utah. Foreign Relations. Japan. King, William. Thomas, Elbert. ca 1922-40. 782
Utah (Salt Lake City). Archival Catalogs and Inventories. China. Genealogical Society of Utah. 15c-20c. 509
Utah (Topaz). Daily Life. Internment. Japanese Americans. Personal narratives. Uchida, Yoshiko. World War II. 1942-43. 942
Uyeda, Clifford I. (account). Citizenship. Ford, Gerald R. Hada, John. Japanese American Citizens League. Pardon. Tokyo Rose (Iva Toguri d'Aquino). 1973-77. 949

V

Values. Attitudes. Japanese Americans. Sociology. World War II. 1940's-70's. *915*
—. Baseball. Democracy. Japan. 1920-41. *637*
—. Civil-Military Relations. Combat. Korean War. 1950-53. *1135*
Vance, Cyrus. China. Taiwan. 1972-77. *129*
Vandenberg, Arthur Hendrick, Sr. China. Foreign Policy. Jiang Jieshi. 1945-50. *255*
Vanderlip, Frank A. American International Corporation. China. 1915-19. *386*
Varg, Paul A. (review article). China. Foreign Relations. 1936-46. *490*
Vatican. China. Diplomacy. World War I. 1918. *145*
Vickers Ltd. Airplane Industry and Trade. China. Embargoes. Great Britain. 1919-21. *448*
Vietnam. Afghanistan. China. Foreign Relations. Invasions. Military cooperation. USSR. 1965-80. *232*
—. Asia, East. Foreign Policy. Japan. Korea. Nixon Doctrine. 1969-73. *90*
—. Cambodia. China. Foreign Relations. USSR. 1978-80. *105*
—. China. Diplomacy. 1975-80. *442*
—. China. Foreign Policy. 1973. *45*
—. Diplomacy. France (Paris). Korea, South (Panmunjom). Peace. 1951-73. *1143*
Vietnam, North. Alienation. China. Cuba. Intellectuals, western. Pilgrimages. USSR. 1930's. 1970's. *296*
—. China. Foreign Relations. Vietnam War. 1970-80. *264*
Vietnam, South. Cambodia. China. Foreign Policy. 1975. *548*
Vietnam War. Afghanistan. Invasions. Korean War. Limited war (concept). USSR. War Powers Act (US, 1973). 1945-79. *104*
—. Air National Guard. Korea, South. Military Reserves. Mobilization. 1968-69. *1036*
—. Air Rescue Service. Korean War. 1961-75. *1133*
—. Air warfare. Korean War. Military Strategy. World War II. 1940-72. *52*
—. Alliances. Korea, South. Military. 1965-73. *1043*
—. Asia, Southeast. China. Foreign Relations. 1973-75. *256*
—. Authoritarianism (theory). Korean War. Personality. Public opinion. Racism. 1950-78. *1046*
—. Balance of Power. China. Foreign Policy. USSR. 1964-76. *512*
—. Bombs (glide, smart). Korean War. Tactics. World War II. 1919-74. *4*
—. Broadcasts. China. USSR. 1968-73. *152*
—. China. Diplomacy. 1964-66. *460*
—. China. Foreign policy. International Trade. Pacific Area. 1960's-70's. *166*
—. China. Foreign relations. 1960's-73. *454*
—. China. Foreign relations. 1973. *228*
—. China. Foreign Relations. Political Commentary. 1960's-70's. *419*
—. China. Foreign Relations. USSR. 1949-74. *511*
—. China. Foreign Relations. Vietnam, North. 1970-80. *264*
—. Communism. Korean War. Prisoners of war. Propaganda. Public opinion. 1950-74. *1021*
—. Daily Life. Korean War. Public Opinion. 1950-73. *1114*
—. Defense spending. Korean War. Military. Minutemen. Political Attitudes. 1784-1979. *1077*
—. Economic aid. Japan. 1960-75. *696*
—. Europe. Foreign policy. Japan. Military strategy. 1970's. *910*
—. Foreign Policy. Japan. 1965-73. *742*

—. Foreign policy. Korean War. 1950-53. 1961-73. *1095*
—. Foreign Relations. Japan. 1964-73. *750*
—. Great Britain. Korean War. Navies. Suez Crisis. USA. 1950-76. *1119*
—. Japan. Public opinion. 1960's-70's. *909*
—. Korean War. Leadership. Military General Staff. Technology. 1950-73. *1085*
—. Korean War. Limited war. Military training. 1945-73. *1131*
—. Korean War. Marines. Transportation, Military. 1945-73. *1108*
—. Korean War. Military rescue concepts. World War II. 1941-74. *11*
—. Korean War. Military Service. National security. 1946-81. *1070*
—. Korean War. Navies. 1945-75. *1120*
—. Korean War. Political Systems. War, limited. 1950-75. *1030*
Vietnamese. China. Communism. Ho Chi Minh. Independence movements. 1942-45. *502*
Villa, Pancho. Korean War. McLain, Raymond Stallings. Military General Staff. Oklahoma. World War I. World War II. 1912-54. *1121*
Vincent, John Carter. Anti-Communist Movements. China. Foreign Policy. May, Gary. McCarthy, Joseph R. 1942-51. *279*
—. China. Diplomacy. Hurley, Patrick J. Jiang Jieshi. Mao Zedong. State Department. 1944-45. *358*
Virginia (Jamestown). Apathy. Colonization. Death and Dying. Korean War. Malnutrition. Prisoners of war. World War II. 1607-24. 1941-53. *74*
Virginia, University of. China. Historiography (Chinese). Jefferson, Thomas. Liu Zuochang. 1770-1826. 1976-81. *321*
Virginia, University of (School of Military Government). Colleges and Universities. Democracy. Japan. Military government. 1944-45. *971*
Voting and Voting Behavior. Australia. Italy. Japan. Netherlands. Political information. 1960's-70's. *716*
—. China. Foreign aid. UN (membership). 1961-68. *144*
Voyages. Brooke, John Mercer. Japan. *Kanrin Maru* (vessel). Navies. Trade. Treaties. 1860. *615*
—. China. Fur trade. South Africa (Cape Colony). 1800-02. *479*
—. China. Shaw, Samuel. Trade. 1784-85. *154*

W

Wages. Europe, Western. Japan. Public services. Trilateral Commission. 1973-79. *925*
—. Great Britain. Japan. ca 1873-1981. *678*
—. Japan. Labor reform. Military Occupation. Working conditions. 1945-60. *918*
Wake Island. China. Japan. Kinney, John F.. Marines. Prisoners of War. World War II. 1941-45. *943*
—. Historiography. Korean War. MacArthur, Douglas. Politics. Public relations. Truman, Harry S. 1950. *1142*
—. Japan. Junghans, Earl A. Marines. Personal narratives. Prisoners of War. War crimes. World War II. 1941-47. *737*
—. Korean War. MacArthur, Douglas. Manchester, William. Military Strategy. Truman, Harry S. 1950. 1980. *1051*
Walker, Walton L. China. Korean War. MacArthur, Douglas. Truman, Harry S. 1950. *1026*
War. *See also* specific kinds of warfare, e.g., Air Warfare, Atomic Warfare.

World War II   289

—. Asia, East. Defense Policy. Military Strategy. 1945-50. *32*

—. Asia, Southeast. Balance of power. China. Communism. USSR. 1920-79. *31*

—. *General Sherman* (vessel). Korea. 1871. *1103*

War crimes. Japan. Junghans, Earl A. Marines. Personal narratives. Prisoners of War. Wake Island. World War II. 1941-47. *737*

War debts. Foreign Relations. Great Britain. Japan. 1920-23. *646*

War, limited. Korean War. Political Systems. Vietnam War. 1950-75. *1030*

War Plan Orange. Japan. Military Strategy. Naval War College. 1900-12. *953*

War Powers Act (US, 1973). Afghanistan. Invasions. Korean War. Limited war (concept). USSR. Vietnam War. 1945-79. *104*

War Relocation Authority. Documentation. Evacuations. Internment. Japanese Americans. Photographs. World War II. 1941-43. *643*

Ward, John Elliot. China. Foreign Relations. 1858-60. *261*

Warren, Earl. California. Japanese Americans. Relocation. World War II. 1941-45. *967*

Warships. *See also* specific warships, e.g., Destroyer Escorts; specific ships by name, e.g., *Wasp* (vessel).

—. Australia. Circumnavigations. Foreign Relations. Japan. 1908. *878*

—. Europe. Japan. 1850-1930's. *845*

Washington. Coffee, John M. Congress. Embargoes. Japan. Schellenbach, Lewis B. 1930's-40. *780*

Washington Conference. Asia, East. Diplomacy. Four-Power Treaty. Karnebeek, Hermann Adriaan van. Netherlands. 1921-22. *9*

—. China (Shandong). Diplomacy. Hughes, Charles Evans. Japan. 1919-22. *863*

Washington (Seattle). Daily Life. Internment. Japanese Americans. Kurose, Aki Kato. World War II. 1930's-50's. *644*

Wasp (vessel). Guadalcanal (battle). *I-19* (submarine). Japan. *North Carolina* (vessel). *O'Brien* (vessel). World War II. 1942. *608*

Watergate trials. China Lobby. Institute of Pacific Relations. McCarran Committee. Public opinion. Thomas, John N. (review article). 1945-75. *58*

Weapons. *See also* terms beginning in "Arms"; Nuclear Arms.

—. China. Economic Conditions. Rhode Island (Providence). Sino-Japanese War. 1894. *36*

Wedemeyer, Albert C. (reminiscences). China. Foreign Relations. World War II. 1920-48. *532*

Wedemeyer, Albert C. (report). China. Communist Party. Foreign Policy. Manchuria. Taiwan. 1946-49. *351*

West, Philip. China (Beijing). Colleges and Universities. Missions and Missionaries. Yanjing University (review article). 1916-52. *161*

Western Nations. Arms Trade (prohibited). China. Civil war. Japan. 1919-29. *17*

—. Developing nations. Economic issues. Japan. Roll-call voting. UN General Assembly. 1970-76. *966*

—. Japan. Navies. Shanghai crisis. 1931-32. *458*

Whiting, Allen S. Buss, Claude A. China. Fairbank, John K. Foreign Relations (review article). 1949-76. *234*

Wildlife Conservation. Canada. Fur trade. Japan. Sea otters. 18c-20c. *988*

William II. Diplomacy (personal). Germany. Meyer, George von Lengerke. Roosevelt, Theodore. Russo-Japanese War. 1902-14. *968*

Williams, Clarence S. Butler, Smedley D. China, North. Marines. Pilots. 1927-28. *410*

Williams, Edward Thomas. China. Disciples of Christ. Missions and Missionaries. 1887-1918. *349*

Williams, George B. Economic development. Japan. Oriental Bank Corporation. Schiff, Jacob. Wilson, James H. Winslow, Edward F. 1872-73. *606*

Williamson, John A. (account). Destroyer escorts. *England* (vessel). Japan. Submarine Warfare. World War II. 1944. *972*

Wilson, James H. Asia, East. China. Development. Foreign Relations. Political Attitudes. 1885-1910. *169*

—. Economic development. Japan. Oriental Bank Corporation. Schiff, Jacob. Williams, George B. Winslow, Edward F. 1872-73. *606*

Wilson, Woodrow. China. Foreign Policy. League of Nations. Paris Peace Conference. Treaties, unequal. 1919. *19*

—. China. Foreign Relations. Loans (consortium). 1910-13. *383*

—. China. Japan. League of Nations. Paris Peace Conference. 1919. *85*

—. Equality (proposed). Hughes, William Morris. Japan. League of Nations Covenant. Paris Peace Conference. Race Relations. 1919. *772*

Winslow, Edward F. Economic development. Japan. Oriental Bank Corporation. Schiff, Jacob. Williams, George B. Wilson, James H. 1872-73. *606*

Wisconsin (Wingspread). China studies (conference). High Schools. 1972. *230*

Wiseman, William. Great Britain. Japan. Military Intelligence. World War I. World War II. 1914-45. *903*

Witte, Sergei. Dillon, Emile Joseph. Portsmouth Peace Conference. Press. Public opinion. Russo-Japanese War. 1904-05. *732*

Women. Atomic bomb. Charities. Japan (Hiroshima). Surgery. World War II. 1945-57. *985*

—. China. Cultural attitudes. Great Britain. Social status. 1840-1927. *243*

—. China. Leftism. Smedley, Agnes (review article). 1930's-50. 1973-76. *329*

Women's liberation movement. China. Ideology. 1960's-70's. *455*

Woods, George W. Diaries. Korea. Naval officers. 1884. *1127*

Working conditions. Japan. Labor reform. Military Occupation. Wages. 1945-60. *918*

World car (concept). Automobile Industry and Trade. Canada. Europe, Western. Gindon, Sam (interview). Japan. Labor. 1945-80. *1006*

World War I. China. Diplomacy. Foreign Investments. Great Britain. Japan. 1915-17. *28*

—. China. Diplomacy. Vatican. 1918. *145*

—. China. International trade. Pacific & Eastern Steamship Company. Ships. USA. 1914-16. *447*

—. Cuba. Decisionmaking. Foreign Policy. Germany. Korean War. 1914-62. *1109*

—. Great Britain. Japan. Military Intelligence. Wiseman, William. World War II. 1914-45. *903*

—. Korean War. McLain, Raymond Stallings. Military General Staff. Oklahoma. Villa, Pancho. World War II. 1912-54. *1121*

World War I (antecedents). Asia, East. Foreign policy. Lansing, Robert. 1914-17. *54*

World War II. Adams, Ansel. California. Internment. Japanese Americans. Lange, Dorothea. Manzanar War Relocation Center. Photography, Journalistic. 1941-45. *840*

—. Adventist Medical Cadet Corps. Armies. Dick, Everett N. (account). Korean War. Military service. 1934-53. *29*

290   World War II

—. Agawa, Hiroyuki. Japan. Military officers. Navies. Yamamoto, Isoroku (review article). 1930's-43. *764*
—. Air Forces. Atomic bomb. Japan (Hiroshima). Military training. Personal narratives. Tibbets, Paul W. 1945. *932*
—. Air Forces. Balloon Force. Documents. Japan. 1942-45. *702*
—. Air Forces. China. 1943-45. *402*
—. Air Forces. F-13 (aircraft). Korean War. 1944-54. *82*
—. Air Forces. Japan. Kenney, George. Rabaul (battle). 1943. *607*
—. Air Forces. Japan. Military Capability. Philippines. 1941. *692*
—. Air Warfare. American Volunteer Group. China. Flying Tigers. Shoulder patches. 23d Fighter Group. 1930's-45. *25*
—. Air Warfare. Army Air Force. China. Flying Tigers. Holloway, Bruce K. (account). P-40 (aircraft). 1942-43. *297*
—. Air Warfare. Balloons. Bombing. Japan. North America. 1940-45. *964*
—. Air Warfare. Bombing. China (Gailan). Coal Mines and Mining. Combs, Cecil E. Personal narratives. 1942. *213*
—. Air Warfare. Bombing. Japan. Personal Narratives. Sims, Jack A. 1942. *905*
—. Air warfare. Chennault, Claire Lee. China. Flying Tigers. Japan. 1941-45. *701*
—. Air Warfare. Chennault, Claire Lee. China. Japan. 1937-45. *98*
—. Air Warfare. Foss, Joseph J. Guadalcanal (battle). Japan. 1942. *795*
—. Air Warfare. Hellcats. Japan. Task Force 58. Truk (battle). 1944. *933*
—. Air Warfare. Japan. Lemay, Curtis. 1940-45. *976*
—. Air Warfare. Japan. Mariana Islands (battle). 1944. *668*
—. Air warfare. Korean War. Military Strategy. Vietnam War. 1940-72. *52*
—. Aircraft carriers. Japan. Submarine Warfare. 1941-45. *865*
—. Airplanes. China (Kunming). Ghana (Accra). Laughlin, C. H. (reminiscences). 1942. *347*
—. Airplanes, Military. Japan. Navies. Productivity. 1941-45. *860*
—. Alaska (Aleutian Islands). *Arthur Middleton* (vessel). Coast Guard. Japan. Laidlaw, Lansing. 1942-43. *769*
—. Alaska (Aleutian Islands). Attu (battle). Japan. 1942. *916*
—. Alliances (review article). British Empire. Japan. Louis, William Roger. Thorne, Christopher. 1941-45. *854*
—. Alperovitz, Gar (review article). Atomic Warfare. Decisionmaking. Historiography. Japan (Hiroshima). 1945-65. *898*
—. Amphibious operations. Japan. 1942-45. *725*
—. Anticolonialism. Asia. Roosevelt, Franklin D. USA. 1941-45. *51*
—. Apathy. Colonization. Death and Dying. Korean War. Malnutrition. Prisoners of war. Virginia (Jamestown). 1607-24. 1941-53. *74*
—. Appeasement (proposal). Diplomacy. Great Britain. Japan. 1941. *680*
—. Arab-Israeli Conflict. Conflict and Conflict Resolution. Decisionmaking. Foreign Policy. Japan. 1941-45. 1967-73. *600*
—. Arizona. Gila River Relocation Center. Japanese Americans. Public Opinion. Race Relations. 1942-45. *627*
—. Arkansas (Rowher Camp). Internment. Japanese Americans. 1942-45. *592*
—. Armies. Japan. Marines. Pelelieu (battle). Sledge, Eugene B. (account). 1944. *907*

—. Armstrong, David M. (personal account). Hawaii. Japan. Pearl Harbor (attack). 1942. *580*
—. Asia. Historiography, US. Japan. Revolutionary movements. USSR. 1930's-49. *862*
—. Atomic bomb. Charities. Japan (Hiroshima). Surgery. Women. 1945-57. *985*
—. Atomic bomb. Documents. Japan (Hiroshima, Nagasaki). 1945. *867*
—. Atomic bomb. Japan. Military Strategy. Truman, Harry S. 1945. *602*
—. Atomic bomb. Japan. Public opinion. 1945-49. *984*
—. Atomic bomb. Japan (Hiroshima, Nagasaki). Truman, Harry S. 1942-47. *605*
—. Atomic energy. Japan. Military Strategy. Smyth Report, 1945. USA. 1940-45. *908*
—. Atomic Warfare. Cold War. Japan (Hiroshima). 1945. *744*
—. Atomic Warfare. Decisionmaking. Japan (Hiroshima, Nagasaki). Military Strategy. 1944-45. *671*
—. Atomic Warfare. History Teaching. Japan. Simulation and Games. 1945. 1978. *658*
—. Atomic Warfare. Japan. Leftists. USSR. 1945. *610*
—. Atomic Warfare. Japan. Military strategy. 1945. *714*
—. Atomic Warfare. Japan. Politics. Surrender. Truman, Harry S. (administration). 1945. *604*
—. Atomic warfare. Japan (Hiroshima, Nagasaki). Military Strategy. 1945. *603*
—. Atomic Warfare. Japan (Hiroshima, Nagasaki). Military Strategy. Surrender, unconditional. 1943-45. *703*
—. Atomic Warfare. Japan (Kyoto). 1945. *848*
—. Attitudes. Authors. Japan. USA. 1940-49. *815*
—. Attitudes. Canada. Internment. Japanese Americans. Japanese Canadians. 1940-80. *642*
—. Attitudes. Japanese Americans. Sociology. Values. 1940's-70's. *915*
—. Attu (battle). Japan. Tatsuguchi, Paul Nobuo (diary). USA. 1941-43. *963*
—. Australia. Japan. Peace settlement. 1942-46. *597*
—. *Awa Maru* (vessel). Japan. Navies. *Queenfish* (submarine). 1945. *912*
—. Balloons, armed. Japan. Project FUGO. South Dakota. 1944-45. *770*
—. Bohme, Frederick G. Census Bureau. Japanese Americans. Letters. Relocation. 1942-45. *640*
—. Bombing. B-29 (aircraft). China-Burma-India Theater. Close, Winton R. Japan. Personal narratives. 1944. *633*
—. Bombing. Japan. 1937-45. *639*
—. Bombing exemption. Japan (Kyoto). Stimson, Henry L. 1940-45. *628*
—. Bombs, balloon-carried. Japan. Pacific Northwest. 1945. *733*
—. Bombs (glide, smart). Korean War. Tactics. Vietnam War. 1919-74. *4*
—. California. Concentration Camps. Japanese Americans. Manzanar War Relocation Center. Riots. Ueno, Harry (arrest). 1942. *691*
—. California. Detention. Japanese Americans. Racism. 1941-45. *818*
—. California. Japanese Americans. Relocation. Warren, Earl. 1941-45. *967*
—. Canada. Ethnicity. Internment. Japanese Americans. Japanese Canadians. Joint Board of Defense. 1941-42. *641*
—. Canada. Internment (conference). Japanese. 1941-45. 1978. *922*
—. Carney, Robert B. Japan. Personal Narratives. Surrender. 1945. *626*
—. Censorship. *Chicago Tribune*. Cryptography. Japan. Midway (battle). Reporters and Reporting. 1942. *679*

World War II   291

—. Censorship. *Chicago Tribune.* Grand Juries. Japan. Midway (battle). Navies. 1942. *669*
—. China. Communist Party. Diplomacy. 1944. *244*
—. China. Diplomacy. Great Britain. Hong Kong. 1941-45. *570*
—. China. Foreign Policy. Japan. Public opinion. 1937-45. *65*
—. China. Foreign Policy. Service, John Stewart. 1945-49. *342*
—. China. Foreign policy. Service, John Stewart (*Lost Chance in China*, excerpts). State Department (Foreign Service). 1945-50's. *483*
—. China. Foreign Relations. Wedemeyer, Albert C. (reminiscences). 1920-48. *532*
—. China. Great Britain. Loan negotiations. 1941-44. *189*
—. China. Historiography. Stilwell, Joseph W. 1942-44. *559*
—. China. Japan. Kinney, John F. Marines. Prisoners of War. Wake Island. 1941-45. *943*
—. China. Jiang Jieshi. Marshall, George C. Military General Staff. Stilwell, Joseph W. 1944. *475*
—. China. Jiang Jieshi. Military strategy. Stilwell, Joseph W. 1942-44. *397*
—. China. *Keys of the Kingdom* (film). Office of War Information. Propaganda. Stereotypes. 1940-45. *172*
—. China. Navies. Sino-American Cooperation Association (SACO). 1942-45. *476*
—. China, north. Civil war. Marines. Military Occupation. 1945-47. *33*
—. China-Burma-India Theater. Emmerson, John K. Memoirs. State Department (Foreign Service). 1941-44. *251*
—. Civil rights. Counterintelligence. Internment. Japanese Americans. Munson, Curtis B. Peiper, N. J. L. 1931-42. *765*
—. Clark Field. Japan. Philippines. 1941-42. *788*
—. Combat Information Unit. Cryptography. Japan. Midway (battle). Navies. 1942. *858*
—. Communications. Great Britain. Japan. Naval Strategy. 1943-45. *652*
—. Concentration Camps. Japanese Americans. 1942-46. *842*
—. Concentration Camps. Japanese Americans. Public schools. 1942-45. *977*
—. Concentration camps. Japanese Americans. Racism. 1940-45. *719*
—. Cryptography. Guadalcanal (battle). Japan. Military Intelligence. Radio. 1942. *810*
—. Daily Life. Internment. Japanese Americans. Kurose, Aki Kato. Washington (Seattle). 1930's-50's. *644*
—. Daily Life. Internment. Japanese Americans. Personal narratives. Uchida, Yoshiko. Utah (Topaz). 1942-43. *942*
—. Destroyer escorts. *England* (vessel). Japan. Submarine Warfare. Williamson, John A. (account). 1944. *972*
—. Diaries. Japan. Norquist, Ernest O. Philippines. Prisoners of War. 1942-45. *837*
—. Diplomacy. Emmerson, John K. Internment. Japanese Peruvians. Memoirs. Peru. 1942-43. *660*
—. Diplomacy. Japan. MacArthur, Douglas. Philippines (Manila). Surrender. 1945. *812*
—. Diplomats. Japanese. Pennsylvania (Bedford). Prisoners of War. 1945. *586*
—. Dixon, Robert E. Japan. Johnston, Stanley. Midway (battle). Military Strategy. Personal narratives. Reporters and Reporting. 1942. *794*
—. Documentation. Evacuations. Internment. Japanese Americans. Photographs. War Relocation Authority. 1941-43. *643*

—. Dull, Paul S. (review article). Japan. Naval Strategy. Pearl Harbor. Yamamoto, Isoroku. 1941-45. *941*
—. Dumas, Harold. Japanese language. Marines. 1944-45. *791*
—. Exports. Great Britain. Japan. Oil Industry and Trade. Roosevelt, Franklin D. 1940-41. *659*
—. Foreign Policy. Japan. Netherlands East Indies. 1941-46. *710*
—. Foreign Policy. Korea. 1941-45. *1083*
—. Foreign Policy. Korea. Partition. 1945. *1082*
—. Foreign Relations. Great Britain. Japan. Thailand. 1942-46. *970*
—. Foreign Relations. Japan. Philippines. Quirino, Elpidio. Treaties. 1945-56. *748*
—. Generations. Internment. Japanese American Citizens League. Patriotism. 1941-42. *913*
—. Great Britain. Japan. Military Intelligence. Wiseman, William. World War I. 1914-45. *903*
—. Great Britain. Japan. Naval Strategy. Pacific Area. 1941-45. *589*
—. *Gregory* (vessel). Japan (Bonin Islands). McCandless, Bruce (reminiscences). Navies. 1945. *798*
—. Guadalcanal (battle). *I-19* (submarine). Japan. *North Carolina* (vessel). *O'Brien* (vessel). *Wasp* (vessel). 1942. *608*
—. Guadalcanal (battle). Japan. 1942-43. *852*
—. Guam (liberation). Japan. 1944. *625*
—. Hawaii. Japan. Naval Vessels. Pearl Harbor. 1941. *1000*
—. Hawaii. Japan. Pearl Harbor. 1941. *885*
—. Herde, Peter (review article). Japan. Pearl Harbor. 1941. *938*
—. Historians, Western. Japan. Military defeat. USSR. 1942-45. *890*
—. Idaho (Minidoka). Japanese Americans. Mukaida, Tomeji (reminiscences). Relocation. 1940's. *789*
—. *Indianapolis* (vessel). *I-58* (vessel). Japan. Submarine Warfare. 1945. *612*
—. Internment. Japanese Americans. Letters. 1942. *914*
—. Internment. Japanese Americans. Martial law. Tule Lake Camp. 1941-44. *843*
—. Internment. Japanese Americans. Mirikitani, Janice ("Lullaby"). Poetry. 1941-45. *609*
—. Internment. Japanese Americans. New Mexico (Clovis). 1942-45. *638*
—. Internment. Japanese Americans. Oral history. Tanaka, Togo. Yoneda, Elaine. Yoneda, Karl. 1941-45. *816*
—. Internment. Japanese Americans. Personal narratives. 1942-81. *1001*
—. Internment. Japanese Americans. Propaganda. 1942-45. *841*
—. Invasions. Japan. Military Strategy. Operation Olympic. 1945. *645*
—. Iwo Jima. Japan. 1944-45. *736*
—. Japan. Junghans, Earl A. Marines. Personal narratives. Prisoners of War. Wake Island. War crimes. 1941-47. *737*
—. Japan. Leyte (battle). Naval Warfare. 1944. *884*
—. Japan. Makin Islands (raid). Marines (2d Raiders). Peatross, Oscar F. (account). Prisoners of War. 1942-47. *853*
—. Japan. Midway (battle). Military Strategy. 1942. *992*
—. Japan. Midway (battle). Navies. 1942. *621*
—. Japan. Military operations. Natural Resources. Oregon (Bly). Project FUGO. 1942-45. *861*
—. Japan. Naval Tactics. Savo Island (battle). 1942. *596*
—. Japan. Naval Tactics. World War II. 1920's-43. *724*
—. Japan. Naval Tactics. World War II. 1920's-43. *724*

World War II

—. Japan. Navies. Philippine Sea (battle). 1944. *619*
—. Japan. Navies. Solomon Islands (Vella Lavella). 1943. *784*
—. Japan. Peace. Potsdam Conference. Surrender, unconditional. 1945. *952*
—. Japan. Pearl Harbor (attack). 1940-41. *846*
—. Japan. Sherrod, Robert (memoirs). Tarawa (battle). 1944. *901*
—. Japanese. Prisoners of war. 1941-45. *759*
—. Japanese Americans (attitudes toward). Sociological theory. Values. 1940's-70's. *915*
—. Korean War. MacArthur, Douglas. Military General Staff. ca 1939-51. *1134*
—. Korean War. McLain, Raymond Stallings. Military General Staff. Oklahoma. Villa, Pancho. World War I. 1912-54. *1121*
—. Korean War. Military rescue concepts. Vietnam War. 1941-74. *11*
—. Korean War. Military Strategy. October War. Pearl Harbor (attack). Surprise attacks. 1941-73. *7*
—. Prisoners of War (German, Japanese, Italian). 1942-45. *620*
World War II (antecedents). Asia, East. Foreign Policy. Japan. 1931-41. *687*
—. Blockades. Chamberlain, Neville. China. Great Britain. Japan. Roosevelt, Franklin D. 1937-38. *686*
—. Butow, R. J. Diplomacy, private. Japan. John Doe Associates. Peace (review article). 1940-41. *723*
—. Congress. Japan. 1940-41. *779*
—. Diplomacy. Emmerson, John K. Japan (Tokyo). Memoirs. State Department. 1941. *662*
—. Diplomacy. Foreign policy. International Trade. Japan. 1937-41. *946*
—. Diplomacy. Hornbeck, Stanley K. Japan. 1937-41. *775*
—. Diplomacy. Hull, Cordell. Indochina. Japan. Philippines. 1941. *616*
—. Diplomacy. Japan. Military Intelligence. Roosevelt, Franklin D. 1940-41. *693*
—. Foreign Policy. Japan. 1940-41. *599*
—. Imperialism. Japan. Navigation. Pacific Area. Pearl Harbor. Prehistory-1941. *648*
—. Japan. 1930's. *1007*
World War II (antecedents; review article). Diplomacy. Europe. Japan. 1930's-41. *700*
—. Europe. Foreign policy. Japan. Offner, Arnold A. 1917-41. *829*
World's fair. Arts and crafts. China. Exhibits and Expositions. Missouri (St. Louis). 1904. *216*
Wyoming (vessel). Americans (protected). Japan (Shimonoseki Strait). McDougal, David. Naval battles. 1863. *683*

Y

Yale University Library (collection). Archives. China. Missions and Missionaries. Protestantism. Yale-in-China Association. 1901-51. *237*
Yale-in-China Association. Archives. China. Missions and Missionaries. Protestantism. Yale University Library (collection). 1901-51. *237*
—. Canton Christian College. China. Church Schools. Revolution. 1925-27. *300*

Yamamoto, Isoroku. Dull, Paul S. (review article). Japan. Naval Strategy. Pearl Harbor. World War II. 1941-45. *941*
Yamamoto, Isoroku (review article). Agawa, Hiroyuki. Japan. Military officers. Navies. World War II. 1930's-43. *764*
Yangtze Rapid Steamship Company. China. Foreign policy. Intervention. Shipping. 1924-36. *302*
Yanjing University (review article). China (Beijing). Colleges and Universities. Missions and Missionaries. West, Philip. 1916-52. *161*
Yasukawa, Takeshi (speech). Foreign Relations. Japan. 1975. *983*
Yasuteru, Aoki. Attitudes. High Schools. Japan. 1970's. *814*
Yoneda, Elaine. Internment. Japanese Americans. Oral history. Tanaka, Togo. World War II. Yoneda, Karl. 1941-45. *816*
Yoneda, Karl. Internment. Japanese Americans. Oral history. Tanaka, Togo. World War II. Yoneda, Elaine. 1941-45. *816*
Yoshida Shigeru. Alliances. Dulles, John Foster. Japan. Political Theory. Treaties. 5c BC-20c. 1951. *653*
—. Foreign policy. Japan. 1945-78. *835*
Yōsuke, Matsuoka. Diplomacy. Japan. 1940-41. *738*
Young, John Russell. China. Diplomacy. 1882-85. *494*
—. China. Diplomacy. Manufacturing. 1882-83. *221*
Young Men's Christian Association. California (Pasadena). China (Shanghai). Daughters of the American Revolution. 1916-57. *422*
Youth. Japan. Mysticism. Religion. 1976. *767*
Yrissari and Co. Bank of England. China. Economic crises. International Trade. Magniac and Co. 1823-27. *18*
Yuan Shikai. China. Constitutional development. Goodnow, Frank Johnson. 1913-15. *449*
—. China. Great Britain. Presidency. 1911-12. *363*

Z

Zhang Yinhuan. China. Diaries. Diplomacy. 1886-89. *159*
Zhou Enlai. China. Foreign policy. Military. Political Factions. USSR. 1970-71. *263*

7th Infantry Division, US (31st Field Artillery Battalion). Armies. Dill, James. Korean War. Personal narratives. 1950-51. *1027*
8th Army, US. Korea. Military Service, Professional. Personal narratives. Ridgway, Matthew B. 1917-52. *1047*
23d Fighter Group. Air Warfare. American Volunteer Group. China. Flying Tigers. Shoulder patches. World War II. 1930's-45. *25*

AUTHOR INDEX

A

Abegglen, James C. 573
Acharkan, V. 996
Agnew, James B. 138
Ahn, Byung-Joon 1
Aigrain, Pierre 574
Alexandrov, A. 833
Alexandrov, I. 139
Alexeyev, I. 140 141
Aliev, R. 575
Allen, T. Harrell 142
Alpern, Stephen I. 143
Alpert, Eugene J. 144
Alvarez, David J. 145
Alvarez, Donato 576 624
Alvi, Naheed 146
Amakawa, Akira 577
Amin, Samir 147
Amody, Francis J. 1008
Anderson, David L. 2 148 149 150
Anderson, Irvine H., Jr. 578
Ano, Masaharu 579
Apalin, G. 141
Aplington, Henry, II 151
Ardoin, Birthney 152
Armentrout-Ma, L. Eve 153
Armstrong, David M. 580
Armstrong, Oscar V. 154
Arnold, Joseph C. 3
Aronsen, Lawrence R. 155
Aruga, Tadashi 581
Aspaturian, Vernon D. 156 565
Auer, J. E. 582
Auw, David C. L. 157 1149

B

Bacchus, Wilfred A. 1009
Baerwald, Hans H. 583
Baker, Edward J. 1010
Ballard, William T. 158
Ballendorf, Dirk Anthony 584
Balsam, Jerome M. 585
Banno, Masataka 159
Barbeau, Arthur E. 586
Barbeiro, Heródoto S. 587
Barié, Ottavio 160
Barnett, Suzanne Wilson 161
Barnouw, Erik 588
Baron, Michael L. 162
Barsegov, Iu. 163
Bartlett, Merrill 589 590
Bayley, David H. 591
Bays, Daniel H. 164
Bearden, Russell 592
Beatty, Roger Dean 593
Beaumont, Roger A. 4
Becker, James M. 999
Bedeski, Robert E. 594
Beer, Lawrence W. 5
Beers, Burton F. 165
Behnam, M. Reza 595
Bel'chuk, A. 996
Bell, Charles 596
Bell, Roger 597
Bellows, Thomas J. 1150
Benaerts, Pierre 6
Benson, Larry 1011
Benz, Wolfgang 598
Ben-Zvi, Abraham 7 599 600
Beresford, Melanie 166

Berman, Jeffrey 340
Bernos, Roger 601
Bernstein, Barton J. 602 603 604 605 1012 1013 1014
Bernstein, Samuel J. 144
Berry, Mary 167
Bert, Wayne 168
Best, Gary Dean 169 606
Bickerton, Ian J. 170
Billa, Krupadanam J. B. 171
Birdsall, Steve 607
Bishop, Donald M. 1015
Black, Gregory D. 172
Blechman, Barry M. 8
Blee, Ben W. 608
Blicksilver, Edith 609
Bobrow, Davis B. 571
Bohm, Fred C. 1127
Boller, Paul F., Jr. 610
Bootsma, N. A. 9
Borg, Dorothy 162 274 289 315 355 562 564 1176
Borisova, K. 611
Bourne, Peter G. 1151
Bowie, Robert R. 910
Boyd, Carl 612
Brach, Hans Günter 173
Bradford, Richard H. 174
Brady, Erika 175
Brahm, Heinz 176
Brandon, Donald 177
Brecher, Charles 675
Briggs, Philip J. 178
Britsch, R. Lanier 613
Bronfenbrenner, Martin 614
Brooke, George M., Jr. 615
Brooks, James L. 1016
Brown, Roger Glenn 179
Brun, Ellen 1017
Brune, Lester H. 616
Buck, Peter 180
Buckley, Roger 617
Buhite, Russell D. 10 181
Bullard, Monte R. 182
Bur, Lawrence J. 618
Burton, Bruce 235
Butera, J. L. 11
Buxbaum, David C. 183
Byrd, Martha H. 619 620 621

C

Cadart, Claude 184
Calder, Kent E. 622
Cameron, Allan W. 623
Capdevielle, Patricia 624
Capie, Susan A. 185
Carano, Paul 625
Carbonneau, Robert 186
Carney, Robert B. 626
Caruso, Samuel T. 627
Cary, Otis 628
Catley, Bob 166
Chan, F. Gilbert 12 187
Chan, Jeffery Paul 13
Chan, K. C. 188 189
Chan, King-yuh 190 1153
Chan, Kit-cheng 570
Chan, Steve 571
Chandler, Alfred 629
Chang, David W. 1152
Chang, Hwa-Bao 191
Chang, Parris H. 192
Chang, Shu Yuan 14

Chang, Y. C. 15
Chang, Yü-fa 193
Chang Chung-tung 194
Chari, P. R. 195
Chary, Srinivas 16
Chen, Robert P. 1154
Ch'en, Ts'un-kung 17
Cheng, Joseph Y. S. 196
Cheng Yu-p'ing 1166
Cheong, W. E. 18 197
Chern, Kenneth S. 198
Chevallier, François-Xavier 630
Chi, Madeleine 19
Chiba, Motoko 670
Chih Meng 199
Chin, Frank 13
Chiu, Hung-dah 200
Cho, Soon Sung 20
Chou, S. H. 201
Choudhury, Golam W. 202
Christopher, Robert C. 631
Chu, John 203
Chu, Yung-Deh Richard 204
Chung, Yong Hwan 1018
Chyba, Christopher F. 205
Ciccarelli, Orazio 632
Cigliani, Carlo 1019
Clark, Ian 206
Clark, Malcolm, Jr. 21
Close, Winton R. 633
Clough, Ralph N. 22
Clubb, O. Edmund 23 207 208
Cohen, Jerome Alan 568
Cohen, Warren I. 24 208 209 210 211 562
Cohen, Yehudi A. 634
Cole, James L., Jr. 1020
Cole, Robert E. 635
Colebrook, Joan 1021
Coleman, Michael C. 212
Combs, Cecil E. 213
Coolidge, T. Jefferson, Jr. 1022
Cooling, B. Franklin 1023
Cooper, Brian 576 624
Cooper, Richard N. 997
Cope, Jesse D. 214
Copper, John F. 215 1155
Cornelius, Wanda 25
Corsi, Matteo 636
Cortinovis, Irene E. 216
Cox, Thomas R. 1156
Crepeau, Richard C. 637
Crone, Ray H. 217
Culley, John J. 638

D

Dallek, Robert 26
Dalton, Verne 1046
Daniels, Gordon 639
Daniels, Roger 640 641 642
Danovitch, Sylvia E. 643
Davidson, Frederic 218
Davidson, Sue 644
Davies, John Paton 27
Davis, Clarence B. 28 219
Davis, Frank 645
Dayer, Roberta Albert 646
Dean, Britten 220 221 222
Dean, David M. 223
Deane, Hugh 224
DeAngelis, Richard C. 225
Dearing, Albin 226
DeBary, William Theodore 227

Author Index

DeCecco, Marcello 647
deDubnic, Vladimir Reisky 228 229
deKeijzer, Arne J. 230
delaSierra Fernández, Luis 648
Delmas, Claude 1024 1025
Delmas, J. 1026
Delpech, Jean Laurens 649
Denicoff, Todd 650
Denoon, David B. H. 651
Deshazo, E. A. 919
DeSimone, Silvio 231 232
Devane, Richard T. 233
Dial, Roger 234
Dick, Everett N. 29
Dickson, W. David 652
Diebel, Terry L. 30
Diem, Bui 31
Dill, James 1027
Dillon, Linda D. 235
Dingman, Roger 32 236 653
Dobbs, Charles M. 33
Dojka, John 237
Dominguez, Jorge I. 238
Donahue, William J. 239 240
Donaldson, Robert H. 241
Donnelly, J. B. 34
Donneur, André 242
Dorwart, Jeffery M. 35 36 37 38 1028
Douglas-Home, Alex 1005
Dove, Kay L. 39
Doyle, James H. 1029
Dreisch, Andrew 654
Drucker, Alison R. 243
Dubinski, A. M. 244
DuBoff, Richard 655
Duke, David C. 245 246
Durden, Robert F. 656
Dutt, Gargi 247

E

Ebel, Wilfred L. 657
Eckstein, Alexander 248 249
Edgerton, F. Van 40
Eggert, Gerald G. 250
Eggleston, Noel C. 658
Eismeier, Dana L. 659
Eldredge, Michael S. 1000
Elowitz, Larry 1030
Emmerson, John K. 251 660 661 662
Endicott, Stephen L. 1031
English, H. Edward 41
Entov, R. 996
Estes, Donald H. 663
Etō, Juiz 664
Etzold, Thomas H. 42
Evans, P. M. 252
Evensen, Jens 1005

F

Fabritzek, Uwe G. 253
Fairbank, John K. 1157
Faramazian. R. 415
Farmer, James H. 1032
Feaver, John H. 254
Feld, Werner J. 665
Fendrich, James M. 760
Ferretti, Valdo 666
Fetzer, James 255
Finn, Dallas 667 1004
FitzGerald, C. R. 256
Flick, Alvin S. 668

Foot, Rosemary 1033
Forcier, Pierre 257
Frank, Larry J. 669
Franz, Margaret-Mary 670
Fraser, A. M. 258 1158
Freedman, Lawrence 671
Frisbee, John L. 1034
Frost, Edwin C. 259
Funnell, Victor C. 260
Fyfield-Shayler, B. A. 672

G

Gabard, William M. 261
Gabriele, Mariano 673
Gaddis, John Lewis 43 564
Garner, William V. 262
Garver, John 263 264
Gay, James Thomas 44
Gayn, Mark 45
Gelm, George E. 265
George, Brian T. 266
Gettys, James W., Jr. 567
Geyer, Hans Martin 674
Ghosh, Partha S. 267 268 269 270
Ghosh, Suchita 271
Giddes, Paul H. 272
Ginneken, Jaap van 46
Ginzberg, Eli 675
Gittings, John 1035
Goldstein, Jonathan 47 100 273
Goldstein, Steven M. 274
Goodman, Grant K. 999
Gordon, Bernard K. 48 676 677
Gordon, Robert J. 678
Goren, Dina 679
Gough, Barry M. 49 275
Grace, Richard J. 680
Graebner, Norman A. 276
Graham, Edward D. 277
Grant, Julia Dent 1004
Grebennikova, E. 681
Greenhut, M. L. 682
Gregor, A. James 1159
Griffiths, William E. 683
Grigor'ev, L. 996
Gross, Charles J. 1036
Gumpel, Werner 50
Gupta, Sisir 278
Gupta, Surendra K. 279

H

Habib, Philip C. 1037
Habibuddin, S. M. 51
Hacker, David A. 691
Hadley, Eleanor M. 684
Haering, George 52
Haga, Shōji 685
Hagiwara, Shigeru 729
Haight, John McVickar, Jr. 686
Haines, Gerald K. 687
Hall, James L. 152
Halliday, Jon 688 1038
Hamilton, David Mike 689
Hamm, Michael J. 1039
Hammond, James W., Jr. 690
Han, Sungjoo 1040 1041 1042 1043
Han, Yung-Chul 1044
Hansen, Arthur A. 691
Hardin, Thomas L. 53
Harding, Harry 280 281
Harrington, Daniel F. 692
Harris, Ruth R. 693

Harrison, Selig S. 1045
Hartgen, Stephen 282
Hartig, Thomas H. 54
Hartmann, Frederick H. 283
Hartwell, Charles K., Mrs. 284
Harvey, Thomas H., Jr. 694
Hata, Ikuhiko 695
Hatakeda, Shigeo 696
Hauptman, Lawrence M. 70 1160
Havens, Thomas R. 697
Hawkins, John N. 285
Hayes, Harold B., III 55
Heath, Laurel 698
Heaton, William R., Jr. 286
Heimann, Bernhard 287
Heininger, Janet E. 288
Heinrichs, Waldo 162 274 289 315 355 562 564 1176
Hellwig, David J. 699
Henrikson, Alan K. 700
Henry, Ernst 290
Henson, Curtis T., Jr. 291
Hersh, Jacques 1017
Herzon, Frederick D. 1046
Hettig, David 292
Hetzel, Frederick A. 1047
Hibel, Franklin 701
Hidagi, Yasushi 702
Hikins, James W. 703
Hilgenberg, James F., Jr. 704
Hinckley, Caryl C. 705
Hinckley, Ted C. 705
Hinton, Harold C. 56 293
Hitchens, Harold L. 1047
Hochman, Steven H. 321
Hoddeson, Lillian 706
Holbo, Paul S. 57
Holbraad, Carsten 294
Holbrook, Francis X. 295
Hollander, Paul 296
Hollerman, Leon 707 708 709
Holloway, Bruce K. 297
Holmes, John W. 58
Homan, Gerlof D. 710
Homma, Nagayo 711 712 999
Hong, Zhu 298
Hooper, Paul F. 713
Horder, Mervyn 714
Hosoya, Chihiro 715
Hou, Chi-ming 193
Houchins, Chang-su 1048
Houchins, Lee 1048
Hout, Thomas M. 573
Howell, Susan E. 716
Hoxie, R. Gordon 1161
Hoya, Thomas W. 299
Hoyt, Frederick B. 59 60 300 301 302 303 304
Hsing Kuo-ch'iang 305 306
Hsu, King-yi 61 62 307
Hsueh, Chun-tu 308
Huan Xiang 309
Huang, Chia-mo 310 312
Huang, Robert Chu-kua 311
Hungdah, Chiu 63 568
Hunt, Michael H. 313 314 315 316
Hyndman, Vance 568

I

Ichioka, Yuji 717
Idanov, I. 944
Idéo, Rosella 718
Iiyama, Patty 719
Ijiri, Hidenori 317

Author Index

Inada, Lawson 13
Ingersoll, Robert S. 720
Inglis, Alex I. 318
Inoue, Shigenobu 64
Ion, A. Hamish 721
Iriye, Akira 722 723
Isby, David C. 724 725
Ishikawa, Hirotomo 726
Israel, Jerry 319 320
Israel, John 321
Ito, Hiroshi 727
Itō, Toshikatsu 1003
Itō, Tsuneo 728
Iwao, Sumiko 729

J

Jablon, Howard 730
Jackson, Hermione Dannelly 322
Jaffe, Philip J. 323
James, D. Clayton 1049
Jan, George P. 65
Janke, Peter 731
Javits, Jacob K. 1162
Jervis, Robert 1050
Jessup, Philip C. 1051
Jobert, Michel 1005
Johnson, Paul W. 732
Johnson, Randall A. 733
Johnson, Ronald W. 1052
Johnson, Sheila K. 324
Jorgenson, Dale W. 734 735
Josephy, Alvin M., Jr. 736
Ju, Woo Jung 325
Juhnke, James C. 326
Jun, Li 399
Jundanian, Brendan F. 327
Junghans, Earl A. 737

K

Kahn, B. Winston 738
Kamachi, Noriko 328
Kamei Shunsuke 739
Kanda, Fumito 740
Kanda, James 741
Kao, Charles H. C. 1163
Karashchuk, E. V. 742
Kashima, Tetsuden 743
Kaspi, André 744 1053
Katz, Naomi 329
Kawagoe, Keizō 1054
Kawahito, Kiyoshi 745
Keatley, Robert 66
Keene, Donald 746
Keeton, Morris T. 330
Kehoe, Barbara B. 331
Keith, Ronald C. 332
Kelley, Ronald R. 747
Kesavan, K. V. 748 749 750
Khesin, E. 944 996
Khlynov, V. 751
Kihl, Young Whan 67
Kil, Soong-Hoom 68
Kim, Hong N. 752
Kim, Ok-Yul 1055
Kim, Paul Sunik 753
Kim, Samuel 333 334
Kim, Won Mo 69 1056 1057
Kim, Young C. 1058
Kimbara, Samon 754
Kimura, Kenji 1003
Kincaid, John 1046
Kinter, William R. 335
Kirk, Merlin 100
Kishi, Masaaki 755

Kissinger, Henry A. 756 1005
Kit-Ching, Chau Lau 336
Klein, Sidney 337
Klimes, Rudolf E. 757
Klimp, Jack W. 1059
Knapp, Ronald G. 70 1160
Knight, Charlotte 1060
Kobak, Cantius J. 1061
Kodama, Masaaki 1003
Koji, Motoo 997
Kolko, Gabriel 1147
Kolko, Joyce 1147
Korsunskii, A. 758
Kosaka, Masataka 910
Kosobud, Richard 71
Kotch, John Barry 1062
Koval, M. 338
Kraft, Carl 1000
Kraft, Nell 1000
Krammer, Arnold 759
Krause, Walter 72
Krauss, Ellis S. 760
Krebs, Edward S. 339
Krummel, John W. 761 762 763
Kua, Michael Y. M. 340
Kuan, John C. 341
Kubek, Anthony 342 343
Kuczewski, André G. 764
Kulikov, V. I. 73
Kumamoto, Bob 765
Kunadze, G. 766
Kupperman, Karen Ordahl 74
Kurihara, Akira 767
Kyrychenko, V. P. 768

L

LaFeber, Walter 75
Lai, H. Mark 344
Laidlaw, Lansing S. 769
Lampton, David M. 345
Langley, Harold D. 1164
Lanier, William D. 972
Laptev, V. 346
Larsen, Judith K. 876
Larsen, Lawrence H. 770
Larson, Sarah 771
Lasater, Martin L. 1165
Laughlin, C. H. 347
Lauren, Paul Gordon 653 772
Lawcock, Larry 773
Lawrie, Gordon G. 572
Lazarev, V. I. 348
Lazo, Dimitri D. 349
Ledovsky, A. 350 351
Lee, Chin-Chuan 352
Lee, Chong-Sik 1063 1064
Lee, Jae Won 1163
Lee, Raymond S. H. 1065
Lee, Sang-Chul 353 774
Lee, Young-Ho 1066 1067
Lee, Yur-Bok 76
Lei, Joanna C. 1166
Leonard, Thomas M. 775
Lester, Richard K. 776
Levine, Steven I. 354 355 356
Levy, Walter J. 777 778
Li, Victor H. 77 357
Li, Wen L. 1167
Liang, Chin-tung 358
Liao, Hollis S. 359
Libby, Justin H. 779 780 781 782
Lien Chan 360
Lin, Sein 361
Lin Kuo-hsiung 362
Lin Ming-te 363

Linde, Gerd 364
Linden, W. H. van der 1068
Lindsay, Michael 365 366
Lindsey, David 783
Litvak, I. A. 367
Liu, Alan P. L. 368
Liu, Ben-Chieh 1168
Liu, Paul 369
Lo, Clarence Y. H. 1069
Lomykin, V. 370
London, Ivan D. 371
London, Miriam 371
Long, Charles H. 372
Longmuir, D. Gordon 78
Lord, Walter 784
Love, Robert William, Jr. 589
Lovelace, Daniel 373
Lovell, John P. 1070
Lumley, Frederick 1071
Lummis, C. Douglas 785
Luo Rongqu 374
Lyon, Jessi Sanders 786
Lyu, Kingsley K. 1072 1073

M

Macdonald, Donald 1074 1075 1076
MacEachron, David 787
MacIsaac, David 1077
MacKinnon, Jan 375
MacKinnon, Steve 375
Maddox, Robert 788 1078
Maeda, Laura 789
Magdoff, Harry 790
Mahajani, Usha 376
Mahler, Oldřich 377
Makela, Lee A. 378
Malloy, Michael P. 568
Manchester, William 791
Manoff, Robert Karl 792
Marinov, V. 1079
Marks, John D. 1080
Marsh, Susan H. 340
Martellaro, Joseph A. 379
Martin, Ben L. 380
Marumoto, Masaji 793
Mason, Robert 794
Massey, Joseph A. 920
Mates, Leo 381
Mathis, F. John 72
Matlock, Jack F. 382
Matray, James I. 1081 1082 1083 1084
Matsuda, Takeshi 383
Matsulenko, V. 1085
Mattiace, John M. 795
Matveev, V. 796
May, Gary 384
Mayer, Arthur J. 1029
Mayers, David 385
Mazuzan, George T. 386 1086
McAlmon, George 797
McCabe, Carol 387
McCandless, Bruce 798
McCoart, J. J. 799
McCormack, Gavan 688
McDermott, Jeanne 800
McGee, Gale W. 388
McKinnon, Ronald I. 801
McLain, Glenn A. 1087
McMillan, C. H. 367
McMorris, Penny 802
McNeil, W. K. 803
McNelly, Theodore 804
Mechling, Charles, Jr. 805
Medvedev, Roy 389

Author Index

Mei, June 390
Melby, John F. 391 392
Melis, Giorgio 393
Meltzer, Ronald I. 806
Mendel, Douglas H., Jr. 807
Mendl, Wolf 808
Merdinger, Charles J. 1000
Mérigot, J. G. 809
Merillat, Herbert Christian 810
Merlo, Vittorio 992
Meserve, Ruth I. 394
Meserve, Walter J. 394
Metallo, Michael V. 395
Metzger, Thomas A. 406
Meyer, Armin H. 79
Meyer, Susan E. 396
Mieczkowski, Bogdan 811
Mieczkowski, Seiko 811
Mikesh, Robert C. 812
Mikulín, Antonín 377 813
Millar, T. B. 80
Miller, Alan 814
Miller, John R. 397
Miller, Milton H. 1169
Mills, William 398
Milton, Nancy 329
Minear, Richard H. 815
Mingde, Tsou 399
Miracle, Ralph 400
Mishra, Pramod Kumar 401
Mitson, Betty E. 816
Miura, Yō-ichi 817
Miyamoto, S. Frank 818
Modelski, George 1088
Molesworth, Carl 402
Moon, Chang Joo 1089
Moore, Jamie W. 819
Moore, John Allphin, Jr. 403
Moore, Ray A. 820
Morgan, William Michael 821
Morita, Akio 822
Morken, Hubert 404
Morley, James William 81
Morrison, Charles E. 1124
Morrow, James 823
Morse, David B. 82
Moseley, H. Stephens 402
Moy, Joyanna 911
Mughal, N. A. 83
Murray, Douglas P. 405
Mushakoji, Kinhide 824 825
Myers, Ramon H. 406 1170

N

Nagai, Yōnosuke 84 826
Najita, Tetsuo 999
Napierała, Jerzy 827
Nass, Matthias 407
Nastri, Anthony D. 408
Navarro, Vicente 828
Nayar, Baldev Ray 409
Neu, Charles E. 829
Neufeld, Gabrielle 410
New, Mary Louie 411
New, Peter Kong-Ming 411
Newman, John Michael, Jr. 412
Newman, Robert P. 413 414
Ney, Virgil 830
Nezadorov, G. V. 831
Nickel, Herman 832
Nikolaenko, S. 996
Nikolayev, N. 833
Nikol'skaia, E. 163
Nikonov, A. 415
Niksch, Larry A. 834 1090
Nilson, Sten Sparre 1148

Ninkovich, Frank 416
Nishihara, Masashi 835
Nishimizu, Mieko 734 735
Nogee, Joseph L. 417
Nolley, Kenneth S. 836
Norquist, Ernest O. 837
Nossal, Kim Richard 418
Notehelfer, F. G. 838
Nuernberger, Richard 85

O

Ogburn, Robert W. 1091
Ogram, Ernest W., Jr. 86
Ohira, Masayoshi 839 1005
Ohrn, Karin Becker 840
Ojha, Ishwer C. 419
Okamura, Raymond Y. 841
Okihiro, Gary Y. 842 843
Okita, Saburo 87 844
Oksenberg, Michel 420 421
Okun, Nathan 845
Oldag, Andreas 407
Oliver, Lucile Cummings 422
Olsen, Edward A. 88 89 90
Oman, Ralph 423
O'Neill, Robert 1092
Oppenheimer, Peter M. 997
Orange, Vincent 846
Osipov, B. 847
Otis, Cary 848
Ovendale, R. 424
Overholt, William H. 91
Owen, Joseph R. 1093
Ozaki, Robert S. 849

P

Packard, George R. 850
Pacy, James S. 425
Palmer, Norman D. 426
Panda, Rajaram 92
Pant, H. G. 93
Papageorge, Linda Madson 427
Pappas, Anna Mamalakis 1171
Park, Bong-Shik 1094
Park, Chang Jin 1095 1096
Park, Han Shik 94
Park, Hong-Kyu 1097 1098
Park, Kyoung-Suh 1099
Park, Tong-jin 1100
Park, Yung H. 95
Paterson, Thomas G. 428
Patokallio, Pasi 851
Patrick, Stephen B. 852
Patterson, Wayne 1101
Paulsen, George E. 429 430 431 432
Payer, Cheryl 1102
Peake, Louis A. 1103
Pearson, Alden B., Jr. 96
Peatross, Oscar F. 853
Peeples, Dale H. 433
Pelz, Stephen E. 97 1104
Peragallo, James L. 98
Perkins, Bradford 854
Perrolle, Pierre M. 340
Pestana, Harold R. 99
Peters, Gayle 100
Petras, James 855
Petrov, D. 101
Petukhov, V. 434 1172
Pevzner, Ia 996
Pfaltzgraff, Robert L., Jr. 435 436
Phillips, Elizabeth M. 856

Phongpaichit, Pasuk 102
Pickler, Gordon K. 437 438
Pilkington, Francis 166
Pilkington, Luann Foster 439
Pillsbury, Michael 440
Poliakov, N. 103
Poll, F. G. van der 1105
Ponnwitz, A. J. 104
Pool, Ithiel de Sola 729
Poropat, Liviana 441 1106
Porter, Gareth 105 442 1107
Potapov, I. 1108
Potis, Michael J. 857
Potter, E. B. 858
Poulose, T. T. 443
Powell, Robert 8
Powles, Cyril 859
Pozzetta, George E. 292
Prados, John 860
Price, Thomas J. 1109
Prioli, Carmine A. 861
Prisco, Sal 444 445
Pronin, V. 862
Pruden, George B., Jr. 567
Prybyla, Jan S. 446
Pugach, Noel H. 447 448 449 450 863
Purka, Joseph W. 864
Pushkin, A. 865
Puślecki, Zdzisław 866

Q

Quester, George H. 451
Quo, F. Quei 106

R

Ramachandran, K. N. 452
Ramsey, Norman F. 867
Ranard, Donald L. 1110 1111
Rapp, William V. 868
Ray, Dennis M. 453
Raymond, David A. 454
Record, Jane Cassels 455
Record, Wilson 455
Reed, Steven R. 869
Reynolds, Bruce 249
Rhee, T. C. 107 108 456
Rhodes, Robert 855
Rice, Edward E. 457
Richardson, John R. 870
Rigin, Y. 871
Risedorph, Gene 1112
Roberts, Brad 872
Roberts, John G. 873
Roberts, Stephen S. 458
Robinson, Thomas W. 459
Roden, Donald 874
Roemer, John E. 875
Rogers, Everett M. 876
Rogers, Frank E. 460
Rosenstone, Robert A. 877
Rosholt, Malcolm 461
Rowe, David N. 109 462 463 464
Rubin, Julius 465
Rubinstein, Murray A. 466 467
Rushkoff, Bennett C. 468
Russell, Hilary 469
Ryder, Richard C. 878
Rylance, Daniel F. 566

# Author Index

S

Saeki, Shōichi 879
Saitō, Makoto 880
Saitō, Yoshifumi 110
Sakamoto, Yoshikazu 111 1113
Sakata, Yasuo 881
Salaff, Janet W. 470
Salaff, Stephen 882
Salin, Pascal 997
Sánchez, G. Walter 471
Sanders, Sol W. 472 883
Sandler, Shmuel 1114
Santelli, James S. 410
Santoni, Alberto 884 885
Sato, Hideo 886 887
Satō, Seizaburo 888
Satoh, Yukio 889
Savin, A. 890
Scalapino, Robert A. 112 113 114 473 565 891
Schaller, Michael 474 475 476 892
Scheel, Walter 1005
Schloss, Ruth 477
Schmidt, Helmut 1005
Scholin, Allan R. 1115
Schonberger, Howard 893 894 895
Schroder, Norma 1170
Schroeder, Paul E. 478
Schuhmacher, W. Wilfried 479
Schwab, Susan C. 896
Schwartz, Harry 480
Segal, Gerald 481
Seidensticker, Edward 897
Seith, Alex R. 482
Service, John S. 483 563
Seth, S. P. 484
Sewall, Arthur F. 485
Shanker, Albert 167
Shapiro, Edward S. 898
Sharpston, Michael 899
Shaw, Yu-ming 115 486
Shellenberger, Jack H. 900
Shen, I-Yao 487
Shenaev, V. 944 996
Shergin, S. O. 488
Sherrod, Robert 901
Shewmaker, Kenneth E. 489 490
Shiba, Yoshinobu 1003
Shiozaki, Hiroaki 902 903
Short, Thayne R. 25
Shrader, Grahame F. 1000
Shuja, Sharif M. 491
Shulman, Frank Joseph 1116 1117
Shunsuke, Tsurumi 904
Sim, Yawsoon 492
Simon, Jeffrey D. 1148
Sims, Jack A. 905
Singh, L. P. 493
Sinha, R. P. 906
Siu, Victoria M. 494
Sizer, Nancy 495
Skaggs, David Curtis 1118
Škvařil, Jaroslav 496
Sledge, Eugene B. 907
Slonim, Shlomo 497
Smith, Gerard C. 116
Smith, M. J. J. 117
Smylie, Robert F. 118
Smyth, H. D. 908
Snow, Edgar 498
Snyder, William P. 499
Sodei, Rinjirō 909
Soderlund, Walter C. 235

Soglian, Franco 500
Solomon, Richard H. 119 501
Sommer, Theo 910
Sormani, Piero 120
Sorrentino, Constance 911
Spanier, John W. 417 1030
Spector, Ronald 502
Speer, R. T. 912
Speicher, Jacob 503
Spickard, Paul R. 913
Sprague, Claire D. 914
Srivastava, H. P. 257
Stacey, John A. 504
Stalbo, K. 1119
Stanley, Peter W. 505
Stebbins, Robert A. 915
Steeds, David 121
Steigleder, Horst 1120
Stewart, Roy P. 1121
Stilwell, Richard G. 1122
Stokes, Houston 71
Stokesbury, James 916
Strauss, William L. 917
Stuart, Angela 506
Stueck, William 1147
Stunkel, Kenneth R. 747
Suffrin, Mark 1123
Sugihara, Kaoru 1003
Sugimoto, Yoshio 918
Suhrke, Astri 1124
Sullivan, Alfred B. 919
Sullivan, Denis G. 920
Sumiya, Mikio 921
Sun Yü-t'ang 507
Sunahara, M. Ann 922
Surrey, Walter S. 568
Sutter, Robert 122 508 1173
Suzuki, Zenji 923
Swartout, Robert, Jr. 1125 1126 1127
Sysoev, I. 924

T

Tabb, William 925
Takemae, Eiji 926
Takeyman, Yasuo 927
Tarpey, John F. 1128
Taylor, Sandra C. 928 929
Telford, Ted A. 509
Temple, Harry 1129
Thach, John S. 1130
Theroux, Eugene A. 568
Thode, Frieda Oehlschlaeger 510
Thomas, James A. 1131
Thompson, Mark E. 1132
Thompson, William R. 930
Thomson, Sandra Caruthers 931
Thornton, Richard C. 511 512
Thurston, Anne F. 513
Tibbets, Paul W. 932
Tikhvinskii, S. L. 123
Tilford, Earl H., Jr. 514 1133
Tillman, Barrett 933
Toinet, Marie-France 1134
Tolley, Kemp 124
Tomabechi, Toshihiro 934
Toner, James H. 1135 1136 1137
Toshitani, Nobuyoshi 935
Tow, William T. 515 516 936 937
Tozer, Warren W. 517
Treadgold, Donald W. 125
Trefousse, Hans L. 938
Triska, Jan F. 565
Trofimenko, G. 939

Ts'ai, Shih-Shan H. 518 519
Tsai Wei-ping 126 520 521
Tsien Tsuen-hsuin 127
Tsou, Tang 522
Tsuchimochi, Gary H. 940
Tsumoda, Jun 941
Tsunoyama, Sakae 1003
Tuchman, Barbara 563
Tucker, Nancy Bernkopf 523 1176

U

Uchida, Kazutomi 941
Uchida, Yoshiko 942
Uhalley, Stephen Jr. 524
Unger, Leonard 1174
Urwin, Gregory 943
Usoskin, V. 944
Utkin, I. 945
Utley, Jonathan G. 946 947 948
Uyeda, Clifford I. 949

V

Van Alstyne, Richard W. 525
VanEdgerton, F. 128
Varg, Paul A. 526
Varma, Lalima 950
Vernant, Jacques 129
Vidich, Arthur J. 527
Vidov, A. 130
Vigny, Georges 528
Viksnins, George J. 951
Villa, Brian L. 952
Vivian, James F. 566
Vlahos, Michael 953
Volokhova, A. A. 529
Vorontsov, G. A. 954

W

Wabuda, Susan 955
Wagner, David H. 956
Wakaizumi, Kei 131
Wakatsuki, Yasno 957
Waldner, George W. 958
Walker, Richard L. 132
Wallerstein, Immanuel 959
Walsh, James P. 530
Wang, James C. F. 531
Warner, Geoffrey 1138
Warren, Shields 960
Watanabe, Masao 961
Watanabe, Toshio 962
Watkins, Floyd C. 963
Webber, Bert 964
Wedemeyer, Albert C. 532
Weems, John E. 1139
Weiner, Charles 965
Weinstein, Martin E. 133
Weintraub, Sidney 966
Weiss, Ruth 533
Welch, William 534
Wells, Samuel F., Jr. 1077
Werking, Richard Hume 535
Wescott, Richard R. 747
Westerfield, H. Bradford 1140
Whetten, Lawrence L. 536
White, G. Edward 967
White, John Albert 537
Whiting, Allen S. 134 538 539 540
Wiegand, Wayne A. 968
Wilhelm, Alfred D., Jr. 135
Wilkins, Mira 969

Williams, J. E. 970
Williams, Justin, Sr. 971
Williamson, John A. 972
Wilson, David A. 541
Wilson, R. C. 542
Wiltz, John Edward 1141 1142
Winiecki, Jan 973 974
Wittner, Lawrence S. 975
Witze, Claude 1143
Wolk, Herman S. 976
Wollenberg, Charles 977
Wong, J. Y. 543
Wong, Leslie 544
Wong, Shawn 13
Worden, Robert L. 545
Wright, Christopher C. 978
Wu Chen-tsai 546

X

Xiang Rong 547

Y

Yagisawa, Mitsuo 979
Yahuda, Michael B. 548
Yamaguchi, Yasuko 593
Yamamura, Kozo 980
Yang, Caroline A. 981
Yang Chih-hung 549
Yao, Richard 982
Yao Meng-hsüan 550
Yasuba, Yasukichi 1003
Yasukawa, Takeshi 983
Yavenditti, Michael J. 984 985
Yeats, A. J. 986
Yee, Albert 551
Yee, Herbert S. 1175
Yen, Susan Morrison 552
Yim, Yong Soon 1144 1145
Yin Ch'ing-yao 553 554 555 556
Yodfat, Aryeh 557 558
Yonekawa, Shin'ichi 987

Yonge, C. M. 988
Yoshitsu, Michael M. 989
Yoshizawa, Tetsutarō 136
Young, Dana B. 990
Young, Kenneth Ray 559
Yu, Linda 1167
Yu, Suk-Ryul 1146
Yu, Tzong-shian 193
Yü, Yüh-chao 991
Yu-ming Shaw 137
Yung Wei 560

Z

Zancardi, Pietro 992
Zanegin, B. N. 561
Zimmerman, E. C. 993
Zobrist, Benedict K. 994
Zook, Benjamin M. 565
Zorgbibe, Charles 995
Zuk, Gary 930